Family Therapy
CONCEPTS AND METHODS
Second Edition

MICHAEL P. NICHOLS, Ph.D.
Albany Medical College

RICHARD C. SCHWARTZ, Ph.D.
Institute for Juvenile Research, Chicago
University of Illinois College of Medicine

With a Foreword by

CARLOS E. SLUZKI, M.D.
Berkshire Medical Center

ALLYN AND BACON
Boston London Toronto Sydney Tokyo Singapore

Executive Editor: Susan Badger
Editorial Assistant: Dana Lamothe
Production Administrator: Susan McIntyre
Editorial-Production Service: Spectrum Publisher Services, Inc.
Text Designer: Suzanne Harbison
Cover Administrator: Linda Dickinson
Composition Buyer: Linda Cox
Manufacturing Buyer: Megan Cochran

The publisher gratefully acknowledges permission from the following sources to reprint material in
this book:

For material on pages 83, 84, 85, 88, and 137: From *Family Therapy Networker*, edited by Richard
Simon.

For material on pages 101, 102, and 105: Copyright © 1984 by M. Davidson. From the book
Uncommon Sense and reprinted with permission from Jeremy P. Tarcher, Inc., Los Angeles, CA.

For material on page 116: From *Family Therapy in Clinical Practice* by Murray Bowen, M.D.,
copyright © 1985, 1983, 1978 by Jason Aronson Inc. Reprinted with permission of the publisher.

For material on pages 481, 482, and 485: From *In Search of Solutions, A New Direction in Psychotherapy*, by William Hudson O'Hanlon and Michele Weiner-Davis, by permission of W.W. Norton
& Company, Inc. Copyright © 1989 by William Hudson O'Hanlon and Michele Weiner-Davis.

For material on pages 487, 488, 491, and 492: From *Schizophrenia and the Family*, by C. Anderson,
D. Reiss, and B. Hogarty. Copyright © 1986. Reprinted by permission of The Guilford Press.

For material on pages 496, 497, 498, and 499: From *Selected Papers*, by Michael White, copyright ©
1989 by Michael White. Reprinted with permission of the author.

Library of Congress Cataloging-in-Publication Data
Nichols, Michael P.
    Family therapy: concepts and methods / Michael P. Nichols.
    Richard C. Schwartz; with foreword by Carlos Sluzki.—2nd ed.
      p. cm
    Includes bibliographical references and index.
    ISBN 0-205-12887-4
    1. Family psychotherapy.   I. Schwartz, Richard C.   II. Title.
    [DNLM: 1. Family Therapy.   WM 430.5.F2 N621f]
RC488.5.N53   1991
616.89'156—dc20
DNLM/DLC
for Library of Congress   90-14569
                                           CIP

Printed in the United States of America

10 9 8 7 6   95 94

To our wives, Melody Nichols and Nancy Schwartz,
and our children, Sandy and Paul Nichols, Jessie, Sarah,
and Hali Schwartz, for their support and instruction

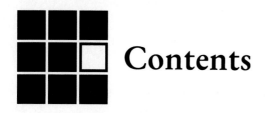

Contents

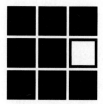# Foreword

The history of the field of family therapy is the history of the language developed to talk about it. Thus, our discipline was born when some therapists began naming what they were doing "family therapy." Until then, interviews that included more than one family member took place, when they occurred at all, as supplementary meetings for individual therapy and were not specifically labeled, structured, or defined. Instead, they were called (and hence they *were*) parental guidance conversations, supportive couple's sessions, information-seeking interviews, or the like. Although there were therapists who consistently conducted therapeutic interviews with couples or families, they kept it under wraps due to the concept's heterodoxy.

The miracle of naming this new practice "family (or couple) therapy"—catalyzed by cybernetics, systems theory, information theory, and related sciences—triggered a dramatic evolution of the field. In the beginning, the language was so sparse that, to refer to what they were doing, those pioneers had to resort to *showing* their methods rather than talking or writing about them: they borrowed from Arnold Gessell (and from the CIA) the one-way mirror. Permeating the patient-therapist sanctum constituted an iconoclastic, revolutionary testimony of the field's willingness to observe itself. Then came the words. This naming fervor created many new observables, made tangible many new ideas, and enabled people to talk about them. Thus, the language of family therapy evolved out of the dialectic spiral between generative models, creative practices, challenging training programs, and multifaceted research. The exponential growth of the specialized literature is evidence of this generativity.

In an editorial titled "Family Process: Mapping the journey over twenty-five years" (*Family Process*, 26(2):149–152, 1987) I mused about all this, weighing only one of many possible parameters to measure the field's growth—the number of journals devoted to family therapy. It has ballooned from one (arguably three) in 1962 to fifteen in 1987 (since then, four more were added!) *plus* eight family therapy-oriented newsletters *plus* seventeen journals in the specialty published abroad. Should I add to this the number and diversity of interesting books being published on a yearly basis? I have long since abandoned any hope of catching up with them. And what about the number of informative, even groundbreaking, workshops, conferences, and symposia? Well.

It is said that Descartes, in the seventeenth century, was the last of the great minds able to sum up in a cogent and articulate fashion all the branches and layers of (occidental) human knowledge. Or perhaps it was Leonardo da Vinci or Gianbattista Vico, one hundred years before that. Or maybe that precious synthesis occurred for the last time in an obscure medieval monk sequestered in a cloister, never identified in the register of history. One way or another, the expansion of human knowledge exceeded centuries ago the mind's capacity to embrace it, organize it, and use it. *Mutatis mutandis*, the same may be said of the evolution of the young field of family therapy: perhaps in its beginnings there were many who could talk cogently about each and every research project done in the field, each and every conceptual design, each and every practice modality. Even ten years ago there were a few specialists who seemed able to encompass it. But in the past decade the field's fund of knowledge has exceeded by far any one practitioner's grasp. And it is not only a matter of sheer number of books and papers, or the vast diversity of the models proposed, or the richness of the praxis spelled out for each of them, or the wealth of research aimed at disproving them. The very boundary of the field has expanded and, in the process, unavoidably blurred. It has expanded in a dialogue with other disciplines in the field of health and human services, as well as in the gallery of mirrors of a self-reflective epistemological inquiry. And in expanding it has nourished and been nourished (and in the process, sometimes rarified) by the language of the philosophy of science, semiotics, hermeneutics, ethics, the new physics, and so on.

The systemic awareness of this, and any, discipline as an interactive whole of ideas requires an acknowledgment of the ever-expanding boundaries of the other sciences that interact with (and therefore, in a sense, are a part of) ideas about 'family,' of the sciences interacting with those, and so on. Correspondingly, the conceptual field evolving from this process of intertwining with other disciplines generates a pressing need for a new *kind* of mapping effort, one radically different from that of the hypothetical enlightened medieval monk. It is important to acknowledge that mapping itself constitutes a creative (constructive) activity because *mapping is also naming*, and thus, it affects both territory and journey.

All this is being tackled in Michael Nichols' and Richard Schwartz's massive synthesis. This welcome new *mapa mundis* of our field-in-context provides a stock-taking that is comprehensive without trivializing; that acknowledges the turbulent, complex nature of systemic thinking while offering a clear synopsis of it; that recognizes the contributions of different trends, orientations, and alternative views of a controversial and politicized field. And, by including the description of our collective journey and the cross-disciplinary spiral of premises that continually nourishes us, it pays tribute to the complexity of our field while offering glimpses of the many intriguing and still uncharted territories that lie beyond its current frontiers. Thus, while allowing us to plant our feet firmly on the ground, it provides us with the space to exercise the wings of our scientific imagination.

Carlos E. Sluzki, M.D.
Chair, Department of Psychiatry
Berkshire Medical Center
Pittsfield, MA
August 1990

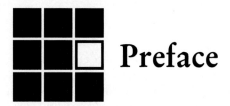 Preface

Writing the first edition of this book was a monumental task; it took seven years of very hard work. I read prodigiously and did my utmost to shape and organize the material into a coherent structure. It was a lot of work, but I was lucky too; there were a lot of rewards. By reading such a vast literature, I learned a good deal more about family therapy, and fortunately the book was generously received. When I met Jay Haley at a party and he told me he liked my book, I felt like a kid whose jump shot Michael Jordan had praised. It's also meant a lot to me that a number of people have written to thank me for writing the book because it was useful to them in graduate school or in practice. So, since I'm a sucker for praise, I agreed to write a second edition.

Working on the second edition was a very different task. For one thing, the field has changed. Today there is less clear distinction between the schools of family therapy. There are still very different ways of doing therapy, but most experienced therapists now borrow some of the concepts and methods from other schools. So, while there are still a variety of approaches to family therapy, there is also much more cross-fertilization among them. In addition, I have changed. I'm a little older, a little more experienced, and in writing the second edition I was able to talk to many of the leading figures in the field about what they do, rather than relying on published accounts. I hope this makes for a more balanced treatment, and I hope it has enabled us to make the second edition a little more informative about clinical technique.

In this second edition, my new co-author, Richard Schwartz, and I have updated and expanded the original text, with special emphasis on describing the various approaches to family therapy as they are actually practiced. We have also taken pains to examine the most important intellectual trends and controversies of the 1980s and 1990s, including constructivism, the post-Milan movement, the psychoeducational approach, and the feminist critique—significant challenges to complacency that raise large questions about the nature of the family and the therapies designed to treat it. But perhaps the most important feature of this edition is its thorough presentation of the new therapies on the leading edge of the field. Included are Salvador Minuchin's latest techniques, the work of Michael White, solution-based therapies, the latest applications of Bowenian theory, the internal family systems model, and a variety of approaches that integrate the self and the system. Both new and traditional approaches are described in detail, then measured against each other in a comparative analysis section.

We have also included a comprehensive guide to family therapy training centers, a summary of family therapy research, and a glossary of terms. With our recommended reading list we went out on a limb to recommend what we think are the most useful books available for understanding and treating families at various stages of the life cycle.

Another important difference in writing the second edition was my collaboration with Dick Schwartz; I asked him to work with me on the second edition because his interests and expertise complement my own. He's more directly familiar with some of the strategic approaches than I am; he's more knowledgeable about who's who and what's what in the field today; and his own work is in the forefront of exciting new developments in family therapy. But all that could be true and he could still be an unpleasant guy to work with—slow, lazy, or dogmatic. He isn't. In fact, working with Dick was the best part of doing this revision. Whenever you tackle a big job, it's nice to do so with another person who does his share. Dick is a demon worker who did his share and then willingly helped me with mine. He's a fine writer and he has a very balanced way of seeing things. More than once, he pointed out places where I had allowed myself to be opinionated (moi?) and he helped me—and this second edition—to become a little broader. (I'd say "kinder and gentler," but that's too much of a cliché.)

So many people have contributed, directly and indirectly, to my development as a family therapist and to the writing of this book that it's impossible to thank them all. But I would like to single out a few for special thanks. The people who taught me family therapy were Rodney Shapiro, Lyman Wynne, Murray Bowen, Michael Kerr, and Salvador Minuchin. To every one of them: thank you. Next, I owe an enormous debt of gratitude to Gardner Spungin, publisher of Gardner Press, who believed in me when no one else did. He took a chance on me, and when the original manuscript was finished he took a pile of scribblings and turned it into a book. And then he did all the things a publisher can do to help make it a success. No author could ask for more. But Gardner gave more. In addition to making this book a success, he provided me with steadfast and generous encouragement. In midlife, I discovered a dream in my heart that I hadn't dared to pursue before: the wish to be a writer. Thank you, Gardner, for helping me recognize the dream and for encouraging me to act on it.

Some of the people who went out of their way to read drafts of this manuscript or to meet with me to discuss family therapy are: Murray Bowen, Betty Carter, Stuart Golan, Phil Guerin, Rachel Hare-Mustin, Judith Lieb, Florence Kaslow, David Keith, Michael Kerr, Howard Liddle, Robert Noone, Jack O'Connor, Fred Sander, Virginia Satir, David Scharff, Jill Savege Sharff, and Salvador Minuchin.

I'm grateful to Bill Barke, Susan Badger, and Dana Lamothe at Allyn and Bacon who were patient enough to wait a little longer than they wanted for the manuscript and understanding enough to make a hard job a little easier.

Finally, I would like to thank the teachers of my post-graduate course in the family: my wife Melody and my kids Sandy and Paul. In the brief span of twenty-three years Melody has helped transform me from a shy young man, totally ignorant of how to be a husband and father, into a shy middle-aged man who at least knows he's ignorant. Sandy and Paul have already taught me about diapers and hiking and tolerance (theirs and mine), and are now in the process of teaching me about marathon telephone calling, MTV, and what's going on in the twentieth century—"*Dad . . .* don't be a dork, nobody does that anymore." Thanks guys.

Michael P. Nichols
Albany, New York, September 1990

Nearly twenty years ago I became infatuated with a revolutionary set of ideas called systems thinking, and the psychotherapy practices that evolved from them which came to be known as family therapy. Unlike most love affairs, my passion for this field never waned; it remains a constant source of intellectual and personal gratification. When *Family Therapy: Concepts and Methods* emerged in 1984 I was pleased that the field finally had an overview book that was well-written, comprehensive, and deep. I was glad to see that it sold well and was used by many as the basic text for the field.

When Mike Nichols asked me to co-author the second edition, I was shocked and honored. I didn't know Mike and I was daunted by the quality of his writing and scholarship. How could I maintain those high standards? Also, why would he want to bring on someone else when he could do the updating of each chapter himself? How would he tolerate changes I might want to make in material he had already written? Would he be flexible enough to allow me to express opinions in the book even if they differed from his? My desire to express some of the passion I have for family therapy overrode these concerns and, warily, I plunged in.

As I worked with Mike this year, his openness, generosity, and supportiveness calmed my fears. He is committed to excellence in whatever he does and he recognized that the number of new and important issues and models that arose in family therapy's turbulent 1980s called for the "binocular" view of two observers. He gave me a free hand to rewrite the chapters for which I was primarily responsible (2, 3, 9, and 11) as I saw fit. Not only has he tolerated my expression of differences, he has fostered a rich exchange of ideas between us that I hope continues long beyond this collaboration. He also encouraged me to include my internal family systems model in Chapter 11. I am grateful to Mike for all this and for sharing with me this book, in which he had invested so much, and which has already achieved such a fine reputation and large readership. I am proud to be associated with it and with him.

If there is one truth that family therapy has come to grips with this decade, it's that there is no absolute truth—at least none that can be known objectively. There are only perspectives of reality, each of which is biased and distorted. This book is a perspective on family therapy, not the truth about family therapy. We have tried to provide a fair representation of the concepts and methods of the models we cover but also to openly discuss our opinions of them, rather than pretending to be totally objective. I hope readers will use these opinions to define and clarify their own.

The field of family therapy has become so large and complex that even a book of this size can't do justice to all those who have contributed to it. An awareness of the responsibility that accompanied my acceptance of this task grew each day, as did my panic at the thought that, inevitably, important people and ideas would be slighted. I apologize to those people.

As Frank Pittman said recently, you can have all kinds of interactions with people, but until you have been edited by them, you don't really know them. I want to thank all the people, in addition to Mike, that I have gotten to know in this way while working on this project. Their comments and support have been invaluable. They include: Lee Combrinck Graham, Debbie Gorman-Smith, Reggie Goulding, Rachel Hare-Mustin, Robert Noone, Nancy Schwartz, Rich Simon, Doug Sprenkle, and Michael White. Additional thanks go to Joel Van Dyke for his help tracking down obscure references and to Debbie Gorman-Smith for all her help on the research section of Chapter 3.

In addition, I'm eternally grateful to the faculty of the Family Systems Program at the Institute of Juvenile Research for creating, over the past ten years, an intellectual incubator in which the best opinions or perspectives in my sections of this book were born. They include: Doug Breunlin, Rocco Cimmarusti, Betty Karrer, and Howard Liddle. I have also learned from and with a host of remarkable clients, students, teachers, and friends too numerous to mention. Special thanks, however, are due Reggie Goulding, Rich Simon, Doug Sprenkle, and Ted and Gen Schwartz.

Finally, I thank my wife Nancy and our daughters, Jessie, Sarah, and Hali, for all their sacrifice, support and instruction. They lived with my panicked achievement part for the past year and didn't see much of me, even when I was home. They still love me and I am very lucky.

Richard C. Schwartz
Chicago, Illinois, September, 1990

1

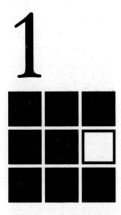

The Historical Context of Family Therapy

We are by now so used to hearing about "family therapy" that we may be beguiled into thinking of it as a monolithic enterprise, a programatic approach to treatment with a coherent set of concepts and methods. As family therapists are well aware, however, there is not one, but many family therapies, each with distinctly different ways of conceptualizing and treating families. Still the general impression persists that the history of family therapy is one continuous line of development with subsequent specialization. Yes, today we have a proliferation of competing approaches, but aren't they all variations on a common theme? And weren't the early family therapists pretty much in agreement about the general principles of treatment? In fact, such consensus never existed. Family therapy was developed by a heterogeneous group of investigators working in distinctly different contexts and with different purposes. These pioneers discovered family therapy before they discovered each other. While it is true that there are unifying principles that most family therapists share, variety, not unity, has always been a major theme of the story of family therapy.

Like the country family therapy grew up in, the field is a melting pot in which the ingredients never really melted. Family therapy's rich history of diversity complicates the task of the historian. The challenge is to describe the differences among various approaches without losing track of the common threads uniting them. Our response to this challenge is to divide the task among the first three chapters. In this chapter, focusing on the 1950s and 1960s, we describe the rivulets that fed into what was to become the mainstream of family therapy. In Chapter 2 we take a closer look at the ideas that shaped the field's identity, especially during the 1960s and 1970s. In Chapter 3, which covers the turbulent 1980s, we discuss the controversies and rude awakenings of that decade.

PSYCHOTHERAPEUTIC SANCTUARY

It is tempting to look back at the days before family therapy and see those who insisted on segregating individual mental patients from their families as naive and wrongheaded, exponents of a fossilized view of mental disorder according to which psychiatric maladies are firmly embedded in the heads of individuals. When we consider that clinicians didn't begin treating whole families together until the mid 1950s, we may be tempted to ask, what took them so long?

For one thing, there are very good reasons for conducting psychotherapy in private, in isolation from distressed and distressing relationships.

The two most influential approaches to psychotherapy in the middle of the twentieth century, Freud's psychoanalysis and Rogers's client-centered therapy, were both predicated on the assumption that psychological problems arose from unhealthy interactions with others and could best be alleviated in a private relationship between patient and therapist.

Freud's discoveries indicted the family, first as a breeding ground for childhood seduction, and later as the agent of cultural repression. Since the natural child is oriented toward pure pleasure, the family must stand for antipleasure. Ideally this dialectic tames the animal underside of our natures, making us fit to live in society and able to find healthy gratification without undue conflict with others. All too often, though, repression is excessive; instead of learning to express our needs in moderation, we bury them, settling for security instead of satisfaction. Unfortunately a life without pain is a life without passion. When we grow up a little bit neurotic—unconsciously afraid of our natural drives—whom else do we blame except our parents?

Given that neurotic conflicts were spawned in the family, it seemed only natural to assume that the best way to undo the family's influence was to isolate the family from treatment, to keep its contaminating influence out of the psychoanalytic operating room.

Freud also discovered that the less he revealed of his own personality and feelings, the more his patients reacted toward him as though he were a significant figure from the patient's family. At first these *transference* reactions seemed a hindrance, but Freud soon realized that they provided an invaluable glimpse into the past. Thereafter, fostering and analyzing transference became the cornerstone of psychoanalytic treatment, which meant that since the analyst was interested in the patient's memories and fantasies about the family, having the real family present in the treatment room would only obscure the subjective truth of the past. Freud was not interested in the living family; he was interested in the family-as-remembered, locked away in the unconscious.

By conducting treatment in private, Freud safeguarded the patient's trust in the sanctity of the therapeutic relationship and thus maximized the likelihood that the patient would repeat, in relation to the analyst, the understandings and misunderstandings of early childhood.

Carl Rogers also believed that psychological problems stemmed from destructive early interactions with others. Each of us, Rogers said, is born with an innate tendency toward *self-actualization*, an idea that became the premise of all humanistic psychotherapies. Left to our own devices, we tend to follow our own best interests. Since we are curious and intelligent, we explore and learn; since we have strong bodies, we play and exercise; and since being with others brings us joy, we tend to be outgoing, loving, and affectionate.

Unhappily, said Rogers, our healthy instinct toward actualization gets warped and subverted. We crave the approval of others so badly that we learn to do what we think others want, even when it may not be what is best for us. Little boys may act tough in order to please daddies who wish they were tougher themselves, and little girls may subdue their competitive strivings to conform to what they think their parents expect.

Gradually this conflict between self-fulfillment and the need for approval leads to denial and distortion of our inner promptings and even of the feelings that signal them. Thus we learn to deny feelings of anger when we are unfairly criticized, lest we encounter disapproval. In fact, some people spend their whole lives in vocations that were selected as a means of getting approval, rather than as a means of fulfilling what is best in their own natures. It has been said that marriage is the most important and most neurotic choice that most people make. That may be, but choosing a career, too, is often influenced, directly or indirectly, more by the expectations of others than by following one's own inclinations and talents. Young men and women often fall into careers that their parents encourage, or choose the opposite sort of careers their parents would wish, confusing counter-conformity with independence. The consequences of this decision may be a life of vague unhappiness, with or without more obvious psychological symptoms, but the real cause of unhappiness—the unfulfilled basic needs—may never be recognized.

The therapy that Rogers developed was designed to help patients rediscover their real feelings, urges, and basic self-actualizing tendencies. Given his faith that people will find their own best interests, Rogers's view of the proper role of the therapist was that of a midwife—passive, but supportive. The therapist does not do anything to the patient, but rather provides conditions to help the patient discover what needs to be done, primarily by providing *unconditional positive regard.* The therapist listens carefully and sympathetically, communicating understanding, warmth, and respect. In the presence of such an accepting listener, the patient is gradually able to get in touch with his or her own feelings and inclinations. Although this sounds simple, it is a unique relationship. If you doubt that, try telling a friend about a problem. Most likely you will find that the friend soon interrupts to tell you a similar story or to give you some advice—advice which may suit the friend more than it does you.

The client-centered therapist, like the psychoanalyst, maintains absolute privacy in the therapeutic relationship in order to avoid any situations in which patients' feelings and impulses might be denied or distorted to win the approval of others. Only a specially trained person can communicate the unconditional acceptance that helps patients rediscover their basic selves; therefore family members and other outsiders have no place in the work of client-centered therapy.

When one of the authors finished giving a talk on family therapy to a group of psychiatrists, the question was asked: "But does this brief family intervention result in lasting change, or does the patient's personality reassert itself?" It was a good question. What is needed for real change: a brief intervention in the family or a long-term exploration of personality? Actually family therapy is not simply predicated on changing the individual patient in context. Family therapy can exert change on the entire family and therefore improvement can be lasting because each and every family member changes, and continues to exert synchronous change on each other. Still there are some basic aspects of personality—say, a father's oversensitiveness, or a mother's insecurity—that may be best treated in individual psychotherapy.

As we have seen, then, there are and continue to be valid reasons for conducting psychotherapy in a private, safe, confidential relationship. But individual therapy also plays a political role, serving as another social institution that displaces the family's function as the primary agency for the support and guidance of its members.

Ordinarily the question of individual versus family therapy is posed as a technical one—which approach works best with a given problem? But the choice between individual and family therapy also reflects a philosophical understanding of human nature. Although most therapists are too busy trying to help people to contemplate philosophical questions about their work, they are, nevertheless, shaped by the context in which they work, an important aspect of which is the prevailing climate of opinion about the place of the individual and the role of the family.

The rise of individualism and the legitimization of selfhood led many people to place the needs of the individual over those of the group. "Authenticity" was once equated with radical individualism, just as it often is among adolescents struggling to define identities as individuals separate from their families. Perhaps family therapy has flourished at the close of the twentieth century, not only because of its proven clinical effectiveness, but also because American society is rediscovering the interconnectedness that characterizes our planet.

One of the cherished myths of psychotherapy is that it is value-free: Psychotherapists don't impose solutions; they only help people discover their own solutions. That sounds good, but psychotherapy is inevitably a moral enterprise. The type of treatment we choose to help people reflects our view of the proper balance between individualism and group membership. Most people value the claims of the individual *and* the group. Still, there is almost inevitably a greater emphasis on one or the other, and this emphasis is reflected in a greater or lesser tendency to turn to individual or family therapy to solve life's problems.

THE IMPACT OF THE FAMILY ON HOSPITALIZED PATIENTS

Except for purposes of footing the bill, hospital psychiatrists have generally kept families of patients at a distance. Although the family's role in the etiology of psychiatric problems has long been widely acknowledged, most clinicians believed that excluding the family was a necessary condition for undoing their destructive influence. Eventually, however, therapists were forced to acknowledge the family's continuing power to influence the course of treatment, especially for patients who go mad and require hospital care. Individual psychotherapy is predicated on the patient's having a stable, dependable, and relatively constant environment, so that the therapist can take a continuing family context for granted and concentrate on the individual's personality, unconscious, and past. This approach is less reasonable when the patient's environment is itself undergoing crisis, conflict, and change. All too often the hospitalized individual is an emotional prisoner of a chaotic environment.

Two consistent observations betrayed the reciprocal influences between psychiatric patients and their families. First, many therapists noticed that when the patient got better, someone else in the family got worse. It was almost as though the family *needed* a symptomatic member, and that any member would do. In the early fifties Don Jackson documented the dramatic effects psychotherapy had on other members of the patient's family (Jackson, 1954). In one case Jackson was treating a woman for depression; when she began to improve, her husband called to complain that her emotional condition was getting worse. When she continued to improve, the husband lost his job. Eventually he killed himself. Apparently this man's stability was predicated on having a sick wife.

In another case a husband urged his wife to seek psychotherapy for frigidity. When, after several months of treatment, she became less inhibited and more sexually responsive, he became impotent. Another example of dysfunctional balance is a marriage in which one spouse is an alcoholic and the other spouse subtly encourages the drinking. Some people seem better able to accept a needy, dependent partner than one who is a competent and capable adult.

A similar pattern of shifting disturbance was discovered in families with an identified schizophrenic patient. When the patient improved, disruptions often occurred at home. The behavior of other family members changed in such a way as to push the patient back into psychosis; or if the patient recovered, others in the family began to show pathological distress (Bateson, 1959; Haley, 1959; Jackson, 1961; Jackson and Weakland, 1959). Otto Will (quoted in Stierlin, 1977, p. 12) noted, "Frequently it is at the first sign of progress with schizophrenics that their relatives want to take them out of treatment."

The impact of a patient's improvement on the family is not always negative. Fisher and Mendell (1958) reported a spread of positive changes from patients to other family members. However, whether the nature of the effect that patient change has on the family is positive or negative is not the point. The fact is, change in one person changes the system.

The validity of these clinical observations was first corroborated in a study conducted at the Maudsley Hospital in England, in which a group of schizophrenic patients who were discharged either to their parents' homes or to live with their spouses was compared to a similar group of patients who lived alone. A significantly higher relapse rate was observed in the group who returned to their families (Brown, 1959). At least in this sample, the disrupting influence of living with families outweighed any positive effects of family support and nurturance. Furthermore the fact that family visits may disturb psychiatric patients is so well documented that to this day many hospitals do not allow patients to have family visitors, at least during the initial period of their hospital stay.

The shortsightedness of isolating mental patients from their families in psychiatric hospitals has recently been movingly documented in *Institutionalizing Madness* by Joel Elizur and Salvador Minuchin (1989). Through the stories of four disturbed young people, the authors explore the consequences of labeling people as sick and then treating them as such— "a mode of therapy based on seclusion and forced contact with an insane world"—instead of supporting families in caring for their members. In one of the cases a sixteen-year-old boy tragically drifts into the status of chronic mental patient, in part because of a progression of uncoordinated institutional vested interests. "Although he could act competently in many ways, the diagnosis of madness organized a rocklike reality that constrained possibilities, restricting his life so that the most morbid expectations were fulfilled (p. 61)."

As we enter the 1990s, over forty years after the development of family therapy, most psychiatric hospitals still segregate patients from their families. True, there are some enlightened hospitals with enough trained staff to work with patients *and* their families; and there are some patients (battered women, for example, and severely abused children) whose families are pernicious and from whom the patient needs shelter. However, in the vast majority of hospitals, the pressure to stabilize patients on medication and return them as quickly as possible to the community (in order to free beds for the next round of admissions) means that patients are released into the same chaotic environments that helped precipitate hospitalization in the first place. Moreover even in those hospitals that make some attempt to recognize that patients have families, efforts at family therapy often mean no more than conducting family meetings with some attempt to help family members "communicate," when often as not the problem in these families is that family members communicate too much and need to develop more independence.

SMALL GROUP DYNAMICS

Those who wished to understand and treat families found a ready parallel between families and small groups; the similarities are obvious, the differences few. This led some therapists to begin treating families as though they were just a special type of small group. Later they were to discover that a few significant differences limit the transfer of technologies directly from one arena to the other. Before considering the limitations of group methods as applied to family therapy, let us examine some of the principles of group dynamics and group psychotherapy.

One reason that studies of group dynamics are so relevant to family therapy is that group life is a complex blend of individual personalities and superordinate properties of group structure. The bitter battle between Rousseau and Diderot throughout the middle of the eighteenth century about which had priority—society or the individual—is echoed among social scientists who periodically argue that groups and families are a product of *either* the individual *or* the collective forces of the larger system. In groups are met the province of the psychologist—individuals and what makes them tick—and the sociologist or social psychologist—the laws of group structure and interaction.

During the 1920s social scientists began studying natural groups in society, hoping to learn how to solve social problems by coming to understand social interaction in normal social groupings. They did casework with various groups and social welfare projects; they held group discussions with patients which, in the 1930s, led to the development of group psychotherapy; and they investigated small group dynamics. In 1920 the pioneering social psychologist William McDougall published *The Group Mind*, in which he described how a group's continuity depends in part on the group being an important idea in the minds of its members, the need for boundaries and structures in which differentiation and specialization of function could occur, and the importance of customs and habits developing so that member-to-member relations could be fixed and defined. A more scientific and empirical approach to group dynamics was ushered in during the 1940s by Kurt Lewin, whose *field theory* (Lewin, 1951) guided a generation of researchers, industrial psychologists, group therapists, and agents of social change. In fact Lewin, with his collaborators and students, was preeminent in developing the laboratory method that produced first T-groups and then the encounter group movement.

Lewin's field theory described the organic interactions between individuals and their environment. Drawing on ideas from the Gestalt school of perceptual psychology, Lewin emphasized the interdependence of part-whole relationships. He developed the notion that the group is a psychologically coherent whole, rather than merely a collection of individuals. The group as a whole is different from, and more than, the sum of its parts. This transcendent property of groups has obvious relevance to family therapists who must work not only with individuals but also with a family system. Many of Lewin's other concepts will already be familiar. They include: *life space, tension, energy, need, valence,* and *vector.* Using these concepts people can be described (and diagrammed) as occupying more or less *life space,* experiencing varying degrees of *tension,* and being driven by fluctuating amounts of *energy* in pursuit of a variety of *needs* whose salience at the moment provides the *valence* for movement along certain *vectors.*

Another of Lewin's important discoveries is that group discussions are superior to individual instruction or lecturing for changing ideas and social conduct. Applied to psychotherapy, this suggests that conjoint family meetings may be more effective in changing each family member's behavior than separate meetings with individuals. Trying to coach a wife by herself to behave more assertively at home, for example, is far less likely to succeed than working with the couple. By meeting with both partners the therapist can help the wife deal better with her spouse's counterreactions and at the same time can make the husband more aware of the need to accept the new assertiveness.

Analyzing what he called *quasi-stationary social equilibrium,* Lewin pointed out that change in group behavior requires "unfreezing" and "refreezing." First something must shake up and unsettle the group's accustomed beliefs and behavior; only then will group members be prepared to accept change. Lewin's ideas have been confirmed by the experience of successful family therapists. In individual therapy the unfreezing process is initiated by the disquieting experiences that lead a person to become a patient. Once he or she accepts the status of patient and meets individually with a therapist, the person has already begun to unfreeze habitual group ties. When families come for treatment, it's quite a different matter. Many of the members may not have been sufficiently unsettled by the symptomatic member's behavior to be prepared to change their own behavior. Furthermore family members bring their own primary reference group with them, with all its traditions, mores, and habits. Consequently much more effort is required to unfreeze, or shake up, a family than an individual before therapeutic change can take place. Examples of unfreezing maneuvers include Minuchin's promotion of crises in family lunch sessions, Norman Paul's use of cross-confrontations, and Peggy Papp's family choreography. The idea of unfreezing foreshadows early family therapists' great concern with disrupting family *homeostasis*—a notion that dominated family therapy for decades.

Wilfred Bion is another major figure in the study of group dynamics who emphasized the group as a whole, with its own dynamics and hidden structure. He is best known for his description of three basic assumptions of groups (Bion, 1948). According to Bion, most groups become diverted from their primary tasks by engaging in patterns of *fight-flight*, *dependency*, or *pairing*. In *fight-flight* groups, members become so preoccupied with interpersonal conflict that battling or avoiding it, rather than problem-solving, becomes the real purpose of most meetings. In *dependency* groups, maintaining a dependent relationship with the leader is actually more important to the members than the content of group discussions or even the group's avowed goals. This kind of dependency is operating when students select courses in order to be entertained by witty instructors or to be enthralled by attractive ones. Finally, in *pairing* groups, members are more interested in being with each other than they are in working toward the group's goals. Even in therapy groups, members may be more involved with meeting weekly to socialize than with personal exploration and change.

Bion's basic assumptions are easily extrapolated to family therapy. Some families are so afraid to face conflicts that, session after session, they scrupulously avoid dealing with the issues that concern them. Others use therapy sessions just to vent their anger, preferring to fight endlessly rather than to contemplate compromise, much less change.

Both Lewin and Bion have greatly influenced students of group dynamics. There are two major centers today devoted to analysis and change of small group behavior—The National Training Laboratory (NTL) in the United States and the Tavistock Institute of Human Relations in Britain.

Other concepts from group dynamics also apply to family treatment. Warren Bennis, a student of Lewin's, described group development as going through two main phases, each with three subphases (Bennis, 1964): Phase I *Dependence* (1) dependence-flight, (2) counterdependence-flight, and (3) resolution-catharsis; Phase II *Interdependence* (4) enchantment-flight, (5) disenchantment-flight, and (6) consensual validation. Understanding that groups go through stages of development has been translated by family therapists who plan therapy in stages, and later into notions about the family life cycle. Bennis's conception of dependence and interdependence as the central problems in group life antedates similar notions among family therapists, among them Minuchin's description of families as varying from enmeshment to disengagement.

The *process/content* distinction in group dynamics has likewise had a major impact on family treatment. Many family therapists have learned to attend more to *how* families talk than to the content of their discussions. Strategic therapists even go so far as to say that the ways that family members try to solve their difficulties become problem-maintaining behavior and thus more troublesome than the original difficulties.

Students of small group behavior have also explored the factors involved in developing a productive atmosphere in groups (group cohesiveness); the effectiveness of high- and low-structured groups; implications of authoritarian and democratic groups; scapegoating; the sociometric assessment of how friendship choices dictate channels of communication more than does formal structure; leadership and power, formal and informal, autocratic, democratic, or laissez faire; and effective leadership as it contributes to the emotional needs and tasks of the group (Luft, 1970; Lakin, 1985).

Role theory, explored in the literatures of psychoanalysis and group dynamics, has had particularly important applications to the study of families. The expectations that roles provide bring regularity to complex social situations. A narrowing of roles shrinks the possibilities of family life; too many roles may lead to conflicting loyalties. At the beginning of the century the sociologist Charles Cooley described differing roles in various groups as having a prepotent impact on behavior (Cooley, 1902). According to this role analysis, multiple roles and multiple group affiliations are keys to understanding individual motives. We often think of family members in terms of a single role (wife or husband), but we need to remember that a wife may also be a mother, a friend, a daughter, and an employee. (Some husbands should remember this too.) Furthermore even those roles that are not currently performed are potential and therefore important. A mother who is a single parent is also potentially a wife or lover. Her neglect of these potential roles may impoverish her life and cause her to smother her children. When members of unhappy families become bogged down in few and rigid roles, they develop interpersonal arthritis, a disease that leads to family rigidity and the atrophy of unused life.

Sherif (1948) and others have shown that multiple roles, required to belong to various groups, can create problems. Dutifully doing what you are told and patiently waiting for recognition and reward may work when you are in the role of son or daughter, but these attitudes do not work for a lover or an employee, where more outgoing and assertive action is called for.

Roles tend to be stereotyped in most groups and so there are characteristic behavior patterns of group members. Bales (1950) described twelve broad categories of group behavior, including: "shows solidarity" (raises others' status, gives help); "shows tension-release" (jokes, laughs); "agrees" (passive-accepting compliance); "gives suggestions"; and "asks for suggestions." Similar role patterns also characterize family members, most of whom learn roles in the family that become more or less fixed. Sometimes these roles are transferred to extrafamilial relationships where they are generally less appropriate. Virginia Satir (1972) described family roles, such as the placator or the disagreeable one, in her book *Peoplemaking*. If you think about it, you may be able to recognize that you played a fairly regular role in your family while you were growing up. Perhaps you were "the good boy," "mother's helper," "the quiet one," "the family joker," "the counselor," "the thinker," or "the successful one." The trouble is that a role once learned is hard to put aside. The result is often a limited range of behavior in which we continue to do what's come to be expected of us. You may have noticed that even such simple changes as growing a beard, losing weight, or changing hairstyles discomfits some people—they just aren't comfortable adapting their expectations to your change.

The encounter group movement, which had such enormous clinical and social consequences, was a direct offshoot of studies of group dynamics. T-groups, forerunners of encounter groups, were begun in 1946 by Kurt Lewin and his colleagues Leland Bradford, Kenneth Benne, and Ronald Lippit (Benne, 1964). These groups were begun as a means of using participant observation to study small group dynamics. The aim gradually shifted from simply understanding group behavior to helping members clarify their goals and learn methods by which to realize these goals in group interactions. These modest aims proved very successful in increasing effectiveness and satisfaction; as a result, T-groups evolved into encounter groups, the main purposes of which were personal growth and enrichment. Influential as the encounter group movement has been (Nichols and Zax, 1977), it came too late to have any impact on the early history of family therapy. However, the experiential school of family therapy has been influenced by the encounter group movement, as we shall explain in Chapter 6.

Group therapy has also had a definite influence on the course of family therapy. The man credited with beginning group therapy in this country was not a psychiatrist but an internist, Joseph Hershey Pratt, who in July 1905 assembled a group of tubercular patients for encouragement and supervision. Subsequently, two psychiatrists, L. Cody Marsh and Edward Lazell, met with groups of hospitalized psychiatric patients for didactic discussions and mutual support (Kaplan and Sadock, 1983). Group treatment remained largely an inspirational, persuasive, and supportive technique until the psychoanalytic conceptual framework was applied by Trigant Burrows, Louis Wender, and Paul Schilder (Nichols and Zax, 1977). Their new approach, which incorporated the dynamics of small groups with the dynamics of personality structure, was consolidated into a coherent theory and technique by Samuel Slavson (1943), who was also a founder of the American Group Psychotherapy Association in 1948.

These analytic group leaders regarded the group as a re-creation of the family, with the therapist as an object of transference and other group members as sibling figures. Thus, ironically, analytic group therapy, which later became one of the prototypes for family treatment, began by treating the group as an ersatz family. Analytic groups were designed to be frustratingly unstructured, in order to arouse latent unconscious conflicts and revive problems from the original family group. Group members' basic motives were considered to be dynamic equilibria between love and hate, pain and pleasure, and strictures of the superego versus demands of primitive impulses. The developing ego was seen as the basic coping mechanism, and the growth and dissolution of psychological defenses the battleground on which these forces met. Notice that the emphasis was on the individual, rather than the group as a whole.

In the group dynamics approach, developed by Foulkes, Bion, Ezriel, and Anthony in Great Britain, the focus shifted from individuals to the group itself, seen as a transcendent entity with its own inherent laws. These therapists studied group interaction not only for what it revealed about individual personalities but also to discover overall themes or dynamics common to all patients. This *group process* was considered a fundamental characteristic of social interaction and a major vehicle for change.

Another clear departure from psychoanalytic group therapy was the existential or experiential model. Experiential group therapy, stimulated by existential psychiatrists Ludwig Binswanger, Medard Boss, and Rollo May in Europe and by Carl Rogers, Carl Whitaker, and Thomas Malone in the United States, emphasized deep personal involvement with patients as opposed to dissection of people as objects. Phenomenology took the place of objective analysis, and immediate experience, especially emotional experience, was seen as the royal road to personal growth. Instead of transference, experiential therapists emphasized the profoundly real aspects of the therapeutic relationship conceived as an authentic "I-thou" encounter.

Moreno's psychodrama, in which patients act out their conflicts instead of discussing them, was one of the earliest approaches to group treatment (Moreno, 1945). Psychodramas are dramatic enactments from the lives of participants, using a number of techniques to stimulate emotional expression and clarify conflicts. Because the focus is on interpersonal action, psychodrama is a direct and powerful means of exploring family relationships and resolving family problems. Although psychodrama has remained tangential to the mainstream of group therapy, Moreno's role-playing techniques have been widely adopted by group leaders and family therapists. Minuchin, for example, conducts family treatment as though he were a theatrical director, and insists that dramatic enactments are essential for capturing the real drama of family life. Family sculpting and choreography are even more direct applications of psychodrama.

Fritz Perls's Gestalt psychotherapy aims to enhance patients' awareness in order to increase spontaneity, creativity, and personal responsibility. Even though it is frequently used in groups, Gestalt therapy discourages other group members from interacting with the patient while he or she is working with the therapist. Although more widely used in individual than in group or family treatment, Gestalt techniques have been borrowed by encounter group leaders, such as William Shutz, to stimulate emotional interaction among group members. Family therapists have also adopted some Gestalt techniques (Kempler, 1974); these will be discussed in Chapter 6.

Like Gestalt therapy, behavior therapy is aimed at individuals even when practiced in group settings. Behavioral groups are usually made up of members who share a single habit disorder, such as social phobia. The meetings are conducted as practice sessions for trying out new forms of behavior. Assertive training groups are probably the most widespread and familiar form of behavioral group therapy.

Given all these extensive and diverse procedures for exploring interpersonal relationships developed by group therapists, it was natural that some family therapists would apply group treatment models to working with families. Family group therapy was an application of small group theory and group therapy technique to the natural group of the family. After all, what are families but collective groups with various subgroups? The first to apply group concepts to family treatment were John Elderkin Bell and Rudolph Dreikurs. Bell, whose work is well-known and influential among family therapists, first described family group therapy in 1955. Dreikurs, whose work is less well known, began publishing his ideas in the late forties and early fifties. Bell and Dreikurs's work will be considered at length in Chapter 4.

Before examining the question of how suitable the group treatment model is for family therapy, we must mention one more historical fact. Even before Bell and Dreikurs began to apply group psychotherapy to families, a number of workers had used the group format to enlist cooperation from family members in planning treatment for individual patients. Marsh, for instance, lectured to groups of relatives at Worcester State Hospital (Marsh, 1935); and Low also used this technique in his work (Low, 1943). Other therapists concentrated on group meetings with mothers whose children were in treatment (Amster, 1944; Burkin, Glatzer, and

Hirsch, 1944; Lowrey, 1944). Some, including Ross at McGill, held weekly discussion groups for families of adult patients (Ross, 1948). In all these group meetings relatives were treated like helpers who were not themselves in need of therapy. The "real" patients were not involved in the meetings, and the therapists who conducted the groups did not work with the patients. In this way the group sessions were kept separate from the patients' psychotherapy. This work was similar to the long tradition of group counseling with parents, especially in child welfare agencies (Grunwald and Casell, 1958), and is still the way most adolescent inpatient units try to involve families.

One step closer to family therapy is "family group counseling" (Freeman, Klein, Riehman, Lukoff, and Heisey, 1963). This is a sociological, problem-solving approach on the level of external interactions. Counselors facilitate communication but de-emphasize individual goals and change. Intrapsychic conflicts are avoided. Family counselors try to foster understanding at the social level of external reality by helping family members recognize and modify social role conflicts. They aim for change in the social functioning of the family unit, rather than in its individual members. Although changes in the social functioning of whole families can effect profound changes in individuals, Freeman and his colleagues did not try or claim to achieve anything more than superficial support. Refreshing modesty.

Family group counselors promote and guide communication in the group. They also help formulate goals and solve problems. By limiting the goals to those of whole families, rather than separate members, they seek to minimize individual strivings. A similar approach was reported by Knoblochova and Knobloch (1970), who developed and practiced what they called family therapy in Czechoslovakia from 1949 to 1953. They used a group-centered approach and conducted family meetings as a supplement to treatment of individual patients.

By the 1970s when family therapy had become thoroughly sophisticated and thoroughly systemic, these early group counseling approaches seemed naive, treating as they did individuals as the real patients and families only as playing a supporting role in patients' recovery. However, in the 1980s there was a growing recognition that some problems may, in fact, be primarily problems of individuals—or at least best treated that way. Carol Anderson and her colleagues at the University of Pittsburgh developed a program of *psychoeducation* for families with schizophrenics (Anderson, Reiss, and Hogarty, 1986). Consistent with mainstream psychiatry, this approach treats schizophrenia as a disease that can best be dealt with using medication, and counseling for families faced with the terrible ordeal of coping with a schizophrenic member. Alcohol and drug abuse is another area where many believe that treatment must be directed primarily at individuals and secondarily at families (Kaufman and Kaufmann, 1979; Steinglass, 1987). Where once family group counseling, which preserved the primacy of the individual patient, seemed naive, today treating schizophrenia or alcohol and drug abuse exclusively as byproducts of psychological stress now seem equally naive.

The psychoeducation approach was prefigured by the work of Kirby and Priestman (1957), who described a group that went on for fourteen months with six young schizophrenic women and their mothers at Brooklyn State Hospital. When the group began, the patients were quiet and withdrawn, while the mothers talked on and on about all they tried to do for their children. This behavior is typical in psychotic families. Gradually, however, the young patients overcame their submissiveness and began to speak up to their mothers, using words instead of symptoms. Encouraged by the support of the therapists and other patients with similar concerns, the daughters became able to voice their own feelings and complaints. Eventually another significant shift also took place—the mothers gave up their defensive preoccupation with their daughters' problems and began to discuss their own needs. This shift from the usual scapegoating pattern greatly benefitted the daughters. Even though this group closely approximated conjoint family therapy, its focus still remained on individual expression. The daughters were encouraged to speak up, but the therapists neither sought nor sustained interaction; and though the mothers finally spoke about their own problems, no attempt was made to resolve their marital problems, nor were their husbands ever invited to be present.

All these approaches to group treatment were available to family therapy. Some of the techniques were useful, some not. It was a short step, for instance, from observing a patient's reactions to others in a group— some of whom may be similar to siblings, parents, or other children—to observing interactions with real, rather than transference, families.

Furthermore, from a technical point of view, group and family therapies are similar. Both involve several people. Both are more complex and amorphous, more like everyday social reality, than individual therapy. In groups and families each patient must react to a number of people, not just the therapist, and therapeutic use of this interaction is a definitive mechanism of change in both settings. Consequently, many group and family therapists endeavor to remain relatively inactive and decentralized so that patients in the room will relate to each other.

In individual treatment the therapist is a safe but somewhat artificial confidant. Patients expect their therapists to be understanding and accepting, an audience of one friendly person. It is not so with groups and families. In both, the situation is more naturalistic, more threatening perhaps, but also more like everyday experience. Transfer to life outside the consulting room is therefore more direct.

On closer examination, however, we can see that the differences between families and groups of strangers are so many and so significant that group therapy only has limited application for family treatment. Families are different from therapy groups: Family members have a long history and, more important, a future together. Groups are comprised of strangers, families of intimates. Revealing yourself to strangers is easier and safer than exposing yourself to members of the family. In fact great harm can be done to patients by therapists who are so naive as to push family members always to be "completely honest and open" with each other. Once blurted out, there's no taking back thoughts that, perhaps, better remain private—the affair, long since over, or the revelation that a woman cares more about her career than her children. Continuity, commitment, and shared distortions all mean that treatment for families has to differ from therapy for groups.

In one of the few small group studies using families, Strodtbeck (1954) tested a variety of propositions derived from groups of strangers and found major differences, which he ascribed to the enduring relationship of family members. Strodtbeck (1958) later substantiated the opinion that family interactions, unlike those in ad hoc groups, can only be understood in terms of the history of the family group.

Group therapy is predicated on a few basic conditions inherent in the structure of the group (Yalom, 1985). Some of the differences between family structure and that of groups are trivial, others are significant enough to make group therapy techniques inappropriate for families. Therapy groups are designed to provide an atmosphere of warmth and support. By being with others, patients feel less alone. They may have felt isolated before, but now they see the group as a place where they are to be helped and where they can help others. This feeling of safety among sympathetic strangers cannot be part of family therapy, for instead of separating treatment from a stressful environment, the stressful environment, itself, is brought into treatment. Furthermore in group therapy all patients can have equal power and status, but this is not appropriate in families. The official patient in the family, for instance, is likely to remain isolated, and to feel unique and stigmatized. After all, he or she is "the problem." The sense of protection felt in being part of a therapeutic group made up of strangers, who will not have to be faced tomorrow, cannot be part of family therapy, where it isn't always safe to speak openly because no therapist will be there to protect you from retaliation on the ride home.

Another basic therapeutic mechanism of groups is that they stimulate typical patterns of social interaction which then can be analyzed and changed. This function of groups has been likened to a "laboratory for social change" or a "social microcosm" (Nichols and Zax, 1977). Families, however, are less flexible and open to experimentation. They have a complex shared mythology that dictates certain roles and ways of behaving. These highly developed and patterned communications make families far less able to experiment with new social responses.

Family therapy is a less productive context for testing social reality than group therapy. Groups are specifically designed to provide opportunities for reality testing in a relatively nonthreatening atmosphere (Handlon and Parloff, 1962) so that distorted perceptions may be corrected and new ways of behaving tried out. But families share distortions of reality which must be maintained for the sake of family equilibrium. Individual members are thus less able to re-examine their perceptions than they are when they receive feedback from observers who have different points of view.

Therapy groups also provide therapeutically useful opportunities for members to display transference distortions through the variety of the group members (Handlon and Parloff, 1962). The family therapy situation is different; the real figures are actually present. Transference still occurs, but it is less amenable to exploration and correction. Parents may see their adolescent children in ways that fit the past better than the present. Children may see their parents accurately but transfer these perceptions on to the therapists. Therapists are generally hamstrung by powerful countertransference reactions when dealing with families. Furthermore, transference distortions are often supported by family mythology. "Daddy is such a monster!" is a myth that pervades the thinking of some mother-child coalitions—that he isn't is a myth in others. Such distortions and misperceptions are certainly available as grist for the therapeutic mill, but they are more difficult to deal with in families.

Although group therapy was used as a model for family therapy by some early practitioners, only the process/content distinction and role theory had any lasting impact on the mainstream of family therapy. One application of group methods that has persisted in family therapy are couples groups, and we shall examine this form of treatment in Chapters 4 and 5.

THE CHILD GUIDANCE MOVEMENT

Early in this century major social reforms and changes in the legal status of children led to universal compulsory education, attempts to control juvenile delinquency, restrictions on child labor, and a greater respect for children's rights. This new concern for children also extended to emotionally disturbed children and thus led to the child guidance movement.

The child guidance movement was founded on the belief that since emotional disorders begin in childhood, treating problems of children is the best way to prevent mental illness in the population. It was Freud who introduced the idea that psychological disorders of adulthood were the consequence of unsolved problems of childhood. Among his followers, Adler was the principal one to pursue the implication that treating the growing child might be the most effective way to prevent adult neuroses from developing. To this end Adler organized child guidance clinics in Vienna where not only children but also families and teachers were counseled. Adler's approach was to offer encouragement and support in an atmosphere of optimism and confidence. His technique helped to alleviate the child's feeling of *inferiority* so that he or she could work out a healthy *life-style*, directed toward achieving competence and success through *social usefulness*. Adler's methods are still practiced in child guidance clinics in Europe and America.

By 1909 the psychiatrist William Healy had founded the Juvenile Psychopathic Institute in Chicago, a forerunner among child guidance clinics (now known as the Institute of Juvenile Research). By 1917 Healy had moved to Boston and established the Judge Baker Guidance Center, devoted to diagnostic evaluation and treatment of delinquent children.

When the child guidance movement in the United States expanded in the 1920s, under a grant from the Commonwealth Fund (Ginsburg, 1955), Rudolph Dreikurs, one of Adler's students, was one of its most effective proponents. In 1924 the American Orthopsychiatric Association was organized to work toward the prevention of emotional disorders in children. Although they remained few in number until after World War II, child guidance clinics now exist in every city in the United States. American child guidance clinics provided a setting for the study and treatment of childhood psychological problems and of the complex social and family forces contributing to these problems. Treatment was carried out by psychiatrist-psychologist-social worker teams, who focused much of their attention on the child's family environment.

Gradually child guidance workers concluded that the real problem was not the obvious one brought to the clinic, the child's symptoms, but the tensions in the family that were their source. At first there was a tendency to blame the parents, especially the mother, for the child's problems. Mothers were viewed as enemies to be vanquished and fathers were generally ignored (Burgum, 1942). The usual arrangement was for a psychiatrist to treat the child and a social worker to see the mother. Treatment of the mother was secondary to the primary goal of treating the child. The major purposes for seeing the mother were to reduce emotional pressure and anxiety, redirect hostility away from the child, and modify childrearing attitudes. In this model the family was viewed as an extension of the child, rather than the other way around.

Although the importance of the family's influence was recognized, mothers and children were treated as separate individuals. They were not seen together, and discussion between therapists was discouraged on the grounds that it might impair the privacy of the separate therapeutic relationships. Under the reigning influence of psychoanalysis, there was a tremendous emphasis on the individual psyche, with its unconscious conflicts and irrational motivations. Attempts to apply a social approach to disturbances in family life were dismissed as "superficial"—the ultimate indictment from psychoanalytic clinicians.

In this climate much was learned about individual childhood development, but clinicians often lost sight of the interpersonal context. It was assumed that resolution of the child's problems would also resolve family problems. Occasionally this happened, but more often it did not. Neurotic problems in individuals are only one problem in relationships, the others are interactional. Unfortunately, individual therapy may cause patients to increase their preoccupation with themselves, exclusive of others in the family. After analysis the patient may be wiser, but sadder—and lonelier.

Researchers in child guidance clinics tended to focus on parental psychopathology throughout the 1940s and 1950s. David Levy (1943) was among the first to establish a relationship between pathogenic traits in parents and psychiatric disturbances in their offspring. The chief cause of childhood psychological problems, according to Levy, was *maternal overprotectiveness*. Mothers who themselves had been deprived of love while growing up became overprotective of their children. Some did so in a domineering manner, others were overly indulgent. Children with domineeringly overprotective mothers were submissive at home but had difficulty making friends; children with indulgent mothers were disobedient at home but well behaved at school.

During this period Frieda Fromm-Reichmann (1948) introduced her famous concept of the *schizophrenogenic mother*, a domineering, aggressive, rejecting, and insecure mother. Such women, especially when they were married to inadequate, passive, and indifferent men, were thought to provide the pathological parenting that produces schizophrenia. Adelaide Johnson's description of the transmission of *superego lacunae* was another example of how parents were blamed for causing their children's problems (Johnson and Szurek, 1954). According to Johnson, antisocial behavior in delinquents and psychopaths was due to defects in their superegos, passed on by their parents.

Eventually the emphasis in the child guidance movement shifted from seeing parents as noxious agents to the view that pathology was inherent in the relationships that developed among patients, parents, and significant others. This shift had profound consequences. No longer was psychopathology located within the individual; no longer were parents seen as villains, and patients as victims. Now the nature of the interaction was seen to be the problem, which resulted in a more optimistic prognosis and changed the very nature of treatment. The goal shifted from weaning patients from their families to clarifying the relationships between parents and patients in hopes of improving them. Instead of trying—in vain—to separate children from their families, child guidance workers began to help families support their children.

John Bowlby's work at the Tavistock Clinic exemplified the transition from an individual to a family approach. Bowlby (1949) was treating a child psychoanalytically and making very little progress. Feeling frustrated, he decided to see the child and his parents together for one session. During the first half of this two-hour session, child and parents took turns complaining, each blaming the other. During the second half of the session, Bowlby interpreted to each of them what he thought their contributions to the problem were. Eventually, through this process, all three members of the family developed some sympathy for the others' points of view.

Although he was intrigued by the possibilities of these conjoint interviews, Bowlby was still wedded to the one-to-one format, which he believed should precede and follow joint sessions. For Bowlby, family meetings were a useful catalyst but only as an adjunct to the *real* treatment— individual psychoanalytic therapy. Nevertheless by eliminating the strict separation of the child's treatment from the mother's treatment, and pioneering the use of conjoint family interviews, Bowlby began the transition from what had been individual therapy to what would become family therapy.

What Bowlby began as an experiment, Nathan Ackerman carried through—family therapy as the major form of treatment in child guidance clinics. As early as 1938 Ackerman went on record as suggesting the clinical utility of viewing the family as a single, whole entity when dealing with disturbance manifest in any of its members (Ackerman, 1938). Subsequently he (Ackerman and Sobel, 1950) recommended studying the family as a means of understanding the child—instead of the other way around. Once he saw the need to understand the family in order to diagnose problems, Ackerman soon took the next step—family treatment. Before we get to that, however, let us examine a parallel development in research on schizophrenia that led to the beginning of family therapy.

THE INFLUENCE OF SOCIAL WORK

No history of family therapy would be complete without mention of the enormous contribution of social workers and their tradition of social service. (We are indebted to Donald Bardhill and Benjamin Sanders [1988] for pointing out earlier omissions of this important contribution.) Since the beginning of the profession, social workers have been concerned with the family, both as the critical social unit and the focus of intervention (Ackerman, Beatman, and Sherman, 1961).

The profession of social work grew out of the charity movements in Great Britain and the United States in the late nineteenth century. Then, as now, social workers were dedicated to improving the condition of society's poor and underprivileged. In addition to ministering to basic needs for food, clothing, and shelter, social workers have also tried to relieve emotional distress in their client families and to address the social forces responsible for extremes of poverty and privilege.

The *friendly visitor* was a social worker who visited clients in their homes in order to assess their needs and offer help. By bringing helpers out of their offices and into the homes of the helped, these visits served to break down the artificiality of the doctor-patient model that prevailed for so long. Friendly visitors were directly involved in treating problems of troubled marriages and difficulties of childrearing. Workers at *settlement houses* offered social services, not only to individuals, but to family groups as well.

Family casework was probably the most important focus of early social work training. In fact the first course taught by the first school of social work in the United States was entitled "The Treatment of Needy Families in Their Own Homes" (Siporin, 1980). Friendly visitors were taught the importance of interviewing both parents at the same time to get a complete and accurate picture of a family's problems, this at a time when mothers were considered responsible for family life, and long before traditional mental health workers began experimenting with conjoint family sessions.

These turn of the century family caseworkers were well aware of something that it took psychiatry fifty more years to discover—that families must be considered as whole units. Thus, for example, Mary Richmond (1917) in her classic text *Social Diagnosis* prescribed treatment of "the whole family" and warned against isolating family members from their natural context. Richmond's concept of *family cohesion* also had a strikingly modern ring, anticipating, as it did, later work by role theories, group dynamics research, and, of course, structural family therapy. According to Richmond the degree of emotional bonding between family members was a critical determinant of their ability to survive and flourish.

Richmond also anticipated developments that family therapy became concerned with in the 1980s by viewing families as systems within systems. As Bardhill and Saunders pointed out (1988, p. 319),

> She recognized that families are not isolated wholes (closed systems), but exist in a particular social context, which interactively influences and is influenced by their functioning (i.e. they are open). She graphically depicted this situation using a set of concentric circles to represent various systemic levels from the individual to the cultural. Her approach to practice was to consider the potential effect of all interventions on every systemic level, and to understand and to use the reciprocal interaction of the systemic hierarchy for therapeutic purposes. She truly took a systemic view of human distress.

Ironically, social workers, who pioneered in treating the family as the unit of intervention, retreated to a more traditional individual-as-patient approach as they came under the sway of psychiatry in the 1920s. Social workers in the mental health wing of the profession were strongly influenced by the prevailing psychoanalytic model, which emphasized individuals, not families.

When the family therapy movement was launched, social workers were among the most numerous and most important contributors. Among the leaders of family therapy who are social workers have been: Virginia Satir, Ray Bardhill, Celia Mitchell, Peggy Papp, Lynn Hoffman, Harry Aponte, Betty Carter, Braulio Montalvo, and Monica McGoldrick. Incidentally, even starting such a list is difficult because unless it went on for pages it would have to omit a host of important names.

RESEARCH ON FAMILY DYNAMICS AND THE ETIOLOGY OF SCHIZOPHRENIA

Families with schizophrenic members proved to be an especially fertile area for research because their strange patterns of interaction were so dramatic and striking. Human nature is exaggerated under stress. However, as we shall see, the fact that family therapy emerged from research on schizophrenia led to an overly optimistic hope that family therapy might be the way to cure this baffling form of madness. Moreover, because abnormal families are so resistant to change, the early family therapists probably exaggerated the homeostatic properties of family life.

Family therapists did not discover the role of the family in schizophrenia, but, by actually observing families interacting, they witnessed patterns that their predecessors had only speculated about. Recognition of family influences on schizophrenia has existed at least since Freud's famous account (1911) of Dr. Schreber. In this first psychoanalytic formulation of psychosis, Freud discussed psychological factors in paranoia and schizophrenia, and also suggested how the patient's bizarre relationship with his father played a role in his fantastic delusions.

Harry Stack Sullivan focused on interpersonal relations in his brilliant work with schizophrenics. Beginning in 1927 he emphasized the importance of the "hospital family"—physicians, nurses, and aides—as a benevolent substitute for the patient's real family. Sullivan did not, however, take his ideas one step further and directly involve families in treatment. Frieda Fromm-Reichmann also believed that the family played a part in the dynamics of schizophrenia and considered the hospital family important to the resolution of schizophrenic episodes; however, she also failed to recommend family treatment. Although these interpersonal psychiatrists recognized the importance of family life in schizophrenia, they continued to treat the family as a pathogenic environment from which patients must be removed.

In the 1940s and 1950s research on the link between family life and the development of schizophrenia led to the pioneering work of the first family therapists.

Gregory Bateson—Palo Alto

One of the groups with the strongest claim to originating family therapy was Gregory Bateson's schizophrenia project in Palo Alto, California. There were actually two Palo Alto groups. The first was the "Project for the Study of Schizophrenia," under the direction of Gregory Bateson. Project members—Jay Haley and John Weakland, with Don Jackson and William Fry as principal consultants—were primarily interested in the study of communication, secondarily interested in families, and only tangentially interested in treatment. The other group was the Mental Research Institute, directed by Don Jackson, who was primarily interested in treating families. Bateson's project was thus mainly devoted to scientific study, and Jackson's group to the problems of treating families.

A scientist in the classic mold, Gregory Bateson did research on animal behavior, learning theory, evolution, and ecology, as well as in hospital psychiatry. He worked with Margaret Mead in Bali and New Guinea; then, becoming interested in cybernetics, he wrote *Naven*, and worked on synthesizing cybernetic ideas with anthropological data. He entered the psychiatric field when he worked with Jurgen Ruesch at the Langley Porter Clinic. Together they wrote *Communication: The Social Matrix of Psychiatry*. In 1962 Bateson shifted to studying communication among animals, and after 1963 worked at the Oceanographic Institute in Hawaii until his death in 1980.

The Palo Alto project began in the fall of 1952 when Bateson received a grant from the Rockefeller Foundation to study the general nature of communication in terms of its levels. All communications, Bateson had written (Bateson, 1951), have two different levels or functions—*report* and *command*. Each message has a stated content, as, for instance, "Wash your hands, it's time for dinner"; but, in addition, the message carries how it is to be taken. In this case the second message is that the speaker is in charge. This second message—*metacommunication*—is at a higher level and often goes unnoticed. Bateson's idea about levels of communication was derived from Bertrand Russell's *Theory of Logical Types* (Whitehead and Russell, 1910), which dealt with hierarchies in levels of abstraction, or logical types. Russell pointed out that a class cannot be a member of itself, nor can a member of the class be the class. That is, classes and members are of different logical types. For example, the class of chairs is not a chair, but neither is it some *thing* other than a chair; the class of chairs is a different level of abstraction. Another illustration is that the noun *university* is a higher-level, more abstract, or collective, noun than the separate buildings subsumed as members of the class "university." Bateson wanted to analyze a variety of phenomena using this insight.

Bateson was joined in early 1953 by Jay Haley and John Weakland. Haley was primarily interested in social and psychological analysis of fantasy; Weakland was a chemical engineer who had become interested in cultural anthropology. Later that same year, a psychiatrist, William Fry, joined them; his major interest was the study of humor. This group of eclectic talents and catholic interests began a number of different studies: otters at play, the training of guide dogs, the meaning and uses of humor, and the social and psychological significance of popular movies and the utterances of schizophrenic patients. Jay Haley (1976) has explained that Bateson gave the project members free rein, but although they investigated many kinds of complex human and animal behaviors, all their studies had to do with possible conflicts between messages and qualifying messages.

In 1954 Bateson received a two-year grant from the Macy Foundation to study schizophrenic communication. Shortly thereafter they were joined by Don Jackson, who served as a clinical consultant and supervisor of psychotherapy with schizophrenics.

The group's interests turned to developing a communication theory that might explain the origin and nature of schizophrenic behavior, particularly in the context of families. Worth noting, however, is that in the early days of the project none of them thought of actually observing schizophrenics and their families.

Bateson and his colleagues hypothesized that family stability is achieved by feedback that monitors the behavior of the family and its members. Whenever the family system is threatened—that is, disturbed—it moves toward balance or *homeostasis*. Thus, apparently puzzling behavior might become understandable if it were perceived as a homeostatic mechanism. For example, if whenever two parents argue one of the children exhibits symptomatic behavior, the symptoms may be a way to interrupt the fighting by uniting the parents in concern for the child. In this manner the symptomatic behavior serves the cybernetic function of preserving the family's equilibrium by keeping the parents from fighting. Unhappily, in the process, one of the family members may have to assume the role of "identified patient."

In addition to applying systems ideas to explain the overall nature and purpose of family interaction, the group used communications theory to analyze specific sequences of family interaction. Even animals, Bateson had observed (1951), metacommunicate. Notice, for example, how two dogs or cats or monkeys play-fight. One leaps at the other, they tussle, they nip each other, but neither fights seriously and inflicts damage. How do they know they're playing? Clearly they must have some way of metacommunicating, of indicating that the attack is only playful. Humans achieve considerable complexity in framing and labeling messages and meaningful actions. Typically the qualifying metamessages are conveyed through nonverbal signals, including gesture, tone, posture, facial expression, and intonation. "I hate you," may be said with a grin, with tears, or with a fixed stare and clenched teeth. In each case the metacommunication alters the message.

Hypothesizing that schizophrenia may be a result of family interaction, Bateson's group wanted to identify sequences of experience that might induce such symptomatology. They were not interested in traumatic childhoods, but in characteristic family patterns of communication. Their basic premise was at this time simply conjecture; only later was it supported by observation (Bateson, Jackson, Haley, and Weakland, 1963). Once they agreed that schizophrenic communication had to be a product of what was learned inside the family, the group looked for the kind of circumstances that could lead to such confused and confusing patterns of speech. In 1956 they published a preliminary report on their findings, "Toward a Theory of Schizophrenia," in which Bateson, Jackson, Haley, and Weakland (Fry was off doing military service) introduced the concept of the *double-bind*.

They assumed that psychotic behavior might not be the result of a collapse ("breakdown") of one's ability to deal with reality, but may stem from having to learn how to cope with a reality of disturbed communication. Consider someone who has an important relationship where escape is not feasible and response is important; when he or she receives two related but contradictory messages on different levels, but finds it difficult to detect or comment on the inconsistency or leave the relationship (Bateson, Jackson, Haley, and Weakland, 1956), that person is in a double-bind.

Because this difficult concept is often misused as a synonym for paradox or simply contradictory messages, it is worthwhile to review each feature of the double-bind as the authors listed them. The double-bind has six characteristics:

1. Two or more persons are involved in an important relationship;

2. The relationship is ongoing;

3. A primary negative injunction is given, such as "Do not do X or I will punish you," or "If you don't do X, I will punish you";

4. A second injunction is given that conflicts with the first, but at a more abstract level; this injunction is also enforced by punishment or perceived threat. The second injunction is often nonverbal and frequently involves one parent negating the injunction of the other;

5. A tertiary negative injunction prohibits escape from the field, and demands a response. Without this crucial factor the "victim" will not feel bound and therefore there will be no bind;

6. Finally, once the victim is conditioned to perceive the world in terms of a double-bind, the necessity for every injunction to be present disappears, and almost any part is enough to precipitate panic or rage.

Most of the examples of double-binds in the literature are inadequate because they don't include all the critical features of the definition. Skynner, for instance, cites (1976): "Boys must stand up for themselves and not be sissies"; but "Don't be rough . . . don't be rude to your mother." These two messages are confusing and may cause conflict, but they hardly constitute a double-bind; they are merely a contradiction. Faced with those two statements, a child is free to obey either one, to alternate, or even to complain that there is a contradiction. This and many similar examples neglect the specification that the two messages exist on different levels of communication. A better example is the one given in the original article by Bateson, Jackson, Haley, and Weakland (1956). A young man, recovering in the hospital from a schizophrenic episode, was visited by his mother. When he put his arm around her, she stiffened. But when he withdrew, she asked, "Don't you love me anymore?" He blushed, and she said, "Dear, you must not be so easily embarrassed and afraid of your feelings." Following this exchange, the patient became upset; after the visit with his mother was over he assaulted an aide and had to be put into seclusion. Notice that all the features of the double-bind were present in this conversation and also that the young man was obviously caught. There is no bind if the subject is not bound. The concept is interactional.

Furthermore we may say that this mother was made anxious by intimacy with her son, but couldn't accept her feelings; consequently she behaved overtly as a loving mother who always does the right thing. Typically in such a family, there is no one else, such as a strong and insightful father, who can intervene and support the child. The mother tries to control her anxiety by controlling the closeness between herself and her child. But because she can't admit her anxiety, even to herself, she has to hide important aspects of her communication, that is, her own anxiety or hostility. In addition she forbids comments about her messages. Hence the child grows up unskilled in the ability to communicate about communication, unskilled in determining what people really mean, and unskilled in the ability to relate. Although it sounds esoteric, people need to metacommunicate in order to get along. It is often necessary to ask such questions as "What do you mean?" or "Are you serious?" In the double-binding family, however, such questions are not possible; comment and questioning are threatening to the parents, and the contradictory injunctions are obscure, occurring on different levels of communication.

We're all caught in occasional double-binds, but the schizophrenic has to deal with them continually—and the effect is maddening. Unable to comment on the dilemma, the schizophrenic must respond defensively, perhaps by being concrete and literal, perhaps by speaking in disguised answers or in metaphors. Eventually the schizophrenic, like the paranoid, may come to assume that behind every statement is a concealed and hidden meaning; alternatively, he or she may gradually withdraw from the external world and grow progressively detached.

This 1956 double-bind paper has proved to be one of the most influential and controversial in the history of family therapy.

Members of the Bateson group continued to clarify the concept of double-bind and tried to document its occurrence in schizophrenic families. Other researchers created laboratory analogues of the double-bind so they might test its effects under controlled conditions. Among the laboratory situations designed to imitate the double-bind have been studies on: inconsistent reward and censure (Ciotola, 1961); nonzero sum games, such as the prisoner's dilemma (Potash, 1965); the shifts and evasions that occurred when mothers of schizophrenics were asked about their feelings (Beavers, Blumberg, Tinken, and Weiner, 1965); schizophrenics rating the frequency with which their mothers had used a list of double-binding verbal-nonverbal contradictions (Berger, 1965); double-binds in written communications (Ringuette and Kennedy, 1966); incongruent instructions for a task (Sojit, 1969); impossible tasks with helpers who wouldn't help (Kingsley, 1969); tasks in which anxiety was generated but denied (Schreiber, 1970), written tests of parent-to-child messages (Phillips, 1970); channel-discrepant messages and paradoxical injunctions (Guindon, 1971); training schizophrenics and neurotics to recognize double-binds (Schaeffer, 1972); punishment and contradictory material (Smith, 1972); and paradoxical alternatives in a testing situation (Ables, 1975). All of these efforts were confident attempts to bring laboratory precision to the evaluation of a highly complex construct, but most of these researchers failed to document the destructive effects of the double-bind.

The problem with these double-bind studies was that they all failed to include one or more of the essential ingredients. A genuinely crucial relationship such as child/parent or patient/therapist must be involved; otherwise the victim can simply ignore the situation and walk away from the relationship. Laboratory experiments rarely involve anything like a critical relationship. In fact, the atmosphere tends to be one of gamesmanship and skepticism. And even if all the essential conditions seem to be met, what is being studied is merely a potential bind, because a bind is not a bind unless it binds. Some studies present contradictions between verbal and nonverbal messages, paradigms of the double-bind, but this situation, too, is an inadequate substitute, since the levels in a true double-bind are, by definition, different *logical* levels, not simply different ways to communicate. In the final analysis it appears that the essential features of the double-bind have eluded operationalism.

Those who studied the double-bind tended to look for evidence that it does or does not cause schizophrenia. But this approach is based on linear causality—A's response causes B's response. A more appropriate approach is to use the systems idea of *circular causality* and ask what's going on in schizophrenic families—A's response, then B's response, then A's response. It's more useful to think of the double-bind as a pattern of relationships than as a discrete event, and we concur with those reviewers (Ables, 1976) who have suggested that a natural-history approach (observing without attempting to control) may be the most fruitful means of understanding the phenomenon.

The double-bind theory undeniably offered us an enormously productive way to look at schizophrenia. Since its introduction the concept has been extended to humor, creativity, poetry, fiction, delinquency, hypnosis, religion, art, and psychotherapy—that is, to both creative and productive behavior as well as to pathological—on the basis of the response of the person who is the victim. There are four possible ways to respond to double-binds or, indeed, to disqualifying messages of any kind: comment; withdrawal from the relationship; acceptance; or counterdisqualification (Sluzki, Beavin, Tarnopolsky, and Veron, 1967). The first two avoid or offset the double-bind, and if these responses are able to circumvent the bind, they may lead to creativity (Bateson, 1978). The reason for this is that an adaptive solution to a double-bind involves stepping out of the frame, recognizing the different logical types. The ability to step back like this is a creative act, based on the rare capacity to take an objective view of one's own context. Although the double-bind was originally described as dependent on the motivation of one person (the mother's need to mask her anxiety or hostility), a comprehensive description would involve interaction with the other person's motivation. To describe interchanges between two people, one must postulate functions (motives, intentions, behavior) that involve both of them.

Bateson's original paper focused on a two-person interaction, essentially between mother and child. Father was described only in a negative way, as being unable to help the child resist being caught in the bind. Family analyses limited to two persons, although frequent (notably among child behavior therapists and couples therapists), are inadequate. A mother's relationship with her child is shaped by her relationship with her husband and, in turn, reshapes that relationship. So, too, a therapist's relationship with a patient is mutually defined by and defines the therapist's relationship with supervisors and administrators. In 1960 Weakland attempted to extend the double-bind from two- to three-person interactions (Weakland, 1960) and discussed the fact that three people are involved in the double-bind, even though one may not be immediately apparent. However, in general, the Bateson group was more concerned with broad applications than with the intricacies of three-person systems. Thus they suggested that the double-bind concept may be useful for analyzing three-person systems in the family, clinic, business world, government, and organized religion, but they dealt with the father's effect on the mother-child dyad in a fairly superficial fashion. Indeed, the Bateson group, as well as their communications therapy and strategic therapy offspring, have persistently failed to deal effectively with three-person systems. In a similar way, although they espoused open systems concepts, their analyses have always tended to be limited to closed systems.

The Bateson group did not stop with their work on double-binds. In 1956 members of the project began seeing parents jointly with their schizophrenic offspring. These meetings were held to observe and explore rather than to treat, but they were nonetheless an attempt to study actual behavior rather than speculate about it. Live observation of families was so revealing that it could be considered the beginning of the family therapy movement.

After 1956 the project went in several directions at once. The group continued to observe and try to understand double-binds and, at the same time, to compile descriptions of communication and families. Haley began making regular visits to Phoenix to consult with Milton Erickson about the nature of hypnosis (Haley, 1976). Haley was fascinated by issues of power and control, and he considered the struggle for control between people as the relationship context—that is, the motive—for double-binding. His ideas on this subject will be developed below.

In 1959 the group received one grant from the National Institute of Mental Health for a family therapy project and another from the Foundations Fund for Research in Psychiatry for a series of experimental studies on family dynamics. A good deal of this work was done by Haley who, as a result, became skeptical about the possibility of doing meaningful controlled research with families.

In 1959 Don Jackson also founded the Mental Research Institute (MRI) and invited Virginia Satir to join him. Although the Bateson group and MRI staff shared the same building in downtown Palo Alto for a while, there was never any formal connection between them (Haley, 1976). Bateson, always more interested in theory than treatment, wrote: "As regards psychotherapy, all I would claim as a contribution from double-bind theory is greater insight; and I do not mean insight for the patient which some practitioners think useless or harmful. I mean that the theory gives the therapist who works with schizophrenics or with families more insight into his patients and perhaps more insight into his own actions—if that be desirable" (Bateson, 1978, p. 42). Although clinical work was never a major goal for the project, Bateson, Haley, and Weakland did do psychotherapy with families; so, naturally, did the psychiatrists of the group, Jackson and Fry.

All the diverse efforts of the Bateson group were united on one point, the importance of communication on the organization of families; but within this point of view there was also considerable disagreement. Bateson, for example, was most interested in pursuing the double-bind, while others were more interested in the varying patterns of communication in different types of families. Therapists have also been attracted to the appealing notion that different kinds of symptoms might be linked to different kinds of families. Thus, in the 1950s, there was great interest in the characteristics of psychotic families; in the 1960s, families of delinquent boys; in the 1970s, psychosomatic families. The hunt for family types is linked to the linear idea that families *cause* symptomatic behavior in their members, rather than the circular idea that family patterns and symptoms are circular, each one affecting the other.

Members of the project also disagreed about what constitutes the central motivating forces of families. Haley thought it was control; Bateson and Weakland thought it was concealment of unacceptable feelings. They all agreed that to understand families they had to use systems theory to identify the patterns of rules and stability; they also agreed that to understand interaction, they had to identify levels of messages, rules, and governing processes. All believed that schizophrenic behavior was, in some way, adaptive to the family context and that family members respond in error-activated ways to each other and so govern each other's behavior. However, given the diversity of talents and interests, it was not surprising that the output of this group was more a collection of ideas than a homogenous theoretical presentation. Some of their ideas are summarized in *Pragmatics of Human Communication* (Watzlawick, Beavin, and Jackson, 1967), but to get any clear idea of the full scope of their work it is necessary to examine their papers individually. In 1962 the group disbanded.

Theodore Lidz—Yale

Theodore Lidz's investigations of the family dynamics of schizophrenia were grounded in psychoanalytic theory, and he sought the roots of schizophrenia in family object relationships. Much of his work focused on two traditional psychoanalytical concerns: rigid roles of family members and the effects of faulty parental models on identification and incorporation.

When Lidz began his studies of the families of schizophrenics in 1941, while he was completing his residency at Johns Hopkins, he and his colleagues surveyed the gross features of the family environment in which schizophrenics were reared. This original study, published in 1949 (Lidz and Lidz, 1949), surveyed fifty case histories. They exhibited a prevalence of broken homes and seriously disturbed family relationships. Forty percent of the young schizophrenic patients in the sample had been deprived of at least one parent by death, divorce, or separation; 61 percent of the families exhibited serious marital strife; 48 percent of the families contained at least one extremely unstable parent (psychotic, seriously neurotic, or psychopathic); and 41 percent of the families exhibited bizarre or unusual patterns of childrearing. In all, only five of fifty randomly selected schizophrenic patients appeared to have come from stable homes, raised by two well-adjusted and compatible parents. Lidz challenged the then current belief that maternal rejection is a major distinguishing feature of schizophrenic families, and in one of his most notable findings, observed that the father's influence was frequently more destructive than the mother's.

Lidz followed up this initial exploration with an extensive longitudinal study of a group of sixteen families containing a schizophrenic member. These intensive studies on a relatively small number of cases over the course of several years yielded an intimate glimpse of the environment in which young schizophrenics grew up. The primary method of study was to interview repeatedly all available family members over periods ranging from six months to several years. Additional information was gleaned from observing the interaction between families and hospital staff. Finally, projective testing was done with all members of the families. Since each of the patients in the sample had been hospitalized at the Yale Psychiatric Institute, a private hospital, they were all from middle- and upper-class families. Thus there was a bias in the sample toward a relatively high socioeconomic status, which meant there was a greater likelihood that the families were intact and better integrated than typical schizophrenic families. In the face of this bias toward better functioning, the consistent observation of severe family disruption and psychopathology is all the more striking.

Findings were categorized by parent-child relationships, marital interaction and its influence on the child, the dynamics of the family as a small group, the manner in which the family fosters ego integration, and the nature of family communication. And although Lidz was firmly rooted in the traditional psychoanalytic way of thinking about families, and many of his concepts focused on individuals and their roles, some of his observations went beyond one- and two-person systems and ideas about identification and incorporation to include consideration of three-person systems and the whole family as a unit. Thus Lidz bridged older theories about the impact of individual parents' personalities on their children and the more modern interest in families as systems.

Lidz believed that the major psychodynamic explanations of schizophrenia were too narrow. He rejected Freud's idea that schizophrenia was due to fixation at an early oral level and subsequent regression in the face of stress during young adulthood. Lidz did not find overt rejection of their children by any of the mothers he studied; consequently he also rejected the idea propounded by Frieda Fromm-Reichmann and John Rosen that severe and unqualified rejection by mothers was a major cause of schizophrenia. Furthermore Lidz considered the entire period of maturation, not just infancy, and tried to correct the tradition of ignoring the role of fathers.

Early in his studies Lidz's attention was drawn to the fathers who were as frequently and severely disturbed as the mothers (Lidz, Parker, and Cornelison, 1956). In a landmark paper entitled "Intrafamilial Environment of the Schizophrenic Patient II: The Father" (Lidz, Cornelison,

Fleck, and Terry, 1957a), Lidz and his colleagues described five patterns of pathological fathering in families of schizophrenics.

The first group was domineering and rigidly authoritarian, constantly in severe conflict with their wives. Having failed to establish intimate relationships with their wives, they sought to win over their daughters, who thus abandoned their mothers as objects of identification and tried to follow their fathers' inconsistent, unrealistic demands.

The second group of fathers were hostile toward their children rather than toward their wives. These men rivaled their sons for the mother's attention and affection, and behaved like jealous siblings rather than parents. They strutted and bragged, belittling their sons' achievements and sabotaging their self-confidence.

The third group of fathers exhibited frankly paranoid grandiosity. They were aloof and physically distant. The sons of these men were too weak to be like their fathers, but they continued desperately to emulate the parent's bizarre characteristics.

The fourth group of fathers were failures in life and nonentities in their homes. Children in these families grew up as though fatherless. They could hardly look up to the pathetic figures who were treated with such disdain by their wives.

The fifth group of fathers were passive and submissive men who acted more like children than parents. They were pleasant, almost motherly, but offered weak models of identification. These submissive fathers failed to counterbalance the strong domineering influence of their wives. Lidz concluded that it may be better to grow up without a father than with one who is too aloof or too weak to serve as a healthy model for identification.

After elucidating some of the characteristics of the fathers in schizophrenic families, Lidz turned his attention to defects in the marital relationship. The theme underlying his findings was an absence of *role reciprocity*. The partners in these marriages did not function cooperatively as a unit. In a successful marriage it's necessary first to fill one's own role and then to support the role of the spouse. In these families the spouses were inadequate to fulfill their own roles and disinclined to support their mate's. Lidz followed Parsons and Bales in saying that the father's role is primarily *adaptive-instrumental* while the mother's is primarily *integrative-expressive*. If each parent fulfills a version of one of these roles, then they can fit together harmoniously. However, if fathers are unsuccessful at their instrumental tasks, or mothers reject expressive nurturing, difficulties will arise in their relationship.

(Notice how wedded to traditional sex roles the investigators' assumptions were: Fathers should be "masculine," not "motherly," and a good marriage is rigidly complementary—fathers were forceful and made their way in the world; women were soft and selfless; they stayed home, serving children, and the men.)

Lidz found highly disturbed parental relationships in all cases that he studied (Lidz, Cornelison, Fleck, and Terry, 1957b). In focusing on the failure to arrive at reciprocal, interrelating roles, Lidz identified two general types of marital discord. In the first, *marital schism*, there is a chronic failure of the spouses to accommodate to each other or to achieve role reciprocity. These husbands and wives chronically undercut each other's worth and compete aggressively and blatantly for their children's loyalty and affection. Their marriages are combat zones in which every member of the family is wounded and scarred. The second pattern, *marital skew*, involves serious psychopathology in one marital partner who dominates the other. Thus one parent becomes extremely dependent while the other appears to be a strong parent figure but is, in fact, a pathological bully. The weaker spouse, in Lidz's cases usually the father, goes along or even supports the pathological tendencies and distortions of the dominant one. In all these families, unhappy children are torn by conflicting loyalties and weighted down with the pressure to balance their parents' precarious marriages.

Lyman Wynne—NIMH

Lyman Wynne also examined the effects of communication and family roles on schizophrenia. What distinguishes his work is his focus on pathological thinking in the families of schizophrenics. He is also unique in being the only pioneer investigator of family dynamics and schizophrenia who has not given up this challenging field of study.

In 1952 Wynne joined the National Institute of Mental Health (NIMH), where he remained until the early seventies, serving as Murray Bowen's replacement as chief of the family research section. During his tenure at NIMH, Wynne also received training at the Washington Psychoanalytic Institute and was on the faculty of the Washington School of Psychiatry. From the fifties through the seventies Wynne published many research reports; he also trained several talented researcher-clinicians, including Shapiro, Beels, and Reiss. In 1972 Wynne left NIMH to become Professor and Chairman of the Department of Psychiatry in Rochester. He is still actively pursuing his research at Rochester, although he stepped down from the chair in 1978.

Wynne's study of families of schizophrenics began in 1954 when he started seeing the parents of his hospitalized patients in twice-weekly psychotherapy. He was fascinated by the chaos he observed in these families, and sought to make sense out of it by extending psychoanalytic concepts and role theory to the systems level. What struck Wynne most forcefully about disturbed families were the strangely unreal qualities of both positive and negative emotions within them, which he labeled *pseudomutuality* and *pseudohostility*, and the nature of the boundaries around them—*rubber fences*—apparently yielding, but actually impervious to outside influence (especially from therapists).

Pseudomutuality (Wynne, Ryckoff, Day, and Hirsch, 1958) is a facade of togetherness that masks conflict and blocks intimacy. Such families have an unnatural dread of separateness. They are preoccupied with fitting together so closely that there is no room for the differentiation of separate identities, and no room for recognition and appreciation of any divergence of self-interests. The family cannot tolerate either deeper, more honest relationships, or independence. This surface togetherness submerges deep affectionate and sexual feelings, and keeps both conflict and greater intimacy from emerging.

Pseudohostility is a different guise for a similar collusion to obscure *alignments* and *splits* (Wynne, 1961). Sequences of splits and alignments may be observed during family sessions; they are used to maintain a kind of dynamic equilibrium in which change in any part of the system, either an alignment or a split, reverberates to produce change in other parts of the system. A typical situation may be an alignment between one parent and the patient, with a split between the parents. But the truth of these coalitions is threatening and, therefore, often covered up.

Pseudohostility is a self-rescuing operation. Although noisy and intense, it signals only a superficial split. Like pseudomutuality, it blurs intimacy and affection as well as deeper hostility and, like pseudomutuality, pseudohostility distorts communication and impairs realistic perception and rational thinking about relationships.

In disturbed families various mechanisms are employed to quell any sign of separateness, either inside or outside the family. The *rubber fence* is an invisible barrier that stretches to permit essential extrafamilial involvement, such as going to school, but springs back tightly if the involvement goes too far. The family's rigid role structure persists, protected by the family's isolation. The most damaging feature of the rubber fence is that precisely those who most need outside contact to correct family distortions of reality are the ones who are allowed it least. Instead of being a subsystem of society (Parsons and Bales, 1955), the schizophrenic family becomes a complete society, with a rigid boundary and no openings.

In a context where togetherness is everything and no significant outside relationships are tolerated, recognition of personal differences may be impossible, short of the blatantly bizarre behavior seen in schizophrenic reactions. The person may thus finally achieve the status of separateness but is then labeled schizophrenic and extruded from the family; and like mud oozing back over the place where a rock has been removed from a swamp, the family's pseudomutuality is thereupon restored. In these terms, acute schizophrenia may be considered a desperate attempt at individuation which not only fails but also costs the person membership in the family.

If acute schizophrenia becomes chronic, the now defeated patient may later be reaccepted into the family.

Wynne also linked the new concept of *communication deviance* with the older notion of *thought disorder*. He saw communication as the vehicle for transmitting thought disorder, the defining characteristic of schizophrenia. Communication deviance is a more interactional concept than thought disorder and more readily observable than double-binds. By 1978 Wynne and his colleagues had studied over six-hundred families, and had gathered incontrovertible evidence that disordered styles of communication are a distinguishing feature of families with young adult schizophrenics. Similar disorders also appear in families of borderlines, neurotics, and normals, but they are progressively less severe (Singer, Wynne, and Toohey, 1978). This observation—that communication deviance is not confined solely to schizophrenic families, but exists on a continuum (greater deviance with more severe pathology)—is consistent with other studies that describe a "spectrum of schizophrenic disorders."

Role Theorists

Other researchers and clinicians used role theory to explain the deviant patterns in schizophrenic families. In 1934 Kasanin, Knight, and Sage described the parent-child relationships of schizophrenics and suggested that family relationships were an important and specific etiological factor of schizophrenia. In forty-five cases of schizophrenia, they found *maternal overprotection* in twenty-five and *maternal rejection* in two. Kasanin described a pair of identical twins discordant for schizophrenia and suggested that the differences in their relationships with family members were responsible for the differences in their fates (Kasanin, Knight, and Sage, 1934). David Levy (1943) found that *maternal overprotection* was much more frequently associated with schizophrenia than was *rejection*. While the mother's overprotection was generally more obvious, Levy also found many cases of paternal overprotection. Moreover, he observed that overprotection was not simply imposed by parents on their children; children in these families met their overprotecting parents more than halfway. Thus Levy introduced an interactional dimension to what had previously been regarded as another way that parents victimize their children.

In 1951 the Group for the Advancement of Psychiatry (GAP) decided that families had been neglected in the field of psychiatry. They therefore appointed a committee, chaired by John Spiegel, to review the field and report their findings. The committee not only went beyond the individual patient, but also beyond the influence of individual persons on individual patients to consider the total family. When they began to think at this level, they were impressed by the degree to which families are embedded in and shaped by culture and society. This illustrates the point that individual behavior can be seen as reflecting progressively wider social influences depending upon the focus of observation. Nevertheless Spiegel's committee decided that limiting their observations to the level of the family would provide data that was optimally comprehensive and pragmatic.

The GAP committee's report (Kluckhohn and Spiegel, 1954) emphasized roles as the primary structural components of families. They concluded that healthy families contained relatively few and stable roles, and that this pattern was essential to teach children a sense of status and identity. There were norms for every role, and children learned these norms by imitation and identification. Family roles do not exist independently from each other; each role is circumscribed by other, reciprocal roles. Role behavior on the part of two or more people involved in a reciprocal transaction defines and regulates their interchange. The committee explained roles as a function, not of external social influences, but also of inner needs and drives. Thus role theory served as a link between *intra*personal and *inter*personal structures.

Spiegel went on to Harvard Medical School in 1953 where he followed up his interests in role theory and family pathology. He observed that symptomatic children tend to be involved in their parents' conflicts; non-symptomatic children may also have parents in conflict, but these children do not get directly involved. Spiegel (1957) described his observations in psychoanalytic terms: The child identifies with the unconscious wishes of the parents and acts out their emotional conflict. The child's acting out serves as a defense for the parents, who are thereby able to avoid facing their own conflicts and each other.

R.D. Laing's analysis of family dynamics was often more polemical than scholarly, but his observations helped popularize the family's role in psychopathology. Laing (1965) borrowed Marx's concept of *mystification* (class exploitation) and applied it to the "politics of families." Mystification refers to the process of distorting children's experience by denying or relabeling it. One example of this is a parent telling a child who is feeling sad, "You must be tired" (*Go to bed and leave me alone*). Similarly, the idea that "good" children are always quiet breeds compliant, but lifeless, children.

According to Laing's analysis, labeling behavior as pathology, even "family pathology," tends to mystify it. The prime function of mystification is to maintain the status quo. Mystification contradicts perceptions and feelings—and, more ominously, reality. When parents continually mystify a child's experience, the child's existence becomes inauthentic. Because their feelings are not accepted, these children project a *false self*, while keeping the *real self* private. In mild instances this produces unassertiveness, but if the real self/false self split is carried to an extreme, the result is madness (Laing, 1960).

Murray Bowen at NIMH and Ivan Boszormenyi-Nagy at the Eastern Pennsylvania Psychiatric Institute also studied family dynamics and schizophrenia, but since they are better known for their clinical contributions, their work will be considered below.

MARRIAGE COUNSELING

The history of professional marriage counseling is a less well known contributory to family therapy because much of it took place outside of the mainstream of psychiatry. For many years there was no apparent need for a separate profession of marriage counselors. People with marital problems are likely to discuss them with their doctors, clergy, lawyers, and teachers before they seek out professional mental health workers. Some students in courses on marriage and the family stay after class to talk to their instructors about personal as well as academic problems, and many women discuss sexual problems in marriage with their gynecologists.

The first professional centers for marriage counseling were established in about 1930. Paul Popenoe opened the American Institute of Family Relations in Los Angeles and Abraham and Hannah Stone opened a similar clinic in New York City. A third center for marriage counseling was the Marriage Council of Philadelphia, begun in 1932 by Emily Hartshorne Mudd (Broderick and Schrader, 1981). Members of this new profession started meeting annually in 1942 and formed the American Association of Marriage Counselors in 1945 in order to share ideas, establish professional standards, and foster research.

In the 1940s the movement spread from the initial three centers to fifteen, located throughout the country. Between then and now the profession has evolved from an informal service-oriented group to an organized profession, with a code of ethics and several training centers (Nichols, 1979).

At the same time these developments were taking place there was a parallel trend among some psychoanalysts leading to conjoint marital therapy. Although the majority of psychoanalysts have always followed Freud's prohibition against contact with the patient's family, a few have broken the rules and experimented with concomitant and conjoint therapy for married partners.

The first report on the psychoanalysis of married couples was made by Clarence Oberndorf at the American Psychiatric Association's 1931 convention (Oberndorf, 1938). Oberndorf advanced the theory that married couples have interlocking neuroses and that they are best treated in concert. This view was to be the underlying point of agreement among those in the analytic community who became interested in couples. "Because of the continuous and intimate nature of marriage, every neurosis in a married person is strongly anchored in the marital relationship. It is a useful and at times indispensable therapeutic measure to concentrate the analytic discussions on the complementary patterns and, if necessary, to have both mates treated" (Mittleman, 1944, p. 491).

In 1948 Bela Mittleman of the New York Psychoanalytic Institute became the first to publish an account of concurrent marital therapy in the United States. Previously Rene LaForgue had reported in 1937 on his experience analyzing several members of the same family concurrently. Mittleman suggested that husbands and wives could be treated by the same analyst and that by seeing both it is possible to disentangle their irrational perceptions of each other from rational ones (Mittleman, 1948). This was truly a revolutionary point of view from an analyst: that the reality of object relationships may be at least as important as their intrapsychic representations. Nathan Ackerman (1954) agreed that the concomitant treatment of married partners was a good idea and also suggested that mothers and children could profitably be treated together.

Meanwhile in Great Britain, where object relations were the central concern of psychoanalysts, Henry Dicks and his associates at the Tavistock Clinic established a Family Psychiatric Unit. Here couples referred by the divorce courts were helped to reconcile their differences (Dicks, 1964). Subsequently the Balints affiliated their Family Discussion Bureau with the Tavistock, adding the prestige of that clinic to their marital casework agency and, indirectly, to the entire field of marriage counseling.

In 1956 Victor Eisenstein, Director of the New Jersey Neuropsychiatric Institute, published an edited volume entitled *Neurotic Interaction in Marriage*. In it were several articles describing the state of the art in marital therapy. Frances Beatman, Associate Executive Director of Jewish Family Services in New York, described a casework treatment approach to marital problems (Beatman, 1956); Lawrence Kubie wrote a psychoanalytic analysis of the dynamics of marriage (Kubie, 1956); Margaret Mahler described the effects of marital conflict on child development (Mahler, 1956); and Ashley Montague added a cultural perspective to the dynamic influences on marriage (Montague, 1956). In the same volume Mittleman (1956) wrote a more extensive description of his view on marital disorders and their treatment. He described a number of complementary marital patterns, including aggressive/submissive and detached/demanding. These odd matches are made, according to Mittleman, because courting couples distort each other's personalities through the eyes of their illusions; she sees his independence as strength, he sees her dependency as sexy and giving. Mittleman also pointed out that the couple's reactions to each other may be shaped by their relationships to their parents. Without insight, unconscious motivation may dominate marital behavior, leading to patterns of reactive neurotic circles. For treatment, Mittleman believed that 20 percent of the time one therapist could handle all members of the family but, in other cases, separate therapists may be better.

At about this time Jackson and Haley were also writing about marital therapy within the framework of communications analysis. As their ideas gained prominence among marital therapists, the field of marital therapy was absorbed into the larger family therapy movement.

FROM RESEARCH TO TREATMENT: THE PIONEERS OF FAMILY THERAPY

We have seen how family therapy was preceded by clinical and research developments in several areas, including hospital psychiatry, group dynamics, interpersonal psychiatry, the child guidance movement, research on schizophrenia, and marriage counseling. But who actually started family therapy? Although there are rival claims to this honor, the distinction should probably be shared by John Elderkin Bell, Don Jackson, Nathan Ackerman, and Murray Bowen. In addition to these originators of family therapy, Jay Haley, Virginia Satir, Carl Whitaker, Lyman Wynne, Ivan Boszormenyi-Nagy, James Framo, Gerald Zuk, Christian Midelfort, and Salvador Minuchin were also significant pioneers of family treatment. Of these, Don Jackson, Jay Haley, and Virginia Satir in Palo Alto, Murray Bowen in Washington, DC, and Nathan Ackerman in New York probably had the greatest influence on the first decade of the family therapy movement. Among the others, those with the most lasting influence on the field are Carl Whitaker (Chapter 6), Salvador Minuchin (Chapter 10), and John Bell (Chapter 4).

John Bell

John Elderkin Bell, a psychologist at Clark University in Worcester, Massachusetts, who began treating families in 1951, occupies a unique position in the history of family therapy. Although he may have been the first family therapist, he is mentioned only tangentially in two of the most important historical accounts of the movement (Guerin, 1976; Kaslow, 1980). The reason for this is that although he began seeing families in the 1950s, he did not publish his ideas until a decade later. Moreover, unlike the other parents of family therapy, he had few offspring. He did not establish an important clinical center, develop a training program, or train well-known students. Therefore, although he was a significant early figure, his influence on the first decade of family therapy was not great.

Bell's approach (Bell 1961, 1962) to treating families is based on group therapy. In "family group therapy," Bell relied primarily on stimulating an open discussion in order to help families solve their problems. Like a group therapist he intervenes to encourage silent participants to speak up, and he interprets the reasons for their defensiveness.

Bell believed that family group therapy goes through certain phases just as do groups of strangers. In his early work (Bell, 1961) he carefully structured treatment in a series of stages, each of which concentrated on a particular segment of the family. Later he became less directive and allowed families to evolve through a naturally unfolding sequence of stages. As they did so, he would tailor his interventions to the needs of the moment. For a more complete description of Bell's family group therapy, see Chapter 4.

Palo Alto

While conducting their landmark studies of family dynamics and schizophrenia, the Bateson group stumbled into family therapy. Once the group began to meet with schizophrenic families in 1954, hoping to better understand their patterns of communication through unobtrusive, naturalistic observation, project members found themselves drawn into helping roles by the pain of these families (Jackson and Weakland, 1961). While Bateson was the undisputed scientific leader of the group, Don Jackson and Jay Haley were most influential in developing family therapy.

Jackson's work offers a rare example of the development of psychotherapy following the development of a theory—and secondary to theory. As a therapist, Jackson rejected the intrapsychic role theory and psychoanalytic concepts he learned in training and focused instead on the dynamics of interchange between persons. Analysis of communication was always his tool for understanding and treatment. Like Bateson, Don Jackson believed that behavior and communication are synonymous.

Jackson's thinking about family therapy was first stimulated by encounters with patients' relatives in his private practice and by occasional visits to the homes of individual schizophrenic patients (Jackson and Weakland, 1961). Observing the impact of families on patients—and vice versa—was not new, but Jackson's conclusions were. Since Freud, the family was understood to be the critical force in shaping personality, for better or worse. But the family was dealt with by segregation, physical and emotional, like removing a sick person from a germ-ridden environment. Jackson began to see the possibility of treating patients in the family as an alternative to trying to eliminate the family's influence.

By 1954 Jackson had developed a rudimentary family interactional therapy, which he reported in a paper, "The Question of Family Homeostasis," delivered to the American Psychiatric Association convention in St. Louis. His main emphasis was still on the effect of patients' therapy on their families, rather than on the prospect of family treatment (Jackson, 1954). Borrowing ideas from biology and systems theory, Jackson described families as homeostatic units that maintain relative constancy of internal functioning.

Jackson's concept of *family homeostasis*—families as units that resist change—was to become the defining metaphor of family therapy's first three decades. This view underestimates how families evolve and change shape as they move through the life cycle, and how families undergo sudden change at times of disequilibrium. Looking back we can see that Jackson's emphasis on family homeostasis was partly a function of the families he studied and partly a function of his efforts to change them. Abnormal families highlight homeostasis because they are the ones most likely to resist change. And therapists who see families as pathological and who try to rescue "family scapegoats" by challenging the way the family operates are certainly likely to provoke resistance.

Although Jackson and his colleagues probably overemphasized the homeostatic nature of families, their theoretical papers became increasingly sophisticated. Consistency, they realized, does not necessarily mean rigidity. Instead, family homeostasis is a nonstatic dynamic state, an equilibrium within which the family may be at point A on Monday and point B on Tuesday. Families seek to maintain or restore the status quo; family members function as governors, and the family is said to act in error-activated ways (Haley, 1963). The result is not invariance, but stability in variance of behavior. A clinical illustration of homeostasis is to be found in families in which the symptomatic behavior of children serves to restore the status quo. Frequently, parental argument is followed by disturbed behavior from one of the children, after which the parents stop arguing and become concerned about the now "identified patient's" symptoms. (We'll take a closer look at some of the problems with the homeostasis concept in Chapters 2 and 3.)

In "Schizophrenic Symptoms and Family Interaction" (Jackson and Weakland, 1959) Jackson illustrated how patients' symptoms preserve stability in their families. In one case a young woman diagnosed as a catatonic schizophrenic had as her most pronounced symptom a profound indecisiveness. However, when she did behave decisively her parents fell apart. Mother became helpless and dependent; father became, literally, impotent. In one family meeting the parents failed to hear the patient when she made a simple decision. Only after listening to a taped replay of the session *three times* did the parents finally hear their daughter's statement. The patient's indecision was neither crazy nor senseless but protected the parents from facing their own difficulties. This case is one of the earliest published examples of how schizophrenic symptoms are meaningful in the family context. The paper also contains the shrewd observation that this patient's symptoms were often an exaggerated version of her parents' problems. The parents simply had established better social covers. In addition the case demonstrates how parents obscure and mystify feelings and conflicts. Jackson noted that often when the parents were asked to discuss their own thoughts and feelings, they quickly returned the focus to the patient, lest disagreements emerge.

In moving away from mentalistic inference to behavioral observation of communicational sequences among family members, Jackson found that he needed a new language of interaction. His basic assumption was that all people in continuing relationships develop patterns of interaction. This patterning he called "behavioral (or communicational) redundancy" (Jackson, 1965). The term *redundancy* not only captures an important feature of family behavior but also reflects Jackson's phenomenological stance. Traditional psychiatric terms like *projection*, *defense*, and *regression* imply far more about inner states of motivation than the simple descriptive language of early family therapists. Even when using concepts that imply prescription, Jackson remained committed to description. Thus his *rules hypothesis* was simply a means of summarizing the observation that within any committed unit (dyad, triad, or larger group) there were redundant behavior patterns. Rules (as any student of philosophy learns when studying determinism) can describe regularity, rather than regulation. A second part of the *rules hypothesis* was that family members use only some of the full range of behaviors available to them. This seemingly innocent fact is precisely what makes family therapy possible. Families who come to therapy can be seen as stuck within a narrow range of options—unnecessarily rigid rules. Since the rules in most families are not spelled out, no one ratifies them and they are hard to change. The therapist, however, as an outsider can help families see—and re-examine—the rules they live by.

By 1963 Jackson had delineated three types of family rules: (1) norms, which are covert; (2) values, which are consciously held and openly acknowledged; and (3) homeostatic mechanisms, which are rules about how norms and values are enforced (*metarules*). Many of these rules are inculcated by families of origin, but Jackson generally did not look beyond the nuclear family.

Since families operate by rules, and rules about rules, Jackson concluded that family dysfunction was due to lack of rules for change. Therefore he sought to make explicit and to change the rules by which family transactions are governed. This is, in fact, a fancy way of describing interpretation, a technique that characterizes the treatment of communications therapists far more than their writings suggest. Although he denied that pointing out family patterns of interactions is useful (Jackson and Weakland, 1961), this technique was, in fact, part of his style and part of his influence.

Jackson's therapeutic strategies were based on the premise that psychiatric problems resulted from the way people behave with each other in a given context. He saw human problems as interactional *and* situational. Problem resolution involves shifting the context in which problems occur. Although Jackson had more to say about understanding families than treating them, many of his explanatory concepts (*homeostatic mechanisms*, *quid pro quo*, *double-bind*, *symmetry*, and *complementarity*) informed his strategies and tactics of therapy, and became the early language of systems-oriented family therapists. He sought first to distinguish interactions ("redundant behavior patterns") that were functional from those that were dysfunctional or *problem-maintaining*. To do this, he observed routine behavior patterns and noted when problems occurred and in what context, who was present, and what the people did about the problems. Given the belief that symptoms are homeostatic mechanisms, Jackson also considered how the family might *get worse* if the problem got better. The individual may want to get better, but the family may need someone to play the sick role. Sometimes progress is a threat to the defensive order of things.

Jackson's model of the family as a homeostatic system emphasized the equilibrium-maintaining qualities of symptomatic behavior. This led directly to the idea that deviation or deviance, including symptomatic and irrational behavior, was not necessarily negative—at least if you abandon the point of view of those who want to correct it. A child's symptoms, for example, might distract the parents from conflict between them, and unite them in concern for the child. Unfortunately, following Jackson, some family therapists jumped from the observation that symptoms may serve a purpose to the assumption that some families *need* a sick member—which often led, in turn, to a view of parents victimizing *scapegoated* children. Unfortunately when early family therapists thought of themselves as avenging knights out to rescue innocent victims by slaying family dragons, they often took up an adversarial stance, which only exaggerated family resistance.

Among Jackson's most popular and trenchant papers was "Family Rules: Marital Quid Pro Quo" (Jackson, 1965). In a marriage, husband and wife play a variety of different roles. Jackson denied that these roles are the result of sexual differences; instead he considered that they result from a series of *quid pro quos*, worked out in a long-term collaborative relationship. The traditional view is that marital roles stem from sex role differences; it thus ascribed behavior to individual personalities instead of recognizing that relationships depend in large measure upon the interactions and rules for interaction worked out between people. Jackson's view is not that sexual differences don't exist, but that they are relatively unimportant. The major differences in marriages were worked out, not given. (In their enthusiasm for newly discovered interactional forces, early family therapists may have underestimated the importance of gender and the effect of gender bias on families.) *Quid pro quo* refers to the bargains struck between husband and wife, analogous to a legal contract. The rights and duties of each are established in a mutual exchange. Jackson cites as one of the major quid pro quos among middle-class families the arrangement where the husband plays an instrumental role, dealing with things in a logical and practical manner, and the wife plays an emotional role, dealing more with people than with things. This division of labor is highly practical because the dyad then contains two specialists who combine their talents. The fact that such quid pro quos are not overt or conscious is significant for family therapists who must ferret out these agreements in order to help couples modify those that are not serviceable.

Another construct important to Jackson's thinking was the dichotomy between relationships that are *complementary* and those that are *symmetrical*. (Like so many of the seminal ideas of family therapy, this one was first articulated by Bateson.) *Complementary* relationships are those in which people are different in ways that fit together; if one is dominant, for instance, the other is submissive; if one is logical, the other is emotional; if one is weak, the other is strong. *Symmetrical* relationships are based on equality and similarity. Marriages between two people who both have careers and share housekeeping chores are symmetrical. (Once, the complementary marriage was the norm in this country, giving families stability if not equality. Perhaps the most profound change in family life in the second half of the twentieth century has been the advent of the symmetrical pattern in two-paycheck families. Unfortunately, in the process of transition from a norm of complementarity toward a more egalitarian, symmetrical norm, the American family has undergone a great deal of instability and conflict on the road to equality.)

Most of Jackson's descriptive concepts (*complementary/symmetrical, quid pro quo, double-bind*) describe relationships between only two people. Although his intent was to develop a descriptive language of whole family interactions, Jackson's major success was in describing relationships between husband and wife. This limited focus on the marital dyad is one of the shortcomings of work done by the Palo Alto group. Their sophisticated interest in communication led to an adult-centered bias, and they tended to neglect the children as well as the various triads that made up families. As a consequence many of their students tend to reduce family problems even, or especially, where small children are presented as the patients to marital problems.

Like the other members of the Palo Alto group, Jay Haley's major focus was on the marital pair. Symptoms in a marriage partner, Haley argued, represent an incongruence between levels of communication. The symptomatic spouse does something, such as touching a doorknob six times before turning it, while at the same time indicating that he or she is not doing it, because he or she cannot help it. Haley goes on to argue that the patient's symptoms are perpetuated both by the way the patient behaves and how others respond. From this follows Haley's basic tactic of psychotherapy: to persuade family members to change their behavior in relation to the patient.

Control in relationships is the constant theme which underlies all of Haley's work. He describes everyday relationships as significantly determined by people struggling to achieve control over each other, and the therapeutic relationship as one in which patients attempt to control what is to happen with the therapists (Haley, 1961). Therapists, therefore, according to Haley, need to outwit and manipulate patients in such a way as to defeat their resistance and subtle uncooperativeness. Haley, who borrowed many of his maneuvers from Milton Erickson, the renowned hypnotherapist, treats symptoms just as he treats resistance. Since symptoms are seen as ways of dealing with people, therapy must provide other ways of dealing with people. Thus Haley analyzed patients' manipulative and rebellious ways of dealing with family members. For example, a wife's handwashing compulsion may be seen as a means of rebelling against a tyrannical husband. A psychoanalyst would describe this as "secondary gain"; Haley sees this interpersonal payoff as the primary gain. As he put it, "From the point of view offered here, the crucial aspect of the symptom is the advantage it gives the patient in gaining control of what is to happen in a relationship with someone else" (Haley, 1961, p. 151).

Haley's analysis of the struggle for control between therapist and patient was shrewd, as so many of his analyses are. It was also, however, simplistic. He was sharp enough to realize that the initial contact with the patient often involves subtle and not so subtle maneuvering for position. Thus when the patient says, "I work days and can only meet with you in the evenings," the therapist will respond either by accepting the control or resisting it. While such struggles indeed take place—as most therapists realize—it may be simplistic to see them as the major, or even as a major, feature of the psychotherapeutic relationship. True, if the patient gains control of what happens in therapy, he or she may lose by winning—perpetuating difficulties by continued reliance on a destructive pattern. But it does not follow that therapists can succeed merely by achieving control themselves.

Haley (1963) defined his therapy as being a directive form of treatment, and acknowledged that many of his methods were developed by Milton Erickson. Indeed it is sometimes difficult in Haley's early writings to determine where Erickson leaves off and Haley begins. In what he called "brief therapy," Haley zeroed in on the patient's context and the possible function of the patient's symptoms. His first moves were often designed to gain control of his own relationship with the patient. Thus Haley cites Erickson's device of advising the patient that since this is only the first interview there will be things that the patient may be willing to say and other things that the patient will want to withhold, and that these, of course, should be withheld. Here Erickson is directing patients to do precisely what they will do anyway and thus, subtly, gaining the upper hand.

Even while gaining initial information, the brief therapist begins to establish a context for therapeutic change. Accordingly a history may be taken in such a way as to suggest that progressive improvement has and will continue to occur. Alternatively, with a pessimistic patient, the therapist accepts the pessimism and says that since things have become so terribly bad it is time for a change. In either case the therapist gathers information while at the same time encouraging a commitment to change.

The decisive technique in brief therapy (then and now) is the use of directives. As Haley put it, it isn't enough to explain problems to patients; what counts is getting them to *do* something about them. However as he points out, "One of the difficulties involved in telling patients to do something is the fact that psychiatric patients are noted for their hesitation about doing what they are told" (Haley, 1963, p. 45). Haley's solution was to use directives so cleverly that patients can't help but do what's wanted. Typical of this procedure is to prescribe symptomatic behavior, but add something in the instructions so that the symptoms come under therapeutic direction, and may slowly be modified. In one instance Haley was asked to treat a freelance photographer who compulsively made silly blunders which ruined every picture. Naturally this person became so preoccupied with avoiding mistakes that he was too tense to take satisfactory pictures. Haley instructed him to go out and take three pictures, making one deliberate error in each. While seeming to perpetuate the patient's problem, Haley was, in fact, paradoxically directing symptomatic behavior in such a way that the patient gained control over it. In another case Haley prescribed that an insomniac spend his wakeful late night hours performing arduous, unpleasant tasks, like going for long walks or polishing floors. The patient reported that he dared not suffer from insomnia once he knew that if he failed to fall asleep immediately he had to spend the night polishing floors. Apparently psychiatric patients, like the rest of us, will do almost anything to get out of doing housework.

Central to Haley's thinking is the idea that people develop problems when they are bound by paradoxical directives from their parents, yet they can be helped to overcome these problems by a therapist's benign use of paradox. Haley cites John Rosen as a therapist who used therapeutic paradoxes in an authoritarian manner, and Frieda Fromm-Reichmann as one who used paradoxes in a warm, gentle manner. In one famous instance Rosen dealt with a young schizophrenic patient who claimed to be God by having the ward attendants force the patient to his knees before Rosen, thus demonstrating vividly that he, Rosen, was in charge. The patient was, therefore, in a paradoxical dilemma. He could not deny that he was relating to the therapist by calling himself God; yet, once on his knees he had to acknowledge either that God was subservient to the therapist, or that he was not indeed God.

Frieda Fromm-Reichmann's more gentle approach is described in her book *Principles of Intensive Psychotherapy* (Fromm-Reichmann, 1950). She once treated a patient who said that everything she did occurred in relation to her own private and powerful God rather than in relation to other people. This, of course, provided a convenient excuse for her refusing to relate to Dr. Fromm-Reichmann. Here's what Fromm-Reichmann said to the patient: "Tell him that I am a doctor and you have lived with him in his kingdom now from 7 to 16—that's nine years—and he has not helped you. So now he must permit me to try and see whether you and I can do that job." This patient too was caught in a position where she had to respond to the therapist whatever she did. She could either go to her God and repeat what she was told, thereby conceding that the doctor was in charge; or she could rebel against the doctor, which meant she was relating to her, an action which also renders questionable the existence of her God. Hence, in order to acknowledge her God, she must deny him; similarly if she defies Fromm-Reichmann, she must acknowledge her. What Haley salutes in these examples is the use of *therapeutic paradox* to maneuver patients into responding to their therapists. Once that happens the patients can no longer deny that they are responding to another human being; and Haley believes that is the necessary first step for treating schizophrenic patients.

In describing marriage therapy, Haley devoted most of his attention to analyzing the dynamics of marital relationships, leaving little room for discussion of the actual techniques of therapy. As we shall see, Haley has written several extremely informative books on doing therapy; his early writing, however, left the reader intrigued and fascinated, but uninformed as to how to proceed technically. One may infer from Haley's description of marital dynamics, and from those few techniques he did describe, that he pointed out to couples some of the dynamics of their interaction and encouraged them to communicate openly about how they are dealing with each other. In one place he said, "One of the functions of a marriage therapist might be to provoke a couple to fight and say what is on their minds so they do not continue to punish each other indirectly for crimes which have never been brought up as accusations. When a couple cannot fight, all issues which require defining an area of the relationship are avoided" (Haley, 1963, p. 125).

Haley based his recommendations for therapy with whole families on an amalgam of concepts from the Bateson group. As in traditional individual psychotherapy, conflict was a major focus; but conflict was seen as occurring *between*, rather than within, people. The model was cybernetic: One person's behavior was seen as provoking a response in other family members; family members set limits on one another's behavior in a self-corrective process by responding in error-activated ways when any individual goes beyond the acceptable limits. This process of mutually responsive behavior defines rules in the family system. Haley relied on the metaphor of a power struggle when describing who sets the rules. The therapeutic task was to help families resolve power struggles.

Virginia Satir was another member of the Palo Alto group who played a major role in the development of family therapy. Satir saw troubled family members as trapped in narrow family roles like *victim, placator, defiant one*, and *rescuer*. Her concern with identifying such life-constricting roles and freeing family members from their grip was consistent with her major focus, which was always on the individual. Thus Satir was always a humanizing force, even in the early days of family therapy, when many were so enamored of the new systems metaphor that they sometimes neglected the emotional life of families—their disappointment, pain, and hope.

In her work with families Satir concentrated on clarifying communication, expressing feelings, and fostering a climate of mutual acceptance and warmth. The 1964 publication of Satir's book *Conjoint Family Therapy* did much to popularize the family therapy movement. This book, along with *Pragmatics of Human Communication* (Watzlawick, Beavin, and Jackson, 1967), helped spread the influence of the Palo Alto group's brand of systemic thinking. Eventually Satir went on from family therapy to become a major force in the human potential movement, and we will consider her work more fully in Chapter 6, Experiential Family Therapy.

Murray Bowen

Murray Bowen began treating families while he was directing a research project on the interaction in schizophrenic families. In the first year of this project (1954) Bowen treated each family member with individual psychotherapy. However, after concluding that the family was the unit of disorder, he began to hold therapy sessions with all family members assembled together. Thus in 1955 Bowen became one of the first to invent family therapy.

Beginning in 1955 Bowen also held large group therapy sessions open to all project staff members and all families. In this early form of network therapy, Bowen assumed that togetherness and open communication would be therapeutic, for problems within families and between family members and staff.

The history of Bowen's methods of therapy mark the evolution of his thinking. At first he used four therapists to manage the large multifamily meetings, but he became dissatisfied when he noticed that the therapists tended to pull in different directions. So he put one therapist in charge, with the others consigned to supporting roles. However, just as multiple therapists tended to pull in different directions, so did the other families. As soon as a crucial point was being developed within one family, someone from another family became anxious and changed the subject. Finally Bowen decided that families would have to take turns—one family was the focus for each session, while the others were silent auditors.

At first Bowen's approach to single families was the same as the one he employed with the large meetings. He did what many people do when they are new to family therapy: just brought the family members together and tried to get them talking. He reasoned that simply by being together and discussing mutual concerns families would improve. Although Bowen soon rejected this idea, many people continue to approach family treatment this way. Nondirective, participant observation has little utility beyond getting family members started talking together and perhaps resolving relatively transient problems. Bowen soon learned this, and he developed a structured and directive approach which paralleled the evolution of his theory.

When he brought family members together and encouraged them to define their problems and discuss solutions, Bowen was most struck by their intense *emotional reactivity*. Feelings overwhelmed thinking and tended to involve the whole group in a process whereby no one retained a separate identity. Bowen felt the family's tendency to pull him into the center of this *undifferentiated ego mass*, and he had to make a concerted effort to stay objective and detached (Bowen, 1961). He believed that if they were forced to solve their problems, the family would become more responsible and competent. So Bowen sat with them, remaining neutral and detached, while he observed the process of family interactions. His major active efforts during the sessions were to discourage scapegoating by pointing out to family members when they used the patient as an excuse for avoiding other problems. At the end of each session he summed up what he observed, emphasizing the process by which the family went about trying to solve their problems.

Parallel to the formal research project on families of schizophrenics, Bowen also conducted a larger clinical operation for families of children with a wide range of problems. Although he initially believed that the pathological mechanisms in schizophrenic families were exclusive to schizophrenic families—and were the *cause* of schizophrenia—he discovered that the same phenomena were present in all families, although to a lesser degree.

Bowen found that observing entire family units was invaluable as a source of information, but he was disappointed with the results of therapy with whole families. Beginning in 1960 he began meeting with just the parents of symptomatic children. His purpose was to block scapegoating and help the parents focus on problems in their own relationship, without being distracted by their children. He was much happier with the results of seeing the parents alone, and has continued to do so, only rarely including children. When he first began interviewing parents, Bowen analyzed the intrapsychic processes in one spouse at a time, focusing heavily on dreams for his interpretations. He soon abandoned this intrapsychic focus and shifted to explore the relationship system between spouses. Bowen experimented with different methods of working with couples until about 1964, when he developed his present method which has not been modified since:

1. Defining and clarifying the relationship between the spouses
2. Keeping self detriangled
3. Teaching the spouses about how emotional systems function
4. Demonstrating differentiation by taking "I-position" stands

1. Defining and Clarifying Relationships between Spouses. Bowen encourages each spouse to talk directly to the therapist, not to his or her mate. In this way the therapist, not the couple, controls the affect in the interchange. The Bowenian therapist tries to keep things calm, low-keyed, and objective. A spouse who is neither speaking nor being spoken to is less emotionally reactive and, therefore, better able to listen. The therapist focuses on cognition—thoughts and ideas, rather than feelings. Only after a couple makes a great deal of progress towards understanding each other rationally, does the therapist invite them to talk about their emotional reactions and feelings. When feelings are stirred up, the therapist encourages the couple to discuss the issues about which they have feelings, not the feelings themselves. Emotions that do emerge from these issue-oriented discussions are probably more spontaneous than those elicited when couples are encouraged to express feelings.

2. Keeping Self Detriangled. Bowen believes that a prerequisite to avoiding emotional entanglement with client families is a mature resolution of emotional conflicts within one's own family and emotional system at work. In the absence of such personal maturity, a therapist is liable to react emotionally to family members who restimulate conflicts and blind spots. To avoid emotional entanglement, therapists should focus on process, not content, and avoid taking sides, being charmed, or getting angry. The Bowenian therapist remains calm at all times.

3. Teaching Spouses about the Functioning of Emotional Systems. This should only be attempted when anxiety is reduced. Otherwise whatever the therapist says is liable to be interpreted as siding with one or the other spouses. When anxiety in the couple is moderately low, Bowen may discuss progress made in other cases, to illustrate certain points. When the anxiety between the spouses is very low, he teaches them directly about functioning of emotional systems. If they are motivated, he also encourages them to work on differentiating themselves in relation to their families of origin.

4. Taking "I-Position" Stands. The more the therapist can define him- or herself in relationship to the family, the more family members can follow suit and define themselves in relation to the rest of the family. Defining oneself means to become clear about and express convictions, beliefs, and actions in relation to other people. By knowing what one believes and saying so in a calm, straightforward manner, one can avoid *fusion*, or *undifferentiation*.

The goals of Bowen's work with parents is to help them achieve a reasonable level of differentiation of self, from each other and from their families of origin, to learn enough about family systems to handle future crises, and to develop the motivation to continue working towards further differentiation after therapy is terminated.

Besides treating couples Bowen has also used two other methods of treatment: couples groups and individual sessions.

When he found himself covering similar issues with different couples in session after session, Bowen decided that he might save time by working with several families at once. This seemed particularly appropriate for Bowen's therapy since it is relatively didactic. So beginning in about 1965 (Bowen, 1976) he began treating couples in groups. Bowen's use of Multiple Family Therapy was paradoxical because his major emphasis had been to avoid the fusion inherent in social and emotional togetherness. When he worked with groups, though, Bowen minimized emotional interaction between families and forbid contact outside the group sessions. Although he found it no easier to teach families about emotional systems and much harder to remain neutral, the couples in these groups made rapid progress. Apparently families learned a great deal about the process of emotional systems, with less anxiety, as they listened to discussions of other people's problems. For several years the Multiple Family Therapy method was the bulk of Bowen's practice.

In addition to couples and couples groups, Bowen also worked frequently with single family members. This is a unique approach, and it challenges facile assumptions about family therapy. Family therapy is both a method and an orientation. As an orientation, it means understanding people in context of significant emotional systems; as a method, it usually means working with whole families. But some might argue that Bowen's work with individual family members is more exclusively focused on family issues, systems concepts, and emotional process than is almost any other family therapy approach.

In 1966 there was an emotional crisis in Bowen's family and his personal experience in resolving that crisis was a formative event in teaching him about changing families.

Murray Bowen was the oldest of five children from a tightly knit family that for several generations resided in the same small town in Pennsylvania. After growing up, he kept a formal distance from his parents and maintained family relations on a comfortable but superficial basis. Like many of us, Bowen mistook avoidance for emancipation. But as he later realized, emotional tension in the family remains with us, making us vulnerable to repeat similar patterns in new relationships, until our family conflicts are actually resolved.

Bowen's personal resolution of emotional reactivity in his family was as significant for his work as Freud's self-analysis had been for psychoanalysis. In neither case was it easy. Bowen spent twelve years trying to understand his family, using the framework of his theory, and seven or eight years of active effort to modify himself in relation to the family before the major breakthrough occurred. The going is usually slower for explorers of unknown territory than for those who come later with maps to guide them.

In his attempt to understand and improve relationships with his own family, Bowen turned first to his nuclear family and only later to his family of origin. Although this seems a natural sequence, Bowen's experience convinced him that the most productive course is to begin with the original family. Only then is it possible to make genuine progress in reducing tension in the more significant, but more emotionally reactive, nuclear family. *Differentiation of self* in the family of origin is begun by developing an individual, person-to-person relationship with each parent and with as many members of the family as possible. If visiting is difficult, letters and phone calls help re-establish relationships, particularly if they are personal and intimate. Differentiating one's self from the family is completed when these relationships are maintained without fusion or triangulation. Differentiated people can talk about the full range of personal issues between them without getting anxious and detouring the conversation to a third person or impersonal subject.

Bowen's most important achievement was detriangling himself from his own parents. His parents had been accustomed to complaining to him about unresolved tension and conflict between them. Most of us are flattered to receive these confidences and consider them a form of intimacy born of respect for our judgement. Bowen recognized this triangulation for what it was, and when his mother complained about his father, he told his father: "Your wife told me a story about you; I wonder why she told me instead of you." Naturally father discussed this with mother and, naturally, she was annoyed. Moves to differentiate oneself violate family norms and cause emotional upheaval. If there is no upheaval, then the differentiation effort is probably insignificant. Although his mother fussed about it, Bowen's maneuver was effective in keeping his parents from trying to get him to take sides—and it made it harder for them to avoid discussing things between themselves. Telling the third person what a second person says to you about him or her is one of the most effective detriangling moves.

Bowen also discovered that it is important to define self around significant issues. Since emotionally significant issues are usually dormant, the most productive visits home are during a crisis or stressful occasion, such as a death, serious illness, wedding, or birth. At these times the family's emotional reactivity is at high tide. It was at such a point that Bowen returned home for a carefully orchestrated effort to differentiate himself from a series of interlocking family triangles. The details of that venture are complex but make rewarding reading for the serious student (Anonymous, 1972).

Bowen's trip came on the heels of a family squabble over problems with the family business. He prepared the way by writing a series of intimate and provocative letters to the major players in the family drama. These letters were designed to open hidden conflicts and promote a lively confrontation. Thus, he wrote to his brother, a family scapegoat, and told him all the stories and gossip about him. That did the trick.

When Bowen arrived home, the whole family was present—and hopping mad. Every segment of the family tried to engage him in an emotional tug of war. But differentiation requires thinking, instead of hasty reaction, and remaining objectively neutral about conflicts between others. Although his letters had provoked the showdown, the issues were among the family members who lived together in Pennsylvania. Bowen saw his task as stirring things up, but not taking sides. Armed by his understanding of family systems theory and knowing what to expect from the family, Bowen was able to remain absolutely neutral. This forced the feuding parties, all of whom were present, to work things out among themselves.

The trip was a great success. Bowen was able to remain in personal contact with each member of his family at a time of crisis, but without becoming triangled or emotionally reactive.

After he told them about his experience with his own family, many of Bowen's trainees began to return to their own families and work on differentiating themselves. They did so even though Bowen had not directly encouraged them. When he noted how productive these trainees became as therapists, as compared with those who had not returned to their own families, Bowen decided that the best way to become a family therapist is to resolve emotional problems in the family of origin. Thus, beginning in 1971, studying one's own family became the core of Bowen's approach to training. The major emphasis is on returning to the family of origin, making contact, and developing a viable working relationship with every possible member of the family, while remaining detriangled.

Nathan Ackerman

Nathan Ackerman came to family therapy from psychoanalysis, and his thinking about families continued to reflect that background. He emphasized psychodynamic issues more than the behavioral sequences, communications, and interaction that systems-oriented family therapists stressed, but he had a keen sense of the overall organization of families. Families, Ackerman said, give an appearance of unity, but underneath they are emotionally divided into competing factions. This you may recognize as similar to the psychoanalytic model of individuals who, despite apparent unity of personality, are actually minds in conflict, driven by the interplay of drives and defenses and competing structural forces. Just as an individual expresses the dynamic conflicts of id, ego, and superego, so too are families dynamic coalitions, sometimes of mother and daughter against father and son, sometimes of one generation against the next.

Ackerman was a psychoanalytically trained child psychiatrist. After completing his residency training during the Depression, he joined the psychiatric staff at Southard School, a facility for disturbed children at the Menninger Clinic in Topeka, Kansas. In 1937 he became chief psychiatrist of the Child Guidance Clinic. At first he followed the child guidance model of having a psychiatrist treat the child and a social worker see the mother. But by the mid 1940s he began to experiment with having the same therapist see both. Unlike Bowlby, however, Ackerman did more than use this as a temporary expedient to resolve treatment impasses. Instead he re-evaluated his whole conception of psychopathology and began to see the family as the basic unit for diagnosis and treatment.

In 1955 Ackerman organized and led the first session on family diagnosis at a meeting of the American Orthopsychiatric Association. Two years later, in 1957, he opened the Family Mental Health Clinic of the Jewish Family Service in New York City and taught at Columbia University. From there he founded the Family Institute, in 1960, which was renamed the Ackerman Institute following his death in 1971.

In addition to his clinical innovations, Ackerman also published several important articles and books. As early as 1938 he wrote "The Unity of the Family," and some consider his article, "Family Diagnosis: An Approach to the Preschool Child" (Ackerman and Sobel, 1950), as the beginning of the family therapy movement (Kaslow, 1980). In 1962 Ackerman, with Don Jackson, cofounded the field's first journal, *Family Process*. Under the editorial leadership of Jay Haley (1962–1969), Donald Bloch (1969–1982), Carlos Sluzki (1983–1990), and Peter Steinglass (1990–present), *Family Process* has for many years been the major scholarly and scientific vehicle through which family therapists communicate their ideas.

While other family therapists de-emphasized the psychology of individuals in favor of systemic organization and processes, Ackerman was always concerned with what goes on inside one person, as well as what goes on between persons. Ackerman never lost sight of the individual's feelings, hopes, and desires. In fact, Ackerman's model of the family was like the psychoanalytic model of an individual writ large; instead of conscious and unconscious issues, Ackerman talked about how families confront some issues while they avoid and deny others, particularly conflictual ones involving sex and aggression. He described his role as therapist as one of stirring up the family and bringing the family's secrets into the open.

Ackerman recommended that everyone living under the same roof be present in all family interviews. As Ackerman put it, "It is very important at the outset to establish a meaningful emotional contact with all members of the family, to create a climate in which one really touches them and they feel they touch back" (Ackerman, 1961, p. 242). Once contact was made, Ackerman encouraged an open and honest expression of feeling. As a therapist he was a dynamic *agent provocateur*, stirring up revelations and confrontations with his legendary wit, ebullience, and willingness to stick his nose into personal family issues.

Ackerman pointed out that identity has various aspects: one has identity as an individual, a member of various family subsystems, and as a member of the family as a whole. In order to pinpoint these various components of identity, he was alert to the coalitions revealed in family interviews. One clue to such coalitions is found in the seating arrangement; that is, as family members enter the room they tend to pair off in ways that reveal alignments. But to see these various alignments and their conflicts clearly, Ackerman recommended mobilizing spontaneous interaction among family members. Once family members are interacting among themselves and with the therapist, it is possible to see how the family is emotionally divided, as well as what problems and prohibitions are present. He also paid close attention to nonverbal cues, because he believed that disguised feelings were conveyed in body language far more eloquently than in words.

In order to promote more honest emotional interchange, Ackerman "tickled the defenses" of family members—his phrase for teasing, provoking, and stimulating people to open up and say what is really on their minds. The phrase nicely reflects Ackerman's charismatic and provocative style.

What are thought to be family secrets, Ackerman said, generally turn out to be known by all family members but are simply not spoken of. Children generally know a good deal more than parents think. They also know what they're not supposed to talk about. However, as long as the therapist is in control, the family is reassured and, therefore, feels free to speak more plainly about matters that they usually avoid.

According to Ackerman, the therapist should be neither neutral nor passive. Ackerman himself was spontaneous, lively, and outspoken, which put him in the center of things. He didn't hesitate to confront, provoke, challenge, or even argue with family members. According to him it's more therapeutic for the therapist to become a target for anger and hostility than other family members.

In order to encourage families to give up their own emotional restraint, Ackerman himself was unrestrained. He willingly sided first with one part of the family and later with another. He didn't think it was necessary—or possible—to be always neutral and objective; instead, he believed that an impartial balance was achieved in the long run by moving about and giving support now to one, and now to another family member. He was also unabashedly straightforward and blunt with family members. If he thought someone was lying, he said so. To critics who suggested this bluntness might produce too much anxiety in patients, Ackerman replied that people derive more reassurance from honesty than from bland support.

Ackerman also made use of psychoanalytic processes like transference, resistance, and interpretation. He used the feelings aroused in counter-transference because he thought therapy was lifeless unless the therapist was fully and feelingly engaged.

Ackerman explained many family events as the product of conflict. He said that conflicts within individuals, among family members, and between families and the larger community must be identified and resolved if psychological hurts are to be mended. Conflicts between family members and within the mind of an individual family member are related in a circular feedback system—that is, personal conflict affects intrapsychic conflict and vice versa (Ackerman, 1961). Conflicts of identity, values, and strivings may produce rifts among family members or subsystems, mobilizing one segment against the other. Likewise, conflicts between segments of the family may produce subsequent disturbance within family members. Ackerman considered symptoms to be products of the internalization of persistent pathological family conflict. To reverse symptomatic disturbances, the therapist must bring conflicts into the open, into the field of family interaction, where new solutions can be found. As long as conflicts remain locked within individuals, Ackerman believed, psychopathology remains fixed.

Ackerman's treatment procedure was problem-oriented rather than technique-oriented (Ackerman, 1970a). Rather than approach families with a preordained plan, he preferred to use procedures determined by the needs of the family group and its individual members. He was not wedded to seeing any particular family unit; he might begin by seeing the nuclear family, but then subsequently meet with parents and grandparents, parents alone, or parents with their children. This creative flexibility makes it very difficult to describe or to teach Ackerman's approach. He was a clinical artist, not a systematizer.

While it may be impossible to neatly characterize Ackerman's method, there were clear themes. One was the necessity for depth of commitment and involvement with families. He himself became quickly and deeply emotionally involved with the families he treated, in contrast, say, to Murray Bowen, who consistently cautioned therapists to remain uninvolved in order to avoid being triangulated. Depth also characterized the type of material on which Ackerman focused—family analogues of the kinds of conflicts, feelings, and fantasies that lie buried in the individual unconscious. Ackerman believed that there are similar currents of highly significant conflict, feeling, and fantasy excluded from the family's awareness—a kind of interpersonal unconscious of the family group. Ackerman's psychoanalytic orientation sensitized him to these hidden themes, and his flamboyant, provocative, therapeutic style enabled him to help families vividly enact them.

In one very interesting paper, "The Art of Family Therapy" (Ackerman, 1970b), Ackerman reflected on the fact that in previous descriptions of his approach he had never really related much about his personal style. He had never mentioned his use of first names, his humor, and how he tried to make family encounters interesting and pleasant for himself and for the family, apparently because his long training as a psychoanalyst had inculcated certain taboos against informality and intimacy with patients. He concluded that if teachable principles did underlie his work, they were probably inextricably bound up with his personal performance as a therapist. Thus Ackerman came to see family therapy as a unique and spontaneous expression of the therapist's personality in a therapeutic role.

Ackerman's contributions to the field of family psychotherapy were extensive and important: He was one of the first to envision whole family treatment, and he had the personal inventiveness and energy to initiate it. As far back as the late forties he was pointing out that treating family members in individual therapy without considering the configuration of the family was often futile. Very early Ackerman (1954) recommended that family groups be evaluated as wholes, and that these evaluations be followed by therapy of the family group and individual therapy for selected family members.

Ackerman's second major impact was as a brilliant artist of family therapy technique. He was one of the great geniuses of the movement. Those who studied with him and observed his treatment of families all attest to his clinical wizardry. He was a dynamic catalyst, active, open, and forthright, never rigid or shy. He interacted with families in a highly emotional and effective manner. Nor was he content to remain always in the office, for he recommended and made frequent home visits (Ackerman, 1966).

Despite his brilliance as a therapist, however, Ackerman's theoretical papers don't go much beyond pointing out that individuals are intricately involved in families. Moreover his clinical writings offer little in the way of systematic strategy for working with families. He is often colorful, but rarely concrete or explicit. Some of his recommendations are vague; for instance, that the therapist must evaluate the outer and inner reality of the family and then stir family members to open up (Ackerman, 1966).

Finally there are Ackerman's contributions as a teacher, which may be his most important legacy. On the East Coast his name was synonymous with family therapy throughout the late 1950s and 1960s. Among those fortunate enough to study with him was Salvador Minuchin, who openly acknowledges his debt to Ackerman's genius for innovation.

Ackerman consistently urged therapists to be emotionally involved with families, and work in a highly confrontive manner to transform dormant conflicts into open discussions. How does a therapist provoke candid disclosures? Ackerman did it by calling attention to avoidance and emotional dishonesty ("tickling the defenses"), challenging cliches, and interrupting fruitless bickering over unimportant matters. Ackerman's techniques suggest that he was somewhat more concerned with the content of family conflicts than with the process by which family members dealt with them, and more interested in secrets and hidden conflicts (particularly those involving sex and aggression) than in emotional distance and proximity among family members and their patterns of communication. Perhaps his major enduring contribution was his consistent stress on individual persons and whole families; he never lost sight of the fact that people are both individuals and members of a family.

Carl Whitaker

Even among the strong-willed and colorful founders of family therapy, Carl Whitaker stands out as the most dynamic and irreverent. His approach to psychotherapy has always been radical and provocative, and he brought this same style to his innovative work with families. Whitaker's view of psychologically troubled people is that they are alienated from their emotions and frozen into devitalized routine (Whitaker and Malone, 1953). Whitaker turns up the emotional temperature. His "Psychotherapy of the Absurd" (Whitaker, 1975) is a blend of warm support and unpredictable emotional goading, designed to loosen people up and help them get in touch with their immediate experience.

Given his bold and inventive approach to treatment, it is not surprising that Whitaker was one of the first to break with psychiatric tradition in order to experiment with family treatment. In 1943 he and John Warkentin, working as cotherapists in Oakridge, Tennessee, began including spouses and, eventually, children in their patients' treatment. Whitaker also pioneered the use of cotherapy for treatment, and he continues to feel that a supportive cotherapist is essential to enable family therapists to react spontaneously without fear of unchecked countertransference.

In 1946 Whitaker accepted the chair of psychiatry at Emory University in Atlanta, where he was joined by Warkentin and Thomas Malone. Together they continued to experiment with family treatment and shifted their interest to working with schizophrenics and their families. During this period Whitaker initiated a series of conferences that eventually led to the first major meeting of the family therapist movement. Beginning in 1946 Whitaker, Warkentin, and Malone began twice-yearly conferences during which they observed and discussed each other's work with families. The group found these sessions to be enormously helpful, and mutual observation, using one-way vision screens, has since then been one of the hallmarks of family therapy.

In 1953 Whitaker invited John Rosen, Albert Scheflen, Gregory Bateson, and Don Jackson to participate in the semiannual conference on families, which was held that year in Sea Island, Georgia. Each took turns demonstrating his own approach with the same family, while the others observed and, afterwards, joined in for a group discussion and analysis. The cross-fertilization of ideas that occurred has continued to characterize the family therapy movement; family clinicians openly display their work, both for teaching and for mutual enrichment.

Whitaker resigned from Emory's Department of Psychiatry in 1955 and entered private practice with Warkentin, Malone, and Richard Felder. He and his partners at the Atlanta Psychiatric Clinic developed an "experiential" form of psychotherapy, utilizing a number of highly provocative techniques, as well as the force of their own personalities, in the treatment of families, individuals, groups, and couples (Whitaker, 1958).

In 1965 Whitaker left Atlanta to become a professor of psychiatry at the University of Wisconsin. Since he has been in Madison he has worked exclusively with families and is now one of the elder statesmen of the family therapy movement. He travels widely, giving workshops and presentations at conventions, and he has been on the Editorial Board of *Family Process* since its inception.

When the family therapy movement first began, Whitaker was less well known to students than were many of the other first generation family therapists. Perhaps this was due to his atheoretical position. Whereas Jackson, Haley, and Bowen developed theoretical concepts that were intriguing and easy to grasp, Whitaker always eschewed theory in favor of creative spontaneity. His work has, therefore, been less accessible to students than that of his colleagues. Nevertheless he has always had the respect of his peers, and people who have had the chance to observe his work can see that there is method to his madness.

To begin with, Whitaker deliberately creates tension by teasing and confronting families, in the belief that stress is necessary for change. In the process he does not have an obvious strategy nor does he use structured techniques, preferring, as he says, to let his unconscious run the therapy (Whitaker, 1976). Although his work seems completely spontaneous, even outrageous at times, there is a consistent theme. All of his interventions have the effect of promoting flexibility and change. He views the core problem in families as emotional sterility, and his treatment is to open individuals up to their own feelings and help them share these feelings within the family.

Ivan Boszormenyi-Nagy

Ivan Boszormenyi-Nagy came to family therapy from psychoanalysis, and he has been one of the seminal thinkers in the family therapy movement since its earliest days. In 1957 he founded the Eastern Pennsylvania Psychiatric Institute (EPPI), in Philadelphia, as a center for research and training in families and schizophrenia. Because he was a respected scholar-clinician and an able administrator, Nagy was able to attract a number of highly talented colleagues and students. Among these were James Framo, one of the few psychologists in the early family therapy movement; David Rubenstein, a psychiatrist who later conducted a separate family therapy training program; and Geraldine Spark, a social worker who worked with Nagy as a cotherapist, codirector of the unit, and coauthor of *Invisible Loyalties* (Boszormenyi-Nagy and Spark, 1973). This group was joined by Gerald Zuk, a psychologist who became interested in families while working with mentally retarded persons. Zuk later developed a "triadic-based" approach to family therapy (1971), in which he conceptualized the therapist as a member of the system in treatment. In triadic-based family therapy, the therapist begins as a mediator but then takes sides in order to shift power alignments in the family. According to Zuk (1971, p. 73), "By judicious siding, the therapist can tip the balance in favor of more productive relating, or at least disrupt a chronic pattern of pathogenic relating."

In 1960 Albert Scheflen moved from Temple University to EPPI and joined with Ray Birdwhistell to study body language in the process of psychotherapy. Ross Speck, who did his psychiatric residency in the early 1960s, developed, along with Carolyn Attneave, "network therapy," which broadened the context of treatment far beyond the nuclear family. In this approach as many people as possible who are connected to the patient are invited to attend therapy sessions. Frequently as many as fifty people, including the extended family, friends, neighbors, and teachers, are brought together for approximately three 4-hour sessions and helped by a minimum of three therapists to discuss ways to support and help the patient change (Speck and Attneave, 1973).

Aside from his sponsorship of these students and colleagues, Nagy himself has made major contributions to the study of schizophrenia (Boszormenyi-Nagy, 1962) and family therapy (Boszormenyi-Nagy, 1966, 1972; Boszormenyi-Nagy and Spark, 1973). Nagy described himself as a therapist who went from being an analyst, prizing secrecy and confidentiality, to a family therapist, fighting the forces of pathology on an open battlefield. One of his most important contributions was to introduce the criterion of morality to therapeutic goals and techniques. According to Nagy, neither the pleasure-pain principle nor transactional expediency are sufficient guides to human behavior. Instead, he believes that family members have to base their relationships on trust and loyalty, and that they must balance the ledger of entitlement and indebtedness.

Salvador Minuchin

Although he was not one of the very first family therapists, Minuchin was an early entry into the field and his accomplishments rank him as one of the most influential of all family therapists. Salvador Minuchin is a psychiatrist, trained in his native Argentina, who developed a family approach to treating delinquents at the Wiltwyck School for Boys in New York. The use of family therapy with urban slum families was a new development, and publication of his ideas (Minuchin, Montalvo, Guerney, Rosman, and Schumer, 1967) led to his being invited to become the director of the Philadelphia Child Guidance Clinic. Minuchin brought Braulio Montalvo and Bernice Rosman with him, and they were joined in 1967 by Jay Haley; together they set about transforming a traditional child guidance clinic into one of the great centers of the family therapy movement.

Minuchin's first notable achievement at the Philadelphia Child Guidance Clinic was a unique program for training indigenous members of the local black community as paraprofessional family therapists. The reason for this special effort is that cultural differences often make it very difficult for white middle-class therapists to understand and relate successfully to urban blacks and hispanics.

In 1969 Minuchin received a grant to support his training program. This helped launch an intensive two-year program in which Minuchin, Haley, Montalvo, and Rosman developed a highly successful approach to training as well as one of the most important systems of family therapy. According to Haley, one of the advantages to training people with no previous experience as clinicians to become family therapists is that they have less to unlearn, and are, therefore, less resistant to thinking in terms of systems. Minuchin and Haley sought to capitalize on this by developing an approach with the least possible number of theoretical concepts. Conceptual elegance became one of the hallmarks of "structural family therapy."

The major features of the training were hands-on experience, on-line supervision, and extensive use of videotapes. Minuchin himself is a practical, technique-oriented clinician, and he believes that therapists are best taught by experience. Once they have seen a few families, therapists, he believes, are ready to appreciate and utilize systems theory. Traditional psychotherapy supervision is done after the session and takes the form of telling students what they should have done. In contrast Minuchin and Haley supervised by actually observing sessions and interrupting to provide redirection when necessary. Instead of learning afterwards what they did wrong, therapists learned, on the spot, how to do it right. Later the group studied videotapes for a more in-depth analysis of what works and what doesn't.

The structural family therapy that Minuchin and his colleagues developed (Minuchin, 1974) begins with the observation that family transactions, when they are repeated, develop a patterned regularity, or *structure*. For example, when new parents bring home their first baby from the hospital, they must work out a system for parenting. Since they have no previous experience, their initial interactions are unprogrammed and somewhat unpredictable. When the baby cries in the middle of the night, will the mother get up and nurse him in his room or will the father get up and bring him to her; who will change the baby's diapers when both parents are present; and how early and often will the new parents leave the baby with a babysitter in order to resume their relationship as husband and wife? These questions are soon answered, and the results shape the family's structure.

The nature of the family's structure is determined by emotional *boundaries* which keep family members either close or distant. Either pattern, closeness leading to *enmeshment*, or distance leading to *disengagement*, may be more or less functional for any particular family. This is a point frequently missed by beginning family therapists, who often assume that any family pattern that differs from their own should be changed. Problems begin, according to Minuchin, when a family fails to modify its structure to fit changing circumstances. When this happens, the family needs help.

The techniques of structural family therapy fall into two general strategies. First the therapist must accommodate to the family in order to join them. To begin by confronting and challenging the family's preferred mode of relating is to insure that they will resist. If instead the therapist begins by trying to understand and accept the family, they will be more likely to accept treatment. Once this initial *joining* is accomplished, the structural family therapist begins to use *restructuring* techniques. These are active and directive maneuvers designed to disrupt dysfunctional structures by strengthening diffuse boundaries and softening rigid ones (Minuchin and Fishman, 1981).

In the 1970s, under Minuchin's leadership, the Philadelphia Child Guidance Clinic became one of the outstanding centers for family therapy and training. The clinic itself is a large and marvelously equipped building with excellent facilities for videotaping, "live supervision," workshops, and conferences, and they even have small apartments for hospitalizing whole families. When Minuchin stepped down as director in 1975, he was succeeded first by Harry Aponte, then by Ron Liebman, and recently by Bernice Rosman. This left Minuchin free to pursue his special interest in treating psychosomatic families, especially those with anorexia nervosa (Minuchin, Rosman, and Baker, 1978).

Since 1981 Minuchin has moved to New York where he runs The Family Studies Institute and pursues his dedication to teaching family therapists from all over the world and his burning commitment to social purpose by working with the foster care system, as well as continuing to turn out a steady stream of the most influential books in the field. His 1974 *Families and Family Therapy* is deservedly the most popular book ever written in family therapy, with sales (as of 1990) around two hundred thousand.

Other Early Centers of Family Therapy

In New York, Israel Zwerling, who had been analyzed by Nathan Ackerman, and Marilyn Mendelsohn, who was analyzed by Don Jackson, organized the Family Studies Section at Albert Einstein College of Medicine and Bronx State Hospital. Andrew Ferber was named Director in 1964, and later Philip Guerin, a protege of Murray Bowen's, joined the section. Nathan Ackerman served as a consultant to the group, and they assembled an impressive array of family therapists with diverse orientations. These included Chris Beels, Elizabeth Carter, Monica Orfanidis (now Mc-Goldrick), Peggy Papp, and Thomas Fogarty (Guerin, 1976).

Philip Guerin became Director of Training of the Family Studies Section in 1970 and in 1972 established an extramural training program in Westchester. Shortly afterward, in 1973, he founded the Center for Family Learning in New Rochelle, New York. Here Guerin developed one of the strongest family therapy training programs in the nation.

In Galveston, Texas, Robert MacGregor and his colleagues developed "multiple impact therapy" (MacGregor, 1967). It was a case of necessity being the mother of invention. The clinic where MacGregor was located served a large population scattered widely over southeastern Texas, and many of his clients had to come from hundreds of miles away. Because they had to travel such distances, most of these people were unable to return for weekly therapy sessions. Therefore, in order to make the maximum possible impact in a short time, MacGregor assembled a large team of professionals who worked intensively with the families for two full days. The treatment team consisted of psychologists, social workers, psychiatric residents, and trainees. They met with the family together and in various subgroups in a series of sessions; between sessions the treatment team discussed their findings and refined their strategies of intervention. Although few family therapists have used such marathon sessions, the team approach to treating families has continued to be one of the hallmarks of the field.

In conservative and proper Boston the two most significant early contributions to family therapy were both in the existential-experimental wing of the movement. Norman Paul developed an "operational mourning" approach to family therapy designed to uncover and ventilate unresolved grief. According to him, this cathartic approach is useful in almost all families, not only those who have suffered an obvious recent loss.

Also in Boston, Fred and Bunny Duhl set up the Boston Family Institute, where they developed "integrative family therapy." The Duhls, along with David Kantor and Sandy Watanabe, combined ideas from several family theories and added a number of expressive techniques, including *family sculpting*.

In Chicago, the Family Institute of Chicago and the Institute for Juvenile Research were important parts of the early scene in family therapy (Guerin, 1976). At the Family Institute, Charles and Jan Kramer developed a clinical training program, which was later affiliated with the Northwestern University Medical School. The Institute for Juvenile Research also mounted a training program under the leadership of Irv Borstein, with the consultation of Carl Whitaker.

Some of the important developments in family therapy outside the United States included: Robin Skynner's (1976) use of psychodynamic family therapy at the Institute of Family Therapy in London; British psychiatrist John Howells's (1975) system of family diagnosis as a necessary step for planning therapeutic intervention; West German Helm Stierlin's (1972) integrative efforts bringing together psychodynamic and systemic ideas to bear on understanding and treating troubled adolescents; and Mara Selvini-Palazolli and her colleagues who founded the Institute for Family Studies in Milan in 1967.

We will conclude this section by mentioning the contributions of Christian Midelfort.

Even more than was the case with John Bell, Midelfort's pioneering work in family therapy was slow to gain recognition. He began treating families of hospitalized patients in the early 1950s; delivered what was probably the first paper on family therapy at a professional meeting in 1952, at the American Psychiatric Association Convention; and published one of the first complete books on family therapy in 1957. Nevertheless he remained isolated from the rest of the family therapy movement, while he continued to practice as a staff psychiatrist at a clinic in LaCrosse, Wisconsin. Only recently are his pioneering efforts being recognized (Broderick and Schrader, 1981). Midelfort's method of treating families was based on the group therapy model and its combined psychoanalytic insights with techniques of support and encouragement. At first his concern was to counsel family members on the best ways to help the identified patient, but gradually he evolved a systems viewpoint and conceived of the family as the patient. His technique, which is described in Chapter 4, was to encourage family members to give each other the love and support that was initially provided by the therapist.

SUMMARY

As we have seen, family therapy has a short history but a long past. For many years therapists resisted the idea of seeing members of a patient's family, in order to safeguard the privacy of the patient-therapist relationship. (That this arrangement also preserved the shame associated with psychological disorder as well as the myth of the individual as hero was not noticed, or at least not mentioned.) Freudians excluded the real family in order to uncover the unconscious, introjected family; Rogerians kept the family away in order to provide the unconditional positive regard they thought necessary to help clients rediscover their own inner promptings; and hospital psychiatrists discouraged family visits which might disrupt the benign milieu of the ersatz hospital family.

Several converging developments in the 1950s led to a new view, namely that the family is a living system, an organic whole. Hospital psychiatrists noticed that often when a patient improved someone else in the family got worse. Moreover despite good reasons for keeping family members isolated from an individual's therapy, there were also distinct disadvantages to this approach. To begin with, individual treatment is predicated on relative stability in the patient's environment—otherwise, trying to change the individual, but then returning him or her to a destructive environment, would not make sense. When families were undergoing crisis and conflict, the patient's improvement sometimes made the family worse. Thus it became clear that change in any one person changes the whole family system. Eventually it also became apparent that changing the family might be the most effective way to change the individual.

Although practicing clinicians in hospitals and child guidance clinics prepared the way for family therapy, the most important breakthroughs were achieved in the 1950s by workers who were scientists first, healers second.

In Palo Alto, Gregory Bateson, Jay Haley, Don Jackson, John Weakland, and William Fry, studying communication, discovered that schizophrenia made sense in the context of pathological family communication. Schizophrenics are not crazy in some meaningless way; their apparently bizarre behavior can be understood as an extension of their crazy families. At Yale, Theodore Lidz found a striking pattern of instability and conflict in the families of schizophrenics. *Marital schism* (open conflict) and *marital skew* (pathological balance) had a profound effect on the pathological development of children. Murray Bowen's observation of how mothers and their schizophrenic offspring go through cycles of closeness and distance was the forerunner of the *pursuer-distancer* dynamic. Behind these cycles, Bowen believed were cycles of anxiety: separation anxiety and incorporation anxiety. By hospitalizing whole families at Menninger's for observation and treatment, Bowen implicitly located the problem of schizophrenia in an *undifferentiated family ego mass* and even extended it beyond the nuclear family to three generations. Lyman Wynne, at NIMH and later Rochester, linked schizophrenia to the family by demonstrating how communication deviance contributes to thought disorder. *Pseudomutuality* described the maddening unreality of some families, and the *rubber fence* described the psychological membrane that surrounds them, like a thick skin surrounding a living organism.

These observations launched the family therapy movement, but the excitement they generated blurred the distinction between what the research teams observed and what they concluded. What they observed was that the behavior of schizophrenics *fit* with their families; what they concluded was far more momentous. First it was implied that since schizophrenia fit (made sense) in the context of the family, then the family *must be the cause* of schizophrenia. A second conclusion was even more influential. Family dynamics—double-binds, pseudomutuality, undifferentiated family ego mass—began to be seen as products of a "system," rather than features of persons who share certain qualities because they live together. Thus was born a new creature, "the family system."

Once the family became the patient, there was a need for new ways to think about and treat human problems. The systems metaphor was the pivotal concept in this radical new endeavor. And, though neither could be considered the founder of family therapy, no one had any greater influence on how we think about families than Gregory Bateson and Milton Erickson. The anthropologist and the alienist, Bateson and Erickson, epitomized the two traditions that came to dominate the new family therapy movement.

Although his reputation was limited until Haley's brilliant exposition of his ideas in *Uncommon Therapy* (Haley, 1973), Milton Erickson had an enormous influence on the field's development. Erickson's legacy to family therapy was the pragmatic, problem-solving approach. He helped us learn to figure out what keeps families stuck, how to get them unstuck—using creative, sometimes counterintuitive ideas—and then get out, letting families get on about their business, rather than incorporating a therapist into the family as an expensive crutch. But Erickson's mesmerizing artistry also promoted a tradition of the quick fix, done *to* rather than done *with* families.

Inspired by Bateson's scientific commitment to observation and study, early family therapists spent a good deal of time watching and listening. They were willing to observe and learn because they knew they were going into unknown territory. Unfortunately, many family therapists have gotten away from this receptive openness. So much has been written about family dynamics and technique that therapists too often approach families with a set of precooked techniques and generic preconceptions that they impose on the family's reality.

Bateson is also the patron saint of the intellectual wing of family therapy. His ideas were so profound that they are still being mined by the most sophisticated thinkers in the field. On the other hand, Bateson also set an example of overly abstract theorizing and importing ideas from other—"more scientific"—disciplines. In the early days of family therapy, perhaps we needed models from fields like cybernetics to help us get started, but when so many family therapists continue to lean so heavily on the intellectual underpinnings of physics and biology, one wonders, why this physics envy? Perhaps, after all this time, we are still insecure about the legitimacy of psychology and about our own ability to observe human behavior in human terms without losing our objectivity. Or, perhaps, as we shall see in Chapter 2, the advance of family therapy has involved a series of pendulum shifts, which began with a radical shift away from the psychodynamic past and a search for new metaphors to characterize a new way of thinking.

Another reason family therapists gravitated to abstract theories from mechanics and the natural sciences is that they totally rejected the major body of literature about human psychology: psychoanalysis. The psychoanalytic establishment was none too enthusiastic about this new challenge to their way of thinking, and in many quarters family therapists had to fight to win a place for their beliefs. Perhaps it was this resistance that pushed family therapists into a reactive position. The extreme hostility between family therapists and psychodynamic therapists cooled off in the 1970s, after family therapy established itself as a powerful part of the mental health establishment. One reason family therapy gained acceptance was that it carved out its domain in areas traditionally neglected by the psychiatric establishment—services to children and the poor. An unfortunate legacy of this early antagonism, however, was a prolonged period of ignorance and neglect. Now, in the 1990s, the pendulum is beginning to shift. Family therapists are beginning to discover that at the same time we are trying to understand hidden forces in the family, it may also be useful to pay attention to the hidden forces in the individuals who make up the family (see Chapters 5 and 11). Perhaps the fullest appreciation of human nature lies in the fullest understanding of self *and* system.

Obvious parallels between small groups and families led some family therapists to treat families as though they were just another form of group. They were well served in this endeavor by a large volume of literature on group dynamics and group therapy. Some even saw therapy groups as models of family functioning, with the therapist as father, group members as siblings, and the group collectively as mother (Schindler, 1951). While group therapists experimented with married couples in groups, some family therapists began to conduct group therapy with individual families. Among these John Bell was the most significant and his family group therapy was one of the most widely imitated of the early models (see Chapter 4).

As therapists gained more experience with families, they discovered that the group therapy model was not entirely appropriate for families. Therapy groups are made up of separate individuals, strangers with no past or future outside the group. Families, on the other hand, consist of intimates who share the same myths, defenses, and points of view. Moreover, family members are not peers who can relate democratically as equals; generational differences create hierarchical structures which cannot be ignored. For these reasons family therapists eventually abandoned the group therapy model, replacing it with a variety of systems models.

The child guidance movement contributed the team approach to family therapy. At first members of interdisciplinary teams were assigned to different family members, but, gradually, as they came to appreciate the interlocking behavior patterns of their separate clients, they started integrating and later combining their efforts. The child guidance movement began in this country in 1909 as a creation of the juvenile courts, in order to treat delinquent children who were considered disturbed. Soon these clinics broadened the scope of their population to include a wide range of disorders, and at the same time they broadened the unit of treatment from the child to include the family. At first family therapy was seen as a better means of helping the patient; later it was conceived as a way to serve the needs of the entire family.

Who was the first to practice family therapy? This turns out to be a difficult and controversial question. As in every field there were some visionaries who anticipated the recognized development of family therapy. Freud, for example, occasionally saw "Little Hans" together with his father in 1909. However, such experiments were not sufficient to challenge the hegemony of individual therapy until the climate of the times was receptive. In the early 1950s family therapy was begun independently in four different places: John Bell began family group therapy at Clark University (Chapter 4), Murray Bowen started treating families of schizophrenics at the Menninger Clinic and later at NIMH (Chapter 8), Nathan Ackerman began his psychoanalytic family therapy in New York (Chapter 5), and Don Jackson and Jay Haley started communications family therapy in Palo Alto (Chapters 4 and 10).

All of these pioneers had distinctly different backgrounds and clinical orientations. Not surprisingly, therefore, the approaches they developed to family therapy were also quite different. This diversity still characterizes the field today. Had family therapy been started by a single person, as was psychoanalysis, it is unlikely that there would have been so much creative competition so soon.

In addition to those people just mentioned, others who made significant contributions to the beginning of family therapy include Wynne, Lidz, Satir, Whitaker, Nagy, Midelfort, MacGregor, and Minuchin. Even this list leaves out a number of important figures for what began after a long period of incubation quickly grew and spread. By the 1960s there were literally hundreds of family therapists. Today the field is so large and complex that it will take an entire chapter (Chapter 3) just to provide a descriptive overview.

All the complexity of the family field should not, however, obscure its basic premise: The family is the context of human problems; and, like all human groups, the family has emergent properties—the whole is greater than the sum of its parts. Moreover, no matter how many and varied the explanations of these emergent properties, they all fall into two categories: structure and process. The structure of families includes triangles, subsystems, and boundaries. Among the processes that describe family interaction—emotional reactivity, dysfunctional communication, etc.—the central concept is *circularity*. Rather than worrying about who started what, family therapists understand and treat human problems as a series of moves and countermoves, in repeating cycles.

REFERENCES

Ables, G. 1975. The double-bind: Paradox in relationships. Ph.D. diss., Boston University.

Ables G. 1976. Researching the unresearchable: Experimentation on the double-bind. In *Double-bind: The foundation of the communication approach to the family*, C.E. Sluzki and D.C. Ransom, eds. New York: Grune and Stratton.

Ackerman, N.W. 1938. The unity of the family. *Archives of Pediatrics. 55*:51–62.

Ackerman, N.W. 1954. Interpersonal disturbances in the family: Some unsolved problems in psychotherapy. *Psychiatry. 17*:359–368.

Ackerman, N.W. 1954. Interpersonal disturbances in the family: Some unsolved problems in psychotherapy. *Psychiatry. 17*:359–368.

Ackerman, N.W. 1961. A dynamic frame for the clinical approach to family conflict. In *Exploring the base for family therapy*, N.W. Ackerman, F.L. Beatman and S.N. Sherman, eds. New York: Family Services Association of America.

Ackerman, N.W. 1966. Family psychotherapy—theory and practice. *American Journal of Psychotherapy. 20*:405–414.

Ackerman, N.W. 1970b. The art of family therapy. In *Family therapy in transition*, N.W. Ackerman, ed. Boston: Little Brown.

Ackerman, N.W., Beatman, F., and Sherman, S.N.,eds. 1961. *Exploring the base for family therapy*. New York: Family Service Assn. of America.

Ackerman, N.W., and Sobel, R. 1950. Family diagnosis: An approach to the preschool child. *American Journal of Orthopsychiatry. 20*:744–753.

Amster, F. 1944. Collective psychotherapy of mothers of emotionally disturbed children. *American Journal of Orthopsychiatry. 14*:44–52.

Anderson, C.M., Reiss, D.J., and Hogarty, G. E. 1986. *Schizophrenia and the family*. New York: Guilford Press.

Andres, F.D. 1971. An introduction to family systems theory. Paper presented at Georgetown Family Symposium, Washington, DC.

Anonymous. 1972. Differentiation of self in one's family. In *Family interaction*, J.L. Framo, ed. New York: Springer.

Bales, R.F. 1950. *Interaction process analysis*. Cambridge, MA: Addison-Wesley.

Bardhill, D.R., and Saunders, B.E. 1988. In *Handbook of family therapy training and supervision*, H.A. Liddle, D.C. Breunlin, and R.C. Schwartz, eds. New York: Guilford Press.

Bateson, G. 1951. Information and codification: A philosophical approach. In *Communication: The social matrix of psychiatry*, J. Ruesch and G. Bateson, eds. New York: Norton.

Bateson, G. 1959. Cultural problems posed by a study of schizophrenic processes. In *Schizophrenia: An integrated approach*, A. Auerbach, ed. New York: Ronald Press.

Bateson, G. 1978. The birth of a matrix or double-bind and epistemology. In *Beyond the double-bind*, M.M. Berger, ed. New York: Brunner/Mazel.

Bateson, G., Jackson, D.D., Haley, J., and Weakland, J. 1956. Toward a theory of schizophrenia. *Behavioral Science. 1*:251–264.

Bateson, G., Jackson, D.D., and Weakland, J.H. 1963. A note on the double bind—1962. *Family Process. 2*:154–161.

Beatman, F.L. 1956. In *Neurotic interaction in marriage*, V.W. Eisenstein, ed. New York: Basic Books.

Beavers, W.R., Blumberg, S., Timken, K.R., and Weiner, M.F. 1965. Communication patterns of mothers of schizophrenics. *Family Process. 4*:95–104.

Bell, J.E. 1961. *Family group therapy*. Public Health Monograph #64. Washington, DC: U.S. Government Printing Office.

Bell, J.E. 1962. Recent advances in family group therapy. *Journal of Child Psychology and Psychiatry. 3*:1–15.

Benne, K.D. 1964. History of the T-group in the laboratory setting. In *T-group theory and laboratory method*, L.P. Bradford, J.R. Gibb, and K.D. Benne, eds. New York: Wiley.

Bennis, W.G. 1964. Patterns and vicissitudes in T-group development. In *T-group theory and laboratory method*, L.P. Bradford, J.R. Gibb, and K.D. Benne, eds. New York: Wiley.

Berger, A. 1965. A test of the double-bind hypothesis of schizophrenia. *Family Process. 4*:198–205.

Bion, W.R. 1948. Experience in groups. *Human Relations. 1*:314–329.

Boszormenyi-Nagy, I. 1962. The concept of schizophrenia from the point of view of family treatment. *Family Process. 1*:103–113.

Boszormenyi-Nagy, I. 1966. From family therapy to a psychology of relationships; fictions of the individual and fictions of the family. *Comprehensive Psychiatry. 7*:408–423.

Boszormenyi-Nagy, I. 1972. Loyalty implications of the transference model in psychotherapy. *Archives of General Psychiatry. 27*:374–380.

Boszormenyi-Nagy, I., and Spark, G.L. 1973. *Invisible loyalties: Reciprocity in intergenerational family therapy*. New York: Harper and Row.

Bowen, M. 1960. A family concept of schizophrenia. In *The etiology of schizophrenia*, D.D. Jackson, ed. New York: Basic Books.

Bowen, M. 1961. Family psychotherapy. *American Journal of Orthopsychiatry. 31*:40–60.

Bowen, M. 1965. Family psychotherapy with schizophrenia in the hospital and in private practice. In *Intensive family therapy*, I. Boszormenyi-Nagy and J.L. Framo, eds. New York: Harper and Row.

Bowen, M. 1976. Principles and techniques of multiple family therapy. In *Family therapy: Theory and practice*, P.J. Guerin, ed. New York: Gardner Press.

Bowen, M., Dysinger, R.H., and Basamania, B. 1959. The role of the father in families with a schizophrenia patient. *American Journal of Psychiatry*. *115*:1017–1020.

Bowlby, J.P. 1949. The study and reduction of group tensions in the family. *Human Relations. 2*:123–138.

Broderick, C.B., and Schrader, S.S. 1981. The history of professional marriage and family therapy. In *Handbook of family therapy*, A.S. Gurman and D.P. Kniskern, eds. New York: Brunner/Mazel.

Brown, G.W. 1959. Experiences of discharged chronic schizophrenia patients in various types of living groups. *Milbank Memorial Fund Quarterly. 37*: 105–131.

Burgum, M. 1942. The father gets worse: A child guidance problem. *American Journal of Orthopsychiatry. 12*:474–485.

Burkin, H.E., Glatzer, H., and Hirsch, J.S. 1944. Therapy of mothers in groups. *American Journal of Orthopsychiatry. 14*:68–75.

Ciotola, P.V. 1961. The effect of two contradictory levels of reward censure on schizophrenics. Ph.D. diss., University of Missouri.

Cooley, C.H. 1902. *Human nature and the social order*. New York: Scribners.

Dicks, H.V. 1964. Concepts of marital diagnosis and therapy as developed at the Tavistock Family Psychiatric Clinic, London, England. In *Marriage counseling in medical practice*, E.M. Nash, L. Jessner, and D.W. Abse, eds. Chapel Hill, NC: University of North Carolina Press.

Elizur, J., and Minuchin, S. 1989. *Institutionalizing madness: Families, therapy, and society*. New York: Basic Books.

Fisher, S., and Mendell, D. 1958. The spread of psychotherapeutic effects from the patient to his family group. *Psychiatry. 21*:133–140.

Freeman, V.J., Klein, A.F., Riehman, L., Lukoff, I.F., and Heisey, V. 1963. Family group counseling as differentiated from other family therapies. *International Journal of Group Psychotherapy. 13*:167–175.

Fromm-Reichmann, F. 1948. Notes on the development of treatment of schizophrenics by psychoanalytic psychotherapy. *Psychiatry. 11*:263–274.

Fromm-Reichmann, F. 1950. *Principles of intensive psychotherapy*. Chicago: University of Chicago Press.

Ginsburg, S.W. 1955. The mental health movement and its theoretical assumptions. In *Community programs for mental health*, R. Kotinsky and H. Witmer, eds. Cambridge: Harvard University Press.

Greenberg, G.S. 1977. The family interactional perspective: A study and examination of the work of Don D. Jackson. *Family Process. 16*:385–412.

Grunwald, H., and Casell, B. 1958. Group counseling with parents. *Child Welfare. 1*:1–6.

Guerin, P.J. 1976. Family therapy: The first twenty-five years. In *Family therapy: Theory and practice*, P.J. Guerin, ed. New York: Gardner Press.

Guindon, J.E. 1971. Paradox, schizophrenia and the double bind hypothesis: An exploratory study. Ph.D. diss., University of Washington.

Haley, J. 1959. The family of the schizophrenic. *American Journal of Nervous and Mental Diseases*. *129*:357–374.

Haley, J. 1961. Control in brief psychotherapy. *Archives of General Psychiatry*. *4*:139–153.

Haley, J. 1963. *Strategies of psychotherapy*. New York: Grune & Stratton.

Haley, J. 1973. *Uncommon therapy*. New York: Norton.

Haley, J. 1976. Development of a theory: A history of a research project. In *Double-bind: The foundation of the communication approach to the family*, C.E. Sluzki and D.C. Ransom, eds. New York: Grune & Stratton.

Haley, J., and Hoffman, L., eds. 1968. *Techniques of family therapy*. New York: Basic Books

Handlon, J.H. and Parloff, M.B. 1962. Treatment of patient and family as a group: Is it group therapy? *International Journal of Group Psychotherapy*. *12*:132–141.

Hare-Mustin, R.T., and Marecek, J. 1988. The meaning of difference: Gender theory, postmodernism, and psychology. *American Psychologist*. *43*:455–464.

Hirsch, S.R., and Leff, J.P. 1975. *Abnormalities in parents of schizophrenics: A review of the literature and an investigation of communication defects and deviances*. London: Oxford University Press.

Howells, J.G. 1971. *Theory and practice of family psychiatry*. New York: Brunner/Mazel.

Jackson, D.D. 1954. Suicide. *Scientific American*. *191*:88–96.

Jackson, D.D. 1957. The question of family homeostasis. *The Psychiatric Quarterly Supplement*. *31*:79–90.

Jackson, D.D. 1961. Family therapy in the family of the schizophrenic. In *Contemporary psychotherapies*, M. Stein, ed. Glencoe, IL: The Free Press.

Jackson, D.D. 1965. Family rules: Marital quid pro quo. *Archives of General Psychiatry*. *12*:589–594.

Jackson, D.D., and Weakland, J.H. 1959. Schizophrenic symptoms and family interaction. *Archives of General Psychiatry*. *1*:618–621.

Jackson, D.D., and Weakland, J.H. 1961. Conjoint family therapy, some considerations on theory, technique, and results. *Psychiatry*. *24*:30–45.

Johnson, A.M., and Szurek, S.A. 1954. Etiology of anti-social behavior in delinquents and psychopaths. *Journal of the American Medical Association*. *154*:814–817.

Kaplan, H. and Sadock, B. 1983. *Comprehensive group psychotherapy*. Baltimore: Williams & Wilkins.

Kasanin, J., Knight, E., and Sage, P. 1934. The parent-child relationships in schizophrenia. *Journal of Nervous and Mental Diseases*. *79*:249–263.

Kaslow, F.W. 1980. History of family therapy in the United States: A kaleidoscopic overview. *Marriage and Family Review*. *3*:77–111.

Kaufman, E., and Kaufmann, P., eds. 1979. *Family therapy of drug and alcohol abuse*. New York: Gardner Press.

Kempler, W. 1974. *Principles of Gestalt family therapy.* Salt Lake City: Desert Press.

Kingsley, V.C. 1969. The effects of the double-bind conflict and sex of the experimenter on the conceptual functioning and visual discrimination of male good and poor premorbid schizophrenics. Ph.D. diss., New York University.

Kirby, K., and Priestman, S. 1957. Values of a daughter (schizophrenic) and mother therapy group. *International Journal of Group Psychotherapy.* 7:281–288.

Kluckhohn, F.R., and Spiegel, J.P. 1954. *Integration and conflict in family behavior.* Group for the Advancement of Psychiatry, Report No. 27. Topeka, Kansas.

Knoblochova, J., and Knobloch, F. 1970. Family therapy in Czechoslovakia: An aspect of group-centered psychotherapy. In *Family therapy in transition*, N.W. Ackerman, ed. Boston: Little, Brown.

Kubie, L.S. 1956. Psychoanalysis and marriage. In *Neurotic interaction in marriage*, V.W. Eisenstein, ed. New York: Basic Books.

Laing, R.D. 1960. *The divided self.* London: Tavistock Publications.

Laing, R.D. 1965. Mystification, confusion and conflict. In *Intensive family therapy*, I. Boszormenyi-Nagy and J.L. Framo, eds. New York: Harper & Row.

Lakin, M. 1985. *The helping group: Therapeutic principles and issues.* Reading, MA: Addison-Wesley.

Levy, D. 1943. *Maternal Overprotection.* New York: Columbia Unversity Press.

Lewin, K. 1951. *Field theory in social science.* New York: Harper.

Lidz, R.W., and Lidz, T. 1949. The family environment of schizophrenic patients. *American Journal of Psychiatry.* 106:332–345.

Lidz, T., Cornelison, A., Fleck, S., and Terry, D. 1957a. Intrafamilial environment of the schizophrenic patient. I: The father. *Psychiatry*, 20:329–342.

Lidz, T., Cornelison, A., Fleck, S., and Terry, D. 1957b. Intrafamilial environment of schizophrenic patients. II: Marital schism and marital skew. *American Journal of Psychiatry.* 114:241–248.

Lidz, T., and Fleck, S. 1960. Schizophrenia, human integration, and the role of the family. In *The etiology of schizophrenia*, D.D. Jackson, ed. New York: Basic Books.

Lidz, T., Parker, B., and Cornelison, A.R. 1956. The role of the father in the family environment of the schizophrenic patient. *American Journal of Psychiatry.* 113:126–132.

Low, A.A. 1943. *The technique of self-help in psychiatry after-care.* Vol. 3, *Lectures to relatives of former patients.* Chicago: Recovery, Inc.

Lowrey, L.G. 1944. Group treatment for mothers. *American Journal of Orthopsychiatry.* 14:589–592.

Luft, J. 1970. *Group processes.* Palo Alto, CA: National Press Books.

MacGregor, R. 1967. Progress in multiple impact theory. In *Expanding theory and practice in family therapy*, N.W. Ackerman, F.L. Beatman, and S.N. Sherman, eds. New York: Family Services Association.

Mahler, M.S. & Rabinovitch, R. 1956. The effects of marital conflict on child development. In *Neurotic interaction in marriage*, V.W. Eisenstein, ed. New York: Basic Books.

Marsh, L.C. 1935. Group therapy and the psychiatric clinic. *American Journal of Nervous and Mental Diseases*. 82:381–393.

Midelfort, C.F. 1957. *The family in psychotherapy*. New York: McGraw-Hill.

Minuchin, S. 1974. *Families and family therapy*. Cambridge, MA: Harvard University Press.

Minuchin, S., and Fishman, H.C. 1981. *Family therapy techniques*. Cambridge, MA: Harvard University Press.

Minuchin, S., Montalvo, B., Guerney, B.G., Rosman, B.L., and Schumer, F. 1967. *Families of the slums*. New York: Basic Books.

Minuchin, S., Rosman, B.L., and Baker, L. 1978. *Psychosomatic families: Anorexia nervosa in context*. Cambridge, MA: Harvard University Press.

Mittleman, B. 1944. Complementary neurotic reactions in intimate relationships. *Psychoanalytic Quarterly*. 13:474–491.

Mittleman, B. 1948. The concurrent analysis of married couples. *Psychoanalytic Quarterly*. 17:182–197.

Mittleman, B. 1956. Analysis of reciprocal neurotic patterns in family relationships. In *Neurotic interactions in marriage*. V.W. Eisenstein, ed. New York: Basic Books.

Montague, A. 1956. Marriage—A cultural perspective. In *Neurotic interaction in marriage*, V.W. Eisenstein, ed. New York: Basic Books.

Moreno, J.L. 1945. *Psychodrama*. New York: Beacon House.

Nichols, M.P., and Zax, M. 1977. *Catharsis in psychotherapy*. New York: Gardner Press.

Nichols, W. 1979. Doctoral programs in marital and family therapy. *Journal of Marital and Family Therapy*. 5:23–28.

Oberndorf, C.P. 1938. Psychoanalysis of married couples. *Psychoanalytic Review: 25*, 453–475.

Parsons, T., and Bales, R.F. 1955. *Family socialization and interaction*. Glencoe, IL: Free Press.

Phillips, M. 1970. Response to "double-bind" messages in relation to four dimensions of personality and two maternal child rearing attitudes: A study of interpretational and feeling preferences of late adolescents. Ph.D. diss., New York University.

Potash, H.M. 1965. Schizophrenic interaction and the concept of the double-bind. Doctoral diss., Michigan State University.

Richmond, M.E. 1917. *Social diagnosis*. New York: Russell Sage.

Ringuette, E.L., and Kennedy, T. 1966. An experimental study of the double-bind hypothesis. *Journal of Abnormal Psychology*. 71:136–141.

Ross, W.D. 1948. Group psychotherapy with patient's relatives. *American Journal of Psychiatry*. 104:623–626.

Satir, V. 1964. *Conjoint family therapy*. Palo Alto, CA: Science and Behavior Books.

Satir, V. 1972. *Peoplemaking*. Palo Alto, CA: Science and Behavior Books.

Schaeffer, R.L. 1972. Training schizophrenics and neurotics to recognize double-binds: A comparison. Ph.D. diss., Adelphi University.

Schindler, W. 1951. Counter-transference in family-pattern group psycho-therapy. *International Journal of Group Psychotherapy*. *1*:100–105.

Schrieber, A.W. 1970. An experimental double-bind and communicativeness. Ph.D. diss., City University of New York.

Sherif, M. 1948. *An outline of social psychology*. New York: Harper and Brothers.

Singer, M.T., Wynne, L.C., and Toohey, M.L. 1978. Communication disorders and the families of schizophrenics. In *The nature of schizophrenia*, L.C. Wynne, R.L. Cromwell, and S. Matthysse, eds. New York: Wiley.

Siporin, M. 1980. Marriage and family therapy in social work. *Social Casework*. *61*:11–21.

Skynner, R. 1976. *Systems of family and marital psychotherapy*. New York: Brunner/Mazel.

Slavson, S.R. 1943. *An introduction to group therapy*. New York: The Commonwealth Fund.

Sluzki, C.E., Beavin, J., Tarnopolsky, A., and Veron, E. 1967. Transactional disqualification. *Archives of General Psychiatry*. *16*:494–504.

Smith, E.K. 1972. The effect of double-bind communications upon the state of anxiety of normals. Ph.D. diss., University of New Mexico.

Sojit, C.M. 1969. Dyadic interaction in a double-bind situation. *Family Process*. *8*:235–259.

Speck, R., and Attneave, C. 1973. *Family networks: Rehabilitation and healing*. New York: Pantheon.

Spiegel, J.P. 1957. The resolution of role conflict within the family. *Psychiatry*. *20*:1–16.

Steinglass, P. 1987. *The alcoholic family*. New York: Basic Books.

Stierlin, H. 1972. *Separating parents and adolescents*. New York: Quadrangle/New York Times Books.

Stierlin, H. 1977. *Psychoanalysis and family therapy*. New York: Jason Aronson.

Strodtbeck, F.L. 1954. The family as a three-person group. *American Sociological Review*. *19*:23–29.

Strodtbeck, F.L. 1958. Family interaction, values, and achievement. In *Talent and society*, D.C. McClelland, A.L. Baldwin, A. Bronfenbrenner, and F.L. Strodtbeck, eds. Princeton, NJ: Van Nostrand.

Uzoka, A.F. 1979. The myth of the nuclear family. *American Psychologist*. *34*:1095–1106.

Watzlawick, P.A., Beavin, J.H., and Jackson, D.D. 1967. *Pragmatics of human communication*. New York: Norton.

Weakland, J.H. 1960. The 'double-bind' hypothesis of schizophrenia and three-party interaction. In *The etiology of schizophrenia*, D.D. Jackson, ed. New York: Basic Books.

Whitaker, C.A. 1958. Psychotherapy with couples. *American Journal of Psychotherapy*. *12*:18–23.

Whitaker, C.A. 1975. Psychotherapy of the absurd: With a special emphasis on the psychotherapy of aggression. *Family Process*. *14*:1–16.

Whitaker, C.A. 1976. A family is a four-dimensional relationship. In *Family therapy: Theory and practice*, P.J. Guerin, ed. New York: Gardner Press.

Whitaker, C.A., and Malone, T.P. 1953. *The roots of psychotherapy.* New York: Balkiston.

Whitehead, A.N., and Russell, B. 1910. *Principia mathematica.* Cambridge, MA: Cambridge University Press.

Wynne, L.C. 1961. The study of intrafamilial alignments and splits in exploratory family therapy. In *Exploring the base for family therapy*, N.W. Ackerman, F.L. Beatman, and S.N. Sherman, eds. New York: Family Services Association.

Wynne, L.C. 1978. Knotted relationships, communication deviances, and metabinding. In *Beyond the double bind*, M.M. Berger, ed. New York: Brunner/Mazel.

Wynne, L.C., Ryckoff, I., Day, J., and Hirsch, S. I. 1958. Pseudomutuality in the family relationships of schizophrenics. *Psychiatry. 21*:205–220.

Yalom, I.D. 1985. *The theory and practice of group psychotherapy.* 3rd ed. New York: Basic Books.

Zuk, G.H. 1971. *Family therapy: A triadic-based approach.* New York: Behavioral Publications.

2

The Conceptual Context
of Family Therapy

One of family therapy's greatest contributions to the mental health field is to stress the importance of understanding people's behavior in their natural context. As Bateson (1979) wrote, "It is the context that fixes the meaning." Prior to this recognition, the symptoms of a psychiatric patient were examined in isolation, apart from his or her network of family relationships, so the only available explanation for them was that the person was defective. Once therapists began to view the person's behavior within the context of the family, the behavior not only seemed less strange but it could also be understood as an inevitable and necessary aspect of the way the family had evolved.

Similarly when viewed apart from the context of the evolution of our scientific culture, the field of family therapy seems a strange and radical departure from the direction of the field of psychotherapy, generated by iconoclastic pioneers. The purpose of this chapter is to do more than simply introduce the reader to family therapy's concepts and methods but also to provide some context for evolution of these ideas and techniques. Once viewed in this context, family therapy also can be seen as an inevitable or necessary development in the evolution of psychotherapy.

EVOLUTION OF IDEAS _____

Before exploring the specific case of family therapy, we would like to discuss the way science in general evolves so we can have a larger perspective on the emergence of family therapy and, perhaps, have some idea of where the field is headed.

Science historian Thomas Kuhn (1977) traced the evolution of scientific disciplines. He found that most disciplines begin in what he called a "preparadigmatic period," during which the practitioners of a science are split into many competing schools, each of which approach the same subject differently, while claiming that theirs is the best way. This stage lasts until a major scientific breakthrough makes most of the schools obsolete, after which, in the "postparadigmatic period," the discipline is dominated by one school.

Kuhn cites many examples from the physical sciences of this evolutionary process. One of these relates to our understanding of the nature of light. Before Newton's work there was no scientific consensus regarding the nature of light.

> From remote antiquity . . . many men advanced a large number of different views about the nature of light. Some of these views found few adherents, but a number of them gave rise to continuing schools of optical thought. Although the historian can note the emergence of new points of view as well as changes in the relative popularity of older ones, there never was anything resembling consensus. As a result, a new man entering the field was inevitably exposed to a variety of conflicting viewpoints; he was forced to examine the evidence for each, and there always was good evidence (p. 231).

Eventually Newton's idea that light consisted of material corpuscles won out and became the agreed-upon view, until that paradigm was replaced in the early nineteenth century by the view of light as wave motion which, in turn, was replaced early this century by the quantum-mechanical view of light as photons, which have some characteristics of waves and some of particles.

Kuhn proposes that this pattern of evolution of science, from a period during which there are many competing schools to the dominance of one school which is subsequently overthrown by a new one, is characteristic of all fields. Different disciplines reach their first consensus during different centuries, and Kuhn suggests that "This century appears to be characterized by the emergence of a first consensus in parts of a few of the social sciences" (p. 232).

Psychotherapy is not one of those social sciences to have reached consensus. Instead, the current state of psychotherapy is a classic example of the preparadigmatic or preconsensual phase, in which there are a number of competing schools and subschools, each claiming validity. This state of the art can be accounted for, in part, by the relative youth of the field but also by the complexity of the phenomena that theories of psychotherapy are trying to explain or predict. Unlike the physical sciences, the social sciences are faced with more diverse and changing variables and have few and imprecise instruments with which to measure these variables.

To illustrate the difference between the physical and biological sciences, Gregory Bateson (1979) used the example of kicking a stone versus kicking a dog. The effect of kicking a stone can be predicted precisely by measuring the force and angle of the kick and the weight of the stone. If a man kicks a dog, on the other hand, the effect is far less predictable. The dog may respond to the kick in any number of ways, from cringing and running away to turning and biting the man, depending on the temperament of the dog and how it interprets the kick. In response to the dog's reaction, the man may modify his behavior in any number of ways, and so on, so that the number of possible outcomes is immense.

Given this complexity it is difficult for a field like psychotherapy to test the validity of its theories. Kuhn's (1977) description of astrology hits uncomfortably close to psychotherapy's home: "The occurrence of failures [of prediction] could be explained, but particular failures did not give rise to research puzzles, for no man, however skilled, could make use of them in a constructive attempt to revise the astrological tradition. There were too many possible sources of difficulty, most of them beyond the astrologer's knowledge, control, or responsibility" (p. 276).

In the absence of iron-clad validity tests and solid conclusions, how are schools within a preparadigmatic field born or retired? Richard Schwartz (1985) proposed a framework for understanding the differentiation of the field of psychotherapy, as well as the subfield of family therapy and the various schools of family therapy. We elaborate on this framework below to help the reader understand how family therapy arrived at its present state.

The marketplace of models in psychotherapy can be compared to the evolution of biological systems. Stephen Jay Gould (1985), a leading scholar of evolution, summarizes the process this way: "When systems first arise, they probe all the limits of possibility. Many variations don't work; the best solutions emerge, and variation diminishes" (p. 220). For example, mollusks now exist as snails, clams, octopuses, and a few other groups, but early in their history there were ten to fifteen fundamental variations.

The same process applies to theories in a field like psychotherapy. When this new approach to human problems arose, i.e., the idea that people could be helped through some form of contact with a "therapist," all the limits of possibility were probed. Many models were generated. Eventually they should either merge or die from lack of popularity or success and, ideally, we would be left with a few models that represent the most effective ways to do psychotherapy, within the limitations imposed by the premises and metaphors of our particular age and culture.

In this early stage of the evolution of psychotherapy, there is not only great variation but also a high degree of polarization. One model will be countered by a rival that is based on opposite assumptions from the first. This pendulum-swinging process seems to be useful in that the extremes are quickly explored, allowing for a gradually increasing drift toward a middle ground. For example, Freud's extreme focus on the power of the psyche was countered by the behaviorist movement that discounted the intrapsychic and overemphasized environmental reinforcers. Next the reductionistic focus on the individual of the Freudian and behaviorist schools was countered by family therapy's extreme emphasis on the power of the family system. It is only lately that any common ground among these three extreme approaches is being explored.

Stages within a Model

Essentialistic.   This pendulum-swinging process seems a natural artifact of the way people react to new ideas or innovations. The proponents or discoverers of an advance usually consider it the long-sought understanding that captures the *essence* of the phenomenon being investigated. This begins an *essentialistic stage* in the model's development, which is often characterized by tunnel vision, zeal, and chauvinism—enthusiasms that are understandable and even useful, if they do not persist indefinitely. Tunnel vision seems necessary temporarily in order to fully explore the complex possibilities of the new approach without the distraction of old or alternative points of view. Zeal and chauvinism arise from the belief that the essence has finally been found, and also provide a defense against attacks from the establishment that new models provoke.

An essentialistic stage is often a period of high productivity and creativity, fueled by the excitement and commitment that accompanies the belief that one is on the brink of something big. This stage can have a down side, however, because essentialistism breeds either/or thinking: the model is right and all others are wrong. Any failure of the model is explained away by essentialists as a misapplication of its principles or as faulty documentation of outcome.

The duration and extremism of the essentialistic stage is likely to depend on (1) how long it takes to explore the model to the point where its limitations begin to emerge, and (2) the degree to which the established orthodoxy accepts or accommodates to the new model. The more the essentialists must defend their model, the more they feel like enlightened crusaders, the less able they are to examine their discoveries critically. The less they can examine their results critically, the longer it takes to discover that their model is limited or flawed.

Transitional.   The *transitional stage* begins when some essentialists start to recognize that their model is limited or flawed. This can be a tumultuous period, depending upon how extreme the essentialistic period was. If hopes of having found the essence were raised high, they have a long way to fall when prophecies fail. When this happens, the transitional period is marked by intramodel polarization, with some adherents defending the model while others desert in disillusionment.

Thus we can see how the zealousness and naive optimism of an essentialistic stage generates the pendulum-swinging process; as disillusioned former adherents of the model and outsiders, polarized by the essentialists' chauvinism and zeal, spin off new, opposite, but equally extreme models.

Some of those who remain loyal to the original model through this transitional stage will be inclined to retrench in the face of the chaos and polarization and become even more rigidly dogmatic about the model's assumptions and methods. Others, however, gradually accept the model's limitations—that it may not have full essentialistic power or universality—and can begin to see it in context. They are able to drop the tunnel vision that was necessary earlier and see the commonalities as well as the differences with other models. Their zeal is replaced with a new openness and modesty as they become comfortable with a shift in goal from finding the blockbuster discovery to contributing a piece to a larger puzzle.

Ecological.   This opening of the boundaries of the model is often accompanied by the fear that its unique qualities will dissipate or will be co-opted by the establishment. This can be a real danger and adherents walk a tightrope in trying to maintain the model's integrity while considering other possibilities. Ideally the tension of this process forces theorists to a "meta" position—a perspective from which they can look down upon the larger field, and see their model as one among an ecology of models. From this meta and modest state of mind they are better able to see the "pattern that connects" (Bateson, 1979) their model with other models that they once believed to be contradictory or incompatible. This period is characterized by increased communication and cooperation among models. In this way the *ecological period* may produce a new metatheory that is able to account for and deal with a much wider range of phenomena than any of the individual models within the ecology.

CONTEXTUAL INFLUENCES ON THE EVOLUTION OF FAMILY THERAPY

The field of family therapy emerged as part of this pendulum-swinging, stage-wise process within the larger mental health field, and the various schools of family therapy emerged as a subpart of that process. This explains why family therapy, and many of its schools, have often been characterized by tunnel vision, zeal, and chauvinism. In the 1980s family therapy emerged from its essentialistic stage, survived the disillusionment, retrenchment, and challenge of the early transitional stage, and is now showing some of the modesty and openness characteristic of the late transitional period. This characterization also applies to some schools of family therapy while, as we shall see, others remain relatively essentialistic and isolated.

Let us now take a more careful look at how family therapy has arrived at this stage. Accounts that summarize the emergence and evolution of the field fit well with our pendulum-swinging, stages framework. Consider Lynn Hoffman's (1981) observations:

> The family movement in therapy resembles the Protestant movement in religion. It follows on the heels of a highly organized body of ideas and practice which has a well-recognized founding father, Sigmund Freud. Despite multiple heresies and schisms, psychoanalysis has formed the basis for a mental health establishment. Some pioneers in the family therapy field have mounted a revisionistic assault, almost amounting to revolution, against the ideas of this Freudian establishment . . . (p. 219).

Many family therapy pioneers were disillusioned psychoanalysts, frustrated by the limits of psychoanalytic orthodoxy and its focus on the individual out of context, its overemphasis on intrapsychic and historical factors, its pessimistic and pathological assumptions about people, its esoteric theorizing, its impracticality for the majority of Americans and for many syndromes, and its rigid dogmatism.

In fairness to psychoanalysis, many of these criticisms may apply more to its essentialistic stage than to its current practice. Nevertheless the extreme essentialism of psychoanalysis helped generate the extreme essentialism of early family therapy, with its overemphasis on the power of the family context; its exclusion of intrapsychic and historical considerations; its overly optimistic assumptions; its overemphasis on pragmatism, simplicity, brevity; and its own dogmatism. When the pendulum swings, it swings all the way.

During this early period family therapy's rhetoric reflected the need to differentiate from mainstream thought and recruit converts. There existed an us-versus-them mentality characteristic of revolutionary groups: We are systemic, they are linear; we can cure all problems, they can cure none; we are the therapy of the people, they are for the wealthy; we are good, they are bad. In a book chapter titled "Family Therapy: A Radical Change," Jay Haley (1971a), probably the most radical and polemical of the pioneers, wrote "[when there is a discontinuous change in a field,] the ideas of the past are not building blocks but become stumbling blocks in grasping a new way of thinking" (p. 272). While this essentialism and polarization are part of the natural evolution of the field of psychotherapy, they also take a toll on the quality of theorizing. A decade later the same Jay Haley said in reflecting on this period,

> At one time I thought I had more freedom because I was an outsider. I didn't have to think in a restricted way like the insiders. Then I realized I was not free because I was not allowed to think like an insider if I was to be on the outside. (Simon, 1982b, p. 36).

As family therapy became more widely accepted as a valid orientation to human problems, much of the extreme dogma and essentialistic thinking abated. It is less necessary to attack the establishment now because there are fewer attacks from the establishment and more converts. As the field moves through its transitional phase and communicates with the establishment, the fear of co-option grows. As Minuchin lamented,

> The psychiatric field has incorporated family therapy as a modality of treatment—without, of course, changing the diagnostic categories of individual patients . . . This is the way society works. It co-opted a movement that was challenging basic ways of thinking about human problems by making it official. (Simon, 1984, p. 30).

Indeed, versions of family therapy, such as the psychoeducation movement, have emerged and become increasingly popular. They seem more closely tied to the assumptions of the medical model than to the systemic paradigm that Minuchin and others want to protect. Other models, like the psychoanalytic and behavioral schools of family therapy (see Chapters 5 and 7, respectively), which have always been considered outgrowths of the establishment rather than part of the systems revolution, have also been gaining in popularity as they develop clarity.

Whether these trends represent a fatal dilution of the essence of family therapy or steps toward an ecological stage in the field that will result in a valuable synthesis or metatheory is yet to be determined.

DIFFERENTIATION WITHIN FAMILY THERAPY

The process by which family therapy differentiated into competing models parallels the pendulum-swinging, stages framework by which family therapy as a whole differentiated from the psychiatric establishment. In the 1950s family therapy was a radical, new experiment practiced in relative isolation by a small number of clinician-researchers around the country. During that period these theorists shared a sense of awe at the magnitude of the task they faced in making sense of phenomena that no one before them had studied and a sense of solidarity against the establishment that all revolutionary groups start out with. Carlos Sluzki (1983, p. 24) likened these early family therapists to pioneers of the old west:

> During its first ten or fifteen years, the situation in the family therapy field was akin to that of the western frontier of the U.S. during the mid-1800s. There was a lot of territory to occupy and explore, an undeclared war with the previous inhabitants (in family therapy's case, psycho-dynamically-oriented and classical psychiatrists) and a prevailing spirit of adventure and expansionism. Back then, family therapists were, for the most part, not too preoccupied with staking out their personal domains since like-minded neighbors were few and far between and they were concerned with developing common defenses against the unfriendly elements in the mental health establishment.

Minuchin's description of the same time period also emphasized their co-operation, excitement, and shared anxiety:

> The old timers knew that their private truths were only partial, and when they met around a cup of coffee, they gossiped about the beginnings and shared their uncertainties and hopes (Simon, 1984, p. 68).

Gradually, and from the perspective of our pendulum-swinging, stages framework, naturally, the field began to differentiate and polarize. Systems theory was abstract and had a number of different versions so that it could be, and was, translated in a number of ways, depending on the inclination of the theorist. As with the proverbial blind men exploring different parts of an elephant, many of the family therapy pioneers studied and stressed the importance of different aspects of family systems, and each began believing that their aspect was the essence of what caused problems in families. These early essences, which will be described later in this chapter, were encapsulated in terms like *incongruent communication*, lack of *differentiation*, poorly defined *boundaries, function of the symptom*, and *positive feedback loops*. Differences in theory translated into ever larger differences in technique and, in this way, a series of idiosyncratic models of family therapy entered their essentialistic stage.

Economic Influences

There are a number of factors that contributed to the length and competitiveness of this essentialistic period within each model, not the least of which is money. Since family therapy was an antiestablishment movement, it was not born, nor could it take root, within the traditional establishment institutions like medical schools or universities. Students who wanted training in family therapy could not get it through traditional academic avenues and, instead, looked to the private training institutes that sprang up around the country and to private workshops put on by the peripatetic pioneers. This privatization of family therapy training released it from the economic constraints of academia and made it a very lucrative enterprise. During family therapy's boom period of the late 1970s and early 1980s a big name presenter could make ten thousand dollars in a weekend workshop.

Sluzki (1983) colorfully described the effect this profit motive has had on the differentiation of the field.

> Over the last 10 years . . . there has been a population explosion within the field as well as a dramatic increase in the commercial advantages of having control of part of its territory. As a result, people have been known to surreptitiously move fences, erect huge stockades, dispute certain areas and even claim as their own territories that were previously defined as common grounds. During the past 10 years, we have witnessed a Balkanization of the field into sectors based on political rather than scientific boundaries. We have also seen the rise of a "star" system, based on maintaining those artificial boundaries for politico-economic reasons. The consequence of all this has been the development of more and more "brand-name" models and increased bickering about whose technique washes whiter (p. 24).

Minuchin also recognized that the motives of the various schools to maintain their essentialistic differences were not scientifically pure. In describing the pioneers (some of which may be autobiographic) he stated that,

> . . . lo and behold, their institutions grew and they needed large buildings to accommodate all their students. Slowly, before anyone realized it, the buildings became castles with turrets and drawbridges, and even watchmen in the towers. The castles were very expensive and they had to justify their existence. Therefore, they demanded ownership of the total truth (Simon, 1984, p. 68).

Today there are still many different castles. Some inhabitants guard them as ferociously as ever and rarely venture out. One harbinger of the transitional stage, however, is the increasing number of family therapists who, having gone through the essentialistic stage with one model, have traveled far enough to see their castle in perspective and are living on the borders between conceptual kingdoms. This is a generation of therapists with less direct allegiance to the charismatic royalty of the castles and, therefore, less constrained by personal loyalties.

The leaders of this transitional generation are less likely to erect impenetrable castles of their own. Castle building requires the zeal and single-mindedness that come with the belief that one "knows" while others do not, and this group seems beyond that stage. They also seem less able to generate, or less interested in generating, the big money that would en-

encourage castle building. There is less patience with simplistic, unidimensional descriptions of families or with all-purpose techniques. As Minuchin observed, "When I first began to teach family therapy, I did so with a deceptive simplicity. Today I talk a lot more about the complexities" (Simon, 1984, p. 68). Thus as the field matures more is written about the variation among families and less about a universal family pattern against which all families are measured.

The Influence of Free Market Research

Another effect of the field's development outside academia is that the pioneering theorists were relatively immune to traditional academic publication standards. They could (and some did) make dramatic outcome claims without the scrutiny that traditional institutions and review processes afford. Alan Gurman, former editor of the *Journal of Marital and Family Therapy*, complained that,

> The prominent purveyors of family therapy often seemed to be making across-the-board assertions about what their methods could accomplish— it is as if they were saying they had the cleanest wash no matter what the dirt was. Mostly this has been communicated indirectly by rarely reporting failures and not providing clear research data (quoted in Schwartz and Perrotta, 1985, p. 20).

On the other hand, subjecting the field to standard professional constraints might have stifled creativity and innovation. Seminal ideas and practices might have been watered down if the goal had been to reduce family therapy to the kind of easily controlled or operationalized studies that academic journals demand—where the findings are often rigorous but trivial. Perhaps a few questionable notions and inflated claims is the price to be paid for creative freedom.

Don Ransom, associate editor of *Family Systems Medicine*, provides another rationale for exaggerated claims during the essentialistic stage:

> Creating a climate of enthusiasm is a stage in the sociology of any new profession. The early claims made by family therapy—the idea that it might be the panacea—were important in turning many of us on, getting us involved in the field (quoted in Schwartz and Perrotta, 1985, p. 20).

The flaw in these ends-justify-the-means arguments lies in the damage done to those clients whose problems were oversimplified and whose hopes were raised and dashed, as clinicians around the country rushed to try out the latest exciting techniques.

The danger of naive enthusiasm is exemplified by the actions of a fledgling therapist who, in 1974, discovered *Change: Principles of Problem*

Formation and Problem Resolution (Watzlawick, Weakland, and Fisch, 1974), the classic text for strategic family therapy. This eager convert embraced this book as the solution to all his therapeutic muddles.

> This attitude was not discouraged by the authors who made statements like ". . . second-order change through paradox—is undoubtedly the most powerful and elegant form of problem resolution known to us," and "We see our basic views on problem formation and resolution, persistence and change, as usefully and appropriately applicable to human problems generally."
>
> He seized on what amounted to a small footnote in the book that said a wide range of psychiatric problems were at least significantly improved in 73 percent of nearly 100 cases, and in an average of less than 10 sessions. Taking this as compelling proof of the validity of the paradoxical approach, he brazenly prescribed that all kinds of psychiatric morasses he encountered in his crisis work remain the same.
>
> On one occasion he made a home visit to a chronically depressed older man who had an established pattern of becoming bedridden for weeks, being hospitalized, getting better, returning to work, then getting depressed and returning to bed for weeks . . . With barely hidden sarcasm, [the therapist] told the now bedridden man that he should continue in his current helpless state because his wife was a retired nurse and needed to have a patient to care for. Enraged, the man bounded out of bed, grabbed a broomstick, and chased the well-meaning young therapist out of his house.
>
> Did this incident point towards a positive outcome? After all, the man was activated to get out of bed and express his anger directly. But the couple never wanted to see the therapist again and quickly fell back into their old pattern (Schwartz and Perrotta, 1985, p. 21).

The point of this story is not that paradoxical techniques are without value (see Chapter 9 for a discussion of paradox), but that in the excitement of discovery, these authors oversold them.

This has been the case with the debut of other models. Therapists around the world have been inspired to try and replicate the methods of the Milan Associates based on their book *Paradox and Counterparadox* (Selvini Palazzoli, Cecchin, Boscolo, and Prata, 1978), which contains few warnings or guidelines, while promoting paradoxical technique with some very impressive anecdotal outcome claims. Indeed the Italians confessed in the introduction to this book that they felt pressured into publishing their work "despite the fact that publication is undoubtedly premature" (p. xi). A decade later, Selvini Palazzoli has totally abandoned this paradoxical approach which had seemed so miraculous, stating that "I had too many failures using paradoxical methods with psychotic and anorectic families" (Simon, 1987, p. 26).

Now she has a new method, the *invariant prescription*, for which she claims equally miraculous results. Based on ten cases in which she claims there was a complete alleviation of symptoms in anorexic and schizophrenic patients, she concludes that "the therapeutic power of the invariable prescription, when obeyed, had now been confirmed beyond all doubt" (Simon, 1987, p. 20).

The same criticism applies to Haley's (1980) "Leaving Home Model," a very difficult and risky approach, based on a handful of anecdotal successful outcome reports and accompanied by few guidelines or warnings. It was packaged, instead, as an instrument that "causes positive change and has a low risk of doing harm" and suggested that it could be applied to most troubled young adults regardless of diagnosis or symptoms. Years later, after hearing about how therapists had been misapplying this model, Haley confessed that "sometimes what you write for therapists spills into the community in unfortunate ways and then you're sorry you ever wrote it" (Simon, 1984).

We aren't suggesting here that family therapy outcome research in general is shoddier than that of other schools of psychotherapy. There have been some rigorous outcome studies in the family therapy literature. Moreover the frequency of seemingly exaggerated claims seems to have decreased considerably. Perhaps the field has begun to follow Braulio Montalvo's advice: "We have to learn how to lower our sights and realize what we can accomplish. I think our effort now needs to be highlighting the various areas in which we have some honest knowledge and away from clinical myth-making" (quoted in Schwartz and Perrotta, 1985, p. 24).

Returning to our stages framework for the evolution of models, a model that rises rapidly on the wings of big promises is more likely to crash and burn when its performance doesn't match its promise. This then triggers the pendulum swings and polarizations that perpetuate the field's essentialistic stage. Over the years, models of family therapy have gone in and out of fashion at remarkable rates and, undoubtedly, some babies have been thrown out with the bathwater. Some ideas and techniques have survived, however, and have become the enduring concepts and methods that will be described later in this chapter. Before we get there, we will examine some other important contextual influences on family therapy's concepts and methods.

Gender and Class Bias

While it is true that different models of family therapy emerged in part because theorists selected different aspects of family interaction to emphasize, it is also true that because of the idiosyncrasies of personality and background, various theorists viewed the families they studied through entirely different lenses. If, for example, Nathan Ackerman and Virginia Satir were observing the same family and were asked to focus on the same aspect of the family's interaction, their observations, assessments, and interventions would have been very different. That is because the assumptions and beliefs we hold about the world color the way we see it.

Family therapy has struggled to give up the Lockean notion that there is a reality out there that we can objectively perceive and, with the help of both the feminists and constructivists (two groups that otherwise are often in conflict), now realizes the importance of understanding the belief systems of the observers and the contextual influences on those belief systems.

Let us briefly examine the personalities, backgrounds, and cultural contexts of the family therapy pioneers and speculate as to how these factors might have affected what they saw. With few exceptions, these pioneers were white, male psychiatrists, who were exploring and writing during a very conservative period of American history, the late 1950s. As might be expected, they share many of the biases of their times. Beginning in the early eighties, feminist family therapists re-examined many of the premises and techniques that two generations of family therapists held sacred (see Chapter 3). Their critique stunned a field that prided itself on its liberalism, compassion, and openness. It was as if the feminists switched on a light in a dark room; once the bias in the original theories was pointed out, it is hard to understand how we had been so blind. Perhaps the length of family therapy's essentialistic stage accounts for some of this blindness. It took a while for the insecurity and excitement of exploring unknown territory and making new discoveries to wear off to the point that we could take another look at our theories.

At any rate, it seems clear now that sexism had an impact on the field. Deborah Luepnitz, in *The Family Interpreted* (1988), recently presented a scathing yet scholarly feminist critique of the thinking of the pioneers. Luepnitz states that the patriarchal belief system of someone like Nathan Ackerman (1958) (see Chapter 5), who has been called "the father of family therapy," is easy to identify. Luepnitz cites the following passage where Ackerman writes:

> In certain families, there is a reversal of sexual roles. The woman dominates and makes the decisions; she "wears the pants." The father is passive and submits to avoid argument. The mother pushes the father towards many of the maternal duties . . . Such trends as these have had an immeasurable effect in distorting the functions of mothering and in confusing the sexual and emotional development of the child . . . He [the father] has been stripped of all semblance of arbitrary authority in the family. His power to discipline and punish family offenders, whether wife or child, has been sharply undercut.

Patriarchal assumptions in other models are less blatant but still evident. For example, Luepnitz (1988) criticized Bowen's (1978) overimplication of the mother in the development of pathology in her child. Additionally, she and others (Hare-Mustin 1978; Lerner, 1986) criticize

Bowen's emphasis on male-oriented adjectives like "autonomous," "goal-directed," or "intellectual" in describing the "differentiated" way people should strive to be, while he uses qualities that, traditionally, women have been socialized for, like "seeking love and approval," "relatedness," and "being-for-others," to describe the poorly differentiated person. Finally Bowen's thesis that to differentiate one should separate the emotional from the intellect and put the intellect in control can also be seen as reflective of a male value system that reveres reason and fears feelings.

Salvador Minuchin, the founder of structural family therapy (see Chapter 10), one of the field's most popular models, has not escaped the feminist critique. In watching tapes of Minuchin work, feminists noticed the frequency with which he tried to disengage what he considered to be an enmeshed mother and child by getting the father to be more involved in taking over for the mother, rather than encouraging and supporting the mother to become more competent (Luepnitz, 1988). As we discuss further in the next chapter, many of these pioneers saw mothers as incompetent or enmeshing people because they were viewing families in isolation—out of their social-political context. They did not see that our culture can turn families into places that are dangerous to the health of mothers.

Strategic family therapists as a group, including the MRI contingent, Haley and Madanes, and the Milan associates (see Chapter 9), are indicted by Luepnitz (1988) for acts of omission. While there is little overt sexism in their writing or technique, they show limited concern over how their techniques might be used in the service of, rather than in opposition to, patriarchy. In striving to be pragmatic, using any means to solve the presenting problem, strategic therapists have shown little interest in examining the larger implications of their solutions. The result of their attempt to be apolitical and value-free is that therapists are given free reign to use the powerful strategic technology without thought to the consequences. As Luepnitz (1988) asserts, "there is nothing in strategic therapy that would rule out making a wife more submissive to her husband if such a change would remove a symptom" (p. 77).

This attempt on the part of strategic therapists to be value-free is directly related to the thinking of Gregory Bateson (see Chapters 1 and 3), who has had an extraordinary influence on the basic assumptions underpinning family therapy theory. Bateson's distaste for the metaphor of power led him to imply that all parts of a system are mutually (and equally) influential. This idea has been rejected by feminists and those who work with victims of sexual or physical abuse, because it can be used to excuse the abuser. In addition, Bateson led the group that constructed the famous double-bind theory of schizophrenia (Bateson, Jackson, Haley, and Weakland 1956; see also Chapter 1), which seemed to blame mothers for the schizophrenia of their children. Despite the fact that this group later refuted this theory as too linear, it has had an impact on the field.

It is interesting to note that Bateson's caveats about the use of power metaphors have not prevented many family therapy theorists (most notably Haley) from emphasizing the importance of power relations between the generations, otherwise known as family hierarchy. Yet these same theorists ignore the power differential between the sexes in families, except to the extent that it interferes with parenting (Goldner, 1988).

By presenting elements of the feminist critique of some pioneers, we do not intend to diminish their contributions, but to highlight the power of a theorist's cultural and intellectual context and background on his or her observations. We're all subject to the blind spots of our time and we can only hope that future generations will recognize that what will seem so obvious to them is difficult for us to see now.

Our culture not only affected the way the pioneers saw (or didn't see) gender relations within families, but also had an impact on what these theorists considered to be a normal or ideal family structure. Family therapy received another jolt in the early 1980s, this time from clinicians who had worked with families from other cultures and recognized that many characteristics of these ethnic families would be considered dysfunctional by conventional family therapy maps (McGoldrick, Pearce, and Giordano, 1982). Practitioners in the field were awakened to their ethnocentric and absolutist ideas of what normal and pathological structures are like by the recognition that families from other cultures have different values and structures, and that these differences do not necessarily represent dysfunction. When we work with a family from southern Italy, for example, we are now aware of the importance of family loyalty. Thus, we do not assume that they are sick simply because they seem more inclined than middle-class American families to sacrifice their own desires for the interests of "the family."

Salvador Minuchin probably has been the most influential cartographer for the family therapy field because he presents a clear and understandable normative model of how families should look (see Chapter 10). The implied ideal family, with its clear divisions between the generations, its emphasis on the primacy and smooth functioning of the *executive subsystem* (usually the parents), its advocacy of an "age-appropriate" parenting style designed to create autonomous, independent children, and its valuing of an open boundary around the family, is a family that fits well in our American middle-class culture. Therapists routinely compare the families they treat to this structural ideal and gear their therapy toward creating a better match. While many family therapists use this map flexibly and with respect for the variety in family forms, some will see pathology in families from different cultures or classes because they will not fit this ideal.

Celia Falicov (1983) draws on the work of anthropologist Francis Hsu (1971) to point out that in many cultures the dominant or governing dyad in a family is not the husband/wife, but instead, it is intergenerational, e.g., husband/son in some cultures, wife/son in others, or even brother/brother in still others. Thus the very *cross-generational coalitions* that we seize upon as a root of a family's problem and strive to dissolve may well be normative or adaptive in that family's culture. As the feminists remind us, however, just because a family structure is normative does not mean that it is balanced or fair and should be preserved.

Returning to family therapy's normative map, it can be seen as promoting a streamlined, nuclearized family structure and values that fit well with our highly mobile, materialistic society, but might create problems for families in nonmobile societies. We will present briefly some elements of our middle-class American culture that make this structural model the family-of-best-fit with it.

First and foremost ours is a capitalist society in which corporations need a large pool of middle-level employees who are willing to put the corporation, and their advancement within it, ahead of the interests of their families. To reverse the strong "family first" doctrine that governs families from more stable cultural contexts, we are bombarded through the media with materialistic messages. This creates a striving for personal success that can override the interests of relationship networks.

In their climb up the corporate ladder, families routinely moved, and still move, every two or three years. As Robert Bellah and his colleagues (1985) reported in *Habits of the Heart*, their study of American values, "Being tied to one particular job, in one particular location, is tantamount to being stuck, trapped, denied the opportunity for personal fulfillment" (p. 186). The not-so-funny joke among IBM employees is that the initials stand for "I've Been Moved." The roots of relational networks have barely grown before they are dug up and transplanted a thousand miles away or more.

The isolation resulting from this repeated uprooting tends to reinforce a materialistic orientation to life because, as the family is perpetually having to present an image to strangers and getting fewer rewards from emotional connections, issues of status and appearance come to dominate. In turn, the materialistic, rather than relational, striving reinforces mobility, which again reinforces materialism, and we get caught in an American vicious circle. Young and Willmott (1957) saw this same phenomenon in their classic study of the effects on families who moved from a highly stable, homogenous working-class borough in East London to a housing development outside London.

> One might even suggest, to generalize, that the less the personal respect received in small group relationships, the greater is the striving for the kind of impersonal respect embodied in a status judgement. The lonely man, fearing he is looked down on, becomes the acquisitive man;

possession the balm of anxiety; anxiety the spur to unfriendliness (p. 164).

The lonely husband, wife, and children also are more likely to make television the centerpiece of their family which, in turn, increases materialism.

In our highly mobile middle-class society, we are expected to leave our parents at an early age and, likewise, our children are expected to leave us. The only constant relationship amid all these transitional ones is marriage. Thus in lieu of a stable network of emotionally satisfying relationships, we put most of our emotional eggs in one basket. Spouses are expected to be far more than just partners in parenthood, or in the struggle for economic survival, or a bridge connecting two extended families, as is the case in many other cultures. The ideal middle-class marriage is a union of soulmates who selected each other and who enjoy a consistently high level of intellectual, emotional and sexual intimacy throughout their long lives together.

We stay with our marriage partners because they satisfy us, turn us on, more than any other, and if that were to change, we want to be free to change partners. Thus, not only does the modern middle-class marriage carry unprecedented emotional expectations, it also has an unprecedented lack of traditional obligation. All this is in keeping with the need in a capitalistic society for a professional and managerial workforce that is willing to put materialistic and achievement values in front of family commitments or considerations. Bellah and his colleagues (1985) interviewed "Brian" who exemplifies this ethic.

> Still rising toward the peak of a career that has defined his identity by its progress, Brian looks back on his twenties and thirties, devoted to advancing his career at the expense of tending his marriage and family life, and concedes, "I got totally swept up in my own progress, in promotions and financial success." Yet even now, Brian's definition of success revolves around an open-ended career on the upswing. . . "Where I come as close as I can to performing at the absolute limits of my capacity. That's success" (p. 68).

With a multitude of Brians, and a culture that reinforces them, love and marriage must accommodate accordingly.

American childrearing values, too, have conformed to the needs of our corporate culture. More than in any other culture, American children are encouraged to negotiate with parents for what they want, to compete with peers in all arenas, to desire and expect material possessions, and to think for themselves rather than rely on tradition or authority. Middle-class children are expected to leave home at eighteen, to enter and succeed in a harsh survival economy. In many ways childhood is a long proving and training ground for a reality that is very different from life in cultures where children are socialized for obedience, loyalty, conformity, and to put the interests of the family before personal advancement.

Seen in light of these national values, American models of therapy have evolved that reinforce many of the same values responsible for creating problems in the first place. Psychoanalysis is an obvious target of this critique in its view that anyone who cannot cope with this extreme world of competitive striving is maladjusted and its measure of growth being the degree to which people can separate from their families.

Because family therapy does attempt to view people's problems in context, it is a less obvious culprit in the maintenance of our culture's extremes. But the goal of differentiating individuals from their families so they can rely on themselves, so they do not have to live up to their family's expectations, so they can leave home and pursue their individual interests, are no less products of and contributions to the American middle-class value system. To varying degrees the models of pioneers like Minuchin, Haley, and Bowen seem designed to reduce the sense of social or family obligation or guilt that constrains clients from achieving their personal ambitions. We have been helping people shed baggage and streamline so that they are better able to compete, without considering whether these extremely competitive, individualistic values themselves are healthy for our clients or for the global ecology.

This is not to suggest that normative family maps haven't been useful. We need a template of the family-of-best-fit for our society so that we can help families decide if they want to fit into it. What has been largely missing in family therapy, with the exception of the feminist critique, however, is a critical evaluation of the society we are helping people fit into that could enable us to help clients make educated decisions about their value systems.

Another cultural bias in many family therapy models, which stems from our individualistic heritage, is the belief that families are inherently able to find their own best solutions, and that when they fail to do so, it is because of the interference of social control agents or because they have tripped over a bump in their life cycle. In a feminist critique of this belief, Virginia Goldner (1988) summarized this position: "Were it not for developmental snags and external meddlers, families would 'naturally' grow and develop, and in the process emerge as more complex forms of life" (p. 26). The implication is that if we just get the control agents and other "helpers" off the family's back and jump-start its natural problem-solving mechanisms, the family will heal itself.

This view of the family is consistent with the image of the American family that grew out of the industrial revolution of the first half of the nineteenth century when one's home and workplace became separated. Since then middle-class Americans have viewed their families as "havens in a heartless world," private retreats where one can find respite from the selfish, competitive, and immoral jungle of the business world (Hareven, 1982; Lasch, 1977).

The instinct to idealize and protect these havens from meddlers is deeply rooted in conservative American politics and is reflected most directly in the brief, strategic, and systemic schools of family therapy (see Chapter 9). Running throughout the literature from these schools are the themes: (1) that therapy should not be political, therapists should not be agents of social control; (2) that families should be left alone as quickly as possible; and (3) that after minimal intervention, families can be trusted to find their own best solutions. As Boscolo, Cecchin, Hoffman, and Penn (1987) assert, "If you let them alone, they improve" (cited in Luepnitz, 1988, p. 115).

This trust in the healing resources of people and focus on their strengths was a refreshing counterpoint to the pessimistic orientation of the analytic establishment that turned therapists into "psychopathologists," and led to "parentectomies" (the long-term hospitalization of children) or other disrespectful intrusions into families. Carried too far, however, an optimistic, minimalistic orientation blinds therapists to the political or ecological impact of their interventions (Goldner, 1987; Luepnitz, 1988; Keeney and Sprenkle, 1982) and encourages the tendency of some families to deny the existence of problems (as, for example, violence, sex abuse, and addictions).

Finally we cannot ignore the impact of the pioneers' personal characteristics on their theories and techniques. It has often been suggested that therapists find out what they like to do in therapy and then construct elaborate theories to rationalize these preferences. Anyone who saw Salvador Minuchin present, particularly in the 1970s or early 1980s, would not be surprised to learn that structural family therapists were taught to be highly directive, dramatic, and provocative. Likewise those who have experienced Murray Bowen first-hand are not surprised that therapists using this model are to be rational, low-key, and controlled.

Along these lines it is interesting to contrast the language and concepts used by the late Virginia Satir, the only woman among the pioneers, with those of her male colleagues (Luepnitz, 1988). Satir was no less exposed to the exciting new ideas of systems theory and was closely associated with the men who infused the field with those concepts, yet she spoke of the importance of self-esteem, compassion, and the congruent expression of feelings, while her colleagues spoke of feedback loops, homeostasis, and hierarchy. She touched and nurtured her clients while her colleagues strategized to trick them into changing or used their authority to command change. As a result Satir was viewed as a fuzzy thinker, who was too "touchy-feely" and naive for the real systems thinkers. Ironically some of these same systems thinkers are currently re-evaluating the authoritarian, distant therapist-client relationships of their prior models and moving toward Satir-like collaborative, supportive positions (see Chapter 6).

Returning to our earlier example, not only did each blind man and woman have personal idiosyncrasies and preconceptions that made the elephant seem different to them, they were also seeing different elephants. The families struggling with schizophrenia, that formed the basis of the concepts introduced by Bowen, the Bateson group, Wynne, Lidz, and Whitaker (see Chapter 1), were very different from the families of the slums studied by Minuchin and his colleagues, or even from the families of Italian schizophrenics upon which the Milan group based their model (see Chapter 9). What works with a family organized around one kind of syndrome, in one cultural context, may be totally ineffective with another kind of syndrome or culture, yet, for the most part, these early models became generalized and applied universally (Breunlin, Cornwell, and Cade, 1983).

Furthermore these models of family functioning were developed from observations of families that had problems or were in crisis. A family that is organized around their child's recent schizophrenic break may look entirely different from the same family one or two years before or later. Crises tend to exaggerate conflict and rigidity, and it is probably unfair to base generalized models of "psychosomatic families" or "schizophrenic families" on observations made when these families were at their worst.

In sum, we highlight the influence of the personalities, and cultural contexts and backgrounds, of the field's founding parents on what they saw and did, not to denigrate their approaches or assumptions, but to remind the reader that their theories do not describe some objective reality of family process. Each theorist has made valuable contributions, but it is important to see their ideas in context. Thus instead of trying to compare the models in this book based on which best describes "real" family process, we recommend using such standards as how effective, ethical, ecologically or politically sensitive an approach is and how well it fits the values, personal style, and intuition of the reader. The first section of this chapter has been presented to help readers consider those assessments.

CONCEPTUAL INFLUENCES ON THE EVOLUTION OF FAMILY THERAPY

If we were to poll family therapists as to the biggest conceptual influence on the development of the field, the winner by a landslide would be something called "systems theory." It is probably also true that if we followed up that survey and asked many of those family therapists to describe this systems theory, they might mumble phrases like "the whole is greater than the sum of its parts," or words like *equifinality* or *homeostasis*, while feeling uneasy about their inability to articulate this theory that they believe they should know by heart.

While many clinicians probably don't pay enough attention to the conceptual foundations of their therapy models, the inarticulateness of family therapists is not entirely their fault. Systems theory is not really a coherent, standardized theory, but is more like a way of thinking, and there are many variations on the systemic theme. This incoherence has been reflected in much of the writing regarding the application of systemic thinking to family therapy, and systemic ideas are abstract enough to provide a wide variety of disparate interpretations. What we describe below is no less an interpretation, but we hope it is one that provides some coherence and clarity.

Many family therapists do not fully realize that a large number of the concepts the pioneers used to try to understand families were not developed by those pioneers, but instead were imported into the field under the general rubric of systems theory. These concepts were taken from a number of fields of study, all of which were changing in a similar direction at the time family therapy emerged. Jay Haley (1971) summarized some of those changes:

> The idea of trying to change a family appeared in the 1950s at the same time as other happenings in the social sciences in America. At midcentury the social sciences became more social: the study of small groups flourished, animals were observed in their natural environments instead of in the zoo or laboratory, psychological experiments were seen as social situations in experimenter-bias studies, businesses began to be thought of as complex systems, mental hospitals were studied as total institutions, and ecology developed as a special field, with man and other creatures looked upon as inseparable from their environments (p. 1).

Functionalism

Of these fields, the changes within anthropology most closely parallel the changes brought to psychotherapy by family therapy. This is not surprising when we consider that the person most responsible for bringing systems ideas into psychotherapy was Gregory Bateson, an anthropologist.

Until the turn of the century anthropology was dominated by the cultural evolutionists. They tried to apply Darwinian theory to cultures, and theorized about the various stages through which humankind evolved from primitive savagery to modern civilization. Their theories were based on the artifacts brought back by archaeologists, and the tales of travelers or merchants, so they were more like philosophers than scientists.

Beginning around the turn of the century, but not dominating the anthropological scene until the 1930s, an approach known as *functionalism* emerged as a reaction against the evolutionist's tendency to tear cultural traits out of their context and to disregard cultures as meaningful wholes. British anthropologists, like Bronislaw Malinowski and A. R. Radcliffe-Brown, took the position that historical studies were futile because the data were scant and unverifiable. They were interested in studying cultures as social systems in the present and had little concern for the history of the cultures they studied. Thus they studied cultures ethnographically, as "participant observers" in the field, and tried to make sense out of the various customs or social institutions they observed. In this endeavor, they wanted to understand cultural ceremonies or customs in their context and tried to discern the function that a cultural practice served for the larger social organism.

These functionalists were as affected by Darwin's theory as the historical evolutionists against whom they reacted, only in a different way. They speculated about the function that certain kinds of social behavior served for the larger group in much the same way that Darwinians speculated about the survival value of an aspect of an organism. Thus functionalists believe that the adaptive function of any behavior can be found if the behavior is viewed in the context of the larger environment into which the organism or family or culture has had to fit.

The parallels between this shift in anthropology and a later shift in the field of psychotherapy are striking. Psychoanalysts tried to reconstruct a person's history by searching for and studying, out of context, events in the person's past. Like the evolutionary anthropologists, they developed theories based on historical speculation. Indeed Freud was fascinated by archaeology and compared his psychological explorations to archaeological expeditions.

Family therapy's reaction against the historical and out-of-context theorizing of psychoanalysis was similar to the earlier reaction by anthropological functionalists against the same historical and out-of-context qualities of evolutionism in anthropology. Like the functionalists, systems-based schools of family therapy were not interested in history and, instead, tried to become participant-observers of families in the present. Like the functionalists, family therapists were interested in understanding the function that the behavior of family members served for the family system.

One of the hazards of family therapy's functionalist inclination is to view *any* behavior as potentially adaptive. As Luepnitz (1988) asserts, "Functionalist explanations can justify almost anything in terms of some putative social need. Functionalist historians have even argued that lynchings and witch hunts serve a social need, i.e., a cathartic or 'therapeutic' need. Therapeutic for whom? one might well ask" (p. 65).

An example relevant to family therapy is the assertion by Talcott Parson (Parsons and Bales, 1955), probably the most influential functionalist sociologist, that the mother's proper role in a family is *expressive* and the father's *instrumental*. The *expressive role* involves emotional support, management of tensions, and care and support of the children. The *instrumental role* involves managerial decisions, solution of group tasks, and discipline of the children. In this case, Parsons took an observation of the sex-role polarity that existed in many families in the 1950s and used functionalism to imply that this division was adaptive, serving the needs of the family and society.

As family therapist Lynn Hoffman (1971, 1981) has pointed out, this functionalist bent entered sociology through the work of Emile Durkheim. Durkheim studied modern society and speculated that many kinds of behavior that society considers deviant or pathological may perform a socially useful role in bringing the larger group together. Later, sociologists who studied social deviance, like Erving Goffman, took Durkheim's ideas even further and suggested that social groups may *need* deviants for their stability or survival. Delinquency, suicide, and psychiatric patient status are all behaviors that have been the focus of this sociological functionalist interpretation.

Before moving on, another sociological study bears mentioning because its findings closely paralleled and corroborated the function-of-the-symptom ideas of family therapists. Alfred Stanton and Morris Schwartz (1954) studied the interaction among patients and staff in a mental hospital. As Hoffman (1981) observed, Stanton and Schwartz's description of the process by which a mental patient sometimes got caught in a power struggle between two staff members, that escalated the patient's symptoms, is remarkably similar to the process of *triangulation* or *cross-generational coalition* that family therapists were reporting.

In these hospital triangles, one staff member tried to uphold the rules of the institution and didn't want patients to have any special treatment, while another staff member resented this rigidity and thought that rules should be flexible enough to accommodate individual needs. A patient who stumbled into this polarization would become the battlefield over which this staff conflict was played out and would immediately have a permissive ally pitted against a restrictive antagonist. The more the one staff member protected the patient, the more the other would punish him or her, and the whole hospital unit might be pulled into the escalating polarization, forced to take sides. As the tension mounted, the patient would become increasingly disruptive on the unit.

Functionalist Influence in Family Therapy

In the early 1930s, the period when functionalism began to dominate anthropology, Gregory Bateson was in New Guinea observing the Iatmul culture. In studying that society as a system, he was interested in the Iatmul's hierarchy, or remarkable absence of hierarchy relative to our culture, and the role a particular ceremony, known as the Naven, played in settling conflicts within the group (Bateson, 1956). Thus, the person who brought systems thinking into the field of psychotherapy was, twenty years earlier, studying societies in the present as hierarchical systems and trying to understand the function of their unusual behaviors.

Family therapists took the functionalist notion that deviant behavior may serve a protective function for a social group and applied it to the symptoms of family members. Initially their view of a family's "identified patient" was similar to Stanton and Schwartz's view of the patient in the hospital. The family's "identified patient" was a scapegoat, a victim on whom the other family members focused, or over whom they fought, to avoid having to deal with each other. Later, family therapists suspected that many of these scapegoats were active volunteers for the position. It was thought that these "symptom-bearers" were willingly sacrificing their own welfare for the greater good. This idea that the symptom served a function for the family became a cornerstone of family therapy theory that, more recently, has been challenged and will be discussed in more detail in the next chapter.

To summarize functionalism's influence on family therapy, families were viewed as living organisms that had needs to survive and thrive, but also had to adapt to their environment. The behavior and traits of the family organism were examined in this context to see how they helped the family adapt or better meet its needs. Symptoms among family members were viewed as signs that the family was not adapting well to its environment or was, for some reason, unable to meet its needs. Descriptions and techniques based on these basic assumptions can be found throughout the early and current family therapy literature. Functionalism has proven useful in understanding how families try to adapt but, like Darwin, functionalists saw the environment as a given that the organism must fit into, and, consequently, turned the field's attention away from questioning whether the environment that the family was trying to adapt to was healthy. Thus, functionalism could be used to support a conservative political agenda.

General Systems Theory

Because the functionalists used the metaphor of an organism to understand families, this organismic metaphor itself has been criticized (Luepnitz, 1988). We believe that this is a case of guilt by association. There are ways to use the organismic metaphor that do not create the blind spots associated with functionalism and are more systemic or ecological.

Ludwig von Bertalanffy was a prominent biologist who began to wonder if the laws that applied to biological organisms might also apply to other areas, from the human mind to the global ecosphere. He developed a model that was mistranslated from the German as General Systems Theory (GST), the last word of which he intended to have been "teaching," because it is not so much a theory as an approach, a way of thinking or a set of assumptions that can be applied to all kinds of systems (Davidson, 1983).

Bertalanffy published widely and had some influence on all the social sciences, but, unlike Bateson, he had no extended direct contact with the pioneers of family therapy (although Dick Auerswald [1969] was excited by Bertalanffy's ideas and, in turn, strongly influenced Minuchin's thinking). In addition, as will be discussed later, Bertalanffy had a lifelong disdain for mechanism and was highly critical of cybernetics, the mechanistic systems approach that, through Bateson, came to dominate family therapy. Consequently, while many of the concepts of GST seem to have seeped into the family therapy literature, Bertalanffy's work is rarely cited, and where it is noted, it is often described as being basically the same as cybernetics (Bateson, 1971; Becvar and Becvar, 1988). In the following we will devote considerable attention to Bertalanffy's ideas for two reasons. First, we believe that this contribution to family therapy is underappreciated and, second, in discussing his ideas we can introduce the reader to a host of systems principles that will reappear throughout the book.

Part of Bertalanffy's obscurity in family therapy may be because he was a generalist, spreading his ideas over the fields of medicine, psychiatry, psychology, sociology, history, education, philosophy, and biology, and also because GST is not a clear-cut theory with a list of testable hypotheses. Until Mark Davidson's thoughtful biography of Bertalanffy, *Uncommon Sense*, in 1983, there was no overview or summary of his voluminous work that could help us recognize the immensity of his contribution. In explaining Bertalanffy, we will draw heavily upon Davidson's book and recommend it to the reader. Davidson (1983) summarized Bertalanffy's definition of a system as

> any entity maintained by the mutual interaction of its parts, from atom to cosmos, and including such mundane examples as telephone, postal, and rapid transit systems. A Bertalanffian system can be physical like a television set, biological like a cocker spaniel, psychological like a personality, sociological like a labor union, or symbolic like a set of laws . . . A system can be composed of smaller systems and can also be part of a larger system, just as a state or province is composed of smaller jurisdictions and also is part of a nation. Consequently, the same organized entity can be regarded as either a system or a subsystem, depending on the observer's focus of interest (p. 26).

Bertalanffy pioneered the idea that a system was more than the aggregate of its parts, in the sense that a watch is more than a pile of machine parts or a piece of music is more than a cluster of notes. There is nothing mysterious or mystical about this assertion, just the idea that when things are organized into a pattern, something emerges out of the pattern and the relationship of the parts within it that is more or different, "the way wetness emerges from the interaction of two parts of hydrogen and one part of oxygen" (Davidson, 1983, p. 28). Thus Bertalanffy conveyed the importance of focusing on the pattern of relationships within a system, or among systems, rather than on the substance of their parts.

For these reasons Bertalanffy believed that science had become far too *reductionistic* in its tendency to analyze phenomena by breaking whole systems up and studying their parts in isolation. While he believed that such analysis has a place in science and has led to certain advances, the study of whole systems had been grossly neglected and he urged scientists learn to "think interaction" rather than striving to find and study the basic elements of a system.

Applied to family therapy, these ideas—that a family system should be seen as more than just a collection of people, and that therapists should focus on interaction or relationships among family members rather than the qualities of the individual family members—became central tenets of the field.

Like the functionalists, Bertalanffy used the metaphor of an organism for social groups, but an organism that was an *open system*, an entity continuously interacting with its environment. Open systems, as opposed to closed systems (which are nonliving), sustain themselves by continuously exchanging substances—e.g., taking in food and oxygen and exporting carbon dioxide and nitrogenous waste—with their environment.

One difference in Bertalanffy's view of organisms from the functionalist view, implied in this open systems concept, is his stress on the importance of the relationship between an organism and its environment which, of course, includes other organisms, rather than seeing organisms simply as reactors to a given environment. He believed that the sciences must recognize that organisms do not just passively react to stimuli, but rather autonomously initiate much creative activity to enhance themselves.

Indeed Bertalanffy was a life-long crusader against the passive automaton or machine view of living systems, particularly of those living systems called people. He believed that, unlike machines, living organisms demonstrate *equifinality*,

> the ability of organisms to reach a given final goal from different initial conditions and in different ways. (In nonliving systems, the final state and the means of that state are fixed by the initial conditions.) He and other biologists used that term to identify the organism's inner-directed ability to protect or restore its wholeness, as in the human body's mobilization of antibodies and its ability to repair skin and bone (Davidson, 1983, p. 77).

Thus living organisms were creatively, spontaneously active and could use many methods to maintain their organization, but were not solely motivated to maintain the status quo. As we will discuss later, family therapy picked up on the concept of *homeostasis*, that is the tendency of a system to regulate itself so as to maintain a constant internal environment in response to changes in external environment. This term, coined by French physiologist Claude Bernard in the nineteenth century to describe the regulation of such conditions as body temperature or blood sugar level, does describe some of the behavior of Bertalanffy's organisms, but he believed that an overemphasis of this reactive, homeostatic aspect of an organism reduced it to the level of a machine. Bertalanffy wrote that "If [this] principle of homeostatic maintenance is taken as a rule of behavior, the so-called well-adjusted individual will be [defined as] a well-oiled robot" (quoted in Davidson, p. 104), "In the sense of homeostasis, Michelangelo should have followed his father's advice and gone into the stonecutting business. He would have had a much happier life than the one he led painting the Sistine Chapel in a very uncomfortable position" (quoted in Davidson, p. 127).

As we shall discuss later, homeostasis is a more central concept in cybernetics, which is the study of self-regulating systems like thermostats, endocrine systems, or guided missiles, than it is in GST. The concept was introduced into family therapy by Don Jackson (1957), as a way to explain the tendency of families to resist change. While it remains a central concept in family therapy, its limited ability to account for the wide variety of human and family behavior has been repeatedly acknowledged by family therapists, in ways that echo Bertalanffy's concerns (Hoffman, 1981; Speer, 1970; Dell, 1982). The cyberneticians had to propose new concepts like "morphogenesis" (Speer, 1970) to account for what Bertalanffy believed was simply a property of organisms—to seek, in addition to resist, change.

One of Bertalanffy's chief quarrels with the mechanistic view of people was that it led to valuelessness, a concern that foreshadowed the feminist critique of family therapy discussed in Chapter 3. If families are like machines, then we simply study how they work, determine how they become "dysfunctional," and repair the dysfunction. None of this activity requires any consideration of the desirability of the system's functional state or the desirability of the state of its environment.

For example, when a family mechanic encounters a rebellious adolescent daughter embedded in a striving American family, where father is never home because of his job and mother fights bitterly with the girl about her friends and her appearance, the mechanic might try to break the covert alliance between the father and daughter against mother and encourage father to support mother's attempts to discipline the girl. This structural repair might, at least temporarily, calm the situation and decrease the girl's defiance, so that the family could become more "functional." The therapist, however, would not have helped the family examine or question the effect of the father's job and the values that are associated with it on the health of the family members. A Bertalanffian therapist might encourage the family to weigh the economic benefits of father's job next to the effects of his lack of involvement with the family and high level of stress.

If one thinks ecologically, one cannot avoid considering values because it becomes clear that certain values are ecological and others are not, whether they are held by an individual, a family, a nation, or the planet. A balance must exist among the parts of a system, and whenever one part strives for unrestrained growth or power within a system, the system and those systems above and below it, will lose this healthy balance. Despite Bateson's admonition that certain ways of thinking, for example, using power metaphors, were "epistemological errors," family therapists, by and large, have tried to remain value-free mechanics.

Bertalanffy sought to raise these kinds of ecological and ethical questions at all levels of human endeavor because he saw that there are systems of beliefs or values that have as much or more life and power as systems of living beings. Thus, like the Bertalanffian therapist's questions to a family, the Bertalanffian politician would ask us to weigh the economic benefit of an industrial plant next to the long-term damage of its pollution. Thus, by underscoring our interconnectedness and the ecological impact of our decisions, he sought to broaden our loyalties beyond ourselves or our families or our nations to our planet, and in that sense he predated and influenced the environmental movement that emerged in the 1960s.

Bertalanffy's insistence on the importance of human belief systems also predated the recent shift in family therapy's focus from behavior to belief, a shift that will be discussed in Chapter 3. Bertalanffy's emphasis on values and beliefs, as well as family therapy's, is the result, in part, of his understanding of the inadequacies of logical positivism, the philosophy that has dominated western science since the nineteenth century. This philosophy holds that the only valid data are those derived from experience or observations which can be empirically verified. This paradigm divorced science from the fields of philosophy or ethics with the assumption that only through the empirical sciences can we truly know reality. Logical positivism and its assumptions about our ability to know reality was wounded by the discovery in physics earlier this century that subatomic particles did not really exist, in the sense that we are used to thinking about things existing. Fritzjov Capra (1982), whose book *The Turning Point* provides a good overview of systems thinking among the sciences, describes the discovery this way: "At the subatomic level, matter does not exist with certainty at definite places, but rather shows 'tendencies to exist' . . . subatomic particles have no meaning as isolated entities but can be understood only as interconnections, or correlations, between various processes of observation and measurement" (p. 80). Thus, it seems that there are no elementary particles to be found and analyzed. This discovery, captured by the famous Heisenberg uncertainty principle, led theorists in many fields to question the absolutist position on reality.

To counter logical positivism, Bertalanffy (1968) coined the term "perspectivism" to characterize his belief that while reality exists, the reality one *knows* can never be fully objective because their view of it is filtered through their particular perspective. To a man with a hammer, everything looks like a nail. To a physicist, a table is a collection of electrons; a chemist sees the same table as organic compounds; the biologist sees a set of wood cells; and the art historian sees a baroque object. To Bertalanffy, all those views have some validity but each is incomplete and none should be seen as more authentic than the others.

Bertalanffy's perspectivism is quite similar to a philosophy, derived from Kant, known as *constructivism*, that has had a major impact recently on the field of family therapy and will be discussed further in Chapter 3. In fact the following Bertalanffian quote might just as well have come from Paul Watzlawick or Heinz von Forrester or any of the other constructivist writers that have influenced, in particular, the strategic or systemic family therapies (see Chapter 9).

> There are no facts flying around in nature as if they are butterflies that you put into a nice orderly collection. Our cognition is not a mirroring of ultimate reality but rather is an active process, in which we create models of the world. These models direct what we actually see, what we consider as fact (quoted in Davidson, 1983, p. 214).

Bertalanffy also recognized that the act of observation has an effect on he phenomena being observed. This strengthened his perspectivist conviction that one should be humble about one's observations and theories, rather than believing that they are the absolute truth. This keeps one's mind open to valuable new ideas.

Some family therapists have interpreted constructivism to mean that since no one has the corner on absolute reality, any interpretation is as valid as any other and, therefore, the therapist is free to "reframe" reality in any way he or she wants as long as the family seems to buy the reframe and it produces a change (Duncan and Solovey, 1989). In all likelihood, Bertalanffy would have objected to this relativistic position. Instead, he believed the opposite: that our inability to know absolute reality implies that we should be increasingly concerned with values and assumptions because some perspectives are far more ecologically destructive than others. This implies that therapists should carefully scrutinize their own values and those of their theories and should not become too attached to the truth or objectivity of their observations. Bertalanffy had this to say to the theorists and philosophers of the world: "It is we who, in the last resort, manufacture the glasses through which people look at the world and at themselves—

little as they may know it. . . . I dare say we are the great spectacle makers in history" (quoted in Davidson, 1983, p. 69).

To summarize, through this section on Bertalanffy we have encountered many of the concepts and issues that have shaped, and still are shaping, family therapy. These include:

- *concept of a system as more than the sum of its parts;*
- *emphasis on interaction within and among systems versus reductionism;*
- *human systems as ecological organisms versus mechanism;*
- *concept of equifinality;*
- *homeostatic reactivity versus spontaneous activity;*
- *importance of ecological beliefs and values versus valuelessness;*
- *perspectivism or constructivism versus logical positivism.*

Many of these issues will reappear both in the ensuing discussion of cybernetics and throughout the book. Bertalanffy's position on them was profound and deserved more attention.

Cybernetics of Families

Cybernetics was developed and named (from the Greek word for helmsman) by Norbert Wiener, a mathematician at MIT. During World War II, Wiener was asked to work on the problem of how to get guns to hit moving targets. From this work, he expanded his ideas about cybernetic systems—that is, systems that are self-correcting—to the way people or animals operate.

At the core of cybernetics is the concept of the *feedback loop*, the process by which a system gets the information necessary to self-correct in its effort to maintain a steady state or to move toward a preprogrammed goal. This feedback may be regarding the system's performance relative to its external environment or regarding the relationship among the system's parts. Feedback loops can be *negative* or *positive*. This distinction refers to the effect they have on deviations from a steady, homeostatic state within the system, not to whether they are beneficial or not. *Negative feedback* reduces deviation or change; *positive feedback* amplifies it.

Because cybernetics arose from the study of machines, where positive feedback loops led to destructive "runaways" in which the machinery would break down, the emphasis was on negative feedback and the maintenance of homeostasis in the face of change. The system's environment would change—the temperature outside a house would go up or down exceeding a certain temperature range—and this change would trigger the negative feedback mechanisms to bring the system back to homeostasis—the air-conditioning or heat would go on.

Translated to the study of families then, one becomes interested in several phenomena: (1) *family rules*, which govern the range of family behaviors that the family system can tolerate, i.e., the family's homeostatic range; (2) *negative feedback* processes that families use to enforce those rules (e.g., guilt, double messages, symptoms); (3) *sequences of family interaction* around a problem that characterize the system's reaction to it; that is, the feedback loops around a deviation; and (4) what happens when the system's traditional negative feedback is ineffective, triggering *positive feedback loops*.

For example, in a family with a low threshold for the overt expression of anger, Johnny, the adolescent son, blows up at his parents over their insistence that he not stay out past curfew. Mother is shocked and begins to cry. Father is outraged and responds by grounding Johnny for a month. Rather than reducing Johnny's deviation, i.e., stifling his anger back within homeostatic limits, this negative feedback from the parents produces the opposite effect. Johnny explodes and challenges their authority. They respond with more of the same crying and punishing, which further escalates Johnny's anger. In this way the parents' original negative feedback (crying and punishing) becomes positive feedback in the sense that it begins to amplify rather than diminish his deviation. The family is caught in a positive feedback "runaway," otherwise known as a vicious cycle, that threatens to destroy the family, much as positive feedback loops, if unabated, break cybernetic machines.

Later cyberneticians like Walter Buckley and Ross Ashby recognized that positive feedback loops are not all bad and can help systems adjust to changed circumstances if they don't get out of hand. Thus Johnny's family needed to recalibrate their rules for anger to accommodate an adolescent; the crisis that this positive feedback loop produced could lead to a reexamination of the family's rules, if the family could step out of the loop long enough to get some perspective. In so doing they would be *metacommunicating*, that is communicating about their ways of communicating, a process that can lead to a change in communication rules (Satir, 1972). This recognition, that positive feedback loops could lead to change, paved the conceptual foundation for some of the crisis-inducing forms of family therapy like the Milan (Chapter 9) or structural (Chapter 10) models. As Haley (1971b) suggested, "If a treatment program subdues and stabilizes the family, change is more difficult. . . . To change a stabilized, miserable situation and create space for individual growth of family members, the therapists often must induce a crisis which creates instability" (p. 8).

Such a change in family rules is what cybernetically-oriented family therapists strive for and call *second-order change*, to distinguish it from *first-order change*, in which the family changes some behaviors but those behaviors are still governed by the same rules (Watzlawick, Weakland, and Fisch, 1974).

As should be clear by now, family cyberneticians were highly interested in the feedback loops within families, otherwise known as patterns of communication or interaction. Hence the family theorists most influenced by cybernetics came to be known as the communications school, and they advocated an interactional view (see Chapter 4). Faulty or unclear communication results in inaccurate or incomplete feedback so the system cannot self-correct (change its rules) and, consequently, overreacts or underreacts to change.

Cybernetics was introduced to family therapy by Gregory Bateson. Bateson encountered Wiener and cybernetics shortly after World War II during the Macy Conferences, a series of gatherings of high-level thinkers from different disciplines who tried to apply their theories to the problems of the other field. Bateson became interested in the feedback processes of systems and pioneered a conceptual shift that has become central to family systems thinking, the shift from *linear* to *circular causality*. Before the advent of family therapy, explanations of psychopathology were based on linear models—medical, psychodynamic, and behavioral. In all of these, etiology was conceived in terms of prior events—disease, emotional conflict, or learning history—which caused symptoms in the present. The patient is the locus of malfunction in all of these models.

Using the concept of circularity, Bateson helped psychotherapists change the way they think about psychopathology from something caused by events in the past to something that is a part of ongoing, circular feedback loops. The concept of linear causality is based on a Newtonian model, in which the universe is like a billiard table where the balls act unidirectionally on each other. Bateson believed, while linear causality was useful for describing the nonliving world of forces and objects, it was a poor model for the world of living things because it neglects to account for communication and relationships as well as force, as illustrated by the example of the man kicking the dog, mentioned earlier.

In addition to observable circular feedback loops, Bateson was also quite interested in how communicative behaviors are interpreted by those receiving the communication. The mechanistic cyberneticians believed one could understand systems simply by studying their behavioral inputs and outputs and, in that sense, as Bertalanffy asserted, they were basically behaviorists but with the addition of the feedback loop. Bateson, however, did not limit his interest to behavioral sequences, but studied the meaning people derived from communication and its context.

Bateson's interest in context and meaning led him to try to apply Bertrand Russell's Theory of Logical Types to animal and human communication (see Chapter 1). This focus on the context of communication—that any act can only be understood in its context, which may have several layers—directed Bateson and his research group to speculate about the communicative context of schizophrenia, one of humanity's most puzzling forms of communication.

One result was the famous "double-bind" hypothesis (see Chapter 1) which, in contradiction to Bateson's ethnographic training, was developed deductively, without observing any families directly.

When they began to study families directly, the Bateson group split into two camps (Haley, 1981; Simon, 1982). On one side was Bateson, continuing to focus on the way the receiver of communication processes it, and interested in the way individuals learn and perceive; on the other side, the others in the group were taken by the cybernetic metaphor and wanted to focus exclusively on the observable interaction patterns among family members.

The Bateson project ended in 1962, and Bateson shifted his interests away from psychiatric phenomena. The legacy of the project to psychotherapy was left to the other Bateson project and MRI members who, with the exception of Satir, advanced the mechanistic notions of homeostasis and feedback loops, keeping a logical positivistic focus on observable behavior sequences, and ignoring for the most part Bateson's concerns about the individual's perception and learning (Breunlin, Schwartz, and Karrer, in press). These theorists borrowed the "black box" metaphor to justify their mechanistic position:

> The impossibility of seeing the mind "at work" has in recent years led to the adoption of the Black Box concept from the field of telecommunication. . . . The concept is more generally applied to the fact that electronic hardware is by now so complex that it is sometimes more expedient to disregard the internal structure of a device and concentrate on the study of its specific input-output relations. . . . This concept, if applied to psychological and psychiatric problems, has the heuristic advantage that no ultimately unverifiable intrapsychic hypotheses need to be invoked, and that one can limit oneself to observable input-output relations, that is, to communication (Watzlawick, Beavin, and Jackson, 1967, pp. 43–44).

Viewing people as black boxes seemed the ultimate expression of the mechanistic tendencies that Bertalanffy lamented. This metaphor had the behavioristic advantage of simplifying one's field of study by eliminating concerns about the mind and emotions of the individual, as well as the history of the family. In addition, one could judge the outcome of therapy equally simply—if the problem was solved, the system returned to a functional state, the outcome was positive, and therapy could end. Hence the evolution of brief, strategic therapy. ▪

Control and Power

Another important rift developed in this group that, by the early 1960s, was theorizing from the Mental Research Institute (MRI) in Palo Alto.

Haley believed that these black boxes were wired to move in a certain direction; i.e., that people's communication was motivated by the desire to control each other. His first law of relationships states that "when one person indicates a change in relation to another, the other will act upon the first so as to diminish and modify that change" (Haley, 1963, p. 189). Bateson strongly objected to the use of control and power metaphors, and the other family cyberneticians at the MRI strove to avoid imputing any motivation to people's behavior and, instead, to simply observe feedback loops (Haley, 1981).

Haley's view of social behaviors as attempts to control others led him, more than any other family therapy pioneer, to maintain the functionalist legacy from anthropology and sociology described earlier. Therapists who use the brand of strategic therapy developed by Haley and his later collaborator, Cloe Madanes, search for the function that a symptom serves, not only for the symptom-bearer, but also for the family.

Considering Haley's interest in interpersonal control, it's not surprising that he was also drawn to hypnosis. During the years of the Bateson project, as the emphasis shifted from doing research only to also doing therapy, Haley, along with John Weakland, began traveling periodically to Phoenix to consult with and study the work of a well-known hypnotherapist who also was working with couples and families in addition to individuals, Milton Erickson. Haley (1985) reports, "As we sought consultation and supervision, Dr. Erickson was the only person who could advise us on interview technique with couples and families" (p. 32).

Bateson had strong reservations about psychotherapy and was wary of changing systems in general. Haley remembers that

> Bateson was an anthropologist to his soul and an anthropologist doesn't believe you should tamper with the data or change it in any way. . . . After I met Erickson and began to go into a very directive style of therapy in which you produce a change, Bateson got more and more uncomfortable, particularly when I began describing the therapy relationship as a struggle for control or power (Simon, 1982, p. 22).

Thus with the exception of Bateson himself, the interests of Bateson Project members were shifting from studying people's behavior in context to using people's interpersonal context to influence their behavior, and Erickson was a master at manipulating interpersonal contexts.

Haley (1985) again explains, "At that time we were studying communication, focusing on how messages are classified and the paradoxes that occur when levels of messages conflict. Erickson's work was replete with deliberate use of paradox" (p. 32) (see Chapter 9 for more on using paradox and Erickson's influence on technique). Thus through Erickson these researchers-cum-therapists were introduced to a wide array of powerful and unorthodox techniques, including such famous maneuvers as paradoxical directives, reframing, and using the client's language, that they applied to families. Paul Watzlawick has suggested that the MRI model (see Chapter 9) of brief therapy is essentially an elaboration of Erickson's techniques (Bogdan, 1983).

Erickson's beliefs about people, however, also had a strong impact on family therapy and countered some of the pessimistic assumptions that the group was deriving from cybernetics. Haley (1985) relates that "As we applied the notion [of homeostasis] to families in therapy, it took the form of resistance to change. When we offered these ideas to Dr. Erickson, he responded with polite irritation. He thought, correctly I believe, that a theory that encouraged the notion that people resist change was a noxious theory for a therapist, since expecting resistance encourages it" (p. 32). Erickson's optimistic view of people—that they wanted to change and possessed the resources to do so—was, perhaps, his most important contribution to the family therapy movement. At a time when the psychotherapy establishment was extremely pessimistic about change and was long term, interpretive, nondirective, and highly suspicious of symptom-removal, Erickson's approach was optimistic, brief, directive, problem-focused, and at times, included the client's family or others in treatment (Bogdan, 1983). Erickson offered Haley, Weakland, and their colleagues in Palo Alto, an antidote to all the things they didn't like about psychoanalysis and to the pessimism of the homeostatic model they had been adopting.

From Cybernetics to Structure

Haley's interest in power led him to focus on the hierarchy, or generational power structure, of families. He pioneered the understanding of child problems as being the result of coalitions between family members that cross the boundary between children and parents, much like the stressful coalitions that crossed the line of authority between patients and staff in Stanton and Schwartz's mental hospital. With these concepts of hierarchy and boundary, Haley's interest was moving toward the structure of families rather than just their communication circuits. In 1967 he left the MRI and joined and influenced the developers of structural family therapy, Salvador Minuchin and Braulio Montalvo at the Philadelphia Child Guidance Clinic.

In contrast to the focus of the family cyberneticians at the MRI, structural family therapy owes a debt to the organismic (Bertalanffy and cellular biology) and structural-functional (Malinowski, Radcliffe-Brown, Levi-Strauss, and Parsons) trends in the social sciences mentioned earlier. The family is viewed as an organism, an open system, made up of subsystems each of which is surrounded by a semipermeable *boundary*, which is really a set of rules governing who is included within that subsystem and how they can interact with those outside it.

To appreciate structural family therapy's functionalist heritage, consider this passage by Talcott Parsons (Parsons and Bales, 1955):

> That the [nuclear family] is itself a subsystem of a larger system is of course a sociological commonplace. But to break it in turn down into subsystems is a less familiar way of looking at it. Yet we will treat the family in this way and say that, in certain crucially important respects, the very young child does not participate in, is not fully a "member," of his whole family, but only of a subsystem of it, the mother-child subsystem. The marriage pair constitute another subsystem as may, for certain purposes, also the child with all his siblings, all the males in the family, all the females, etc. In fact, any combination of two or more members as differentiated from one or more other members may be treated as a social system which is a subsystem of the family as a whole (p. 37).

Thus, as early as 1955, families were viewed in this structural way—as having subsystems with boundaries separating them.

According to structural family theory, a healthy structure for meeting the needs of this family organism requires clear boundaries, particularly generational boundaries. Deviations from this healthy structure create a dysfunctional family structure, one manifestation of which is the symptomatic family member. If the structural flaw is corrected, the family organism will return to health (Bertalanffian equifinality).

Thus where the family cyberneticians saw circular sequences of interaction that maintained problems, structural family therapists saw boundary violations that resulted in inappropriate alliances and coalitions among family members. Where family cyberneticians were interested in the temporal (tracking sequences over time), structural family therapists were interested in the spatial (the proximity of family members to one another). The structuralists' spatial orientation is reflected in their use of two-dimensional diagrams on which the closeness and distance of family members can be mapped.

Concerns with generational boundaries, and the importance of the proper functioning of the parental subsystem, predate Minuchin's creative application of these ideas to family treatment. Theodore Lidz (1963), who frequently cited his debt to functionalist sociologist Talcott Parsons, said in a lecture in 1961, "Failure to achieve a parental coalition will often lead to infractions of the generation boundaries within the family" (p. 62). Lidz elaborated that violations of this boundary lead to the entanglement of the child in the parent's struggle. "Often, the child becomes a scapegoat. His difficulties are magnified into the major source of dissent between the parents, and he comes to feel responsible for it. At times, the child falls in with the assignment and obliges by creating further unhappiness that masks the friction between the parents" (p. 57). Structural family therapy theory echoes these ideas that Lidz espoused more than a decade before publication of the classic structural text, *Families and Family Therapy* (Minuchin, 1974).

Nathan Ackerman, the most influential figure in family therapy on the East Coast, undoubtedly had an impact on both the theory of structural family therapy and Minuchin's therapeutic style, since Minuchin studied with Ackerman for a period. As described in Chapter 1, Ackerman focused on the hidden conflicts among family members and saw the job of the therapist as surfacing these conflicts so that they could be resolved. Indeed, structural family therapy was originally called "conflict-resolution family therapy." Like Minuchin, and unlike the family cyberneticians, Ackerman was not afraid to use his personal relationship with family members to evoke and resolve family conflict in a blunt and straightforward way.

A final influence on structural family theory that we will identify here comes from the client population with which it was developed. Both in New York and in Philadelphia, Minuchin and his colleagues worked with "families of the slums," low socioeconomic families of delinquent children. Dick Auerswald, who worked with Minuchin in New York at the Wiltwyck School for Boys, was interested in Bertalanffy's ecological ideas and noticed that by connecting isolated Puerto Rican immigrants with their cultural networks, their psychotic symptoms abated (Duhl, 1983). Minuchin's group became increasingly impressed with the degree to which changes in external context (family or community structure) could produce remarkable changes in individual family members. They also experimented with action-oriented techniques, finding the traditional verbal, insight-oriented techniques ineffective with this population.

The structural philosophy can be best characterized by this premise: the key to changing an individual is to change his or her context—the network of current relationships in which the individual is embedded. A related assumption within this philosophy is that no matter how incompetent or pathological a family member appears, an improvement in family structure will elicit a more competent "partial self" of that family member which, in turn, will reinforce the family change. Thus, the structural view of people is essentially optimistic.

To summarize our speculations on the development of structural family therapy, it seems that in his struggle to find a model effective with a disadvantaged population, Minuchin borrowed the Bertalanffian view of systems as open and organismic and the Parsonian concepts of structure and emphasis on generational boundaries, concepts that were in the social science air at that time and had been adopted to varying degrees by more psychoanalytically oriented family theorists (Lidz and Ackerman). Minuchin, however, deleted the psychoanalytic aspects of their theories and techniques, and, in the process of experimenting with action-oriented techniques, discovered the power of an individual's external context as well as ways to harness that power.

In doing this, Minuchin provided the first clear map to understanding and reorganizing families, a map that was received as a godsend by the legions of bewildered therapists who were lost amid a confusing jungle of family entanglements. As a therapist and a presenter, Minuchin was charismatic and authoritative at a time when the field was hungry for dynamic leadership. He was the street fighter who would stand up to the psychiatric establishment for the rest of us, eventually armed with outcome data that could not be dismissed. For all these reasons, structural family therapy became the most popular and influential brand of family therapy in the 1970s.

Satir's Humanizing Effect

Structural family therapy is often associated with the concept of hierarchy because of its emphasis on motivating parents to become effective disciplinarians. Through the work of Minuchin and Haley, the disciplinary, power, or authority aspect of hierarchy has been the primary focus of systems based family therapists, including the MRI family cyberneticians. Virginia Satir was the only family therapy pioneer to promote and focus on the other side of family leadership or hierarchy. She was devoted to getting parents to be more affectionate and loving to each other and to their children, in addition to being more firm.

As an early member of the MRI, Satir was exposed to the same functionalist and cybernetic influences that produced the MRI model of Watzlawick and Weakland and Haley's version of strategic therapy. Thus her theorizing included the idea that children's symptoms can serve the function of distracting from an unhappy marriage and that communication is key in family process. Satir's philosophy of therapy, however, was very different from those of the influential men we have described thus far. She brought some yin into what was becoming an overly yang field through her attraction to the humanistic movement, pioneered by Abraham Maslow and Carl Rogers.

In contrast to the MRI model's view of people as cybernetic black boxes, Haley's view of people as power-game players, and Minuchin's view of people as context reactors, Satir saw people as motivated primarily by the desire for self-esteem, that is to feel good about themselves and to get close to others. "The critical factor in what happens both inside and between people is the picture of individual worth that each person carries around with him" (Satir, 1972, p. 21). Her interest in promoting the self-esteem of each family member led her to maintain a focus on the humanity of individuals at a time when her contemporaries were actively ignoring individual feelings in their struggle to understand families.

Her humanistic view of people led Satir to try to change families into incubators for the positive, loving qualities that she believed to be at the core of each family member. Thus her interest in family communication was not so much to track and break the dysfunctional interaction sequences that surrounded a problem, but instead to encourage family members to drop the protective masks they show each other and to discover and express their real feelings and thoughts.

To illustrate the differences between Satir and the other models, suppose a father says angrily to his teenage daughter, "You can't go out tonight!" The MRI cyberneticians might see this as the beginning of an escalating positive feedback loop; in the father's outburst, Haley might hear the command message of "I am in control of you; I am still one up in relation to you"; and Minuchin might hear father's anger as a reaction to a mother-daughter coalition that renders him powerless. Satir, on the other hand, might hear the father as wanting but afraid to say, "I want you to stay home tonight because I miss you and feel you slipping away from me."

Father does not say this because he's afraid of being rejected, which would be a blow to his self-esteem. If father could be honest, however, daughter would have a chance to express her mixed feelings about growing up and away from him, and they'd both feel good about themselves for having leveled with each other. Thus, Satir believed that the relationship between self-esteem and communication was circular. Low self-esteem begets protective, incongruent communication, which elicits similarly protective communication from others, which in turn, engenders low self-esteem, and so on. Fortunately, however, the cycle can be virtuous as well as vicious: honest communication engenders high self-esteem which encourages more honesty and so on (Satir, 1972, 1988).

The key then to increasing the self-worth of each family member is through direct, straight-from-the-heart communication regarding each family member's life predicament, regarding the impact they have on each other, and regarding the family communication rules (metacommunication). To achieve this, therapists must be able to create an atmosphere within sessions that allows each family member to feel safe and accepted so they will risk this kind of openness. The therapist must be able to challenge people without threatening their self-esteem and so must be a model of honesty and acceptance.

To summarize, Satir deviated from the norms being established by the systems family therapy theorists in Palo Alto. She focused on nurturance where they were interested in control and feedback loops. She focused on qualities of individuals where they believed that such a focus distracted from seeing interactional patterns within the larger family. She worked with whatever imbalances she found that affected communication and self-esteem where they remained problem-focused. She generated and advocated a close collaborative relationship with clients where they remained distant and expert. While Satir was seen by many of these theorists as a fuzzy and naive thinker, it may be that she was ahead of her time.

Bowen and Differentiation of Self

Up to this point all of the seminal family therapy theorists we have described, the MRI group, Haley, Minuchin, and Satir, had at least indirect contact with Bateson and his cybernetic/functionalist epistemology. Thus, despite the differences among them that we have been highlighting, they all had in common an interest in changing the current interaction patterns of the primary family system, which they generally viewed as the nuclear family, rather than the family-of-origin. Murray Bowen, the last family therapy pioneer we will consider here, evolved a version of systems theory apart from this cybernetic/functional influence, so his ideas are quite different from these other models.

Bowen also disavowed the GST of Bertalanffy, although his ideas fit better with GST than cybernetics. To bolster the originality of his ideas, Bowen (1978) wrote,

> There are those who believe family systems theory [the name he originally gave to what is now known as Bowen theory] was developed from general system theory. Back in the 1940s, I attended one lecture by Bertalanffy, which I did not understand, and another by Norbert Wiener, which was perhaps a little more understandable. . . . The degree to which I heard something in those lectures that influenced my later thinking is debatable (p. 359).

What did influence Bowen's ideas was the biological sciences, hence the compatibility with GST. In describing his reasons for looking to biology, Bowen (1978) wrote:

> On the premise that psychiatry might eventually become a recognized science, perhaps, a generation or two in the future, and being aware of the past conceptual problems of psychoanalysis [that used metaphors from literature and hydraulics] . . . I therefore chose to use only concepts that would be consistent with biology and the natural sciences. It was easy to think in terms of the familiar concepts of chemistry, physics, and mathematics, but I carefully excluded all concepts that dealt with inanimate things. . . . The concept of differentiation was chosen because it has specific meaning in the biological sciences. When we speak of "differentiation of self," we mean a process similar to the differentiation of cells from each other. The same applies to the term fusion (p. 354).

Thus Bowen's theory can be seen as the application of cell biology and evolution to the understanding of human beings and the families in which they live. Initially Bowen was struck by the amount of "fusion" between schizophrenic patients and their mothers; that is, that they were highly emotionally reactive to each other. He later noticed that this was the case with the whole family and coined the phrase "undifferentiated family ego mass" to suggest that, because of their emotional reactivity, the whole family was like one undifferentiated cell. Similarly he found that each family member had a low level of *differentiation of self*; that is, their emotions and their intellect were not separated enough to prevent them from reacting automatically and emotionally. Thus the goal of Bowen's therapy became the differentiation of self of key family members such that they could help differentiate the whole family.

This concept of differentiation, which also seems to mean control of reason over emotion, betrays Bowen's psychoanalytic roots. Freud's famous quote "Where id is, there ego shall be," fits this concept of differentiation quite well. Indeed Bowen (1978) saw the emotional system as "an intimate part of man's phylogenetic past which he shares with all lower forms of life" while the intellectual system was "a function of the cerebral cortex which appeared last in man's evolutionary development and is the main difference between man and the lower forms of life" (p. 356).

Unlike many of the other family therapy theorists discussed earlier, Bowen saw a person's level of differentiation as a relatively fixed trait that took a long time to change. He also believed that about 90 percent of the population is not well differentiated. In this, too, we hear Freud's echo.

The theory of evolution reappears in Bowen's speculations about how people arrive at a level of differentiation. He called this the *multigenerational transmission process* and believed that most children emerge from their families with the same level of differentiation that their parents had, while some emerge with lower and some with higher levels. Thus the transmission of differentiation follows a "genetic-like pattern" (Bowen, 1978, p. 410) across generations.

With these beliefs about people, it is understandable that Bowen was less interested in family communication patterns than the other theorists since such patterns are seen as the product of the level of differentiation of each family member and are unlikely to change lastingly until their differentiation levels change. Along these lines, Bowen (1978) asserted that while approaches that work with the whole family to improve their communication "can produce dramatic shifts in the feeling system, and even a period of exhilaration . . . I have not been able to use this as a long-term method for resolving underlying problems" (p. 151).

Like the other family therapy pioneers, Bowen believed that child problems were related to the parents' marriage and, in his theory, the concept of *family triangles* is central. He saw the forming of triangles as a natural human tendency in the face of anxiety. That is, when a two-person relationship, particularly where those two people are not highly differentiated, experiences stress, a third person will become involved. "The two-some might 'reach out' and pull in the other person, the emotions might 'overflow' to the third person, or the third person might be emotionally programmed to initiate the involvement. With the involvement of the third person, the anxiety level decreases" (p. 400). From this we can see that Bowen made many of the same function-of-the symptom observations that became the centerpieces of other models, but, like the psychoanalysts, he saw these patterns as manifestations of an underlying process that had to be changed, rather than as direct targets of change.

Bowen believed that if people became educated to the existence of the emotional triangling process within their nuclear and extended families and learned to avoid being pulled into it, they would gradually differentiate. Bowen's interest in the evolution of levels of differentiation made him one of the few pioneers who paid much attention to a family's history. This was one area where he differentiated from Freud, because Bowen's focus was not on a client's childhood trauma or early relationships; instead, it was on the multigenerational history of the extended family. In his interest in family history, Bowen also differentiated from the other pioneers, most of whom viewed history as an explanatory background for problems in a family's current structure or feedback loops.

Family Life Cycle

The concept of the *family life cycle* was borrowed from sociology to become this explanatory background to the structural and strategic approaches. Sociologists Evelyn Duvall and Reuben Hill began applying a developmental framework to families in the 1940s that is characterized by dividing a family's development into discrete stages with different tasks to be performed at each stage (Duvall, 1957, 1977; Hill and Rodgers, 1964) (see Table 2.1). Duvall's eight stages of family development set the tone, although later theorists have come up with different frameworks by adding or subtracting stages (Solomon, 1973; Barnhill and Longo, 1978).

Family therapists Elizabeth Carter and Monica McGoldrick (1980) enriched this framework by adding a multigenerational point of view and by considering stages of divorce and remarriage. Their book, *The Family Life Cycle*, with chapters on the various stages, greatly popularized the family life cycle concept within family therapy. They have recently completed a second edition (Carter and McGoldrick, 1989) which updates the developments in this area over the decade. Other family therapists injected systems ideas into the family life cycle framework so that the transitions between stages are not so discrete and the family as a whole can be characterized. Lee Combrinck-Graham (1983, 1985, 1988) views the three-generational family as alternating between centrifugal and centripetal states as events in their life cycle alternately call for more interdependence or

TABLE 2.1 Duvall's Stages of the Family Life Cycle

Stage	Developmental tasks
1. Married couples without children.	Establishing a mutually satisfying marriage. Adjusting to pregnancy and the promise of parenthood. Fitting into the kin network.
2. Childbearing families (oldest child birth–30 months).	Having, adjusting to, and encouraging the development of infants. Establishing a satisfying home for both parents and infants.
3. Families with preschool children (oldest child 2½–6 years).	Adapting to the critical needs and interests of preschool children in stimulating, growth-promoting ways. Coping with energy depletion and lack of privacy.
4. Families with children (oldest child 6–13 years).	Fitting into the community of school-age families. Encouraging children's educational achievement.
5. Families with teenagers (oldest child 13–20 years).	Balancing freedom with responsibility. Establishing postparental interests and careers.
6. Families launching young adults (first child gone to last child's leaving home).	Releasing young adults with appropriate rituals and assistance. Maintaining a supportive home base.
7. Middle-aged parents (empty nest to retirement).	Rebuilding the marriage relationship. Maintaining kin ties with older and younger generations.
8. Aging family members (retirement to death of both spouses).	Coping with bereavement and living alone. Closing the family home or adapting it to aging. Adjustment to retirement.

individuation among family members. Douglas Breunlin's (1983, 1988) oscillation theory provides a sophisticated understanding of the transitions
among family and individual life cycle stages. Breunlin demonstrates how
such transitions are never clean, discontinuous shifts, but instead occur as
gradual oscillations between stages or levels of functioning.

Like so many other new ideas, the concept of the family life cycle
was first introduced to the field of family therapy by Jay Haley (1973)
who, in his book *Uncommon Therapy*, also presented Milton Erickson to
the field. Haley saw symptoms as the result of a family becoming stuck at
a transition between life cycle stages because the family was unable or afraid
to make the transition. Later Haley (1980) focused on one particular life
cycle stuck-point in his book *Leaving Home*, which provided strategies
for working with families having difficulty launching their young adults.

The formulations of Minuchin (1974; Minuchin and Fishman, 1981)
were also influenced by the life cycle concept. The structural model contained many of the ideas from sociology regarding stages and tasks, but
couched in terms of the development of various subsystems within the
family system and changes in hierarchy and parenting style as children
mature. Problems develop when a family with a dysfunctional structure
encounters a transition point to another stage and, because of their structural
problems, cannot make the transition adequately.

The MRI group (Watzlawick, Weakland, and Fisch, 1974) also used
the life cycle in their theory of problem formation. Life cycle transitions
present a family with predictable difficulties which become problems because of the family's ill-fated attempted solutions. They used this life cycle
understanding as a way to reframe the family's problem as normal rather
than pathological.

As we will discuss in the next chapter, this use of historical, life cycle
material as a reframe for current family problems was expanded by the
Milan Associates, who would explore a family's history in some detail to
find information with which to build a "positive connotation" of each
family member's behavior. In addition, the Milan Associates pioneered the
use of *family rituals* for facilitating the transitions between life cycle stages.
The use of ritual in family therapy was later elaborated on and has become
a prominent interest of many family therapists (Imber-Black, Roberts, and
Whiting, 1989).

For reasons discussed above, Bowen was less interested in the life
cycle of a nuclear family he treated than the longer-term development of
the parents' extended family. Other psychodynamically oriented family
therapists, however, proposed family life cycle models that were influenced
by psychoanalytic models of individual development. According to these
theorists, the development of families can become fixated or arrested at
earlier stages, just as it can with individuals (Wachtel and Wachtel, 1986;
Skynner, 1981; Paul, 1969; Barnhill and Longo, 1978). The goal becomes

to help families recognize and work through these developmental arrests by, for example, mourning an unresolved loss.

In summary, most of the schools of family therapy have at least paid lip service to the concept of the family life cycle in their theorizing, if not in their therapy. Structural and strategic therapists, with their primary interest in changing current family processes, did not see much value in accompanying the family in historical investigations, other than to find life cycle information with which to "normalize" the problems. Thus the major schools have not taken the concept far beyond the original sociological frameworks. Others have refined and improved the thinking about the family life cycle and, while there remains little consensus as to the best way to use the concept, it has recently received renewed interest and more sophisticated treatment (Falicov, 1988; Pittman, 1987; Carter and McGoldrick, 1989).

SUMMARY OF CONCEPTUAL INFLUENCES

To summarize the conceptual influences on the field, each of these pioneers was faced with the same set of questions for which there were no previous answers:

- How do families operate?

- How do families develop?

- What is the difference between healthy and pathological families?

- What is the relationship between a family member's symptom and the family's operation?

- How can families change the way they operate?

- Why do families sometimes resist taking obvious steps toward improvement?

As we have seen, despite the similarity of many of their initial observations, the pioneers' answers to these questions varied enormously and the therapeutic techniques derived from their answers varied even more. This variation is due in part to differences among the metaphors or conceptual traditions to which each pioneer turned for help. We have seen the influence of a panoply of disparate ideas on the development of the field: functionalism and structuralism, General Systems Theory, Ericksonian hypnotherapy, cybernetics and Bateson's interpretation of it, communication theory, the humanistic movement, cell biology and evolutionary theory, family life cycle theory from sociology, and psychoanalysis.

Each of these traditions conveys a different view of the nature of people and how they can change. We agree with Bertalanffy's assertion that a theory's basic assumptions regarding the human personality will dictate, to a large degree, the practices of its adherents. Those who view people as mechanistic black boxes will try anything to alter the communications among these boxes, and do so from a position of distance, like the expert repairman. Those who understand people through a lens of power and see people's symptoms as power operations, also work from a strategic distance and develop strategies to diffuse the power of the symptom or the power arrangements in the family that made it necessary.

Those who see people as chameleon-like in the degree to which they change when family relationships change, use their own relationship with the family to change its structure and, consequently, work from a position of proximity. Those who believe people basically want intimacy and love, will get close to family members in order to help them feel and share these tender feelings. Those who see people as dominated by irrational emotionality will create a reflective atmosphere in which clients learn to stay rational in the face of family upset.

In family therapy's attempt to focus on the system, rather than the individuals who comprise it, these fundamental assumptions about people, at times, have not been clearly articulated. Given the degree to which the methods of each model of family therapy are driven by its basic view of people, we recommend that those assumptions be examined carefully when evaluating a model.

ENDURING CONCEPTS AND TECHNIQUES

In this chapter we have presented our interpretation of the contextual factors that influenced the early development of family therapy. These factors included the general nature of change within a field; free market opportunism relative to money and research; the personalities, cultural biases, and target populations of the pioneers; and the conceptual traditions from which they drew.

Given the complexity of these ideas, we will summarize what we believe to be the concepts and methods that endured from this early period and continue to shape the field.

The Importance of Family Context

For a long time, individual therapists recognized the importance of family influences in shaping the personality, but assumed that the internal representations of childhood events exerted a more dominant influence than ongoing family interactions. Consistent with this viewpoint, psychotherapists isolated patients from their natural environment in order to manipulate aspects of their internally organized behavior. Family therapists, on the contrary, believe that the dominant forces in personality development are located externally in current interactions in the family system. This is the fundamental premise of family therapy as an orientation: that people are products of their social context, and that any attempt to understand them must include an appreciation of their families.

A corollary of the family orientation is that the most effective way to treat people is to alter their family interactions. As a method, family therapy usually, but not always, involves bringing the family together for treatment. But even those therapists—for example, Bowen and strategic therapists—who do not necessarily meet with whole families, design their interventions to affect family interactions.

In summary, a person's or problem's context is central to family therapy in two ways. The first is related to understanding people and their problems—that they can be understood best when their family context is considered. The second is related to treatment—that changes in family context can create powerful changes in people and their problems.

Dyads to Triads

In attempting to organize observations of family context, family therapy passed through a series of conceptual stages, from regarding individuals as the units of pathology, to dyadic and triadic models, and finally to models that tried to include the whole family's structure. Locating pathology in the individual personality did not begin with psychoanalysis; it has always been a natural way to think about psychological problems. If someone has a problem, something inside must be bothering them. This point of view has been maintained in Freudian theory, as well as in most other theories of psychotherapy. The *monadic* model was later extended by social psychiatrists and object relations theorists to include the dyadic concept of interlocking pathology or *object relations*. Behavior therapists also extended their view to include two people and how they reinforce each other.

Family therapists demonstrated that the dyad's relationship also reflects the influence of third parties. A boy's behavior depends on his relationship with his father and that, in turn, depends on father's relationship with his wife. As family therapy's view expanded to include more family members, the need increased for metaphors for understanding how groups of people interact.

Family Structure

The field selected metaphors of *subsystems* and *boundaries* from cell biology and functionalism in sociology. The idea that families can be understood best by assessing the boundaries around the various subsystems within them, with particular importance given to the boundaries between generations, has become a cornerstone of the field. There is an ideal level of permeability to the boundaries around a subsystem. When boundaries are too open, relationships are described as *enmeshed* or *fused*, and when boundaries are too closed, relationships are *disengaged* or *cut off*. Therapists informed by these ideas are interested in who is close to or distant from whom in families and how to reorganize those alliances or coalitions.

Boundaries around the "executive subsystem," i.e., the leadership in the family, are of particular import because the *hierarchy* of the family is seen as crucial to its well-being. Therapists concerned with family hierarchy assess how well those who are supposed to be leading the family, commonly the parents, are able to work together and how much children are being thrust into that position inappropriately, creating *incongruent hierarchies*.

Psychopathology as Serving a Function in Families

Severely disturbed families provide a magnified focus on processes that operate in all families, but are not always easy to observe. Studies on the etiology of schizophrenia led to the conclusion that deviance was not necessarily negative, but that, on the contrary, the symptoms of schizophrenics made sense when seen in the light of their family contexts and served a function in those families.

Another important finding was that often when the patient got better, someone else in the family got worse. This, and the tenacity with which these families seemed to resist change, led Jackson to coin the term *family homeostasis*. The concept of homeostasis emphasized the sanctions that family members imposed on each other, referred to as *negative feedback*, to keep the system from changing.

Eventually most schools of family therapy subscribed in one way or another to the idea that a family member's problems may be functional somehow for the larger system. The idea was that when a family dyad is stressed they will "triangulate" a third person to diffuse the stress. That person may become the object of concern or criticism, and may actively seek the distractive role or have it imposed upon him or her. Following this logic, symptoms become *homeostatic mechanisms*, or ways to help the system avoid changes that are threatening. As we discuss in the next chapter, these concepts have been re-examined and challenged as the field develops, but they still exert a powerful influence.

Circular Sequences of Interaction

Our language trains us to think *linearly*, that is, to think that there is a specific cause for a specific effect or problem. If Johnny is withdrawn and shy, something inside must be bothering him—he probably has low self-esteem. Before family therapy, explanations of psychopathology were based on linear models—medical, psychodynamic, and behavioral. In all of these, etiology was conceived in terms of prior events—disease, emotional conflict, or learning history—which caused symptoms in the present. The patient was the locus of malfunction in all of these models. Linear thinking is not limited to a focus on one person. It is also linear to assume that one person caused another to behave or think in a problematic way. Johnny is withdrawn and shy because father overprotects him.

Using the concept of *circularity*, family therapists changed the way we think of psychopathology, from something caused by events in the past or inside the person, to something that is a part of ongoing, circular causal sequences of behavior. Johnny is withdrawn and shy because father overprotects; father overprotects because Johnny is so withdrawn and shy.

A family therapist may be able to expand this circular sequence, involving other family members or people outside the family that fit into this vicious circle (*positive feedback loop*). No matter how many people or levels of system are involved in a family therapist's understanding of a problem, however, the formulation will be arranged in a circular rather than linear way. For many family therapists, then, assessment involves tracking or observing the circular sequences of interaction that surround a problem or illustrate the family's structure.

In taking the concept of circularity seriously, family therapists had to include themselves in their assessments of problems. No longer could we see the therapist as an active subject and the client as a passive object. Therapist and family react to each other in circular ways too and, consequently, family therapists began to consider themselves as elements in the fields they were trying to change.

Family Life Cycle

The idea that families evolve over time as they enter and leave different stages of their life cycle added depth to these systemic formulations. A family's inability to successfully navigate one of these predictable stages could initiate the kinds of circular sequences that eventually lead to problems. Shy and withdrawn Johnny reaches the age where, by American middle-class standards, he should be living on his own. He has been overprotected by both parents and caught up in their marital differences. He fears for himself and for his parents if he were to leave home, and his parents are also ambivalent. The family is stuck at the launching stage of their life cycle. Johnny gets and loses several jobs, has a few aborted attempts to live on his own and, with each failure, feels increasingly incompetent and dependent. His parents are increasingly concerned about and embarrassed by his failures, and the stage is set for some sort of chronic symptom that might excuse Johnny's failures and diffuse the growing pressure.

Multigenerational Patterns

Bowen's idea that a family's problems are not simply the result of the current malfunctioning of the family or the result of bumps along the family's life cycle, but instead evolve over many generations, was not of interest to many of the other pioneers covered above who were enamored by the power of current circular family interactions. Gradually, however, the field began to conclude that the evolution of a family system over generations can explain many of their present circular knots. Today, many structural or strategic therapists routinely take a family's genogram to detect multigenerational patterns and to help the family understand their problems in a longitudinal perspective that reduces the blame and guilt they feel.

Views of the Individual

Family therapy has presented a wide array of portraits of personality, some of which are original to the field and some are borrowed. Each school of family therapy carries different fundamental assumptions about the nature of people and, earlier, we reviewed several conceptions of personality: the black box, the power motivated, the self-esteem motivated, the context reactor, the undifferentiated (between reason and emotion), and the psychodynamic (impelled by basic drives). All of these views continue to have some impact on the field, just as each of the schools upon which they are based continue to have some following, and none has emerged as the prevailing view.

These fundamental assumptions about people will determine many of the concepts and methods of a family therapy model. For example, the first four of those views, all of which are optimistic about the possibilities of rapid internal change, informed models that tend to be brief and active, and have more in common than the last two, which are pessimistic about rapid change and, consequently, are long-term and less directive.

FUNDAMENTALS OF TREATMENT _____

The first people to actually treat families began with few established principles and techniques. Necessity mothered a vast array of inventions for treating human problems. Many of these have lost their identity to a particular school of family therapy and, instead, are in a barrel of techniques from which family therapists of every ilk now draw. We will classify them into three categories.

Dealing with Resistance

If people do not feel respect or caring from a therapist they will be more likely to resist. The process by which therapists convey these feelings to all family members has come to be known as *joining* with the family and, particularly for those therapists who rely heavily on their relationships with clients for leverage, joining underpins all the other methods. To join with clients, therapists are taught to be themselves; that is, to relate in a friendly rather than stilted way. This freedom to be genuinely oneself is one of the qualities that initially attracts students to family therapy.

Hypnotists are masters of circumventing and using client resistance, and family therapists borrowed several techniques from one of the most famous hypnotherapists, Milton Erickson. These include what have come to be known as paradoxical techniques like *restraining*, wherein the therapist urges the family to move slowly toward any change, or even to consider not changing, in the hope that the family will do the opposite. *Paradoxical techniques* became a mainstay of strategic family therapy but also have been incorporated into the repertoire of many nonstrategic therapists. Paradoxical techniques can be valuable aids but, as will be discussed in the next chapter, too often they accompany a conception of families as objects of intervention, and as opponents to be outwitted, instead of as partners in a collaborative effort.

Changing Interaction

Family therapists often encourage family members to speak directly to each other and then try to change the way they are interacting. These *enactments* allow the therapist to observe the family's process directly, rather than having to rely on the family's report and to intervene directly into that process and see the results of their interventions.

One common type of enactment, pioneered by Satir, is to direct family members to communicate the more vulnerable feelings or desires that often lie behind their hostility and to listen empathically to each other. Thus, family therapists often strive to change the style of communication of the family. Along these lines, some therapists will send clients on *family-of-origin voyages*, in which they are to meet with extended family members outside of sessions and try to communicate in a new, more differentiated, way with them.

As we mentioned above, the structural concept of boundaries around subsystems has become widely used, and so the technique of *boundary-making* is also widespread. This phrase encompasses a large number of therapist directives designed to separate family members who are too close or bring together those who are too distant. For example, when two disengaged family members start to speak to each other, the therapist will strengthen the boundary around them by preventing others from interrupting.

Similarly, family therapists may *prescribe the symptom*; that is, ask the family to act out the sequences around their problem, with the hope that they will not be able to comply, will change their pattern or, at least, will become more aware of these sequences. All of these action-changing techniques require skill in *giving directives* clearly and with some authority, while remaining joined with the family. This directive stance is another quality that differentiates many forms of family therapy from many forms of individual therapy, and it often takes students time before they are comfortable with this directiveness.

The use of directives has become one of the most widespread techniques of family therapy. Experientialists use directives to promote affective experiences in therapy sessions; behaviorists use directives to teach parents new ways of disciplining their children; structural family therapists use directives to change the boundaries in sessions; Bowen therapists use directives to advise patients how to be different with their parents; and strategic therapists give directives in the form of between-session tasks and also use directives to outwit resistance. This directiveness of early family therapy reflects the belief of many of the pioneers that they were primarily responsible for getting families to change. As we will see later, this belief, and the directiveness it fosters, has also been challenged.

Changing Meaning

The primary method for this purpose to emerge from this early period has been called variously, *reframing, relabeling*, or *creating a workable reality*. These terms refer simply to the process in which a therapist restates the family's problems or presents a family member, in a new way, a way that allows for more possibilities. For example, if the family considers Johnny a depressed person, they will feel powerless to help him other than to take him to doctors for medication. If, on the other hand, the therapist reframes his depressive behaviors as his way of saying he does not feel a part of the family, then the family can reorganize to include him.

Initially family therapy was more focused on changing action than meaning, as is reflected in the larger number of action-oriented techniques discussed above. As we will see in the next chapter, one of the major changes in the field in the last decade has been a reversal of these emphases, with meaning becoming an increasingly important target of change.

Miscellaneous Contributions

In this chapter we have tried to summarize the major contextual and conceptual influences on family therapy during its formative years. In focusing this summary on only a few of the most influential theorists, we have not done justice to the contribution of several other theorists whose work had an impact but did not develop into a distinct school of family therapy. John E. Bell treated families as groups, helped parents learn to negotiate with their children, and introduced the idea that therapy can be conducted in planned stages. Christian Midelfort worked with families in order to help them mobilize latent forces of love and support. Norman Paul's technique of *operational mourning* was another attempt to stimulate healing emotional experiences in families.

Ivan Boszormenyi-Nagy's work initially drew little attention outside the scholarly wing of family therapy. Recently, however, his combination of psychoanalytic, systems, and ethical principles has become more influential, as increasing numbers of family therapists are becoming interested in integrating psychoanalytic theory and family therapy.

Carl Whitaker is one of the major figures in the field, but his impact has been more personal than conceptual, in part because he argues against therapists having a preconceived theory that might interfere with their intuitions. His contributions include emphasizing the value of cotherapy, and teaching—by example—that family therapy can be a spontaneous and provocative experience. Theodore Lidz and Lyman Wynne also made early conceptual contributions derived from their work with schizophrenic families, which are described in Chapter 1.

Finally, no summary of influences would be complete if it did not include the impact of the *one-way mirror* and *videotaping*. The one-way mirror opened a window to the world of family process and therapy that had never existed before. It, and the videotaping of sessions, offered the ability to directly observe families in action, an ability that accounts in part for the rapid conceptual and technical strides that family therapy has made.

In addition, these technologies allowed students to directly observe and emulate the technique of master therapists and allowed supervisors to give direct and immediate feedback to students struggling with families. So-called "live" and video supervision have become standard training practices in institutes around the country. These technologies have also promoted the more recent "team" work approaches to family therapy, in which a team of therapists watch a session from behind the mirror and work with the therapist in treating the family (see Liddle, Breunlin, and Schwartz, 1988, for more on how training influenced family therapy).

REFERENCES

Ackerman, N. 1958. *The psychodynamics of family life.* New York: Basic Books.

Auerswald, E. H. 1969. Interdisciplinary versus ecological approach. In *General systems theory and psychiatry*, W. Gray, F. J. Duhl, and N. D. Rizzo, eds. Boston: Little, Brown and Co.

Barnhill, L., and Longo, D. 1978. Fixation and regression in the family life cycle. *Family Process.* *17*:469–478.

Bateson, G., Jackson, D.D., Haley, J., and Weakland, J.H. 1956. Towards a theory of schizophrenia. In *Steps to an ecology of mind*, G. Bateson, ed. New York: Ballantine.

Bateson, G. 1956. *Naven.* Stanford, CA: Stanford University Press.

Bateson, G., Jackson, D.D., Haley, J., and Weakland, J. 1963. A note on the double-bind. *Family Process.* *2*(1):154–161.

Bateson, G. 1971. *Steps to an ecology of mind.* New York: Ballantine.

Bateson, G. 1979. *Mind and nature.* New York: E.P. Dutton.

Bateson, M.C. 1984. *With a daughter's eye.* New York: William Morrow.

Becvar, D.S., and Becvar, R.J. 1988. *Family therapy: A systemic integration.* Boston: Allyn and Bacon.

Bellah, R.N., Madsen, R., Sullivan, W.M., Swidler, A., and Tipton, S.M. 1985. *Habits of the heart: Individualism and commitment in American life.* New York: Harper & Row.

von Bertalanffy, L. 1968. *General system theory.* New York: George Braziller.

Bogdan, J. 1983. The Ericksonian Rorshach. *Family Therapy Networker.* *7*(5):36–38.

Bogdan, J. 1987. "Epistemology" as a semantic pollutant. *Journal of Marital and Family Therapy.* *13*(1):27–36.

Boscolo, L., Cecchin, G., Hoffman, L., and Penn, P. 1987. *Milan systemic family therapy.* New York: Basic Books.

Bowen, M. 1978. *Family therapy in clinical practice.* New York: Jason Aronson.

Breunlin, D. 1983. Therapy in stages: A life cycle view. In *Clinical implications of the family life cycle*, H. Liddle, ed. Rockville, MD: Aspen Systems Corporation.

Breunlin, D. 1988. Oscillation theory and family development. In *Family transitions*, C. Falicov, ed. New York: Guilford.

Breunlin, D.C., Cornwell, M., and Cade, B. 1983. International trade in family therapy: Parallels between societal and therapeutic values In *Cultural perspectives in family therapy*, C.J. Falicov, ed. Rockville, MD: Aspen.

Breunlin, D.C., and Schwartz, R.C. 1986. Sequences: Toward a common denominator for family therapy. *Family process.* *25*:67–87.

Breunlin, D.C., Schwartz, R.C., and Karrer, B.M. In press. *Metaframeworks for Systemic Therapy.* San Francisco: Jossey-Bass.

Capra, F. 1982. *The turning point.* New York: Simon & Schuster.

Carter, E., and McGoldrick, M., eds. 1980. *The family life cycle: A framework for family therapy.* New York: Gardner Press.

Carter, E., and McGoldrick, M., eds. 1989. *The changing family life cycle: A framework for family therapy. 2nd Ed.* Needham Heights, MA: Allyn and Bacon.

Combrinck-Graham, L. 1983. The family life cycle and families with young children. In *Clinical implications of the family life cycle*, H. Liddle, ed. Rockville, MD: Aspen Systems.

Combrinck-Graham, L. 1985. A model for family development. *Family Process.* *24*:139–150.

Combrinck-Graham, L. 1988. Adolescent sexuality in the family life cycle. In *Family transitions*, C. Falicov, ed. New York: Guilford.

Davidson, M. 1983. *Uncommon sense*. Los Angeles: J.P. Tarcher.

Dell, P.F. 1982. Beyond homeostasis: Toward a concept of coherence. *Family Process*. *21*(1):21–42.

Duhl, B.S. 1983. *From the inside out and other metaphors: Creative and integrative approaches to training in systems thinking*. New York: Brunner/Mazel.

Duncan, B.L. and Parks, M.B. 1988. Integrating individual and systems approaches: Strategic-behavior therapy. *Journal of Marital and Family Therapy*. *14*(2):151–162.

Duncan, B.L. and Solevey, D. 1989. Strategic-brief therapy: An insight-oriented approach. *Journal of Marital and Family Therapy*. *15*(1), 1–10.

Duvall, E. 1957. *Family Development*. Philadelphia: Lippincott.

Falicov, C.J., ed. 1983. *Cultural Perspectives in Family Therapy*. Rockville, MD: Aspen.

Falicov, C.J., ed. 1988. *Family Transitions*. New York: Guilford.

Goldner, V., 1987. Instrumentalism, feminism and the limits of family therapy. *Journal of Family Psychology*. *1*(1):109–116.

Goldner, V. 1988. Generation and gender: Normative and covert hierarchies. *Family Process*. *27*(1):17–33.

Gould, S.J. 1985. *The flamingo's smile: Reflections in natural history*. New York: Norton.

Haley, J. 1963. *Strategies of psychotherapy*. New York: Grune and Stratton.

Haley, J. 1971. Family therapy: A radical change. In *Changing Families: A family therapy reader*, J. Haley, ed. New York: Grune and Stratton.

Haley, J., ed. 1971. *Changing families: A family therapy reader*. New York: Grune and Stratton.

Haley, J. 1973. *Uncommon therapy: The psychiatric techniques of Milton H. Erickson*. New York: Norton.

Haley, J. 1976. *Problem-solving therapy*. San Francisco: Jossey-Bass.

Haley, J. 1980. *Leaving home*. New York: McGraw Hill.

Haley, J. 1981. *Reflections of therapy and other essays*. Chevy Chase, MD: The Family Therapy Institute of Washington, DC.

Haley, J. 1985. Conversations with Erickson. *Family Therapy Networker*. *9*(2): 30–43.

Hare-Mustin, R.C. 1978. A feminist approach to family therapy. *Family Process*. *17*:181–194.

Hareven, T. 1982. American families in transition: Historical perspectives on change. In *Normal family processes*, F. Walsh, ed. New York: Guilford Press.

Hill, R., and Rodgers, R. 1964. The developmental approach. In *Handbook of marriage and the family*, H.T. Christiansen, ed. Chicago: Rand McNally.

Hoffman, L. 1971. Deviation-amplifying processes in natural groups. In *Changing families: A family therapy reader*, J. Haley, ed. New York: Grune and Stratton.

Hoffman, L. 1981. *Foundations of family therapy*. New York: Basic Books.

Hsu, F.K., ed. 1971. *Kinship and culture.* Chicago: Aldine.

Imber-Black, E., Roberts, J., and Whiting, R. 1989. *Rituals in families and family therapy.* New York: Norton.

Jackson, D. 1957. The question of family homeostasis. *Psychiatric Quarterly Supplement.* 3(1):79–90.

Keeney, B.P., and Sprenkle, D.H. 1982. Ecosystemic epistemology: Critical implications for the aesthetics and pragmatics of family therapy. *Family Process.* 21(1):1–20.

Kuhn, T.S. 1977. *The essential tension: Selected studies in scientific tradition and change.* Chicago: The University of Chicago Press.

Lasch, C. 1977. *Haven in a heartless world.* New York: Basic Books.

Lerner, H. G. 1986. Dianna and Lillie: Can a feminist still like Murray Bowen? *Family Therapy Networker.* 9 (16):36–39.

Liddle, H.A., Breunlin, D.C., and Schwartz, R.C., eds. 1988. *Handbook of family therapy training and supervision.* New York: Guilford.

Lidz, T. 1963. *The family and human adaptation.* New York: International Universities Press.

Luepnitz, D.A. 1988. *The family interpreted: Feminist theory in clinical practice.* New York: Basic Books.

McGoldrick, M., Pearce, J.K., and Giordano, J. 1982. *Ethnicity and family therapy.* New York: Guilford.

Minuchin, S. 1974. *Families and family therapy.* Cambridge, MA: Harvard University Press.

Minuchin, S., and Fishman, H.C. 1981. *Family therapy techniques.* Cambridge, MA: Harvard Unversity Press.

Parsons, T., and Bales, R.F. 1955. *Family, socialization and interaction process.* New York: Free Press.

Paul, N. 1969. The role of mourning and empathy in conjoint marital therapy. In *Family therapy and disturbed families,* G. Zuk and I. Boszormenyi-Nagy, eds. Palo Alto: Science and Behavior Books.

Pittman, F. 1987. *Turning points: Treating families in transition and crisis.* New York: Norton.

Satir, V. 1972. *Peoplemaking.* Palo Alto, CA: Science and Behavior Books.

Satir, V. 1988. *The new peoplemaking.* Palo Alto, CA: Science and Behavior Books.

Schwartz, R.C. 1985. Has family therapy reached the stage where it can appreciate the concept of stages? In *Stages: Patterns of change over time,* D.C. Breunlin, ed. Rockville, MA: Aspen.

Schwartz, R.C., and Perrotta, P. 1985. Let us sell no intervention before its time. *Family Therapy Networker.* 9(4):18–25.

Selvini Palazzoli, M., Boscolo, L., Cecchin, G., and Prata, G. 1978. *Paradox and counterparadox.* New York: Jason Aronson.

Simon, R. 1982a. Reflections on family therapy: An interview with Jay Haley, part I. *Family Therapy Networker.* 6(5):18–26.

Simon, R. 1982b. Reflections on the one-way mirror: An interview with Jay Haley, part II. *Family Therapy Networker.* 6(6):32–36, 49.

Simon, R. 1984. Stranger in a strange land: An interview with Salvador Minuchin. *Family Therapy Networker.* 8(6):20–31, 66–68.

Simon, R. 1987. Good-bye paradox, hello invariant prescription: An interview with Mara Selvini Palazzoli. *Family Therapy Networker. 11*(5):16–33.

Skynner, R. 1981. An open systems, group analytic approach to family therapy. In *Handbook of family therapy*, A. Gurman and D. Kniskern, eds. New York: Brunner/Mazel.

Sluzki, C. 1983. Interview on the state of the art. *Family Therapy Networker. 7*(1):24.

Solomon, M. 1973. A developmental, conceptual premise for family therapy. *Family Process. 12*:179–188.

Speer, D.C. 1979. Family systems: Morphostasis and morphogenesis, or "Is homeostasis enough?" *Family Process. 9*(3):259–278.

Stanton, A., and Schwartz, M. 1964. *The mental hospital*. New York: Basic Books.

Wachtel, E.F., and Wachtel, P.L. 1986. *Family dynamics in individual psychotherapy*. New York: Guilford.

Watzlawick, P., Beavin, J.H., and Jackson, D.D. 1967. *Pragmatics of human communication*. New York: Norton.

Watzlawick, P., Weakland, J., and Fisch, R. 1974. *Change: Principles of problem formation and problem resolution*. New York: Jason Aronson.

Young, M., and Willmott, P. 1957. *Family and kinship in East London*. London: Routledge and Kegan Paul.

3

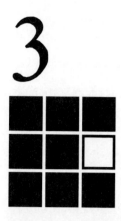

The Contemporary
Context: Rude Awakenings

During the 1960s and 1970s family therapy grew from a radical new experiment to an established force complete with its own journals, conferences, and thousands of adherents. Unlike other fields that were relatively homogeneous because they were organized around one theory or approach (behavior therapy, psychoanalysis, hypnotherapy), or by professional degree (psychology, psychiatry, social work), family therapy had a wide variety of leaders and theories and drew followers from many backgrounds.

If differences in their professional degree or in their orientation to therapy were apparent in the way clinicians looked, then family therapy conferences might resemble the bar scene in *Star Wars*. Family therapy gatherings attracted refugees and renegades from all over the psychotherapy universe, with precious little in common beyond a dissatisfaction with their former haunts and a hope that involving families might be the answer. They tried out one or another of the handful of pioneering models but, unless they received training directly from one of these pioneers, their loyalty to any one model, while intense, was changeable.

As discussed in Chapter 2, the 1960s and 1970s were the decades of family therapy's essentialistic stage. The systems-oriented family therapy models had differentiated from each other in large pendulum swings and were equally polarized from the psychoanalytic or behavioral establishments (though both behaviorism and analysis had their representative models of family therapy). Boundaries around each model were rigid. If, for example, you were a structuralist and met someone at a conference who, after a period of conversation, identified himself as being interested in Bowen or Satir, the conversation was not likely to last much longer.

In the early 1970s family therapy was like the American auto industry in the 1950s. Just as the "big three" automakers competed among themselves but, otherwise, dominated the booming market, the big four or five models of family therapy competed with each other, also in a booming market. As a result, both the automakers and the schools of family therapy experienced the chauvinism and complacency that exist within organizations on the rise—organizations that, because of their prosperity, do not have to challenge their own beliefs or practices.

"The family" that each of these models was trying to understand was not well differentiated. Most descriptions related to two-parent nuclear family systems, with scant attention paid to the importance of ethnic or class differences among families, or to family variations (single parent or stepfamilies), and even less attention given to the power differences between men and women within families. In addition, the pioneers rarely considered the possibility that their observations might not be totally objective. They explored a family as if they were dissecting a specimen to discover its structure—as if that structure was unaffected by their behavior or presuppositions, by the strange context in which they observed it, or, possibly, by the crisis state it was in.

In these early days family therapists saw themselves as experts who would override the family's homeostatic tendencies and reorganize their structure or bestow upon them the best way to view their problems. In their enthusiasm for family patterns, family therapists often lost sight of the personal experience of individual family members and viewed their expression of feelings as homeostatic distractions from the crucial family pattern. In addition, just as individual therapists had ignored the importance of the family system, the primacy of our interest in it kept us relatively ignorant of the impact on people's problems of larger systems like schools, social agencies and institutions, peer groups, and work settings.

The eighties ushered in a new stage in the field's development during which family therapy's biases and blind spots were challenged. In this chapter we will try to capture the flavor of this period and speculate on some reasons for it.

RUDE AWAKENINGS

During the eighties, with far fewer attacks from the establishment to unite and distract the field, family therapy took a good look at itself in the mirror and found the image wasn't entirely pleasing. As we described in Chapter 2, some family therapists began to question whether their model really captured the essence—whether there might be more limitations in effectiveness or application than they had thought. Braulio Montalvo, one of the principle developers of structural family therapy, summarized these sentiments when he said, "We have to learn how to lower our sights and realize what we can accomplish. I think our effort now has to be highlighting the various areas in which we have some honest knowledge and away from clinical myth-making" (Schwartz and Perrotta, 1985).

One result of this reappraisal was a movement to integrate or take what was thought to be the best and most compatible elements of different family therapy models and blend them together. Perhaps an alloy would prove stronger than any pure model by itself. Structural and strategic family therapies were the most frequent candidates for such syntheses because of their common allegiance to systems ideas (Stanton, 1981). While none of these attempts has generated a major new model so far, they do demonstrate how the castle drawbridges began to drop during this period, allowing some cross-exploration of territory among models.

The Milan Revolution

While the existing American models were checking each other out, a new, radically different model was gaining adherents in Europe. Promoted as a cure for the most difficult cases (chronic schizophrenics and anorexics) and as being a more pure translation of Bateson's thinking into practice, the Milan model took the field by storm following the publication of the book *Paradox and Counterparadox* (Selvini Palazzoli, Boscolo, Cecchin, and Prata, 1978). It emerged at a time when structural family therapy and Haley's version of strategic family therapy were the dominant influences in the field. Because the emphasis of these models was on assessing and changing a family's current structure, therapists paid scant attention to a family's history, or to conflicts within family members, in order to focus on the interactions occurring in sessions. Therapists were encouraged to size up a family's dysfunctional structure or problem-maintaining sequences very quickly, often in the first session, and then use the power of their personalities or paradoxical techniques to attack these sequences.

Structural and strategic therapists, then, focused basically on assessing and changing interactional behavior and were less interested in the beliefs family members held that might govern their behavior. Therapists were highly directive and active, telling family members what to do in and out of sessions, and deliberately siding, at least temporarily, with one member against another. The therapist was responsible for getting families to change, and to change in a certain way. This was a uniquely American form of therapy—highly pragmatic and impatient for change, believing that the therapist-as-expert could quickly understand, take command of, and solve any family's problem.

Apparently there were many therapists who, while trying hard to be structural or strategic therapists, didn't feel entirely comfortable with what they were doing. To these therapists the Milan model, with its emphasis on thoroughly and systematically understanding the family's evolution over time and how it came to need the problem; its focus on meaning, not just behavior; its view of therapist as distant and neutral asker of "circular questions," rather than as opinionated, pushy giver of directives; therapist as perturber of the system which will change as it sees fit, rather than as forger of new family structures or sequences, was a welcome change. Peggy Papp, a prominent strategic therapist, described her excitement when she tried the Milan model: "Instead of trying too hard to persuade people to change, I was sitting back, throwing out messages, and watching families react in remarkable ways. . . . In some way, I was leaving the decision to change up to the family. I thought to myself, 'Oh what a relief. . . .' " (quoted in Simon, 1987, p. 23).

It was such a relief to so many therapists that the model spread with amazing speed across Europe and then North America, promoted and interpreted here by other former strategic therapists Carl Tomm and Lynn Hoffman. The field woke up to several new ideas. Therapists didn't have to try so hard. They could take some time to explore and ask questions before acting. They didn't have to be powerfully persuasive or clever to be effective. Families could figure out and change some things on their own if asked the right questions. Questions were powerful.

It also didn't hurt the popularity of the Milan model that it had an exotic and mysterious shape. Therapists worked in nonhierarchical teams and strove for a sort of "group mind" in which the therapist was simply the extension of that mind in the room. The therapist asked strange, sometimes convoluted, questions and through most of any session did very little else. During sessions the therapist would leave the family and go behind the one-way mirror for long stretches to brainstorm with the team. Sessions were scheduled with long intervals (a month or more) between them and the team was to have no contact with the family between sessions. Once the team had a hypothesis they felt good about, it would be delivered by the therapist to the family in a dramatic oration, often read from a letter that the family was to take home and reread regularly. Every family member's intentions were positively connoted in this dramatic message.

Thus not only was the Milan model a relief from the aggressive American approaches, it also appealed to the more cerebral therapists who liked to work from a safe distance, who liked to discuss and solve puzzles, and who liked the camaraderie and shared responsibility of being part of a treatment team. In addition, because it claimed to be more systemic—truer to Bateson's ideas—than the American models, Milan adherents could look down on their structural and strategic colleagues, in much the same way that those therapists used to look down on individual therapists. What Liddle and Saba (1981) called "systemic chic" was in the air.

While many of the Milan ideas and practices were revolutionary, this original version of the model shared some elements with American approaches that would later be seen as undesirable. First, while the team tried to be relatively leaderless and democratic, their relationship to families was distinctly hierarchical. The therapist remained distant and authoritarian; families weren't privy to the mysterious discussions that these teams of experts were having about them behind the mirror. Instead the therapist imposed the team's verdict on the family at the end of a session and declined to discuss it further with them.

Second, these pronouncements usually attributed a sacrificial function to the identified patient's symptoms. The rationales Milan therapists gave for the family's need to have the symptoms were usually far more elaborate, often involving a whole network of people or events in the family's history, than the simple distracting-from-parents'-marriage function assumed in American models. In addition the team was careful to positively connote every family member's motives for their role in the network of relationships that led to the need for the symptom. In this way the team reduced resistance to the message, implying that it was the system that needed the symptom, not its individual members. As we shall see later in this chapter, however, this functionalist idea that symptoms serve a purpose in families is not without problems.

The Milan model's view of people was strongly influenced by the belief that people try to manipulate each other. Despite positively connoting the motives of family members in sessions, the Milan Associates depicted family members as power game players, whose objective is to win at the expense of others in the family. For example, when a family member expressed an emotion, Milan therapists were trained to say to themselves, "He is showing sadness" rather than "He is sad" to highlight the interpersonal manipulative aspect—the function—of showing emotions.

Third, the Milan model's emphasis on remaining neutral and letting the family find its own solutions runs afoul with feminist thinking (discussed later in this chapter) because, in the words of Laurie MacKinnon and Dusty Miller (1987), it

> assumes that families are voluntary organizations functioning for the ultimate good of all members. This does not take into consideration the fact that families have "found their own solutions" for centuries and that these solutions have been primarily at the expense of women and children (p. 150).

That is, the attempt to simply perturb family systems without a map of how they should change ignores the influence of extreme elements of the socio-political context that *will* influence the direction of families' solutions if the therapist does not.

Finally, the original Milan model shared the American fascination, (particularly in strategic models), with technology. Questioning was a prelude to the powerful part of the therapy that was the "positive connotations" delivered at the end of the sessions, like weapons to stop families in their tracks.

In fairness, the Milan fascination with big bang interventions shifted in the early 1980s and they began giving the questioning process more credit for producing change. Matteo Selvini (1988), Selvini Palazzoli's son, describes the period after the Milan group's "interventionist" phase,

> The focus of attention was now shifted to what happens *during* the session, to the interviewing techniques and to the strategies and tactics of conducting the session. The therapeutic effectiveness of the entire course of the therapy, during and between the sessions, was being taken into account, when the earlier view had been that all the team's work was a mere preliminary to the elaboration of the final intervention, of the resolving counterparadox. With this transformation, the therapeutic atmosphere, too, became changed: it was now less "athletic" and competitive (p. 413).

It may be that the focus on perfecting the big intervention kept the Milan Associates (Selvini Palazzoli, Cecchin, Boscolo, and Prata) together as a theorizing group, because it was around the time of this shift out of the interventionist phase that the group split up. The two male members (Gianfranco Cecchin and Luigi Boscolo) pursued their interest in the questioning process and also became intrigued with and influenced by another set of ideas that took the field by storm, variously referred to as the *new epistemology, constructivism,* or *second-order cybernetics*—ideas which will be discussed later in this chapter. Cecchin and Boscolo focused their efforts on training and giving workshops and, consequently, their ideas continue to influence the systemic wing of the field; although, in the face of criticism from feminists (MacKinnon and Miller, 1987), disenchantment because of disappointing results (Coleman, 1987; Mashal, Feldman, and Sigal, 1989), and the emerging popularity of less hierarchical models (Hoffman, 1988), their influence may be waning.

The two women (Mara Selvini Palazzoli and Giuliana Prata), and later Selvini Palazzoli with a new group, moved in an entirely different direction. Turning their backs on paradoxical methods and therapist neutrality, Selvini Palazzoli and her new colleagues began studying schizophrenic and anorexic families with an eye toward uncovering and disrupting the basic pattern that underlies such families. In so doing Selvini Palazzoli seems to have shifted away from the revolutionary changes the Milan Associates brought the field and back to assumptions and techniques akin to Haley's brand of strategic therapy.

Selvini Palazzoli believes she has found the basic "dirty games" that underlie these severe symptoms. Patients in these families are caught up in a struggle between their parents to covertly control each other and, through a series of stages, the child-patient ultimately becomes obsessed with using symptoms to win the dirty game, which often means to show one parent how to defeat the other. To disrupt this pattern, the group developed what they call the *invariant prescription*, which they gave to all families in their research project. In this intervention, parents are coaxed to sneak away together from their children without warning or contact with the children from varying periods of time (Selvini Palazzoli, 1986; Simon, 1987).

Selvini Palazzoli's new approach has been criticized for its negative image of family members (as power game players) and for problems with the research on which her hypotheses and strategies are based (Anderson, 1986). This approach has not had a major impact on the field at this point for two reasons. First, because Selvini Palazzoli's primary interest is in research, very few therapists have been trained in the approach and very little has been written about it. Second, its assertion of a basic pattern underlying severely disturbed families and its standardization of approach to them, runs counter to the trends in family therapy, ironically, trends initiated by the Milan revolution, which are away from preconceiving and directing families, and toward collaborating with and asking questions of families to let them change themselves. It remains to be seen whether, once their research and approach is published, it inspires a second Milan revolution.

When all is said and done, the most important impact of the Milan movement may be the permission it gave a generation of systems-oriented therapists to break away from the narrow rules and aggressiveness of models developed in the United States. In the process, the pendulum may have swung too far, with therapists doing nothing but asking questions of families and giving them license to reorganize themselves in any way they see fit. The lasting contributions of the Milan movement are: (1) recognizing the importance of the historical evolution of problems within family systems; (2) increasing therapists' trust in families to come up with their own solutions and, consequently, decreasing their need to force families to change in preconceived ways; (3) increasing the field's appreciation of and focus on the meanings that are behind family behaviors; and (4) elevating the art of interviewing, in particular, of asking questions.

This fourth contribution merits some elaboration. The Milan Associates introduced a type of interviewing called *circular questioning*, which generates the kind of systemic information that enables families to see their problems differently. The basic method involves asking questions that highlight differences among family members or define relationships, rather than asking for the beliefs or feelings of any one family member without reference to another. For example, a mother might be asked to describe the relationship between her son and husband, or the family in general might be asked which of them would suffer the most if the son were to leave home, or the son might be asked who would worry the most if he left.

When asked questions that force them to define positions relative to each other, family members have to think in new ways, and the network of relationships surrounding problems becomes undeniably clear to all. Because the therapist is eliciting this information through sincerely curious questioning, and because family members are describing each other rather than themselves, these discussions are often less inhibited or defensive.

CHALLENGING FAMILY THERAPY'S PHILOSOPHICAL ROOTS

It is not coincidental that the spread of the Milan movement coincided with a period during which the field's basic philosophical premises were being questioned and, in many cases, rejected by some of its more intellectual practitioners. Until the late 1970s the energy in family therapy had been concentrated on developing pragmatic techniques. As we described in Chapter 2, the pioneers were struggling to try to find ways to understand and tame this strange family animal and to convert a skeptical psychotherapy field. Having succeeded to varying degrees in both arenas by the end of the 1970s, family therapy had a chance to catch its breath and take a look at the foundation upon which it rested. Finally, family therapists could afford the luxury of self-criticism, and it came in two forms: the feminist critique and the new epistemology.

This reappraisal began with a series of attacks on the narrow pragmatism of family therapy models, calling into question such basic concepts as *homeostasis, resistance,* and *paradox* (Keeney and Sprenkle, 1982; Keeney, 1983; Dell, 1982, 1985). The general thrust of these brash articles was that the field had gone astray, had become too results- and technique-oriented and, in the process, had lost touch with broader considerations when thinking about families. The pragmatists in the field took strong exception to this criticism and countered with ridicule, calling these papers "epistobabble" (Coyne, 1982).

This antipragmatism critique can be seen as the beginning of a reaction against the influence of cybernetics and functionalism, described in Chapter 2, that influenced the field to view families as machines to be repaired. With this mechanistic view there was little need to consider the effect on the family of the act of observing, or of the influence of the observer's preconceptions on what they were observing. That is, therapists were too often making the mistake of believing that their map was the territory;

believing that the *structural flaws*, *positive feedback loops*, and *undiffer-entiated ego masses* somehow existed in reality, rather than in their maps.

Thus, rather than give up on the cybernetic metaphor, the cyberne-ticians presented what has come to be known as *second-order cybernetics*; a new, improved version of cybernetics that tries to accommodate these concerns by turning attention from "observed systems" to "observing sys-tems." Essentially this critique has functioned as a crowbar to pry family therapy away from its belief in objectivity—the belief that what one *sees* in families is what *is* in families. To bolster their position, these critics imported the ideas of neurobiologists (Heinz von Foerster, Humberto Ma-turana, and Francisco Varella) and a cognitive psychologist (Ernst von Glaserfeld) (Dell, 1985; Watzlawick, 1984). What seems to be emerging out of the smoke of all this debate and exotic theorizing are some assump-tions that have led groups of clinicians to adventure in new directions.

Constructivism

The first of these is that reality does not exist as a "world out there" but, instead, is a mental construction of the observer. The implications for therapy of this position, called *constructivism*, are that therapists should not consider what they're seeing in families as existing in the family but, instead, should understand that what they are seeing is the product of their particular set of assumptions about people, families, and problems, and their interactions with the family. In other words, we should be less certain about the reality of our observations and should examine carefully the assumptions that we bring to our encounters with families.

This concern about the influence of therapists' preconceptions on their observations expanded to become an increased interest in belief systems in general. Through Bateson's influence, family therapy adopted the term *epistemology* as a synonym for belief system, perspective, or world view, even though the term properly refers to the branch of philosophy concerned with the development of knowledge. Family therapy has always shown some interest in changing meanings—witness the popularity of reframing techniques or the value put on "creating a workable reality"—but these meaning changes were generally in the service of changing behavioral se-quences, which remained the primary target.

Instead of focusing on family interaction patterns, constructivism has shifted the focus of many therapists toward understanding and changing the sets of assumptions that all the people involved with a problem have about the problem. Meaning, itself, has become the primary target. Ex-tending this thinking, some writers have proposed that we jettison our arbitrary focus on family systems and, instead, examine the total meaning systems in which problems are embedded. This might include family mem-bers, but may also include all the other helpers, including the therapist (Anderson, Goolishian, and Winderman, 1986).

While the idea that our belief systems influence what we see may not come as a great revelation to students of philosophy and had been a cliche within family therapy from the beginning—Bateson frequently cited Alfred Korzybski's (1942) saying, "the map is not the territory"—until this philosophic midlife crisis, many structural and strategic family therapists were acting as if their maps *were* the territory. For this reason constructivism has had a large impact on clinical theory and practice in the 1980s, triggering several new pendulum swings.

One clinical impact of constructivism has been to make therapists more humble in their dealings with families. For example, many structural family therapy maneuvers, such as unbalancing or creating intensity, require a high level of confidence in the correctness of one's assessment and interventions. If the therapist wavers, intensity will be lost and, theoretically, the family's homeostasis will not be perturbed. But if therapists believe that their assessment is a reality that they have created arbitrarily, it is hard to avoid wavering. Lynn Hoffman (1988) describes her initial reaction to constructivism this way: "One suddenly doesn't know how to 'teach' therapy, much less how to 'do' it. One loses one's status, one loses one's expert position" (p. 124).

Thus many constructivist therapists have gravitated toward a kinder, gentler therapy in which they are more like collaborators with the family than like experts or directors. Many of the groups in North America and Europe that have moved in this direction began as Milan-style teams, fertilized by visits from Cecchin and Boscolo. As the constructivist bug spread, the resulting collaborative, meaning-focused family therapy became known as the post-Milan movement to differentiate it from the strategic, hierarchical aspects of the original Milan model.

The post-Milan teams have invented several techniques for engaging with families in "conversations" about their problems, during which the constructions of each member of the system, including therapist and team members, are examined and critiqued collectively and nonjudgementally. Rather than presupposing that family members' views are incorrect and in need of change, post-Milan therapists try to promote an understanding of everyone's private reality and create an atmosphere of respect in which the various viewpoints can be discussed nondefensively (Anderson and Goolishian, 1988; Anderson, Goolishian, and Winderman, 1986; Hoffman, 1985, 1988). Toward these ends team members have openly conveyed their views to the family in various formats, including having the family come behind the one-way mirror and watch the team conference (Andersen, 1987).

These post-Milan groups are, in some ways, circling family therapy back toward a Rogerian, nondirective position, although Carl Rogers gets little citation in their literature. The therapy teams strive to create an atmosphere of acceptance and empathy in which it is hoped the defensiveness or aggressiveness of family members can recede, allowing the whole group to brainstorm creatively and flexibly about the problem. Hoffman (1988) summarizes this brand of therapy this way:

> It avoids the implication of fixing something that has been broken down or is not functioning and comes closer to being some kind of hopeful discourse. It is, as far as possible, nonjudgemental, and nonpejorative. It is not control-oriented. It is lateral rather than hierarchical in structure. It is wary of an instructive stance. It shrinks away from an influence that is primarily intentional. It is pluralistic in nature, focusing on many views rather than one. There is no assumption of objectivity or truth (p. 126).

As Hoffman's quote illustrates, at this point the post-Milan movement, like many new approaches that emerge as reactions to an establishment, seems clearer about what it isn't than what it is.

This movement seems to be more of an attitude than a model. Harlene Anderson, who, with Harry Goolishian, is leading the development of one post-Milan variant, says in an interview:

> I try to learn about [the family's] views and create through learning an "in there together" process that leads to new meaning, narrative, and agency. . . . In the therapy room I am a learner. I adopt a "puzzling" position. This flips the position of the client and the therapist. The client is now the knower and the therapist is the not-knower. . . . It is not just the therapist trying to understand the client, collecting information and data and placing it on some kind of cognitive map in a unilateral way. Rather, it is a mutual search in which client and therapist puzzle together in search for understanding, to develop a story that has not been told before (Winderman, 1989, p. 12).

With Anderson's last phrase about developing a story, we segue into another emphasis of some constructivist approaches. The post-Milan approaches mentioned above hope that, out of these "conversations" with a family, a new, more optimistic or empowering story about the problem or the family will emerge. There are other constructivist approaches which also emphasize the importance of new stories or narratives about the family, the problem, or the patient, but have less faith in a democratic conversational process to achieve this re-storying and, therefore, actively lead families to new stories.

Australian Michael White, an increasingly influential writer and presenter, helps families "externalize" their problems; that is, view the problem as a separate entity, external to the person who has it. For example, an encopretic child is asked how his "poo" is affecting his life and when he had been able to resist "sneaky poo." Similar questions are put to other family members regarding the influence of poo in their lives and when they were able to not let it have these consequences. After a round of these questions, White (1989) reports that ". . . Nick could recall a number of occasions during which he had not allowed Sneaky Poo to outsmart him. These were occasions during which he could have cooperated by 'smearing,' 'streaking,' or 'plastering,' but then he declined to do so. He had not allowed himself to be tricked into this" (p. 10).

This externalizing allows families new options for escaping the oppression of problems because they can work together to defeat the problem rather than blame each other for it. White (1989) describes the way families usually view problems this way:

> Although the problem was usually defined as internal to the child, all family members were affected by it, and often felt overwhelmed, dispirited, and defeated. In various ways, they took the ongoing existence of the problem, and their failed attempts to solve it, as a reflection on themselves, each other, and/or on their relationships (p. 5).

In this sense, families with problems present a story about themselves that is, in White's words, "problem-saturated"; it focuses on their impotence and frustration. By externalizing the problem and asking family members to focus on "unique outcomes," that is, times in the patient's or other family members' lives when the problem did not defeat them, White helps people identify how they were able to beat the problem. In the process people are able to separate from the dominant, problem-saturated story that had been shaping their lives and, thereby, see alternative or neglected aspects of themselves that leads them to "redescribe" themselves in a new, empowered story.

Steve de Shazer (1985, 1988) and his colleagues, such as Bill O'Hanlon and Michele Weiner-Davis (1989), have developed another popular constructivist approach that is remarkably similar to White's in that it is solution-focused, rather than problem-focused. De Shazer has clients focus on exceptions—times when their problems did not occur—and helps them find ways to expand those exceptions. By shifting their focus away from the functionalist analyzing of problems to an emphasis on familial or personal strengths and resources, White and de Shazer are helping the field revise the story it had regarding the inherent abilities of families to change and of therapists to help them.

Where will constructivism ultimately take the field? It's hard to tell. Much as was the case when the pioneers shifted their focus from individuals to families, this recent shift from action to meaning opened a whole new world of possibilities for doing therapy. It is likely that the pendulum will continue to swing until these possibilities have been explored.

We believe, however, that this shift has already led to some valuable general changes that will last whether the specific models do or do not.

These changes include: (1) the elevation of meaning to a position equal in importance to behavioral interaction patterns; (2) increased humility about our theoretical models, and concomitantly, increased attention to the values behind our assumptions; and (3) decreased urgency to change or control people, and increased trust in their own resources.

While many have attributed these positive changes to constructivism, it is unclear whether this philosophy created these changes or whether the field was ready to turn in this direction and would have seized any theoretical position that could justify or facilitate such a change. (Of course a good constructivist would say that neither of those possibilities is "correct"; both are equally valid constructions.) We raise this question because we believe there are some problems with using constructivism as a clinical foundation and hope the field takes the time to examine the implications of its story regarding how human beings operate.

For example, if one believes that our maps bear no resemblance to an "out there" reality, but instead are arbitrary constructions, then any reality one can create about a problem is as good as any other, and therapists are granted license to use any "reframe" or interpretation that they can concoct and sell to the family, as long as it seems to make them change or feel better. Such an "anything goes," valueless relativism has already been proposed by some clinical constructivists (Duncan and Solevey, 1989) and takes us in the direction opposite to the assumption-examining that the post-Milan movement advocates.

In addition there is the tendency within most troubled families to want to deny their problems or their pain. If, for example, one has a nondirective "conversation" with many alcoholic or abusive families it is possible to cocreate with them a reality that their problems are not as bad as they think and everyone will walk away, at least temporarily, feeling much better. President Reagan told us that the homeless enjoy their independent life styles and that the contras were freedom fighters. There are those who wanted to believe him because they did not like to think about those problems and if they believed him, in a constructivist world, those problems do indeed disappear. This is not to imply that constructivist therapists routinely cocreate problem-denying realities with families, but instead to suggest that there is nothing in the theory that precludes such a possibility.

Finally, Barbara Held, in collaboration with philosophy professor Ed Pols (Held and Pols, 1987; Held, 1990), pointed out that constructivism contains a logical contradiction that renders it impossible to maintain as a clinical theory. She argues that if one believes that an "out there" reality, or even approximations of it, can't be known, then one cannot make any "reality claims" about, for example, how the mind works, how people change, or how best to do therapy. In other words, constructivists cannot have it both ways. If we cannot know reality, then we cannot assert anything about it. If we want to make reality claims, then, by definition, we are saying we have a more or less distorted and incomplete map of reality, in which case we are no longer constructivists, at least as constructivism has come to be defined within family therapy. This latter position—that we can know approximations of reality, but we must remain humble about them because of our awareness that they are distorted and incomplete— allows for all the aforementioned improvements credited to constructivism and eliminates the "anything goes" or the denial problems we have associated with constructivism. This approximation position is close to the Bertalanffian perspectivism discussed in Chapter 2.

THE FEMINIST CRITIQUE OF FAMILY THERAPY

Further evidence that, even without the constructivist movement, the field was ready to shift away from the aggressive, hierarchical, mechanistic style of family therapy developed by its pioneers, was the powerful infusion of feminist thinking during the early 1980s. Feminist family therapists not only criticized existing models, they advocated a style of therapy that, like the post-Milan movement, is collaborative, respectful, and interested in meaning. Unlike some constructivists, however, feminist family therapists don't advocate valueless neutrality and have trouble with the idea of trusting the family, steeped as it is in patriarchal values, to find its own solutions. For feminists, all realities are not created equal.

The feminist critique was family therapy's rudest awakening. The field's increasing popularity through the 1970s left us feeling a little smug. We were the progressive avant-garde whose theories and techniques were going to revolutionize psychotherapy. It was inconceivable that we could have been blind to these problems along the way. As Lois Braverman (1988) confessed,

> As long as we thought systemically and did not buy into a traditional linear long-term psychotherapy approach to treatment, we considered ourselves to be far ahead of other helping professionals. So while other therapeutic frameworks and treatment modalities of the 1970s were marked by feminist critiques . . . which questioned traditional psychodynamic theory and practice, we, as family therapists, had our heads buried in the sand (p. 6).

Heads came out of the sand in the early 1980s and began to look around at our model of the functional family and at our precious systems theory. It became increasingly and painfully clear that cybernetics and functionalism had led us astray. Cybernetics encouraged us to view a family system as a flawed machine, a machine which, according to Judith Meyers Avis (1988),

. . . functions according to special systemic rules and is divorced from its historical, social, economic, and political contexts. By viewing the family out of context, family therapists locate family dysfunction entirely within interpersonal relationships in the family, ignore broader patterns of dysfunction occurring across families, and fail to notice the relationship between social context and family dysfunction (p. 17).

Thus the mechanistic philosophy of cybernetics narrowed our vision and made us oblivious to the parallels between disharmonies in our culture and in our families.

Additionally the Batesonian version of cybernetics was strongly opposed to the use of power metaphors and, relatedly, asserted that unilateral control in systems was impossible because all elements are continually and circularly influencing each other in repetitious feedback loops. The implication of this is that all parts of a system are equally involved in its problems and, therefore, no one is to blame. This idea had great appeal for family therapists because family members often enter therapy pointing fingers at each other unproductively and failing to see their own steps in their circular dances.

To feminists, however, this idea of equal responsibility for problems looked "suspiciously like a hypersophisticated version of blaming the victim and rationalizing the status quo" (Goldner, 1985, p. 33). This critique was particularly evident in crimes against women, such as battering, incest, and rape, for which psychological theories have long been used to imply that the woman either wanted or consented to the crime (James and Mackinnon, 1990).

But those crimes are only the most obvious instances in which the systemic doctrine of equal responsibility is troublesome. The larger issue is that if one accepts the feminist premise that in our patriarchal society marriage and family life inherently subjugates women, then to suggest that husbands and wives have contributed equally to, and have equal responsibility for, changing their problems is to collude with the rules of these patriarchal microcosms of society.

For example, the dysfunctional family constellation most commonly cited by family therapists as contributing to problems is the peripheral but dominant father, the mother who is overinvolved with her children, and the symptomatic child who is overly involved in his or her parents' issues. For years psychodynamic therapists blamed mother's attachment to the child for the symptoms. Family therapy's apparent advance was to show how father's lack of involvement contributed to mother's overinvolvement, and so therapists tried to pry mother loose by inserting father in her place. This, however, was not the advance for women that it might seem because, in too many cases, mothers were viewed no less pathologically. Mothers were still enmeshed and incompetent, but now we had a new solution—to bring competent, rational fathers to the children's rescue.

What the feminists contend we failed to see, and to help our client families see, is that "the archetypal 'family case' of the overinvolved mother and peripheral father is best understood not as a clinical problem, but as the product of a historical process two hundred years in the making" (Goldner, 1985, p. 31). Women are overinvolved, insecure, controlling, ineffectual, and overemotional—not because of psychopathology, but because they are put in, and encouraged by society to desire, emotionally isolated, economically dependent, overresponsible positions in families, positions that are crazy-making.

Feminist family therapists help families reorganize so that no one, male or female, remains stuck in such positions. Thus instead of further diminishing an insecure mother's self-esteem by replacing her with peripheral father (who is likely to have been critical of her parenting all along), a feminist family therapist might help the family examine and change the rules and roles that kept mother down and father out. During this process, fathers may be encouraged to become more involved with parenting—but not because mothers are incompetent. Rather, because it is a father's responsibility as a parent and because it will allow the mother to begin to move out of that crazy-making position (Ault-Riche, 1986; Goodrich, Rampage, Ellman, and Halstead, 1988; Walters, Carter, Papp, and Silverstein, 1988; McGoldrick, Anderson, and Walsh, 1989).

Feminist family therapists, then, are not simply asking us to be more sensitive to gender issues in working with families. Instead they assert that issues of gender or, more specifically, patriarchy, permeate all of our work as therapists, even though we have been conditioned not to notice them. They believe, therefore, that gender should be a primary organizing concept for family therapists, on a par with the concept of generation (Goldner, 1988).

Only when we look through this lens of gender can we effectively stop blaming mothers, or stop looking to them to do most of the changing simply because they are the most invested in change or the most cooperative. Only then will we be able to fully counter our unconscious biases toward seeing women as primarily responsible for childrearing and housekeeping, as needing to support their husbands' careers by neglecting their own, as needing to be married, or at least, to have a man in their lives. Only then can we stop relying on traditionally male traits like rationality, independence, and competitiveness as our standards of health and stop denigrating or ignoring traits traditionally encouraged in women like emotionality, nurturance, and relationship focus.

In essence, the feminist revolution in family therapy differs from the Milan or constructivist revolutions because it is not just asking that we try on some new concepts or techniques; it's not just technical or theoretical—

it's personal. It forces us, as therapists, to look in the mirror at our attitudes and our lives outside of the professional safety of our offices. It forces us to re-examine the values and structure of our society and evaluate how we are helping to perpetuate or change those values and that structure. It tarnishes the haloes of many of family therapy's pioneers, and it challenges the foundation of the field's fundamental framework, systems theory.

For these reasons, as one might anticipate, the feminist critique was not immediately welcomed or accepted by the established models in the field. The early to mid eighties was a period of polarization and tension between male and female therapists at conferences, as feminists tried to exceed the establishment's "threshold of deafness." By the 1990s that threshold has been exceeded, in the sense that many of the major feminist points are no longer debated, and the field is evolving toward a more collaborative, but socially enlightened, form of therapy. It is less clear, however, that the larger implications of the critique regarding the patriarchal nature of our society have been fully appreciated. We still flinch from questions of power inequities. As Morris Taggert (1989) observed recently, "By continuing to produce 'family therapy' as if the feminist critique did not exist, family therapy theorists intensify the patriarchal project of presenting as comprehensive and normative that which is partial and atypical" (p. 101).

THE DIFFERENTIATION OF THE FAMILY

The eighties brought another related assault on our comfortable image of how families should look. It turned out that the map of the "healthy family" we bought from the pioneers not only contained patriarchal but also ethnocentric biases. Family therapy was disabused of some of its ethnocentric biases by the recognition that families from different cultures and social classes, or having different compositions, will have different values and structures, and that those differences are not necessarily problematic just because they do not match the American middle-class ideal.

Ethnicity

Monica McGoldrick and her colleagues (McGoldrick, Pearce, and Giordano, 1982) dealt one of the first blows to our ethnocentricity with an edited book, each chapter of which described the characteristic values and structure of a different ethnic group. Due to this book and a spate of similar articles, we are now more sensitive to the importance of knowing some of the characteristics of the ethnic group from which a family descends and we don't assume they're sick just because they're different. For example, many non-American, middle-class families have a strong rule that each family member is to think of what is good for the family before attending to what might be good for him or herself. In navigating by the early maps, family therapists were likely to view this self-sacrificial belief and behavior pathologically—as demonstrating a lack of differentiation or as creating enmeshment or overprotectiveness—and would challenge it.

Now, when encountering such a family value, therapists are more likely to consider, or even explore with the family, the ethnic heritage of the family's belief while evaluating its functionality.

In taking off our ethnocentric glasses, we had to look again at many of our pathology markers. For example, Celia Falicov (Falicov and Brudner-White, 1983) drew from the work of anthropologist Francis Hsu to point out that in many cultures the dominant or governing dyad in a family is not the husband or wife. Instead, the primary dyad is often intergenerational—husband/son in some cultures, and wife/son in others. Thus the very cross-generational coalitions that we have been trained to seize upon as being the root of a family's problem, may well be normative in that family's culture. This same kind of critique can apply also to many of our other ideas about family life, such as the importance of democratic versus autocratic parenting styles; of open, expressive communication; and of encouraging autonomy versus loyalty in children.

Just as the constructivist and feminist critiques did, this ethnicity critique raises many issues about how we should understand the beliefs and behaviors of family members; issues which are not yet resolved and, in some areas, conflict with the assertions of the other two critiques. For example, just because a belief or behavior pattern is normative in another culture, does that mean that it's healthy and shouldn't be challenged? Many cultures are at least equally patriarchal to our own. Should we respect the husband's domination simply because it is customary in their native country? When a family has immigrated, should we not try to help them change habits that are not adaptive in the host culture, even if it is normative in their native culture? Finally, are not those who write about what is and is not normative in various cultures constructing realities that are subject to the same bias and overgeneralization that produces ethnic stereotypes?

Underlying many of these questions is the conflict between a relativistic or pragmatic position which asserts that any family structure is fine if it's adaptive or functional for the family versus what might be called an ecological or aesthetic position which asserts that there are some basic universal principles that determine a system's health or illness. The tension between these two positions fueled many of the debates in family therapy during the eighties. We still seem far from finding a middle ground. In the meantime, as is the case in families that harbor powerful unresolved issues, we are likely to continue to experience the repeated flaring of this conflict, perhaps over new content areas, as we've seen over cybernetics, ethnicity, feminism, and constructivism.

Specialization

Another trend in the eighties, one that is related to the recognition of ethnicity as an important consideration, was the increased specification of treatment models. Books emerged that focused on how to do family therapy with specific types of problems and family constellations. This trend pre-dated the eighties (for example, Minuchin and his colleagues had written books on "families of the slums" and on "psychosomatic families"), but this decade witnessed a large number of specialized texts and articles that reflect a maturing and differentiating of the field.

There are books on working with families of people who abuse drugs (Stanton, Todd, and Associates, 1982; Kaufman, 1985), abuse alcohol (Steinglass, Bennett, Wolin, and Reiss, 1987; Bepko and Krestan, 1985; Treadway, 1989; Elkin, 1984), abuse food (Root, Fallon, and Friedrich, 1986; Schwartz, in preparation), and abuse each other (Trepper and Barrett, 1989; Madanes, 1990).

In addition there are books for treating stepparent families (Visher and Visher, 1979, 1988); divorcing families (Isaacs, Montalvo, and Abelsohn, 1986; Sprenkle, 1985; Wallerstein and Kelly, 1980; Ahrons and Rogers, 1987), blended families (Hansen, 1982; Sager, Brown, Crohn, Engel, Rodstein, and Walker, 1983), families in transition among these states (Pittman, 1987; Falicov, 1988), and for all combinations of relationships within families (Walters, Carter, Papp, and Silverstein, 1988). There are also books for families with young children (Zilbach, 1986; Combrinck-Graham, 1989), with troubled adolescents (Mirkin and Koman, 1985) and young adults (Haley, 1980), problems among siblings (Bank and Kahn, 1982; Kahn and Lewis, 1988), as well as a book about "normal families" (Walsh, 1982), and for working with schizophrenic families (Anderson, Reiss, and Hogarty, 1986). Extending the ethnicity theme, there is a book for working with black families (Boyd-Franklin, 1989) and with minority families in general (Saba, Karrer, and Hardy, 1989).

In addition to these specialized books, the field has broadened its scope and extended systems thinking beyond the family to include the impact on families and their problems of larger systems like other helping agents, social agencies, and schools (Schwartzman, 1985; Berger, Jurkovic, and Associates, 1984; Imber-Black, 1988; Minuchin, 1984; Elizur and Minuchin, 1989), and the impact of the absence of family rituals and their use in therapy (Imber-Black, Roberts, and Whiting, 1988).

One point to be made about this trend is that many of these books transcend individual models. The author may have a particular orientation but that orientation takes enough of a backseat to the specific content that the book can be read by therapists from other orientations without engendering rivalry. Thus as opposed to the sixties and seventies, during which the followers of a particular model read little but what came out of that school and eagerly awaited the next offering from the school's leadership, this recent trend toward specialization by content area, rather than by model, has further decreased factionalism and increased communication among the models.

THE IMPACT OF SYMPTOMS ON FAMILIES

Emerging out of one of these specialized movements, however, is an approach that, rather than increasing harmony in the field, represents yet another powerful challenge to the field's basic assumptions. This challenge comes out of work with schizophrenics, the symptom group that launched the family therapy field and, ironically, generated many of the assumptions that this approach now challenges. Rather than seeing families as causing or needing the schizophrenia in their offspring, the "psychoeducational" approach sees schizophrenics as having a disease that impedes their ability to process information and makes them hypersensitive to environmental stimulation.

Family stress, according to this way of thinking, may cause problems for schizophrenic members, but families don't cause schizophrenia. Families don't need the symptoms for a scapegoat or distraction—they themselves are victims of the disease. Families exacerbate the schizophrenia because they are stressed by its impact and do not understand how to deal with it. The disease itself generates high levels of "expressed emotion" among family members which, in turn, makes it worse. Family therapists who use the approach developed by Carol Anderson and her colleagues (Anderson, Reiss, and Hogarty, 1986) join forces with families to help them understand the nature of schizophrenia, to alleviate their guilt, and to help them work together to help the patient (see Chapter 11).

This is in contrast to traditional family therapy approaches that, because of the belief that families either caused the schizophrenia or were invested in its maintenance, may have antagonized family members and increased their guilt. The psychoeducational approach boasts impressive outcome reports (see Chapter 11) which, unlike previous family therapy schools such as the Milan model or Haley's Leaving Home approach, do not claim to cure schizophrenics, but do decrease their rate of rehospitalization.

This psychoeducational approach is significant in several respects, not the least of which is that it represents a reconciliation with (some would say a throwback to) the medical model that the pioneers of family therapy fought so hard against. Psychoeducation asserts that schizophrenia is a biological disease that is to be treated, at least in part, by medication, and reserves the role of therapy to educating families on how to cope with it. This is like a knife into the heart of those who saw family therapy as a revolutionary approach to mental problems. These revolutionaries strove to rescue schizophrenics from what they saw as the misguided and disabling psychiatric attempted solutions that unwittingly colluded with schizophrenics' families in their need to focus on the patient as the problem. Family therapists who talk the psychiatric language and advocate limited psychiatric goals must be viewed by the revolutionaries as traitors to the cause and represent the co-option of the revolution, the beginning of the end of a dream.

Not surprisingly, Jay Haley (1988) has spoken out against the psychoeducational movement. What is somewhat surprising, however, is that this attack did not release a floodgate of pent-up antagonism within the field toward the psychoeducational challenge. For example, Minuchin (Elizur and Minuchin, 1989) chooses a middle, mediative position:

> When Jay Haley made it clear that he had not deviated from a position he has held for decades—that schizophrenia is a sociopsychological entity and that hospitalization and drug treatment produce iatrogenic results— Carol Anderson and Michael Goldstein . . . responded with a broadside: Haley was blind not to see the importance of joining with a family's pain at having a schizophrenic member. Immediately the lines were drawn, and family therapists of different persuasions chose up sides, joining one of the parties and becoming deaf to what the other was saying (p. 65).

It may be that the revolutionary zeal within the field has gradually diminished to the point that these psychoeducational assertions no longer seem so outrageous. Have all but the diehards given up on the original dream or have we become more realistic and mature in the field's middle age?

Indeed family therapy's original family-blaming position alienated patient and family support groups, such as the National Alliance for the Mentally Ill, to the point that they successfully lobbied against the use of federal money to support family therapy studies. Many see psychoeducation as family therapy's ticket back into the good graces of such groups and the psychiatric establishment, which has increasingly adopted the biomedical view of mental problems.

Family therapy has had a similarly difficult time reconciling itself with the disease metaphor for alcoholism, a metaphor that has a powerful and growing grip on the consciousness of the American public. Through the popularity of the twelve-step Alcoholics Anonymous (AA) model, the idea that an alcoholic has an incurable illness, from which he or she can recover but never be cured, has become so pervasive that all mental health professions are forced to take it seriously. Indeed the disease metaphor has expanded to apply to all the people around an alcoholic. An alcoholic's spouse has "codependency" and goes to Codependency Anonymous groups and an alcoholic's child becomes an Adult Child of an Alcoholic and goes to twelve-step groups for ACoAs.

In the case of alcoholism, the disease metaphor has different implications for treatment than it does for schizophrenia, implications that perhaps are more palatable for family therapists. For example, unlike that for schizophrenia, the primary intervention for alcoholism, codependency, or ACoA, is not medication or long-term psychiatric involvement. Instead the primary intervention is often the support of fellow sufferers. In addition many of the principles advocated in twelve-step programs complement or echo principles outlined in this book and help family members differentiate from each other and break up dysfunctional patterns.

Thus there is a growing number of books written by family therapists about alcoholism that incorporate or suggest the use of AA support and language (Bepko and Kresten, 1985; Elkin 1984; Treadway, 1989). In addition, Sharon Wegscheider-Cruse (1985) borrowed Virginia Satir's (1972) typology of family roles (blamer, placater, distracter, and computer) and applied it to children in alcoholic families (hero, scapegoat, lost child, and mascot). Thus, far from ignoring this amazingly powerful movement, family therapy, despite its ambivalence about the disease metaphor, is keeping pace with and contributing to the AA, ACoA movement.

At another level, the psychoeducational movement is but one of many recent challenges to the functionalist base of family therapy that was described in Chapter 2. In particular, the notion that symptoms serve a function for families, one of the cornerstones of the field, has been under attack. Psychoeducators, and those in the addictions field who subscribe to the disease model, believe that family therapy's search for the hidden function that the patient's behavior serves for others in the family has done both patients and their families a terrible disservice by implying that the patient's behavior is voluntary and that family members either want or need it. As a result, these groups say, family members have felt unnecessarily guilty and inept and the patients have felt unnecessarily angry with themselves or their families.

On the opposite side of the family therapy spectrum, many of the constructivists we mentioned have also expressed opposition to functionalism. The following assertion is typical of these complaints:

> . . . we reject the notion that symptoms are "signals" alerting one to conflict, stress, imbalance, or other dysfunction. . . . Nor do we believe that children's problems indicate or reflect the presence of marital conflict or a structural/organizational dysfunction in the family. . . . To hold such hypotheses, however lightly, is to introduce unwarranted deductions and imperatives into the negotiation process, and (most importantly) to introduce prerequisites about what has to happen first before the therapeutic outcome can be reached (O'Hanlon and Wilk, 1987, pp. 98–99).

In their view, why should we entertain these function-of-the-symptom hypotheses when we can choose realities or reframes that are simpler and less blaming from the universe of equally valid constructions?

Michael White (1989) believes that people always feel oppressed, rather than protected, by the symptoms in their family. His "externalizing" approach, described earlier in this chapter and in Chapter 11, turns the functionalist focus on its ear. Rather than examine the effect the family has on the symptom, White focuses on the effect the symptom has on the family and tries to get family members to unite in an effort to wrestle control of their lives from the oppressive symptom.

Despite these and other attacks, the idea that symptoms serve protective functions in families remains a prevalent and powerful one in the field. In a recent survey of family therapists, over three-quarters of the sample responded "often" or "almost always" to the question: "Do you believe that symptoms arise to serve an interpersonal function in families?" (Rait, 1988). While it is difficult to imagine that the family therapy field will ever totally divorce itself from this seminal belief, the strong functionalist position seems to be on the wane.

Antifunctionalist sentiment, while valuable and warranted, may also represent a pendulum swing in reaction to the many unfortunate consequences of the way that family therapy has incorporated functionalism. Schwartz (1990) suggested that while our functionalist baby has soiled its bathwater, we may be able to save it if we clean it up. There is no question that family therapists have done damage by presupposing and conveying to families, overtly or covertly, that they are so selfish as to be willing to have their children suffer rather than face scary issues. In addition, the emphasis on functionalism too often has turned therapists into pathology detectives, hunting for clues to the underlying function and suspicious that the family's reports about their problems are attempts to mislead or obfuscate. Such detectives also will not trust improvements in the problem until the putative function or structural flaw has been rooted out and corrected.

These negative consequences, rather than being inherent in the notion that symptoms sometimes play a protective role in families, are the result of the way that observation has been interpreted. Recognition of the protectively functional nature of symptoms was such a revelation to many therapists that they came to some essentialistic conclusions like: all symptoms or problems serve protective functions in families; the function that a symptom serves in a family is the only, or the primary, factor maintaining it; the patient's sole or primary intention in behaving as they do is to distract or protect other family members; the family's need for a distraction was the sole or primary cause of the onset of the symptom.

All of these extreme beliefs tend to make the function-of-the-symptom element of assessment and treatment overshadow all others and put the therapist into the pathology detective role. It is possible to believe, instead, that in some cases families are so distressed that they will need a distraction and that, sometimes, they will focus on a child's symptoms as one distraction. This belief makes several important distinctions that can eliminate many of the negative consequences of family therapy's functionalism (Schwartz, 1990).

First, the idea that families may need a distraction is different from the idea that they need or want the symptom. Desperately scared or miserable people will often need or want to be distracted and will seize anything available for that purpose. Since their child's symptoms are there and are available, they may use those symptoms, along with any number of other distractions. They may not make the connection between their use of the symptom and its maintenance or exacerbation and, instead, strongly wish it were not there; but since it is, they use it.

Second, this distractive process is involved only in some cases—many, if not most, problems are not attempts to protect other family members. Where evidence suggests that such a protective process is involved, many other processes are also at work on which it may be better to focus. In other words, even where a therapist believes such distractive or protective sequences are involved, this does not have to be pointed out to or admitted by a family for the symptom to be lastingly resolved. If people can lift themselves out of their fear and desperation in other ways then the need for the distraction will vanish, if it ever existed.

With this position about symptoms and their relationship to families, we no longer need to make functionalist investigations the centerpiece of our therapy. Nor, on the other hand, do we have to deny or ignore the protective operation of symptoms when this information emerges and where the family may benefit from discussing this nondefensively. We also do not have to minimize the oppressive impact that symptoms have on family life while insinuating or covertly believing that they want things that way. Instead we can genuinely empathize with the predicament they all are in.

The Self in the System

The final trend in the field that we want to describe and comment on is related to nearly all of the other trends of the eighties that we have described thus far. The pendulum that swung family therapy away from intrapsychic, individual models of psychotherapy finally began to swing back. There are, no doubt, many reasons for this backswing and we will speculate on some of them below.

The first of these reasons is developmental. Family therapy has become accepted enough as a valid discipline that it no longer has to maintain the us-versus-them attitude of its early days. Like an adolescent who is taking a second look at parents she initially rejected, the field has grown strong and confident enough to admit that it may not have all the answers after all, and that intrapsychic considerations may be important.

A second reason is related to the Milan, constructivist, and feminist influences cited above. These movements have led the field from a focus on behavioral sequences, in which insight or awareness is discounted, to an emphasis on the importance of the meanings that individual family members have about each other and their problems. It is a short step from this focus on meaning to an interest in how individuals make and change meaning; a step that takes us inside people.

A third factor has to do with the immigration of increasing numbers of psychodynamically trained clinicians into the family therapy field as family therapy became more popular and less polarized from the psychotherapy establishment. This influx has created an increasing demand for models that can bridge the gap between the self and the system.

Finally, several offshoots of psychoanalysis have evolved to the point that they seem more compatible with family therapy. Classic Freudian drive theory gives people's environment little credit for their problems, and, consequently, gives little justification for working with their families (see Chapter 5). Freud taught us that human nature is propelled by unconscious forces buried deep within the psyche. Both object relations theory and self psychology put more emphasis on a person's early interactions with family.

The essence of object relations theory is quite simple: We relate to people in the present partly on the basis of expectations formed by early experience. For the more interpersonally oriented object relations theorists like Ronald Fairbairn and Donald Winnicott, interpersonal relatedness replaces drives, such as the pleasure principle, as the driving force in human personality.

Object relations theory says that the past is alive—in memory—and it runs people's lives more than they know. From our early relationships with caretakers, we formed mental images, called internal objects, that interact within us. As adults, we react to other people based in large part on how much those people resemble these internal objects, rather than on the real characteristics of the people.

As applied to family therapy then, the idea is that the dysfunctional patterns that family therapists have identified are often maintained by the internal object relations of key family members. Through a process called projective identification, the images of certain internal objects are projected onto other family members. Object relations family therapists often try to interpret these projections to the family when they see them so that family members can be more aware of the unseen forces behind their patterns and more able to change them.

A growing number of books have been written regarding object relations and family therapy (Nichols, 1987; Luepnitz, 1988; Wachtel and Wachtel, 1986; Kirshner and Kirshner, 1986; Slipp, 1984; Scharff and Scharff, 1987) and, currently, it seems to be the theory of choice for those looking to add an intrapsychic perspective to their interpersonal one. In addition, however, the self psychology of Heinz Kohut (1971, 1977) has had a big impact on the psychoanalytic world and, indirectly, on family therapy. Kohut replaces Freud's raging id with an insecure self at the core of human nature. Thus, he believes, our lives are organized around a striving for fulfillment and longing for acceptance and admiration, more than around sex and aggression.

These ideas have strong implications for the nature of the relationship between therapist and patient. Therapists are to be more nurturant and empathic—are to provide a safe, warm envelope known as a *holding environment*—rather than remaining distant, passive, and neutral. This is a big and controversial step for psychoanalysis, and also for family therapy. Virginia Satir had emphasized these very ideas—the importance of self-esteem and of creating a nurturant therapeutic environment—many years earlier, but family therapy had been so enamoured with cybernetic gamesmanship that her impact was not what it might have been.

The attempted marriage of even these more interpersonally oriented psychoanalytic theories with family therapy is a delicate matter. These models still contain concepts and assumptions that do not blend well with systems thinking, and different writers have handled this problem in different ways. Some advocate giving up on systems theory and replacing it with object relations as a basis for family therapy. Others try to use both, but keep them separated and use them sequentially or to complement each other. Still others have tried to integrate the concepts and methods of the two paradigms, a process that, it seems to us, has proven as barren as trying to mate animals across species.

One model has taken a different tack. Instead of trying to work with the incompatibilities between object relations and systems thinking, Schwartz (1987) extended systems principles and techniques inside, applying them to the interaction of internal subpersonalities. In the process he stumbled on to a new method of working intrapsychically and an empowering language for therapy, as well as a way to move fluidly from family to internal considerations (see Chapter 11).

Many family therapists maintain the "external-only" position of the pioneers and view this return to the individual as the inevitable selling-out of the revolution. For many of them, the discovery of systemic concepts and techniques was as clarifying as turning on a light in a dark room. Where there was only chaos and confusion, they could now see triangles, boundary violations, and circular interaction sequences. The idea of going back into the murky, speculative, and emotional intrapsychic arena, from which they were rescued by family therapy, is quite unsavory.

We agree that there are dangers in this swingback. It is easy to get lost in the fascinating inner life of individuals and, once again, to minimize the importance of their external context. It is easy to become daunted by stories of pathological interactions in a person's early life and underestimate the ability to change in the present. It is easy to become overwhelmed by the complexity of trying to understand the many psyches that comprise a family system.

If the field proceeds carefully toward a systemic appreciation of individuals, then these dangers can be addressed. When this is achieved, our models will be enriched and blind spots will be cleared up; we will be able to appreciate both internal and external levels of the system and shift between them as needed. We will respect the power of family systems without losing sight of the abilities of individuals to control their own lives. We will be able to identify problematic interaction patterns in the family while also knowing each family member as a flesh and blood person rather than as a cog in the machine. That is an exciting prospect.

THE FAMILY THERAPY ESTABLISHMENT

Having introduced the reader to the evolution of family therapy's concepts and methods, we will, in this section, present something of a consumer's guide to the field as it appears in the spring of 1990. In the four decades since its inception, family therapy has had a tremendous influence on the psychotherapeutic community and has grown so large that it is impossible to cover it adequately in a few pages. Nonetheless we will attempt to orient readers to some of what is available.

Professional Organizations

The American Association for Marriage and Family Therapy (AAMFT), located in Washington, DC, was organized in 1942 by Lester Dearborn and Ernest Graves as a professional organization to set standards for marriage counselors. In 1970 it was expanded to include family therapists and has become the credentialing body for the field of family therapy. Through its requirements for membership, standards have been set for becoming a family therapist that are used by the various states that regulate the profession. AAMFT also lobbies state and federal governments for the interests of family therapists, interests such as state licensing.

AAMFT's membership has grown enormously, reflecting the growth of the field. In the seven years since the first edition of this book, membership has almost doubled, from 9,000 in 1983 to 17,500 in 1990. This kind of membership and the money generated from it has made AAMFT a powerful player in mental health politics, and has aided in public and governmental recognition of family therapy as a distinct field.

The American Family Therapy Association (AFTA) was organized in 1977 to serve the needs of the field's advanced clinicians and trainers who wanted a smaller, more intimate context for sharing ideas and developing common interests. Despite high standards for membership regarding years of teaching and clinical experience, and an interest in remaining small, AFTA's membership has also nearly doubled since 1983, going from 500 to 940. AFTA is a high-level think tank focused around its annual conference, described below, and its newsletter.

Conferences

Besides the multitude of workshops and conferences privately sponsored or put on by local chapters of AAMFT, there are four main national meetings. By far the largest is AAMFT's annual conference each October which has grown to the point (between four and five thousand) that only a few cities have the facilities to accommodate it. With over two hundred presentations on various family therapy topics to select from, there is something for everyone. In addition, the conference features the Masters Series, in which well-known therapists interview a family while an audience watches, as well as a series of plenary addresses by leaders in the field.

The second largest (over 2,000) is the Family Therapy Network Symposium each March in Washington, DC. Sponsored by the *Family Therapy Networker* magazine described below; all presenters are invited so that quality throughout the eighty workshops is ensured. Each year the symposium has a theme, and invited plenary speakers are often famous for work done outside the field of family therapy; one of these is always a writer such as, in recent years, Tom Wolfe, Maya Angelou, and John Updike.

AFTA's annual meeting deliberately has a different flavor from these other conferences. Because of its small size (usually around 300—it is not open to nonmembers), it is the one place where many of the leaders of the field can gather in a relatively informal setting to discuss ideas. Rather than workshops, the meeting is organized around interest groups and brief presentations designed to promote interaction.

The other conference where many family therapists can be found is not devoted exclusively to family therapy. The American Orthopsychiatric Association is a multidisciplinary organization whose annual conference usually contains a sizable percentage of presentations devoted to family therapy or to issues that would interest systems-oriented clinicians.

Publications

The first book devoted entirely to the diagnosis and treatment of families was Nathan Ackerman's, *The Psychodynamics of Family Life*, published in 1958. The field's first journal, *Family Process*, was founded in 1962. Since these early publications, the family therapy literature has proliferated to the point where it is virtually impossible to stay on top of it. We count over twenty journals or newsletters devoted to some aspect of family therapy published in the United States, with many other countries publishing their own journals. The number of books is equally overwhelming, so we refer the reader to the *Recommended Reading* section in the back of this volume for a selective guide to some of the classic books and articles in the field. Below we will describe some of the major publications.

Family Process continues to exert a powerful influence on the field. Many of the debates and developments described in the first three chapters of this book appeared first in its pages. Founded in 1962 by Don Jackson and Nathan Ackerman, its editors have included Jay Haley, Don Bloch, Carlos Sluzki, and starting in 1990, Peter Steinglass. The *Journal of Marital and Family Therapy* is a close second in prestige and, as the official journal of AAMFT, it has a large readership. Under the editorship of Alan Gurman during the eighties, JMFT increased its focus on research and improved its standards. Douglas Sprenkle took over as editor in 1990.

The *Family Therapy Networker*, a magazine devoted to issues related to family therapy and psychotherapy in general, also has a strong influence. Its huge readership (upwards of 40,000—two to three times larger than any other family therapy publication) has been won through tackling provocative issues with high-quality writing. Rich Simon has turned what began as a small newsletter into the most widely read publication on psychotherapy and, in so doing, has introduced many of family therapy's ideas to therapists throughout the country.

There are a number of other well-established journals that, like *Family Process* and *JMFT*, are devoted to general issues in the field. These include the *American Journal of Family Therapy*, *Journal of Family Psychotherapy*, *The International Journal of Family Therapy*, *Contemporary Family Therapy*, and *Family Therapy Collections*. In addition, a number of specialized journals have emerged. For example, the *Journal of Strategic and Systemic Therapies* is widely read by therapists who use those adjectives to describe themselves, while Bowenian therapists read *The Family*, and those interested in Michael White's work subscribe to the *Dulwich Centre Review* and *Family Therapy Case Studies*.

The cross-fertilization of family therapy with other fields is represented by *Family Systems Medicine*, a journal devoted to the collaboration between family practice medicine and family therapy, by the new *Journal of Family Psychology*, published by a division of the American Psychological Association, and by the new *Feminism and Family Therapy*, which reflects the growing influence of feminist thought on the field.

News within the field and digests of important developments are conveyed through AAMFT's newsletter, *Family Therapy News*, and through the *Marriage and Family Review* and the new *Brown University Family Therapy Newsletter*. Those interested in the branch of sociology called family studies have much in common with family therapists and read *Family Relations* and the *Journal of Marriage and the Family*.

Training Centers

As we have already discussed, family therapy developed primarily outside of academia. There are, however, a handful of doctoral programs and a larger number of masters programs specializing in marital and family therapy in universities around the country. The American Association for Marriage and Family Therapy accredits these academic programs and can provide a list of them. Because we are aware of no comparable list of the major nonacademic training centers, we will provide below a description of some of the best known centers in the United States. There are other major centers throughout the world, but our space is limited. The reader may notice that the large majority of these are clustered in the northeast where family therapy is most strongly rooted. We will begin there and move west.

The *Boston Family Institute*, founded in 1969, is the oldest free-standing family therapy institute in New England. Its director, Fred Duhl, was strongly influenced by Virginia Satir and by general systems theory. He has expanded his model of training to a multilevel, multitechniqued approach tailored to each family problem. The institute offers a one- or two-year, part-time, clinically based program in the "problematic child" (children who disturb families), as well as in marriage and family therapy at a postgraduate level. For further information, write to: Frederick J. Duhl, Director, B.F.I., 315 Dartmouth Street, Boston, MA 02116.

The *Family Institute of Cambridge*, in Massachusetts, was founded in 1976 by David Kantor, Barry Dym, and Carter Umbarger. Kantor left in 1980, and since then four additional codirectors have been added: Richard Chasin, Sallyann Roth, Caroline Marvin, and Charles Verge. The institute is a nonprofit center that offers training and research in applied systems theory. While the faculty is strongly interested in family therapy, they also do systems-oriented work with individuals, couples, organizations, and communities. They offer four one-year training sequences: (1) foundations (for beginners, and not requiring clinical practice), (2) intensive clinical, (3) couples therapy, and (4) Milan systemic. In addition to these training programs, the institute offers a wide variety of workshops, seminars, group supervision, and conferences. They also have some money set aside for research stipends and training scholarships. For more information contact: Lee Moonogian, 51 Kondazian St., Watertown, MA 02172.

The *Kantor Family Institute*, in Somerville, Massachusetts, was founded by David Kantor after he left the Family Institute of Cambridge in 1980, and is informed by his structural/analytic model of therapy, as well as psychodynamic and other family therapy influences. The institute offers a sequence of three one-year training programs that build upon each other but can be taken independently. They also offer a specialized program in couples treatment and in organizational consultation, as well as a variety of apprenticeships, internships, and courses. For more information contact: Julie Wood, Kantor Family Institute, 7 Shepard Street, Cambridge, MA 02138.

Family Studies, Inc. is a small private training institution in New York City, founded in 1983 by Salvador Minuchin. The faculty includes Evan H. Bellin, Anne L. Brooks, Jorge Colapinto, Ema Genijovich, and Patricia Minuchin. Special programs are designed for on-site training in agencies. There is a year-long extern training program for beginning family therapists, for more experienced therapists, and for administrators and supervisors, as well as workshops on subjects including couples therapy, working with poverty-stricken families, family therapy in the school setting, and so on. Although principles of structural family therapy are emphasized, the faculty maintains a systemic perspective. Inquiries may be directed to Salvador Minuchin, P.O. Box 1035, Cooper Station, New York, NY 10276.

The *Ackerman Institute for Family Therapy* in New York City was founded as the Family Institute by Nathan Ackerman in 1965. Following Ackerman's death in 1971, the center was renamed in his honor and the directorship was assumed by Donald Bloch, who has recently passed the baton to Peter Steinglass. In addition to Donald Bloch, the current editor of *Family Systems Medicine*, the institute also has such noted family therapists and theorists as Peggy Penn, Peggy Papp, Olga Silverstein, Marcia Scheinberg, Virginia Goldner, and Gillian Walker.

The institute offers training in systemic family therapy using a structural-strategic and intergenerational model of theory and practice. They offer a one-year introductory training program and a two-year clinical externship program for more experienced family therapists. In addition, the institute offers biweekly, weekend workshops throughout the year. For further information contact: Peggy Penn, Director of Training, 149 East 78th St., New York, NY 10021.

The *Family Institute of Westchester* is located in Mount Vernon, New York, and is directed by Elizabeth Carter, with other notable staff including Fredda Hertz, Monica McGoldrick, and Evan Imber-Black. All of these people were trained in extended family systems theory, but they teach an integrated model which includes aspects of structural and strategic techniques as well. The institute has been in operation since 1977 and is primarily known for its training program. The training offered includes a comprehensive program of supervision, seminars, and small groups which takes three years to complete. There is also a two-year externship which meets weekly. In addition to the training offered on site, members of the teaching staff speak at workshops and conventions throughout the country. Additional information is available from: Lillian Fine, Administrator, 147 Archer Ave., Mount Vernon, NY 10550.

The *Center for Family Learning* in Rye Brook, New York was

founded in 1973 by Philip Guerin, who was trained by Murray Bowen. The center provides a three-year training program in family systems therapy which includes a clinical externship year for experienced clinicians, followed by a fellowship year with center faculty working on the Child and Adolescent Project. The third year is a fellowship spent with faculty who have worked together for the past ten years to study marital conflict. Currently they are working on the treatment of families recovering from alcoholism. The center also offers a wide variety of seminars and workshops, as well as a Community Education Program which is given on a yearly basis throughout the Westchester county area and is taped for cable television. For addition information contact: Eileen Guerin Pendagast, Director of Postgraduate and Community Education, 16 Rye Ridge Plaza, Rye Brook, NY 10573.

The *Family Therapy Training Program at the University of Rochester* was established in 1983 by Judith Landau-Stanton and Duncan Stanton. It presents an integration of structural, strategic, and experimental approaches in a series of postgraduate externships and seminars. This program is unusual in that academic credit is available for participation and cases are provided to trainees. The faculty also includes such notable family therapists as Lyman Wynne and Susan McDaniel. For more information contact: Patricia Atkins, Family Therapy Training Program, Department of Psychiatry, University of Rochester Medical Center, 300 Crittenden Blvd., Rochester, NY 14642.

The *Family Therapy Institute of Washington, DC* is the training center and clinic codirected by Jay Haley and Cloe Madanes. Haley and Madanes teach, supervise, and conduct therapy emphasizing their strategic, problem-focused approach. A variety of training programs are offered in which Haley and Madanes present seminars, videotaped examples of therapy, and live supervision. The institute's clinic offers treatment provided by a multidisciplinary staff, all of whom have previously trained with Haley and Madanes. In recent years Haley and Madanes have become noted for their work with problems of adolescents, including a special emphasis on sexual offenders. Haley and Madanes offer workshops and seminars to professionals throughout the United States and Europe. Inquiries may be made to: David Eddy, Executive Director, Family Therapy Institute of Washington, DC, 5850 Hubbard Dr., Rockville, MD 20852.

The *Georgetown Family Center*, located in Washington, DC, was organized to teach family systems theory as developed by Murray Bowen. Bowen founded and directed this center, affiliated with Georgetown University Medical School, until his death in October 1990. The training programs include a weekly, three-year postgraduate program, and a special program for out-of-towners that meets for three consecutive days, four times a year, over a three-year period. There is also a full-time fellowship for psychiatrists and part-time internships for graduates of their other training programs. A description of these programs is available from: Michael Kerr, Director of Training, The Georgetown Family Center, 4380 MacArthur Blvd. N.W., Washington, DC 20007.

The *Family Therapy Practice Center of Washington, DC* was founded in 1980 by Marianne Walters after she left the Philadelphia Child Guidance Clinic. The center has a strong structural family therapy base and offers a postgraduate externship. In addition, the center develops programs for dealing with at-risk populations and changing family structures such as their adolescent foster care project, family violence assistance project, and runaway youth/multiple family group project. For more information contact: Marcia Pollard, 2153 Newport Place N.W., Washington, DC 20037.

The *Philadelphia Child Guidance Clinic* became one of the leading centers of family therapy in the world during the 1970s. It was here that Salvador Minuchin and his colleagues defined and promulgated the concepts of structural family therapy. As a family-centered institution, it provides the full range of children's services: outpatient, home-based, day hospital, and inpatient. The outpatient specialty services include: early childhood intervention, sexual abuse (victims and offenders), divorce and remarriage, and pain control. Two home-based programs serve children and adolescents at risk for placement and provide specialized foster care. The inpatient service includes family apartments so that families are maximally involved in the treatment process. The treatment models used in the services have been refined from major federal- and state-funded research, most recently in the areas of home-based services, childhood depression, and remarriage, and previously in the areas of divorce, teen pregnancy, single-parent families, foster care, schizophrenia, drug abuse, eating disorders, and psychosomatic disorders.

Unlike most of the other centers of family therapy training, which are located in some clinics and old houses, PCGC is a large, modern, well-equipped facility that is physically part of the Children's Hospital of Philadelphia. The clinic is affiliated with the Departments of Psychiatry and Pediatrics of the University of Pennsylvania School of Medicine. There is an elaborate network of videotaping equipment, and over 300 staff are involved in the clinic's activities. PCGC probably has trained more family therapists than any other center in the world. The training programs include internships and externships for psychology, social work, child psychiatry, and postgraduate students, workshops, conferences, plus off-site contacts to agencies and states throughout the United States and abroad. Additional information can be obtained by writing to: Marion Lindblad-Goldberg, Director, Family Therapy Training Center, Philadelphia Child Guidance Center, Two Children's Center, 34th Street and Civic Center Blvd., Philadelphia, PA 19104.

The *Atlanta Institute for Family Studies* was founded in 1977 by Carrell Dammann, who is no longer there. The current director, Michael

Berger, and faculty, including Tom Russell and Douglas Carl, teach an integration of structural, strategic, Bowen, and Milan approaches in externships. The institute also is doing research on developing support networks for families struggling with AIDS or with handicapped children. For more information contact: Michael Berger, 3715 Northside Parkway, 300 Northcreek, Suite 100, Atlanta, GA 30327.

The *Brief Family Therapy Center* in Milwaukee is known for its specialization in the research, training, and clinical practice of brief therapy for a wide range of clinical symptoms. The center provides short-term and long-term training and their week-long and month-long training attracts many postmasters level clinicians from across the United States and around the world. The center's commitment to a systemic focus for brief treatment is elaborated by its codirector, Steve de Shazer, and his staff, in three books and over seventy papers. For further information contact: Brief Family Therapy Center, 6815 W. Capitol Drive, Milwaukee, WI 53216.

The *Family Institute* (of Chicago, formerly) was founded in 1968 by Charles Kramer to provide training, research, and clinical services in family, marital, and child therapy. William Pinsof, the president of the institute, and the large faculty, including Jay Lebow, expose trainees to four theoretical models of family therapy: Integrative Problem Centered (Pinsof's model), Structural/Strategic, Experiential/Family of Origin, and Psychoanalytic/Object Relations. They offer a one-year clinical training practicum, a two-year postgraduate training program in marital and family therapy, seminars and workshops, a psychology internship, and a postdoctoral fellowship. As a result of a recently completed affiliation with Northwestern University, they plan to offer a masters in family therapy and a doctorate in family psychology. For more information contact: Noble Butler, The Family Institute, 680 N. Lake Shore Drive, Suite 1306, Chicago, IL 60611.

The *Family Systems Program* at the Institute for Juvenile Research in Chicago was founded in 1974 by Irv Borstein, who was succeeded as director by a series of well-known family therapists: Celia Falicov, followed by Howard Liddle, and then Doug Breunlin. The current faculty includes Director Betty Karrer, Richard Schwartz, and Rocco Cimmarusti, with input from Doug Breunlin and Lee Combrinck-Graham, who is Director of the Institute for Juvenile Research, and from a large adjunct faculty. This group has developed and teaches "metaframeworks" for understanding and using the various family therapy models; that is, principles that transcend the limits of each model and apply to all of them.

They offer a variety of postgraduate training experiences including six-week courses, one-year introductory and clinical externships, advanced training in supervision or in Schwartz's Internal Family Systems model, and in collaboration with Rich Simon, editor of the *Family Therapy Networker*, an international studies program which sponsors the training of foreign practitioners. In addition, they are connected to the internships for psychology, social work, and child psychiatry students at the Institute for Juvenile Research. For more information contact: Betty Karrer, 907 South Wolcott, Chicago, IL 60612.

The *Galveston Family Institute* is a private, nonprofit organization that was founded in 1977 to formalize the research effort begun by Multiple Impact Therapy in the 1950s. The current theoretical orientation of the institute is a "language systems approach" that draws upon the philosophical concepts of hermeneutics and social constructionism. The educational program emphasizes openness and sharing of clinical experiences. This is exemplified by group learning, teamwork, live consultation, and observation of faculty work. Programs include: (1) residential (fellowship and apprenticeship program); (2) external programs (postgraduate education for practicing clinicians such as externships, seminars, supervision, and workshops); and (3) visitor study program. For more information contact: Harlene Anderson, Director, or Harold Goolishian, Director Emeritus, 4115 Yoakum, Houston, TX 77006.

The *Mental Research Institute* in Palo Alto, California, was founded in 1969 by the late Don Jackson and is considered one of the locations of the birth of family therapy. Today, MRI's focus is on research and training from an interactional or systemic point of view. Some of the most well-known staff members of the MRI are Paul Watzlawick, John Weakland, Richard Fisch, and Arthur Bodin. The MRI accepts master's level and above candidates into a wide variety of training programs, including workshops, continuing seminars, month-long residency programs, clinical externships, and supervisory groups. For further information about MRI's training programs you may write to: Director of Training, 555 Middlefield Rd., Palo Alto, CA 94301.

RESEARCH IN FAMILY THERAPY

Family therapy has a lot of intuitive appeal. It makes sense that if you don't deal with a person's context then it will be difficult for them to achieve or maintain change. It also makes sense to harness and coordinate the strength of a family to overcome its members' problems. The rapid growth of family therapy was based largely on this intuitive appeal and on the personal experiences of large numbers of therapists after they tried it and found it to be effective and enjoyable. A few of the many outcome studies reviewed in this section particularly hastened the spread of family therapy because they provided its adherent with dramatic evidence to bolster their anecdotal claims.

The earliest of these important studies compared the effectiveness of outpatient, family-centered crisis therapy to conventional, inpatient treatment. Three hundred acutely disturbed patients who had been recommended for hospitalization were randomly assigned to one or the other treatment. Family treatment was clearly superior to hospitalization in terms of length, frequency of readmissions, and ability to avert future hospitalizations (Langsley, Flomenhaft, and Machotka, 1969; Langsley, Pittman, Machotka, and Flomenhaft, 1968). Later, the field was boosted when Minuchin and his colleagues reported dramatically better results with anorexia nervosa than had any former approach (Minuchin, Baker, Rosman, Liebman, Milman, and Todd, 1975; Minuchin, Rosman, and Baker, 1978). Soon after that, Stanton and Todd and their associates (1979) reported impressive success with heroin addicts in a well-designed study. Most recently psychoeducational family approaches have received widespread attention for successfully preventing the rehospitalization of schizophrenics (Falloon, Boyd, McGill, Razani, Moss, and Gilderman, 1982; Falloon, Boyd, and McGill, 1985; Anderson, Reiss, and Hogarty, 1986).

What made each of these studies so useful in promoting family therapy was that they used convincing measures of outcome (e.g., weight gain for anorexics, urine samples for heroin addicts, levels of rehospitalization for schizophrenics) and demonstrated that family therapy was significantly more effective with very difficult populations than traditional approaches. They provided the credibility that a radical new movement needs to be taken seriously.

The clinical effectiveness of family therapy has been a major focus of the research conducted in the field over the last two decades. A number of review articles have been published in an attempt to summarize the large number of outcome studies completed during this time (Gurman and Kniskern, 1978; Dewitt, 1978; Borduin, Henggeler, Hanson, and Harbin, 1982; Ulrici, 1983; Gurman, Kniskern, and Pinsof, 1986; Hazelrigg, Cooper, and Borduin, 1987; Bednar, Burlingame, and Masters, 1988; and Piercy and Sprenkle, in press).

As discussed previously, family therapy encompasses a variety of treatment models including systems-oriented and behavioral approaches. Systems-oriented approaches vary from one model to the next and include structural, strategic, solution-focused, and the Milan model of family therapy. While some authors have argued that the results of different approaches can be combined because all define "symptoms and adjustment difficulties as maladaptive patterns of interaction between people" and all are "designed to alter the behavioral and interactional patterns of members in a system" (Hazelrigg, Cooper, and Borduin, 1987, p. 430), the theoretical differences between these different approaches are great enough that the effectiveness of each approach should be considered separately. This has seldom been the case, however, because few studies have completely defined what they mean by family therapy. As a result many of the reviews have combined the results of all forms of family treatment. While we would agree that combining these approaches might provide information about the overall effectiveness of treatment that requires more than one person to be in the therapy room at some point in the treatment process, it provides little specific information regarding the most effective type of treatment for specific symptoms and populations.

In spite of the lack of specificity within the field, there are enough studies to support the overall effectiveness of systems-oriented family therapy. The major reviews conclude that (1) systemic family therapy is based on concepts, assumptions, and procedures that are different from traditional forms of psychotherapy; (2) family therapy is a useful treatment for a variety of problems; (3) family therapy is at least as effective as other types of therapy; and (4) research directed at the process of therapy and the mechanisms of change is needed (Gurman and Kniskern, 1978; Dewitt, 1987; Jacobson and Bussod, 1983).

Behavioral marital and family therapy is the primary conceptual alternative to systems-oriented approaches that has been heavily researched. The behaviorists strive to propose specific, observable, measurable, and empirically verifiable propositions and provide a treatment package of interventions matched to specific target behaviors. The quantity and quality of research based on behavioral models is greater than that of systems-oriented approaches; however, the overall conclusions of the studies based on behavioral treatments are much the same as those using systems-oriented models. The reviewers of this literature conclude that while behavioral treatment produces improvement at a rate better than chance, it is unclear whether behavioral or systemic treatments are more effective, and there seem to be no major differences in the overall effectiveness when the entire treatment package or only components of the package are used (Jacobson and Bussod, 1983; Baucom and Hoffman, 1985; Gurman, Kniskern, and Pinsof, 1986).

While it is clear that family therapy is at least as effective as other forms of treatment, there is little information available on the effectiveness of family therapy when working with specific presenting problems and populations or on the specific factors that influence family therapy outcome. What information there is will be reviewed briefly in the following sections. The reader is referred to other sources for a more comprehensive review of this literature (Gurman, Kniskern, and Pinsof, 1986).

Juvenile Delinquency

Tolan, Cromwell, and Brasswell (1986) reviewed the family therapy literature on juvenile delinquents. They examined the wide variety of treatments that have been used with delinquents including behavioral contracting, communication skills training, role playing, education about family process, parenting, behavioral management training, family sculpting, symptom prescription, and paradoxical injunctions. Most treatment approaches used a combination of techniques with behavioral contracting and strategic techniques the most common.

While the studies varied greatly in quality of design and outcome measurement, the results clearly indicate that family therapy has a positive effect on delinquent behavior. Studies reported a decrease in delinquent behavior and positive change in family process. The studies that compared family therapy with individual therapy found family therapy to be more effective in reducing recidivism. When compared to interventions other than individual psychotherapy (e.g., traditional probation services and work programs), family therapy was also more effective in reducing recidivism.

There are few studies comparing types of family therapies; however, one study (Alexander, Barton, Schiavo, and Parsons, 1977) compared client-centered, psychodynamic-eclectic family treatment and a behavioral-communication approach and found the behavioral-communication approach to be more effective in improving family process and reducing recidivism. Alexander also examined therapist variables related to effectiveness of treatment and found that therapists possessing adequate relationship skills (humor, warmth, self-disclosure) were more likely to engage patients in therapy. Therapists possessing technical skills (directness, self-confidence, clear communication, treatment strategies), in addition to relationship skills, tended to have successful treatment experiences. While the results of this study are not a surprise, they emphasize the importance of the combination of skills.

Conduct Disorders

The treatment of children and adolescents with a conduct disorder, both aggressive (e.g., physical violence against another person) and nonaggressive (e.g., lying, stealing, truancy), has been evaluated in hundreds of studies. The interventions most often used with this population can be classified within the broad category of "parent management training"(Patterson, Chamberlain, and Reid, 1982; Kazdin, 1984). Parent training involves a variety of treatment procedures including didactic instruction of the parents in social learning principles. Patterson and his colleagues at the Oregon Social Learning Center have conducted the most research in this area, evaluating the treatment of over two hundred families during the last twenty years. Treatment outcome is based on parent and teacher ratings of the child's behavior, as well as observation of parent-child interaction in the home.

Patterson and colleagues have found parent management training to be more effective than no treatment (Patterson, 1974; Patterson, Chamberlain, and Reid, 1982), and the effects of treatment have been maintained at follow-up of up to eighteen months (Fleishmann, 1981; Fleishmann and

Szykula, 1981). Teachers reported changes in classroom behavior as a result of in-home interventions (Patterson, Cobb, and Ray, 1973). In addition the deviant behaviors of siblings of the identified patient have been reduced as a result of parent management training (Arnold, Levine, and Patterson, 1975) and reports indicate a reduction of maternal psychopathology, particularly depression, and an increase in mothers' self-esteem (Patterson and Fleishmann, 1979).

While the results of the Oregon group are impressive, not all parent management training programs have been as effective. Kazdin (1984) discussed a number of factors that appear to influence treatment. Treatment does not appear to be as effective for families where the father is absent, families of low socioeconomic status, families with extreme marital discord, parental psychopathology, or lack of maternal social support. It is likely that families presenting with one or more of these factors will need services, in addition to parent management training.

Psychosomatic Disorders

Much of the work in the area of psychosomatic disorders and family therapy has been conducted by those using structural family therapy (Minuchin and Fishman, 1981) at the Philadelphia Child Guidance Clinic. The most comprehensive report by this group is on the outcome of the treatment of fifty-three anorexics and their families (Minuchin, Rosman, and Baker, 1978). The average length of treatment was six months, with follow-up from one to eighty-four months. Outcome criteria included objective measures of weight gain, rehospitalization, and psychosocial functioning of the patient at home, school, and with peers. The investigators reported that 86 percent of the identified patients were rated as substantially improved or recovered, with rare instances of rehospitalization. The group at Philadelphia Child Guidance Clinic (Minuchin, Baker, Rosman, Liebman, Milman, and Todd, 1975) also reported on the treatment of families with adolescents with either "brittle" diabetes mellitus or chronic asthma and reported that 90 percent of the sample improved as measured by psychosocial functioning and physiological measures (blood sugar levels, respiratory functioning).

Schwartz, Barrett, and Saba (1985) reported on the treatment of bulimic patients and their families using a structural-strategic model. They followed the treatment of thirty consecutive referrals and found 76 percent were at least much improved.

Schizophrenia

Much of the research on the treatment of schizophrenia comes out of the psychoeducational branch of family therapy (see Chapter 11). Psychoeducators try to help family members cope with their schizophrenic offspring and try to reduce the levels of "expressed emotion" (EE) (e.g., hostile or critical interaction, overinvolvement) in the patient's living environment. In addition to outpatient sessions, psychoeducators use medication and present workshops for family members designed to help them know what to expect.

Leff, Kuipers, Berkowitz, Eberlein-Vries, and Sturgeon (1982) randomly assigned twenty-four high-risk families of schizophrenic patients to one of four treatment conditions. The conditions included outpatient drug treatment; psychosocial interventions including educating the family about the etiology, symptoms, course, and management of schizophrenia; groups for relatives of the identified patient; and in-home family therapy. Over a nine-month period, 9 percent of the patients in the psychosocial condition relapsed compared with 50 percent in the medication condition. The families that participated in the family intervention showed significant reductions in level of criticism with near-significant reductions in level of involvement. Expressed emotion was reduced in 73 percent of the families treated. There was no change in the level of EE in families in the medication condition (Berkowitz, Kuipers, Eberlain-Frief, and Leff, 1981; Leff, Kuipers, Berkowitz, Eberlein-Vries, and Sturgeon, 1982).

Falloon and colleagues (1982, 1985) reported on the treatment of thirty-six high-risk schizophrenic patients who were randomly assigned to in-home behavioral family therapy (which included education, problem-solving, and contingency management procedures) or individual supportive psychotherapy. Patients in both conditions continued to receive medication. Over a nine-month period, 6 percent of the patients in the family therapy condition versus 44 percent of the patients in the individual psychotherapy condition were reported to have had a relapse. Patients in the family therapy condition were also rated higher on level of symptomatology and social functioning, both based on blind ratings.

Anderson, Reiss, and Hogarty (1986) had comparably impressive reductions in relapse rates with a larger sample, using a combination of family therapy and educational modalities. It seems clear at this point that psychoeducational family therapy can delay schizophrenic relapse and readmission to hospital better than exclusively individual or medication approaches.

Addictions

Stanton, Todd, and Associates (1982) tried structural-strategic therapy with male opiate addicts and their families. Patients were randomly assigned to one of four treatment groups: (1) paid family therapy, (2) unpaid family therapy, (3) paid movie placebo, or (4) individual therapy combined with methadone treatment. The results indicated that paid family therapy was slightly more effective when measured by days free of drug use and a number of other measures of drug use and both paid and unpaid family therapy were more effective than the placebo conditions.

Marital Therapy

A number of comprehensive reviews of the research on marital therapy have been published recently (Beach and O'Leary, 1985; Baucom and Hoffman, 1985; Jacobson, Follette, and Elwood; 1984). Because of the large body of literature available in this area, only the major trends will be reported here. The interested reader is referred to other reviews for a complete summary of the research in marital therapy.

A number of studies have compared behavioral marital therapy to control groups, as well as other forms of marital therapy. When compared with wait-list control groups, couples receiving behavioral marital therapy demonstrated improvement in the presenting problem, decreases in negative verbal behavior, and increased marital satisfaction (Baucom, 1982; Hahlweg, Schindler, Revenstorf, and Brengelmann, 1984; Jacobson, 1977).

The studies that compared behavioral marital therapy to other types of marital therapies suggest that behavioral marital therapy is as effective as other forms of systemic therapy and psychodynamic marital therapies (Baucom, 1982; Borlens, Emmelkamp, MacGillarry, and Markvoort, 1980; Emmelkamp, vander Hulm, MacGillarry, and van Zanten, 1984). These studies have been criticized, however, because the other therapies have either been inadequately defined or there is some question regarding whether the treatment meets the standards of the treatment model described (Gurman, Kniskern, and Pinsof, 1986).

Process Research

Research examining variables that influence the process of therapy has received increasing attention. Historically, process research referred to an attempt to understand and describe what happens within the therapy session. More recently researchers have suggested that process research relate these in-session factors to the outcome of therapy—i.e., to what happens to the individual or family outside of the therapy session (Kiesler, 1971; Grunberg and Pinsof, 1985). Gurman, Kniskern, and Pinsof (1986) refer to this as the "new process perspective" that looks at both the process and outcome of treatment over time. "Psychotherapy research then becomes the analysis of the interaction between processes that occur within treatment (conventionally defined as process variables) and outside treatment (conventionally defined as outcome variables)" (p. 599).

Patterson and his colleagues recently began looking at the process of treatment of families with aggressive children. Chamberlain, Patterson, Reid, Kavanaugh, and Forgatch (1984) developed a coding system which targets resistant and cooperative behavior of clients during family sessions. The initial study reported that there were significantly more resistant behaviors during the middle phase of treatment, which is when therapists are teaching parents behavior management skills, and that families who eventually dropped out of treatment were more resistant to treatment than those who continued. The current research focuses on the relationship between therapist behaviors, phase of treatment, and client resistance.

Pinsof and his colleagues have also been working on research on the process of family treatment and training. They have developed a number of coding instruments, including the Family Therapist Coding System (Pinsof, 1981), which targets verbal behavior of the therapist and can be used for therapists from a variety of theoretical orientations, and a number of scales designed to assess the therapist-client relationship (alliance). Much of the research conducted to date has focused on the development of these instruments and on obtaining reliability and validity data on these instruments.

Future Directions

While research in family therapy has become increasingly sophisticated both in terms of the questions posed and the methods used to address these questions, there are a number of issues that need to be addressed. Family interaction and the process of treatment are extremely difficult variables to measure. The conventional research methods that have been used don't adequately reflect the nature of this complicated interaction. The first challenge will be to develop new methodologies that will provide qualitative as well as quantitative data which more adequately reflect the nature of family process. The second challenge will be to allow ourselves to use these methods which means straying from the traditional process of scientific research (Schwartz and Breunlin, 1983).

The research clearly indicates that family therapy is an effective form of treatment. Questions remain, however, as to what type of family interventions are most effective with specific populations and presenting problems. More importantly, what factors affect treatment (i.e., therapist variables, family variables) and in what ways. In addition to studying the effectiveness of family therapy for the treatment of specific populations and presenting problems, the complicated relationship between family process and the symptoms of family members should be further examined, if for no other reason than to help resolve the function-of-the-symptom controversy described earlier.

In addition, more prospective research which examines the variables likely to predict the absence or presence of specific problems should be conducted. Studies of this nature not only provide a great deal of information regarding current family functioning, but also provide direction for the development of early intervention and prevention programs which can have an impact at a larger, societal level.

REFERENCES

Ahrons, C., and Rogers, R. 1987. *Divorced families: A multidisciplinary developmental view.* New York: Norton.

Alexander, J. F., Barton, C., Schiavo, R. S., and Parsons, B. V. 1977. Systems-behavioral intervention with families of delinquents: Therapist characteristics, family behavior and outcome. *Journal of Consulting and Clinical Psychology. 44*:656–664.

Andersen, T. 1987. The reflecting team: Dialogue and metadialogue in clinical work. *Family Process. 26*:415–428.

Anderson, C. M. 1986. The all-too-short trip from positive to negative connotation. *Journal of Marital and Family Therapy. 12*(4):351–354.

Anderson, C. M. 1988. Psychoeducational model different than paradigm. *Family Therapy News. 19*(3).

Anderson, C. M., Reiss, D., and Hogarty, G. E. 1986. *Schizophrenia and the family: A practitioner's guide to psychoeducation and management.* New York: Guilford.

Anderson, H., and Goolishian, H. 1988. Human systems as linguistic systems: Preliminary and evolving ideas about the implications for clinical theory. *Family Process. 27*:371–394.

Anderson, H., Goolishian, H. and Winderman, L. 1986. Problem determined systems: Toward transformation in family therapy. *Journal of Strategic and Systemic Therapies. 5*:14–19.

Arnold, J., Levine, A., and Patterson, G. R. 1975. Changes in sibling behavior following family intervention. *Journal of Consulting and Clinical Psychology. 43*:683–688.

Ault-Riche, M., ed. 1986. *Women and family therapy.* Rockville, MD: Aspen Systems.

Avis, J. M. 1988. Deepening awareness: A private study guide to feminism and family therapy. In *Women, feminism, and family therapy*, L. Braverman, ed. New York: Haworth Press.

Banks, S., and Kahn, M. 1982. *The sibling bond.* New York: Basic Books.

Baucom, D. H. 1982. A comparison of behavioral contracting and problem-solving/communications training in behavioral marital therapy. *Behavior Therapy. 13*:162–174.

Baucom, D. H., and Hoffman, J. A. 1985. The effectiveness of marital therapy: Current status and application to the clinical setting. In *Clinical handbook of marital therapy*, N. Jacobson and A. Gurman, eds. New York: Guilford.

Beach, S. R., and O'Leary, K. D. 1985. The current status of outcome research in marital therapy. In *Handbook of family psychology and psychotherapy*, L. L'Abate, ed. Pacific Grove, CA: Wadsworth Inc.

Bednar, R. L., Burlingame, G. M., and Masters, K. S. (1988). Systems of family treatment: Substance or semantics? *Annual Review of Psychology. 39*:401–434.

Bepko, C., and Krestan, J. 1985. *The responsibility trap.* New York: The Free Press.

Berger, M., Jurkovic, G., and Associates, eds. 1984. *Practicing family therapy in diverse settings.* San Francisco: Jossey-Bass.

Berkowitz, R., Kuipers, L., Eberlain-Frief, R., and Leff, J. 1981. Lowering expressed emotion in relatives. In *New developments in interventions with families of schizophrenics*, M. J. Goldstein, ed. San Francisco: Jossey-Bass.

Borduin, C. M., Henggeler, S. W., Hanson, C., and Harbin, F. 1982. Treating the family of the adolescent: A review of the empirical literature. In *Delinquency and adolescent psychopathology. A family-ecological systems approach*, S. W. Henggeller, ed. Boston: John Wright.

Borlens, W., Emmelkamp, P., MacGillarry, D., and Markvoort, M. 1980. A clinical evaluation of marital treatment: reciprocity counseling versus system-theoretic counseling. *Behavioral Analysis and Modification.* 4:85–96.

Boyd-Franklin, N. 1989. *Black Families in Therapy: A Multisystems Approach.* New York: Guilford Press.

Braverman, L., ed. *Women, feminism, and family therapy.* New York: Haworth Press, 1988.

Chamberlain, P., Patterson, G., Reid, J., Kavanaugh, K., and Forgatch, M. 1984. Observation of client assistance. *Behavior Therapy. 15*, 144–155.

Coleman, S. 1987. Milan in Bucks County. *Family Therapy Networker. 11*(5), 42–47.

Combrinck-Graham, L. 1989. *Children in family contexts.* New York: Guilford.

Coyne, J. 1982. A brief introduction to epistobabble. *Family Therapy Networker. 6*(4), 27–28.

Dell, P. 1982. Beyond homeostasis: Toward a concept of coherence. *Family Process. 21*(1), 21–41.

Dell, P. 1985. Understanding Bateson and Maturana. *Journal of Marital and Family Therapy. 11*, 1–20.

de Shazer, S. 1984. The death of resistance. *Family Process. 23*(1), 11–16.

de Shazer, S. 1985. *Keys to solutions in brief therapy.* New York: Norton.

de Shazer, S. 1988 *Clues: Investigating solutions in brief therapy.* New York: Norton.

DeWitt, K. N. 1978. The effectiveness of family therapy: A review of outcome research. *Archives of General Psychiatry. 35*, 549–561.

Duncan, B. L. and Solevey, D. 1989. Strategic-brief therapy: An insight-oriented approach. *Journal of Marital and Family Therapy. 15*(1), 1–10.

Elizur, J. and Minuchin, S. 1989. *Institutionalizing madness: Families, therapy and society.* New York: Basic Books.

Elkin, M. 1984. *Families under the influence.* New York: Norton.

Emmelkamp, P., vander Hulm, M., MacGillarry, D., and van Zanten, B. 1984. Marital therapy with clinically distressed couples: A comparative evaluation of system-theoretic, contingency contracting and communication skills approaches. In *Marital therapy and interaction*, K. Hahlweg and N. Jacobson, eds. New York: Guilford.

Everett, C. A. 1987. *The divorce process: A handbook for clinicians.* New York: Haworth Press.

Falicov, C. 1988. *Family transitions: Continuity and change over the life cycle.* New York: Guilford.

Falicov, C., and Brudner-White, L. 1983. The shifting family triangle: The issue of cultural and contextual relativity. In *Cultural perspectives in family therapy,* C. Falicov, ed. Rockville, MD: Aspen Systems.

Falloon, I., Boyd, J. L., and McGill, C. W. 1985. *Family care of schizophrenia.* New York: Guilford.

Falloon, I. R. H., Boyd, J. L., McGill, C. W., Razani, J., Moss, H. B., and Gilderman, A. M. 1982. Family management in the prevention of exacerbations of schizophrenia. *New England Journal of Medicine. 306*:1437–1440.

Fleishmann, M. J. 1981. A replication of Patterson's "Intervention for boys with conduct problems." *Journal of Consulting and Clinical Psychology. 49*:343–351.

Fleishmann, M. J., and Szykula, S. A. 1981. A community setting replication of a social learning treatment for aggressive children. *Behavior Therapy. 12*:115–122.

Goldner, V. 1985. Feminism and family therapy. *Family Process. 24*:31–47.

Goldner, V. 1988. Generation and gender: Normative and covert hierarchies. *Family Process. 27*:17–33.

Goldstein, M. 1988. Correction on views offered by awardee. *Family Therapy News. 19*(3):7–8.

Goodrich, T. J., Rampage, C., Ellman, B., and Halstead, K. 1988. *Feminist family therapy: A casebook.* New York: Norton.

Grunberg, L., and Pinsof, W., eds. 1985. *The psychotherapeutic process: A research handbook.* New York: Guilford.

Gurman, A. S., and Kniskern, D. P. 1978. Reserach on marital and family therapy: Progress, perspective, and prospect. In *Handbook of psychotherapy and behavior change,* S. L. Garfield and A. E. Bergin, eds. New York: Wiley.

Gurman, A. S., Kniskern, D. P., and Pinsof, W. M. 1986. Research on marital and family therapies. In *Handbook of psychotherapy and behavior change.* S. L. Garfield and A. E. Bergin, eds. 3rd Ed. New York: Wiley.

Hahlweg, K., Schindler, L., Revenstorf, D., and Brengelmann, J. C. 1984. The Munich marital therapy study. In *Marital interaction: Analysis and modification,* K. Hahlweg and N. Jacobson, eds. New York: Guilford.

Haley, J. 1980. *Leaving home.* New York: McGraw-Hill.

Haley, J. 1988. Schizophrenics deserve family therapy, not dangerous drugs and management. *Family Therapy News. 19*(2):000.

Hansen, J. C. 1982. *Therapy with remarriage families.* Rockville, MD: Aspen Systems.

Hare-Mustin, R. T. 1986. The problem of gender in family therapy theory. *Family Process. 26*:15–27.

Hazelrigg, M. D., Cooper, H. M., and Borduin, C. M. 1987. Evaluating the effectiveness of family therapies: An integrative review and analysis. *Psychological Bulletin. 101*:428–442.

Held, B. S. 1990. What's in a name? Some confusions and concerns about constructivism. *Journal of Marital and Family Therapy. 16*:179–186.

Held, B. S. and Pols, E. 1987. Dell on Maturana: A real foundation for family therapy. *Psychotherapy. 24*(3): 455–461.

Hoffman, L. 1985. Beyond power and control: Toward a second-order family systems therapy. *Family Systems Medicine. 3*:381–396.

Hoffman, L. 1988. A constructivist position for family therapy. *The Irish Journal of Psychology. 9*(1):110–129.

Imber-Black, E. 1988. *Families and larger systems: A family therapist's guide through the labyrinth.* New York: Guilford.

Imber-Black, E., Roberts, J., and Whiting, R., eds. 1988. *Rituals in families and family therapy.* New York: Norton.

Isaacs, M., Montalvo, B., and Abelsohn, D. 1986. *The difficult divorce: Therapy for children and families.* New York: Basic Books.

Jacobson, N. S. 1977. Problem-solving and contingency contracting in the treatment of marital discord. *Journal of Consulting and Clinical Psychology. 45*:92–100.

Jacobson, N. S., and Bussod, N. 1983. Marital and family therapy. In *The clinical psychology handbook*, M. Herson, A. E. Kazdin, and A. S. Bellack, eds. New York: Pergamon.

Jacobson, N. S., Follette, W. C., and Elwood, R. W. 1984. Outcome research on behavioral marital therapy: A methodological and conceptual reappraisal. In *Marital interaction: Analysis and modification*, K. Hahlweg and N. Jacobson, eds. New York: Guilford.

James, K., and MacKinnon, L. 1990. The "incestuous family" revisited: a critical analysis of family therapy myths. *Journal of Marital and Family Therapy. 16*:71–88.

Kahn, M., and Lewis, K. G. 1988. *Siblings in therapy.* New York: Norton.

Kaufman, E. 1985. *The power to change.* New York: Gardner Press.

Kazdin, A. E. 1984. Treatment of conduct disorders. In *Psychotherapy research: Where are we and where should we go?* J. Williams and R. Spitzer, eds. New York: Guilford.

Keeney, B. P. 1983. *Aesthetics of change.* New York: Guilford.

Keeney, B. P., and Sprenkle, D. H. 1982. Ecosystemic epistemology: Critical implications for the aesthetics and pragmatics of family therapy. *Family Process. 21*(1):1–20.

Kiesler, D. J. 1971. Experimental designs in psychotherapy research. In *Handbook of psychotherapy and behavior change: An empirical analysis*, A. Bergin and S. Garfield, eds. New York: Guilford.

Kirshner, D. A., and Kirshner, S. 1986. *Comprehensive family therapy: An integration of systemic and psychodynamic models.* New York: Brunner/Mazel.

Kohut, H. 1971. *The analysis of the self.* New York: International University Press.

Kohut, H. 1977. *The restoration of the self.* New York: International University Press.

Korzybski, A. 1942. *Science and sanity: An introduction to non-Aristotelian systems and general semantics, 2nd Ed.* Lancaster, PA: Science Books.

Langsley, D., Flomenhaft, K., and Machotka, P. 1969. Follow-up evaluation of family crisis therapy. *American Journal of Orthopsychiatry. 39*:753–759.

Langsley, D., Pittman, F., Machotka, P., and Flomenhaft, K. 1968. Family crisis therapy—results and implications. *Family Process. 7*:145–158.

Leff, J., Kuipers, L., Berkowitz, R., Eberlein-Vries, R., and Sturgeon, D. 1982. A controlled trial of social intervention in the families of schizophrenic patients. *British Journal of Psychiatry. 141*:121–134.

Luepnitz, D. 1988. *The family interpreted: feminist theory in clinical practice.* New York: Basic Books.

Liddle, H. A., and Saba, G. W. 1981. Systemic chic: Family therapy's new wave. *Journal of Strategic and Systemic Therapies. 1*(2):36–39.

MacKinnon, L. K., and Miller, D. 1987. The new epistemology and the Milan approach: Feminist and sociopolitical considerations. *Journal of Marital and Family Therapy. 13*(2):139–156.

Madanes, C. 1990. *Sex, love and violence.* New York, Norton.

McGoldrick, M., Anderson, C., and Walsh, F., eds. 1989. *Women in families: A framework for family therapy.* New York: Norton.

McGoldrick, M., Pearce, J. K., and Giordano, J., eds. 1982. *Ethnicity and family therapy.* New York: Guilford.

Marshal, M., Feldman, R., and Sigal, J. 1989. The unraveling of a treatment paradigm: A followup study of the Milan approach to family therapy. *Family Process. 28*:457–470.

Minuchin, S. 1984. *Family kaleidoscope.* Cambridge, MA: Harvard University Press.

Minuchin, S., Baker, L., Rosman, B., Liebman, R., Milman, L., and Todd, T. 1975. A conceptual model of psychosomatic illness in children. *Archives of General Psychiatry. 32*:1031–1038.

Minuchin, S., and Fishman, H. C. 1981. *Techniques of family therapy.* Cambridge, MA: Harvard University Press.

Minuchin, S., Montalvo, B., Guernery, B., Rosman, B., and Schumer, F. 1967. *Families of the slums.* New York: Basic Books.

Minuchin, S., Rosman, B., and Baker, L. 1978. *Psychosomatic families.* Cambridge, MA: Harvard University Press.

Mirkin, M. P., and Koman, S. L., eds. 1985. *Handbook of adolescents and family therapy.* New York: Gardner Press.

Nichols, M. 1987. *The self in the system.* New York: Brunner/Mazel.

O'Hanlon, W., and Wilk, J. 1987. *Shifting contexts: The generation of effective psychotherapy.* New York: Guilford.

O'Hanlon, W., and Weiner-Davis, M. 1989. *In search of solutions.* New York: Norton.

Patterson, G. R. 1974. Interventions for boys with conduct problems: Multiple settings, treatment and criteria. *Journal of Consulting and Clinical Psychology. 42*:471–481.

Patterson, G. R., Chamberlain, P., and Reid, J. B. 1982. A comparative evaluation of a parent-training program. *Behavior Therapy. 13*:638–650.

Patterson, G. R., Cobb, J. A., and Ray, R. S. 1973. A social engineering technology for retraining families of aggressive boys. In *Issues and trends in behavior therapy*, H. Adams and I. Unkel, eds. Springfield, IL: Charles C. Thomas.

Patterson, G. R., and Fleishmann, M. J. 1979. Maintenance of treatment effects: Some considerations concerning family systems and follow-up data. *Behavior Therapy.* 10:168–185.

Piercy, F. P., and Sprenkle, D. H. Marriage and family therapy: A decade review. *Journal of Marriage and the Family,* In press.

Pinsof, W. M. 1981. Family therapy process research. In *The handbook of family therapy,* A. S. Gurman and D. Kniskern, eds. New York: Brunner/Mazel.

Pinsof, W. M. 1982. Integrative problem-centered therapy: Toward the synthesis of family and individual psychotherapies. *Journal of Marital and Family Therapy.* 9(1):19–36.

Pittman, F. 1987. *Turning points: Treating families in transition and crisis.* New York: Norton.

Raitt, D. 1988. The family therapy survey. *Family Therapy Networker.* 12:52–57.

Root, M., Fallon, P., and Friedrich, W. 1986. *Bulimia: A systems approach to treatment.* New York: Norton.

Saba, G., Karrer, B., and Hardy, K. 1989. *Minorities and family therapy.* New York: Haworth.

Sager, C., Brown, H. S., Crohn, H., Engel, T., Rodstein, E., and Walker, L. 1983. *Treating the remarried family.* New York: Brunner/Mazel.

Satir, V. 1972. *Peoplemaking.* Palo Alto, CA: Science and Behavior Books.

Scharff, D., and Scharff, J. 1987. *Object relations family therapy.* New York: Jason Aronson.

Schwartz, R. C. 1987. Our multiple selves. *Family Therapy Networker.* 11:23–31, 80–83.

Schwartz, R. C. 1990. The concept of the function of the symptom in family therapy. Unpublished manuscript.

Schwartz, R. C. (in preparation). *The individual and family treatment of bulimia.* New York: Guilford.

Schwartz, R. C., Barrett, M. J., and Saba, G. 1985. Family therapy for bulimia. In *Handbook for the psychotherapy of anorexia nervosa and bulimia,* D. Garner and P. Garfinkel, eds. New York: Guilford.

Schwartz, R. C., and Breunlin, D. C. 1983. Research: Why clinicians should bother with it. *Family Therapy Networker.* 7(4):22–27, 57–59.

Schwartz, R. C., and Perrotta, P. 1985. Let us sell no intervention before its time. *Family Therapy Networker,* July-August, 18–25.

Schwartzman, J. 1985. *Families and other systems: The macrosystemic context of family therapy.* New York: Guilford.

Selvini Palazzoli, M. 1986. Towards a general model of psychotic family games. *Journal of Marital and Family Therapy.* 12(4):339–349.

Selvini Palazzoli, M., Boscolo, L., Cecchin, G., and Prata, G. 1978. *Paradox and counterparadox.* New York: Jason Aronson.

Selvini, M., ed. 1988. *The work of Mara Selvini Palazzoli.* Northvale, NJ: Jason Aronson, Inc.

Simon, R. 1986. An interview with Cloe Madanes. *The Family Therapy Networker.* 10(5):64–65.

Simon, R. 1987. Good-bye paradox, hello invariant prescription: An interview with Mara Selvini Palazzoli. *Family Therapy Networker.* 11(5):16–33.

Slipp, S. 1984. *Object relations: A dynamic bridge between individual and family treatment*. New York: Jason Aronson.

Sprenkle, D. 1985. *Divorce therapy*. New York: Haworth Press.

Stanton, M. D. 1981. Strategic approaches to family therapy. In *Handbook of family therapy*, A. Gurman and D. Kniskern, eds. New York: Brunner/Mazel.

Stanton, M. D., Todd, T., and Associates, 1982. *The family therapy of drug abuse and addiction*. New York: Guilford.

Steinglass, P., Bennett, L., Wolin, S. J., and Reiss, D. 1987. *The alcoholic family*. New York: Basic Books.

Taggert, M. 1989. Epistemological equality as the fulfillment of family therapy. In *Women in families: A framework for family therapy*, M. McGoldrick, C. Anderson, and F. Walsh, eds. New York: Norton.

Tolan, P. H., Cromwell, R. E., and Brasswell, M. 1986. Family therapy with delinquents: A critical review of the literature. *Family Process. 25*:619–649.

Treadway, D. 1989. *Before it's too late: Working with substance abuse in the family*. New York: Norton.

Trepper, T. S., and Barrett, M. J. 1989. *Systemic treatment of incest: A therapeutic handbook*. New York: Brunner/Mazel.

Ulrici, D. 1983. The effects of behavioral and family interventions on juvenile recidivism. *Family therapy. 10*:25–36.

Vaughn, C., and Leff, J. 1976. The measurement of expressed emotion in the families of psychiatric patients. *British Journal of Psychology. 15*:157–165.

Visher, E., and Visher, J. 1979. *Stepfamilies: A guide to working with step-parents and stepchildren*. New York: Brunner/Mazel.

Visher, E., and Visher, J. 1988. *Old loyalties, new ties: Therapeutic strategies with stepfamilies*. New York: Brunner/Mazel.

Wachtel, E. F. and Wachtel, P. L. 1986. *Family dynamics in individual psychotherapy: A guide to clinical strategies*. New York: Guilford.

Wallerstein, J., and Kelly, J. 1980. *Surviving the breakup: How children and parents cope with divorce*. New York: Basic Books.

Walsh, F. 1982. *Normal family processes*. New York: Guilford.

Walters, M., Carter, B., Papp, P., and Silverstein, O. 1988. *The invisible web: Gender patterns in family relationships*. New York: Guilford.

Watzlawick. P., ed. 1984. *The invented reality*. New York: W. W. Norton.

Wegscheider-Cruse, S. 1985. *Choicemaking: For co-dependents, adult children and spirituality seekers*. Pompano Beach, FL: Health Communications.

White, M. 1989. *Selected papers*. Adelaide, Australia: Dulwich Centre Publications.

Winderman, L. 1989. Generation of human meaning key to Galveston Paradigm: An interview with Harlene Anderson and Harold Goolishian. *Family Therapy News. 20*(6):11–12.

Zilbach, J. 1986. *Young children in family therapy*. New York: Brunner/Mazel.

4

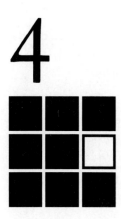

Early Models:
Group Family Therapy and Communications Family Therapy

Those of us who practiced family therapy in the 1960s could often be seen engaged in a strange ritual. When a family filed in for their first session, all anxious and uncertain, the therapist, all smiles, would go over and kneel in front of one of the small children. "Hi! And what's your name?" Then, often as not, "Do you know why you're here?" meanwhile ignoring the parents. The most common answers to this question were: "Mommy said we were going to the doctor's," in a frightened voice; or, in a confused tone, "Daddy said we were going for a ride." Then the therapist, pretending not to be scornful, would turn to the parents and say, "Perhaps you could explain to Johnny why you *are* here."

The reason for this little charade was that before they understood how families were structured, many therapists treated the family as a group, in which the youngest members were presumed to be the most vulnerable and, therefore, in need of "expert" help to express themselves—as though the parents weren't in charge, as though everybody's opinion was equal.

Another common scene was therapists making solemn comments about patterns of communication: "I notice that when I ask Suzie a question, she first turns to Mom to see if it's okay to answer. . ." Very clever. Not only did we expect families to be impressed by such brilliant remarks, we imagined that they'd somehow instantly reform and start communicating according to some ideal model in *our* heads—"I-statements" and all the rest. *And* we thought that such clear communication would somehow magically resolve their problems.

Are we being a little snotty here? Yes. The first family therapists turned somewhat naively to models from group therapy and communications analysis because there were no other models available.

Early family therapists availed themselves of the theories of group dynamics and the techniques of group therapy because, after all, families are groups, aren't they? It was certainly convenient to have a ready-made set of principles and procedures to rely on, and for a long time the group therapy model was one of the most widely used approaches to families. Even today, when therapists with little understanding of systems dynamics or family structure see families, they often treat the family as though it were a group of equals.

The communications model that emerged from Palo Alto in the 1950s had an enormous impact on the entire field of family therapy. Communications family therapy was no mere application of individual psychotherapy to families; it was a radically new conceptualization that altered the very nature of imagination. What was new was the focus on the process, the form of communication, rather than its content. The communications family therapists developed techniques of treatment, but their lasting contribution was a whole new way of thinking about families.

Communications theory is an intellectual tradition with its roots outside of psychiatry. It is closely tied to and derived from *general systems theory, cybernetics*, and *information theory*. Gregory Bateson, the leading figure in communications theory, was an anthropologist; the fact that his work led to family therapy was largely an artifact of the context in which he worked. His research was funded by psychiatry, and he chose schizophrenia as his field of study. At that time schizophrenic symptoms were thought to be crazy and senseless, just as neurotic symptoms had been before Freud. But just as Freud used psychoanalysis to unravel the meaning of neurotic symptoms, the Bateson group used communications analysis to demystify schizophrenic behavior. The fact that schizophrenia was neglected by mainstream psychiatry as a hopeless condition meant that there were fewer vested interests to oppose innovations, such as seeing whole families together.

Bateson's observations led to the conclusion that the interchange of messages between people defined their relationships and that these relationships were stabilized by homeostatic processes in families. His interest was scientific, not therapeutic, and his goal was to develop a general model of human behavior. When Jay Haley and Don Jackson began interviewing families, they were more interested in studying them than in treating them.

Gradually, however, they began to intervene in order to help these families overcome their problems. At first they used interpretations because they still believed that awareness would bring about change. But, finding that this didn't work, they developed new techniques to fit their new ways of thinking. Directives replaced interpretations as the major technique to change family systems by changing the way that family members communicate with one another.

The paradigms of communications theory were so well received that they were adopted by other schools of family therapy. Virtually every approach now treats communication as synonymous with behavior, and concepts like the *double-bind* and *family homeostasis* have been absorbed in the literature. In fact it might be said that communications family therapy died of success. Not only have many of its precepts been universally adopted, but, in addition, its proponents have branched off to form new schools, especially strategic, experiential, and structural approaches to family therapy.

SKETCHES OF LEADING FIGURES

Group therapy influenced the beginnings of family therapy in two ways. First, many of the early family therapists turned to the group therapy and group dynamics literature to guide their efforts at treating families. Second, many of the pioneers of family therapy were themselves products of group therapy training. By far the most influential of these pioneers was John Elderkin Bell.

Bell (1975) credits his start as a family therapist to a fortunate misunderstanding. When he was in London in 1951, Bell heard that Dr. John Bowlby of the Tavistock Clinic was experimenting with group therapy for families. This remark caught Bell's interest and stimulated him to try this approach as a means of dealing with behavior problems of children. It turned out that Bowlby had only interviewed one family as an adjunct to treating a troubled child; but Bell didn't learn this until years after. As Bell later put it, if so eminent an authority as John Bowlby was using family therapy, it must be a good idea.

When Bell started treating families he was encouraged by the success of his newly devised method. As he began to report on his work (Bell, 1961), he gained wide influence in the 1960s, and he is now recognized as one of the fathers of family therapy and one of its most thoughtful spokesman.

While none of the early pioneers of family group therapy are as well known as John E. Bell, their work had a direct impact on many of those who took up family therapy in the late 1950s and early 1960s, among them: Rudolph Dreikurs, Christian Midelfort, S.H. Foulkes, and Robin Skynner.

Rudolph Dreikurs was a student of Alfred Adler's who put Adler's ideas into practice in child guidance clinics in Chicago. Dreikurs translated Adler's ideas about the need to overcome *feelings of inferiority* by developing *social interest* in a variety of formats, including children's groups, community groups, parents' groups, and family therapy groups. His techniques with families combined emotional support and encouragement with interpretations and suggestions about modifying unhappy interactions. He encouraged families to discuss their mutual problems in an open, democratic spirit; and he urged them to institute regular "family councils," in order to carry the model of family group therapy into the family's daily life.

Christian Midelfort is another early figure in family therapy whose influence was largely restricted to his own place and time. He practiced at the Lutheran Hospital in LaCrosse, Wisconsin. Charged with responsibility for treating fairly seriously disturbed patients, Midelfort decided that the only way to achieve lasting results was to include the patients' families in treatment. Although he still considered the patient as the focus of treatment, Midelfort (1957) developed an array of family therapy techniques that anticipated many later developments.

S.H. Foulkes was an English psychoanalyst and one of the organizers of the group therapy movement in Great Britain. Although he began conducting conjoint family therapy interviews early in the 1940s, his work is little known to family therapists because his major interest and publications were in analytic group therapy. Among Foulkes' students was Robin Skynner, whose work overlaps the psychoanalytic (Chapter 5) and group approaches to families. More of a synthesizer than an innovator, Skynner has written a useful guide to analytic and group-oriented family therapy (Skynner, 1976). His orientation to families is revealed in the following remark: "The family, like the small group of strangers, is seen as possessing inherent potentials for constructive understanding and for facilitating growth and positive change, as well as for creating confusion and blocking development" (Skynner, 1976, p. 192).

Communications therapy was one of the earliest approaches to family therapy, and the history of this approach is inextricably intertwined with the history of the first decade of the family therapy movement (see Chapter 1). The leading characters in this history were the members of Bateson's schizophrenia project and the Mental Research Institute (MRI) in Palo Alto. Don Jackson and Jay Haley were the leaders who created and popularized the communications approach to treating families. Nothing in Jackson's traditional psychiatric background portends his radical departure from conventional psychotherapy. He graduated in 1943 from Stanford University School of Medicine where the major influences were Freudian and Sullivanian. He completed his residency training at Chestnut Lodge in Rockville, Maryland in 1949 and remained there as a member of the staff until 1951.

During this period he was also a candidate at the Washington-Baltimore Psychoanalytic Institute. In 1951 Jackson moved to Palo Alto, California, where he maintained a private practice and worked as Chief of the Psychiatric Department of the Palo Alto Medical Clinic. He also was a candidate at the San Francisco Psychoanalytic Institute until 1954, and was associated with the Department of Psychology at Stanford University from 1951 until 1960. He became a consultant to the Palo Alto Veterans Administration Hospital in 1951, which led to his association with the Bateson project.

Jackson established the Mental Research Institute in November 1958, and received his first grant in March 1959. The original staff consisted of Jackson, Jules Riskin, and Virginia Satir. They were joined later by Jay Haley, John Weakland, and Paul Watzlawick. Gregory Bateson served as a research associate and teacher.

When he died tragically in 1968 at the age of 48, Don Jackson left behind a legacy of seminal papers, the leading journal in the field, *Family Process*, which he cofounded with Nathan Ackerman, and a great sadness at the passing of such a vibrant and creative talent.

Jay Haley has always been somewhat of an outsider. He entered the field without clinical credentials, and first established his reputation as a commentator and critic. His initial impact came from his writing, in which he infused irony and sarcasm with incisive analysis of psychotherapy. In "The Art of Psychoanalysis" (reproduced in Haley, 1963), Haley redefined psychoanalysis, not as a search for insight, but as a game of "oneupmanship" (Haley, 1963, pp. 193–194):

> By placing the patient on a couch, the analyst gives the patient the feeling of having his feet up in the air and the knowledge that the analyst has both feet on the ground. Not only is the patient disconcerted by having to lie down while talking, but he finds himself literally below the analyst and so his one-down position is geographically emphasized. In addition, the analyst seats himself behind the couch where he can watch the patient but the patient cannot watch him. This gives the patient the kind of disconcerted feeling a person has when sparring with an opponent while blindfolded. Unable to see what response his ploys provoke, he is unsure when he is one-up and when one-down. Some patients try to solve this problem by saying something like, "I slept with my sister last night," and then whirling around to see how the analyst is responding. These "shocker" ploys usually fail in their effect. The analyst may twitch, but he has time to recover before the patient can whirl fully around and see him. Most analysts have developed ways of handling the whirling patient. As the patient turns, they are gazing off into space, or doodling with a pencil, or braiding belts, or staring at tropical fish. It is essential that the rare patient who gets an opportunity to observe the analyst see only an impassive demeanor.

In this same paper Haley (1963, p. 198) also tossed a few barbs at other popular forms of psychotherapy.

> There is, for example, the Rogerian system of ploys where the therapist merely repeats back what the patient says. This is an inevitably winning system. When the patient accuses the therapist of being no use to him, the therapist replies, "You feel I'm no use to you." The patient says, "That's right, you're not worth a damn." The therapist says, "You feel I'm not worth a damn." This ploy, even more than the orthodox silence ploy, eliminates any triumphant feeling in the patient and makes him feel a little silly after a while (a one-down feeling). Most orthodox analysts look upon the Rogerian ploys as not only weak but not quite respectable. They do not give the patient a fair chance.

Haley saw patients and families during the year he worked on the Bateson project, but retired from clinical practice in 1962 when the project disbanded. Since that time he's concentrated on studying families and teaching and supervising family therapy. His writing continues to be witty and critical, and his relationship to the rest of the field continues to be adversarial and iconoclastic.

Haley was studying for a master's degree in communication at Stanford University when he met Gregory Bateson, who hired him to work on the communications project. Haley began to interview schizophrenic patients in order to analyze the strange style of their communication. From these analyses, Haley, along with Bateson, Jackson, and Weakland, came up with the famous double-bind theory of schizophrenia, and only then actually began to see families in order to confirm their speculations.

As a therapist Haley was greatly influenced by Milton Erickson, with whom he began studying hypnosis in 1953. Then, after the Bateson project broke up in 1962, Haley worked in research at MRI until 1967 when he joined Minuchin at the Philadelphia Child Guidance Clinic. It was here that Haley became especially interested in training and supervision, areas in which he may have made his greatest contribution to the field of family therapy. At present Haley codirects the Family Therapy Institute of Washington, DC, with Cloe Madanes.

Bateson himself had a superbly analytic mind, nurtured from an early age in a variety of scientific disciplines, and his scientific background shaped the character of the group's approach to families. Under Bateson's influence, the orientation of the project was anthropological. Members of the group relied on naturalistic observation, rather than experimentation, to form their ideas. Their forte was generating hypotheses, not testing them. Even the famous double-bind concept was arrived at by deductive conjecture. Given the incongruous nature of schizophrenic communication, Bateson reasoned (Bateson, Jackson, Haley, and Weakland, 1963) it *must* have been learned in the family. Only later was this conclusion supported by observation.

The group didn't set out to develop a clinical approach: their goal was to observe, not to change families. In fact they stumbled onto family therapy more or less by accident. When Bateson developed the double-bind hypothesis in 1954 he had never seen a family. It wasn't until 1956 or 1957 that the group began seeing families. At first the group merely wanted to observe patterns of communication; only later were they moved to try to help the unhappy people they had been studying.

(Virginia Satir was another prominent member of the MRI group, but because her emphasis shifted to emotional experiencing, we will consider her in Chapter 6.)

THEORETICAL FORMULATIONS

Although he's better known for studying the psychology of individuals, Freud was also interested in interpersonal relationships, and many would consider his *Group Psychology and the Analysis of the Ego* (Freud, 1921) the first major text on the dynamic psychology of the group. According to Freud, the major requirement for transforming a collection of individuals into a group is the emergence of a leader. In addition to manifest tasks of organization and direction, the leader also serves as a parent figure on whom the members become more or less dependent. Members *identify* with the leader as a parent surrogate, and with other group members as siblings. *Transference* occurs in groups when members repeat unconscious attitudes formed in the process of growing up. Freud's concept of *resistance* in individual therapy also applies to groups, because group members, seeking to ward off anxiety, may oppose the progress of treatment with silence, hostility, refusing to attend sessions, or avoiding painful topics. Family groups resist treatment by scapegoating, superficial chatting, prolonged dependency on the therapist, refusal to follow therapeutic suggestions, and allowing difficult family members not to show up.

Like Freud, Wilfred Bion (1961) also attempted to develop a group psychology of the unconscious, and he described groups as functioning on *manifest* and *latent* levels. The group's official task is on the manifest level, but people also join groups to fulfill powerful, but unconscious, primal needs. At the latent level groups seek a leader who will permit them to gratify their needs for *dependence*, *pairing*, and *fight-flight*.

Freudian concepts, extrapolated from the individual to the group, remain part of group dynamics theory, but most of the working concepts focus less on individuals than on the interactions among them. Whole groups, including families, are usually defined by structure; subgroups, by function. Most of the time groups, including families, operate as subgroups.

The Family doesn't clean the house—Mom-and-the-kids do. The Family doesn't plan a move, Dad-and-Mom do.

According to Kurt Lewin's (1951) *field theory*, conflict is an inevitable feature of group life, as members vie with one another for adequate *life space*. Just as animals need their own territory, people seem to need their own "space" (or turf), and for this reason there is an inherent tension between the needs of the individual and those of the group. The amount of conflict generated by this tension depends upon the amount of restriction imposed by the group, compared with the amount of mutual support it gives in exchange. (People who give up a lot for their families expect to get back a lot in return.)

What distinguished Lewin's model of group tensions from earlier theories is that it was *ahistorical*. Instead of worrying about who did what to whom in the past, Lewin concentrated on what was going on in the *here-and-now*. This focus on *process* (how people talk), rather than *content* (what they talk about), is one of the keys to understanding the way a group (or family) functions.

Role theory, which influenced so many branches of psychology, also played a prominent place in theories of group functioning. Every position in a group structure has an associated role, which consists of expected and prohibited behavior for the occupant of that position. In family groups some roles are biologically determined, while others depend on the specific dynamics of the group. Sex roles; kinship roles of mother, father, son, and daughter; and age roles of infant, child, teenager, and adult, are obvious, but not necessarily more significant than such assigned roles as "the strong one," "the scapegoat," or "the baby."

The number and character of role conflicts provide a basis upon which to evaluate the functioning of social groups (Brown, 1965). In families, role conflicts can occur within or between roles; some are chronic, while others develop in the face of changing circumstances. *Intra-role* conflict exists when a single role calls for contradictory performances, such as when a child is expected to be both independent and obedient. *Inter-role* conflict exists when two or more roles are incompatible, as, for example, when a woman is expected to be strong as a mother but helpless as a wife. Notice that the notion of role conflict makes no reference to personalities. The problem isn't in the person but in the design of the system.

There can also be problems in how well roles and personalities fit each other. An introverted, narcissistic man may have trouble filling the role of a warm and loving father. Thus personality and role are not exclusive or independent; they're mutually determinative. Talcott Parsons (1950), speaking as an analytically oriented sociologist, emphasized the internalization of family roles as a determining influence on the formation of character. Over time roles tend to become stereotyped, and thus limit flexibility in individuals and in the group (Bales, 1970). Clinicians like Spiegel (1971) and Bell (1975) developed the therapeutic implications of role theory and applied them to the diagnosis and treatment of families. Spiegel made conflict and complementarity central to his conception of role theory; Bell emphasized the impact of role rigidity on family dysfunction.

Communications therapists adopted the *black box* concept from telecommunications and applied it to the individuals within the family. This model disregards the internal structure of individuals in order to concentrate on their input and output—that is, communication. It isn't that these clinicians denied the phenomena of mind—thinking and feeling—they just found it useful to ignore them. By limiting their focus to what goes on between, rather than within, family members, communications theorists qualify as "systems purists" (Beels and Ferber, 1969).

Communications theorists also disregarded the past, leaving speculation about the genesis of behavior to the psychoanalysts, while they searched for patterns with which to understand behavior in the present. They considered it unimportant to figure out what's cause and what's effect, preferring to use a model of circular causality in which chains of behavior are seen as effect-effect-effect.

Families were treated as error-controlled, goal-directed systems, and their interactions were analyzed using cybernetic theory, general systems theory, and games theory. For example, interactions can be described using a games analogy. Someone who doesn't know how to play chess could discover the rules by watching the game being played and noting the pattern of moves, and this is precisely the strategy used by communications theorists in their analyses of family communications. Beginning with schizophrenic families and branching out to a wide variety of families, these workers observed the patterns of communication to discover regularities, which acted as "rules" of family interactions (Jackson, 1965).

Human communication can be analyzed according to *syntax*, *semantics*, and *pragmatics* (Carnap, 1942; Morris, 1938). *Syntax* refers to the way words are put together to form phrases and sentences; it is the manner in which information is transmitted. Errors of *syntax* are particularly likely in the speech of persons who are learning a new language. This is the domain of the information theorist, who is concerned with encoding information; channels of communication; the capacity, variability, redundancy, and noise inherent in the communication; and the patterning of speech over time. In families this would relate to who speaks to whom, the percentage of speaking time for each member, the parsimony of speech, and the ratio of information to noise. Scheflen (1966) elaborated on channels of communication by including nonlanguage modalities: kinesic and postural, tactile, olfactory, territorial, and artifactual (dress, make-up, props). Thus *syntax* is concerned with the stylistic properties of language, not with its meaning. Meaning is the realm of *semantics*. In families, *semantics* refers to the clarity of language, the existence of private or shared communicational systems, and concordance versus confusion of communication. Finally there is the *pragmatics*, or behavioral effect, of communication. In order to evaluate the effects of communication, it's necessary to take into account nonverbal behavior and the context of communication, as well as the words used. The pragmatics of communication (Watzlawick, Beavin, and Jackson, 1967) is the primary concern of communications therapists, and is their basis for understanding behavior in any family system.

In *The Pragmatics of Human Communication*, Watzlawick, Beavin, and Jackson (1967) sought to develop a "calculus" of human communication, which they stated in a series of axioms about the interpersonal implications of communication. These axioms are an aspect of *metacommunication*, which means communicating about communication. The first of these axioms is that people are always communicating. Since all behavior is communicative, and one cannot *not* behave, then it follows that one cannot *not* communicate. Consider the following example.

> Mrs. Snead began the first family therapy session by saying, "I just don't know what to do with Roger anymore. He's not doing well in school, he doesn't help out around the house; all he wants to do is hang around with those awful friends of his. But the worst thing is that he refuses to communicate with us."
>
> At this point, the therapist turned to Roger and said, "Well, what do you have to say about all of this?" But Roger said nothing. Instead he continued to sit slouched in a chair at the far corner of the room, with an angry sullen look on his face.

The problem is not that Roger isn't communicating. In fact, he's communicating that he's angry, mistrustful, and that he refuses to negotiate. Communication may also take place when it isn't intentional, conscious, or successful—that is, in the absence of mutual understanding.

A second major proposition is that all messages have a *report* and a *command* function (Ruesch and Bateson, 1961). The report (or content) of a message conveys information, while the command is a statement about the definition of the relationship. Every time people speak, they're not only sending messages, but also defining relationships. The speaker's message conveys some content, and also how the speaker views him- or herself, and how he or she views the hearer. For example, the message, "Mommy, Sandy hit me," conveys information but also suggests a command—"Do something about it." Notice, however, that the implicit command is ambiguous. The reason for this is that the printed word omits nonverbal and contextual clues. This statement shrieked by a child in tears would have a different command value than if it were spoken by a giggling child. The command aspect of the communication would also be quite different if it were spoken by a small child about a babysitter than if it were said by an older sibling playing in the backyard.

The relationship between speakers is another factor that significantly affects how the command aspects of communication are responded to. For example, a therapist whose aim is to help patients express their feelings would be likely to respond to a husband who is crying by listening sympathetically and encouraging him to continue to express his thoughts and feelings. The man's wife, on the other hand, might well be threatened and upset by his display of "weakness," and try to "cheer him up" by telling him that the problem doesn't really exist or by suggesting ways for him to solve it. In this instance the therapist can listen to the man's feelings without hearing (or responding to) a command to "do something about them." The wife feels threatened and obligated by the inferred command, and so cannot simply listen.

The command aspect of communications functions to define relationships. "Mommy, Sandy hit me" suggests that the speaker accepts a one-down relationship with Sandy, but insists that mother will intercede to settle any problems. This defining is often obscured because it's usually not deliberate or done with full awareness, and, as we have seen, it depends upon how it's received. In healthy relationships this aspect recedes into the background. Conversely, problematic relationships are characterized by frequent struggles about the nature of the relationship: "Don't tell me what to do!"

In families, command messages are patterned as *rules* (Jackson, 1965). The regular patterning of interactions stabilizes relationships. These patterns, or rules, can be deduced from observed redundancies in interaction. Jackson used the term *family rules* as a description of regularity, not as a causal or determining concept. Nobody "lays down the rules." In fact, families are generally unaware of them.

The rules, or regularities, of family interaction operate to preserve family *homeostasis* (Jackson, 1965, 1967), an acceptable behavioral balance within the family. Homeostatic mechanisms bring families back to a previous balance in the face of any disruption, and thus serve to resist change. Jackson's notion of family homeostasis describes the conservative aspect of family systems and is similar to the general systems theory concept of *negative feedback*. Thus, according to a communications analysis, families operate as goal-directed, rule-governed systems.

Communications theorists found in *general systems theory* (von Bertalanffy, 1950) a number of ideas useful in explaining how families work. Some of these ideas have been described in Chapters 1 and 2; their application will be further considered in following sections of this chapter. At this time we would only like to point out that while the communications theorists (Watzlawick, Beavin, and Jackson, 1967) described families as *open systems* in their theoretical statements, they tended to treat them as *closed systems* in their clinical work. Thus they concentrated their therapeutic efforts on the nuclear family, with little or no consideration of inputs from the community or extended family.

Relationships between communicants are also described as being either *complementary* or *symmetrical. Complementary* relationships are ones in which one person is one-up, superior, or primary, while the other is one-down, inferior, or secondary. A common complementary pattern is where one person is assertive and the other submissive, with each mutually reinforcing and sustaining each other's position. It's important to understand that one-up and one-down are descriptive terms, not evaluative. Moreover, it's a mistake to assume that one person's position *causes* the other's, or that the one-down position is any weaker than the one-up. As Sartre (1964) pointed out, it is the masochist as well as the sadist who creates the possibility of a sado-masochistic relationship.

Symmetrical relationships are based on equality; the behavior of one person mirrors that of the other. Symmetrical relationships between husbands and wives, where both are free to pursue careers and share housekeeping and childrearing responsibilities, are often thought of as ideal by today's standards. However, from a communications analysis, there's no reason to assume that such a relationship would be any more stable or functional for the system than a traditional, complementary one.

Another aspect of communication is that it can be *punctuated* in various ways (Bateson and Jackson, 1964). An outside observer may hear a dialogue as an uninterrupted flow of communication, but each of the participants may believe that what he or she says is caused by what the other says. Thus punctuation organizes behavioral events and reflects the bias of the observer. Couples therapists are familiar with the impasse created by each spouse saying, "I only do X, because he (or she) does Y." A common example is the wife who says she only nags because her husband withdraws; while he says he only withdraws because she nags. Another example is the wife who says she'd be more in the mood for sex if her husband was more affectionate; to which he counters that he'd be more affectionate if she'd have sex more often.

As long as couples punctuate their interactions in this fashion, there is little likelihood of change. Each insists that the other causes the impasse and each waits for the other to change. The impasse is created by the universal tendency for people to punctuate a sequence of interactions so that it appears the other one has initiative, dominance, or dependency—in other words, power. Children illustrate this when they have a fight and run to a parent, both crying, "He started it!" Their mutual illusion is based on the mistaken notion that such sequences have a discrete beginning, and that one person's behavior is caused by another's in linear fashion.

Communications theory doesn't accept linear causality or look for underlying causes of behavior; instead, this model assumes circular causality and analyzes specific behaviors occurring at the present time. Considerations of underlying causality are treated as conceptual noise, with no practical therapeutic value. The behaviors that the communications theorist observes are patterns of communications linked together in additive chains of stimulus *and* response. This model of sequential causality enables therapists to treat behavioral chains as *feedback loops*. When the response to one family member's problematic behavior exacerbates the problem, that chain is seen to be a *positive feedback loop*. The advantage of this formulation is that it focuses on interactions that perpetuate problems, which can be changed, instead of inferring underlying causes, which aren't observable and often not subject to change.

NORMAL FAMILY DEVELOPMENT

Now that we have rich literatures on child development and the family life cycle, it doesn't seem particularly fruitful to turn to the group dynamics literature to help us understand normal family development. Nevertheless, in the early days of family therapy, many therapists borrowed concepts of group development and applied them to families. Among the most notorious of these was Talcott Parsons' idea (1950) that groups needed an *instrumental* leader and an *expressive* leader to look after the *social-emotional* needs of the group. Guess who was elected to which roles—and consider how that helped to legitimize an artificial and unfair division of labor.

A more useful discussion was found in William Schutz's (1958) discussion of three phases of group development: *inclusion*, *control*, and *affection*. Many other studies in the group dynamics literature called attention to the critical need for *cohesiveness* in any group that is to function cooperatively as a unit. One factor that helps determine cohesiveness is *need compatibility* (Shaw, 1981). If members of a group have compatible needs, they tend to function well together; if not, not. Likewise, compatible needs—compatible, not identical—make good marriages. This assumption has been supported by studies demonstrating that need compatibility predicts marital choice (Winch, 1955) and marital adjustment (Meyer and Pepper, 1977).

As "systems purists," communications family therapists treat behavior as ahistorical. Whether they're describing or treating family interactions, their attention is on the here-and-now, with very little interest in development. Normal families are described as functional systems, which like all living systems, depend upon two important processes (Maruyama, 1968). First, they must maintain constant integrity in the face of environmental vagaries. This is accomplished through *negative feedback*, which is often illustrated by the example of the thermostat on a home heating unit. When the heat drops below a set point, the thermostat activates the furnace, until the heat returns to the desired temperature.

No living system can survive without a regular pattern or structure. On the other hand, too rigid a structure leaves the system ill-equipped to adapt to changing circumstances. This is why normal families must also have mechanisms of *positive feedback*. Negative feedback minimizes change to maintain a steady state; positive feedback alters the system to accommodate to novel inputs. As children grow older, they change the nature of their input to the family system. The most obvious instance of this is adolescence, at which time children seek more involvement with peers and demand more freedom and independence. A family system limited to negative feedback can only resist such changes in order to maintain its inflexible structure. Normal families, on the other hand, also have positive feedback mechanisms and can respond to new information by modifying the structure of the system.

Normal families become periodically unbalanced (Hoffman, 1971); they do so to permit relationships to shift during transition points in the family life cycle. No family passes through these changes in a totally harmonious fashion; all experience stress, resist change, and develop vicious cycles. But normal families aren't trapped into perpetuating destructive patterns which can develop; they're able to engage in positive feedback mechanisms to modify themselves. Symptomatic families remain stuck, using a symptomatic member to avoid change; normal families are able to change and, thus, don't require any such sacrifice.

Concepts from general systems theory, such as positive feedback, have the virtues of wide applicability and theoretical elegance, but often seem esoteric and abstract. When we recognize that the channel for positive feedback is communication, it's possible to state the case more plainly. Healthy families are able to change because they communicate clearly and are flexible. When their children say they want to grow up, healthy parents listen.

Most of the research on family communication was done with disturbed families, and only recently have researchers begun to pay attention to healthy family communication and interaction. One attempt to correct this comes from an unlikely source. Researchers studying children at "high risk" for psychiatric disorders have begun to examine elements of family interaction and communication that provide high-risk children with resources that promote healthy functioning. These researchers have concluded that clear and logical communication on the part of the parents is most important in promoting healthy adjustment in children, providing them with a model for developing cognitive capacities of attending, focusing, remaining task-oriented, and communicating ideas and feelings clearly and directly (Wynne, Jones, and Al-Khayyal, 1982). Lyman Wynne and his colleagues have found that mothers' healthy communication predicted successful school adjustment. The same was true for fathers' communication, but the effect was less powerful. When parents communicate clearly in a focused, well-structured, flexible manner, their children are regarded as competent academically and socially by their teachers and peers.

DEVELOPMENT OF BEHAVIOR DISORDERS

From a group theory perspective, symptoms were considered products of disturbed and disturbing group processes. But groups weren't thought to *cause* disturbance in their members; rather, the behavior of the members was part of the disturbance of the group. Thus group researchers and therapists rejected linear causality in favor of a form of circular causality that they called "group dynamics." John Bell (1961, p. 48) expresses this point of view by contrasting his circular, group view with the linear, psychoanalytic view that parents cause problems in their children.

> Because psychoanalysis has emphasized the importance of early childhood and its genetic processes in personality formation, there has grown up a tendency to ask about the nature of the parent in relation to the child, to single out the more significant influences of the parent on the child that occur at particular stages of child development, and to evaluate the parents in terms of certain value systems that have been implicit in or the product of such conceptions as the oral and anal phases of development or the Oedipus complex. Thus the evaluation is made from the standpoint of the child, as though the interpreter were looking at the parents through the child's eyes.
>
> In family group therapy it is not possible to empathize with a child to the extent of evaluating parents only from his perspective. To do so would lead to thinking of the parent primarily in terms of his contribution to the child's pathology. It is not hard to see how parents would be offended at being reminded that the sins of the fathers are visited upon the children. In family therapy we have to think, also, that the sins of the children are visited upon the parents.

Family group therapists are less concerned with the origins of psychopathology than with the conditions that support and maintain it. These include stereotyped roles, breakdowns in communication, and blocked channels for giving and receiving support.

Rigidity of roles forces group interactions to occur in a narrow, stereotyped range. When the number of options are reduced for individuals, their flexibility as a group is constrained. Groups stuck with inflexible roles and unvarying structures tend to malfunction when called upon to handle changed circumstances. Moreover, if flexibility is threatening, such groups don't risk communicating about unmet needs; the result is often frustration and sometimes symptomatic disturbance in one of the group's members. If the needs that generate acute disturbance continue to go unmet, the symptoms themselves may be perpetuated as a role, and the group organizes itself around a "sick" member.

Communications theorists developed their conception of behavior disorder by observing patterns of communication in schizophrenic families. In earlier, monadic views the peculiarities of schizophrenic speech were believed to be the result of the patient's thought disorder, not the family's pathological communication (Bleuler, 1950). Later this viewpoint was modified by interpersonal theories of psychopathology, which emphasized the effect of disordered relationships on disordered speech. Sullivan (1944), for example, wrote, "The schizophrenic's speech shows characteristic peculiarities because of recurrent severe disturbances in his relationships with other people and the result is a confusion of the critical faculties concerning the structure of spoken and written language." In Sullivan's *interpersonal theory of psychiatry*, schizophrenic disturbance was no longer considered to be the product of one person's pathology, but was viewed as the result of pathological relationships. Nevertheless, the disturbance was still located in the individual. The relationships may be disturbing, but it was the patient who is disturbed.

The Bateson group carried this line of reasoning a step further. According to them, schizophrenic disturbance is a disturbance of the entire family. Symptoms may be observable in only one member, but they are a function of the whole family system. Moreover, symptoms are seen as communicated messages. At one level they are statements made by the person with the symptoms; at another level, they are statements made by the system.

According to communications family therapists, the essential function of symptoms is to maintain the homeostatic equilibrium of family systems. (As we have seen, the notion that symptoms are functional—implying that families *need* their problems—was to become controversial.) Pathological families were considered to be enmeshed in dysfunctional, but very strong, homeostatic patterns of communication (Jackson and Weakland, 1961). Their interactions may seem odd, and they may be unsatisfying, yet they are powerfully self-reinforcing. These families cling to their rigid and inflexible structures and respond to signs of change as negative feedback. That is, change is treated not as an opportunity for growth but as a threat and a signal to change back. Changes that threaten stability are labeled as "sick," as the following example illustrates.

> Tommy was a quiet, solitary boy, the only child of East European immigrant parents. The parents left their small farming community and came to the United States, where they both found factory work in a large

city in the Northeast. Although they were now safe from religious persecution and their standard of living improved, the couple felt alien and out of sympathy with their new neighbors. They kept to themselves and took pleasure in raising Tommy.

Tommy was a frail child with a number of peculiar mannerisms, but to his parents he was perfect. Then he started school. He began to make friends with other children, and, eager to be accepted, he picked up a number of American habits. He chewed bubble gum, watched television cartoons, and rode his bicycle whenever he had the chance. His parents were annoyed by the gum chewing and by Tommy's fondness for television, but they were genuinely distressed by his eagerness to play with his friends. They began to feel that he was rejecting their values, and that "something must be wrong with him." By the time they called the child guidance clinic, they were convinced that Tommy was disturbed, and they asked for help to "make Tommy normal again."

In their theoretical papers, communications theorists maintained the position that pathology inheres in the system as a whole (Hoffman, 1971; Jackson, 1967; Watzlawick, Beavin, and Jackson, 1967). The *identified patient* was considered a role with complementary counterroles all of which contribute to the maintenance of the system. The identified patient may be the victim, but in this framework "victim" and "victimizer" are seen as mutually determined roles—neither is good or bad, and neither causes the other. However, although this circular causality was a consistent feature of their theorizing, communications therapists often lapsed into linear causality in their research on psychopathology.

The foundations for a family theory of the etiology of schizophrenia, focusing on disturbed patterns of communication, were laid down by Gregory Bateson (Bateson, Jackson, Haley, and Weakland, 1956), Theodore Lidz (Lidz, Cornelison, Terry, and Fleck, 1958), and Lyman Wynne (Wynne, Ryckoff, Day, and Hirsch, 1958). All of these researchers believed in circular causality, but their observations emphasized the pathological effect of parents' irrationality on their offspring, suggesting that the disordered thinking observed in the schizophrenic offspring was caused by their parents.

Lyman Wynne's concept of *communication deviance* reflects cognitive and attentional deficits as well as affective and relational deficits. He found that the severity of parental psychopathology was correlated with communication deviance and with the severity of psychiatric disorder in their late-adolescent and young-adult offspring (Wynne, Singer, Bartko, and Toohey, 1977). Communication in such families isn't focused, and it includes frequent nihilistic, derogatory, disparaging, and critical remarks.

Despite the enthusiastic response to the idea that schizophrenia might be caused by disordered communication in the family, the fact is, it isn't. Communication deviance isn't found in all schizophrenic families, nor is it limited to families so diagnosed. Wynne's view (1968, 1970) is that communications patterns can be regarded as building upon attention-response deficits which probably have an innate, genetically determined component.

It's difficult to judge a single communication as normal or pathological. Instead the judgment must be made on a series or sequence of communications. One can look at syntax and semantics, that is the content of speech, for clarity or confusion. This approach is exemplified by Lyman Wynne's studies in which he found that schizophrenics' speech could be differentiated from that of normals or delinquents (Wynne and Singer, 1963). Alternatively one can look at the pragmatics of communication, as did the members of the Palo Alto group. Here the emphasis wasn't on clarity or content, but on the *metacommunication* or command aspects of language.

Symptoms were seen as messages in response to persistent communicational quandaries. The nonverbal message of a symptom is: "It is not I who does not (or does) want to do this, it is something outside my control—my nerves, my illness, my anxiety, my bad eyes, alcohol, my upbringing, the Communists, or my wife" (Watzlawick, Beavin, and Jackson, 1967, p. 80). As the group became more sophisticated, they tried to get past blaming parents for victimizing their children. Symptoms were no longer considered to be *caused* by communication problems in the family; they were seen as embedded in a pathological context, within which they may be the only possible reaction. Among the forms of pathological communication identified by the Palo Alto group were: denying that one is communicating, disqualifying the other person's message, confusing levels of communication, discrepant punctuation of communication sequences, symmetrical escalation to competitiveness, rigid complementarity, and paradoxical communication.

The most pervasive feature of pathological family communications is the use of *paradox*. A paradox is a contradiction that follows correct deduction from logical premises. In family communications, paradoxes usually take the form of *paradoxical injunctions*. A frequent example of paradoxical injunction is to demand some behavior which by its very nature can only be done spontaneously—"Be spontaneous!" "You should have more self-confidence." "Tell me you love me." A person exposed to such paradoxical injunctions is caught in an untenable position. To comply—to act spontaneous or self-confident—means to be self-consciously deliberate or eager to please. The only way to escape the dilemma is to step outside the context and comment on it, but such metacommunication rarely occurs in families. It's difficult to communicate about communication.

Paradoxical communications are a frequent feature of everyday life. They are relatively harmless in small doses, but when they take the form of double-binds the consequences are malignant. In a double-bind the two contradictory messages are on different levels of abstraction, and there is an implicit injunction against commenting on the discrepancy. A common example of a double-bind is the wife who denounces her husband for not showing feelings but then attacks him when he does.

Continual exposure to paradoxical communication is like the dilemma of a dreamer caught in a nightmare. Nothing the dreamer tries to do in the dream works. The only solution is to step outside the context by waking up. Unfortunately, for people who live in a nightmare, it isn't easy to wake up.

GOALS OF THERAPY

The goal of treating family groups was the same as treating stranger groups: promoting individuation of group members and improving their relationships. Individual growth is promoted when unmet needs are verbalized and understood, and when overly confining roles are explored and expanded. When family members are released from their inhibitions, it was assumed that they would develop greater family cohesiveness. Notice the difference in emphasis between this—considering families as groups of individuals, each of whom must be helped to develop—and the systemic view of the family as a unit. Treating families as though they were groups, like other groups, failed to appreciate the need for hierarchy and structure.

In practice, however, sophisticated clinicians like John Bell moved from the model of the family as group in the direction of more systemic goals. Bell (1975) believed that treatment should lead to families resolving or learning to cope with their presenting symptoms; showing increased cooperation, independence, and humor; interactions becoming freer and more open; all family members experiencing greater security; and there being greater flexibility in family roles. Again, although these sound like worthy goals, notice that it is a way of thinking of the family as though it were a collection of individual personalities, rather than a unit, linked together in complex ways.

Improved communication was seen as the primary way to meet the goal of improved group functioning. The aims of this approach reflect the fairly simple view of families and their problems that was prevalent among clinical practitioners before they learned to think systemically. While Bateson and his colleagues were laboring with their complex systems analyses, the average therapist still thought that the way to help troubled families was simply to have them sit down and talk to one another. In fact, as most families begin to converse, they have enough communication problems to keep therapists busy for a long time correcting their "mistakes," without getting to the individual and systems dynamics that generate them.

The goal of communications family therapy was to take "deliberate action to alter poorly functioning patterns of interaction. . ." (Watzlawick,

Beavin, and Jackson, 1967, p. 145). Because "patterns of interaction" are synonymous with communication, this meant changing patterns of communication. In the early days of communications family therapy, especially in Virginia Satir's work, this translated into a general goal of improving communication in the family. Later the goal was narrowed to altering those specific patterns of communication that maintained the symptom. By 1974 Weakland wrote that the goal of therapy was resolving symptoms, not reorganizing families: "We see the resolution of problems as primarily requiring a substitution of behavior patterns so as to interrupt the vicious, positive feedback circles" (Weakland, Fisch, Watzlawick, and Bodin, 1974, p. 149).

In this model therapists identified symptoms as communicative messages and then looked for behavioral sequences that were maintaining the problems. Once this antecedent behavior was discovered, the goal of interventions was to substitute behaviors that weren't destructive—that is, that didn't support the symptoms. In communications theory terms, this amounts to interrupting positive feedback loops.

The goal of the communications therapist is, like that of the behavior therapist, to interdict behaviors that stimulated and reinforced symptoms. These two models also share the assumption that once pathological behavior is blocked, it will be replaced by constructive alternatives, instead of other symptoms. The limitation of the behavioral model is that it treats the symptomatic person as the problem, and conceives of the symptom as a response rather than as both a response and a stimulus in a chain of interaction. The limitation of the communications model is that it isolates the sequence of behavior that maintains the symptoms, and focuses on two-person interactions without considering triangles or other structural problems. If, for example, a child is fearful because her overinvolved father yells at her, and her father yells at her because his wife isn't emotionally involved, then changing the father's behavior might result in a different form of a symptomatic behavior in the child, unless the relationship with the wife is addressed.

CONDITIONS FOR BEHAVIOR CHANGE

As we've already indicated, group family therapists thought the way to bring about change was to help family members open up and talk to each other. The therapist encourages them to talk openly, supports those who seem reticent, and then critiques the process of their interaction. It is the power of the therapist's support that often helps family members open up where they have once held back, and this, in turn, often shows them in a new light, which enables others in the family to relate to them in new ways. For example, children who aren't accustomed to being listened to by grown-ups, tend to make themselves "heard" by disruptive behavior. But if the therapist demonstrates a willingness to listen, the children may learn to express their feelings in words rather than in actions. As they begin to interact with someone who takes them seriously, they may suddenly "grow up."

Group-oriented therapists promote communication by concentrating on *process* rather than *content* (Bion, 1961; Yalom, 1985; Bell, 1975). This is an important point, and one easy to lose sight of. The minute a therapist gets caught up in the details of a family's problems or thinks about solving them, he or she may lose the opportunity to discover the process of what family members are doing that prevents them from working out their own solutions.

One of the ways therapists influence the process of family dialogue is to model listening. As the family members talk, the therapist listens intently, demonstrating to the speaker what it feels like to be heard and understood, and to other family members how not to interrupt, argue, or blame. After expression comes analysis. Once members of the family have a chance to express their feelings—and to be listened to—the family group therapist begins to explore why those feelings are present, and why they were held back. The assumption is that what families can understand they can change.

If behavior is communication, then the way to change behavior is to change communication. According to the communications theorists, all events and actions have communicative properties: Symptoms can be considered as covert messages, commenting upon relationships (Jackson, 1961). Even a headache that develops from prolonged tension in the occipital muscles is a message, since it is a report on how the person feels and also a command to be responded to. If a symptom is seen as a covert message, then by implication making the message overt eliminates the need for the symptom. Therefore one of the important ways to change behavior is to bring hidden messages out into the open.

As we pointed out above, an essential ingredient of the double-bind is that it is impossible to escape or look at the binding situation from the outside. But no change can be generated from within; it can only come from outside the pattern. So, according to communications theorists (Watzlawick, Beavin, and Jackson, 1967), the paradigm for psychotherapy is an intervention from the outside to resolve relational dilemmas. The therapist is an outsider who supplies what the relationship cannot, a change in the rules.

From the outside position the therapist can either point out problematic sequences or simply manipulate them to effect therapeutic change. The first strategy relies on the power of insight and depends upon cooperation and willingness to change, but the second does not; it's an attempt to beat families at their own games, with or without their cooperation.

Included in the second strategy are many of the most clever and interesting tactics of communications therapy, and much more is written about these than about simple interpretation. Nevertheless, in the early days of family therapy, therapists relied more on the pointing out of communicational problems than on any other technique.

The first strategy, simply pointing out communicational problems, was represented in Virginia Satir's work and was widely practiced by those who were new to family therapy. The second, less direct, approach was always more characteristic of Haley and Jackson and eventually it became the predominant strategy. By the time they wrote *Pragmatics of Human Communication*, Watzlawick, Beavin, and Jackson (1967, pp. 236–237) believed that

> Therapeutic communication, then, must necessarily transcend such counsel as is customarily but ineffectually given by the protagonists themselves, as well as their friends and relatives, [because] bona fide patients—by which we simply mean persons who are not deliberately simulating—usually have tried and failed in all kinds of self-discipline and exercises in will power long before they revealed their distress to others and were told to "pull themselves together." It is in the essence of a symptom that it is something unwilled and therefore autonomous.

Therefore they recommended interventions to *make* people behave in ways that would produce change. These manipulative strategies formed the basis of strategic family therapy (Chapter 9), which is an offshoot of communications theory.

Jackson and Haley's early work with families was influenced by the hypnotherapy they learned from Milton Erickson. The hypnotherapist works by giving explicit instructions whose purpose is often obscure. However, before patients will follow directions the therapist must gain control of the relationship. Haley was especially concerned with power and control in relationships. According to him (1963), everyday relationships are dominated by a struggle to achieve control. The same is true in therapeutic relationships.

The first task is to force the patient to concede that he or she is relating to the therapist. But this isn't always easy. Patients insist that their symptoms are not things they do, but things that happen to them. They say, "I have a handwashing compulsion," not "I compulsively wash my hands." Although symptoms affect relationships, they usually do so outside of awareness—otherwise the symptoms wouldn't "work"; they would be recognized as manipulative ploys and thereby lose their power. A wife's handwashing compulsion may be a rebellion against a tyrannical husband, but it only works as long as it is seen as involuntary.

Jackson sometimes began by giving patients advice about their symptoms. He did so to point up the problem area, just as interpretation would do; but at the same time his comments forced an intellectual understanding into action and made the patient focus on the relationship with the therapist—regardless of whether the patient accepted or rejected the advice. Haley (1961) recommended asking certain kinds of patients to do something in order to provoke a rebellious response, which served to make them concede that they were relating to the therapist. He mentions, as an example, directing a schizophrenic patient to hear voices. If the patient hears voices, then he is complying with the therapist's request; if he doesn't hear voices, then he can no longer claim to be crazy.

Once they established a measure of control of the therapeutic relationship, communications theorists used paradox to break the "games without end" that their patients were caught up in. Haley argued that therapeutic paradoxes—used wittingly or unwittingly—underlie most successful psychotherapy. In "The Art of Psychoanalysis," Haley (1963) took the position that psychoanalysis worked, not by discovering profound truths locked in the unconscious, but by ingeniously creating therapeutic paradoxes from which patients could only escape by giving up their symptoms.

Haley's (1961) direction to hear voices illustrates the technique of *prescribing the symptom*. By instructing the patient to enact a symptomatic behavior the therapist is demanding that something "involuntary" be done voluntarily. This is a paradoxical injunction which forces one of two changes. Either the patient performs the symptom and thus admits that it isn't involuntary, or the patient gives up the symptom. Prescribing the symptom is a form of what the communications theorists called *therapeutic double-binds* (Jackson, 1961). The same technique that drives people crazy is used to drive them sane.

Actually "therapeutic double-bind" is somewhat loose usage because it doesn't necessarily involve two levels of message, one of which denies the other. To illustrate what he meant by a therapeutic double-bind, Jackson (1961) cited the following case report.

> The patient was a young wife with a martyr complex, who felt that despite her best efforts to please her husband he just would not be satisfied. Jackson sensed that she was probably just "acting nice" in order to cover her intense, but unacceptable, rage at her husband. But the patient bridled when he even suggested that she might be "dissatisfied." In the face of this resistance, Jackson suggested that since her marriage was so important and since her husband's mood had such a profound effect on her, that she should learn to be really pleasing.
>
> By accepting the therapist's suggestion, the patient was admitting that she wasn't really pleasing. Moreover, she was forced to change.

In the above example, the patient was directed to change by doing more of the same. The object was to force the patient to step outside the frame set by her dilemma, with or without her awareness. In order to succeed, therapeutic double-binds, or paradoxical injunctions, must be so cleverly designed as to leave no loopholes through which a patient can escape.

According to Jackson's notion of family homeostasis, family systems regulate themselves by using symptoms as negative feedback to maintain their equilibrium. In this way symptomatic families become caught in an increasingly inflexible set of patterns. The task of therapy is to loosen them up by introducing positive feedback to break up stability and equilibrium. The goal is to change the family system so that deviance is no longer necessary to preserve homeostasis. Timing is considered to be an important factor in how the family will respond to attempts to change them. At a period of steady-state equilibrium, families will resist change; at times of crisis, they are more likely to accept change.

The tactics of change employed by the communication therapists focused on altering discrete sequences of interaction that perpetuate symptomatic behavior. Despite their claims to include triadic sequences in their analyses (Sluzki, 1978), most of their interventions were limited to dyadic interactions.

TECHNIQUES

The techniques of family group therapy were similar to those of analytic and supportive group therapy. The role of the therapist was that of a *process leader*. The model of the family was a democratic group, and the therapist related to the family members democratically, just as the members are expected to do with each other. The therapist saw all of them as people with something to say, often in need of help saying it, and the therapist encouraged everyone in the family to open up and express their points of view. There was little concern with structure and few attempts to reinforce the parents' hierarchical position. If anything, there was a tendency to give extra support for children and encourage them to assume a more equal role in family interactions.

John Bell's original approach (1961) was orchestrated in a series of stages. First was a *child-centered phase*, in which children were helped to speak up and express their wishes and concerns. Bell was so anxious to help children participate that he held advanced meetings with parents to encourage them not only to listen but also to go along with some of the children's requests for changes in family rules as a means of gaining their trust and cooperation in the process of negotiating to solve family problems.

After the children spoke up and were rewarded with some additional privileges, then it was the parents' turn. In the *parent-centered stage*, parents usually began by complaining about their children's behavior. During this phase, Bell was careful to soften the harshest of parental criticisms and to focus on problem-solving. In the final, or *family-centered*, stage, the group family therapist equalized support for the entire family while they continued to improve their communication and work out solutions to their problems. The following vignette illustrates Bell's (1975, p. 136) directive style of intervening.

> After remaining silent for a few sessions, one father came in with a great tirade against his son, daughter, and wife. I noticed how each individual in his own way, within a few minutes, was withdrawing from the conference. Then I said, "Now I think we should hear what Jim has to say about this, and Nancy should have her say, and perhaps we should also hear what your wife feels about it." This restored family participation without closing out the father.

It also kept the therapist in charge, preventing him from seeing how the family handled their own confrontations, and from possibly being in a position to point out problems in their way of handling things.

Anything that interfered with balanced self-expression was considered resistance and dealt with accordingly. Often this meant confronting non-verbal signs of unexpressed feeling. "Mr. Brown, you've been silent, but I wonder if your drumming your fingers is trying to tell us something."

Bell (1961) described four varieties of process interpretations: *Reflective interpretations* describe what's going on at the moment—"I notice that when your wife says something critical, you just hang your head as if to say 'Poor me.' " *Connective interpretations* point out unrecognized links between different actions among family members—"Have you noticed that Jenny starts to misbehave the minute you two start to argue?" *Reconstructive interpretations* explain how events in the family's history provide the context for some current experience. *Normative interpretations* are remarks designed to support or challenge a family member by comparing that person to what most people do—"Big deal, most teenagers are sassy with their parents. It's part of growing up."

In the early days of family therapy, family group therapy was often the model chosen by beginners. It required little familiarity with systems dynamics, and, back then, although few clinicians had much experience with families, most had some training in group therapy. Simply helping families talk over their problems often does help them get through a crisis. But if this approach is going to work, it's going to do so quickly.

Three specialized applications of group methods to family treatment were *multiple family group therapy*, *multiple impact therapy*, and *network therapy*.

Peter Laqueur began *multiple family group therapy*, in 1950, at Creedmore State Hospital in New York, and he refined this approach as Director of Family Therapy at Vermont State Hospital (Laqueur, 1966, 1972a, 1972b, 1976). Multiple family group therapy involved the treatment of four to six families together for weekly sessions of ninety minutes. Laqueur and his cotherapists conducted multiple family groups like traditional therapy groups with the addition of encounter group and psychodrama techniques. Structured exercises were used to increase the level of interaction and intensity of feeling; families were used as "cotherapists" to help confront members of other families from a more personal position than therapists could take.

Although multiple family therapy lost its most creative force with Peter Laqueur's untimely death, it is still occasionally used, especially in hospital settings, both inpatient (McFarlane, 1982) and outpatient (Gritzer and Okum, 1983).

Robert MacGregor and his colleagues at the University of Texas Medical Branch in Galveston developed *multiple impact therapy* as a way to have maximum impact on families with a disturbed adolescent in crisis (MacGregor, Richie, Serrano, Schuster, McDonald, and Goolishian 1964; MacGregor, 1967, 1972). These families came from all over Texas to Galveston to spend several days in intense therapy with a large team of professionals. Team members met with several combinations of family members and then assembled in a large group to review findings and make recommendations. Although multiple impact therapy is no longer practiced, its intense but infrequent meetings were a powerful stimulus for change and prefigured later developments in experiential therapy (Chapter 6) and the Milan model (Chapter 9).

Network therapy was an approach developed by Ross Speck and Carolyn Attneave for assisting families in crisis by assembling their entire social network—family, friends, neighbors—in gatherings of as many as fifty people. Teams of therapists were used to work with these large groups, and their emphasis was on breaking up destructive patterns of relationship and mobilizing support for new options (Speck and Attneave, 1973; Ruevini, 1975).

Like multiple family group therapy, network therapy is conducted with a variety of group techniques. According to Speck and Attneave (1973), networking has six phases:

1. *Retribalization*, which involves reacquaintance and awareness of the presenting problems. It begins with the first telephone call inviting people to assemble and lasts throughout the meetings.

2. *Polarization*, in which conflicting positions, primarily generational conflicts, are activated.

3. *Mobilization*, during which tasks are assigned and active efforts to help are inaugurated by concerned group members.

4. *Depression*, which regularly seems to follow initial enthusiasm.

5. *Breakthrough*, when the efforts begun during mobilization start to pay off.

6. *Exhaustion and elation*, which occurs following each meeting as members experience hope and relief. It also occurs following a successful series of network meetings.

Therapeutic teams meet with networks in meetings lasting from two to four hours; groups typically meet three to six times. Encounter group techniques are used to alleviate defensiveness and foster a climate of warm involvement. After five or ten minutes of shaking hands, jumping up and down, shouting, huddling together, and swaying back and forth, the group experiences a release of tension and a sense of cohesiveness.

The polarization phase begins when the leader identifies and activates conflicting points of view in the network. These may be dramatized by arranging people in concentric circles and inviting them to confront their differences. Under the guidance of the leaders, confrontation is moved toward compromise and synthesis. During the mobilization phase, tasks are presented, and subgroups of involved and active members are asked to develop plans for solving concrete problems. If the identified patient needs a job, a committee might be formed to help; if young parents are stuck at home fighting over who's going to take care of the baby, a group might be asked to develop babysitting resources and allow the couple to get out together.

After the initial enthusiasm wears off, network groups often fall into exhaustion and despair as members begin to realize just how entrenched certain problems are and how difficult it is to resolve them. Uri Ruevini (1975) described one case in which a period of depression set in, and the problem family felt isolated and abandoned by the network. Ruevini broke through this impasse by prescribing a cathartic encounter group exercise, "the death ceremony." Family members were asked to close their eyes and imagine themselves dead. The rest of the network members were asked to share their own feelings about the members of the family: their strengths, their weaknesses, and what each of them meant to their family and friends. This dramatic device produced an outpouring of feeling and support which roused the network out of depression.

Speck and Attneave (1973) described breaking the network into problem-solving subgroups, using action instead of affect to move beyond despair. In one case they assigned a group of friends to watch over an adolescent patient who was abusing drugs and another group to arrange for him to move out of his parents' house. Breakthrough is achieved when the network's energies are unleashed and directed toward active resolution of problems. Network sessions often produce what Speck and Attneave called the "network effect"—a feeling of euphoric connectedness and the satisfaction of solving problems once thought to be overwhelming. Once a network has been activated, there's always someone to call when the need arises.

In communications family therapy, technique followed theory more so than in almost any other treatment approach. These therapists wrote a great deal about the theory of human communications before they began applying their ideas to treatment, and even after they began to describe their work with families, most of their publications had a distinctly theoretical flavor. As a result, communications family therapists appear to have had an intellectual stance and more emotional distance from the families they worked with than other early family therapists. Communications therapy seems to have been done *to* families, more than *with* them.

Formal assessment was typically not used by communications therapists, although Watzlawick (1966) did introduce a *structured family interview*. In this procedure, families were given five tasks to complete, including:

1. Deciding their main problem
2. Planning a family outing
3. The parents discussing how they met
4. Discussing the meaning of a proverb
5. Identifying faults and placing the blame on the correct person

While the family worked on these tasks, the therapist, watching behind a one-way mirror, observed the family's patterns of communication, methods of decision making, and scapegoating. Although it was useful for research, the structured family interview never gained wide acceptance as a clinical tool.

Most of the actual techniques of communications family therapy consisted of teaching rules of clear communication, analyzing and interpreting communicational patterns, and manipulating interactions through a variety of strategic maneuvers. The progression of these three strategies from more straightforward to more strategic reflected the growing awareness of how families resist change.

In their early work (Jackson and Weakland, 1961), communications therapists opened by indicating their belief that the whole family was involved in the presenting problem. Then they explained that all families develop habitual patterns of communication, including some that are problematical. This attempt to convert families from seeing the identified patient as the problem to accepting mutual responsibility underestimated the family's resistance to change. Later these therapists were more likely to begin by asking for and accepting a family's own definition of their problems (Haley, 1976).

After the therapists made their opening remarks they asked the family members, usually one at a time, to discuss their problems. While they did so the therapist listened, but concentrated on the process of communication, rather than the content. When someone in the family spoke in a confused or confusing way, the therapist would point this out and insist that the family members follow certain rules of clear communication. Satir (1964) was the most straightforward teacher. When someone said something that was unclear, she would question and clarify the message, and as she did so she impressed on the family some basic guidelines for clear speaking.

One rule is that people should always speak in the first person singular when saying what they think or feel. For example:

HUSBAND: We always liked Donna's boyfriends.

THERAPIST: I'd like you to speak for yourself; later your wife can say what she thinks.

HUSBAND: Yes, but we've always agreed on these things.

THERAPIST: Perhaps, but you are the expert on how you think and feel. Speak for yourself, and let her speak for herself.

A similar rule is that people should make personal statements ("I-statements") about personal matters. Opinions and value judgments must be understood as that, not passed off as facts or general principles. Owning opinions, as such, is a necessary step to discussing them in a way that permits legitimate differences of opinion, much less the possibility of changing opinions.

WIFE: People shouldn't want to do things without their children.

THERAPIST: So you like to bring the kids along when you and your husband go out.

WIFE: Well yes, doesn't everybody?

HUSBAND: I don't. I'd like to go out, just the two of us, once in a while.

Another rule is that people should speak directly to, not about, each other. This avoids ignoring or disqualifying family members and prevents the establishment of destructive coalitions. For example:

TEENAGER: (To therapist) My mother always has to be right. Isn't that so, Dad?

THERAPIST: Would you say that to her.

TEENAGER: I have told her, but she doesn't listen.

THERAPIST: Tell her again.

TEENAGER: (To therapist) Oh, okay. (To mother) Sometimes I get the feeling . . . (Shifts back to therapist) Oh, what's the use!

THERAPIST: I can see how hard it is, and I guess you've kind of decided that it's no use trying to talk to your mom if she isn't going to listen. But in here, I hope we can all learn to speak more directly to each other, so that no one will give up on having their say.

As this exchange illustrates, it's often quite difficult to teach people to communicate clearly just by telling them how to. It seemed like a good idea, but it didn't work very well. The reason a directive approach to family therapy persists at all is that, with enough insisting, most people will follow therapeutic directions, at least for the moment. However, in the face of longstanding habits resistant to change, the new behavior often lasts only as long as the therapist is there to insist.

In the early days of communications family therapy, Virginia Satir was probably the most transparent and directive therapist, and Jay Haley was the least; Don Jackson occupied a position somewhere in between.

When he began treating families of schizophrenics, Jackson thought he needed to protect patients from their families (Jackson and Weakland, 1961) but came to realize that parents and children were all bound together in mutually destructive ways. Even now those who are new to family therapy, especially if they themselves haven't yet become parents, tend to identify with the children and see the parents as the bad guys. Not only is this wrong, as Jackson himself later realized, it alienates parents and drives them out of treatment. Young therapists often begin "knowing" that parents are responsible for most of their children's problems. Only later, when these therapists become parents themselves, do they achieve a more balanced perspective—family problems are all the children's fault.

Jackson emphasized the need for structure and management in family therapy sessions. He began first sessions by saying, "We are here to work together on better understanding one another so that you all can get more out of your family life" (Jackson and Weakland, 1961, p. 37). Not only does this remark structure the meeting, it also conveys the idea that all members of the family are to become the focus of discussion. Furthermore it reveals the therapist's goal and may, therefore, precipitate a struggle with parents who have generally come only to help the patient and who may resent the implication that they are part of the problem. Thus we see that Jackson was an active therapist who set the rules right at the outset and explained fairly openly what he was doing in order to fight resistance, scapegoating, and obfuscation. His style was to anticipate and disarm resistance openly. Today most family therapists find it more effective to be subtler, meeting the families' resistance not with psychological karate but with jujitsu—using their own momentum for leverage, instead of opposing them head on.

Jackson may have found it so difficult to deal with schizophrenic families that he became active and intrusive to avoid being caught up in the families' craziness. In any case, there is a suggestion of combativeness in his writings, as though he saw himself battling against families. He spoke of beating families at their own game (Jackson and Weakland, 1961) by using dual or multiple messages, provoking them to do something in defiance of therapeutic directives whose real purpose may be concealed (therapeutic double-binds). This is a model of a therapist who conspires to outwit families in a distanced sort of way.

Jackson may have been subtly combative with families; Jay Haley wasn't subtle about it. He was clear and explicit in defining therapy as a battle for control between therapist and patients.[1] Haley believed that therapists need to maneuver into a position of power over their patients in order to manipulate them into changing. Although the notion of manipulation may have unpleasant connotations, moral criticism should be reserved for those who use patients covertly for their own ends, rather than used against those who seek the most effective means of helping patients achieve their goals.

Haley's most significant early publication of his ideas was in *Strategies of Psychotherapy* (Haley, 1963). In it he claimed that therapeutic paradoxes underlie what therapists of all different persuasions do, and then he ingeniously reanalyzed a number of different therapeutic modalities. His critiques are always lucid and clever. Haley described the marital relationship in terms of conflicting levels of communication. Conflicts occur not only over what rules the couple will follow in dealing with each other, but also over who sets the rules. Complexity is introduced because couples may be complementary in some spheres and symmetrical in others. But the complexity goes still further; although it may appear that a wife dominates a dependent husband, the husband may, in fact, provoke the wife to be dominating, thus himself dominating the type of relationship they have. It takes a coward to make a bully.

Although Haley's analysis of human relations was highly intellectual and rational, he believed that family members can't be rational about their problems. In fact he still tends to exaggerate people's inability to understand their own behavior. His therapy therefore tends to be done *to* patients rather than done *with* them. Although Haley criticizes to the point of

---

[1]Haley has continued to develop and revise his thinking and, today, he is far from this blunt and provocative. See Chapter 9 on strategic family therapy for a description of Haley's contemporary work.

ridicule the idea that insight is curative, he used to put a lot of faith in simple openness of communication as a way of dealing with problems in couples and marriages.

According to Haley the mere presence of a third person, the therapist, helps couples solve their problems. By dealing fairly with each spouse and not taking sides, the therapist disarms the usual blaming maneuvers; in other words, the therapist serves as a referee. In addition to being a referee, the communications therapist relabeled or redefined the activity of family members with each other. At first the therapist should be permissive and encourage family members to express themselves freely. This is the time for making explicit accusations and protests, so that they can be responded to. Once family members begin to express themselves, the therapist's comments can be directed toward helping participants communicate in problem-solving rather than in destructive ways. One strategy is to redefine what family members say, stressing the positive aspects of their relationship. "For example," Haley says, "if a husband is protesting his wife's constant nagging, the therapist might comment that the wife seems trying to reach her husband and achieve more closeness with him. If the wife protests that her husband constantly withdraws from her, the husband might be defined as one who wants to avoid discord and seeks an amiable relationship." (Haley, 1963, p. 139.) This technique was later to be called *reframing* and to become a central feature of strategic therapy.

One of Haley's major strategies was to make explicit the implicit or covert rules which govern family relationships. Dysfunctional rules made explicit become more difficult to follow. For example, some wives berate their husbands for not expressing themselves, but the wives talk so much and criticize so loudly that the husbands hardly have a chance. If the therapist points this out, it becomes more difficult to follow the implicit rule that the husband should not talk. Haley believed that disagreements about which rules to follow are relatively easily solved through discussion and compromise. Conflicts about who is to set rules are stickier and require that the therapist be less straightforward. Because the issue of control is too explosive to be dealt with openly, Haley recommends subtle directives.

Haley's directives are of two sorts: suggestions to behave differently and suggestions to continue to behave the same. Straightforward advice, he says, rarely works. When it does, it's likely that the conflict is minor or that the couple is moving in that direction anyway. Some of Haley's directives are for changes that seem so small that the full ramifications aren't immediately apparent. In a couple, for example, where the wife seems to have her own way most of the time, the husband is asked to say "no" on some minor issue once during the week. This seems trivial, but it accomplishes two things: It makes the husband practice speaking up for himself, and it makes the wife aware that she's been domineering. (Unfortunately, it also seems to blame the wife for problems in the relationship.) This small beginning gives both spouses a chance to work on changing their part of the interaction. The fact that they're doing so under therapeutic direction often, though not always, makes them more likely to follow the advice.

Haley's suggestion that family members continue to behave in the same way was, in fact, a therapeutic paradox. If people do something under the therapist's direction, the therapist gains control over that behavior. It's the therapist, then, who's laying down the rules for the relationship. Moreover, when they're told to continue their dysfunctional behavior, family members may spontaneously change. When a teenager who is rebellious against his parents is instructed to "continue to rebel," he or she is caught in a paradoxical position. Continuing to rebel means following the direction of an authority figure (and admitting that what you're doing is "rebellious"). Only by giving up this behavior can the teenager maintain the illusion of freedom. Meanwhile the problematic behavior ceases. Sometimes it's more effective to have one spouse suggest that the other continue symptomatic behavior. This may produce a major shift because it alters who defines the nature of the relationship.

EVALUATING THERAPY THEORY AND RESULTS

Family group therapy was a pragmatic, clinical approach. Its practitioners were concerned, not with theory building or research, but with clinical effectiveness. Both John Bell (1961) and Christian Midelfort (1957) reported successful outcomes in the majority of cases they treated with this approach, but such reports can only be considered anecdotal support for these therapists and their early form of family therapy.

One reason why it's difficult to assess family group therapy is that some of its methods have been appropriated by so many people that it hardly exists any longer as a separate approach. Once it was possible to evaluate the work of those who did or didn't use paradoxical injunctions, or considered family structure, or commented on the process of group interactions. Today it's hard to find family therapists who don't use all of these ideas. Group family therapy met the fate of most innovations: its limitations were corrected in models that took more account of the systemic structure and dynamics of families; its workable ideas were absorbed in almost all forms of family therapy.

Communications family therapy was an intellectual and scholarly approach, but one not founded on empiricism. Bateson and his colleagues in Palo Alto used the natural history method of observation to generate their ideas. Their major theories, including family homeostasis and the double-bind, were based on deductive reasoning—given the nature of their communication, schizophrenics *must* have been exposed to double-binds. Only later did they attempt to verify these conclusions by studying family interactions.

The first concern of the communicationists was theory, not therapy. Therapy came later and was very much a product of the theory. This reverses the usual case, where clinicians develop theories to describe what they have found to be true in therapy. Theories of therapy are thus usually ways of organizing the data of clinical experience. In communications family therapy, theory preceded clinical experience and was often given more prominence.

The first major publication of communications theory was the double-bind paper (Bateson, Jackson, Haley, and Weakland, 1956). Initially it was met with great enthusiasm and wide acceptance. This was followed by a period of intense analysis and research (see Chapter 1), which culminated in serious challenge and criticism. It turns out that many of the concepts of communications theory, like the double-bind, are not operationalizable and thus not subject to empirical confirmation. Instead, these concepts are useful metaphors, much like the propositions of psychoanalysis.

Haley actually did quite a bit of careful research on family interactions. Most of it was done not to evaluate therapy, or even a theory of therapy, but to test for differences in communication between schizophrenic and normal families. At one time the finding that verbal communication in families of schizophrenics can be differentiated from communication in other families (Wynne and Singer, 1963) was taken as support for a family etiology theory of schizophrenia. The problem with this conclusion is that most of the studies in which communications disorders were observed were made after the offspring had already been diagnosed as schizophrenic. It's therefore just as likely that the observed disorders of communication were a response to schizophrenia rather than a cause of it.

Two studies by Haley (1968) and Waxler (1974) cast serious doubt on the etiological interpretation. Haley found that normal children were just as able to perform a cognitive task when they were instructed by schizophrenic parents as when instructed by normal parents. Schizophrenic children, on the other hand, were less able to perform the task when both groups were instructed by their own parents. Waxler (1974) found that schizophrenic parents had only a minor and indirect influence on the performance of normal children.

Joan Liem (1974) compared the etiological and responsive hypothesis in an experimental design similar to those used by Haley (1968) and Waxler (1974). The subjects of this study were members of eleven families with schizophrenic young adult sons and eleven families with normal young adult sons. Their task was to describe common objects and simple human concepts for other family members to identify. The results supported the responsive hypothesis over the etiological one. The observed communications disorders of schizophrenic sons had an immediate negative effect on all parents, normal as well as schizophrenic, who attempted to respond to them. On the other hand, communications disorders were not observed in parents of the schizophrenic sons, nor were their communications found to have a disruptive effect on any of the sons who responded to them.

As these three studies illustrate, the idea that communications disorders cause schizophrenia has not been supported. Moreover, family therapy has not proven effective with schizophrenic families. However, although communications therapy began as a result of studies of schizophrenia, its validity doesn't rest on its effectiveness with this disorder. Communications concepts have been so widely adopted by family therapists of all theoretical persuasions that it would be difficult to measure their effectivness by comparing one approach to others.

The communications therapists themselves showed little inclination to conduct outcome studies. Whether or not the techniques of communications therapy are effective is a matter of empirical study, not argument. Thus far, however, there is no evidence for the effectiveness of this approach. The only existing outcome study (Weakland, Fisch, Watzlawick, and Bodin, 1974) was too poorly controlled to provide valid conclusions. The absence of controlled outcome studies does not, of course, distinguish communications family therapy from most of the other approaches to family treatment. For the time being, family therapy remains a field where the power of written descriptions is the only source of conviction other than personal experience.

SUMMARY

Group family therapy was developed by clinicians who had a background in group therapy and others who applied ideas of group dynamics to families. It was an approach widely used in the 1960s, but no longer. Today we recognize that although families are groups, they have so many unique properties that they cannot effectively be treated by the methods of group therapy.

The leading practitioner of group family therapy was John Elderkin Bell who, along with Ackerman, Bowen, Satir, and Jackson, should be considered one of the originators of family therapy. Bell first considered family group therapy to be a battle between parents and children, so that his basic strategy was to allow first one and then the other side to express themselves. Except for giving a little extra protection to the children, Bell remained pretty much in the background, confident that open communication would make it possible for families to resolve their own problems.

Interventions in family group therapy focused on the process of interactions and were designed to confront family members with dysfunctional patterns of communication. These *process comments* were designed to engage families in treatment, maximize individual participation, and move families through the stages of group development.

Group family therapists were directive to the extent of encouraging people to speak up when they appeared to have something to say. Otherwise they were relatively passive and confined themselves to describing the processes they saw in families. In therapy groups of strangers with contrasting defenses and personality styles, this approach is effective; moreover therapists in these groups can act as catalysts who stir members to confront and challenge each other. Families, however, share defenses and pathological attitudes, and therapists cannot rely on other group members to challenge family norms. That's why contemporary family therapists, who treat families more actively, confront family patterns of interaction (rather than individual reticence) and look for ways to circumvent defenses that are more powerful in families than in groups of strangers.

The three specialized applications of group methods with families considered in this chapter—multiple family group therapy, multiple impact therapy, and network therapy—were experiments of the sixties and early seventies. Treating more than one family at the same time allows members of one family to see how others deal with similar problems. However when there are other families present to serve as distractions, it makes it hard to focus for any length of time or depth on entrenched or anxiety–arousing problems. What works in group therapy may not work with families.

Both multiple impact therapy and network therapy brought tremendous resources to bear on families stuck in crisis. Although family therapists in clinics often work in teams, today we usually rely on one therapist to treat a family. Perhaps there are times when it makes sense to launch the all-out effort that multiple impact therapy represented. The additional advantage of network therapy was that the resources it mobilized were the natural resources of a family's community. Perhaps this model, too, is still useful: It uses community resources that are still available after treatment is over, and it's a useful antidote to the isolation of many families.

Communications family therapy was one of the first and most influential forms of family treatment. Its theoretical development was closely tied to general systems theory and the therapy that emerged was a systems approach *par excellence*. Therapy was a by-product of Gregory Bateson's schizophrenia project. The main product was a set of ideas about human communication and family systems. The fact that their studies had a profound impact on the entire field of psychotherapy was largely an artifact of the psychiatric context that was the source of their funding. Many of these ideas—homeostasis, double-bind, feedback—were absorbed by the entire field of family therapy, so that there is no longer a separate school of communications family therapy.

Bateson assembled a unique group with diverse talents, and he gave them free rein to develop their interests. Among the many subjects that interested them, communication was the common denominator. Communication was the detectable input and output they used to analyze the black box of interpersonal systems. Communication was described as feedback, as a tactic in interpersonal power struggles, and as symptoms. In fact, all behavior was considered communication. The trouble is, when "communication" is used so broadly, the concept loses precision. If all events and actions are treated as communication, then communications analysis may be taken to mean everything, and therefore nothing. Human relations are not all a matter of communication; communication may be the matrix in which interactions are embedded, but human interactions have other attributes as well—love, hate, fear, conflict.

The Bateson group may be best remembered for the concept of the double-bind, but their enduring contribution was applying communications analysis to a wide range of behavior, including family dynamics. In fact, the idea of metacommunication is a much more useful concept than that of the double-bind, and it has been incorporated not only by family therapists but also by the general public. Whether or not they are familiar with the term *metacommunication*, most people understand that all messages have both report and command functions.

Another of the most significant ideas of communications therapy is that families are rule-governed systems, maintained by homeostatic, negative feedback mechanisms. This accounts for the stability of normal families and the inflexibility of dysfunctional families. Because such families don't have adequate positive feedback mechanisms, they're unable to adjust to changing circumstances.

Communications theorists borrowed the open systems model from general systems theory, but their clinical analyses and interventions were based on the closed systems paradigm of cybernetics. This is another example of how this approach was more useful theoretically, than pragmatically. In their clinical descriptions, relationships were portrayed as struggles for power and control. Haley emphasized the power struggle between spouses, and Watzlawick said that the major problem of control in families is cognitive. The therapy that they developed from these ideas was conceived as a power struggle in which the therapist takes control to outwit the forces of symptom maintenance.

When communication takes place in a closed system—an individual's fantasies, or a family's conversations—there's little opportunity for adjusting the system. Only when someone outside the system provides communicational input can correction occur. This is the premise on which communications family theory was based. The rules of family functioning are largely unknown to the family, and the best way to examine and correct them is to consult an expert in communications.

While there were major differences among the intervention strategies of Haley, Jackson, Satir, and Watzlawick, they were all committed to altering self-reinforcing and mutually destructive patterns of communication. They pursued this goal by direct and indirect means. The direct approach, favored by Satir, sought change by making family rules explicit and by teaching principles of clear communication. This approach could be described as establishing ground rules, or metacommunicational principles, and included such tactics as telling people to speak for themselves and pointing out nonverbal and multileveled channels of communication.

The trouble is, as Haley noted, "One of the difficulties involved in telling patients to do something is the fact that psychiatric patients are noted for their hesitation about doing what they are told." For this reason, communications therapists began to rely on more indirect strategies, designed to provoke change, not to foster awareness. Telling family members to speak for themselves, for instance, may challenge a family rule and therefore meet with strong resistance. With this realization, communications therapy began a treatment of resistance.

Resistance and symptoms were treated with a variety of paradoxical directives, known loosely as therapeutic double-binds. Milton Erickson's technique of prescribing resistance was used as a lever to gain control—for example, when a therapist tells family members not to reveal everything in the first session. The same ploy was used to prescribe symptoms, an action which made unrecognized rules explicit, implied that such behavior was voluntary and placed the therapist in control.

Eventually communications therapy became symptom-focused, brief, and directive. The focus on symptoms is consistent with the general systems concept of *equifinality* which means that no matter where systems change begins the final result is the same. Moreover, even when they convened whole families, the communications therapists focused on the marital pair, and they were always more adept with dyadic than triadic thinking.

Today the theories of communications therapy have been absorbed into the mainstream of family therapy and the symptom-focused interventions are the basis of the strategic school of family therapy.

REFERENCES

Adler, A. 1931. *Guiding the child.* New York: Greenberg.

Bales, R.F. 1950. *Interaction process analysis: A method for the study of small groups.* Cambridge, MA: Addison-Wesley.

Bales, R.F. 1970. *Personality and interpersonal behavior.* New York: Holt, Rinehart and Winston.

Bateson, G., and Jackson, D.D. 1964. Some varieties of pathogenic organization. *Disorders of Communication.* 42:270–283.

Bateson, G., Jackson, D.D., Haley, J., and Weakland, J.H. 1956. Toward a theory of schizophrenia. *Behavioral Science. 1*:251–264.

Bateson, G., Jackson, D.D., Haley, J., and Weakland, J.H. 1963. A note on the double-bind—1962. *Family Process. 2*:154–161.

Beels, C.C., and Ferber, A. 1969. Family therapy: A view. *Family Process. 8*:280–318.

Bell, J.E. 1961. *Family group therapy.* Public Health Monograph No. 64. Washington, DC: U.S. Government Printing Office.

Bell, J.E. 1975. *Family group therapy.* New York: Jason Aronson.

Bell, J.E. 1976. A theoretical framework for family group therapy. In *Family therapy: Theory and practice,* P.J. Guerin, ed. New York: Gardner Press.

Bennis, W.G., and Shepard, H.A. 1956. A theory of group development. *Human Relations. 9*:415–437.

Bion, W.R. 1961. *Experiences in groups.* New York: Tavistock Publications.

Birdwhistell, R.L. 1952 *Introduction to kinesics.* Louisville, KY: University of Louisville Press.

Bleuler, E. 1950. *Dementia praecox or the group of schizophrenias.* New York: International Universities Press.

Brown, R. 1965. *Social psychology.* New York: The Free Press.

Carnap, R. 1942. *Introduction to semantics.* Cambridge, MA: Harvard University Press.

Cartwright, D., and Zander, A., eds. 1968. *Group dynamics: Research and theory.* New York: Harper & Row.

Cooley, C.H. 1902. *Human nature and the social order.* New York: Scribner.

Dreikurs, R. 1951. Family group therapy in the Chicago community child–guidance centers. *Mental Hygiene. 35*:291–301.

Foulkes, S.H. 1965. *Therapeutic group analysis.* New York: International Universities Press.

Foulkes, S.H. 1975. *Group analytic psychotherapy: Method and principles.* London: Gordon & Breach.

Freud, S. 1921. *Group psychology and the analysis of the ego. Standard Edition.* Vol. 18. London: Hogarth Press, 1955.

Gleitman, H. 1981. *Psychology.* New York: Norton.

Gritzer, P.H., and Okum, H.S. 1983. Multiple family group therapy: A model for all families. In *Handbook of family and marital therapy,* B.B. Wolman and G. Stricker, eds. New York: Plenum Press.

Haley, J. 1961. Control in psychotherapy with schizophrenics. *Archives of General Psychiatry. 5*:340–353.

Haley, J. 1963. *Strategies of psychotherapy.* New York: Grune and Stratton.

Haley, J. 1968. Testing parental instructions to schizophrenic and normal children: A pilot study. *Journal of Abnormal Psychology. 73*:559–565.

Haley, J. 1976. *Problem-solving therapy.* San Francisco: Jossey-Bass.

Hearn, G. 1957. The process of group development. *Autonomous Groups Bulletin. 13*:1–7.

Hoffman, L. 1971. Deviation-amplifying processes in natural groups. In *Changing families,* J. Haley, ed. New York: Grune and Stratton.

Jackson, D.D. 1961. Interactional psychotherapy. In *Contemporary psychotherapies,* M.T. Stein, ed. New York: Free Press of Glencoe.

Jackson, D.D. 1965. Family rules: The marital quid pro quo. *Archives of General Psychiatry. 12:*589–594.

Jackson, D.D. 1967. Aspects of conjoint family therapy. In *Family therapy and disturbed families*, G.H. Zuk and I. Boszormenyi-Nagy, eds. Palo Alto: Science and Behavior Books.

Jackson, D.D., and Weakland, J.H. 1961. Conjoint family therapy: Some consideration on theory, technique, and results. *Psychiatry. 24:*30–45.

Laqueur, H.P. 1966. General systems theory and multiple family therapy. In *Handbook of psychiatric therapies*, J. Masserman, ed. New York: Grune and Stratton.

Laqueur, H.P. 1972a. Mechanisms of change in multiple family therapy. In *Progress in group and family therapy*, C.J. Sager and H.S. Kaplan, eds. New York: Brunner/Mazel.

Laqueur, H.P. 1972b. Multiple family therapy. In *The book of family therapy*, A. Ferber, M. Mendelsohn, and A. Napier, eds. Boston: Houghton Mifflin.

Laqueur, H.P. 1976. Multiple family therapy. In *Family therapy: Theory and practice*, P.J. Guerin, ed. New York: Gardner Press.

Lederer, W., and Jackson, D.D. 1968. *Mirages of marriage.* New York: Norton.

Lewin, K. 1951. *Field theory in social science.* New York: McGraw-Hill.

Lidz, T., Cornelison, A., Terry, D., and Fleck, S. 1958. Intra-familial environment of the schizophrenic patient: IV. The transmission of irrationality. *Archives of Neurology and Psychiatry. 79:*305–316.

Liem, J.H. 1974. Effects of verbal communications of parents and children: A comparison of normal and schizophrenic families. *Journal of Consulting and Clinical Psychology. 42:*438–450.

MacGregor, R. 1967. Progress in multiple impact theory. In *Expanding theory and practice in family therapy*, N.W. Ackerman, F.L. Beatman, and S.N. Sherman, eds. New York: Family Service Association.

MacGregor, R. 1972. Multiple impact psychotherapy with families. In *Family therapy: An introduction to theory and technique*, G.D. Erickson, and T.P. Hogan, eds. Monterey, CA: Brooks/Cole.

MacGregor, R., Richie, A.M., Serrano, A.C., Schuster, F.P., McDonald, E.C., and Goolishian, H.A. 1964. *Multiple impact therapy with families.* New York: McGraw-Hill.

Marayuma, M. 1968. The second cybernetics: Deviation-amplifying mutual causal processes. In *Modern systems research for the behavioral scientist*, W. Buckley, ed. Chicago: Aldine.

McFarlane, W.R. 1982. Multiple-family therapy in the psychiatric hospital. In *The psychiatric hospital and the family*, H.T. Harbin, ed. New York: Spectrum.

Meyer, J.P., and Pepper, S. 1977. Need compatibility and marital adjustment among young married couples. *Journal of Personality and Social Psychology. 35:*331–342.

Midelfort, C.F. 1957. *The family in psychotherapy.* New York: McGraw-Hill.

Morris, C.W. 1938. Foundations on the theory of signs. In *International encyclopedia of united science*, O. Neurath, R. Carnap, and C.O. Morris, eds. Chicago: University of Chicago Press.

Parsons, T. 1950. Psychoanalysis and the social structure. *Psychoanalytic Quarterly. 19*:371–380.

Ruesch, J., and Bateson, G. 1951. *Communication: The social matrix of psychiatry.* New York: Norton.

Ruevini, U. 1975. Network intervention with a family in crisis. *Family Process. 14*:193–203.

Ruevini, U. 1979. *Networking families in crisis.* New York: Human Sciences Press.

Sartre, J.P. 1964. *Being and nothingness.* New York: Citadel Press.

Satir, V. 1964. *Conjoint family therapy.* Palo Alto, CA: Science and Behavior Books.

Satir, V. 1971. The family as a treatment unit. In *Changing families*, J. Haley, ed. New York: Grune and Stratton.

Scheflen, A.E. 1966. Natural history method in psychotherapy: Communicational research. In *Methods of research in psychotherapy*, L.A. Gottschalk, and E.H. Auerbach, eds. New York: Appleton-Century-Crofts.

Scheflen, A.E. 1968. Human communication: Behavioral programs and their integration in interaction. *Behavioral Science. 13*:86–102.

Schutz, W.C. 1958. *FIRO: A three-dimensional theory of interpersonal behavior.* New York: Holt, Rinehart and Winston.

Shaw, M.E. 1981. *Group dynamics: The psychology of small group behavior.* New York: McGraw-Hill.

Skynner, A.R.C. 1976. *Systems of family and marital psychotherapy.* New York: Brunner/Mazel.

Sluzki, C.E. 1978. Marital therapy from a systems theory perspective. In *Marriage and marital therapy*, T.J. Paolino and B.S. McCrady, eds. New York: Brunner/Mazel.

Speck, R.V., and Attneave, C.A. 1971. Social network intervention. In *Changing families*, J. Haley, ed. New York: Grune and Stratton.

Speck, R.V., and Attneave, C.A. 1973. *Family networks.* New York: Pantheon.

Spiegel, J. 1971. *Transactions.* New York: Science House.

Sullivan, H.S. 1944. The language of schizophrenia. In *Language and thought in schizophrenia*, J.S. Kasanin, ed. New York: Norton.

Von Bertalanffy, L. 1950. An outline of general system theory. *British Journal of the Philosophy of Science. 1*:134–165.

Watzlawick, P.A. 1966. A structured family interview. *Family Process. 5*:256–271.

Watzlawick, P., Beavin, J.H., and Jackson, D.D. 1967. *Pragmatics of human communication.* New York: Norton.

Waxler, N.E. 1974. Parent and child effects on cognitive performance: An experimental approach to the etiological and responsive theories of schizophrenia. *Family Process. 13*:1–22.

Weakland, J., Fisch, R., Watzlawick, P., and Bodin, A.M. 1974. Brief therapy: Focused problem resolution. *Family Process. 13*:141–168.

Winch, R.F. 1955. The theory of complementary needs in mate selection: A test of one kind of complementariness. *American Sociological Review.* 20:52–56.

Wynne, L.C. 1968. Methodologic and conceptual issues in the study of schizophrenics and their families. *Journal of Psychiatric Research.* 6:185–199.

Wynne, L.C. 1970. Communication disorders and the quest for relatedness in families of schizophrenics. *American Journal of Psychoanalysis.* 30:100–114.

Wynne, L.C., Jones, J.E., and Al-Khayyal, M. 1982. Healthy family communication patterns: Observations in families "at risk" for psychopathology. In *Normal family processes*, F. Walsh, ed. New York: Guilford.

Wynne, L.C., Ryckoff, I.M., Day, J., and Hirsch, S. 1958. Pseudomutuality in the family relations of schizophrenics. *Psychiatry.* 21:205–220.

Wynne, L., and Singer, M. 1963. Thought disorder and family relationships of schizophrenics: I. Research strategy. *Archives of General Psychiatry.* 9:191–198.

Wynne, L.C., Singer, M.T., Bartko, J.J., and Toohey, M.L. 1977. Schizophrenics and their families: Recent research on parental communication. In *Developments in psychiatric research*, J.M. Tanner, ed. London: Hodder and Stoughton.

Yalom, I.D. 1985. *The theory and practices of group psychotherapy.* 3rd ed. New York: Basic Books.

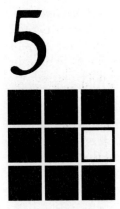

5

Psychoanalytic Family Therapy

Among the pioneers of family therapy many were psychoanalytically trained, including Nathan Ackerman, Ian Alger, Murray Bowen, Lyman Wynne, Theodore Lidz, Israel Zwerling, Ivan Boszormenyi-Nagy, Carl Whitaker, Don Jackson, and Salvador Minuchin. But with the eager enthusiasm so essential to innovation they turned away from the old—psychodynamics—and toward the new—systems dynamics. Some, including Jackson and Minuchin, went far indeed from their psychoanalytic roots. Others, including Bowen, Lidz, and Wynne, retained a distinctly analytic influence in their work.

In the 1960s and 1970s the burgeoning field of family therapy followed the lead of Jackson and Minuchin, not only ignoring, but at times denouncing, psychoanalytic thinking. Jackson went so far as to declare the death of the individual (Jackson, 1967). As Minuchin was to recall, "We understood that the decontexted individual was a mythical monster, an illusion created by our psychodynamic blinders" (Minuchin, 1989). Family therapists saw themselves as forward-looking modern progressives, liberating the field from a fossilized view of mental disorder, namely, that problems are firmly embedded inside people's heads. If at times they sounded a little self-righteous, perhaps that was due to the vehemence of the resistance they encountered from the entrenched powers of the psychiatric establishment. Understandable or not, the result was a prolonged and polarized alienation between family therapists and psychoanalysts.

Then in the 1980s a surprising shift occurred; family therapists took a renewed interest in the psychology of the individual. While the current re-emergence of psychodynamics in family therapy may not be as significant as the crumbling of the Berlin wall, to those who remember the old antagonisms it was equally unexpected.

One reason for the revival of interest in psychodynamics is that there have been a number of recent innovations: within family therapy, a host of voices calling for a reintroduction of psychodynamic ideas; and, within psychoanalysis, the growth of object relations theory and the tremendous popularity of self psychology. Among the books and articles offering an integration of psychoanalytic ideas and family therapy are: *Individual and Family Therapy: Toward an Integration* (Sander, 1979); "Integrating Psychoanalytic Object Relations Understanding with Family Systems Intervention in Couples Therapy" (Friedman, 1980); "Integrative Marital Therapy" (Gurman, 1981); *Object Relations: A Dynamic Bridge Between Individual and Family Treatment* (Slipp, 1984); *The Self in the System* (Nichols, 1987); *Object Relations Family Therapy* (Scharff and Scharff, 1987); and *The Foundations of Object Relations Family Therapy* (Scharff, 1989).

The reason these psychodynamic approaches have found a receptive audience is that many clinicians believe that while family therapists discovered profound truths about systemic interactions, they were wrong to turn their backs on the lessons of depth psychology. There seems to be a paradox here: Psychoanalysis is a theory and therapy of individuals; family therapy is a theory of social systems and a therapy of families. How, then, can there be a psychoanalytic family therapy?

One way of answering this question, illustrated by the object relations family therapy of David and Jill Scharff, is to do psychoanalytic therapy with families. Another solution, suggested by Nichols in *The Self in the System*, is to selectively introduce psychoanalytic insights and interventions in systemic family therapy. In either case, the question—Can there be a psychoanalytic family therapy?—remains a good one.

SKETCHES OF LEADING FIGURES

We can distinguish four distinct groups of contributors to psychoanalytic family therapy: psychoanalytic forerunners; psychoanalytically trained pioneers who helped develop family therapy; the few who pursued psychoanalytic investigations even when mainstream family therapy was vociferously antipsychoanalytic; and those in the forefront of the contemporary resurgence of psychoanalytic family therapy.

It is appropriate to begin by acknowledging Freud's contribution to the psychoanalytic study of family life. Freud was interested in the family, but viewed it as old business—the context where people learned neurotic fears, rather than the contemporary context where such fears are maintained. Presented with a phobic Little Hans, Freud (1909) was more interested in analyzing the child's Oedipus complex than treating the family.

Flugel (1921) also put forth a psychoanalytic view of the family; but, like Freud's, his thinking was limited to intrapsychic processes and his therapy to individuals.

Major advances were achieved in the psychoanalytic understanding of family dynamics by child psychiatrists who began to analyze mothers and children concurrently (Burlingham, 1951). An example of the fruits of these studies is Adelaide Johnson's (Johnson and Szurek, 1952) explanation of the transmission of *superego lacunae*, gaps in personal morality passed on by parents who do things like telling their children to lie about their ages in order to save a couple of dollars at the movies.

Subsequently, the concurrent analysis of married couples revealed the family as a group of interlocking, intrapsychic systems (Oberndorf, 1938); Mittlemann, 1948; Martin and Bird, 1953). The notion of interlinked psyches remains an important feature of the psychoanalytic view of families (Sander, 1989). Most contemporary family therapists view the family as functioning in terms of a single organic unity, but psychoanalytic therapists are concerned with complex interactions among and within individual family members.

From the 1930s to the 1950s more and more psychoanalytic researchers became interested in the family. Erik Erikson explored the sociological dimensions of ego psychology. Erich Fromm's observations about cultural forces and the struggle for individuality foreshadowed later work by Bowen on the process of differentiation within the family. Harry Stack Sullivan's interpersonal theory emphasized the mother's role in transmitting anxiety to her children. Moreover, although he did not treat families, Sullivan transformed the treatment milieu at Sheppard and Enoch Pratt Hospital into a kind of surrogate family for young schizophrenic patients.

The psychoanalysts who helped create family therapy were moving away from psychodynamics, and the analytic influence retained in their work was deliberately muted. Murray Bowen, Lyman Wynne, Theodore Lidz, and Nathan Ackerman have been discussed elsewhere. Among this group, Nathan Ackerman retained the strongest tie to psychoanalytic theory in his approach to families.

In the first two decades of family therapy, Nathan Ackerman was the leading family therapist on the East Coast. Students, among them Salvador Minuchin, flocked to the Family Institute (now Ackerman Institute) in New York to observe this master therapist at work. His book, *The Psychodynamics of Family Life*, published in 1958, was the first one devoted to diagnosis and treatment of families. Classical Freudians assumed that the individuals they treated lived in stable environments. Dreams and fantasies were the royal roads to the unconscious and consequently they didn't think it necessary to know anything about the real family. Ackerman realized, though, that families are rarely stable, dependable, or predictable; rather than quarantine them, however, he believed they could be changed for the better (Ackerman, 1966). Moreover, he wrote (Ackerman, 1958) that accurate understanding of an individual's unconscious requires an understanding of its context in the reality of family interactions. Since people don't live in isolation, Ackerman believed they shouldn't be treated in isolation.

Ivan Boszormenyi-Nagy, also a psychoanalyst, developed another important center of family therapy at the Eastern Pennsylvania Psychiatric Institute (EPPI) in 1957. Among his colleagues and students at EPPI were David Rubenstein, James Framo, Geraldine Spark, and Ross Speck. Nagy's writings (Boszormenyi-Nagy and Framo, 1965; Boszormenyi-Nagy and Spark, 1973; Boszormenyi-Nagy and Ulrich, 1981; Boszormenyi-Nagy, 1987) merit careful study by serious students of family therapy.

Even when family therapy was most inhospitable to psychoanalytic thinking, important, though not well-known, psychoanalytic investigations of the family were being carried out at Tavistock and NIMH.

In the 1940s Henry Dicks (1963) established the Family Psychiatric Unit at the prestigious Tavistock Clinic in England, where teams of psychiatric social workers attempted to reconcile couples referred by the divorce courts. By the 1960s Dicks (1967) was applying object relations theory to the understanding and treatment of marital conflict. Also at the Tavistock, John Bowlby (1949) described conjoint family interviews as an adjunct to individual psychotherapy; he saw the parents of one of his adolescent patients in an effort to resolve a treatment impasse. His report of this case is, like many others, an isolated example of a clinician experimenting with family sessions, but without much notice or lasting influence.

In the 1950s and 1960s American psychoanalysis was dominated by ego psychology (which focuses on intrapsychic structures), while object relations theory (which lends itself to interpersonal analysis) flourished an ocean away in Britain. Edith Jacobson (1954) and Harry Stack Sullivan (1953) were the most influential thinkers who helped bring American psychiatry to an interpersonal point of view. Less well known, but more important to the development of family therapy, was the work carried out at NIMH. When NIMH opened in 1953, Irving Ryckoff jumped at the chance to move from Chestnut Lodge, where he'd been working with chronic schizophrenics isolated from their families, to develop a research project on families of schizophrenics under the leadership of Robert Cohen. He was joined by Juliana Day and Lyman Wynne and later by Roger Shapiro and John Zinner. This group produced a series of well-known papers introducing such concepts as *pseudomutuality* (Wynne, Ryckoff, Day, and Hirsch, 1958), *role stereotyping* (Ryckoff, Day, and Wynne, 1959), *trading of dissociations* (Wynne, 1965), and *delineations* (Shapiro, 1968). But perhaps their most important clinical contribution was the application of the concept of *projective identification* (from Melanie Klein) to the family as a group (from the work of Wilfred Bion). This group also introduced to psychoanalytic researchers the idea of seeing the family as the unit for study, and to clinicians the analytic group-interpretive approach to families (Shapiro, 1979).

In the sixties, Ryckoff and Wynne introduced a course in family dynamics at the Washington School of Psychiatry, which led to a family therapy training program. They were joined by Shapiro and Zinner and Robert Winer. In 1975 they recruited Jill Savege (now Scharff) and David Scharff. By the mid 1980s the Washington School of Psychiatry, under the directorship of David Scharff, had become one of the leading centers of psychoanalytic family therapy. What characterizes the Scharffs' work is its object relations focus and its frank psychoanalytic approach to families.

Among others who have incorporated psychoanalytic theory into family therapy are: Helm Stierlin (1977), Robin Skynner (1976), William Meissner (1978), Fred Sander (1979, 1989), Michael Nichols (1987), Nathan Epstein, Harry Grunebaum, and Clifford Sager. Another influential object relations approach to family therapy is that of Samuel Slipp (1984, 1988), whose work differs from the Scharffs' in attempting to be more of an integration of systems and psychoanalytic concepts and methods.

THEORETICAL FORMULATIONS

The practical essence of psychoanalytic theory is being able to recognize and interpret unconscious impulses and defenses against them—and, adding object relations theory, old expectations that distort current relationships.

It isn't a question of analyzing individuals instead of family interactions: it's knowing where to look to discover some of the basic wants and fears that keep those individuals from interacting in a mature way.

Psychoanalytic theory gets so complex when you get into the specifics that it's easy to get lost. Here are the basics.

Freudian Drive Psychology. At the heart of human nature are the drives—sexual and aggressive. Mental conflict arises when children learn, and mislearn, that expressing these basic impulses will lead to punishment. Conflict is signalled by unpleasant affect: anxiety or depression. Anxiety is unpleasure associated with the idea (often unconscious) that one will be punished for acting on a particular wish—e.g., the anger you're tempted to express would make your partner stop loving you. Depression is unpleasure plus the idea (often unconscious) that the feared calamity *has already occurred*—e.g., the anger you showed your mother long ago made her stop loving you; in fact, nobody loves you.

The balance of conflict can be shifted in one of two ways: by strengthening defenses against a conflicted wish or by relaxing defenses sufficiently to permit some gratification.

Self Psychology.   The essence of *self psychology* (Kohut, 1971, 1977) is that human beings crave appreciation. If, when we're young, our parents demonstrate their appreciation, we internalize this acceptance in the form of strong and self-confident personalities. But to the extent that our parents insufficiently demonstrate admiring appreciation and acceptance, then our craving for it is retained in an archaic manner. As adults we alternately suppress the desire for attention and then allow it to emerge unmodified, whenever we're in the presence of a receptive audience.

Object Relations Theory.   Drive psychology and the psychology of the self describe the basic motives and fears of human nature—and the resultant conflict. Psychoanalysis is primarily the study of individuals and their elemental motives (drives and the need for attachment), and family therapy is the study of social relationships; the bridge between the two is *object relations theory*. While the details of object relations theory can be quite complicated, its essence is simple: We relate to people in the present partly on the basis of expectations formed by early experience. The residue of these early relationships leaves *internal objects*—mental images of self and other, and self in relation to others, built from experience and expectation. The unconscious remnants of those internalized objects form the core of the person—an open system developing and maintaining its identity through social relatedness, present *and* past. The roots of object relations theory lie in Freud's discovery of the Oedipus complex and how it influences treatment through transference and resistance. But although Freud acknowledged the importance of early family relationships, his emphasis was on how the family context affected the evolution of instinctual expression.

Freud's original focus was on bodily appetites, particularly sex. While these appetites obviously involve other people, they are primarily biological needs, and the relationships they involve are secondary matters. Sex cannot be divorced from object relations, but on the other hand sexual relations can be more physical than personal. This is less true of aggression (to which Freud turned his interest in later years), because aggression is not an organic appetite. As Guntrip (1971) put it, aggression is a personal reaction to "bad" object relations. Therefore as Freud's interest shifted from sex to aggression, the interpersonal, object-relational side of his thinking came to the fore. Eventually he ceased to regard anxiety as dammed-up sexual tension and considered it to be the ego's reaction to danger—often, loss of love or rejection.

Subsequently Melanie Klein's observations of the role of aggression in infancy led her to think about object relations. She combined Freud's psychobiological terms and concepts with her own brilliant insights into the mental life of little children to develop psychodynamic object-relational thinking.

Klein's theory (Segal, 1964) stemmed from her observations of the infant's developing relationship with the first significant object, namely the mother. According to Klein, an infant doesn't form impressions of his mother based solely upon real experiences of her, but instead sifts these experiences through an already rich fantasy life. The infant's innate makeup contains forces of love and hate, which are experienced before the real objects themselves. From the start, perception of real objects is filtered through the distortions of an already formed inner world. The infant doesn't develop impressions of a "bad" mother from actual experience; he projects his own aggressive fantasies onto her. The child then reintrojects—that is, internalizes—those objects that cause pain, which leads to a cruel superego and severe anxiety. Unlike orthodox Freudians, Klein believed that super-ego formation and oedipal conflicts begin in the first two years of life. The infant thus never experiences real objects objectively; what he experiences depends more upon his own innate makeup than on the actual behavior of real objects. The environment confirms but does not originate the baby's primary anxieties and inner conflicts (Segal, 1964).

The infant's first internalized objects are fragmented; that is, they are experienced as *part-objects*, and as either "good" or "bad." In place of Freud's instinctual maturational phases—oral, anal, phallic, and genital—Klein postulated two developmental positions which depend on the role of object relations. Introjection of bad objects, such as a dry breast or the angry face of mother, generates anxiety and fear, which leads the baby into what Klein (1946) called the *paranoid position*. If the child also has sufficient positive experiences, the introjection of these good objects helps to alleviate anxieties and fears.

At about the time of weaning, the infant begins to experience the mother as one person, with both good and bad qualities. In addition, the infant discovers that he has the capacity to hurt the ones he loves. In consequence, the baby is depressed at becoming ambivalent toward mother and feels guilty about the capacity to inflict pain upon her. This leads to the *depressive position*, which in turn is instrumental in the development of the oedipal conflict beginning in the second year of life.

Klein has been criticized for her failure to follow her own observations to their logical conclusion—namely, that object relations are more relevant than instincts to personality development. Ronald Fairbairn went much further than Klein in the direction of object relations and away from drive psychology. His radical version of object relations theory stressed the ego as object-seeking and downplayed the role of instincts—making love more important than sex.

Because internal object relations are developed from the earliest and most primitive forms of interpersonal interaction, it's not surprising that the major advances in this field have been made by people like Klein and Fairbairn who treated and studied very young children and disturbed adults. In the late 1930s and 1940s, based on his work with schizoid patients (1952), Fairbairn elaborated the concept of *splitting*. Freud originally mentioned splitting as a defense mechanism of the ego; he defined it as a lifelong coexistence of two contradictory positions that do not influence each other.

Fairbairn's view of splitting is that the ego is divided into structures which contain (a) part of the ego; (b) part of the object; and (c) the affect associated with the relationship. The external object is experienced in one of three ways: (1) an ideal object that is just right, which leads to feelings of satisfaction; (2) a rejecting object that frustrates, which leads to anger; or (3) an exciting object that excites needs, which leads to longing. As a result of internalizing split objects, the resulting structure of the ego is: (1) a *central ego*, conscious, adaptable, satisfied with its ideal object, (2) a *rejecting ego*, unconscious, inflexible, frustrated by its rejecting object, or (3) an *exciting ego*, unconscious, inflexible, in a state of longing for a tempting but unsatisfying object. To the degree that splitting is not resolved, object relations retain a kind of "all good" or "all bad" quality.

The primitive ego uses splitting to keep positive and negative images separate, at first because positive and negative experiences happen separately, and later on as a way to avoid anxiety. Splitting, which prevents the anxiety associated with negative (aggressive) images from being generalized throughout the ego, usually disappears in the second year of life as positive and negative images are integrated. If it's excessive, however, splitting interferes with integration of these images and leads to the dramatic shifts from calm to upset of borderline personalities.

Internalization of object relations starts on a relatively primitive level and, as the child grows, becomes more sophisticated. *Introjection* is the earliest and most primitive form of internalization. The child reproduces and fixates its interactions with the environment by organizing memory traces which include images of the object, the self interacting with the object, and the associated affect. Included are good and bad internal objects, each with images of the object and the self. Thus, if mother yells, images of a bad mother and an unworthy self are stored. Introjection is a crude and global form of taking in, as if those fragments of self-other interaction were swallowed whole.

Identification, a higher level of internalization, involves the internalization of a role. In the earliest introjections, object- and self-images are not clearly differentiated; in identification they are. The result of identification is that the child takes on certain roles and behaves in the same way the parents do. Notice, for example, how two-year-olds love to dress up like Mommy or Daddy.

Ego identity (Erikson, 1956) represents the most sophisticated level of internalization. It is the overall organization of synthesized identifications and introjections. Ego identity involves a consolidation of inner structures, which provides a sense of coherence and continuity of the self. Ego identity includes a consolidated self-concept and a consolidated world of object representations. At the highest level of development, according to Kernberg (1976, p. 73),

> A harmonious world of internalized object-representations, including not only significant others from the family and immediate friends but also a social group and a cultural identity, constitute an ever growing internal world providing love, reconfirmation, support, and guidance within the object relations system of the ego. Such an internal world, in turn, gives depth to the present interaction with others. In periods of crisis, such as loss, abandonment, separation, failure, and loneliness, the individual can temporarily fall back on his internal world; in this way, the intrapsychic and the interpersonal worlds relate to and reinforce each other.

In their observations of infants and young children, Rene Spitz and John Bowlby emphasized the child's profound need for physical attachment to a single and constant object. If this primitive need is denied, the result will be *anaclitic depression* (Spitz and Wolf, 1946), a turning away from the world and withdrawal into apathy. According to Bowlby (1969), attachment is not simply a secondary phenomenon, resulting from being fed, but a basic need in all (including human) animals. We must have a secure and loving human attachment in infancy if we are to become secure adults. Those who do not have this experience are excessively vulnerable to even the slightest lack of support, and become chronically overdependent. This, in psychoanalytic terms, explains the genesis of *enmeshed* families.

Margaret Mahler observed infants and young children and described the essential role of a process of *separation-individuation*. For the first month of life, which Mahler described as the *autistic phase*, infants are concerned primarily with their own bodily needs and sensations. The second, or *symbiotic phase*, lasts from approximately two to six months, during which the good mother relieves the baby's tension by feeding, changing, holding, and smiling. The more adequate the care given during this phase, the higher the child's self-esteem will be. After this the child begins a gradual process of separation from the mother, progressively renouncing symbiotic fusion with her. The result of successful separation and individuation is a well-differentiated and internally integrated organization of the self (Mahler, Pine, and Bergman, 1975). Failure to achieve separation and individuation undermines the development of a cohesive sense of self and a differentiated sense of identity, resulting in an overly intense emotional attachment to the family. Depending upon the severity of the failure to separate, crises are liable to develop when the child reaches school age, enters adolescence, or prepares to leave home as an adult.

The shift in emphasis from drives to object relations can also be seen in the work of Americans such as Karen Horney, Erich Fromm, and Harry Stack Sullivan, whose level of analysis was more social and cultural than depth analytic. In his theory of interpersonal psychiatry, Harry Stack Sullivan (1953) emphasized the ways that individuals function in interpersonal situations; he thought that was more important than how an individual expresses instinctual impulses. In every interpersonal situation the participants interact with each other on the basis of past relations with others. Sullivan pointed out the crucial importance of the early mother-child interaction on the *self-system* or *self-dynamism*. The nature of these interactions leads to three types of personifications which determine the nature of the self-system. When the mother is warm and nurturing, the child feels good; when the mother rebuffs or frustrates the child's need for tenderness, the child feels bad; and when the child is exposed to extreme pain or frustration, he dissociates to escape anxiety which would otherwise be intolerable. These experiences create the self-dynamisms: *good me, bad me*, and *not me*, which then become part of the person's response to future interpersonal situations.

Sullivan has been enormously influential in this country, although he has been criticized for neglecting Freud's insights into the instinctual determinants of behavior (Kernberg, 1976) and for neglecting unconscious conflicts related to internalized object relations, while stressing actual present and past interpersonal relations (Guntrip, 1961). In Sullivanian theory, the child is at the mercy of the environment. The child searches for *security* and *satisfaction*, and develops a self-system derived from interpersonal relations with the parents by repudiating those actions which cause the parents anxiety. Thus, the extent of the parents' anxiety sets the limits on the child's healthy growth and development.

More recently Erik Erikson (1956, 1963) has theorized that introjections and identifications, along with social roles, form the basis of *ego identity*. Erikson never abandoned the instinctual basis of Freudian theory. He recognizes the influence of sexual and aggressive drives, and accepts the importance of the oral stage of development; however, he stresses the importance of *basic trust*. In order for basic trust to develop, the infant needs physical comfort and protection from undue anxiety, frustration, and rejection. Armed with basic trust, the growing person can face new situations with confidence and equanimity; without it, new experiences bring fear and apprehension. The child who successfully negotiates the stages of Eriksonian development emerges with basic trust and a clear sense of ego identity.

To understand object relations theory, it's essential to bear in mind that it isn't objects that are in the psyche, but fantasies of objects. As Edith

Jacobson (1964) pointed out, the object is never perceived exactly as it is; what is perceived is a representation that reflects the subjective experience of the object. Thus object relations are determined not only by how the object behaves toward the subject but also by how the subject perceives and then integrates that behavior. In *The Brothers Karamazov*, Dostoevsky, speaking through the monk Zossima, makes exactly this point.

> From the house of my parents I have brought nothing but pleasant memories, for there are no memories more precious than those of one's early childhood in one's own home, and that is almost always so, if there is any love and harmony in the family at all. Indeed, precious memories may be retained even from a bad home so long as your heart is capable of finding anything precious.

The internal world of object relations never exactly corresponds to the actual world of real people. It is an approximation, strongly influenced by the earliest object images, introjections, and identifications. This inner world gradually matures and develops, becoming progressively synthesized and closer to reality. The individual's internal capacity for dealing with conflict and failure is intimately related to the maturity and depth of the internal world of object relations. Trust in one's self and one's goodness is based on the confirmation of love from internalized good objects.

Although the application of his ideas will be developed in subsequent sections, we cannot leave theory without mentioning Heinz Kohut. Not since Freud's drive psychology has there been as significant an impact on psychoanalysis as Kohut's *psychology of the self*. Kohut believed that at the heart of human desires is a longing for admiring attention. The child lucky enough to grow up with appreciative parents will be secure, able to stand alone as a center of initiative, and able to love. The unhappy child, cheated out of loving affirmation, will move through life forever craving the attention he or she was denied. As we shall see, Kohut's ideas have enormous practical application.

NORMAL FAMILY DEVELOPMENT

The distinction between normal and abnormal development is less clearly drawn by psychoanalytic writers than by family therapists in other schools. Following Freud, they take clinical phenomena and psychopathological developments as starting points from which to retrace the development of personality, normal and abnormal. Bear in mind, therefore, that many of the processes described in this section as normal family development have the potential to produce behavior disorders, and that most of the processes described as behavior disorders also have normal counterparts.

The psychoanalytic model of normal development contains concepts drawn from object relations theory, attachment theory, and theories of the self—all of which are modifications and additions to Freud's psychology of drives. The first stage of object relations is an objectless stage. Freud called this *primary narcissism*; Mahler called it *autistic*. The newborn's responses are limited to conditioned reflexes. Gradually, sensation, perception, and memory develop, shaping the infant's experience and encoding the influence of other people. Thereafter the entire process of growth depends upon the ego's relations with objects, at first as actual interactions with real objects, and later as unconscious residues of these first interactions. According to Freudian models, psychological well-being depends upon: (a) gratification of instincts; (b) realistic control of primitive drives; and (c) coordination of independent psychic structures. According to object relations theory, achieving and preserving psychic wholeness through good object relations is the key to psychological adjustment.

The child's innate potential does not mature in sublime indifference to the interpersonal world. The infant needs a facilitating environment in order to thrive. This environment does not have to be an unattainable ideal; an *average expectable environment* featuring *good-enough mothering* (Winnicott, 1965a) is sufficient. Tender, responsive parents first accept the infant's total dependence; but as time goes on, they support the child's growing autonomy, and eventually ratify the child's finding a life of his own through personal relations with others.

The parents' capacity to provide good-enough mothering and sufficient security for the baby's developing ego depends upon whether they themselves feel secure. To begin with, the mother must be secure and selfless enough to channel most of her energy into supporting and caring for her infant. She drains interest from herself and her marriage and focuses it on the baby. As the baby comes to need less, mother gradually recovers her self-interest, which allows her to permit the child to become independent (Winnicott, 1965b). At the same time she also redevelops an interest in the marital relationship.

If the early relationship with mother is secure and loving, the infant will gradually be able to give her up, while retaining her loving support in the form of a good internal object. In the process, most little children adopt a *transitional object* (Winnicott, 1965b) to ease the loss—a soft toy or blanket that the child begins to cling to during the period when he or she starts to realize that mother is a separate object and can go away. The toy that Mommy gives reassures her anxious baby; it is a reminder that stands for her and keeps alive the mental image of her until she returns. When Mommy says, "Goodnight," the child hugs the teddy bear until morning when Mommy reappears.

The outcome of good object relations in infancy is the emergence of a secure and successfully differentiated identity. The little child who has been cared for by consistently loving and reliably supportive parents develops a sense of *libidinal object constancy* (Kernberg, 1966). The well-loved child feels worthwhile. This sense of worth endows the child with a capacity to delay gratification, tolerate frustration, and achieve competent ego functioning; he or she has a coherent and cohesive sense of self, and is able either to be with others or to be independent. The child with a backlog of good object relations matures with the ability to tolerate closeness as well as separateness.

The child's identity is continually enriched and revised, especially at nodal points of development such as the oedipal period, puberty, and adolescence. But the search for identity does not end with adolescence (Erikson, 1959); the sense of identity continues to be shaped by experiences in adulthood, especially social relations, career development, and family life (Levinson, 1978; Nichols, 1986). Although popular culture treats the search for identity as a narcissistic quest (Lasch, 1978), for Erikson it means finding one's identity in relation to social groups, including the family.

The early attachment between mother and child has been shown to be a critical aspect of healthy development (Bowlby, 1969). Close physical proximity and attachment to a single maternal object are necessary preconditions for healthy object relations in childhood and adulthood. The infant needs a state of total merging and identification with the mother as a foundation for future growth of a strongly formed personal self.

After passing through the normal autistic and symbiotic phases, the child enters a long *separation-individuation period* at approximately six months (Mahler, Pine, and Bergman, 1975). First efforts at separation are tentative and brief, as symbolized playfully in the game of peekaboo. At about eight months, the child begins to experience *stranger anxiety* (Spitz, 1965). (The normalness of stranger anxiety has recently been called into question by Daniel Stern's research, to be discussed shortly.) Exaggerated stranger anxiety is a sign that the child is not secure in separating from mother; absence of stranger anxiety indicates that the child has not established a firm bond to mother as a primary object.

Soon the child begins to creep and then to crawl, first away from and then back to mother. What enables the child to practice separating is the awareness that mother is constantly there for assurance, like a safe harbor. At a similar stage, Harlow's infant monkeys alternately venture out to explore and then return to cling to their mothers. Those without mothers remain huddled in the corner of their cages.

Learning to walk enables the toddler to become very much more independent and separate from mother. The one-year-old child plays a variety of games to practice separation and reunion. Toys and objects are hidden and then found, with shrieks of delight. If all goes well the child achieves a sense of self, separate from mother, by about age three. He or she will have developed a sense of confidence and self-esteem that goes along with realistic recognition of interpersonal boundaries.

The necessary and sufficient condition for successful completion of separation-individuation is the reliable and loving support of a good mother. "Predictable emotional involvement on the part of the mother seems to facilitate the rich unfolding of the toddler's thought processes, reality testing and coping behavior. . ." (Mahler, Pine, Bergman, 1975, p. 79). A *good-enough mother* is physically and emotionally present; her support of separation-individuation results in the child's achieving a firm sense of identity and a lifelong capacity for developing nonsymbiotic object relations.

Recently, Otto Kernberg and Heinz Kohut have brought theories of the self to center stage in psychoanalytic circles. Although both Kernberg and Kohut began with observations of severe character disorders, their work illuminates the organization of the normal, inner psychic world and the integration of the self.

According to Kernberg (1966), pleasure and pain organize good and bad internalized object relations; they are the major motivational system which organizes intrapsychic experience. The earliest introjections occur in the process of separating from mother. If separation is successful and securely negotiated, the child establishes him- or herself as an independent being. When the introjective process is positive and constructive, the child absorbs part of the mother's personality, in modified form, for constructive use. Ideally, part of what the child internalizes is conflict-free and independent of drive pressures and defensive needs.

The mother must have a capacity to tolerate separation and withdrawal in order to accept the child's growing independence. If the child is excessively dependent and clings in fear of separation, or if the mother is made anxious by the loss of the symbiotic relationship, or is excessively rejecting, the process is subverted. In the normal outcome, loving parents are the objects of selective and partial identifications, in which only those features that are in harmony with the image of the self are internalized. As Kernberg (1966, p. 243) says,

> Actually the enrichment of one's personal life by the internal presence of such selective, partial identifications representing people who are loved and admired in a realistic way without indiscriminate internalization, constitutes a major source of emotional depth and well-being.

Normal ego development reaches a stage where positive and negative introjections are synthesized to provide a realistic and balanced view both of others and of the self in relation to others.

In Kohut's (1971, 1977) self psychology, the formation of a strong and cohesive sense of self depends upon the availability of parental *self-objects* who respond with approval to the child's grandiose fantasies, thereby relieving feelings of helplessness. The child, who is thus able to overcome feelings of helplessness, is able to recognize that he or she and mother are separate persons, each with their own needs. In this way the child is able to tolerate separation from the mother and to develop a sense of goodness and strength. Moreover, if mother remains warm and loving during the process of separation, the little child retains a sense of lovableness while achieving individuality and strength. The child who sees approval and acceptance in the mirror of parental eyes develops a strong self, capable of tolerating victory and defeat, as well as acceptance or rejection, throughout adult life.

Unquestionably the most significant recent contribution to the psychoanalytic study of normal family development is the work of Daniel Stern (1985). Stern, a psychoanalyst and infant researcher, has painstakingly traced the development of the sense of self through detailed observations of infants and small children. The infant's *emergent sense of self* begins in the first two months of life as a sense of physical cohesion and continuity in time. Already at this age, the infant has a sense of himself as a person—a distinct and integrated body, an initiator of actions, an experiencer of feelings, and a communicator. From two to six months, infants consolidate the sense of a *core self* as a separate cohesive, bounded physical unit, with confidence in their own agency and worth. At first the sense of self is a physical self, then somewhere between the seventh and ninth month, infants start to develop a second organizing perspective, *intersubjective relatedness*. The most revolutionary of Stern's findings is that child development is *not* a gradual process of separation and individuation. Rather, Stern's meticulous observations reveal that infants differentiate themselves almost from birth, and then progress through increasingly complex modes of relatedness. From *attunement* (reading and sharing the child's affective state) to *empathy*, attachment, trust, and dependency are needs throughout life.

Michael Kahn has begun to establish a theoretical and clinical framework for understanding sibling relationships across the life span (Bank and Kahn, 1982). Since the sibling subsystem comes in so many combinations and variations, Kahn has found concepts of birth order and fixed roles character of each child in the family to be insufficient and reductionistic. He views siblings as existing within a dialectical framework, identifying with and differentiating from one another, influenced by the projections and expectations of their parents, having a secret subsystem in which intensive behaviors and feelings are unleashed. Depending upon their stage in the life cycle, Kahn sees siblings drawing closer or more distant, requiring therapists to be skillful in bringing them together as a viable resource group

(Kahn and Lewis, 1988). Sibling relationships are a previously underutilized but rich resource system, particularly in light of the strain on parental resources in contemporary two-paycheck households.

From the psychoanalytic perspective, the fate of family development is largely determined by the early development of the individual personalities that make up the family. If the spouses are mature and healthy adults, then the family will be healthy and harmonious. According to Skynner (1976) the characteristics of optimally well-developed families are as follows: affiliative, open, reaching out to others; respect for separateness and individuality; open, clear communication; firm parental coalitions, sharing of power, flexible control by negotiation, spontaneous interactions, with humor and wit; initiative and the encouragement of uniqueness; and lively, strong character development.

Some of the most interesting and productive psychoanalytic ideas are contained in descriptions of the psychodynamics of marriage. In the mid fifties, the marital bond was described as a result of unconscious fantasy (Stein, 1956). We marry a blurry blend of real partners and hoped-for partners. But more recently, and more interestingly, psychoanalysts have described the overlapping and interlocking of fantasies and projections (Blum, 1987; Sander, 1989). Some authors have described this as "mutual projective identification" (Zinner, 1976; Dicks, 1967), others as "neurotic complementarity" (Ackerman, 1966), "marital collusion" (Dicks, 1967), "mutual adaptation" (Giovacchini, 1958, 1961), and "conscious and unconscious contracts" (Sager, 1981). One of the most thoughtful contemporary psychoanalytic family therapists, Fred Sander, sums up the analytic position this way.

> Thus, we are noting explicitly what earlier authors from Freud on implicitly noted: the shared participation in neurotic conflicts. The threats of object loss, loss of love, castration, and superego disapproval—the calamities of childhood in all ages and cultures—continue to affect our relations to others, especially those with whom we live and work. The repression of such universal childhood experiences and conflicts leads to their repetition with important others who reciprocally enact similar or complementary unconscious conflicts (Sander, 1989, pp. 165–166).

DEVELOPMENT OF BEHAVIOR DISORDERS

Nonpsychoanalytic family therapists locate problems in the nature of interaction *between* people; psychoanalytic therapists identify problems *within* the interacting people. According to classical psychoanalytic conflict theory, symptoms are attempts to cope with unconscious conflicts and the anxiety which signals the emergence of repressed impulses. Structurally, these conflicts are between the id and the ego: an instinctual drive seeks expression in a struggle against an opposing restraint (Fenichel, 1945). While agreeing that this basic formulation remains valid, object relations theorists have added the notion that not only behavior, but also psychic structure, evolves out of early experiences with others. Therefore, psychopathology is seen as reflecting the consequences of untoward early object relations.

As psychoanalytic thinkers shifted their emphasis from instincts to object relations, infantile dependence and incomplete ego development became the core problems in development, in place of the oedipal complex and repressed instincts. Fear-dictated flight from object relations, which begins in early childhood, is now considered to be the deepest root of psychological problems.

Psychoanalysts trace the roots of behavior disorders to the earliest months of life when parents first begin interacting with their infant. One important reason for psychopathology is that the child develops distorted perceptions by attributing qualities belonging to one person to someone else. Freud (1905) discovered this phenomenon and called it *transference* when his patient Dora displaced her feelings for her father and a family friend onto him, and terminated treatment abruptly just as it was on the threshold of success. Others have observed similar phenomena and called them by other names—"scapegoating" (Vogel and Bell, 1960); "trading of dissociations" (Wynne, 1965); "merging" (Boszormenyi-Nagy, 1967); "irrational role assignments" (Framo, 1970); "delineations" (Shapiro, 1968); "symbiosis" (Mahler, 1952); "family projective process" (Bowen, 1965). Regardless of name, all are variants of Melanie Klein's (1946) concept, *projective identification.*

Projective identification is a process whereby the subject perceives an object as if the object contained elements of the subject's personality *and* evokes behavior and feelings from the object that conform to these projected perceptions. Unlike projection, projective identification is a truly interactional process. Not only do parents project anxiety-provoking aspects of themselves onto their children, the children collude and behave in a way that fulfills their parents' fears. By doing so, they may be stigmatized or scapegoated, but they also gratify aggressive impulses, as, for instance, in delinquent behavior (Jacobson, 1964); they realize their own omnipotent fantasies; they receive subtle reinforcement from their families; and they avoid the terrible fear of rejection for not conforming (Zinner and Shapiro, 1972). Meanwhile the parents are able to avoid the anxiety associated with having certain impulses; experience vicarious gratification of the projected impulses through their children; and still punish the children for expressing them. In this way, an intrapsychic, structural conflict becomes externalized, with the parent acting as the superego, punishing the child for acting on the dictates of the parental id. That's one reason parents overreact: They're afraid of their own impulses.

The J. family sought help controlling 15-year-old Paul's delinquent behavior. Arrested several times for vandalism, Paul seemed neither ashamed of nor able to understand his compulsion to strike out against authority. As therapy progressed, it became clear that Paul's father harbored a deep but unexpressed resentment of the social conditions which made him work long hours for low wages in a factory, while the "fat cats didn't do shit, but still drove around in Cadillacs." Once the therapist became aware of Mr. J.'s strong but suppressed hatred of authority, they also began to notice that he smiled slightly whenever Mrs. J. described Paul's latest exploits.

The descriptions of disturbed family relations made by psychoanalytically trained observers during the 1950s and 1960s focused on identifying features of the family environment conducive to the development of schizophrenia. For the most part these theorists dealt with dyadic concepts— "emotional divorce" (Bowen, Dysinger, and Basamania, 1959), "marital schism" and "marital skew" (Lidz, Cornelison, Fleck, and Terry, 1957); and they emphasized adult roles and communication—"role reciprocity" (Mittlemann, 1948); and "pseudomutuality" (Wynne, Ryckoff, Day, and Hirsch, 1958).

More recent descriptions of family pathology by psychoanalytic clinicians either suggest or are explicitly based on arrested ego development and pathological early object relations. Skynner (1981) listed the following major features of disturbed families: diffuse interpersonal boundaries, unclear identities, satisfaction from fantasy as opposed to reality, difficulty coping with separation and loss, attempts to preserve past states of relationships—often fantasied—and attempts to manipulate others into rigidly held views of them. Many of these concepts are clearly related to the developmental tasks described above.

From an object relations point of view, inadequate separation and individuation as well as introjection of pathological objects are critical determinants of poor adult adjustment. Whether premature or delayed, difficulty in separating creates lasting problems. Guntrip (1969, p. 128) described how separation anxiety weakens the ego, as follows:

> However caused, the danger of separation, whether by desertion or withdrawal, is that the infant, starting life with a primitive and quite undeveloped psyche, just cannot stand the loss of his object. He cannot retain his primitive wholeness for more than a short period in the absence of mother and cannot go on to develop a strong sense of identity and selfhood without an object-relation. Separation-anxiety then is a pointer to the last and worst fear, fear of the loss of ego itself, of depersonalization and the sense of unreality.

Failure to develop a cohesive sense of self and a differentiated identity causes a prolonged and intensely emotional attachment to the family. This dependent attachment to parents handicaps a person's ability to develop a social and family life of his or her own. This, in object relations terms, explains the enmeshment that characterizes so many symptomatic families (Minuchin, 1974).

The parents' own failure to accept the fact that their children are separate beings can take extreme forms, leading to the most severe types of psychopathology. Several investigators have remarked that anorexia nervosa is a problem that results from inadequate separation and individuation (Bruch, 1978; Masterson, 1977). Often the parents' own serious personality disorders prevent them from understanding and accepting their children's need for independence. Such parents cannot tolerate separation or deviation from their rules, and respond to independent ventures with extreme overcontrol. The result is that the children do not differentiate their own needs from those of their parents; and they become overly compliant, "perfect" children. Lidz (Lidz, Cornelison, and Fleck, 1965) described a mother of identical twins who, when she was constipated, would give her two sons an enema or laxative.

The compliant facade of "false self" (Winnicott, 1965b) of these children is adaptive only as long as they remain at home with their parents. That is why poorly differentiated children usually face a crisis in adolescence, a time when developmental pressures for independence conflict with infantile family attachments. The outcome may be continued dependence or a violent adolescent rebellion. But the teenager who rebels as a reaction against strong unresolved dependency needs is ill-equipped for mature social relations—not to mention marriage. Behind a facade of proud self-reliance, such individuals harbor deep longings for dependence and tend to be extremely emotionally reactive. When they marry, they may seek constant approval, or automatically reject control and influence, or both.

> In their first couples therapy session, Mr. and Mrs. B.'s complaints were mirror images. He claimed she was "bossy and demanding," while she said that he "had to have everything his own way and wouldn't listen to anybody." An exploration of Mr. B's history revealed that he was the youngest child in a closely-knit family of five. He described his mother as warm and loving, but said she tried to smother him, and that she discouraged all his efforts to be independent. Subjected to these same pressures, his two older sisters conformed and still remain unmarried, living with their parents. Mr. B., however, rebelled against his mother's domination and left home to join the Marines at 17. As he related his experience in the Marine Corps and successful business ventures, it was clear that he was fiercely proud of his independence.
>
> Once the story of Mr. B.'s success in breaking away from his overcontrolling mother was brought out into the open, both Mr. and Mrs. B. had a clearer understanding of his tendency to overreact to anything he perceived as controlling. Deeper analysis subsequently revealed that

while Mr. B. staunchly rejected what he called "bossiness," he nevertheless was terribly concerned with securing praise and approval. Apparently, he had learned to fear his deep-seated dependency needs, and he protected himself with a facade of "not needing anything from anybody." Nevertheless, the needs were still there, and had in fact been a powerful determinant of his choice of wife.

Much of the current psychoanalytic thinking about the effects of pathological object relations have come from Otto Kernberg's and Heinz Kohut's studies of borderline character disorders and narcissistic personalities. While the majority of persons seeking family therapy are not so severely disturbed, a great many people suffer from similar dynamics.

In treating borderline personality disorders, Kernberg (1966) was struck by the fact that his patients alternately expressed complementary sides of a conflict, one minute expressing libidinal or aggressive impulses, the next minute behaving defensively in just the opposite manner. He deduced that their behavior was the result of marked compartmentalization of ego states due to a *splitting of the ego.* In borderline personalities, early conflict-ridden object relations are easily triggered, resulting in expression of contradictory ego states that are split off from one another. Good and bad partial objects are swallowed whole and remain as potential expressions without being integrated or modified.

The essence of Kernberg's position is that borderline pathology is an object relations disorder. Excessive rage is its cause, and splitting is the defense against it. Borderline patients are liable to sudden outbursts of anger, then equally suddenly will change to warm, friendly, and dependent behavior. When provoked to rage, their image of the hated person corresponds to an early image of mother; their self-image as a rejected or attacked little child corresponds to an image internalized from early interactions.

The cause of pathological introjection is maternal overprotection or rejection, or both. The child who is exposed to inadequate parenting takes in narcissistic grandiosity, or devaluation and narcissistic rage. Moreover, failure to develop positive forms of identification impairs the child's ability to establish a cohesive self, adequately differentiated from others. Instead the emerging self is organized around pathological introjects; this results in a sense of inadequacy and an inability to tolerate frustration or criticism without feeling rejected to the point of threatened destruction.

Kohut (1971, 1977) described the development of narcissistic pathology, which can take extreme forms as in narcissistic personality disorders, but in less severe forms is one of the most significant and widespread problems in human nature. The child whose needs for *mirroring* and *idealization* are not adequately met goes through life forever hungering to be admired. This hunger may be manifest in the showy exhibitionism most people associate with the term "narcissistic," but it is equally likely to be seen as a childlike craving for dependency and appreciation. The child who hungered in vain for praise becomes an adult who alternately suppresses the craving for attention, then lets it break through in an all-or-none form in the presence of anyone who seems to be responsive. If selfishness means unconcern with others, narcissistic personalities are just the opposite. They are obsessed with the opinion of others—and have an inordinate need to be loved and admired.

The more starved for appreciation the child, the less likely the adult will ever be satisfied. The reason is that the under-responded-to child does not modify the *grandiose self* into realistic goals and ambitions, but represses it, where it remains as an impossible standard of unconscious ambition.

To the extent that pathogenic introjections form the core of the self, there is a propensity for projection. Meissner (1978) described this as the *paranoid process;* split-off and repressed parts of the self are externally displaced, distorting object relations. Pathological introjects not only create a poor self-image, they contaminate relations with others as well. This process causes transference reactions, and it seriously affects marital choices and, ultimately, the dynamics of family life.

When it comes to marital choice, psychoanalysts assure us, love is blind. Freud (1921) wrote that the overvaluation of the loved object when we fall in love leads us to make false judgments based on *idealization*. The "fall" of "falling in love" reflects an overflow of narcissistic libido, so that the object of our love becomes a substitute for our own unattained ego ideal. Naturally our own identity glows in an ideal light. It is particularly when we have dark doubts that we seem to need this special lighting.

Psychoanalysts point out that marital choice is based partially on the desire to find an object who will complement and reinforce unconscious fantasies (Dicks, 1963). Depending upon the nature of these fantasies, some people expect their partners always to gratify them, and others expect their partners never to gratify them. Moreover, people tend to seek mates with complementary needs (Meissner, 1978); this point is illustrated in those marriages where one partner is dominant and the other submissive. Such relationships may be both stable and functional; beginning therapists are therefore well advised not to impose their own values, or try to "save" women from doll's-house marriages, or rescue men from being dominated by their wives.

Further complicating marital choice is the fact that we learn early to hide some of our real needs and feelings in order to win approval. Children who are insecure tend to develop an outward appearance of being good, and to deny and repress impulses and feelings they fear may lead to rejection. Winnicott (1965a) dubbed this phenomenon the *false self*—children behave as if they were perfect angels, pretending to be what they are not.

But because they are only acting, their emotional responses lack depth and genuineness. Such children do not trust other people to accept their unbridled selves, and use false selves to protect fragile self-esteem.

In its most extreme form, the development of a false self leads to schizoid behavior (Guntrip, 1969); even in less severe manifestations it affects the choice of a marital partner. During courtship both partners are eager to please and, therefore, present themselves in the best possible light. Powerful dependency needs, narcissism, and unruly impulses may be submerged before marriage; but once married, the spouses reveal themselves without camouflage—warts and all.

Marital choice is heavily influenced by the mutual fit of the two partners' projective systems. Typically each wants the other to be an idealized parent. But since this need was frustrated in childhood, it is defended against, and neither directly felt nor revealed. The honeymoon may therefore turn out to be no honeymoon at all, as a woman realizes that the tower of strength she thought she married is in fact not her father, but a callow young man with dependency needs of his own. Likewise, a new husband may discover that he is now the target of those angry hysterics he had previously seen directed only against his wife's mother.

In addition to feeling freer to be themselves after marriage, many spouses actually regress to an earlier stage of development. While they are teenagers living with their parents, most people react to stress and frustration in immature ways, such as pouting or attacking angrily. Such behavior is not likely to be accepted by peers, so that people tend to suppress it outside their families and while they are living on their own. However, after they marry, so that they are once again in a family situation, many people begin again to act like adolescents. Consequently the first few months of marriage can be very trying.

Families as well as individuals seem to have *general developmental levels* and experience fixation and regression. According to Skynner (1981), families pass on a general level of development from one generation to the next. Developmental failures are part of every family's inheritance; for example, a woman who did not get good-enough mothering will probably fail in this role herself. Often the signs of developmental failure may be manifest in sexual or aggressive acting out; such symptoms often obscure the object relations root of the problem. But Guntrip (1971, p. 40) has cautioned,

> I have never yet met any patient whose overintense sexuality and/or aggression could not be understood in object-relational terms, as resulting from too great and too early deprivations of mothering and general frustration of healthy development in childhood.

Most families function adequately until they are stressed, at which time they become "stuck" in rigid and dysfunctional patterns (Barnhill and

Longo, 1978). When faced with stress, families tend to decompensate to earlier levels of development. The amount of stress a family can tolerate depends upon its level of development and the type of fixations its members may have.

Like individuals, families may pass through one developmental stage and on to the next without having fully resolved the issues of the transition. Thus there may be partial fixations at one or more stages of the family life cycle. When stressed, the family not only re-experiences old conflicts, but also falls back on old patterns of coping. Consequently, family therapists need to identify fixation points and regressive patterns of coping, as well as current difficulties.

Psychiatrists, and especially psychoanalysts, have been criticized (Szasz, 1961) for absolving people of responsibility for their actions. To say that someone has "acted-out" "repressed" sexual urges through an extramarital affair is to suggest that he or she is not to be held accountable for infidelity. One writer, however, Ivan Boszormenyi-Nagy, stresses the idea of ethical accountability within families. Good family relationships include behaving ethically with other family members and considering each member's welfare and interests. Nagy believes that family members owe one another *loyalty*, and that they acquire *merit* by supporting each other. To the degree that parents are fair and responsible, they engender loyalty in their children; however, parents create loyalty conflicts when they ask their children to be loyal to one parent at the expense of disloyalty to the other (Boszormenyi-Nagy and Ulrich, 1981).

Pathological reactions may develop from *invisible loyalties*. These are unconscious commitments that children take on to help their families, to the detriment of their own well-being. For example, a child may get sick to unite parents in concern. Invisible loyalties are problematic because they are not subject to rational awareness and scrutiny. The similarity between invisible loyalties and object relations concepts is not surprising; many of Nagy's concepts redescribe traditional psychoanalytic concepts in the language of relational ethics. Another example is his (1967, 1972) concept of *interlocking need templates*, essentially the same as projective identification.

Nagy believes that symptoms develop when the trustworthiness of relationships breaks down because caring and accountability are absent. But while emphasizing such ethical and transactional considerations, Nagy does not neglect the subjective experience and unconscious dynamics of individual family members (Boszormenyi-Nagy and Ulrich, 1981, p. 160):

> There is no theoretical parsimony in trying to invalidate the significance of drives, psychic development, and inner experience. On the contrary, it appears that the intensive, in-depth relational implications of psychoanalytic theory need to be explored, expanded, and integrated with the other contextual dimensions.

The other contextual dimensions referred to are *facts*, *power alignments*, and *relational ethics*.

While most psychoanalytic thinkers would agree that it's appropriate and necessary to consider individual rights and responsibilities within the family, some have pointed out that individual boundaries are blurred by unconscious connections with other family members. Kernberg (1975), for example, writes that blurring of boundaries between the self and others is a result of projective identification, since part of the projected impulse is still recognized within the ego.

Marriage on the surface appears to be a contract between two responsible people; at a deeper level, however, marriage is a transaction between hidden internalized objects. Contracts in marital relations are usually described using the terms of behavioral or communications theories; but Sager's (1981) treatment of marital contracts also considers the unconscious and intrapsychic factors that are based on earlier introjected childhood influences. Each contract has three levels of awareness: 1) verbalized, though not always heard (!); 2) conscious but not verbalized, usually because of fear of anger or disapproval; and 3) unconscious. Each partner acts as though the other ought to be aware of the terms of the contract, and is hurt and angry if the spouse does not live up to these terms. Spouses who behave like this do not accept each other's real personality and identity; each wants the other to conform to an internalized role model, and punishes the other when these unrealistic expectations are disappointed (Dicks, 1963). Even when such behavior is overtly resisted, it may at the same time be unconsciously colluded with. It is valid and useful to emphasize individual rights and responsibilities in real relationships (Boszormenyi-Nagy, 1972) but it is also true that at an unconscious level a marital pair may represent a single personality, with each spouse playing the role of half self and half the other's projective identifications. This is why people tend to marry those with needs complementary to their own (Meissner, 1978).

A similar dynamic operates between parents and children. Even before they are born, children exist as part of their parents' fantasies (Scharff and Scharff, 1987). The anticipated child may represent, among other things, a more devoted love object than the spouse, someone to succeed where the parent has failed, or a peace offering to re-establish loving relations with grandparents.

Zinner and Shapiro (1972) coined the term *delineations* for parental acts and statements that communicate the parents' images to their children. Pathogenic delineations are based more on parents' defensive needs than on realistic perceptions of the children; moreover, parents are strongly motivated to maintain defensive delineations despite anything the children actually do. Thus it is not uncommon to see parents who insist upon seeing their children as bad, helpless, and sick, or brilliant, normal, and fearless, regardless of the truth.

Any and all of the children in a family may suffer from such distortions, but usually only one is identified as "the patient" or the "sick one." He or she is chosen usually because of some trait that makes him or her a suitable target for the parents' projected emotions. These children should not, however, be thought of as helpless victims. In fact, they collude in the projected identification in order to cement attachments, assuage unconscious guilt, or preserve their parents' shaky marriages. Often the presenting symptom is symbolic of the denied parental emotion. A misbehaving child may be acting out her father's repressed anger at his wife; an overly dependent child may be expressing his mother's fear of leading an independent life outside the home; and a bully may be counterphobically compensating for his father's projected insecurity.

Intrapsychic personality dynamics are obscured by psychological defenses, which mask the true nature of an individual's feelings, both from himself and from others. *Family myths* (Ferreira, 1963) serve the same function in families, simplifying and distorting reality. Stierlin (1977) elaborated on Ferreira's view of family myths and developed the implications for family assessment and therapy. Myths protect family members from facing certain painful truths, and also serve to keep outsiders from learning embarrassing facts. A typical myth is that of family harmony, familiar to family therapists, especially those who have worked with conflict-avoiding families. In the extreme, this myth takes the form of "pseudomutuality" (Wynne, Ryckoff, Day, and Hirsch, 1958) found in schizophrenic families. Often the myth of family harmony is maintained by the use of projective identification; one family member is delegated to be the bad one, and all the others insist they are happy and well-adjusted. This bad seed may be the identified patient or sometimes a deceased relative.

Families often view outsiders, especially family therapists, as intruders who want to stir up painful and embarrassing memories. The more they fear such inquiries, the more they cling to family myths. Therapists must neither be fooled by these myths, nor make the mistake of attacking them prematurely.

GOALS OF THERAPY

The goal of psychoanalytic family therapy is to free family members of unconscious restrictions so that they will be able to interact with one another as whole, healthy persons on the basis of current realities rather than unconscious images of the past. Plainly this is an ambitious task and often therapists will accept less. Families in acute crisis are treated with understanding and support to help them through their crisis. Once the crisis is resolved, the psychoanalytic family therapist hopes to engage the family in long-term reconstructive psychotherapy. Some families accept, but many do not. When the family is motivated only for symptom relief, the therapist should support its decision to terminate, lest the family members drop out and feel that they have failed. Some psychoanalytic family therapists deliberately plan short-term treatment. In these cases, just as in individual short-term dynamic psychotherapy (e.g., Sifneos, 1972), it is considered essential to narrow the field of exploration by selecting a specific focus for treatment. A notable exponent of short-term psychoanalytic family therapy is Christopher Dare, at the Maudsley Hospital in London. Although it is not common, some psychoanalytic family therapists also engage in explicitly crisis-oriented family therapy (Umana, Gross, and McConville, 1980).

When psychoanalytic family therapists opt for crisis resolution with symptom-reduction as the only goal, they function much like other family therapists. Hence, they focus more on supporting defenses and clarifying communication than on analyzing defenses and uncovering repressed needs and impulses. When the goal is personal growth and structural change, more technical psychoanalytic methods are employed and therapy is extended for a year or more.

It is easy to say that the goal is personality change; it is rather more difficult to specify precisely what is meant by "change." The kind of change most commonly sought after is described as separation-individuation (Katz, 1981) or differentiation (Skynner, 1981); both terms emphasize the growth and independence of individuals from their families of origin, and thus reflect the prominent influence of object relations theory. (Perhaps an additional reason for emphasizing separation-individuation is the fact that enmeshed families are more likely to seek and to remain in treatment than are isolated or disengaged families). Individual therapists often think of individuation in terms of physical separation. Thus adolescents and young adults may be treated in isolation from their families in order to help them become more independent. Family therapists, on the other hand, believe that emotional growth and autonomy are best achieved by working through the emotional bonds within the family. Rather than remove individuals from their families, psychoanalytic family therapists convene families to help them learn how to let go of one another in a way that allows each individual to be independent as well as related. Individuation neither requires, nor is achieved by, severing relationship bonds. The following extended example illustrates how the goals of psychoanalytic family therapy were implemented with a particular family.

Three months after he went away to college, Barry J. had his first psychotic break. A brief hospital stay made it clear that Barry was unable to withstand separation from his family without severely decompensating; therefore, the hospital staff recommended that upon discharge he should live apart from his parents with only minimal contact, in order to help him become an independent adult. Accordingly, he was discharged to a supportive group home for young adults and seen twice weekly in individual psychotherapy. Unfortunately, he suffered a second breakdown, and within two months was once again hospitalized.

As the time for discharge from this second hospitalization approached, the ward psychiatrist decided to convene a meeting of the entire family in order to discuss plans for Barry's post-hospital adjustment. During this meeting it became painfully obvious that powerful forces within the family were binding Barry and impeding any chance for genuine separation. Barry's parents were both pleasant and effective people who separately were most engaging and helpful. Towards each other, however, they displayed an icy hatred. During those few moments in the interview when they spoke to each other, rather than to Barry, their hostility was palpable. Only their concern for and involvement with Barry, their youngest, prevented their relationship from becoming a battleground—a battleground upon which Barry feared one or both of them might be destroyed.

At the staff conference following this interview two plans for disposition were advanced. One group, recognizing the powerful pathological influence of the family, recommended that Barry be removed as far as possible from the family and treated in individual psychotherapy. Only by isolating Barry from his parents, they argued, was there hope that he could mature into an independent person. Others on the staff disagreed, arguing that only by treating the family conjointly could the collusive bond between Barry and his parents be resolved. After lengthy discussion the group reached a consensus to try the latter approach.

Most of the early family meetings were dominated by the parents' anxious concern about Barry: about the apartment complex where he lived, about his job, about his friends, about how he was spending his leisure time, about his clothes, about his grooming—in short, about every detail of his life. Gradually, with the therapist's support, Barry was able to limit how much of his life was open to his parents' scrutiny. As he did so, and as they were less able to preoccupy themselves with him, they began more and more to focus on their own relationship. As Barry became more successful at handling his own affairs, his parents became openly combative with each other.

Following a session during which the parents' marital relationship was the primary focus, the therapist recommended that the parents come for a few separate sessions in addition to the regular family meetings. In these separate sessions, unable to divert their attention to Barry, the J.s fought viciously, leaving no doubt that theirs was a seriously destructive relationship. Rather than getting better in treatment, their relationship got worse.

After two months of internecine warfare—during which time Barry continued to improve—Mr. and Mrs. J. sought a legal separation. Once they were separated, both parents seemed to become happier, more involved with their friends and careers, and less worried about Barry. As they further released their stranglehold on their son, both parents began to develop a warmer and more genuine relationship with him. Even after the parents divorced they continued to attend family sessions with Barry.

In place of the original tensely symbiotic bond, a more balanced relationship between Barry and his parents gradually emerged. Resolution of hidden conflicts, and working through of unconscious loyalties, led to genuine autonomy of separate persons—enjoying but no longer needing each other—an outcome far better than isolation.

CONDITIONS FOR BEHAVIOR CHANGE

As any student knows, psychoanalytic therapy achieves personality change and growth through insight; but the idea that insight cures is a misleading oversimplification. Insight is necessary, but not sufficient, for successful psychoanalytic treatment. In psychoanalytic family therapy, family members expand their insight by learning that their psychological lives are larger than their conscious experience, and by coming to understand and accept repressed parts of their personalities. Just as in individual therapy, interpretations, to be effective, should be limited to preconscious material—that which the patient is almost aware of; interpretations of unconscious material arouse anxiety, which means they will be rejected. Whatever insights are achieved, however, must subsequently be *worked through* (Greenson, 1967)—that is, translated into new and more productive ways of behaving and interacting.

Some (Kohut, 1977) have even suggested that psychoanalytic treatment works not as much by insight as by reducing defenses—patients simply experience and express repressed parts of themselves. From this point of view, it may be more important for family members to express their unconscious needs than to learn to understand them better. Regardless of which position is taken, most therapists work to do both—that is, both foster insight and encourage expression of repressed impulses (Ackerman, 1958).

Analytic therapists foster insight by penetrating beneath the surface of behavior to the hidden motives below. In individual therapy, dreams and free associations are considered to be *manifest content*, not to be taken at face value. Likewise, manifest family interactions are thought to be disguised versions of the latent feelings hidden behind them. Nonanalytic family therapists accept the meaning of the family's manifest interactions; analytic family therapists attempt to uncover other material, especially that which is hidden, unconscious, and from the past. According to Framo (1970, p. 158), "The family cannot undergo deep or meaningful change if the therapist deals only with current, immediate interactions among the members."

Naturally, families defend against exposing their innermost feelings. After all, it is a great deal to ask of anyone to expose old wounds and embarrassing emotions. Psychoanalysts deal with this problem by creating a climate of trust and by proceeding very slowly. But the risk of exposure is far greater in family therapy. Not only do family members have to acknowledge painful feelings, they are asked to do so in front of the very people they most want to hide them from. A therapist might offer as an interpretation the idea that a man hates his wife because he blames her for depriving him of the freedom of his lost youth. In individual treatment, the patient may acknowledge this fairly readily, wonder why he has suppressed his feelings, and begin to explore the roots of his reactions. But imagine how much more difficult it is to admit its truth and acknowledge his feelings in front of his wife.

Since patients in family therapy are likely to be concerned about public exposure as well as self-protection, therapists must offer them a great deal of security. Such security is necessary both for uncovering material for analysis, and also for working through this material in family interaction. Once an atmosphere of security is established, the analytic family therapist can begin to identify projective mechanisms and bring them back into the marital relationship. Then the spouses can reinternalize parts of themselves that they projected onto their mates. Once they no longer need to rely on projective identification, they can acknowledge and accept previously split-off, guilt-ridden libidinal and aggressive parts of their own egos. The therapist helps spouses resolve introjects of their parents, so they can see how their present difficulties emerged from unconscious attempts to perpetuate old conflicts from their families of origin. This work is painful and cannot proceed without the continual security offered by a competent and supportive therapist. Nichols (1987) emphasizes the need for *empathy* to create a "holding environment" for the whole family.

Any form of family therapy derived from psychoanalytic principles must establish a climate of sufficient safety to expose and analyze object-relational images, internalized at an early age. Moreover, in order to work through these insights, secure social interactions must be nurtured in family treatment sessions so that unfinished developmental tasks can be uncovered and surmounted. Speaking to this point, Guntrip (1971) wrote that analysts who emphasize instinct theory can blame treatment failures on the great strength of their patients' sexuality and aggression. But from an object-relations perspective, such failures are more likely to be seen as the therapist's failure to make treatment relationships secure. For the therapist, this means listening without becoming overly intrusive; for family members, it means learning to hear each other's complaints as statements of feelings and requests for change, rather than as attacks that threaten their ego integrity.

Transference, the *sine qua non* of individual psychoanalysis, is also considered essential for psychoanalytic family therapy. Individual patients reveal their unconscious assumptions about people by acting them out in the therapeutic relationship. Family members reveal repressed images of past family relationships in their current interactions with family members, as well as with the therapist.

To some, the idea of transference seems relevant only to individual therapy, where in the absence of a real relationship most of the patient's feelings toward the therapist must be inspired by fantasy. What need is there to think of transference in family therapy when the "real" relationships are actually present? In fact, transference is ubiquitous in all emotionally significant relationships. By re-experiencing and acting out repetitious past patterns—towards the therapist, or other family members, or both—a person can begin to view these interactions objectively and, with a therapist's help, begin to break up repititious pathological cycles. According to Boszormenyi-Nagy (1972, p. 378) family therapy offers an even more fertile field of utilizing transference than does individual therapy.

> Beginning family therapists are soon struck with a different climate for therapeutic transference as they begin to see families rather than isolated individuals. The chief reason for this is the fact that family relationships themselves are embedded in a transference context and the family therapist can enter the ongoing transference relationship system rather than having to recreate it as a new relationship in the privacy of an exclusive therapist-patient work relationship.

Elsewhere, Nadelson (1978, p. 123) wrote,

> Since marital conflict may be viewed as a result of the mutual projection, by each partner, of early internalized objects, and thus may become the battleground for past conflict, the therapist must be aware of each spouse's transference projection onto the partner as well as onto the therapist.

When two or more generations of family members are present in treatment it often becomes painfully obvious how certain distortions in one relationship are rooted in repetitions of previous experiences. Here psychoanalytic family therapists have great information, and the leverage to rework developmental experiences in such a way as to modify pathological introjects. In describing the interrelations among family members' pathology, Ackerman (1966) coined the felicitous phrase, "a cluster of interpenetrating illnesses."

By gathering whole families for treatment, the psychoanalytic therapist broadens the number of transference reactions, but mutes their intensity. Transference to the therapist exists, but because the family is present, it is less intense than in individual therapy. As Nagy (1972) has observed, "parentification" of the therapist is antithetical to existing family ties. Both the real and the transference reactions to other family members divert a good deal of emotional energy that otherwise might be focused on the therapist. Furthermore the aloofness and ambiguity of the therapist is less marked in family than in individual therapy.

For most psychoanalytical family therapists, transference is the operative model for understanding family emotional systems. "It is as if the family members evolve a more or less stable transference-countertransference configuration among themselves" (Meissner, 1978, p. 81).

The field of observation is enlarged for the psychoanalytic therapist, who can see not only the real relationship among the generations that are assembled but also the vestiges of previous generations and past interactions encoded as object images and manifest as transference. As in individual therapy, the family therapist ignores transference at his peril. But although awareness of transference, as well as resistance and projection, must guide the therapist's interventions, these reactions need not always, or only, be interpreted. Some psychoanalytically inspired therapists prefer to offset interactions based on transference rather than to interpret them (Boszormenyi-Nagy and Ulrich, 1981).

Two of the major considerations in family therapy are who should be included in the treatment and on whom should the help be focused. Some approaches, as, for instance, strategic and behavioral, focus on helping the identified patient, even though the family may be seen conjointly. Most psychoanalytic family therapists seem to agree that the commitment should be to all family members; however, they are more likely to mean helping individuals to grow and mature, than helping the family as an organic whole. "To help an individual or couple in marital conflict one must help each partner move towards a higher level of personality development" (Blanck, 1967, p. 160).

The nature of this "higher level of personality development" has been defined in both structural and object-relations terms. For example, Nadelson (1978, p. 146) emphasized the structural aim of bringing instinctual drives under the dominion of the ego, when she wrote,

> The ultimate aim of interpretation and working through in psychoanalytically oriented marital therapy is the neutralization and integration of aggressive and libidinal needs so that behavior is motivated more in the service of the ego and less by impulse and intrapsychic conflict.

When aggressive and libidinal impulses are interpreted and experienced, they become conscious. Once they become aware of such impulses, family members are better able to integrate them into their lives and thus overcome their pathological, controlling power.

The personal growth aimed for in psychoanalytic treatment can also be sought in terms of improved object relations. For family members to overcome pathological attachments to each other, they must be helped to become whole individuals. As Guntrip put it, "Psychotherapy is the rein-

tegration of the split-ego, the restoration of lost wholeness" (1971, p. 94).
The split ego, which developed from bad object relations early in life, is
resolved by good object relations, first in psychotherapy and subsequently
in interactions within the family.

TECHNIQUES

For all the complexity of psychoanalytic theory, psychoanalytic technique
is relatively simple—not necessarily easy, but simple. In psychoanalytic
family therapy there are four basic techniques: listening, empathy, interpretation, and maintaining analytic neutrality. Two of these—listening and
analytic neutrality—may not sound terribly profound or different from
what other family therapists do. They are.

Listening is a strenuous but silent activity, rare in our culture. Most
of the time we're too busy waiting to get in a word edgewise to listen more
than superficially. This is especially true in family therapy where therapists
feel a tremendous pressure to Do Something to help the troubled and
troubling families they treat. And this is where the importance of maintaining analytic neutrality comes in. To establish an analytic atmosphere it
is essential to aim for listening and understanding without worrying about
whether or what the family changes. Change may come about as a by-
product of understanding, but the analytic therapist suspends anxious involvement with outcomes. It is impossible to overestimate the importance
of this frame of mind in establishing a climate of analytic exploration.

The psychoanalytic therapist resists the temptation to be drawn in to
reassure, advise, or confront families in favor of a sustained but silent
immersion in their experience. When analytic therapists do intervene, they
express empathic understanding in order to help family members open up,
and they make interpretations to clarify hidden and confusing aspects of
experience. While there is no way to specify the optimal mix of listening
and intervening, most therapists talk too much. There are many reasons
and twice as many rationalizations for this excess activity, but they have a
common result: The therapist remains overly central. Psychoanalytic therapists concentrate instead on careful listening, which, incidentally, also adds
power to the infrequent interpretations they do make.

In classical psychoanalysis, therapeutic change is achieved by analysis:
confrontation, clarification, interpretation, and working through (Greenson, 1967). Even when modifications are made, as in psychodynamic psychotherapy where cathartic techniques, suggestion, and manipulation are
employed (Bibring, 1954), interpretation remains the decisive technique.
This holds true for psychoanalytic family therapy as well. However, psychoanalytic clinicians doing family therapy are more inclined to include
other, not strictly analytic, techniques because in family treatment the

patients can begin to use awareness and start to behave differently in their families without having to leave the treatment room.

Before the therapist can attempt to change families, he or she must formulate an understanding of them. Here, psychoanalytic therapists are particularly well equipped because they have available a comprehensive theory of personality and behavior. Moreover, as some authors (Dare, 1979) have pointed out, psychoanalytic understanding is useful for developing a comprehensive picture of family dynamics even when treatment techniques are drawn from other approaches. Thus the early psychoanalytic family therapists used psychoanalytic concepts for understanding families, but resorted to other methods, especially facilitating communication, for treatment.

What distinguishes psychoanalytic from most other diagnostic formulations of families is that, as we discussed above, they understand the individual family members' intrapsychic dynamics; in fact, the majority of psychoanalytic concepts are about individuals or dyads. But since psychoanalytic family therapists must also deal with larger relationship systems, they also must consider the family's interpersonal dynamics as well as the intrapsychic lives of its members.

The following is an abbreviated sketch of an initial psychoanalytic evaluation of a family.

> After two sessions with the family of Sally G., who was suffering from school phobia, the therapist made a preliminary formulation of the family's dynamics. In addition to the usual descriptions of the family members, the presenting problem, and their history, the formulation included assessments of the parents' object relations and the collusive, unconscious interaction of their marital relationship.
>
> Mr. G. had been initially attracted to his wife as a libidinal object who would fulfill his sexual fantasies, including his voyeuristic propensities. Counterbalancing his sexual feelings was a tendency to idealize his wife, the dynamic reaction of his libidinal impulses. Thus he was deeply conflicted and intensely ambivalent in his sexual relations with her.
>
> At another level, Mr. G. had unconscious expectations that she would be the same long-suffering, self-sacrificing kind of person that his mother was. Thus, he longed for motherly consolation from her. However, these dependent longings were threatening to his sense of masculinity, so he behaved outwardly as though he were tough, self-sufficient, and needed no one. That he had a dependent inner object inside himself was shown by his tender solicitude towards his wife and children when they were ill. But they had to be in a position of weakness and vulnerability to enable him to overcome his defenses enough for him to gratify his own infantile dependency needs vicariously.
>
> Mrs. G. expected marriage to provide her with an ideal father, someone who would be loving, nurturing, and supportive. Given this unconscious expectation, the very sexuality that attracted men to her was

also a threat to her wish to be treated like a little girl. Like her husband, she too was highly conflicted about sexual relations. Raised as an only child, she always expected to come first. She was even jealous of her husband's warmth toward Sally, and attempted to maintain distance between father and daughter by her own intense attachment to Sally.

At the level of her early self-object images, she was a jealous, greedy, demanding little girl. Her introjection of her mother provided her with a model of how to treat a father figure. Unfortunately, what worked for her mother with her father did not work for her with her husband.

Thus, at an object-relations level, both spouses felt themselves to be deprived little children, each seeking automatic gratification of wishes, each wanting to be taken care of without having to ask. When these magical wishes were not granted, both of them seethed with angry resentment. Eventually they reacted to trivial provocations with the underlying rage, and horrible quarrels erupted.

When Sally witnessed her parents' violent altercations, she became terrified that her own hostile and murderous fantasies might come true. Although her parents hated their own internalized bad parent figures, they seemed to act them out with each other. Further enmeshing Sally in their conflict was the fact that the ego boundaries between herself and her mother were blurred. It was almost as though mother and daughter shared one joint personality.

Dynamically, Sally's staying home from school could be seen as a desperate attempt to protect her mother-herself from her father's attacks, and to defend both her parents against her own, projected, murderous fantasies.

Nonanalytic clinicians tend to focus their evaluations on overt communications and interactions, as well as on conscious hopes and expectations. From a psychoanalytic perspective such descriptions only scratch the surface. Unconscious forces constitute the core of family life. However, this doesn't mean that psychoanalytic clinicians deal only with the psychology of individual personality defects. Psychoanalysts who work in family therapy recognize that family dynamics are more than the additive sum of individual dynamics. Thus Henry Dicks (1967, pp. 8–9) wrote, "But such [personality] defects have mainly become organized around the marriage without necessarily invading or disturbing other facets of personality functioning, e.g., the work sphere or the area of social relations." Individuals may bring impaired object relations to family life, but it is the unconscious fit between family members that essentially determines adjustment.

Applying object relations theory to family evaluation, Dicks (1967) proposed three levels upon which to assess the marital relationship: (1) cultural values and norms—race, religion, education, values; (2) central egos—personal norms, conscious judgements and expectations, habits, and tastes; and (3) unconscious forces that are repressed or split off, including drives and object-relations needs. If a couple is in harmony on any two of these three levels, Dicks believed they will stay together, even in the face of constant conflict. However, if they are incompatible on two or more levels, the marriage will probably end in divorce.

Dicks' analysis helps to explain why many couples seem to remain together despite constant fighting, and why other couples who seem content enough suddenly split up. Presumably the battling couples who cleave together fit each other's unconscious needs, and their object-images dovetail. In discussing one such couple, Dicks (1967, p. 119) wrote,

> At the level of social value judgement, I would have no hesitation in rating the marriage of Case Ten as more living, deeper and "truer" than the conventional whited sepulchres in which no sleeping dog is permitted to raise his head, let alone bark.

Analysts do not postpone treatment until they have made an exhaustive study of their cases; on the contrary, psychoanalytic therapists may not complete their evaluations, may not even arrive at a final diagnosis, until the end of treatment. Psychoanalytic family therapists do emphasize assessment, but even so consider it merely begun at the outset of the treatment; its completion comes in the course of therapy itself.

After the preliminary psychodynamic assessment, the therapist must decide who to include in treatment. Psychoanalytic family therapists today work with every possible combination of family members. Perhaps most common, however, is treatment of married couples; most psychoanalytic clinicians will prefer to emphasize the adult nucleus of the family because it is consistent with their own verbal and intellectual level.

From an object relations point of view (Dicks, 1963), marriage is a transaction between hidden, internalized objects. These internal objects, which reflect the parenting and marital relationships in the spouses' original families, are brought into awareness by interpretation of the unconscious bases for the couple's interactions. Frequently, couples are found to have dominant *shared internal objects* (Dicks, 1967), based on unconscious assimilation of parent figures. Such couples do not relate to each other as real persons, but as angry or loving parents, to be tormented or idealized. (See Sander [1989] for a recent version of this view.)

Some aspects of internalized objects are conscious, readily expressed, and easily examined. These are based upon direct identification with consciously perceived parental models, or overcompensation against negative images. A bullying husband may be overcompensating for feeling weak, like his father. His behavior seems to say, "I won't be pushed around the way my Dad was." Such consciously held object images will emerge regardless of therapeutic technique; however, in order to get unconscious images to emerge, psychoanalytic clinicians rely upon a nondirective exploratory style.

Psychoanalytic patients are taught to *free associate*—that is, express their thoughts as they occur spontaneously, without planning or censorship. This technique is the best way to bring unconscious material to the surface. While the patient free-associates, the analyst occasionally asks clarifying questions, but mostly listens with silent interest. Eventually, the analyst begins to interpret material, particularly resistance and transference.

Psychoanalytic family therapists generally follow this basic approach. To begin with, family members are invited to speak freely about their concerns with very little interruption or guidance from the therapist. This may not sound different from what other family therapists do, but psychoanalytic family therapists are far more nondirective than practitioners of other schools. This nondirectiveness comes out in both obvious and subtle ways. Strategic therapists ask pointed questions about behavior sequences surrounding symptoms; structuralists direct family members to engage in extended dialogues; psychoanalytic therapists tend to just listen. This is not to say that they do not ask questions or that their interest is not selective. The point is that they are convinced that the spontaneous flow of their patients' thoughts and feelings provides important clues to their underlying concerns; their free associations also reveals patterns of family interactions. Psychoanalytic therapists intervene very little, much less often than others. Once a new family starts discussing its problems, most psychoanalytic therapists scrupulously refrain from comments or questions until the spontaneous flow of the family's dialogue subsides (Dicks, 1967).

Not only do they generally avoid explicitly directing what their patients say, psychoanalytic therapists are also careful not to be drawn into offering advice; nor do they try to manipulate their patients' lives. Most other family therapists also deny or minimize the amount of advice they give; but some do so frequently, however inadvertently—as in the following case.

Summarizing her fourth session with the Z. family, a psychology intern reported that they had responded quite well to an important interpretation. She then proceeded to review the detailed process notes of the session with her supervisor.

Midway through the session, Mr. Z. described an argument with his wife that took place during the week. He had come home late from work, and his wife began to nag and scold him. Previously when this happened Mr. Z. would feel terribly hurt, and go off sulking and thinking how cruel and unfair his wife was to him. This time, however, her nagging provoked him to fight back, and they had a terrific row. At this point in the narrative, the therapist intervened, saying, "So, this time you stood up for yourself. And no doubt afterwards, you felt better, didn't you?" Mr. Z. said that yes, he did feel better afterwards, and then fell silent.

Listening to this material, the supervisor realized that although Mr. Z.'s fighting back was a step in the right direction, the therapist's intervention was not an interpretation, but a thinly veiled manipulation; furthermore, it closed off exploration of the couple's dynamic interaction. Certainly, Mr. Z was aware that his pouty withdrawal in the face of criticism from his wife was not an adaptive response. What he did not understand were the unconscious reasons for his doing so—what awful consequences he anticipated in his fantasy, who it was his wife reminded him of, and what her conscious and unconscious feelings were about arguing with a man. By simply giving Mr. Z. a verbal pat on the back at this juncture the therapist helped to seal off this crucial data.

The following are examples of advice-giving and persuasion passing as interpretations. Notice that the interventions are statements of widely held beliefs and personal opinions—therapeutic clichés—rather than uncovering comments based on specific material revealed by unique persons.

A husband reported that after feeling anxious and depressed at the office all day, he had stopped on the way home and bought a bouquet of flowers for his wife. She, pleased with the gift, was especially warm and friendly that evening, and the husband felt reassured. The therapist commented, "That's good; you have to give to get."

After several sessions in which he was silent and depressed, a teenage boy finally began to argue with his mother, angrily accusing her of not understanding him and playing favorites with his brother and sister. Just as the mother was about to respond, the therapist intervened, saying, "That's good. It's good to let your feelings out. If you'd express your anger more you wouldn't get so depressed."

In the first example, the therapist, by delivering a hackneyed bit of advice, missed an opportunity to explore the husband's anxiety and the reason he was reluctant to simply tell his wife that he was unhappy. In the second, the therapist's "interpretation" precluded an exploration of what the youngster imagined would happen if he asked for more attention from his mother. Moreover, it also obscured the mother's response and took it out of the session. If she responds to her son's complaints in an angry or rejecting fashion after the session, even if it is reported, the interaction will not be directly available in the session for therapeutic intervention. Thus the advantage of being able to work through and integrate the boy's new behavior was lost.

Psychoanalytic family therapy is certainly more active than classical psychoanalysis; nevertheless, it remains a nondirective uncovering technique. The discipline involved in learning to interfere minimally, and to scrutinize one's responses to eliminate unessential or leading interventions is a critical part of psychoanalytic technique, with individuals or with families. Interpretations should neither reassure nor direct people; they should facilitate the emergence of new material, forgotten or repressed, and mobilize feelings previously avoided (Dicks, 1967).

In addition to limiting interpretations to specific material revealed by their patients, psychoanalytic therapists also limit the number of interpretations they make. Two or three per session is typical. Most of the rest of the analytic therapist's activity is devoted to eliciting material without becoming overly directive. Sessions typically begin with the therapist inviting family members to discuss current experiences, thoughts, and feelings. In subsequent meetings, the therapist might begin either by saying nothing or perhaps, "Where would you like to begin today?" The therapist then leans back and lets the family talk, with minimal direction or interference with the spontaneous flow of their communication. Questions are limited to requests for amplification and clarification. "Could you tell me more about that?" "Have the two of you discussed how you feel about moving to Chicago?"

When the initial associations and spontaneous interactions dry up, the psychoanalytic therapist probes gently, eliciting history, people's thoughts and feelings, and their ideas about family members' perspectives. "What does your father think about your problems? How would he explain them?" This technique underscores the analytic therapist's interest in assumptions and projections.

Although we have repeatedly emphasized the nondirective nature of psychoanalytic technique, it is far from a passive approach. While family members are speaking about whatever is on their minds, the therapist is actively analyzing what is being said for derivatives of drives, defenses, ego states, and manifestations of transference. Psychoanalytic therapists, more than most others, order the raw data of family dialogues by fitting them to their theory. The bare facts are always ambiguous; psychoanalytic theory organizes them and makes them meaningful.

In addition to fitting the raw data to theory, the psychoanalytic therapist also directs it by pursuing the past. Particular interest is paid to childhood memories of and associations to interactions with parents. The following vignette shows how transitions are made from the present to the past.

Among their major disappointments in each other Mr. and Mrs. S. both complained bitterly that the other one "doesn't take care of me when I'm sick, or listen to my complaints at the end of the day." Not only did they share the perceptions of the other one's lack of "mothering," they both steadfastly maintained that they were very supportive and understanding. Mrs. S.'s complaint was typical: "Yesterday was an absolute nightmare for me. The baby was sick and fussy, and I had a miserable cold. Everything was twice as hard for me and I had twice as much to do. All day long I was looking forward to John's coming home. But when he finally did, he didn't seem to care about how awful I felt. In fact he only listened to me for a minute before he started telling some dumb story about his office." Mr. S. responded by telling a similar story, but with the roles reversed.

At this point the therapist intervened to ask both spouses to describe their relationships with their mothers. What emerged were two very different but very revealing histories.

Mr. S.'s mother was a child of the Depression, for whom self-reliance, personal sacrifice, and unremitting struggle were paramount virtues. Though she loved her children, she withheld warmth, affection, and nurturance lest they become "spoiled and soft." Nevertheless, Mr. S. craved his mother's attention and constantly sought it. Naturally, he was often rebuffed. A particularly painful memory for him was of a time he came home in tears after getting beaten by a bully in the school yard. But instead of the loving comfort he hoped for, his mother scolded him for "acting like a baby," and told him he had to learn to fight his own battles. Over the years he learned to protect himself from these rebuffs by developing a rigid facade of independence and strength.

With the second significant woman in his life, his wife, Mr. S. maintained his rigid defensiveness. He never talked about his problems, but since he continued to yearn for compassionate understanding, he resented his wife bitterly for not drawing him out. His own failure to risk rejection by asking for support served as a self-fulfilling prophecy, confirming his expectation, "She doesn't care about me."

Mrs. S.'s background was quite different from her husband's. Her parents were indulgent and demonstrative. They doted on their only child, communicating their love by expressing constant, anxious concern for her well-being. When she was a little girl, the slightest bump or bruise was the occasion for lavish expressions of solicitous concern. She came to marriage used to talking about herself and her problems. At first Mr. S. was enchanted. *Here is someone who really cares about my feelings,* he thought. But when he discovered that she didn't ask him to talk about his own concerns, he became resentful and progressively less sympathetic. This convinced her, *He doesn't care about me.*

After the historical roots of current family conflicts have been uncovered, interpretations are made about how family members continue to re-enact past, and often distorted, images from childhood. The data for such interpretations come from transference reactions to the therapist or to other family members, as well as from actual childhood memories. Even more so than in individual therapy, psychoanalytic therapists who work with families deal less with recollections of the past than with re-enactments of its influence, manifest as transference. For this reason it is considered essential to create and maintain a milieu in which patients feel safe enough to relive some of their crucial unresolved conflicts, and to reactivate their early relationship images.

The following case demonstrates how a therapist's permissive acceptance enables family members to gradually shed their outer defenses and to reveal their basic conflicts and object images, which provide the material for mutative interpretations.

The H.'s were a wealthy, highly educated family, who were concerned with their oldest child's listlessness, irritability, and poor performance in school. Despite the fact the boy showed all the signs of a mild depressive episode, the therapist insisted upon seeing the whole family.

In the first few sessions, the family was very polite and dignified, with each one playing a recognizable role. Alex, the identified patient, described his discouragement and lack of interest in school, while his parents expressed their concern, alternately supportively and critically. Alex's younger sister Susan, a lively and robust child, showed little concern for her brother, and generally spoke much more about her life outside the family than her brother did.

At first the family was so composed and collected that the therapist began to experience reality as they did: namely, that nothing was wrong in the family, except for Alex. After a time, the parents voiced a few disagreements about how to respond to Alex, but they quickly submerged them. Gradually, however, as they felt safer in therapy—safer than they did alone together at home—Mr. and Mrs. H. began to argue more and more openly. During this process the therapist made no interpretations, but concentrated her efforts on accepting the couple's arguing, while gently blocking their efforts to detour their conflict. Because they felt protected by the therapist, the spouses allowed the full fury of their feelings to be expressed, and their arguments became increasingly vituperative.

By uncovering the hidden conflict in the marriage, and blocking the scapegoating of the identified patient, the therapist was following the same course that most nonanalytic therapists would pursue. At this point, she did not simply stay with the couple's conflict, but instead began to explore their separate childhood histories. In short, having uncovered their conflict, she sought to trace its genetic sources.

What emerged from Mr. H.'s portrait of his childhood was a picture of a boy who had learned to appease his hypercritical mother by not openly challenging her. Moreover, since he did not expect much positive reaction from her, he generally avoided her company as much as possible.

For her part, Mrs. H. described her close relationship with a dominant mother and a lifelong disdain for her father, a man who was very successful professionally, but played only a marginal role in her upbringing.

Only after extensive exploration of these early object relations did the therapist begin to interpret the couple's conflictual behavior. Mr. H., she pointed out, believed that he had to mollify his wife (like his mother), but didn't expect any understanding or support from her, so he withdrew from her and lavished his affection on his children. In their early married years, Mrs. H. struck back in self-defense; she demanded that he spend more time with her, talk more, be more attentive. Eventually, however, she accepted his withdrawal (as she had seen her mother do with her father), and redirected her angry disappointments to her son. In short, these two apparently sophisticated adults were behaving, unconsciously, like children; he like a frightened child hiding from a harsh, critical mother, and she like a spoiled daughter hopelessly enraged at the lack of a relationship with her husband.

In this case the therapist analyzed and interpreted the unconscious object representations that played a large part in the family's conflict. In addition, her permissive acceptance of the couple's loud arguments provided them with a permissive superego figure to be incorporated in the holding environment. Psychoanalytic family therapists are aware that their influence is not confined to rational analysis, but also includes a kind of reparenting. Thus therapists may act in a more controlling or permissive fashion depending upon their assessment of the particular needs of the family.

One psychoanalytic family therapist who was acutely aware of his personal influence on families was Nathan Ackerman. His recommendations on technique (Ackerman, 1966) were designed to penetrate family defenses in order to surface hidden conflicts over sex and aggression. To begin with, he advocated a deep personal commitment and involvement with families. His own style was intimate and provocative. Unlike the traditionally reserved and aloof analyst, Ackerman related to families in a very open and personal manner. In this regard he wrote (1961, p. 242):

> It is very important at the outset to establish a meaningful emotional contact with all members of the family, to create a climate in which one really touches them and they feel they touch back.

After making contact, Ackerman encouraged open and honest expression of feeling by being open and honest himself. His spontaneous self-disclosure of his own thoughts and feelings made it hard for family members to resist doing likewise.

Ackerman certainly made full use of his warm and charismatic personality, but did more than simply "be himself" and "let it all hang out" in family sessions. He also made conscious and deliberate use of confrontive techniques to ease family secrets and conflicts from behind their defensive facades. His own memorable phrase to describe this was "tickling the defenses." Always aware of people's tendency to avoid what is painful or embarrassing, he teased, cajoled, and provoked family members to open up and say what was really on their minds.

Naturally, psychoanalytic family therapists emphasize that much of what is hidden in family dialogues is not consciously withheld, but rather repressed into unconsciousness. The approach to this material is guarded by resistance, and when it is manifest it is often in the form of transference. In fact, it is fair to say that the goal of any form of psychoanalytic psychotherapy is to overcome resistance and to work through the past in the transferences of the present.

Resistance is any conscious or unconscious behavior that blocks or impedes therapy. In families, resistance is collusive and more often manifest in overt behavior than it is in private therapy. Frank discussions of problems within the family are often painful, and most people go to great lengths to avoid them. Some of the common forms of resistance include seeking individual therapy or separate sessions to avoid facing family problems; persistently talking to the therapist instead of to other family members; avoiding conflictual topics; scapegoating; becoming depressed to avoid the danger of angry confrontations; and steadfastly refusing to consider one's own role in problematic interactions.

Most psychoanalytic family therapists deal with resistance by interpreting it early in its appearance. The family technique for interpreting resistance is different from that used in individual therapy. In individual therapy the aim is primarily to foster insight into the nature and meaning of resistance; therefore, resistances are generally not interpreted until they become obvious to the patient. Moreover, the most effective interpretations are elicited from the patient, rather than given by the therapist. For example, in individual psychotherapy a psychoanalytic therapist would wait for three or four recurrences before discussing a patient's lateness. Confronting lateness on its first occurrence is merely liable to make the patient defensive, and thus impede understanding of the reason he or she is tardy. After the lateness (or other form of resistance) has become a recognized pattern, the therapist will ask the patient to consider its meaning.

By contrast, family therapists interpret resistance more directly and sooner. The reason for this is that resistance in family therapy is more likely to take the form of acting-out, so that family therapists have to meet resistance with confrontation very early on. The following vignette illustrates the interpretation of resistance.

> Mr. and Mrs. Z. had endured ten years of an unrewarding marriage, with an unhappy sexual relationship, in order to preserve the fragile security that being married offered them. Mrs. Z.'s totally unexpected and uncharacteristic affair forced the couple to acknowledge the problems in their marriage, and so they consulted a family therapist.
>
> Although they could no longer deny the existence of conflict, both spouses exhibited major resistance to confronting their problems openly. Their resistance represented personal reluctance to acknowledge certain of their feelings, and a joint collusion to avoid frank discussions of their relational problems.
>
> In the first session, both partners said that married life had been "more or less okay"; that Mrs. Z. had some kind of "midlife crisis"; and

that it was she who needed therapy. This request for individual therapy was seen as a resistance to avoid the painful examination of the marriage, and the therapist said so. "It seems, Mr. Z., that you'd rather blame your wife than consider how the two of you may both be contributing to your difficulties. And you, Mrs. Z., seem to prefer accepting all the guilt in order to avoid confronting your husband with your dissatisfaction and anger."

Accepting the therapist's interpretation and agreeing to examine their marriage together deprived the couple of one form of resistance, as though an escape hatch had been closed to two reluctant combatants. In the next few sessions both spouses attacked each other vituperatively, but they talked only about her affair and his reactions rather than about problems in their relationship. These arguments were not productive because whenever Mr. Z. felt anxious he attacked his wife angrily, and whenever she felt angry she became depressed and guilty.

Sensing that their fighting was unproductive, the therapist said, "It's clear that you've put each other through a lot of unhappiness and you're both quite bitter. But unless you get down to talking about specific problems in your marriage, there is little chance that you'll get anywhere."

Thus focused, Mrs. Z. timidly ventured that she'd never enjoyed sex with her husband, and wished that he would take more time with foreplay. He snapped back, "Okay, so sex wasn't so great, is that any reason to throw away ten years of marriage and start whoring around!" At this, Mrs. Z. buried her face in her hands and sobbed uncontrollably. After she regained her composure, the therapist intervened, again confronting the couple with their resistance: "It seems, Mr. Z., that when you get upset, you attack. What is it that makes you so anxious about discussing sex?" Following this the couple was able to talk about their feelings about sex in their marriage until near the end of the session. At this point, Mr. Z. again lashed out at his wife, calling her a whore and a bitch.

Mrs. Z. began the following session by saying that she had been extremely depressed and upset, crying off and on all week. "I feel so guilty," she sobbed, "You should feel guilty!" retorted her husband. Once again, the therapist intervened. "You use your wife's affair as a club. Are you still afraid to discuss specific problems in the marriage? And you, Mrs. Z., cover your anger with depression. What is it that you're angry about? What was missing in the marriage? What did you want?"

This pattern continued for several more sessions. The spouses who had avoided discussing or even thinking about their problems for ten years used a variety of resistances to veer away from them in therapy. The therapist persisted in pointing out their resistance, and urged them to talk about specific complaints.

Psychoanalytic family therapists endeavor to foster insight and understanding; they also urge families to consider what they are going to do about the problems they discuss. This effort—part of the process of working through—is more prominent in family therapy than in individual therapy. Nagy, for example, considers that family members must not only be made aware of their motivations, but also held accountable for their behavior. In "Contextual Family Therapy" Boszormenyi-Nagy (1987) points out that the therapist must help people face the intrinsically destructive expectations involved in invisible loyalties, and then help them find more positive ways of making loyalty payments in the family ledger. What this boils down to is developing a balance of fairness among various family members.

Ackerman too stressed an active working through of insights by encouraging families to constructively express the aggressive and libidinal impulses uncovered in therapy. In order to alleviate symptoms impulses must become conscious; but an emotional experience must be associated with increased self-awareness in order for lives to change. To modify thinking and feeling is the essential task of psychoanalytic therapy, but family therapists are also concerned with supervising and analyzing changes in behavior.

EVALUATING THERAPY THEORY AND RESULTS

Psychoanalytic therapists have generally been opposed to attempts to evaluate their work using empirical standards. Since symptom reduction is not the goal, it cannot serve as the measure of success. And since the presence or absence of unconscious conflict is not apparent to family members or outside observers, whether or not an analysis can be considered successful has to depend on the subjective clinical judgement of the therapist. Psychoanalytic clinicians, of course, consider that the therapist's observations are entirely valid as a means of evaluating theory and treatment. The following quotation from the Blancks (1972, p. 675) illustrates this point. Speaking of Margaret Mahler's ideas, they wrote,

> Clinicians who employ her theories technically question neither the methodology nor the findings, for they can confirm them clinically, a form of validation that meets as closely as possible the experimentalist's insistence upon replication as criterion of the scientific method.

Another example of this point of view can be found in the writing of Robert Langs. "The ultimate test of a therapist's formulation," says Langs (1982, p. 186), "lies in the use of the therapist's impressions as a basis for intervention." What then determines the validity and effectiveness of these interventions? Langs does not hesitate; the patient's reactions, conscious and unconscious, constitute the ultimate litmus test. "True validation involves responses from the patient in both the cognitive and interpersonal spheres."

Is the ultimate test of therapy then the patient's reactions? Yes and no. First, the patient's reactions themselves are open to various interpretations—especially since validation is sought not only in direct manifest responses but also in unconsciously encoded derivatives. Moreover, this point of view does not take into account the changes in patients' lives that occur outside the office or consulting room. Occasionally therapists report on the outcome of psychoanalytic family therapy, but mostly as an uncontrolled case study. One such unsubstantiated report is Dicks' (1967) survey of the outcome of psychoanalytic couples therapy at the Tavistock Clinic, in which he rated as having been successfully treated 72.8 percent of a random sample of cases.

SUMMARY

Psychoanalytically trained clinicians were among the first to practice family therapy. However, when they began treating families, most of them traded in their ideas about depth psychology for those of systems theory. The result was most often an eclectic mix of psychoanalytic and systems concepts, rather than a true integration.

Since the mid 1980s, there has been a resurgence of interest in psychodynamics among family therapists, an interest dominated by object relations theory and self psychology. In this chapter we have sketched the main points of these theories, and shown how they are relevant to a psychoanalytic family therapy which integrates depth psychology and systems theory. A few practitioners (e.g., Kirschner and Kirschner, 1986; Nichols, 1987; Slipp, 1984) have combined elements of both; some have developed more frankly psychoanalytic approaches (notably Scharff and Scharff, 1987; and Sander, 1989); none has achieved a true synthesis.

REFERENCES

Ackerman, N.W. 1958. *The psychodynamics of family life*. New York: Basic Books.

Ackerman, N.W. 1961. The emergence of family psychotherapy on the present scene. In *Contemporary psychotherapies*, M.I. Stein, ed. Glencoe, IL: The Free Press.

Ackerman, N.W. 1966. *Treating the troubled family*. New York: Basic Books.

Bank, S., and Kahn, M. D. 1982. *The sibling bond*. New York: Basic Books.

Barnhill, L. R., and Longo, D. 1978. Fixation and regression in the family life cycle. *Family Process*. 17:469–478.

Bibring, E. 1954. Psychoanalysis and the dynamic psychotherapies. *Journal of the American Psychoanalytic Association*. 2:745–770.

Blanck, G., and Blanck, R. 1972. Toward a psychoanalytic developmental psychology. *Journal of the American Psychoanalytic Association.* 20:668–710.

Blanck, R. 1967. Marriage as a phase of personality development. *Social Casework.* 48:154–160.

Blum, H.P. 1987. Shared fantasy and reciprocal identification: General considerations and gender disorder. In H.P. Blum et al. *Unconscious fantasy: Myth and reality.* New York: International Universities Press.

Boszormenyi-Nagy I. 1967. Relational modes and meaning. In *Family therapy and disturbed families,* G.H. Zuk and I. Boszormenyi-Nagy, eds. Palo Alto: Science and Behavior Books.

Boszormenyi-Nagy, I. 1972. Loyalty implications of the transference model in psychotherapy. *Archives of General Psychiatry.* 27:374–380.

Boszormenyi-Nagy, I. 1987. *Foundations of contextual therapy.* New York: Brunner/Mazel.

Boszormenyi-Nagy, I., and Framo, J., eds. 1965. *Intensive family therapy: Theoretical and practical aspects.* New York: Harper and Row.

Boszormenyi-Nagy, I., and Spark G. 1973. *Invisible loyalties: Reciprocity in intergenerational family therapy.* New York: Harper and Row.

Boszormenyi-Nagy, I., and Ulrich, D.N. 1981. Contextual family therapy. In *Handbook of family therapy,* A.S. Gurman and D.P. Kniskern, eds. New York: Brunner/Mazel.

Bowen, M., Dysinger, R.H., and Basamania, B. 1959. The role of the father in families with a schizophrenic patient. *American Journal of Psychiatry.* 115:1017–1020.

Bowen, M. 1965. Family psychotherapy with schizophrenia in the hospital and in private practice. In *Intensive family therapy,* I. Boszormenyi-Nagy and J.L. Framo, eds. New York: Harper and Row.

Bowen, M. 1966. The use of family therapy in clinical practice. *Comprehensive Psychiatry.* 7:345–374.

Bowlby, J. 1949. The study and reduction of group tension in the family. *Human Relations.* 2:123–128.

Bowlby, J. 1969. *Attachment and loss.* Vol. 1: *Attachment.* New York: Basic Books.

Broderick, C.B., and Schrader, S.S. 1981. The history of professional marriage and family therapy. In *Handbook of family therapy,* A.S. Gurman and D.P. Kniskern, eds. New York: Brunner/Mazel.

Bruch, H. 1978. *The golden cage.* Cambridge, MA: Harvard University Press.

Burlingham, D.T. 1951. Present trends in handling the mother-child relationship during the therapeutic process. *Psychoanalytic Study of the Child.* New York: International Universities Press.

Dare, C. 1979. Psychoanalysis and systems in family therapy. *Journal of Family Therapy.* 1:137–151.

Dicks, H.V. 1963. Object relations theory and marital studies. *British Journal of Medical Psychology.* 36:125–129.

Dicks, H.V. 1967. *Marital tensions.* New York: Basic Books.

Dostoyevsky, F. 1958. *The Brothers Karamazov.* New York: Penguin Books.

Erikson, E.H. 1956. The problem of ego identity. *Journal of the American Psychoanalytic Association.* 4:56–121.

Erikson, E.H. 1959. Identity and the life cycle. *Psychological Issues. 1*:1–171.

Erikson, E.H. 1963. *Childhood and society.* New York: Norton.

Fairbairn, W.D. 1952. *An object-relations theory of the personality.* New York: Basic Books.

Fenichel, O. 1945. *The psychoanalytic theory of neurosis.* New York: Norton.

Ferreira, A. 1936. Family myths and homeostasis. *Archives of General Psychiatry. 9*:457–463.

Flugel, J. 1921. *The psychoanalytic study of the family.* London: Hogarth Press.

Framo, J.L. 1970. Symptoms from a family transactional viewpoint. In *Family therapy in transition*, N.W. Ackerman, ed. Boston: Little, Brown.

Freud, S. 1905. Fragment of an analysis of a case of hysteria. *Collected papers.* New York: Basic Books, 1959.

Freud, S. 1909. Analysis of a phobia in a five-year-old boy. *Collected papers.* Vol. III. New York: Basic Books, 1959.

Freud, S. 1921. Group psychology and the analysis of the ego. *Standard edition, 17*:1–22. London: Hogarth Press, 1955.

Freud, S. 1923. The ego and the id. *Standard edition. 19*:13–66. London: Hogarth Press, 1961.

Friedman, L. 1980. Integrating psychoanalytic object relations understanding with family systems interventions in couples therapy. In *Family therapy: Combining psychodynamic and family systems approaches*, J. Pearce and L. Friedman, eds. New York: Grune and Stratton.

Giovacchini, P. 1958. Mutual adaptation in various object relations. *International Journal of Psychoanalysis. 39*:547–554.

Giovacchini, P. 1961. Resistance and external object relations. *International Journal of Psychoanalysis. 42*:246–254.

Greenson, R.R. 1967. *The theory and technique of psychoanalysis.* New York: International Universities Press.

Guntrip, H. 1961. *Personality structure and human interaction.* London: Hogarth Press.

Guntrip, H. 1969. *Schizoid phenomena, object relations theory and the self.* New York: International Universities Press.

Guntrip, H. 1971. *Psychoanalytic theory, therapy, and the self.* New York: Basic Books.

Gurman, A. 1981. Integrative marital therapy. In *Forms of brief therapy*, S. Budman, ed. New York: Guilford.

Jackson, D.D. 1967. The individual and the larger context. *Family Process. 6*:139–147.

Jacobson, E. 1964. *The self and the object world.* New York: International Universities Press.

Johnson, A., and Szurek, S. 1952. The genesis of antisocial acting out in children and adults. *Psychoanalytic Quarterly. 21*:323–343.

Kahn, M.D., and Lewis, K.G., eds. 1988. *Siblings in therapy: Life span and clinical issues.* New York: Norton.

Katz, B. 1981. Separation-individuation and marital therapy. *Psychotherapy: Theory, Research and Practice. 18*:195–203.

Kernberg, O.F. 1966. Structural derivatives of object relationships. *International Journal of Psychoanalysis. 47*:236–253.

Kernberg, O.F. 1975. Countertransference. In *Borderline conditions and patho-logical narcissism*, O.F. Kernberg, ed. New York: Jason Aronson.

Kernberg, O.F. 1976. *Object-relations theory and clinical psychoanalysis.* New York: Jason Aronson.

Kirschner, D., and Kirschner, S. 1986. *Comprehensive family therapy: An integration of systemic and psychodynamic treatment models.* New York: Brunner/Mazel.

Klein, M. 1946. Notes on some schizoid mechanisms. *International Journal of Psycho-Analysis. 27*:99–110.

Kohut, H. 1971. *The analysis of the self.* New York: International Universities Press.

Kohut, H. 1977. *The restoration of the self.* New York: International Universities Press.

Langs, R. 1982. *Psychotherapy: A basic text.* New York: Jason Aronson.

Lasch, C. 1978. *The culture of narcissism.* New York: Norton.

Levinson, D.J. 1978. *The seasons of a man's life.* New York: Ballantine Books.

Lidz, T. Cornelison, A., Fleck, S. 1965. *Schizophrenia and the family.* New York: International Universities Press.

Lidz, T. Cornelison, A., Fleck, S., and Terry, D. 1957. The intrafamilial environment of schizophrenia patients; II: Marital schism and marital skew. *American Journal of Psychiatry. 114*:241–248.

Mahler, M.S. 1952. On child psychosis and schizophrenia: Autistic and symbiotic infantile psychoses. *Psychoanalytic Study of the Child.* Vol. 7.

Mahler, M., Pine, F., and Bergman, A. 1975. *The psychological birth of the human infant.* New York: Basic Books.

Martin, P.A., and Bird, H.W. 1953. An approach to the psychotherapy of marriage partners. *Psychiatry. 16*:123–127.

Masterson, J.F. 1977. Primary anorexia nervosa in the borderline adolescent-and object-relations view. In *Borderline personality disorders: The concept, the syndrome, the patient*, P. Hartocollis, ed. New York: International Universities Press.

Meissner, W.W. 1978. The conceptualization of marriage and family dynamics from a psychoanalytic perspective. In *Marriage and marital therapy*, T.J. Paolino and B.S. McCrady, eds. New York: Brunner/Mazel.

Minuchin, S. 1974. *Families and family therapy.* Cambridge, MA: Harvard University Press.

Minuchin, S. 1989. Personal communication. Quoted from *Institutionalizing madness*, J. Elizur and S. Minuchin. New York: Basic Books.

Mittlemann, B. 1948. The counterpart analysis of married couples. *Psychoanalytic Quarterly. 17*:182–197.

Modell, A.H. 1968. *Object love and reality.* New York: International Universities Press.

Nadelson, C.C. 1978. Marital therapy from a psychoanalytic perspective. In *Marriage and marital therapy*, T.J. Paolino and B.S. McCrady, eds. New York: Brunner/Mazel.

Nichols, M.P. 1986. *Turning forty in the eighties.* New York: Norton.

Nichols, M.P. 1987. *The self in the system.* New York: Brunner/Mazel.

Oberndorf, C.P. 1938. Psychoanalysis of married couples. *Psychoanalytic Review.* 25:453–475.

Ryckoff, I., Day, J., and Wynne, L. 1959. Maintenance of stereotyped roles in the families of schizophrenics. *AMA Archives of Psychiatry.* 1:93–98.

Sager, C. J. 1981. Couples therapy and marriage contracts. In *Handbook of family therapy*, A.S. Gurman and D.P. Kniskern, eds. New York: Brunner/Mazel.

Sander, F.M. 1979. *Individual and family therapy: Toward an Integration.* New York: Jason Aronson.

Sander, F.M. 1989. Marital conflict and psychoanalytic therapy in the middle years. In *The middle years: New psychoanalytic perspectives*, J. Oldham and R. Liebert, eds. New Haven: Yale University Press.

Scharff, D., and Scharff, J. 1987. *Object relations family therapy.* New York: Jason Aronson.

Scharff, J., ed. 1989. *The foundations of object relations family therapy.* New York: Jason Aronson.

Segal, H. 1964. *Introduction to the work of Melanie Klein.* New York: Basic Books.

Shapiro, R.L. 1968. Action and family interaction in adolescence. In *Modern Psychoanalysis*, J. Marmor, ed. New York: Basic Books.

Shapiro, R.L. 1979. Family dynamics and object relations theory. In *Adolescent Psychiatry*, S.C. Feinstein and P.L. Giovacchini, eds. Chicago: University of Chicago Press.

Sifneos, P.E. 1972. *Short-term psychotherapy and emotional crisis.* Cambridge, MA: Harvard University Press.

Skynner, A.C.R. 1976. *Systems of family and marital psychotherapy.* New York: Brunner/Mazel.

Skynner, A.C.R. 1981. An open-systems, group analytic approach to family therapy. In *Handbook of family therapy*, A.S. Gurman and D.P. Kniskern, eds. New York: Brunner/Mazel.

Slipp, S. 1984. *Object relations: A dynamic bridge between individual and family treatment.* New York: Jason Aronson.

Slipp, S. 1988. *Technique and practice of object relations family therapy.* New York: Jason Aronson.

Spitz, R.E. 1965. *The first year of life.* New York: International Universities Press.

Spitz, R., and Wolf, K. 1946. Anaclitic depression: An inquiry into the genesis of psychiatric conditions early in childhood. *Psychoanalytic Study of the Child.* 2:313–342.

Stein, M. 1956. The marriage bond. *Psychoanalytic Quarterly.* 25:238–259.

Stern, D.N. 1985. *The interpersonal world of the infant.* New York: Basic Books.

Stierlin, H. 1977. *Psychoanalysis and family therapy.* New York: Jason Aronson.

Sullivan, H.S. 1953. *The interpersonal theory of psychiatry.* New York: Norton.

Szasz, T.S. 1961. *The myth of mental illness.* New York: Hoeber-Harper.

Umana, R.F., Gross, S.J., and McConville, M.T. 1980. *Crisis in the family: Three approaches.* New York: Gardner Press.

Vogel, E.F., and Bell, N.W. 1960. The emotionally disturbed as the family scapegoat. In *The family*, N.W. Bell and E.F. Vogel, eds. Glencoe, IL: Free Press.

Winnicott, D.W. 1965a. *The maturational process and the facilitating environment.* New York: International Universities Press.

Winnicott, D.W. 1965b. *The maturational process and the facilitating environment: Studies in the theory of emotional development.* New York: International Universities Press.

Wynne, L.C. 1965. Some indications and contradictions for exploratory family therapy. In *Intensive family therapy*, I. Boszormenyi-Nagy and J.L. Framo, eds. New York: Harper and Row.

Wynne, L.C. 1971. Some guidelines for exploratory family therapy. In *Changing families*, J. Haley, ed. New York: Grune and Stratton.

Wynne, L., Ryckoff, I., Day, J., and Hirsch, S. 1958. Pseudomutuality in the family relations of schizophrenics. *Psychiatry.* 21:205–220.

Zinner, J. 1976. The implications of projective identification for marital interaction. In *Contemporary marriage: Structure, dynamics, and therapy*, H. Grunebaum and J. Christ, eds. Boston: Little, Brown.

Zinner, J., and Shapiro, R. 1976. Projective identification as a mode of perception and behavior in families of adolescents. *International Journal of Psychoanalysis.* 53:523–530.

6

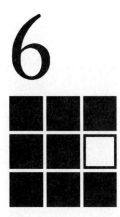

Experiential Family Therapy

An experiential branch of family therapy emerged from the humanistic psychology of the 1960s that, like the individual humanistic therapies, emphasized immediate, *here-and-now* experience. The quality of ongoing experience was both the criterion of psychological health and the focus of therapeutic interventions. Experiential family therapists consider feeling-expression to be the medium of shared experience and the means to personal and family fulfillment.

Experiential therapy was most popular when family therapy was young, when therapists talked about systems change, but borrowed their techniques from individual and group therapies. Experiential family therapists drew heavily from Gestalt therapy and encounter groups. Other expressive techniques, such as *sculpting* and *family drawing*, bore the influence of the arts and of psychodrama. Because experiential treatment emphasizes sensitivity and feeling-expression, it wasn't as well suited to family therapy as were approaches that deal with systems and action; consequently, the experiential approach has lately been used less and some of its early exponents, such as Peggy Papp, have adopted systems concepts and methods. Nevertheless the approach remains vital in the hands of such people as Carl Whitaker, followers of the late Virginia Satir, Walter Kempler, August Napier, David Keith, Leslie Greenberg and Susan Johnson, and Fred and Bunny Duhl; they and other experiential family therapists have introduced a number of expressive techniques that any family therapist may find useful.

SKETCHES OF LEADING FIGURES

Two giants stand out as leaders of experiential family therapy: Carl Whitaker and Virginia Satir. Whitaker is the dean of experiential family therapy, the leading exponent of a freewheeling, intuitive approach aimed to puncture pretense and liberate family members to be themselves. He was among the first in the field to do psychotherapy with families, and he has steadily grown in stature to become one of the most admired therapists in family therapy. Iconoclastic, even outrageous at times, Whitaker has, nevertheless, retained the respect and admiration of the family therapy establishment. He may be their Puck, but he's one of them.

Carl Whitaker grew up on an isolated dairy farm in Raymondville, New York (for those who don't live in New York, that's just outside of nowhere). Rural isolation may have bred shyness and a touch of sadness, but, perhaps, also conditioned Whitaker to be less hemmed in than most of us by social convention. After college in Syracuse and medical school and a residency in obstetrics and gynecology, Whitaker went into psychiatry where he immediately became fascinated by the psychotic mind. Unfortunately—or fortunately—back in the 1940s Whitaker couldn't rely on neuroleptic drugs to blunt the hallucinatory fantasies of his patients; instead he listened and learned to understand thoughts crazy but human, thoughts that the rest of us keep buried.

After working at the University of Louisville College of Medicine and at the Oakridge Hospital, Dr. Whitaker accepted the chairmanship of Emory University's Department of Psychiatry, where he remained from 1946 to 1955, building a first-rate program. In the face of mounting pressure to make the department more psychoanalytic, Whitaker and his entire faculty finally resigned to form the Atlanta Psychiatric Clinic, a productive and creative group, including Thomas Malone, John Warkentin, and Richard Felder. Experiential psychotherapy was born of this union, and the group produced a number of highly provocative and challenging papers (Whitaker and Malone, 1953). In 1965 Whitaker went to the University of Wisconsin Medical School, and also conducted a private practice in Madison. Since his retirement in the late 1980s, Whitaker has traveled frequently to share his wisdom, experience, and himself at conventions and workshops. Among Whitaker's most well-known associates are August Napier, now in private practice in Atlanta, and David Keith, now at the State University of New York in Syracuse.

The other major charismatic figure among experiential family therapists was the late Virginia Satir. Satir, who was one of the well-known members of the early MRI group in Palo Alto, emphasized communication as well as emotional experiencing, and so her work must be considered in both the communications and experiential traditions.

Social worker Virginia Satir began seeing families in private practice in 1951. In 1955 she was invited to set up a training program for residents at the Illinois State Psychiatric Institute. (One of her students was Ivan Boszormenyi-Nagy.) In 1959 Don Jackson invited Satir to join him at MRI, where she became the first director of training and remained until she left MRI in 1966 to become the Director of Esalen Institute in Big Sur, California.

Satir was the prototypical nurturing therapist in a field enamored with experience-distant concepts and tricky strategic maneuvers. Still, her warmth and genuineness gave her a tremendous appeal and a tremendous impact as she traveled all over the country leading demonstrations and workshops. Her ability to move large audiences in experiential exercises made her a legend as family therapy's most celebrated humanist.

In the 1970s Satir's influence waned and she received less recognition than she deserved as one of the innovators of family therapy. This was very painful for her. In Venezuela, in 1974, at a *Family Process* board meeting there was a debate between Salvador Minuchin and Satir about the nature of family therapy. Minuchin argued that it was a science that requires skills rather than just warmth and faith, and that the main job was to fix broken families; Satir stuck to her belief in the healing power of love, and spoke out for the salvation for humankind through family therapy. It turned out that Minuchin was speaking for the field, and Satir felt out of step. After this she drifted away from the family therapy establishment and, instead, became a world traveler and spokesperson for her evangelical approach. Satir died of pancreatic cancer in 1988.

Another Californian who has written a great deal about experiential family therapy is Walter Kempler, who brings many of the ideas and techniques of Gestalt and other emotive therapies to his work with families. He describes procedures commonly found in encounter groups and existential-humanistic individual therapies, which demonstrate the roots of experiential family therapy.

Fred and Bunny Duhl, codirectors of the Boston Family Institute, have introduced a number of expressive techniques into experiential family therapy. They use nonverbal means of communication, such as *spatialization* and *sculpting* (Duhl, Kantor, and Duhl, 1973), as well as *roleplaying* and *family puppets* (Duhl and Duhl, 1981). Their approach, which they call "integrative family therapy," is an amalgam of elements from numerous sources, including psychodrama, experiential psychotherapy, cognitive psychology, structural family therapy, and behavioral psychotherapy. The Duhls are included in this chapter because of their technical contributions, rather than because their work fits neatly into this, or any other, conceptual scheme.

The cofounder of the Boston Family Institute in 1969, along with Fred Duhl, was David Kantor, who brought with him a background in psychodrama and helped emphasize the "family as theater" metaphor in family therapy (Kantor and Lehr, 1975).

Among the most recent experiential approaches to family therapy is the "emotion-focused couples therapy" of Leslie Greenberg and Susan Johnson, which draws on Perls, Satir, and the MRI group (Greenberg and Johnson, 1985, 1986, 1988).

We group such unclassifiable individualists as Virginia Satir and Carl Whitaker together in this chapter because they are united by their investment in spontaneity, creativity, and risk-taking. While they share a commitment to freedom, individuality, and personal fulfillment, experientialists are otherwise relatively atheoretical. The hallmark of this approach is the use of techniques to open individuals to their inner experience and to unfreeze family interactions. Having reached their greatest popularity in the 1960s (Nichols and Zax, 1977), experiential approaches have been largely displaced by new developments in more systems-oriented therapies. Once feeling-expression occupied center stage in psychological therapies; today that place is held by behavior and cognition. Psychotherapists have discovered that people think and act; but that doesn't mean we can ignore the immediate emotional experience that is the main concern of experiential family therapy.

THEORETICAL FORMULATIONS

Carl Whitaker may have best expressed the experientialists' position on theory in his "The Hindrance of Theory in Clinical Work" (Whitaker, 1976a). In this article Whitaker described what he considered the chilling effect of theory on intuition and creativity in psychotherapy. Theory may be useful for beginners, Whitaker says, but his advice is to give up theory as soon as possible in favor of just being yourself. He quotes Paul Tillich's existential aphorism, "being is becoming," to support his own contention that psychotherapy requires openness and spontaneity, not theory and technique; and he cites the fact that technical approaches usually don't work for second-generation therapists (as many people found out when they tried to imitate the "simple" steps of Minuchin's structural family therapy). Perhaps we hamper our own creative efforts by trying to copy our mentors. Although Whitaker doesn't make this point, it may also be that the theories of clinical innovators are only secondary elaborations—afterthoughts and rationalizations—of intuitive methods that express their own convictions and personal styles.

Whitaker says that therapists who base their work on theory are likely to substitute dispassionate technology for caring, and goes on to imply that theory is a refuge from the anxiety-provoking experience of sharing a family's life stress. Instead of having the courage just to "be" with families and help them grapple with their problems, theoretically inclined clinicians use theory to create distance in the name of objectivity.

Most people consider psychotherapy to be a mixture of art and science; for experiential therapists the art is 90 percent, the science 10 percent. The search for theory, according to this viewpoint, arises from an attempt to escape the tension and anxiety of being openly empathic with unhappy families. Whitaker says therapists don't need theories to handle stress and anxiety; what they do need are supportive cotherapists and wise, helpful supervisors. In short, it isn't technique, but personal involvement that enables therapists to do their best. By avoiding theory, Whitaker believes that he forces families to establish their own theoretical way of living. David Keith (1988) echoes this conviction, saying that he often leaves families stewing in ambiguity rather than oversimplifying life by pointing them in a particular direction. This is a therapeutic pattern modeled after benevolent parenting, which carries a deep respect for people's ability to discover their own directions in life.

No theory is, of course, itself a theory. To say that therapy shouldn't be constrained by theory is to say that it should be loose, creative, open, and spontaneous. Therapists should share feelings, fantasies, and personal stories, if that's what they feel like doing, and if that's what it takes to help families become more aware and sensitive. Despite Whitaker's disdain for theory, however, experiential family therapy is very much a child of the existential, humanistic, and phenomenological tradition.

Philosophers like Edmund Husserl and Martin Heidegger (1963) began to work out the implications for clinical practice contained in existential thought. Their ideas were assimilated and developed by Ludwig Binswanger (1967) who formulated a new theory of psychotherapeutic process, but remained tied to the psychoanalytic method. The same may be said of Medard Boss (1963), the developer of "Daseinanalysis," which also differed from psychoanalysis more in theory than in practice. Much of the theorizing of these existential psychologists was in reaction to perceived shortcomings of psychoanalysis and behaviorism. In place of *determinism*, the existentialists emphasized *freedom* and the necessity to discover the essence of one's *individuality* in the immediacy of experience. Instead of being pushed by the past, they saw people as pulled toward the future, impelled by their *values* and *personal goals*. Where psychoanalysts posited a structuralized model of the mind, existentialists treated persons as wholes. Finally, existentialists substituted a positive model of humanity for what they believed was an unduly pessimistic psychoanalytic model. They believed that people should aim at personal fulfillment, rather than settle for partial resolution of their neuroses.

These new ideas—which Maslow (1968) called the "Third Force Psychology"—were translated into new practices of psychotherapy by Victor

Frankl, Charlotte Buhler, Fritz Perls, Rollo May, Carl Rogers, Eugene Gendlin, Sidney Jourard, R. D. Laing, Carl Whitaker, and others. The most influential of these new approaches were Frankl's (1963) *Logotherapy*, Perls' (1961) *Gestalt Therapy*, Rogers' (1951) *Client-Centered Therapy*, and Gendlin's (1962) *Experiencing*. Incidentally, it was probably Whitaker and Malone (1953) who first used the term "experiential psychotherapy."

The theoretical statements of experiential psychotherapists generally consist of a series of loosely connected constructs and statements of position. Most of them are melioristic, and often the language is more colorful and stagy than clear and precise. Take, for instance, the following sample from Whitaker and Keith (1981, p. 190).

> Metacommunication is considered to be an experiential process, an offer of participation that implies the clear freedom to return to an established role security rather than be caught in the "as if" tongue-in-cheek microtheater. That trap is the context that pushes son into stealing cars or daughter into incest with father while mother plays the madame. The whimsy and creativity of the family can even be exaggerated to where family subgroups or individuals are free to be nonrational or crazy.

According to Virginia Satir (1972, p. 21), "So many of the words professional people use to talk about human beings sound sterile and lack life-and-breath images," that she preferred folksy and concrete images. Consequently much of the writing done by experientialists is more evocative than elucidative.

Despite the paucity of elegant theoretical statements, there are a number of basic theoretical premises that define the experiential position on families and their treatment—a basic commitment to individual awareness, expression, and self-fulfillment. Whitaker emphasizes that self-fulfillment depends upon family cohesiveness, and Satir stressed the importance of good communication with other family members; but the basic commitment seems to be to individual growth. Moreover, while there was some talk about family systems (Satir, 1972), the early experiential model of families was more like a democratic group than a system with structure and a hierarchy. (This is less true of more recent work by Whitaker and the highly sophisticated efforts of Gus Napier and David Keith.) Still there is great emphasis on flexibility and freedom with respect to family roles and the distribution of power. Roles are thought to be reciprocal. If one spouse is a quiet, private person, the other is apt to be sociable and outgoing. Treatment is generally designed to help individual family members find fulfilling roles for themselves, without an overriding concern for the needs of the family as a whole. This is not to say that the needs of the family system are denigrated, but they're thought to follow automatically on the heels of individual growth. At times the family was even portrayed as the enemy of individual freedom and authenticity (Laing and Esterson, 1970).

After reading the previous paragraph, David Keith (in a personal letter) helped put into perspective the experiential position about the claims of the individual versus the claims of the family as follows:

> Our thinking is individually focused to the extent that I am very clear that I am the only one inside my skin. No one knows how I feel or how I think. Likewise I am unable to know how anyone else feels or thinks. There is a dialectical tension between the individual and the family— between dependence and independence. To overemphasize either individuality or family connectedness is to distort the human condition. This tension is transcended only by experience, not by thinking or theory. One of my basic assumptions in working with families is that, for better or worse, the family is in charge of itself. A corollary to that idea is that I am suspicious of families in that I know that families will sacrifice members in order to preserve the whole, or to shield certain members.

Theories of families as systems are translated into techniques that facilitate communication and interaction. The emphasis on altering interactions implies an acceptance of whatever level of individual experience and understanding is already present. This is where experiential theory differs (as does psychoanalytic theory) from most systems approaches. Here the emphasis is on expanding experience. The assumption is that such expansion on the individual level is prerequisite to breaking new ground for the family group, and the consequent new material and increased awareness will, almost automatically, stimulate increased communication and sharing of feelings among family members. Families will talk more when their members become more aware of what they have to say.

Underlying much of the work of experiential family therapy is the premise, seldom mentioned, that the best way to promote individual and family growth is to liberate affects and impulses. Efforts to reduce defensiveness and unlock deeper levels of experiencing rest on this basic assumption.

NORMAL FAMILY DEVELOPMENT

Existential family therapists subscribe to the humanistic faith in the natural goodness and wisdom of unacculturated human feelings and drives. Left alone, people tend to flourish, according to this point of view. Problems arise because this innate tendency toward *self-actualization* (Rogers, 1951) runs afoul of social (Marcuse, 1955) and familial (Laing and Esterson, 1970) counterpressures. Society enforces repression in order to tame people's instincts to make them fit for productive group living. Unhappily, socially required self-control is achieved at the cost of "surplus repression" (Marcuse, 1955) and emotional devitalization. Families add their own additional controls to achieve peace and quite, perpetuating outmoded *family myths* (Gehrke and Kirschenbaum, 1967) and using *mystification* (Laing, 1967) to alienate children from their experience.

In the ideal situation, these controls aren't excessive, and children grow up in an atmosphere of support for their feelings and creative impulses. Parents listen to their children, accept their feelings, and validate their experience, which helps the children develop healthy channels for expressing their emotions and drives. Affect is valued and nurtured; children are encouraged to experience things passionately and to express the full range of human emotions (Pierce, Nichols, and DuBrin, 1983).

Mental health is viewed as a continuous process of growth and change, not a static or homeostatic state. "The healthy family is one that continues to grow in spite of whatever troubles come its way" (Whitaker and Keith, 1981, p. 190). Furthermore, the healthy family deals with stress by pooling its resources and sharing problems, not dumping them all on one family member.

Experiential therapists describe the normal family as one which supports individual growth and experience. In so doing, clinicians may unwittingly foster a dichotomy between the individual and the family: "bad" families repress people, "good" ones leave them alone. Neither Carl Whitaker nor Virginia Satir falls into this trap, although Whitaker seems ambivalent about accepting the necessity for an organized family structure. At times he speaks of the need for hierarchy and generational boundaries, while at other times he emphasizes creative flexibility. The following quotation (Whitaker and Keith, 1981, p. 190) shows his vacillation on this point.

> The healthy family maintains a separation of the generations. Mother and father are not children and the children are not parents. The two generations function in these two separate role categories. Members of the same generation have equal rank. However, there is a massive freedom of choice in periodic role selection and each role is available to any member. Father can be a five-year-old, mother can be a three-year-old, the three-year-old can be a father, the father can be a mother, depending upon the situation, with each family member protected by an implicit "as if" clause.

In any case, Whitaker sees the family as an integrated whole, not a confederation of separate individuals. Other experientialists often seem to think of the whole as less than the sum of its parts. Kempler (1981), for example, emphasizes *personal responsibility*, which he defines as each person maximizing his or her own potential. Some call this narcissism (Lasch,

1978), but experientialists assume that enhanced personal commitment automatically leads to greater commitment to others.

Satir (1972) described the normal family as one that nurtures its members. Individual family members listen to and are considerate of each other, enabling them to feel valued and loved. Affection is freely given and received. Moreover, family members are open and candid with each other. "*Anything* can be talked about—the disappointments, fears, hurts, angers, criticisms as well as the joys and achievements" (Satir, 1972, p. 14).

Satir also considered flexibility and constructive problem-solving as characteristics of a functional healthy family. Nurturing parents, she says, realize that change is inevitable; they accept it and try to use it creatively. Her description of the "nurturing family" brings to mind the world portrayed by Norman Rockwell on the covers of *The Saturday Evening Post*: warm and pleasant, but not quite true to life. Perhaps Satir's (1972) idealized version of family life is better taken as a prescription for, rather than a description of, healthy family living.

In general, experiential family therapists describe the family as a place of sharing experience with others. The functional family supports and encourages a wide range of experiencing; the dysfunctional family resists awareness and blunts responsiveness. The vitality of each person's individual experience is the ultimate measure of sanity. Healthy people accept the truth and richness of their experience in each moment. This enables them to stand up for who they are and what they want—and to accept the same from others. Functional families are secure enough to be passionate; dysfunctional families are frightened and bloodless. Neither problem-solving skills nor particular family structures are considered to be nearly as important as expanding open, natural, and spontaneous experiencing. The healthy family offers its members the freedom to be themselves, and supports privacy as well as togetherness.

DEVELOPMENT OF BEHAVIOR DISORDERS

From the experiential perspective, denial of impulses and suppression of feelings are the root of family problems. Dysfunctional families are rigidly locked into self-protection and avoidance (Kaplan and Kaplan, 1978). In Sullivan's (1953) terms, they seek *security*, not *satisfaction*. They're too busy trying not to lose to ever dare to win.

Such families function automatically and mechanically, rather than through awareness and choice. Their presenting complaints are many, but the basic problem is that they smother emotion and desire. Laing (1967) described this as the *mystification* of experience, and he held parents responsible. Parents are, of course, not the villains. The process is circular. Kempler (1981) also speaks of family pressure for loyalty and cohesion as interfering with individuals' loyalties to themselves. The untested premise in these unhappy families is that assertiveness or confrontation would lead to emotional chaos. The sad result is that feelings are never acknowledged openly.

According to Whitaker (Whitaker and Keith, 1981), there's no such thing as a marriage—merely two scapegoats sent out by their families to perpetuate themselves. Each is programmed to recapitulate the family of origin; together they must work out the inherent conflict in this situation. Feeling helpless and frustrated, they cling even more to what is familiar, intensifying, rather than alleviating their problems. Each strenuously resists the other's accustomed ways of doing things. When couples present in this struggle for control, one may appear sicker than the other. But, according to Whitaker (1958), the degree of disturbance in spouses almost always turns out to be similar, even if at first they appear manifestly different.

Couples who remain together eventually reach some kind of accommodation. Whether it's based on compromise or unilateral concession, it lessens the previous conflict. Dysfunctional families, terrified of conflict, cling rigidly to the structures and routines that they work out together. Having experienced being different—and not liking it—they now cling to togetherness. Once again alternatives are dismissed or blocked from awareness.

What distinguishes dysfunctional families is that the flow of their behavior is clogged with unexpressed emotion, robbing them of flexibility and vitality. Clinicians see fixed triangles and pathological coalitions; anyone can see their rigidity.

Avoidance of feelings is described as the cause and effect of family dysfunction. Kempler (1981) lists a number of devices commonly used to avoid feelings: asking questions, instead of stating opinions; using the editorial we ("*We* are worried about Johnny"); and changing subjects. The attention paid to these protective conversational devices, used to avoid intimacy, reflects the experientialists' concern with relatively minor forms of psychic difficulty.

Experiential family therapists believe that a climate of emotional deadness leads to symptoms in one or more family members. However, because they are as concerned with positive health as with clinical pathology, experientialists point to the "normal" casualties that others might overlook. Whitaker (Whitaker and Keith, 1981) speaks of "the lonely father syndrome," "the battle fatigue mother syndrome," "the infidelity syndrome," and "the parentified child syndrome." These "normal" problems concern experiential family therapists just as much as do the symptoms of the identified patient. Experiential family therapists also look for culturally invisible pathologies, such as obesity, heavy smoking, and overwork. These symptoms of family trouble are "invisible," because they're regarded as normal.

Systems-oriented family therapists (see Chapters 8, 9, 10, 11) generally look no deeper than interactions between family members to explain psychopathology. But, experientialists, like psychoanalysts, are concerned as much with individuals as with systems, and consider intrapsychic problems when explaining psychopathology. For example, Kaplan and Kaplan (1978) speak of projection and introjection and intrapsychic defenses which lead to interpersonal problems in the family. Members of such families disown parts of themselves, and fit together by adopting complementary but rigidly limiting roles. One person's "strength" is maintained by the other's "weakness." The ongoing, patterned interactions in such families are described as "confluent," meaning ritualized playing out of roles. The majority of clinical examples from the experiential literature are about families with a depressed or critical wife and a reasonable, but ineffectual husband. Moreover, unlike other family therapists, experientialists describe patterns of family dysfunction using the individual or a dyad as the unit of analysis. Kempler (1981), typical of the Gestalt-and-encounter wing of experiential therapists, describes dyadic patterns of avoiding intimacy with clever names, such as "pouter-shouter," "crier-shrieker," and "shrew and mouse."

Dysfunctional families are made up of people incapable of autonomy or of real intimacy. They don't know themselves and they don't know one another. The root cause is *alienation* from experience, what Kempler (1981) calls "astigmatic awareness." Their communication is restricted because their awareness is restricted. They don't say much to each other because they don't feel much. They don't really experience their own experience, much less share it with other family members.

Many of the experientialists' descriptions of disordered behavior are based on concepts borrowed from other orientations. Perls' notion of *unfinished business* is frequently referred to (e.g., Kempler, 1965). Whitaker, who has worked with almost all of the major figures in family therapy, uses Minuchin's concepts of *enmeshment* and *disengagement* (Whitaker and Keith, 1981), as well as many of Bowen's notions about *triangles* and *emotional cutoffs* from the extended family (Napier and Whitaker, 1978). He also uses the concept of *projective identification*, although not so named (Whitaker and Keith, 1981, p. 196).

> If a mother is guilty about her early sex life, she may pressure the oldest son to be a priest or the oldest daughter to be a nun. If mother was frustrated in her effort to go to medical school, she may pressure son to become a family doctor.

Whitaker also speaks of family pathology as arising from an impasse in a transition in the family life cycle or in the face of changing circumstances. While this is anything but novel, it's certainly consistent with the experientialists' emphasis on the need for change and flexibility. Not to change in the face of changing circumstances can be equally problematic as doing something actively destructive. In this model, the covert is often seen as more dangerous than the overt.

In her portrayal of troubled families, Satir (1972) emphasized the atmosphere of emotional deadness. Such families are cold; they live in a climate of forced politeness; they are bored, sullen, and sad. There's little evidence of warmth or friendship; the family seems to stay together merely out of habit or duty. The adults don't enjoy their children, and the children learn not to value themselves or care about their parents. In consequence of the lack of action in the family, these people avoid each other, and preoccupy themselves with work and other activities outside the family.

It's important to notice that the "dysfunction" Satir described isn't the kind of clinical pathology found in diagnostic manuals. Satir, like others in the experiential camp, was just as concerned with "normal" people who lead lives of quiet desperation as with the more blatantly disturbed people who usually present themselves to clinics. As Satir (1972, p. 12) put it,

> It is a sad experience for me to be with these families. I see the hopelessness, the helplessness, the loneliness. I see the bravery of people trying to cover up—a bravery that can still bellow or nag or whine at each other. Others no longer care. These people go on year after year, enduring misery themselves or in their desperation, inflicting it on others.

Satir stressed the role of destructive communication in smothering feeling, and said that there were four wrong ways people communicate: *blaming*, *placating*, being *irrelevant*, and being *super reasonable*. What's behind these patterns of dishonest communication? Low self-esteem. If we feel bad about ourselves, it's hard to tell the truth about our feelings—and threatening to let others tell us, honestly, what they feel.

GOALS

Growth, not stability, is the goal of experiential family therapy. Symptom relief, social adjustment, and work are considered important, but secondary to increased personal integrity (congruence between inner experience and outer behavior), greater freedom of choice, less dependence, and expanded experiencing (Malone, Whitaker, Warkentin, and Felder, 1961). The painful symptoms that families present with are regarded as tickets of admission (Whitaker and Keith, 1981); the real problem is emotional sterility. The aim is for individual family members to become sensitive to their needs and feelings, and to share these within the family. In this way, family unity is based on lively and genuine interaction, rather than on repression and self-abnegation.

Some experiential therapists have a tendency to focus on individuals and their experience more than on family organization. In Kempler's (1981,

p. 27) case the commitment to the individual is acknowledged: "I consider my primary responsibility to people—to each individual within the family—and only secondarily to the organization called family." This emphasis on the individual over the family is *not* true of the more systems-wise experiential family therapists, such as Carl Whitaker, David Keith, and Gus Napier.

In common with others in the existential-humanistic tradition, experiential therapists believe that the way to emotional health is to uncover deeper levels of experiencing—the potential for personal fulfillment locked inside of all of us. It's what's inside that counts. Virginia Satir (1972, p. 120) stated the goals of family therapy in this way:

> We attempt to make three changes in the family system. First, each member of the family should be able to report congruently, completely, and honestly on what he sees and hears, feels and thinks, about himself and others, in the presence of others. Second, each person should be addressed and related to in terms of his uniqueness, so that decisions are made in terms of exploration and negotiation rather than in terms of power. Third, differentness must be openly acknowledged and used for growth.

When experiential methods are applied to treating family systems (rather than to individuals who happen to be assembled in family groups), the goal of individual growth is merged with the goal of achieving a strengthened family unit. Carl Whitaker's work nicely embodies this dual goal. According to him, personal growth requires family integration, and vice versa. A sense of belongingness and the freedom to individuate go hand in hand. In fact, it's often necessary to bring parents emotionally closer together to enable their children to leave home, since many children can't leave unless they sense that their parents can be happy without them.

In addition to the general goal of increasing the creativity of the family and its members, experiential therapists also try to help every family work out its own particular problems. But this work is done with minimal systematic conceptualization or advanced planning. In fact many of the goals may be unconscious during therapy and can only be acknowledged in retrospect (Napier, 1977). Experiential therapy includes rational and nonrational elements. The former are designed to promote conscious awareness and understanding, the latter to increase spontaneity and sincerity. Conscious experience of inner potentials (affects, fantasies, impulses) deprive them of their pathogenic influence and liberate their life force. The result of this increased awareness is a *reintegration* of repressed or disowned parts of the self.

Most experientialists emphasize the feeling side of human nature: creativity, spontaneity, and the ability to play. Whitaker advocates "craziness," nonrational, creative experiencing and functioning, as a proper goal of therapy. If they let themselves become a little crazy, he believes, families will reap the rewards of zest, emotionality, and spontaneity.

When writing about their treatment goals, experiential clinicians emphasize the value of experience for its own sake. Whitaker (1967), for example, sees all therapy as a process of expanding experience, which he believes leads toward growth.

New experience for family members is thought to break down confluence, disrupt rigid expectancies, and unblock awareness—all of which promotes individuation (Kaplan and Kaplan, 1978). Bunny and Fred Duhl (1981) speak of their goals as a heightened sense of competence, well-being, and self-esteem. In emphasizing *self-esteem*, the Duhls echo Virginia Satir (1964, 1988) who believed that low-self esteem and the destructive communication responsible for it were the major problems in unhappy families. Expanded awareness of self and others is also thought to promote flexible behavior, in place of automatic, stereotyped habits. Because they emphasize behavior change as a consequence of enhanced experiencing, the Duhls define explicit behavioral goals in collaboration with their patients.

Most family therapists consider that an increased sensitivity and growth in individuals serves the broad aim of enhanced family functioning. Some experiential family therapists keep the family-systems goal implicit and devote relatively few of their interventions to promote it; others perceive individual growth as explicitly linked to family growth, and so devote more of their attention to promoting family interactions. The Duhls (1981) espouse "new and renewed integration" within and between family members as mutually reinforcing goals of treatment. Whitaker (1976a) presumes that families come to treatment because they're unable to be close, and therefore unable to individuate. By helping family members recover their own potential for experiencing, he believes he's also helping them recover their ability to care for one another.

CONDITIONS FOR BEHAVIOR CHANGE

Among the misconceptions of those new to family therapy is that families are fragile, and therapists must be cautious to above breaking them. A little experience teaches that the opposite is true. Most families are so rigidly structured that it takes therapeutic dynamite to change them. Effective family therapy requires powerful interventions—and for experiential family therapists that power comes from emotional experiencing.

Experiential clinicians use evocative techniques and the force of their own personalities to create personal therapeutic encounters, regression, and intimate disclosure. The vitality of the therapist as a person is one major force in therapy; the vitality of the *encounter* is another. This powerfully personal experience is thought to help establish caring, person-to-person relationships among all family members. Gus Napier (Napier and Whitaker, 1978) wrote, in *The Family Crucible*, a nice description of what experiential family therapists think causes change. Breakthroughs occur when family members risk being "more separate, divergent, even angrier" as well as "when they risk being closer and more intimate." Outbursts of anger are often followed by greater intimacy and warmth, because the unexpressed anger that keeps people apart also keeps them from loving one another.

Because feeling-expression and intimate experience within sessions are believed to be crucial, anxiety is stimulated and prized. (The opposite is true with more cerebral approaches to family therapy such as Murray Bowen's.) Experiential family therapists are alternately provocative and warmly supportive. In this way they help families dare to take risks that may make them more anxious, at least temporarily. This permits them to drop protective, defensive patterns and really open up with each other.

Existential encounter is believed to be the essential force in the psychotherapeutic process (Kempler, 1973; Whitaker, 1976a). These encounters must be reciprocal; instead of hiding behind a professional role or using devices to maintain distance from families, the therapist must be a genuine person who catalyzes change using his or her personal impact on families. As Kempler (1968, p. 97) said:

> In this approach the therapist becomes a family member during the interviews, participating as fully as he is able, hopefully available for appreciation and criticism as well as he is able to dispense it. He laughs, cries and rages. He feels and shares his embarrassments, confusions and helplessness. He shares his fears of revealing himself when these feelings are a part of his current total person. He sometimes cannot share himself and hopefully he is able to say at least that much.

Virginia Satir said it this way:

> Some therapists think people come into therapy not wanting to be changed; I don't think that's true. They don't think they *can* change. Going into some new, unfamiliar place is a scary thing. When I first begin to work with someone, I am not interested in changing them. I am interested in finding their rhythms, being able to join with them, and helping them go inside to those scary places. Resistance is mainly the fear of going somewhere you have not been (quoted in Simon, 1989, pp. 38–39).

For Satir, demonstrating caring and acceptance was the key to helping people overcome their fear, open up to their experience, and open up to each other. It's a willingness to understand and accept people—rather than an anxious eagerness to change them—that enables experiential family therapists to help people experience and understand deeply held, but poorly understood fears and desires.

Therapists are advised to attend to their own responses to families. Are they anxious, angry, or bored? Once noted, these reactions are to be shared with the family. Whitaker and his colleagues at the Atlanta Psychiatric Clinic (Whitaker, Warkentin, and Malone, 1959) pioneered the technique of spontaneously communicating their feelings *fully* to patients. These therapists often seemed highly impulsive, even falling asleep and reporting their dreams. According to Kempler (1965, p. 61), "By being, as nearly as possible, a total person, rather than playing the role of therapist, the atmosphere encourages all members to participate more fully as total personalities." He translates this into action by being extremely self-disclosing, even in his opening statements to families. At times, this seems more self-indulgent than provocative. For example, he says (Kempler, 1973, p. 37), "If the therapist is hungry he should say so: 'I'm getting hungry. I hope I can make it until lunchtime.' "

The belief is that by being a "real person," open, honest, and spontaneous, the therapist can teach family members to be the same. As Whitaker (1975) said, if the therapist sometimes gets angry, then patients can learn to deal with anger in others and in themselves. While this is a compelling point of view, its validity rests on the assumption that the therapist is a worthwhile model—not only a healthy, mature person, but also one whose instincts are trustworthy and useful to families. Experiential therapists have great faith in themselves as valid barometers against which family members can measure themselves.

This is an attractive idea, and one that seems to work in the hands of experienced practitioners like Carl Whitaker. However, younger and less experienced therapists would be wise not to overestimate the salutary effects of their personal disclosures, nor to underestimate the potential for countertransference in their emotional reactions to families.

Experiential family therapists share the humanistic faith that people are naturally healthy and if left to their own devices they will be creative, zestful, loving, and productive (Rogers, 1951; Janov, 1970; Perls, Hefferline, and Goodman, 1951). The main task of therapy is therefore seen as unblocking defenses and opening up experience.

Some experiential therapists pay more attention to resistance to feeling within family members than to resistance of family systems to change. For example, Kempler's conception of interlocking family patterns is that they are easily resolved by the therapist's pointing them out. "Often in families, merely calling attention to the pattern is sufficient for one or more members to stop their part in it, thereby eliminating the possibility of continuing that interlocking behavior" (Kempler, 1981, p. 113). Kempler believes the objective of experiential therapy is to complete interpersonal encounters. He tries to promote this objective by simply pushing family members through impasses. But, just as is true with encounter groups (Lieberman, Yalom, and Miles, 1973), these changes will probably not be sustained without being repeated and worked through.

Dysfunctional families have strong conservative or homeostatic predilections; they opt for safety rather than satisfaction. Since needs and passions are messy, unhappy families are content to submerge them; experiential therapists are not. Clinicians like Whitaker believe that it is important to be effective, not safe. Therefore he deliberately aims to generate enough stress to destabilize the families he works with.

Just as stress opens up family dialogues and makes change possible, therapeutic regression enables individual family members to discover and reveal hidden aspects of themselves. Once these personal needs and feelings emerge, they become the substance of progressively more intimate, interpersonal encounters within the family.

What sets experiential family therapy apart from most other family treatments is the belief that promoting family interaction is not a sufficient vehicle for change. Most other approaches begin with an interpersonal focus; their aim is to help family members tell each other what's on their minds. But this means that they'll only be sharing what they're conscious of feeling. They'll have fewer secrets from each other, but they'll continue to have secrets from themselves, in the form of unconscious needs and feelings. Experiential family therapists, on the other hand, believe that increasing the experience levels of individual family members will lead to more honest and intimate family interactions. The following example demonstrates this "inside out" process of change.

> After an initial, information-gathering session, the L. family was discussing ten-year-old Tommy's misbehavior. For several minutes Mrs. L. and Tommy's younger sister took turns cataloging all the "terrible things" Tommy did around the house. As the discussion continued, the therapist noticed how uninvolved Mr. L. seemed to be. Although he dutifully nodded agreement to his wife's complaints, he seemed more depressed than concerned. When asked what was on his mind, he said very little, and the therapist got the impression that, in fact, very little *was* on his mind—at least consciously. The therapist didn't know the reason for his lack of involvement, but she did know that it annoyed her, and she decided to say so.

> THERAPIST (To Mr. L.) You know what, you piss me off.

> MR. L. What? (He was shocked, people, he knew, just didn't speak that way.)

> THERAPIST I said, you piss me off. Here your wife is concerned and upset about Tommy, and you just sit there like a lump on a log. You're about as much a part of this family as that lamp in the corner.

MR. L. You have no right to talk to me that way (getting angrier by the minute). I work very hard for this family. Who do you think puts bread on the table? I get up six days a week and drive a delivery truck all over town. All day long, I have to listen to customers bitching about this and that. Then I come home and what do I get? More bitching. *"Tommy did this, Tommy did that."* I'm sick of it.

THERAPIST Say that again, louder.

MR. L. I'm sick of it! I'm sick of it!!

This interchange dramatically transformed the atmosphere in the session. Suddenly, the reason for Mr. L.'s disinterest became clear. He was furious at his wife for constantly complaining about Tommy. She, in turn, was displacing much of her feeling for her husband onto Tommy, as a result of Mr. L.'s emotional unavailability. In subsequent sessions, as Mr. and Mrs. L. spent more time talking about their relationship, less and less was heard about Tommy's misbehavior.

Following her own emotional impulse, the therapist in the example above increased the affective intensity in the session by attacking a member of the family. The anxiety generated as she did so was sufficient to expose a hidden problem. Once the problem was uncovered, it didn't take much cajoling to get the family members to fight it out.

Although the reader may be uncomfortable with the idea of a therapist attacking a family member, it's not at all unusual in experiential therapy. What makes this move less risky than it may seem is the presence of other family members. When the whole family is there, it seems safer for therapists to be provocative with less risk of hurting or driving patients away than is true in individual treatment. And as Carl Whitaker (1975) points out, families will accept a great deal from a therapist, once they're convinced that he or she genuinely cares about them.

While experiential family therapists emphasize expanded experiencing for individuals as the vehicle for therapeutic change, they are now beginning to advocate inclusion of as many family members as possible in treatment. As experientialists, they believe in immediate personal experiencing; as family therapists, they believe in the interconnectedness of the family. The family may be likened to a team in which none of the players can perform adequately without the unity and wholeness of the group.

Carl Whitaker (1976b) believes that it's important to work with three generations. He pushes for at least a couple of meetings with the larger family network, including parents, children, grandparents, and divorced spouses. Inviting these extended family members is an effective way to help them support treatment, instead of opposing and undermining it. It also provides additional information and helps correct distortions.

Whitaker believes that children should always be included, even when they aren't the focus of concern. He finds it difficult to work without children, who, he believes, are invaluable for teaching parents to be spontaneous and honest. In order to overcome possible reluctance to attend, Whitaker invites extended family members as consultants, "to help the therapist," not as patients. In these interviews grandparents are asked for their help, for their perceptions of the family (past or present), and sometimes to talk about the problems in their own marriage (Napier and Whitaker, 1978). Parents may begin to see that the grandparents are different from the images of them they introjected twenty years before. The grandparents, in turn, may begin to see that their children are now adults.

In addition to the increased therapeutic opportunities available when the larger family is present, it seems likely that small changes in the large family group have more powerful repercussions than large changes in one subsystem. Since family therapy is based on the premise that changing the system is the most effective way to change individuals, it follows that a cross-generational group holds the greatest potential for change. (In fact it may be that the real reason many family therapists don't include the extended family is that they lack the nerve or the leverage to bring them in.)

TECHNIQUES

According to Walter Kempler (1968), in experiential psychotherapy there are no techniques, only people. This epigram neatly summarizes the experientialists' emphasis on the curative power of the therapist's personality. It isn't so much what therapists do that matters, but who they are. If the therapist is rigid and uptight, then the treatment is likely to be too cool and professional to generate the intense emotional climate deemed necessary for experiential growth. If, on the other hand, the therapist is an alive, aware, and fully feeling person, then he or she will be able to awaken these potentials in families.

Carl Whitaker also endorses this position, and is himself the paradigmatic example of the spontaneous and creative therapist. The point is: therapists who would foster openness and authenticity in their patients, must themselves be open and genuine. However, this point is at least partly rhetorical. Whoever they *are*, therapists must also *do* something. Even if what they do isn't highly structured or carefully planned, it can nevertheless be described. Moreover, experiential therapists tend to do a lot; they're highly active and some (including Kempler) use quite a number of structured techniques.

In fact, experiential therapists can be divided into two groups with regard to therapeutic techniques. On the one hand, some employ highly structured devices such as *family sculpting* and *choreography* to stimulate affective intensity in therapy sessions; on the other hand, therapists like Carl Whitaker rely on the spontaneity and creativity of just being themselves with patients. Whitaker hardly plans more than a few seconds in advance; and he certainly does not use structured exercises and tactics. However, underlying both these strategies is a shared conviction that therapy should be an intense, moving experience in the here-and-now.

Virginia Satir had a remarkable ability to communicate clearly and perceptively. Like many great therapists, she was a vigorous and dynamic person who engaged clients authoritatively from the first session onward. Where she led, clients followed. But she did not rely merely on spontaneity and personal disclosure. Rather, she worked actively to clarify communication, turned people away from complaining about the past toward finding solutions, supported every member of the family's self-esteem, pointed out positive intentions (long before "positive connotation" became a strategic device), and showed by example the way for family members to touch and be affectionate (Satir and Baldwin, 1983). She was a loving but forceful teacher.

Just as experiential therapists are theoretically eclectic, many of their techniques are also borrowed from a variety of sources. For example, the theatrical and psychodramatic origins of *family sculpting* and *choreography* are quite evident. Similarly, Whitaker's work with the extended family seems to derive from Murray Bowen's work. Experiential family therapists have also drawn on encounter groups (Kempler, 1968), Gestalt-therapy techniques (Kaplan and Kaplan, 1978), psychodrama (Kantor and Lehr, 1975), and art therapy (Bing, 1970; Geddes and Medway, 1977).

Although all the therapists considered in this chapter employ evocative techniques, they differ sharply with regard to how self-consciously they do so. Some plan and structure sessions around one or more well-practiced techniques, while others are deliberately unstructured and nonstrategic; they emphasize *being with* the family rather than *doing* something, and say that techniques shouldn't be planned, but allowed to flow from the therapist's personal style and spontaneous impulses. Principal speaker for the latter view is Carl Whitaker. Techniques, Whitaker believes (Keith and Whitaker, 1977), are a product of the therapist's personality and of the cotherapy relationship. His own numerous published case studies reveal a playful, nonstructured approach. When children are present, Whitaker is a model parent, alternately playing with the kids in an involved, loving manner, and disciplining them with a firmness and strength. Patients learn from being with Carl Whitaker to become more spontaneous and open, and to feel more worthwhile.

Since he favors a personal and intimate encounter over a theory-guided or technique-bound approach, it's not surprising that Whitaker's style is the same with individuals, couples, or groups (Whitaker, 1958). He assiduously avoids directing real-life decisions, preferring instead to open family members up to their feelings and join them in sharing their experience. This may sound trite, but it's a powerful and important point. As long as therapists (or anyone else for that matter) are anxious to change people, it's hard, very hard, to help them feel and understand their fears and desires—and it's impossible to really empathize with them.

A comparison between Whitaker's early work (Whitaker, Warkentin, and Malone, 1959; Whitaker, 1967) and his later reports (Napier and Whitaker, 1978) shows that he changed over years of seeing families. He started out as deliberately provocative and outlandish. He might fall asleep in sessions and then report his dreams; he wrestled with patients; he talked about his own sexual fantasies. Today he is much less provocative—and this seems to be what happens to most therapists as they mature: they have less need to impose their own direction and more willingness to understand and sympathize. Indeed, reading some of Whitaker's early reports makes one wonder how much was genuinely spontaneous and how much a studied pose; how much was for the relationship, how much for himself, and how much for the titillation of observers.

Because Whitaker's treatment is intense and personal, he believes it essential that two therapists work together. Having a cotherapist to share the emotional burden and to interact with keeps the therapist from being totally absorbed in the emotional field of the family. The deep emotional involvement characteristic of experiential family therapy activates powerful countertransference reactions. A detached, analytic stance minimizes such feelings; an intense involvement maximizes them. All family therapy tends to activate the therapist's own feelings toward types of family members; experiential family therapy maximizes such feelings. The trouble with countertransference is that it tends to be unconscious. Therapists are more likely to become aware of such feelings after sessions are over. Easier still is to observe countertransference in others. Consider the example of Dr. Fox. Dr. Fox is a married man who specializes in individual therapy, but occasionally sees married couples in distress. In 75 percent of such cases, Dr. Fox encourages the couple to seek a divorce, and his patients have a high rate of following his advice. Perhaps if Dr. Fox were happier in his own marriage or had the courage to change it, he'd be less impelled to guide his patients where he fears to go.

Whitaker and his Atlanta Psychiatric Clinic colleagues wrote an excellent treatise on countertransference in family therapy (Whitaker, Felder, and Warkentin, 1965), suggesting that experiential family therapists should be emotionally involved—"in" the family, but not "of" the family. The therapist who's emotionally involved in the family should be able to identify with each of the family members. Thinking about experiences you've had that are similar to the family member's or asking yourself, "What would I like or need if I were that person?" facilitates the process of identification.

In order to minimize potential destructive acting out of countertransference feelings, Whitaker recommends sharing feelings openly with the family and always working with a cotherapist. If feelings are expressed to the family they are more useful and less likely to be lived out than if they remain hidden. At times, however, even the therapist may be unaware of such feelings. This is where having a cotherapist is important. Very often the cotherapist recognizes such feelings in a colleague and can discuss them after a session, or counteract them during the session.

Young therapists are especially likely to be critical of parents and sympathetic toward the kids; the best prevention for such countertransference reactions is maturity. A mature person has the freedom to enter intense relationships, personal and professional, without becoming enmeshed or reacting as though to his or her own parents. Adequate training, experience, and supervision also immunize therapists against taking sides. In addition, having a strong and rewarding family life minimizes the likelihood of the therapist seeking ersatz gratification of personal needs with patients.

To prevent countertransference problems, Whitaker recommends that the therapist maintain an overview of the family as a whole, so that he or she will be less likely to get entangled with individuals or subgroups. But the most important method of controlling countertransference is the cotherapy relationship. A strong investment in the cotherapy relationship (or treatment team) keeps therapists from being *inducted* (drawn into families). Therapists who see families without a cotherapist may bring in a consultant to help achieve the emotional distancing necessary to stay objective.

Because of their interest in current thoughts and feelings, most experientialists eschew history-taking (Kempler, 1965) and formal assessment (Kaplan and Kaplan, 1978). Kempler (1973, p. 11) once stated his disdain for diagnosis: "Diagnoses are the tombstones of the therapist's frustration, and accusations such as defensive, resistant, and secondary gain, are the flowers placed on the grave of his buried dissatisfaction." The point of this flowery remark seems to be that the objective distance necessary for formal assessment removes the therapist from a close emotional interaction with families; moreover, since diagnostic terms tend to be perjorative, they may serve to discharge hostility while masquerading as scientific objectivity.

For most experientialists, assessment is implicit. It takes place automatically as the therapist gets to know the family. In the process of getting acquainted and developing an empathic relationship, the therapist learns what kind of people he or she is dealing with. Whitaker begins by asking each family member to describe the family and how it works. "Talk about the family as a whole." "What is the family like; how is it structured?" In this way, he gets a composite picture of individual family members and their perceptions of the family group. Notice also that by directing family members toward the structure of the family as a whole, he shifts attention away from the identified patient and his or her symptoms.

Kempler, who conducts family therapy much like an encounter group, often begins by sitting and saying nothing. This device generates anxiety and helps create an atmosphere of emotional intensity. There is, however, something paradoxical about opening like this; it seems nondirective and it seems to be a way of decentralizing the therapist, but it's neither. In fact, by not saying anything, the therapist calls attention to himself, and is in a very controlling position. Any pretense that this opening device signals a nondirective approach is quickly dispelled by reading the transcripts of encounter-group-style family therapists (Kempler, 1981). Whether they open with silence or by inquiring into specific content areas, they soon become extremely active and directive, asking questions, directing conversations, and actively confronting evasive or defensive family members.

Whitaker's first sessions (Napier and Whitaker, 1978) are fairly structured, and they include the taking of a family history. For him, the first contacts with families are opening salvos in "the battle for structure" (Whitaker and Keith, 1981). He labors hard to gain enough control to be able to exert maximum therapeutic leverage. He wants the family to know that the therapists are in charge, and he wants them to accept the idea of family therapy. This begins with the first telephone call. Whitaker (1976b) insists that the largest possible number of family members attend; he believes that three generations are necessary to ensure that grandparents will support, not oppose, therapy, and that their presence will help correct distortions. If significant family members won't attend, Whitaker may refuse to see the family. Why begin with the cards stacked against you?

Most of what experiential family therapists do is aimed at stimulating emotional experience and interaction. To achieve these ends, they use a combination of their own provocativeness and a number of structured, expressive techniques. Experiential therapists tend to push and confront families from the outset (Kempler, 1973). Their interventions tend to be creative and spontaneous, and are described as letting the unconscious operate the therapy (Whitaker, 1967). Many seem to develop genuine and personal attachments to patients, and don't hesitate to side with first one family member, then another.

Among experiential, if not all family therapists, Carl Whitaker is the most outspoken proponent of therapists using their own personalities to effect change. For Whitaker, the therapist's personal adequacy, ability to be caring, firmness, and ability to be unpredictable are far more effective tools than any therapeutic techniques. He believes that a therapist's wisdom, experience, and creativeness will guide his or her interventions better than any preconceived plan or structure. (This probably works better for therapists who are wise, experienced, and creative than for those who are not.)

Experiential family therapists help families to become more real, direct, and alive by modeling this behavior for them. They don't just point the way, they lead the way. Most are very provocative. Whitaker (Napier and Whitaker, 1978), for example, in one session asked a teenage daughter if she thought her parents had a good sex life. Kempler (1968) describes the therapist as a catalyst and as an active participant in family interactions. As a catalyst, he makes suggestions and gives directives. Typical directives include telling family members to look at each other, speak louder, repeat certain statements, or rephrase a remark to make it more emotional. He (Kempler, 1968) cites an example of telling a husband that he whimpers at his wife and whimpers at the therapist. Moreover, this was said in a sarcastic tone, deliberately designed to arouse the man's anger, "Tell her to get the hell off your back—and mean it!" The decision to become an active participant in family encounters depends largely on the therapist's own level of emotional arousal. If he gets upset or angry, he's liable to say so. "I can't stand your wishy-washy answers!" The avowed purpose of such bluntness is to teach—by example—the use of "I-statements." As Kempler (Kempler, 1981, p. 156) remarks, "The expressed experiential 'I' ness of the therapist is the epitome of experiential intervention." He frequently challenges and even argues with family members, while freely acknowledging that this largely has to do with his own frustration.

Although they can be blunt, these therapists also limit how far they push people. Kempler (1968) says that therapists should be spontaneous, but not impulsive; and most experientialists agree that only a very warm and supportive therapist can afford to risk being pushy and provocative. Napier and Whitaker (1978) also espouse setting limits on the "let it all hang out" credo that sometimes is used to justify permitting family members to engage in destructive fights. Trying to emulate Whitaker's provocativeness without his warmth and power to restrain can lead to disaster.

Whether they are provocative or supportive, experiential family therapists are usually quite active and directive. Instead of being left to work out their own styles of interaction, family members are frequently told, "Tell him (or her) what you feel!" or asked, "What are you feeling now?" Just as the best way to get a school teacher's attention is to misbehave, the best way to get an experiential therapist's attention is to show signs of feeling, without actually expressing it.

Therapists observe nonverbal signs of feeling; they notice how interactions take place; they notice whether people are mobile or rigid; and they try to identify suppressed emotional reactions. Then they try to focus awareness (Kaplan and Kaplan, 1978). By directing attention to what a person is experiencing at the moment, the therapist may induce a breakthrough of affect or a revelation of previously withheld material. When family members appear to be blocked or disrupted, the therapist focuses on the ones who seem most energized.

THERAPIST I see you looking over at Dad whenever you ask Mom a question, what's that about?

JOHNNY Oh, nothing—I guess.

THERAPIST   It must mean something. Come on, what were you feeling?

JOHNNY   Nothing!

THERAPIST   You must have been feeling something. What was it?

JOHNNY   Well, sometimes when Mommy lets me do something, Dad gets real mad. But instead of yelling at her, he yells at me (crying softly).

THERAPIST   Tell him.

JOHNNY   (Angrily, to the therapist,) Leave me alone!

THERAPIST   No, it's important. Try to tell your Dad how you feel.

JOHNNY   (Sobbing hard) You're always picking on me! You never let me do anything!

Experiential therapists use a great number of expressive techniques in their work. With some, this amounts to a kind of eclectic grab bag, as the following remark from Bunny and Fred Duhl (1981, p. 511) suggests.

> For us, we feel free to choose a particular technique or methodology as one chooses a tool from a tool box—that is, the appropriate tool for the specific job—in order to achieve the goal of a changed system interaction in a manner that fits all participants, goals, and processes.

Among the techniques available in the experiential family therapy tool box are *family sculpture* (Duhl, Kantor, and Duhl, 1973), *family puppet interviews* (Irwin and Malloy, 1975), *family art therapy* (Geddes and Medway, 1977), *conjoint family drawings* (Bing, 1970), and *Gestalt therapy techniques* (Kempler, 1973). Included among the accoutrements of experiential therapists' offices are toys, doll houses, clay, teddy bears, drawing pens and paper, and batacca bats. Although these props are commonly used for play therapy, experiential therapists don't limit their use to children.

In *family sculpture*, originated by David Kantor and Fred Duhl, the therapist asks each member of the family to arrange the others in a meaningful tableau. This is a graphic means of portraying each person's perceptions of the family, in terms of space, posture, and attitude. This was also a favorite device of Virginia Satir, who frequently used ropes and blindfolds to dramatize the constricting roles family members trap each other into (Satir and Baldwin, 1983).

The following example of sculpting occurred when a therapist asked Mr. N. to arrange the other members of the family into a scene typical of the time when he comes home from work.

MR. N.   When I come home from work, eh? Okay (to his wife) honey, you'd be by the stove, wouldn't you?

THERAPIST   No, don't talk. Just move people where you want them to be.

MR. N.   Okay.

He guided his wife to stand at a spot where the kitchen stove might be, and placed his children on the kitchen floor, drawing and playing.

THERAPIST   Fine, Now, still without any dialogue, put them into action.

Mr. N. then instructed his wife to pretend to cook, but to turn frequently to see what the kids were up to. He told the children to pretend to play for awhile, but then to start fighting, and complaining to Mommy.

THERAPIST   And what happens, when you come home.

MR. N.   Nothing. I try to talk to my wife, but the kids keep pestering her, and she gets mad and says to leave her alone.

THERAPIST   Okay, act it out.

As the family mimed the scene that Mr. N. had described, each of them had a powerful awareness of how he felt. Mrs. N. acted out trying to cook and referee the children's fights. The children, who thought this a great game, pretended to fight, and tried to outdo each other getting Mommy's attention. When Mr. N. "came home," he reached out for his wife, but the children came between them, until Mrs. N. finally pushed them all away.

Afterwards, Mrs. N. said that she hadn't realized her husband felt pushed away. She just thought of him as coming home, saying hello, and then withdrawing into the den with his newspaper and bottle of beer.

Family sculpture, choreography, or *spatializing* (Jefferson, 1978) is also used to illuminate scenes from the past. A typical instruction is, "Remember standing in front of your childhood home. Walk in and describe what typically happened." With this technique, the idea is to make a sculpture using people and props to portray one's perceptions of family life. It's a useful device to sharpen sensitivity, and it provides useful information to the therapist. It's probably most useful if it suggests changes, which are then acted upon. "Do you like it that way? If not, change it to be the way you want it to be. And if you really care, then do something about it between sessions."

Another structured expressive exercise is *family art therapy*. Kwiatkowska (1967) instructs families to produce a series of sequentially ordered drawings, including a "joint family scribble," in which each person makes a quick scribble and then the whole family incorporates the scribble into a unified picture. Bing (1970) has families draw a picture of themselves as family. Rubin and Magnussen (1974) ask for joint murals, as well as two- or three-dimensional family portraits.

Elizabeth Bing (1970) describes the *conjoint family drawing* as a means to warm families up and free them to express themselves. In family drawings the basic instruction is, "Draw a picture as you see yourselves as a family." The resulting pictures may disclose perceptions that haven't previously been discussed, or may stimulate the person drawing the picture to realize something that he or she had never thought of before.

A father once drew a picture of the family that showed him off to one side, while his wife and children stood holding hands. Although he was portraying a fact well known to his wife and himself, they hadn't spoken openly of it. Once he produced his drawing and showed it to the therapist, there was no avoiding discussion. In another case, when the therapist asked each of the family members to draw the family, the teenage daughter was quite uncertain what to do. She had never thought much about the family, or her role in it. When she started to work, her drawing just seemed to emerge. After she finished, she was somewhat surprised to discover that she'd drawn herself closer to her father and sisters than to her mother. This provoked a lively discussion between her and her mother about their relationship. Although the two of them spent time together, the daughter didn't feel close, because she thought her mother treated her like a kid, never talking about her own concerns, and showing only superficial interest in the daughter's life. For her part, the mother was surprised, and not all displeased, that her daughter felt ready to establish a relationship on a more equal, sharing basis.

Another projective technique designed to increase expressiveness is the *symbolic drawing of family life space* (Geddes and Medway, 1977). First the therapist draws a large circle. Then he or she instructs the family that everything inside the circle is to represent what is inside the family. Persons and institutions thought not to be part of the family are to be placed outside in the environment. Each person in the family is to draw a small circle, representing himself or herself, and place it inside the family circle in a position meaningfully related to the others. As the family complies with these instructions, the therapist reflects their apparent perceptions. "Oh, you feel you are on the outside, away from everyone else." "It looks like you think your sister is closer to your parents than you are."

In *family puppet interviews*, Irwin and Malloy (1975) ask one of the family members to make up a story using puppets. This technique, originally used in play therapy with small children, is supposed to be a vehicle for expression and for highlighting conflicts and alliances. In fact, its usefulness is probably limited to working with small children. Most adults resist expressing anything really personal through such a childlike medium.

Even a frightened eight-year-old knows what's up when a therapist says, "Tell me a story."

Roleplaying is another favorite device of experimental therapists. Its use is based upon the premise that experience, to be real, must be felt and exposed in the present. Recollection of past events and consideration of hoped-for or feared future events can be made more immediate by roleplaying them in the immediacy of the session. Kempler (1968) encourages parents to fantasize and roleplay scenes from childhood. A mother might be asked to roleplay what it was like when she was a little girl, or a father might be asked to imagine himself being a boy caught in the same dilemma as his son is.

Most of the experiential family therapists frequently break off the family dialogues to work with individuals. At times this may be to explore emotional blocks, investigate memories, or even analyze dreams. "The individual intrapsychic work may require a few minutes or it may take an entire session. In some instances it has taken the better part of several sessions" (Kempler, 1981, p. 203). The reason for the individual work is the belief that an individual's unfinished business prevents him or her from encountering others in the family.

When someone is mentioned who isn't present in the session, therapists may introduce Gestalt *there-and-then* techniques (Kempler, 1973). If a child talks about her grandfather, she may be asked to speak to a chair, which is supposed to personify grandfather. These techniques have proven very useful in individual therapy (Nichols and Zax, 1977) to intensify emotional experiencing by bringing memories into focus and by acting out suppressed reactions. Whether or not such devices are necessary or useful in family therapy is open to question. In individual treatment patients are isolated from the significant figures in their lives, and roleplaying may be useful to approximate being with those people. But since family therapy is conducted with at least some of the most significant people present, it seems doubtful that roleplaying or other means of fantasy are necessary. If emotional action is wanted, it seems that plenty of it is available simply by opening the dialogue between family members.

Whitaker (1975) uses a similar roleplaying technique, which he calls "psychotherapy of the absurd." This consists of augmenting the unreasonable quality of a patient's response to the point of absurdity. It often amounts to calling a person's bluff, as the following example illustrates:

PATIENT   I can't stand my husband!

THERAPIST   Why don't you get rid of him, or take up a boyfriend.

At other times this takes the form of sarcastic teasing, such as mock fussing in response to a fussy child. The hope is that patients will get objective distance by participating in the therapist's distancing; the danger is that patients will feel hurt at being made fun of.

EVALUATING THERAPY THEORY AND RESULTS

Experiential family therapists have shown a general lack of interest in verifying their theories of their results. Their writings reflect a concern with providing potent affective experiences in therapy. That emotional expression and interaction produce change is more or less taken for granted. Even Alvin Mahrer (1982), one of the most productive researchers and scholars among experiential psychotherapists, believes that outcome studies of psychotherapy are essentially useless. His position is that studies of outcome might be of interest to administrators or insurance companies, but they will have little impact on practitioners. Instead, he recommends studying "in-therapy outcomes": what therapeutic interventions lead to desired consequences on patients' behavior?

Although Mahrer (1982) and others (Nichols and Zax, 1977) have begun to examine such "in-therapy outcomes" in individual treatment, there are as yet no empirical studies of experiential family therapy. What is offered instead as verification consists of anecdotal reports of successful outcome (Napier and Whitaker, 1978; Duhl and Duhl, 1981) and descriptions of techniques which were observed to be effective in catalyzing emotional expression within sessions (Kempler, 1981).

Experiential family therapists aim to provide a useful experience for the families they treat, but they don't seem to believe that every family member must change overtly to validate their efforts. Moreover, change is believed to frequently come in small ways, which may be difficult to measure. If, as a result of experiential therapy, a family is able to make more direct contact with a schizophrenic son, this would be considered a success.

Whitaker (Whitaker and Keith, 1981) claims little empirical evidence of the success of his approach, but cites the goodwill of the community, referrals from previous patients, and the satisfaction of families after treatment as evidence of success. He also mentions his own satisfaction as a therapist, stating that when therapy is unsuccessful therapists become burned out and bitter.

SUMMARY

Experiential family therapy is designed to change families by changing family members, reversing the direction of effect usually envisioned by family therapists. Among experientialists, families are conceived of and treated as groups of individuals more than as systems. Enhanced sensitivity and expanded awareness are the essential aims of treatment.

In addition to focusing on *intra*personal change, experiential family therapy is also distinguished by a commitment to growth as opposed to problem-solving. Personal growth and self-fulfillment are seen as ingrained human tendencies, which naturally emerge once interferences and defensiveness are reduced. Treatment is therefore aimed at reducing defenses within and between family members. Experientialists challenge and question that which is familiar and automatic. They interrupt automatic behavior and make the familiar strange, believing that once automatic behavior is interrupted, the potential exists for alternative behavior to be more functional and satisfying.

In order to introduce novelty and enhance immediate experiencing, therapists use their own lively personalities as well as numerous structured, expressive techniques. Like encounter group leaders, experiential family therapists act as *agents provocateur* for intense emotional awareness and expression. Therapy is viewed as an existential encounter, conducted by therapists who participate fully and spontaneously. Interventions are said to arise out of the therapist's aliveness and creativity. At various times these interventions take the form of self-disclosure, teasing, sarcasm, humor, personal confrontation, paradoxical intention, and modeling.

These freewheeling responses may seem intimidating, but the risk is minimized by the presence of other family members (and frequently, cotherapists). Nevertheless, any therapy that features personal disclosure from the therapist has the potential to make the therapist—his or her experience, needs, values, and opinions—more important than the patients. The following is an example of "therapeutic candor" from a prominent experiential family therapist. "I'm almost ready for you people. I'm still thinking about the previous session which was quite moving" (Kempler, 1977, p. 91). Such a remark is fraught with problematic implications and seems oblivious to the needs of the family. The rationale sometimes offered for such dumping is that it enables the therapist to be more completely focused on the present. Perhaps so, but it seems equally likely to divert family members from their experience to his.

Experiential therapy derives from existential, humanistic, and phenomenological thought, from which comes the idea that individual freedom and self-expression can undo the devitalizing effects of culture. Beyond this, however, experiential family therapy tends to be relatively atheoretical. The result is an approach with little basis for systematically conceptualizing family dynamics, and instead simply borrows concepts and techniques from other approaches.

The essential vitality of this approach lies in its techniques for promoting and expanding intense experience. As they grow up, most people learn to blunt the full range of their experiencing. Indeed, defensive avoidance of anxiety may be the most prominent motivating force in people's lives. Experiential therapy takes families who have become refractory to emotional experience and puts some of the oomph back in their lives.

At its best, experiential therapy helps people uncover their own potential aliveness. Experience is real, it's a fact. Therapy conducted on the basis of putting people in touch with their own genuine experience has an undeniable validity. Moreover, when this personal discovery is conducted in the context of the family, there is a good chance that family relations can be revitalized by authentic interaction among people who are struggling with becoming themselves.

In order to reduce defensiveness and heighten emotional experience, experiential family therapists can be highly active. Unfortunately, it's difficult to be active without also becoming interpretative and directive. Even the best of those in this tradition (Napier and Whitaker, 1978) find it difficult to resist telling people what they should be, rather than simply helping them find out who they are. Moreover, provocative directions such as "Tell her to get the hell off your back and mean it!" (Kempler, 1968), often seem to produce compliant shows of feeling, rather than genuine emotional responses. When emotional resistance is truly reduced, feelings will emerge, without the direction of a therapist.

In experiential therapy the emphasis is on experience, not understanding. Nevertheless, experiential practitioners seem ambivalent in their attitudes about the utility of insight and understanding. Most, like Whitaker (Whitaker, Felder, and Warkentin, 1965), emphasize the nonrational forces in treatment, so that the intellectual side of human nature is subordinated to the feeling side. Whitaker's (Whitaker and Keith, 1981) statement that insight doesn't work—recognition isn't change—is typical. Elsewhere his treatment is described (Napier, 1977) as providing a complex emotional experience, not "intellectual nagging." However, case studies of experiential family therapy are filled with examples of advice-giving and interpretation. It seems that psychotherapists—of all persuasions—are as prone as the rest of humankind to offer advice and render judgment, and experiential family therapists do so no less often than members of other schools. The Duhls (Duhl and Duhl, 1981), for example, recognize the need for insight to support emotional change, and have criticized what they call "intervention without education."

Once, the idea that families are systems was both novel and controversial; today it is the new orthodoxy. Now that the pendulum has swung so far in the direction of systems thinking, individuals and their private joys and pains are rarely mentioned. Surely one of the major contributions of experiential family therapy is to remind us not to lose sight of the person in the system.

REFERENCES

Bartlett, F.H. 1976. Illusion and reality in R.D. Laing. *Family Process.* *15*:51–64.

Bing, E. 1970. The conjoint family drawing. *Family Process.* 9:173–194.

Binswanger, L. 1967. *Being-in-the-world.* In *Selected papers of Ludwig Binswanger,* J. Needleman, ed. New York: Harper Torchbooks.

Boss, M. 1963. *Psychoanalysis and Daseinanalysis.* New York: Basic Books.

Duhl, B.S. 1983. *From the inside out and other metaphors.* New York: Brunner/Mazel.

Duhl, B.S., and Duhl, F.J. 1981. Integrative family therapy. In *Handbook of family therapy,* A.S. Gurman and D.P. Kniskern, eds. New York: Brunner/Mazel.

Duhl, F.J., Kantor D., and Duhl, B.S. 1973. Learning, space and action in family therapy: A primer of sculpture. In *Techniques of family psychotherapy,* D.A. Bloch, ed. New York: Grune and Stratton.

Frankl, V.E. 1963. *Man's search for meaning.* New York: Washington Square Press.

Geddes, M., and Medway, J. 1977. The symbolic drawing of family life space. *Family Process.* 16:219–228.

Gehrke, S., and Kirschenbaum, M. 1967. Survival patterns in conjoint family therapy. *Family Process.* 6:67–80.

Gendlin, E.T. 1962. *Experiencing and the creation of meaning.* New York: Macmillan.

Greenberg, L.S., and Johnson, S.M. 1985. Emotionally focused couple therapy: An affective systemic approach. In *Handbook of family and marital therapy,* N.S. Jacobson and A.S. Gurman, eds., New York: Guilford.

Greenberg, L.S., and Johnson, S.M. 1986. Affect in marital therapy. *Journal of Marital and Family Therapy.* 12:1–10.

Greenberg, L.S., and Johnson, S.M. 1988. *Emotionally focused therapy for couples.* New York: Guilford.

Heidegger, M. 1963. *Being and time.* New York: Harper and Row.

Irwin, E., and Malloy, E. 1975. Family puppet interview. *Family Process.* 14:179–191.

Janov, A. 1970. *The primal scream.* New York: Dell.

Jefferson, C. 1978. Some notes on the use of family sculpture in therapy. *Family Process.* 17:69–76.

Kantor, D., and Lehr, W. 1975. *Inside the family.* San Francisco: Jossey-Bass.

Kaplan, M.L., and Kaplan, N.R. 1978. Individual and family growth: A Gestalt approach. *Family Process.* 17:195–205.

Keith, D.V. 1988. The family's own system: The symbolic context of health. In *Family transitions: Continuity and change over the life cycle,* C.J. Falicov, ed. New York: Guilford.

Keith, D.V., and Whitaker, C.A. 1977. The divorce labyrinth. In *Family therapy: Full-length case studies,* P. Papp, ed. New York: Gardner Press.

Kempler, W. 1965. Experiential family therapy. *The International Journal of Group Psychotherapy.* 15:57–71.

Kempler, W. 1968. Experiential psychotherapy with families. *Family Process.* 7:88–89.

Kempler, W. 1973. *Principles of Gestalt family therapy.* Oslo, Norway: Nordahls.

Kempler, W. 1981. *Experiential psychotherapy with families*. New York: Brunner/Mazel.

Kwiatkowska, H.Y. 1967. Family art therapy. *Family Process*. 6:37–55.

Laing, R.D. 1967. *The politics of experience*. New York: Ballantine.

Laing, R.D., and Esterson, A. 1970. *Sanity, madness and the family*. Baltimore: Penguin Books.

Lasch, C. 1978. *The culture of narcissism: American life in an age of diminishing expectations*. New York: Norton.

Lieberman, M.A., Yalom, I.D., and Miles, M.B. 1973. *Encounter groups: First facts*. New York: Basic Books.

Mahrer, A.R. 1982. *Experiential psychotherapy: Basic practices*. New York: Brunner/Mazel.

Malone, T.P., Whitaker, C.A., Warkentin, J., and Felder, R.E. 1961. Rational and nonrational psychotherapy. *American Journal of Psychotherapy*. 15:212–220.

Marcuse, H. 1955. *Eros and civilization*. New York: Beacon Press.

Maslow, A.H. 1968. *Toward a psychology of being*. 2nd ed. Princeton, NJ: Van Nostrand.

Napier, A.Y. 1977. Follow-up to divorce labyrinth. In *Family therapy: Full-length case studies*, P. Papp, ed. New York: Gardner Press.

Napier, A.Y., and Whitaker, C.A. 1978. *The family crucible*. New York: Harper and Row.

Neill, J.R., and Kniskern, D.P., eds. 1982. *From psyche to system: The evolving therapy of Carl Whitaker*. New York: Guilford.

Nichols, M.P., and Zax, M. 1977. *Catharsis in psychotherapy*. New York: Gardner Press.

Papp, P. 1976. Family choreography. In *Family therapy: Theory and practice*, P. J. Guerin, ed. New York: Gardner Press.

Perls, F.S. 1961. *Gestalt therapy verbatim*. Lafayette, CA: Real People Press.

Perls, F.S., Hefferline, R. E., and Goodman, P. 1951. *Gestalt therapy*. New York: Delta.

Pierce, R., Nichols, M.P., and DuBrin, J. 1983. *Emotional expression in psychotherapy*. New York: Gardner Press.

Rogers, C.R. 1951. *Client-centered therapy*. Boston: Houghton Mifflin.

Rubin, J., and Magnussen, M. A. 1974. A family art evaluation. *Family Process*. 13:185–200.

Satir, V.M. 1964. *Conjoint family therapy*. Palo Alto, CA: Science and Behavior Books.

Satir, V.M. 1971. The family as a treatment unit. In *Changing families*, J. Haley, ed. New York: Grune and Stratton.

Satir, V.M. 1972. *Peoplemaking*. Palo Alto, CA: Science and Behavior Books.

Satir, V.M. 1988. *The new peoplemaking*. Palo Alto, CA: Science and Behavior Books.

Satir, V.M., and Baldwin, M. 1983. *Satir step by step: A guide to creating change in families*. Palo Alto, CA: Science and Behavior Books.

Simon, R. 1989. Reaching out to life: An interview with Virginia Satir. *The Family Therapy Networker*. 13(1):36–43.

Simon, R.M. (1972). Sculpting the family. *Family Process*. 11:49–51.

Sullivan, H.S. 1953. *The interpersonal theory of psychiatry*. New York: Norton.

Whitaker, C.A. 1958. Psychotherapy with couples. *American Journal of Psychotherapy. 12*:18–23.

Whitaker, C.A. 1967. The growing edge. In *Techniques of family therapy*, J. Haley and L. Hoffman, eds. New York: Basic Books.

Whitaker, C.A. 1975. Psychotherapy of the absurd: With a special emphasis on the psychotherapy of aggression. *Family Process. 14*:1–16.

Whitaker, C.A. 1976a. The hindrance of theory in clinical work. In *Family therapy: Theory and practice*, P.J. Guerin, ed. New York: Gardner Press.

Whitaker, C.A. 1976b. A family is a four-dimensional relationship. In *Family therapy: Theory and practice*, P.J. Guerin, ed. New York: Gardner Press.

Whitaker, C.A., Felder, R.E., and Warkentin, J. 1965. Countertransference in the family treatment of schizophrenia. In *Intensive family therapy*, I. Boszormenyi-Nagy and J.L. Framo, eds. New York: Harper & Row.

Whitaker, C.A., and Keith, D.V. 1981. Symbolic-experiential family therapy. In *Handbook of family therapy*, A.S. Gurman and D.P. Kniskern, eds. New York: Brunner/Mazel.

Whitaker, C.A., and Malone, T.P. 1953. *The roots of psychotherapy*. New York: Blakiston.

Whitaker, C.A., Warkentin, J., and Malone, T.P. 1959. The involvement of the professional therapist. In *Case studies in counseling and psychotherapy*, A. Burton, ed. Englewood Cliffs, NJ: Prentice Hall.

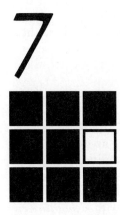

7

Behavioral Family Therapy

Behavioral family therapists started out using learning theory techniques devised for treating individuals and applying them to problems encountered by families; but in the twenty years since its inception, the technology of behavioral family therapy has become increasingly sophisticated and its practitioners increasingly aware that families are more complicated than individuals. Behavior therapists have developed a variety of powerful, pragmatic techniques that they administer to a variety of family problems, but most of the emphasis remains on parent training, behavioral marriage therapy, and treatment of sexual dysfunctions.

The distinctive methods of behavioral family therapy are derived from classical and operant conditioning treatments for individuals. Target behavior is precisely specified in operational terms; operant conditioning, classical conditioning, social learning theory, and cognitive strategies are then used to produce change. As behavior therapists have built up experience treating family problems, they have begun to address such traditionally nonbehavioral concerns as the therapeutic alliance, the need for empathy, the problem of resistance, communication, and problem-solving skills. However, even when dealing with such mainstream issues, behaviorists are distinguished by their methodical and directive approach. More than by any technique, behavioral therapy is characterized by careful assessment and evaluation. Analysis of behavioral sequences prior to treatment, assessment of therapy in progress, and evaluation of its final results are hallmarks of all forms of behavioral therapy.

When behavioral therapists apply their techniques to families, they are explicit and direct; and they measure their results. This is consistent with the credo of behavior therapy, namely that behavior is determined more by its consequences than its antecedents.

SKETCHES OF LEADING FIGURES

Behavior therapy is a direct descendent of the laboratory investigations of Ivan Pavlov, the Russian physiologist whose work on conditioned reflexes led to the development of *classical conditioning*. In classical conditioning, an *unconditioned stimulus* (UCS), such as food, which leads to a reflex *unconditioned response* (UCR), like salivation, is paired with a *conditioned stimulus* (CS), such as a bell. The result is that the conditioned stimulus begins to evoke the same response. Pavlov published the results of his laboratory work with animals and also reported on the application of his techniques to abnormal behavior in humans (Pavlov, 1932, 1934). Subsequently John B. Watson applied classical conditioning principles to experimentally induce a phobia in "Little Albert" (Watson and Raynor, 1920), and Mary Cover Jones successfully resolved a similar phobia in the case of "Peter" (Jones, 1924).

In the 1930s and 1940s extensions and elaborations of Pavlov's conditioning theory were applied to numerous clinical problems. Nevertheless classical conditioning was still viewed as having limited practical utility. Then, in 1948, Joseph Wolpe introduced *systematic desensitization*, with which he achieved great success in the treatment of phobias and generated enormous interest in behavioral treatment. According to Wolpe (1948) anxiety is a persistant response of the autonomic nervous system acquired through classical conditioning. Systematic desensitization deconditions the anxiety through *reciprocal inhibition*, by pairing responses that are incompatible with anxiety to the previously anxiety-arousing stimuli. For example, if Indiana Jones® was frightened of snakes, Wolpe would first teach Dr. Jones how to relax deeply, and then have him imagine approaching a snake in a graded hierarchy of stages. Each time Indy became anxious, he would be told to relax. In this way the anxiety evoked by imagining snakes would be systematically extinguished by reciprocal inhibition.

Systematic desensitization has proven to be a very powerful technique for reducing anxiety, which is even more effective when it includes actual practice in gradually approaching the feared object or situation (*in vivo desensitization*).

The application of classical conditioning methods to family problems has been primarily in the treatment of anxiety-based disorders, including agoraphobia and sexual dysfunctions, pioneered by Wolpe (1958) and later elaborated by Masters and Johnson (1970) at Washington University. Effective behavioral treatments for enuresis have also been developed using classical conditioning (Lovibond, 1963).

By far the greatest influence on behavioral family therapy came from B. F. Skinner's *operant conditioning*. The term *operant* refers to voluntary behavioral responses, as opposed to involuntary or reflex behavior. The frequency of operant responses is determined by their consequences. Those responses that are *positively reinforced* will occur more frequently; those that are *punished* or ignored will be *extinguished*. In 1953 Skinner published an enormously influential book, *Science and Human Behavior*, in which he presented a behavioristic approach to all human behavior.

The operant conditioner carefully observes target behavior, and then quantifies its frequency and rate. Then, to complete a *functional analysis* of the behavior, the experimenter or clinician notes the consequences of the behavior to determine the *contingencies of reinforcement*. For example, someone interested in a child's temper tantrums would begin by observing when they occurred and what their consequences were. A typical finding might be that the child threw a tantrum whenever his parents denied his requests, and that the parents frequently gave in if the tantrums were prolonged. Thus the parents would be discovered to have been reinforcing the very behavior they least wanted. To eliminate the tantrums, they would be taught to ignore or punish them. Moreover they would be told that giving in, even occasionally, would maintain the tantrums, because behavior that is partially or *intermittently reinforced* is the most difficult to extinguish. If the child were aware of the contingencies, he might think, "They're not giving me what I want now, but if I keep fussing they will eventually give in; if not this time, then the next."

Skinner, who first used the term "behavior therapy," argued convincingly that behavior problems can be dealt with directly, not simply as symptoms of underlying psychic conflict. The first professional journal in this field, *Behavior Research and Therapy*, started in 1963, elicited a flood of studies demonstrating dramatic and impressive behavior change. A key question that arose in those early days was, "How permanent were the behavior changes?" Yes, behavior therapists could shape new sequences of behavior; but would such changes last? In learning theory terms, this is a problem of *generalization*, a problem which remains crucial to any form of psychotherapy. Behavior therapists consider this a problem to be solved, rather than a question to be debated. Behavioral family therapists have worked to generalize their results by moving from the consultation room to natural settings (home and school), using naturalistic reinforcers, using family members as therapists, and by *fading* (gradually decreasing) external contingencies. Generalization is now programmed rather than hoped for or lamented.

Among the first reports of effective behavior therapy for family problems was Williams' (1959) successful intervention to reduce bedtime tantrums in a young child. The parents were instructed to put the child to bed in an affectionate manner, to close his bedroom door, and ignore his subsequent protestations. The key principle here is *extinction*.

Operant conditioning is particularly effective with children, because parents have considerable control over their reinforcers and punishments. Boardman (1962) trained parents in the effective use of a punishment paradigm to deal with the aggressive antisocial behavior of their five-year-old. Wolpe (1958) described how to employ spouses as cotherapists in anxiety management. Risley and Wolf (1967) trained parents in the operant reinforcement of speech in their autistic children.

Although no single charismatic figure was responsible for the development of behavior family therapy, three leaders clearly played a dominant role: a psychologist, Gerald Patterson, a psychiatrist, Robert Liberman, and a social worker, Richard Stuart.

Gerald Patterson, at the University of Oregon, was the most influential figure in developing the field of behavioral parent training. Patterson and his colleagues realized that observation of family interactions in a laboratory or consulting room was far removed from the behavior in the natural environment of the home. As a result, they developed methods for sampling periods of family interaction in the home, trained parents in the principles of social learning theory, developed programmed workbooks (e.g., Patterson, 1971b), and worked out careful strategies for eliminating undesirable behavior and substituting desirable behavior. Among others prominent in this field are Anthony Graziano, Rex Forehand, Daniel and Susan O'Leary, and Roger McAuley in Belfast, Ireland.

The second major figure in the development of behavioral family therapy was Robert Liberman. In his 1970 paper, "Behavioral Approaches to Family and Couple Therapy," he outlined the application of an operant learning framework to the family problems of four adult patients with depression, intractable headaches, social inadequacy, and marital discord. In addition to employing contingency management of mutual reinforcers, Liberman introduced the use of *modeling* concepts of Bandura and Walters (1963) to family therapy.

The third major influence on behavioral family therapy was the contingency contracting approach of Richard Stuart (1969). Rather than focus on how the undesired behavior of one family member could be modified, Stuart focused on how the exchange of positive behavior could be maximized. Thus he introduced the principle of *reciprocity*.

In his first efforts, Stuart (1969) transferred operant principles, used to modify children's behavior, to couples in distress. He applied a reciprocal reinforcement paradigm in which couples learned to: (a) list the behavior they desired from each other; (b) record the frequency with which the spouse displayed the desired behavior; and (c) specify exchanges for the desired behavior. In this early work, tokens were used for reinforcers. Mutual exchanges were based on written contracts.

The early work in behavioral family therapy depended almost entirely on applications of operant conditioning and appeared most successful where behavioral problems could be defined in terms of relatively straightforward stimulus-response exchanges.

Ed Katkin (1978) reported success with *charting* in the treatment of a paranoid jealous wife. In charting, the patient is asked to keep an accurate record of the problem behavior. Katkin's ploy was to ask the wife to record the frequency of her irrational accusations. This approach illustrates the early attempts to approach family problems through the treatment of individuals. It also illustrates the adaptation of nonbehavioral techniques— in this case, paradoxical intention.

Other early applications of behavior therapy to couples included teaching spouses how to shape positive behavior in one another (Liberman, 1970) and having them analyze the consequences of their behavior and learn to interrupt negative interaction chains (Friedman, 1972). Mutual behavior change efforts were given even more structure by introducing behavioral contracts, written agreements to exchange desired behavior (Rappaport and Harrell, 1972).

During the 1970s behavioral family therapy was developed into three major packages: parent training, behavioral marital therapy, and sexual therapy. At present the leading figures in behavioral marital therapy include Robert Weiss, Neil Jacobson, Richard Stuart, Michael Crowe, Norman Epstein, and Gayola Margolin. Weiss took over the development of marital therapy from Gerald Patterson and was particularly influential in establishing a substantial body of research in the assessment and treatment of marital discord.

Two additional developments have further increased the popularity and influence of behavior therapy. First, many nonbehavioral family therapists selectively include behavioral interventions in their work. A good example of this was Minuchin's (Minuchin, Rosman, and Baker, 1978) use of operant conditioning in his work with anorexia nervosa. Second, there has recently been a rapprochement between stimulus-response conditioning models and cognitive theories (e.g., Mischel, 1973; Barton and Alexander, 1981; Epstein, Schlesinger, and Dryden, 1988). Now many behavioral therapists are beginning to consider the role of various "internal" processes such as attitudes, thoughts, and feelings. In addition, family systems theory is having an increasing impact on behavioral family therapists. Gerald Patterson, once a pure operant behaviorist, studied systems theory with Salvador Minuchin; as first illustrated in an article published in *Family Process* by Spinks and Birchler (1982), dealing with resistance has become a major concern in behavioral family therapy; and recent books on the state of the art in behavior family therapy (e.g., Falloon, 1988) are very sophisticated in their handling of family systems dynamics.

THEORETICAL FORMULATIONS

Theory follows practice in most family therapies. Successful techniques are developed first, and only later are theories adduced to explain the results. But this is less true of behavioral approaches. The claim that behavior therapy is strictly based upon research and laboratory technology (Barton and Alexander, 1975) has been challenged (Gurman and Knudson, 1978), but it is nevertheless true that behavioral family therapy was developed after the major theories supporting it had already been well developed.

The basic tenets of the behavior therapy were not developed specifically in relation to family problems, but are assumed to be directly applicable to them. Behavioral strategies relate more to how behavior is changed than to how families function, and therefore the theoretical foundations of behavioral family therapy are those of behavioral therapy in general.

Those approaching behavior therapy for the first time are often confused by references to *learning theory, behavior modification, behavior therapy*, and *social learning theory*. Are these terms synonymous or do they mean different things? Although sometimes used interchangeably, each of these expressions has its own meaning. *Learning theory* refers to the general body of principles discovered in laboratory experiments on learning and conditioning. These laws are the scientific foundation upon which behavioral treatment rests. *Behavior modification* and *behavior therapy* have been used interchangeably, although some distinctions have been made between them. Lazarus (1971) suggested that *behavior modification* refers to strict operant procedures, while *behavior therapy* is associated with counterconditioning methods for treating anxiety. *Behavior modification* has lately been less often used and seems to conjure up an image of mindless control among the public, who sometimes confuse the ends of behavior control with the efficiency of methods used to achieve it. Because the term *behavior therapy* is now commonly used to refer to all operant and nonoperant behavioral treatments, we will follow this usage. *Social learning theory* is a broad approach to human behavior, integrating principles from social, developmental, and cognitive psychology along with those principles of learning derived from experimental psychology. In social learning theory, environmental influences are still the primary concern, but private thoughts and feelings are also used to understand behavior. This framework takes into account the pervasive effects of social influences on behavior. *Cognitive-behavior therapy* refers to those approaches inspired by the work of Aaron Beck (1976) and Albert Ellis (1962) that emphasize the necessity for attitude change to promote and maintain behavior change.

The central premise of behavior therapy is that *behavior is maintained by its consequences*. It follows from this that behavior will resist change unless more rewarding consequences result from new behavior (Patterson, 1971b). Elaborating the consequences of behavior as well as the cues that elicit it requires an understanding of *stimuli* and *reinforcements*.

Four different stimulus functions are described by learning theorists: eliciting stimuli, discriminative stimuli, neutral stimuli, and reinforcing stimuli. *Eliciting stimuli* are aspects of a situation that reliably produce a response. These are particularly relevant to classical conditioning, where certain eliciting stimuli are known to produce reflexlike responses. *Discriminative stimuli* signal the occasions when a particular response will be followed by a certain consequence. Because they have been associated with those consequences in the past, discriminative stimuli have acquired a cuing function making particular responses more probable. Children, for example, quickly learn to detect certain discriminative stimuli that indicate their parents "really mean it" when they say something. *Neutral stimuli* have no direct relationship to behavior, but conditioning can establish a link between a previously neutral stimulus and a response. Thus Pavlov's dogs responded to a bell only after it had been paired with feeding. *Reinforcing stimuli* are consequences of behavior that affect the probability of future responses. They are cues that reinforcement will follow.

Responses are usually defined as *respondent* or *operant*. Respondents are those that are under the control of eliciting stimuli, and their consequences do not usually affect their frequency of occurrence. Operants are behaviors that are not automatically elicited by some stimulus, but whose occurrence is affected by their consequences. From a systems point of view, the distinction between respondents and operants is problematic. Operants are causes, while respondents are effects. From a linear viewpoint this is a useful distinction, but when we think in terms of circular causal chains, the usefulness of this distinction breaks down. With a nagging wife and a withdrawing husband, what is cause and what is effect? Is the nagging an operant or a respondent behavior? (Both spouses can give you the answer—and both answers will be different.)

Some responses may not be recognized as operants—something done to get something—just because people aren't aware of the reinforcing payoffs. For example, whining is usually reinforced by attention, although the people providing the reinforcement may not realize it. In fact, a variety of unpleasant behaviors, including nagging and temper tantrums, are reinforced by attention. Even though the attention may be unpleasant—yelling—it may be the most social interaction that the nagging spouse or tantruming child receives. Thus, responses are often maintained under conditions that are counterintuitive.

Reinforcements are consequences that affect the rate of behavior, either accelerating or decelerating it. Consequences which accelerate behavior are called *reinforcers*, while those that decelerate behavior are known as *punishers*. Within the class of reinforcers there are: (a) *positive reinforcers*, positive or rewarding consequences; and (b) *negative reinforcers*, aversive consequences terminated by a response. Thus, parents can positively reinforce their child's cleaning her room by rewarding her after she does it, or negatively reinforce her by nagging until she does it.

Punishment can take the form of (a) *aversive control*, such as yelling or spanking, or (b) *withdrawal of positive consequences*, such as having to sit in the corner or being "grounded" for a week. Punishment and negative reinforcement are often confused, but do have distinctly different meanings.

Reinforcement and punishment may be either primary or secondary. *Primary reinforcers* are natural or biological outcomes, including sex and food; *primary punishments* might be physical pain or loud noises. *Secondary reinforcers* are ones that have acquired a positive meaning through social learning, like praise or eye contact, while *secondary punishers* include criticism or withdrawal of attention. Because attention has such a powerful influence on behavior, focusing attention on undesirable behavior often provides unintended social reinforcement.

Extinction occurs when no reinforcement follows a response. Inattention, as many people know, is often the best response to behavior that you don't like. The reason why many people fail to credit this is because withholding response rarely leads to *immediate* cessation of unwanted behavior. This is because most behavior has been partially or intermittently reinforced, and therefore takes a long time to extinguish.

The relationship between a response and its consequences defines the *contingencies* governing that response. *Reinforcement schedules* describe the relationship between responding and the occurrence of consequences. When reinforcement occurs at irregular intervals, the response becomes more resistant to extinction. Perhaps you can think of a reinforcement schedule with such regular contingencies of reinforcement that even a few occurrences of nonreinforcement would be sufficient to convince you that no further reinforcement is forthcoming.

While it's easy to see how simple responses can be reinforced, it may be less clear how more complicated responses, including responses not yet in someone's repertoire, can be learned. One way for this learning to occur is by successive approximation, or *shaping*. For example, parents can shape a child's learning to play soccer by paying attention to and praising the child's gradual development of the component skills of the game. Negative behavior can also be shaped, as in those families where children only get attention for progressively more angry and destructive behavior. (Children and recalcitrant spouses can also shape yelling by refusing to respond until the volume gets turned way up.)

In addition to shaping, *modeling* is also used to teach complex or new behavior (Bandura, 1969). People often learn by emulating others, particularly if the models are perceived as successful or prestigious, and if their behavior is seen to lead to reinforcing consequences (Bandura and Walters, 1963). Modeling can be used by a therapist or a family member who exhibits a desired behavior which is then imitated by another member of the family. The amount of learning that takes place during modeling depends upon the degree to which the target family member pays attention, has the capacity to understand and rehearse the new behavior, and can reproduce the behavior. Modeling has been found to be an effective way to short-cut the long and tedious process of trial-and-error learning. (Imagine trying to teach someone how to be pleasant without showing them how.)

To many people, behavior therapy seems mindless and mechanistic. With all their talk about "schedules of reinforcement" and "controlling behavior," behavior therapists seem to ignore thoughts and feelings. While this may be true of early behaviorists, it is less true today. Behavior therapists are increasingly aware that people not only act but also think and feel. And the behaviorists are becoming increasingly aware of complications with simply re-educating patients about their behavior. The most frequent form this recognition takes is in efforts to integrate pure stimulus-response behaviorism (Skinner, 1953) and cognitive theories (Mahoney, 1977). Inner events such as cognitions, verbalizations, and feelings are now recognized as events which function as stimuli in controlling overt behavior. This is a point made over and over again by various writers on behavioral family therapy (Weiss, 1978; Jacobson, 1981), but in the opinion of the present authors cognitive events play a more important role in the theory than in the practice of behavior therapy.

As behavior therapists shifted their attention from individuals in isolation to family relationships, they came to rely on Thibaut and Kelley's (1959) *theory of social exchange*. According to social exchange theory, people strive to maximize "rewards" and minimize "costs" in relationships. When applied to marriage, this behavioral economics provides a basis for understanding the reciprocity which develops between spouses. In a successful marriage both partners work to maximize mutual rewards, while minimizing costs. By contrast, in unsuccessful marriages the partners concentrate on minimizing costs, with little expectation of reward. Unhappily married people are too busy trying to protect themselves from being hurt to consider ways to make each other happy. Each person can trim the costs of relating by giving less value (for example by withdrawing) or by shifting to negative reinforcement and punishment. According to Thibaut and Kelley, behavior exchanges follow a norm of reciprocity over time, so that parity or equilibrium is established for the exchange. Aversive or positive stimulation from one person tends to produce reciprocal behavior from another. Pleasantness begets pleasantness; nastiness begets nastiness.

In its early days behavior therapy tended to focus on individuals rather than relationships. This focus is reflected in the early reports of behavioral marital therapy in which therapists treated spouses separately in individual sessions (Goldiamond, 1965) or treated only one spouse. For example, in two of three marital therapy cases reported by Lazarus (1968) only the wife was treated. Typically, wives were offered desensitization and assertiveness training to help them establish a more balanced and effective relationship with their husbands. Other therapists taught wives the principles of reinforcement and extinction so that they could modify their husbands' behavior (Goldstein, 1971; Goldstein and Francis, 1969).

Asked to treat children, behaviorists initially began seeing them individually. Later, like systems theorists, they began to consider other people in the children's environments as part of the problem. But unlike systems theorists, many behaviorists continue to operate with a linear point of view. The parents' behavior is seen as *causing* the children's behavior. Moreover, despite disclaimers to the contrary (Gordon and Davidson, 1981; Liberman, 1970), the unit of behavioral analysis is *dyadic* rather than *triadic*. The focus is on changing interactions between a parent (usually the mother) and a child, or between one spouse and another. Little or no attention is paid to how these relationships are affected by others in the family. Gordon and Davidson (1981, p. 522) acknowledge that deviant child behavior may be related to other problems in the family, but suggest that this is much exaggerated by systems theorists.

> Clinical experience indicates that deviant child behavior occurs in families with *and without* marital discord. The simple presence of marital discord in these families may or may not be causally related to the child's problems.

From a systems point of view, such a statement seems naive; the authors apparently fail to recognize that *overt* marital discord may be absent precisely *because* the spouses have triangulated their conflict onto a child. Social learning theory may be relatively simple, but family dynamics are not.

NORMAL FAMILY DEVELOPMENT

Behaviorists de-emphasize historical data in favor of analyses of current sequences of behavior. As a result, behavioral family therapists have little to say about the development of normal or abnormal behavior. Instead they focus their attention on descriptions of the current state of affairs. Moreover, most of their descriptions of healthy family relationships are extrapolated from descriptions of distressed families.

According to the behavior exchange model (Thibaut and Kelley, 1959), a good relationship is one in which giving and getting are balanced. Another way of stating this is that there is a high ratio of benefits relative to costs.

Put as generally as this, little is added to everyday common-sense notions of family satisfaction. But behaviorists have begun to spell out, in empirical studies, some of the details of what makes for relationship satisfaction. For example, Weiss and Isaac (1978) found that affection, communication, and child care are the most important behaviors leading to marital satisfaction. Earlier, Wills, Weiss, and Patterson (1974), in a pioneering behavioral analysis of satisfaction in marriage, found that affectional and instrumental *dis*pleasures were more important than pleasures in determining marital satisfaction. They found that the exchange of displeasurable responses reduced marital satisfaction significantly more than pleasurable responses increased it. A good relationship, then, is one in which there is an exchange of pleasant behavior and, even more important, minimal unpleasant behavior. Another way of putting this is that good relationships are under positive reinforcing control.

Because behaviorists focus on overt behavior, they have tended to look at the benefits of family life in terms of manifest and tangible events. Thus they tend to overlook the fact that unconscious benefits are among the most important sources of satisfaction and stability in family life. Moreover, the behavior exchange model posits a *comparison level* or evaluation of cost/benefit reward ratio offered by the partner as compared with possible relationships outside the family. Here the behavioral bias may underestimate the importance of one's own self-evaluation of worth. Some people may be satisfied with a low benefit to cost ratio, because they feel that they "don't deserve any better." Furthermore, your own evaluation of the benefits of family life is also influenced by previous models (especially parents), and by images of an ideal partner. Clinical experience demonstrates that some people are dissatisfied despite being married to partners who behave in a very rewarding fashion. Perhaps for these people internal images of what married life "should be" are more important than the overt behavior of their spouses. Put in terms of social learning theory, there is a need to consider not only the stimuli provided by other family members, but also the way these stimuli are perceived. An increasing attention to cognitive variables will allow behavior therapists to take such ideas into account.

Effective communication is also considered by behaviorists as an important feature of good relationships (Gottman, Markman, and Notarius, 1977). Good communication increases the rewards and pleasures of relating by leading to effective stimulus control over behavior. Clear communication enables family members to discriminate among and between behavioral events, and enhances their ability to be understanding and to give support. It's considered important that family members be good listeners, with understanding, although not necessarily agreement.

Families in treatment often express their desire to be free from problems, and many look to therapists to solve their problems for them. Unfortunately, problems are part of life. Therefore healthy families are not problem-free, but have the ability to cope with problems when they arise. Recognizing this, behavioral family therapists stress the need for problem-solving skills and the ability to resolve conflicts as criteria for successful marriages (Jacobson and Margolin, 1979). In a good relationship the partners are able to speak openly and directly about conflicts. They are able to keep issues in perspective and discuss specific behaviors that are of concern to them. Moreover, each is willing and able to understand the other's viewpoint.

When problems arise or when circumstances change, families need the skills to change behavior. Some behaviorists consider communications skills to be the most powerful determinant of marital success (Markman, 1979), while others emphasize sexual gratification (Masters and Johnson, 1970).

Many people assume that good family relationships will occur naturally if people are well matched and if they love each other. Behaviorists, on the other hand, consistently emphasize the need to develop relationship skills. Good marriages, they believe, are not made in heaven, but are a product of learning effective coping behavior. Jacobson (1981, p. 561) described a good relationship as one in which the partners maintain a high rate of rewards.

> Successful couples adapt effectively to the requirements of day-to-day intimacy. In particular, they expend their reinforcement power by frequently acquiring new domains for positive exchange. Spouses who depend on a limited quantity and variety of reinforcers are bound to suffer the ill effects of satiation. As a result, over time their interaction becomes depleted of its prior reinforcement value. Successful couples cope with this inevitable reinforcement erosion by varying their shared activities, developing new common interests, expanding their sexual repertoires, and developing their communication to the point where they continue to interest one another.

Like others, behaviorists emphasize the capacity for adaptability, flexibility, and change; they stress that these are not personality traits but skills that can be learned, most easily in relationships that are under the stimulus control of rules and where there is a consensus about what the rules are (Weiss, 1978). Moreover, the rules should be comprehensive and flexible rather than narrow or rigid (Jacobson and Margolin, 1979). In these happy relationships awards exceed costs; social reinforcement is dispensed equitably and at a high rate. Moreover, these relationships are built upon positive control, rather than negative reinforcement, punishment, and coercion (Stuart, 1975).

DEVELOPMENT OF BEHAVIOR DISORDERS

Behaviorists view symptoms as learned responses, involuntarily acquired and reinforced. Unlike their nonbehavioral colleagues, they don't look for underlying meaning in symptoms, nor do they posit conflict in or between spouses as leading to problems in the children. Instead they concentrate their attention on the symptoms themselves and look for environmental responses that reinforce the problem behavior.

At first glance it would seem unlikely that family members reinforce undesirable behavior. Why, for example, would parents reinforce temper tantrums in their children? Or why would a wife reinforce her husband's withdrawal, when it appears to cause her so much pain? The answer is not to be found in some kind of convoluted motive for suffering, but in the simple fact that people often inadvertently reinforce precisely those responses that cause them the most distress.

Naturally it's easier to see how *other* people cause their own problems. How many times have you seen parents threaten their children with punishment that they don't carry out? And most of us still remember how our own parents failed to reward us for certain skills and achievements. The local shopping mall, American family life's public stage, is a good place to observe how often harried parents both fail to punish misbehavior and to reward good behavior in their children. And while it's a little harder, it's also possible to begin observing yourself and discovering how often you use reinforcement to shape the behavior of people in your own social context.

It's also possible to notice that "punishments" may have the opposite effect from what is intended. Consider the following scenario.

> Five-year-old Sandy is playing quietly with tinker toys while her father reads the newspaper. After a few minutes, she knocks the tinker toys off the table and onto the floor. Her father puts down the paper and tells her to be quiet. A little later she starts singing; again her father tells her to quiet down. Finally, she begins making so much noise that her father slams down the paper, storms into the room where she's playing, and gives her a long lecture on the virtues of playing quietly and not disturbing her parents.

What is Sandy apt to learn from this episode? That if she makes enough noise she'll get her father's attention.

Parents usually respond to problem behavior in their children by yelling at them or spanking them. These reactions may seem like punishment, but they may in fact be reinforcing, because attention—even from an angry parent—is an extremely powerful *social reinforcer* (Skinner, 1953). The truth of this is reflected in the sound advice to "Ignore it and it will go away." The problem is that most parents have trouble ignoring undesirable behavior in their children. Notice, for example, how quickly children learn that certain words get a big reaction from their parents. Moreover, even when parents do resolve to ignore certain misbehavior, they usually don't do so consistently. This can make things even worse, because *intermittent reinforcement* is the most resistant to extinction (Ferster, 1963).

In addition to countless behavior problems unwittingly maintained by parental attention, others persist because many parents are unaware of how to make effective use of punishment. Parents make threats that they cannot or do not follow through on; they punish so long after the fact that the child doesn't associate the punishment with the bad behavior; they use punishments so mild as to have no effect; or they use punishments so severe as to cause fear and anxiety instead of discriminative learning.

Systems thinkers would find the previous discussion wanting, because it's based on a linear view of causality: Children continue to misbehave *because* their parents use ineffective contingencies of reinforcement. While it's true that most behavioral family therapists do operate with a linear model, some have attempted to offer a more complex model. For example, Liberman (1972) has described the family as a system of *interlocking reciprocal behaviors*; Gerald Patterson has described patterns of *reciprocal reinforcement* in families. Consider the behavior of a mother and daughter in the supermarket.

> The little girl asks her mother for a candy bar; the mother says, "No." The child begins crying and complaining, and the mother says, "If you think I'm going to buy you candy when you make such a fuss you have another think coming, young lady!" But the child escalates her tantrum, getting louder and louder. Finally, the exasperated and embarrassed mother gives in, saying, "All right, if you'll quiet down first I'll buy you some cookies."

Obviously, the child has been reinforced for throwing a temper tantrum. Not so obviously, but also true, the mother has been reinforced for giving in—by the child's quieting down after being promised cookies. Thus a spiral of undesirable behavior is maintained by reciprocal reinforcement.

Behavioral family therapists have described a number of defective patterns of reinforcement in cases of marital discord. Azrin, Nester, and Jones (1973) listed the following causes of marital discord:

1. Receiving too little reinforcement from the marriage.
2. Too few needs given marital reinforcement.
3. Marital reinforcement no longer provides satisfaction.
4. New behaviors are not reinforced.
5. One spouse gives more reinforcement than he or she receives.
6. Marriage interferes with extramarital sources of satisfaction.
7. Communication about potential sources of satisfaction is not adequate.
8. Aversive control predominates over positive reinforcement.

The use of *aversive control* is often cited as the major determinant of marital unhappiness. In dysfunctional marriages, spouses react to problems with attempts at aversive control—nagging, crying, withdrawing, or threatening. Rarely do these couples think to shape positive alternatives. So, as a result, the spouses feel more and more negatively about each other. If someone yells at you to stop doing something, you will probably feel upset and anxious; you may understand what the person wants you to do, but you certainly won't feel like going out of your way to please that person. You may not even understand; you may be too anxious or bitter.

In distressed marriages there are fewer rewarding exchanges and more punishing exchanges, verbal and instrumental (Stuart, 1975). Spouses typically reciprocate their partners' use of punishment, and a vicious circle develops (Patterson and Reid, 1970). Partners enter marriage expecting that the rewards of being married will exceed the rewards of remaining single. Marriage provides countless opportunities for rewarding exchanges, and well-functioning couples exchange many benefits. However, when there is a failure to exchange benefits, the reward system shifts from positive to aversive control. The wife whose generosity toward her husband is neither acknowledged nor reciprocated begins to demand her share of exchanged rewards. Unfortunately, as Weiss (1978, p. 189) observed, "Forced rewards, like solicited compliments, lose their value."

People in distressed family relationships also have poor problem-solving skills (Vincent, Weiss, and Birchler, 1975; Weiss, Hops, and Patterson, 1973). When they discuss a problem, they frequently change the subject; they phrase wishes and complaints in vague and critical ways; and they respond to complaints with countercomplaints. The following exchange demonstrates sidetracking, cross-complaining, and name-calling, all typical of distressed marriages.

> "I'd like to talk about all the sweets you've been giving the kids lately."
> "What sweets! Talk about me, you're always stuffing your face. And what do you ever do for the kids? You just come home and complain. Why don't you just stay at the office! The kids and I get along better without you."

According to Patterson and Reid (1970), reciprocity also exists between parents and children: Parents who behave aversively toward their children get the same in return. This also holds true for the use of negative reinforcement. Children as well as parents develop patterns of reinforcement which exert a powerful controlling effect. If the children are consciously aware of these contingencies, they may be called "manipulative," but often they are as oblivious to the consequences of their responses as are their parents.

Most behavioral analyses point to the lack of reinforcement for adaptive strivings in distressed families. The old adage, "The squeaky wheel gets the grease," seems to apply in such families. Depressions, headaches, and temper tantrums tend to elicit concern and therefore more attention than prosocial behavior. Because this process is unwitting, family members are often mystified about their role in maintaining maladaptive behavior. Behavior therapists believe that since abnormal behavior is learned and maintained by the same processes as normal behavior, it can therefore be treated directly, without reference to underlying causes.

GOALS OF THERAPY

The goals of behavioral therapy are quite specific and limited: modifying specific behavior patterns to alleviate the presenting symptoms. There is little concern with systems change or with growth and development. Symptom change is not thought to lead to symptom-substitution, but to inaugurate a positive spiral of behavior, and is dealt with by techniques designed to substitute desirable alternative behaviors.

The behavioral family therapist tailors treatment to fit each family; the goal is to eliminate undesirable behavior or increase positive behavior as defined by the family (Azrin, Naster, and Jones, 1973). Sometimes it may be necessary to redefine a family's goal of decreasing negative behavior in terms of increasing positive and incompatible behavior (Umana, Gross, and McConville, 1980), or to one that is interpersonal rather than centered on one individual. But these changes are essentially strategies to solve the presenting problem and not related to developing broader goals.

Couples often state goals of reducing aversive behavior, but this pain-avoidance strategy only reduces dissatisfaction without increasing positive feelings (Weiss, 1978). Therefore behavioral couples therapists also help spouses increase their satisfaction by accelerating positive behavior. "The goal of behavioral marital counseling is to provide couples with behavior change operations based upon positive control procedures" (Weiss, 1978, p. 206).

The general goals of behavioral therapy are to increase the rate of rewarding interactions by fostering positive behavior change; to decrease the rate of coercion and adversive control; and to teach more effective communication and problem-solving skills (Gurman and Knudson, 1978).

Some of the goals of behavioral family therapy may be shaped by the clientele and setting in which it is practiced. Behavior marital therapy, for example, is most frequently practiced in university teaching clinics. The therapists are often graduate students, and much of the treatment is conducted on an experimental basis. Clients in these settings tend to be relatively young and advantaged; and clients and therapists are often close to each other in age, outlook, and values. Not surprisingly, therapy in such a context often becomes a collaborative effort between people who feel each other to be peers, and a fair amount of teaching goes on. In case studies of behavioral family therapy, many of the interventions take the form of interpretations designed to foster conscious insight. For example, Liberman (1972) reported on his treatment of a couple in which the wife got her husband's attention only when she had headaches. Liberman explained the dynamics of this to the couple; thereafter the husband started paying attention to the appropriate wifely and motherly behavior, while ignoring the headaches. Sounds simple, doesn't it?

What this demonstrates is that behavioral family therapists aim not only to alleviate symptoms, but also to teach skills and foster understanding so that families will be able to solve their own problems in the future. This point is also supported by Robert Weiss (1978) who suggests that many forms of behavioral family therapy are more concerned with prevention than with cure.

CONDITIONS FOR BEHAVIOR CHANGE

The basic premise of behavior therapy is that behavior will change when the contingencies of reinforcement are altered. To begin with, a *functional analysis of behavior* is required to identify the antecedents and consequences of the target behavior. Once this is complete, a specific approach is designed for specific problems. First, they specify family problems in concrete, observable—and measurable—terms. Second, they plan specific strategies based on an empirical theory of behavior change. And third, their efforts are subjected to empirical analysis of their effects in achieving specified behavioral goals. Thus, each family is treated as a unique case, whose therapy program is conceived of as a single-subject experiment.

Careful observation is considered a prerequisite to attempts to control behavior. Great emphasis is placed on measurement and scientific methodology. The first task of the therapist is to observe and record the frequency and duration of problem behavior, as well as the stimulus conditions that precede it and the reinforcement that follows it. This enables the therapist to design an individually tailored treatment program.

Moving out of the playroom and the office into the natural world of the home and classroom enabled behavior therapists to discover that some of their previous notions about child aggression were fundamentally erroneous. Contrary to Skinner's assumptions, punishment *does* have long-term effects. The data show that reinforcement of positive behaviors, such as cooperation and compliance, do not lead to reductions in antisocial behavior. Introducing punishment (time out, point loss) produces long-term reductions in antisocial behavior (Patterson, 1988).

The primary approach in behavioral family therapy is operant rather than classical conditioning (with the exception of treating sexual dysfunctions), and the focus is on changing dyadic interactions (parent-child or spouse-spouse). This dyadic focus differs from the triadic approach of systems-oriented family therapists. Although some behavioral family therapists (Liberman, 1970; Falloon and Lillie, 1988) have disputed this distinction, we believe this is a major difference between behavioral and nonbehavioral family therapists.

Although behavior change remains the primary focus, more and more behavioral family therapists are recognizing the critical role of cognitive factors in determining and resolving relationship problems. Barton and Alexander (1981), for example, maintain that family members' behavior toward each other will only change if their views of themselves and each other change. And Jacobson and Margolin (1979) point out that the establishment of a collaborative attitude in distressed spouses often is a prerequisite for efforts toward positive behavior change.

Barton and Alexander, who call their approach *functional family therapy* (Barton and Alexander, 1981; Morris, Alexander, and Waldron, 1988), point out that members of unhappy families tend to attribute their problems to negative traits (laziness, irresponsibility, poor impulse control) in other members. Such views block therapeutic change by projecting blame in a way that makes it impossible for anyone to change. Such inaccurate, negative, and incomplete views of what's going on leave family members with a limited sense of control over their lives together. Unless such rigid views can be challenged, family members may continue to feel powerless. After all, what can one person do to change another person's "laziness," "irresponsibility," or "poor impulse control"?

Cognitive behavior therapists believe that attributional shifts are necessary to make behavior change possible, but that in turn behavior change is necessary to reinforce new and more productive attributions.

In general, behaviorists de-emphasize the "art" of therapy, treating it instead as a technical procedure dependent largely upon the application of learning theory. Some behavioral writers have argued that change will occur if current behavioral principles are applied regardless of the individual personality or style of the therapist (Stuart, 1969; Hawkins, Peterson, Schweid, and Bijou, 1966). Although a few behavioral therapists have emphasized that complex skills and great tact are required to conduct family therapy, many of the articles in this field imply that one merely needs to read the literature to be equipped to conduct psychotherapy. Moreover, behavioral approaches are typically taught in graduate psychology programs by faculty who have more theoretical knowledge than practical experience.

Behavioral family therapy consists of a number of highly structured procedures, which focus on technique more than on patients or therapists. Little attention is paid to patients' histories, unconscious motivations, or complex family interactions. Traditionally, behaviorists have been little concerned with resistance, despite the fact that systems theorists have established that any ongoing social system resists change, either from within or without. Although behavioral family therapists have lately recognized the importance of resistance (Birchler, 1988), most have tended to assume that people seeking psychotherapy are capable of rational, collaborative effort to change. As Spinks and Birchler (1982, p. 172) put it:

> Most behaviorists view so-called resistance phenomena as the results of ineffective case management. That is, resistance is a sign that the treatment model or the therapist have been unsuccessful, not that the clients inherently resist change, or will not change.

Cognitive behavior therapists have become more concerned with resistance (Birchler, 1988), but their view of it differs from systemic family therapists in two ways. First, they see resistance as primarily a property of individuals, rather than a homeostatic tendency in systems. Second, they assume that although family members may have beliefs or expectancies that interfere with change, these beliefs are relatively straightforward—easily reexamined and re-evaluated. Once an individual's concerns are addressed, therapy can continue for the group. While this happy optimism seems preferable to those systemic therapists who assume family members are blindly driven by mechanical forces they are powerless to resist, it also seems a little naive.

As their experience with families increased in the 1970s and 1980s, behavioral family therapists began to incorporate more principles and techniques from systems theory into their work. Gerald Patterson, for example, studied Minuchin's structural family therapy, and Gary Birchler integrated systems theory and behavioral marital therapy (Birchler and Spinks, 1980; Spinks and Birchler, 1982). According to Birchler, straight behavioral family therapy is overly structured and fails to deal with underlying relationship dynamics. In addition, the elaborate assessment procedure, which may take up three or four sessions, is burdensome to many patients.

Behavioral therapists invariably refer to the people they work with as clients, not patients. Although they are not the only ones who prefer this term, it underlines their skills-oriented approach. Behavioral parent trainers (Gordon and Davidson, 1981) and marital therapists (Stuart, 1969) believe that the goals of treatment can usually be reached without attending to the parents' or spouses' personal difficulties. Only when such problems noticeably interfere with treatment are they addressed (Spinks and Birchler, 1982).

A major tenet of behavioral family treatment is that behavior change is better achieved by accelerating positive behavior than by decelerating negative behavior. Although, as we've seen, there may be a need to introduce punishment to eliminate antisocial behavior in aggressive children, behavior therapists generally try to minimize coercion by aversive control or extinction. It is believed that most distressed families already use these approaches to excess. Therefore only positive reinforcement is consistently and widely used in behavioral family therapy.

Behavioral family therapists directly manipulate contingencies of reinforcement in the families they treat, and may provide reinforcement themselves when the family members comply with their instructions. Once new behaviors are established, therapists counsel family members to use intermittent positive reinforcement and then to fade out material reinforcements in favor of social ones. Following this direct control, therapists teach family members how to observe and modify their own contingencies of reinforcement to maintain their initial gains using self-control procedures.

Learning theory may have been developed by observing white rats in laboratory mazes, but applying learning theory to families is quite a different matter. In behavioral family therapy it is important not to make simplistic assumptions about what may be rewarding and what may be punishing. Instead, it is critical to examine the interpersonal consequences of behavior. The therapist must find out what is reinforcing for each person and each family, rather than assume that certain things are universally rewarding. Moreover, a variety of different behaviors may be aimed at the same payoff. For example, a child might throw tantrums, whine, or drop things at various times, but all of these may be reinforced by parental attention. Therefore, in order to understand how to help families change, the therapist must shift attention from the behavior (R) to the consequences (KC).

TECHNIQUES

Since behavioral family therapy is usually practiced as either parent training, marital therapy, or treatment of sexual dysfunction, we shall describe each of these approaches separately.

Behavioral Parent Training

The process of psychotherapy begins with the therapist redefining the client's conception of the nature of the problem and of the appropriate solution. Most family therapists begin with the assumption that the family, not the individual, is the problem, so that the whole family should be convened to solve it. Behavioral therapists, on the other hand, accept the parents' view that the child is the problem, and generally meet with only one parent (guess which one) and the child, although some behaviorists (Gordon and Davidson, 1981) recommend that both parents and even older siblings be included.

Clients also expect therapy to be a kind of education, and behavior therapists tend to operate as educators (Liberman, 1972). Thus, from the outset, behavioral family therapists employ a model which accords with the typical parents' view of the nature of their problems and the sort of solutions that would be helpful.

The early work of Patterson, Risely, Wolf, and others working with disturbed children was packaged in a diverse array of educationally oriented programs to train parents in the application of behavioral skills. With the aid of instruction and programmed workbooks, parents were taught the application of social learning principles to temper tantrums, bed-wetting, autistic behavior, doing homework, hyperactivity, toilet training, disobedience, phobias, and aggressive behavior. The advantage of these educational efforts was bringing a knowledge of how behavior is reinforced to bear on a large number of problems. The disadvantage is that when therapy is reduced to teaching, therapists fail to uncover and resolve conflicts, within and between people, that are responsible for maintaining problems and bringing them about in the first place. Moreover, as Falloon and Lillie (1988, p. 10) observed:

> Many of these training programs were conducted in workshops attended by large numbers of parents and presented by professionals with limited therapeutic skills and understanding of behavior therapy principles. As a result, the cornerstone of behavior therapy, the behavioral analysis and evaluation of specific goals, was frequently overlooked.

Thus the advantage of behavior therapy—being a straightforward approach with simple strategies—became a disadvantage in the hands of therapists who wrongly assumed that if the principles of reinforcement were simple then therapy, too, could be simple. It isn't.

Behaviorists say that what distinguishes them is not so much a set of techniques, but the fact that they apply principles from experimental and social psychology to clinical problems, and that they carefully verify the results of their procedures. Liberman (1972) expressed this by referring to therapeutic tactics as "behavioral change experiments," and the literature is replete with a variety of behavioral techniques, together with empirical demonstrations of their utility. In fact behavioral parent training has been successfully applied to almost every type of behavioral problem in children (Graziano, 1977; O'Dell, 1974; McCauley, 1988). Graziano (1977) classified these problems in six categories: (1) somatic symptoms (seizures, eating problems, toilet training); (2) complex syndromes (brain damage, retardation, psychosis); (3) negativistic and aggressive behavior (hyperactivity, fighting, physical and verbal abuse); (4) fears and phobias (school phobia, fear of loud noises); (5) language and speech disorders (elective mutism); and (6) common behavior problems in the home (bedroom cleaning, persistent whining, getting dressed).

The many techniques developed to address these various problems can be grouped in three major categories: operant conditioning, respondent conditioning, and cognitive/affective techniques. By far the most commonly used approach is operant conditioning, where the reinforcers employed may be tangible or social. In fact, smiling, praise, and attention have been found to be as effective as money or candy (Bandura, 1969). Operant techniques may be further divided into *shaping, token economies, contingency contracting, contingency management,* and *time out. Shaping* (Schwitzgebel and Kolb, 1964) consists of reinforcing change in small steps that gradually approximate the desired goals. *Token economies* (Baer and Sherman, 1969) use a system of points or stars to reward children for successful behavior. In this very popular approach, children collect some kind of reward once they have accumulated a sufficient number of tokens. *Contingency contracting* (Stuart, 1971) involves agreements by the parents to make certain changes following changes made by their children. *Contingency management* (Schwitzgebel, 1967) consists of giving and taking away rewards and punishments based upon the children's behavior. *Time out* (Rimm and Masters, 1974) is a punishment where children are made to sit in the corner or sent to their rooms.

Respondent conditioning techniques involve modification of physiological responses. Most common of these are systematic desensitization (Wolpe, 1969), assertiveness training (Lazarus, 1971), aversion therapies (Risley, 1968), and sex therapies (Masters and Johnson, 1970). Most of these (particularly the last one) are primarily used with adults but have also been applied to training parents to use with their children. Some commonly used cognitive/affective techniques include thought-stopping (McGuire and Vallance, 1964), rational emotional therapy (Ellis, 1962), modeling (Bandura, 1969), reattribution (Kanfer and Phillips, 1970), and self-monitoring (Rimm and Masters, 1974). Although behaviorists proudly point to the incorporation of cognitive therapy into their procedures, little of this approach is widely used in the field of behavioral parent training. Parents have been trained individually and in groups, through lectures, assigned readings, programmed materials, discussions, modeling, and direct coaching. Practitioners begin by deciding what responses to modify and which techniques to employ. Research literature provides some guidelines, but here as elsewhere clinicians tend to favor the approach they are most familiar with.

In common with other forms of behavioral family therapy, parent training begins with an extensive assessment procedure. While the exact procedure varies from clinic to clinic, most assessments are based upon Kanfer and Phillips' (1970) *SORKC* model of behavior: *S* for stimulus, *O* for the state of the organism, *R* for the target response, and *KC* for the nature and contingency of the consequences. The following example illustrates how this assessment model is applied.

In the case of parents who complain that their son pesters them for cookies between meals and throws tantrums if they don't give him any, the tantrums would be considered the target behavior, $R. O$, the state of the organism, might turn out to be mild hunger or, even more likely, boredom. The stimulus, S, might be the sight of cookies in the cookie jar; and the nature and contingency of the consequences, KC, might be that the parents give in by feeding the boy cookies occasionally, and especially if he makes enough of a fuss.

Like any useful diagnostic scheme, the $SORKC$ model begins to suggest solutions as soon as it is applied.

In simple cases, such as the one above, applying the $SORKC$ model is straightforward, but it quickly becomes more complex with families, where there are long chains of interrelated behavior, and therapists must examine the mutual impact of behavior on each family member. Consider the following.

> Mr. and Mrs. J. complain that their two small children whine and fuss at the dinner table. A home observation reveals that when Mr. J. yells at the children for misbehaving they start to whine and stand by their mother's chair.

Given this sequence it is not difficult to apply the $SORKC$ model. Imagine, however, that the above sequence is only part of a more complex picture.

> In the morning, Mr. J. makes a sexual overture to his wife, but she, tired from taking care of the children, rolls over and goes back to sleep. Mr. J. is hurt and leaves for work after making some unkind remarks to his wife. She, feeling rejected by her husband, spends the entire day playing with the children for solace. By the time she has to cook dinner, Mrs. J. is exhausted and exasperated with the children. Mr. J. comes home after a difficult day at the office and tries to make up with his wife by hugging her. She responds but only perfunctorily because she is busily trying to cook. While she's at the stove, the children and Mr. J. vie for her attention, each one wanting to tell her something. Finally, she blows up—at her husband—"Can't you see I'm busy!" He goes into the den and sulks until dinner is ready. Just as his wife finds it difficult to express her anger at the children and takes it out on him, Mr. J. has trouble directing anger at his wife and so tends to divert it onto the children. At the dinner table he yells at them for the slightest infraction, at which they whine and turn to their mother. She lets one sit on her lap while she strokes the other's hair.

In this longer, but not atypical sequence, what is stimulus and what response? Obviously these definitions become circular, and their application depends upon the perspective of the observer.

Assessment in behavioral parent training entails defining, observing, and recording the frequency of the behavior that is to be changed, as well as the events that precede it and those that follow it. Early reports in this field involved simple, discrete behavior such as temper tantrums and enuresis. But since the late sixties, parent training has been done with more severe and complex problems (conduct disorders, DiGiuseppe, 1988; child abuse, Morton, Twentyman, and Azar, 1988), making a clear definition of the behavior to be assessed an essential first step.

Assessment methods fall into one of three categories: interview, observation, and baseline data collection. Interviews, usually with the mother, are designed to provide basic information, such as a definition of the problem and a list of potential reinforcers. Observations may be conducted behind a one-way mirror or during a home visit. Baseline data, collected prior to the initiation of therapy, may be recorded by therapists or by one or more family members. Typically, parents are trained to pinpoint problem behavior, to observe and record its occurrence, and to note the occurrence and frequency of various events which might serve as stimuli and reinforcers.

Keefe, Kopel, and Gordon (1978) outlined a five-stage model of behavioral assessment consisting of: (1) problem identification, (2) measurement and functional analysis, (3) matching treatment to client, (4) assessment of ongoing therapy, and (5) evaluation of therapy outcome. As this outline illustrates, assessment is an integral part of behavioral treatment, from beginning to end. The problem-identification stage begins with an interview of one or both parents. Gordon and Davidson (1981) recommend that the child not be included, in order to minimize distractions and to maximize the parents' candor. These authors suggest that if the child were present and heard all of his parents' complaints he would be unwilling to participate in therapy. However, it seems that excluding the child supports the parents' view that the child is the problem, and that the parents, not the child, will profit from treatment.

Parents generally find it difficult to pinpoint specific problem behavior; instead their complaints are phrased by attributing the cause and effect of problems to various personality traits. "The problem with Johnny is that he's lazy—shy, hostile, hyperactive, or disrespectful." Therapists respond by probing for descriptions with concrete behavioral referents, and by developing a picture of the interactions between the parents and child. The question, "What does Johnny *do* that indicates his laziness?" helps pinpoint the problem. When this is followed by an inquiry such as, "And what do you do when he does that?" a picture of the interaction emerges. Asking for detailed descriptions elicits information about the frequency, intensity, duration, and social consequences of the problem behavior. Behaviorally oriented checklists and questionnaires are also administered. These provide information that may have been omitted or overlooked in interviews. The final product of this stage of the assessment is the selection of target behaviors for modification.

The measurement and functional analysis stage consists of actually observing and recording the target behavior, as well as its antecedents and consequences. This may be done by the parents at home or by the therapists in the clinic—and, now, more and more, by therapists in the natural setting (Arrington, Sullaway, and Christensen, 1988).

In the next stage the therapist designs a specific treatment package to match the particular needs of the family. Among the factors considered are the degree to which environmental control is possible; whether or not serious interpersonal problems between the parents may preclude their working together collaboratively; possible psychological problems in either parent which might interfere with parent training; and whether or not other forms of treatment might be more effective or economical.

The second consideration, possible conflict between the parents, is usually assumed to be of critical importance by nonbehavioral therapists. Behavioral therapists vary considerably in the degree to which they consider parental conflict to be a problem. Most minimize the role of conflict between the parents, as the following quotation (Gordon and Davidson, 1981, p. 526) illustrates.

> On several occasions we have observed parents whose marriage is characterized by extreme dislike for each other who have, nevertheless, been able to put aside their differences in order that they may work together in a constructive fashion to help their child.

Once the assessment is complete the therapist decides which behaviors should be increased and which decreased. To accelerate behavior, the *Premack principle* (Premack, 1965) is applied; that is, high probability behavior (particularly pleasant activities) is chosen to serve as a reinforcer for behavior with a low probability of occurrence. Where once it was thought that reinforcers must satisfy some basic drive, such as hunger or thirst, it is now known that behaviors chosen more frequently (given a wide variety of choices) can serve as reinforcers for those chosen less frequently. The following example shows how the Premack principle can be applied in parent training.

> Mrs. G. stated that she couldn't get her five-year-old son Adam to clean up his room in the morning. She went to say that she had already tried rewarding him with candy, money, and toys, but "Nothing works!" A functional analysis of Adam's behavior revealed that, given his choice of

things to do, the most probable behaviors were watching television, riding his bicycle, and playing in the mud behind his house. Once these activities were made contingent upon tidying his room he quickly learned to do so.

A variety of material and social reinforcers have been employed to accelerate desired behaviors, but as the Premack principle demonstrates, to be effective, reinforcers must be very popular with the particular child in question. While money or candy may seem like powerful rewards, they may not be as effective as a chance to play in the mud for some children.

Once effective rewards are chosen, parents are taught to shape the desired behavior by reinforcing successive approximation to the therapeutic goals. They are also taught to raise the criteria for reinforcement gradually, and to present reinforcement immediately contingent upon the desired behavior. Once the child is regularly performing the desired response, reinforcement becomes intermittent in order to increase the durability of the new behavior.

Interestingly, although parents are taught to apply operant conditioning principles to their children, behavioral therapists generally do not apply these same principles to the parents whom they are training. Instead they rely on the assumption that the process of training is inherently reinforcing. There are exceptions to this, however, as the following (Rinn, 1978, p. 378) illustrates.

> It is advisable that the clinician be as reinforcing as possible (e.g., praise, smiles, excited voice) whenever the family carries out homework assignments and procedures. Therapists who are not particularly enthusiastic about the importance of data collection have a tendency to reinforce low rates of data presentation from families.

Deceleration techniques apply contingent punishment and extinction. The most common technique for decelerating behavior is *time out* from positive reinforcement. Basically this means ignoring or isolating the child after he or she misbehaves. This procedure has been shown to be effective with a wide variety of child problems (Forehand and MacDonough, 1975). Studies have shown that a duration of about five minutes is the most effective (Pendergrass, 1971). Children are first warned, to give them a chance to control their own behavior, before they are put into time out. Other techniques used to declerate behavior include verbal reprimand, ignoring, and isolation. Simply repeating commands to children has been shown to be a most ineffective way to change their behavior (Forehand, Roberts, Doleys, Hobbs, and Resnick, 1976). Response-contingent aversive stimulation (LeBow, 1972) is little used with families, although it has been used effectively working directly with children (Jacobson and Martin, 1976).

Because of the inconvenience of reinforcing behavior immediately after it occurs, token systems have been very popular with parent trainers. Points are earned for desirable behavior and lost for undesirable behavior (Christophersen, Arnold, Hill, and Quilitch, 1972). The principles of behavioral parent training described above are exemplified and more clearly delineated in the following case study.

Mrs. F. is a twenty-five-year old housewife and mother of two small children who came to the clinic complaining of headaches and crying spells. The intake interviewer found her to be mildly depressed and, although she had symptoms of a passive dependent personality disorder, concluded that the depression was primarily a situational reaction to her difficulty coping with her children. Suzie, age five, was a shy child who rarely played with other children and had frequent temper tantrums. Robert, who was eight, was more outgoing and sociable, but did very poorly in school. Between them the children were a handful, and Mrs. F. felt helpless and resentful in her dealings with them.

A functional analysis of behavior revealed that Suzie's shyness resulted in her getting a great deal of extra attention from her anxious mother. Whenever Suzie declined an invitation to play with other children, her mother spent a great deal of time talking with her and doing special things to make her feel better. The therapist selected social behavior (not shyness) as the first target response, and instructed Mrs. F. to reinforce all efforts at socializing and to ignore Suzie when she avoided social contact. Thereafter, whenever Suzie made any attempt to socialize with other children, Mrs. F. would immediately reinforce her with attention and praise. When Suzie chose to stay home rather than play with other children, her mother ignored her, instead busying herself with her own activities. In three weeks, Mrs. F. reported that Suzie had made remarkable changes and "seemed to have gotten over her shyness."

Following this initial successful experience the therapist felt it was time to help Mrs. F. tackle the more difficult problem of Suzie's temper tantrums. Since the temper tantrums were unlikely to occur while the family was at the clinic or during a home visit, the therapist instructed Mrs. F. to make observational notes for a week. These notes revealed that Suzie generally had her tantrums when either of her parents denied her requests for a treat or some special indulgence, such as staying up an extra half an hour to watch television. Moreover, tantrums were especially likely to occur at the end of the day when Suzie (and her parents) were tired. As for how the parents responded to these maddening temper tantrums, Mrs. F. reported that "We've tried everything. Sometimes we try to ignore her, but that's impossible, she just screams and shrieks until we can't stand it anymore. Then we sometimes spank her, or sometimes give her what she wants—just to shut her up. Sometimes after we spank her she cries so much that we let her stay up and watch television until she calms down. That usually works to quiet her down."

After listening to this description, the therapist explained as gently and carefully as she could how Mr. and Mrs. F. had inadvertently been reinforcing the tantrums, and told them what they would have to do to stop them. For the next week, the F's were instructed to ignore temper tantrums whenever they occurred. If they occurred at bedtime, Suzie was to be put in her bed; if she continued to cry and scream, she was to be left alone until she stopped. Only when she stopped were her parents to talk with her about what was on her mind. The following week Mrs. F. reported that the temper tantrums had indeed decreased, except for one night when they took on a new and more troubling form. When Suzie was told that she would not be able to stay up late to watch television she began to yell and cry as usual. Instead of relenting, Mrs. F. put Suzie in her room and told her to get ready for bed. However, realizing that her parents were going to ignore her, as they had earlier in the week, Suzie began to scream and smash things in her room. "It was awful, she was completely out of control. She kicked and struck out at everything in sight, even smashing the little dog-shaped lamp I bought her. We didn't know what to do, so just that once we let her stay up." Again the therapist described the consequences of such behavior, and explained to Mrs. F. how, should Suzie again become destructive, both parents should hold her until the tantrum subsided.

At the next session, Mrs. F. described how Suzie did "get out of control again." This time, instead of giving in, the parents held her as they had been told. Mrs. F. was amazed at the fury and duration of the resulting tantrum. "But we remembered what you said—there was no way we were going to give in!" It took twenty minutes, but Suzie finally calmed down. This, it turned out, was the last time Suzie ever became so violent during a temper tantrum. Nevertheless she did continue to have an occasional tantrum during the next few weeks of therapy. According to Mrs. F., the few tantrums that did occur seemed to take place in different settings or under different conditions than the usual episodes at home (which Suzie had now learned would not be reinforced). For example, one episode took place in a supermarket, when Suzie was told she could not have a candy bar. By this time, however, Mrs. F. was thoroughly convinced of the necessity of not reinforcing the tantrums, and so she didn't. Because she was embarrassed at all the noise her daughter was making in public, she did find it necessary to take her out of the store. But she made Suzie sit in the car and took pains not to let it be a pleasant experience for her. Very few tantrums followed this one.

Next the therapist turned her attention to the problem of Robert's poor performance at school. A careful assessment revealed that Robert rarely brought assignments home from school and when asked usually denied that he had any homework. After checking with Robert's teacher the therapist discovered that the children generally did have homework, and that they were expected to work between thirty minutes and an hour a night. Mrs. F. selected a high probability behavior, watching television, and made it contingent upon Robert's having first completed his homework assignment. For the first two weeks of this regimen, Mrs. F. found it necessary to call the teacher every night to verify the assignments. But soon this was no longer necessary. Doing homework fairly quickly became a habit for Robert and his grades increased from Ds and Cs to Bs and As by the end of the school year. At this point, everyone was happier, and Mrs. F. felt the family no longer needed help.

A follow-up session in the fall found things continuing to go well. Suzie was now much more sociable and had not had any temper tantrums in months. Robert was doing well in school, although he had begun to neglect some of his more difficult assignments. To address this, the therapist explained to Mrs. F. how to institute a token system, and she was able to use it with excellent results in a short space of time.

The preceding example illustrates a form of behavioral parent training in which the therapist meets with the mother and instructs her in the use of operant conditioning principles. Another format is to observe parent and child interacting behind a one-way mirror in the clinic. In this way, the therapist can get a first-hand look at what actually transpires. With this approach, parents can be taught how to play with their children, as well as how to discipline them, and how to negotiate with them. Sometimes the observing therapist may communicate to the parents through a remote microphone, called a "bug in the ear."

The techniques that have been described are particularly effective with small children and preadolescents. With teenagers the use of *contingency contracting* (Alexander and Parsons, 1973; Rinn, 1978) is a more widely used procedure. Contracting is introduced by the therapist as a way for everybody in the family to get something by compromising. Both parent and teenager are asked to specify what behavior they would like the other to change. These requests form the nucleus of the initial contract. In order to help family members arrive at contracts, the therapist models, prompts, and reinforces: (a) clear communication of content and feelings; (b) clear presentation of demands; leading to (c) negotiation, with each person receiving something in exchange for some concession.

Alexander and Parsons (1973) recommend starting with easy issues while the family is learning the principles of contingency contracting. Success in dealing with minor issues will increase the family's willingness to deal with more difficult problems. Some parents are reluctant to negotiate with their children to "do things that they *should* do anyway, without being bribed." In fact, these parents have a legitimate point, and they should be helped to understand the difference between rules (which are nonnegotiable) and privileges (which can be negotiated).

Behavioral parent training is also conducted in general child training programs, which are designed for preventive education. The content of these programs varies from general principles of operant behavior to specific techniques for dealing with specific problems. They usually begin with an introduction to social learning theory. Following this, parents are instructed how to pinpoint behaviors and to select one or two for modification. After being taught to analyze the antecedents and consequences of the target behavior, parents learn to monitor the frequency and duration of the responses. Many of these programs include instruction in charting, or graphing, the target behavior. Parents are also taught how to state and enforce rules, and the necessity for being consistent. Usually, techniques for accelerating desired behavior are used concomitantly. Training in the use of positive reinforcement includes helping the parents to increase the frequency and range of reinforcers that they apply. In addition to increasing behavior that their children are already engaging in, the parents are taught to develop new behaviors through shaping, modeling, instructing, and prompting.

Behavioral Marriage Therapy

Most forms of psychotherapy begin as art and move toward science; behavioral marriage therapy did the reverse, beginning as science and moving toward art. Early reports in the literature (Goldiamond, 1965; Lazarus, 1968) consisted of relatively straightforward application of learning theory principles to problems of married couples. A strictly operant conditioning approach was common (Goldstein, 1971), and therapists were relatively naive about the interpersonal dynamics of families. Since that time behavioral marriage therapy has become increasingly popular and increasingly sophisticated. Therapists have become aware, not only of the dynamics of the marital relationship, but also of the dynamics of the therapeutic relationship. Robert Liberman, for example, has written (1972, pp. 332–333) about the importance of creating and maintaining a positive therapeutic alliance.

> Without the positive therapeutic alliance between the therapist and those he is helping, there can be little or no successful intervention. The working alliance is the lever which stimulates change. In learning terms, the positive relationship between therapist and patient(s) permits the therapist to serve as a social reinforcer and model; in other words, to build up adaptive behaviors and allow maladaptive behaviors to extinguish. The therapist is an effective reinforcer and model for the patients to the extent that the patients value him and hold him in high regard and warm esteem.

As in other forms of behavioral therapy, marriage therapy begins with an elaborate, structured assessment process. This process usually includes clinical interviews, ratings of specific target behaviors, and standard marital assessment questionnaires. Most widely used of the latter is the Locke-Wallace Marital Adjustment Scale (Locke and Wallace, 1959), which is a twenty-three-item questionnaire, covering various aspects of marital satisfaction including communication, sex, affection, social activities, and values. Rating scales are used to describe and quantify couples' most troublesome problems. Weiss and his colleagues at the Oregon Marital Studies Program ask couples to record their spouse's "pleasing" and "displeasing" behavior during the week.

Assessments are designed to reveal the strengths and weaknesses of the marital relationship and the manner in which rewards and punishments are exchanged. Several relationship skills are evaluated, including the ability to discuss relationship problems, current reinforcement value for one another, skill in pinpointing relevant reinforcers in the relationship, competencies in sex, childrearing, financial management, distribution of roles, and decision-making.

Interviews are used to specify and elaborate target behaviors, first revealed on the structured assessment devices. Some attempt is also made during interviews to understand the etiology of the problems that couples describe as well as to discover problems other than those noted by the spouses themselves. In general, however, behavioral marital therapists deemphasize interviews (Jacobson and Margolin, 1979) in favor of written questionnaires and direct observation of couples' interactions. Jacobson (1981) offers an outline for pretreatment assessment which is reproduced in Table 7.1 (see pages 340–341).

After completing the assessment, the behavioral clinician presents the couple with an analysis of their relationship in social learning theory terms. In doing so, therapists take pains to accentuate the positive, striving to maintain positive expectancies and a collaborative set (Jacobson, 1981). Married partners tend to state their goals negatively, in terms of decelerating aversive behavior: "I want less arguing from him"; or "She nags too much." Most have difficulty describing behavior that they want their spouses to accelerate. To help them do so, some therapists (Azrin, Naster, and Jones, 1973) assign a homework task asking the spouses to make a list of pleasing things their partners do during the week. Reviewing these lists in the following session provides the opportunity to emphasize the importance of giving positive feedback.

Since disturbed marital interaction is viewed as resulting from low rates of positive reinforcement exchanged by couples (Stuart, 1969; Patterson and Hops, 1972), a major treatment strategy is to increase positive control while decreasing the rate of aversive control. This strategy is promoted both while the couple is interacting in the clinic, and by assigning them homework to alter their pattern of interaction at home. A second major strategy is to improve communication, which in turn facilitates couples' abilities to solve problems. Stuart (1975) lists five intervention strategies which summarize the behavioral approach to treating troubled marriages. First, couples are taught to express themselves in clear, behavioral descriptions, rather than in vague and critical complaints. Second, couples

TABLE 7.1 Jacobson's Pretreatment Assessment for Marital Therapy

---

A. *Strengths and skills of the relationship*

What are the major strengths of this relationship?

Specifically, what resources do these spouses have to explain their current level of commitment to the relationship?

What is each spouse's current capacity to reinforce the other?

What behaviors on the part of each spouse are highly valued by the other?

What shared activities does the couple currently engage in?

What common interests do they share?

What are the couple's competencies and skills in meeting the essential tasks of a relationship: problem-solving, provision of support and understanding, ability to provide social reinforcement effectively, sexual capabilities, childrearing and parenting skills, ability to manage finances, household responsibilities, interpersonal skills regarding interaction with people outside the relationship?

B. *Presenting problems*

What are the major complaints, and how do these complaints translate into explicit behavioral terms?

What behaviors occur too frequently or at inappropriate times from the standpoint of each spouse?

Under what conditions do these behaviors occur?

What are the reinforcers that are maintaining these behaviors?

What behaviors occur at less than the desired frequency or fail to occur at appropriate times from the standpoint of each spouse?

Under what conditions would each spouse like to see these behaviors occur?

What are the consequences of these behaviors currently, when they occur?

How did the current problems develop over time?

How are current lines of decision-making authority drawn?

Is there a consensus on who makes important decisions in regard to various areas of the relationship?

What kinds of decisions are made collectively as opposed to unilaterally?

C. *Sex and affection*

Are the spouses physically attracted to one another?

Is either currently dissatisfied with rate, quality, or diversity of sex life together?

If sex is currently a problem, was there a time when it was mutually satisfying?

What are the sexual behaviors that seem to be associated with current dissatisfaction?

Are either or both partners dissatisfied with the amount or quality of nonsexual physical affection?

Are either or both partners currently engaged in an extramarital sexual relationship?

TABLE 7.1 *Continued*

If so, is the uninvolved partner aware of the affair?

What is the couple's history regarding extramarital affairs?

D. *Future prospects*

Are the partners seeking therapy to improve their relationship, to separate, or to decide whether the relationship is worth working on?

What are each spouse's reasons for continuing the relationship despite current problems?

What steps has each spouse taken in the direction of divorce?

E. *Assessment of social environment*

What are each person's alternatives to the present relationship?

How attractive are these alternatives to each person?

Is the environment (parents, relatives, friends, work associates, children) supportive of either continuance or dissolution of present relationship?

Are any of the children suffering from psychological problems of their own?

What would the probable consequences of relationship dissolution be for the children?

F. *Individual functioning of each spouse*

Does either spouse exhibit any severe emotional or behavioral problems?

Does either spouse represent a psychiatric history of his/her own? Specify.

Have they been in therapy before, either alone or together? What kind of therapy? Outcome?

What is each spouse's past experience with intimate relationships?

How is the present relationship different?

—From Jacobson (1981).

---

are taught new behavior exchange procedures, emphasizing positive in place of aversive control. Third, couples are helped to improve their communication. Fourth, couples are encouraged to establish clear and effective means of sharing power and making decisions. Fifth, couples are taught strategies for solving future problems, as a means of maintaining and extending gains initiated in therapy.

In his initial efforts Stuart (1969) employed the operant method of exchanging tokens as rewards for targeted desired behaviors. In this way one person could build up a "credit balance" by performing a high frequency of behaviors desired by other family members, which could later be exchanged when he or she was the recipient of rewarding behavior from others. Refinements of this approach dispensed with tokens. Mutual exchanges were based on written contracts. Although much of Stewart's work has been devoted to marital discord, his contingency contracting and principles of enhancing the mutual positive reinforcement potential of family members has been used widely by behavioral family therapists (Patterson, 1971b).

Behavior exchange procedures are taught to help couples increase the frequency of desired behaviors. Couples are advised to express their wishes and annoyances specifically and behaviorally. A typical device is to ask each spouse to list three things that he or she would like the other to do more often. These can provide the basis for a trade, or *quid pro quo*. While explicitly exchanging "strokes" in this way, spouses are implicitly learning ways of influencing each other through positive reinforcement. An alternative tactic is to ask each partner to think of things the other might want, do them, and see what happens. Weiss and his associates direct couples to have "love days," where one spouse doubles his or her pleasing behaviors toward the other (Weiss and Birchler, 1978). Stuart (1976) has couples alternate "caring days," where one spouse demonstrates caring in as many ways as possible.

The major intent of these procedures is to help couples establish *reinforcement reciprocity*, based on rewarding behavior, in place of coercion. Positive control is doubtless more pleasant and effective than aversive control. However, the concept of reinforcement reciprocity implies a symmetrical relationship. While this pattern may characterize some couples seen in university clinics, it surely does not apply to all; and it certainly does not apply to the majority of couples seen in other settings. Unfairness and inequality in marriage is one of the knottiest problems in American families. Assuming that husbands and wives can nicely negotiate agreements about who does what seems a little like assuming that rich nations will bargain in good faith with poor ones.

Behavioral marriage therapists try to help spouses learn to ask for what they want, rather than to expect the other to intuit it. In fact, the whole field has moved from stressing patterns of reinforcement to working on communication and problem-solving (Weiss, 1978). Unlike some other marital therapists, however, behavior therapists emphasize communication that is agreement-oriented rather than expression-oriented. The stress is always more on negotiating agreements than on expressing feelings. Because of this, some critics (Gurman and Kniskern, 1978) have suggested that behavioral marriage therapists try to eliminate arguing and expressions of anger, in the pursuit of dispassionate problem-solving. The implication is: "Do not complain, criticize, interrupt, disagree harshly, show disinterest, etc. 'Be docile, be quiet, be still,' to borrow a phrase" (Gurman and Kniskern, 1978, p. 133). Indeed, behavior marital therapy often does seems mechanical and dispassionate. For example, Jacobson (1981) recommends that couples not try to solve a problem while they are fighting about it, but postpone the discussion to a prearranged problem-solving session. "Couples report that if they postpone the discussion to the next scheduled problem-solving session, by the time the session occurs the problem seems trivial" (Jacobson, 1981, p. 579). Perhaps, but it also seems likely that the interval of postponement allows for the reconstitution of defensiveness and further, that the feelings involved are suppressed, not resolved. Jacobson (1981) says that angry exchanges occur in all relationships, "but they do not lead to behavior change" (p. 580). On the other hand, many relationships are based on chronic disengagement and a facade of intimacy. Angry feelings are part of being alive; to suppress them is to deaden oneself. Moreover, angry outbursts may often be the prelude to opening up and then solving problems. Couples therapists often need to rekindle smoldering conflicts before open expression or problem-solving can occur.

Training in communications skills may be done in a group format (Ely, Guerney, and Stover, 1973; Hickman and Baldwin, 1971; Pierce, 1973) or with individual couples. The training includes instruction, modeling, roleplaying, structured exercises, behavior rehearsal, and feedback (Jacobson, 1977; Patterson, Hops, and Weiss, 1973; Stuart, 1976). Couples are taught to be specific, phrase requests in positive terms to avoid attacking, respond directly to criticism instead of cross-complaining, talk about the present and future rather than the past, listen without interruption, minimize punitive statements, and eliminate questions that sound like declarations (O'Leary and Turkewitz, 1978).

After explaining these principles, therapists invite the couples to incorporate them in their discussions, during which the therapists provide feedback. Many therapists recommend that couples replay previous arguments, and ask the spouses to paraphrase each other's remarks before replying to them.

Once a couple has been taught to communicate in ways that are conducive to effective problem-solving, they are introduced to the principles of *contingency contracting*. Contingency contracting means changing something contingent on the partner making changes. There are two forms of contract negotiation used in behavioral family therapy. The first of these is the *quid pro quo* contract (Knox, 1971; Lederer and Jackson, 1968), where one spouse agrees to make a change after a prior change by the other. Contracting is highly structured and the agreements are usually written down. Each spouse specifies desired behavior changes, and with the therapist's help they construct agreements. At the end of the session a written list is made and each spouse signs it. According to Rappaport and Harrell (1972) written agreements act as references, obviating the need to rely on memory, they can be easily modified, they act as cues (discriminative stimuli) reminding spouses of their agreements, and they symbolize the couple's commitment to change. Such a contract might take the following form.

Date _____

This week I agree to:

(1) Come home from work by 6 P.M.
(2) Play with the children for half an hour after supper.

_____

Husband's signature

Contingent upon the above changes, I agree to:

(1) Go bowling once a week with my husband.
(2) Not serve leftovers for supper on weeknights.

_____

Wife's signature

This form of contracting substitutes positive for aversive control and ensures that changes in one spouse are immediately reinforced by the other (Eisler and Hersen, 1973). Therapists should guide the couple's choices of reinforcement so that the rewards desired by one spouse are not aversive to the other, and contracts for sexual behavior are avoided (O'Leary and Turkewitz, 1978).

Jacobson and Martin (1976) have argued that *quid pro quo* contracts are more efficient and less time-consuming than other forms. However, the *quid pro quo* arrangement requires one spouse to be the first to change. In an atmosphere of mistrust and animosity neither may be willing to do so. An alternative form of contracting is the *good faith* contract, in which both spouses agree to make changes that are not contingent upon what the other does (Weiss, Hops, and Patterson, 1973). Each spouse's independent changes are independently reinforced. In the example cited above, the husband who comes home each night by six p.m. and plays with the children after supper might reward himself by buying a new shirt at the end of the week, or be rewarded by his wife with a back rub. Stuart (1980) emphasizes training couples to negotiate exchanges in a "two-winner" context, rather than the "win-lose" orientation that typifies many distressed relationships. Knox (1973) has suggested a combined form of contracting, using "good faith" contracts until appropriate changes are initiated and then switching to *quid pro quo* contracts once an atmosphere of trust and confidence is established.

Problem-solving training is initiated to deal with problems that are too conflictual or complicated for simple exchange agreements. The key to successful problem-solving is to develop a collaborative set between the spouses. Negotiations are preceded by a careful and specific definition of problems. Only when the spouses agree on the definition of a problem can they effectively begin to discuss a solution. Discussions are limited to only one problem at a time. Each spouse begins by paraphrasing what the other has said, and they are taught to avoid making inferences about the other's motivation—especially inferences of malevolent intent. They are also encouraged to avoid verbal abuse and other aversive responses. When defining a problem it is most effective to begin with a positive statement; instead of saying, "You never . . . ," spouses are taught to say, "I appreciate the way you . . . and, in addition I want . . ."

Behavior therapists are very active in these discussions, teaching structured procedures for problem-solving and giving feedback. The discussions are frequently punctuated by such therapist comments as "You just interrupted him"; "As soon as she makes a request, you change the subject"; or "When you blamed her for the problem, the two of you started arguing instead of planning. Whenever you accuse each other of being unfair you get sidetracked from solving the problem at hand."

The problem with the activity and directiveness of behavioral marriage therapists is that couples may learn what they're doing wrong, but without having sufficient independent practice to correct it. There is a real danger that such a directive approach will tie couples into a long-term relationship in which they are dependent upon the therapist to referee their fights and tell them how to solve their disagreements. To avoid fostering such dependent relationships most nonbehavioral family therapists remain sufficiently decentralized to promote independent self-sufficiency on the part of their clients (Minuchin, 1974; Ables and Brandsma, 1977; Guerin, Fay, Burden, and Kautto, 1987). It seems to the present authors that behavioral therapists do create highly dependent relationships with the clients. Indeed their literature emphasizes the need to resolve this dependency by gradually tapering off treatment. O'Leary and Turkewitz (1978) describe four stages in the therapeutic relationship: courtship, engagement, marriage, and disengagement. During the disengagement stage, the therapist gradually withdraws direction and control. The skills learned in therapy must be generalized so that couples can use them independently of the therapist. For this reason, most behaviorists recommend that termination be gradual, so that the therapist's influence can be faded out.

As we move into the 1990s the methods employed by most behavioral marital therapists differ very little from those described by Stuart (1969) and Liberman (1970). The contingency contract remains the mainstay of treatment, both in enhancing the quality and quantity of mutually pleasing transactions and diminishing the frequency of negative communication sequences and arguments. The most significant advance in behavioral treatment is the increasing use and sophistication of cognitive-behavioral methods (Epstein, Schlesinger, and Dryden, 1988).

The cognitive mediation model (Beck, 1976) posits that emotions and actions are mediated by specific cognitions. Understanding these cognitions (*beliefs*, *attributions*, and *expectancies*) makes it possible to identify factors that trigger and maintain the dysfunctional emotional and behavioral patterns that families bring to treatment. In Barton and Alexander's (1981) "functional family therapy," it is assumed that members of disturbed families tend to attribute their problems to negative traits; and therefore the therapist's goal is to provide family members with new information that will impel them to new emotional and behavioral reactions in order to maintain cognitive consistency. In practice this boils down to repeatedly ferreting out and confronting negative assumptions that keep people stuck.

Treatment of Sexual Dysfunction

Some people would not consider sex therapy to be a form of family therapy. Even Masters and Johnson (1970), progenitors of this treatment, didn't regard themselves as behavior therapists. However, complaints about sexual problems are so frequently encountered by family therapists that we will summarize the techniques of sex therapy here to give students a basic familiarity with this approach.

It's often difficult to decide whether to focus directly on sexual problems or to treat them as a symptom of underlying problems in the relationship. At times it may be possible to resolve sexual problems indirectly, by working on the interpersonal relationship (Gill and Temperley, 1974). On the other hand, what appear to be intractable interpersonal problems can sometimes be resolved with improvements in a couple's sexual relationship (Kaplan, 1974). After all, sex and affection provide a bond that helps couples endure the inevitable hurts and slights that come into every relationship. In all cases, the decision as to whether or not to treat sexual dysfunction directly should be based upon informed clinical judgement, not ignorance of the techniques available.

Prior to the publication of Masters and Johnson's *Human Sexual Inadequacy* in 1970, the prevailing treatment for sexual dysfunction was a combination of analytic discussion and common-sense suggestions. For example, men suffering from premature ejaculation were often advised to think distracting, nonsexual thoughts during intercourse. For women who failed to reach orgasm the most common advice was to fake it.

Wolpe's (1958) introduction of *systematic desensitization* led to major advances in the treatment of sexual dysfunction. According to Wolpe most sexual problems are the result of conditioned anxiety reactions. His therapy consists of instructing couples to engage in a graded series of progressively more intimate encounters, avoiding thoughts about erection or orgasm. A second behavioral approach that frequently proved effective was *assertive training* (Lazarus, 1965; Wolpe, 1958). In assertive training, socially and sexually inhibited persons were encouraged to accept and express their needs and feelings.

While these behavioral remedies were often effective, the real break-through came with the publication of Masters and Johnson's (1970) approach. This was followed by a number of others who applied and extended Masters and Johnson's basic approach (Lobitz and LoPiccolo, 1972; Kaplan, 1974, 1979).

Although the specific details vary, there is a general approach to treatment followed by most sex therapists. As with other behavioral approaches, the first step is a careful and thorough assessment. Included in the assessment is a complete medical examination to rule out organic problems, and extensive interviews to determine the nature of the dysfunction as well as to establish goals for treatment. In the absence of organic problems, cases involving lack of information, poor technique, and poor communication in the sexual area are most amenable to sexual therapy. Moreover, those people suffering from premature ejaculation, vaginismus, or orgasmic dysfunction generally respond well to brief treatment (five to twenty sessions); cases of ejaculatory incompetence, erectile failure, and longstanding lack of sexual desire are generally more difficult to resolve (Heiman, LoPiccolo, and LoPiccolo, 1981).

Therapists following Masters and Johnson tended to lump sexual problems into one category—anxiety that interfered with couples' ability to relax into arousal and orgasm. Helen Singer Kaplan (1979) pointed out that there are three stages of the sexual response and, hence, three types of problems: disorders of desire, arousal disorders, and orgasm disorders. Disorders of desire range from "low sex drive" to sexual aversion. Treatment of these problems is often successful, with motivated clients. Treatment focuses on (a) deconditioning anxiety, and (b) helping clients identify and stop negative thoughts that interfere with sexual desire. Arousal disorders include decreased emotional arousal and difficulty achieving and maintaining an erection or dilating and lubricating. These problems are often helped with a combination of relaxation techniques and teaching couples to focus on physical sensations involved in touching and caressing, rather than worrying about what comes next. Orgasm disorders include the timing of orgasm (e.g., premature or delayed), the quality of the orgasm, or the requirements for orgasm (e.g., some people only have orgasm during masturbation). Problems with orgasm can also be either chronic or situational. Premature ejaculation usually responds well to sex therapy; lack of orgasm in women may respond to sex therapy, usually involving teaching the woman to practice on her own and learning to fantasize.

Following the assessment, clients are presented with an explanation of the role of conditioned anxiety in problems with sex, and they are told how anxiety developed and is being maintained in their sexual relationship. Insight and attitude change are thus a fundamental part of this "behavioral" therapy. Not only may a couple's ignorance be creating problems, but they may also harbor attitudes about sex that are incompatible with the aims of treatment. John Bancroft, who uses a behavioral approach to treat sexual problems, noted (1975, p. 149) that, "Changing attitudes is an essential part of treatment which has been sadly neglected by behavior therapists." Kaplan (1974) makes extensive use of psychodynamic theory and technique to deal with attitudinal resistance. Attitudes may be changed by confronting clients with discrepancies between their attitudes and reality; by subtly fostering behavior change (sometimes, where the body goes the heart follows); and by facilitating the cathartic expression of feelings.

Although sex therapy must be tailored to specific problems, most treatments are initiated with *sensate focus*. In this phase of treatment couples are taught how to relax and enjoy touching and being touched. They are told to go home and find a time when they are both reasonably relaxed and free from distraction, and then get in bed together naked. Then they take turns gently caressing each other. The person being touched is told to simply relax and concentrate on the feeling of being touched. Later the one being touched will let the partner know which touch is most pleasing and which is less so. At first couples are told not to touch each other in the sensitive breast or genital areas, in order to remove undue anxiety.

After they learn to relax and exchange gentle, pleasant caressing, couples are encouraged to gradually become more intimate—but to slow down and calm down if either should feel anxious. Thus sensate focus is a form of *in vivo desensitization*. Couples who are highly anxious and fearful of "having sex" (which many people reduce to a hectic few minutes of poking and panting) learn to overcome their fears through a gradual and progressively more intimate experience of mutual caressing. As anxiety drops and desire mounts, they are encouraged to engage in progressively more intimate exchanges. In the process of sensate focus, couples are also taught to figure out and communicate to each other what they like and don't like. So, for example, instead of enduring something unpleasant until she finally gets so upset that she yells at her partner or avoids sex altogether, a woman might be taught how to gently but quickly show him, "No, not like that, like this." Sex therapists also emphasize the need to become comfortable with initiating and refusing sexual contact. Couples are taught how to initiate sex without the ambiguity or poor timing that leads to a history of tension, anxiety, and, eventually, dread.

Once sensate focus exercises have gone smoothly, the therapist initiates specific techniques to deal with specific problems. Among women the most common sexual dysfunctions are difficulties with orgasm (Kaplan, 1979), and frequently these problems are rooted in lack of information. The woman and her partner may be expecting her to have orgasms reliably during intercourse without additional clitoral stimulation. In men, the most common problem is premature ejaculation, for which part of the treatment is the *squeeze technique* (Semans, 1956), in which the woman stimulates the man's penis until he feels the urge to ejaculate. At that point, she squeezes the frenulum (at the base of the head) firmly between her thumb and first two fingers until the urge to ejaculate subsides. Stimulation begins again until another squeeze is necessary.

Techniques to deal with erectile failure are designed to reduce performance anxiety and increase sexual arousal. These include desensitization of the man's anxiety; discussions in which the partners describe their expectations; increasing the variety and duration of foreplay; the *teasing technique* (Masters and Johnsons, 1970), in which the woman alternately starts and stops stimulating the man; and beginning intercourse with the woman guiding the man's flaccid penis into her vagina.

Many sex therapy programs have a stated time limit, so that termination is anticipated from the start. Otherwise sex therapy is usually terminated by joint agreement of therapist and clients. In my (M.P.N.) own experience, successful sex therapy usually ends with the couple's sex life much improved, but not as fantastic as frustrated expectations had led them to imagine—expectations that were part of the problem in the first place. As in any form of directive therapy, it's important for sex therapists to gradually fade out their involvement and control. Therapeutic gains are consolidated and extended by reviewing the changes that have occurred; by anticipating future trouble spots; and by planning in advance to deal with problems according to principles learned in treatment.

EVALUATING THERAPY THEORY AND RESULTS

Behavior therapy was born and bred in a tradition of research, and so it's not surprising that behavioral family therapy is the most carefully studied form of family treatment. Almost all reports of behavioral family therapy are accompanied by some assessment of outcome, and there are hundreds of reports of successful parent training, couples' treatment, and sex therapy. However, the majority of these are single case studies, both anecdotal and experimental. They do help substantiate the efficacy of the behavioral approach to problems in family living, but such case reports are probably better considered demonstrations than investigations. In addition, there are also a host of controlled experimental studies of behavior family therapy. Gordon and Davidson (1981) summarized studies of the effectiveness of behavioral parent training, and found that the majority of measures yielded positive results in the majority of cases. They reported hundreds of documented successes with a wide variety of problem children. The outcome criteria in studies of parent training are usually based on parents' and observers' frequency counts of prosocial and deviant behavior. Researchers have found that more advantaged families show distinctly better results from behavior parent training (O'Dell, 1974). This is not surprising, considering the heavy emphasis on theory and education in this approach.

A typical finding is that targeted behavior improves; only marginal changes, however, can be seen for nontargeted problem behavior. Apparently the specific focus on presenting problems in this approach lends leverage to resolving focal complaints, but only minimally generalizes to overall family functioning. Moreover, improvements do not generalize from home to other settings, such as school (Gurman and Kniskern, 1978). Finally, there is a tendency for therapeutic gains to decrease sharply between termination and follow-up.

The behavioral literature also contains a large number of empirical studies of marital therapy. These studies are usually done on brief treatment (approximately nine sessions) and the most common criteria of success are observers' ratings and couples' self-reports. In 1978 Gurman and Kniskern (1978) reported on eight controlled analogue studies; two showed behavioral couples therapy to be significantly better than no treatment; in five controlled analogue studies behavioral couples therapy was found to be more effective than alternative forms of treatment in only one case. In the same survey, Gurman and Kniskern found that six of seven naturalistic comparative studies favored behavioral couples therapy. These findings provide support for the efficacy of this approach; however, as the authors noted, behavioral therapy is still relatively untested on couples with severe marital problems. When they updated their survey in 1981, Gurman and Kniskern (1981) found similar results, and concluded that behavioral marriage therapy appears to be about as effective for mild to moderate marital problems as are nonbehavioral approaches.

Several studies have shown that the most effective ingredient in any form of marital therapy is increasing the couple's communication skills (Jacobson, 1978; Jacobson and Margolin, 1979). Jacobson's studies strongly support his approach, based on observational measures of communication and self-reported marital satisfaction. Liberman and his colleagues (Liberman, Levine, Wheeler, Sanders, and Wallace, 1976) found that on objective measures of marital communication, behavioral marriage therapy in a group setting was more effective than insight-oriented couples groups. However, the two approaches did not differ in effecting increased marital satisfaction. O'Leary and Turkewitz (1979) have shown that behavior exchanges procedures are effective, especially with young couples; older couples tend to respond more favorably to communications training.

Despite the tremendous growth of public and professional interest in sex therapy, there are still few well-controlled studies of its effectiveness. In a careful review, Hogan (1978) found that most of the literature consists of uncontrolled, clinical case studies. These reports are little more than box scores of successes and failures. Absent are pre- and post-measures, detailed specification of techniques, points of reference other than the therapists, and follow-up data. Moreover, since most of these reports come from the same handful of therapists, it is impossible to discern what is being evaluated—the techniques of sex therapy or the skill of these particular therapists. This state of the research hadn't changed much by 1990, according to more recent summary reports (Crowe, 1988; Falloon and Lillie, 1988).

The greatest success rates with sexual therapy have been found in treating vaginismus, orgasmic dysfunction, and premature ejaculation. Vaginismus, the spastic contraction of vagina muscles, has been successfully treated in 90 to 95 percent of cases (Fuchs, Hoch, Paldi, Abramovici, Brandes, Timor-Tritsch, and Kleinhaus, 1973). Eighty-five to 95 percent of the women who had never previously achieved orgasm did so after treatment. Success rates are lower, 30 to 50 percent, when limited to those who had previously reached orgasm during coitus (Heiman, LoPiccolo, and LoPiccolo, 1981). The reported success rates for treatment of premature ejaculation using the squeeze technique (Masters and Johnson, 1970) are uniformly high, 90 to 95 percent.

For men who had never had erectile functioning, the success rates are between 40 and 60 percent—though, as Michael Crowe (1988) has noted, this problem turns out to be medically related more often than we used to think. For those who once had adquate erectile functioning and then developed difficulty, success rates average 60 to 80 percent (Heiman, LoPiccolo, and LoPiccolo, 1981). Retarded ejaculation or failure to ejaculate is relatively uncommon; consequently there are fewer reported treatment cases. Among this small sample, reported success rates range from 50 to 82 percent (Heiman, LoPiccolo, and LoPiccolo, 1981). Treatment of individuals with very low levels of interest in sex is relatively new (Kaplan, 1979) and there are as yet few statistics, but apparently such cases respond well to treatment (LoPiccolo and LoPiccolo, 1978).

The fact that there are relatively few published studies should not obscure the fact that sex therapy appears to be an effective procedure for some very vexing problems. Most observers (Gurman and Kniskern, 1981) agree that it should be considered the treatment of choice when there is an explicit complaint about a couple's sex life.

Currently there are three areas of research in family intervention that seem to be ready to move to a more advanced stage of development. These areas are: conduct disorders in children (Patterson, 1986; Morris, Alexander, and Waldron, 1988), marital conflict (Follette and Jacobson, 1988), and schizophrenic adults (Falloon, 1985).

SUMMARY

Although behavior therapists have begun to apply their techniques to family problems, they have done so, for the most part, within a linear frame of reference. Behavioral problems are regarded as *caused* by dysfunctional patterns of reinforcement between parents and children, or between spouses. Therefore, behavioral family therapy is used to teach parents how to apply learning theory to control their children; to help couples substitute positive for aversive control; and to decondition anxiety in partners with sexual problems. Behavioral family therapists give very little consideration to complex and circular family interactions.

Family symptoms are treated as learned responses, involuntarily acquired and reinforced. Treatment is generally time-limited and symptom-focused. The behavioral approach to families is based on social learning theory, which is a complex and sophisticated model, according to which behavior is learned and maintained by its consequences, and can be modified by altering those consequences.

Behaviorists' systematic analysis of behavior and their insistence on technically sound interventions make it clear that a therapist's personality is not all that's needed to help people change. Behaviorists don't believe that therapists have to *be* something—warm, self-disclosing, forceful—rather, they have to *do* something. Personal skills are required, not personal style; to treat behavioral problems you need to understand behavioral theory.

An essential adjunct to social learning theory is Thibaut and Kelley's exchange theory, according to which people strive to maximize interpersonal "rewards" while minimizing "costs." Social behavior in a relationship is maintained by a high ratio of rewards to costs, and by the perception that alternative relationships offer fewer rewards and more costs (comparison level of alternatives). In this view, marital and family conflicts occur when optimal behavior-maintaining contingencies do not exist, or when dysfunctional behavior change methods are applied. In unhappy families, coercion replaces reciprocity.

The general goals of behavioral family therapy are to increase the rate of rewarding exchanges; to decrease aversive exchanges; and to teach communication and problem-solving skills. Remediation of problem behavior is the primary goal; prevention of future problems is secondary. Specific techniques are applied to target behaviors; in the process, families are also taught general principles of behavior management.

The behaviorists' focus on modifying the consequences of problem behavior accounts for some of the strengths and weaknesses of behavioral family therapy. By narrowly concentrating their attention on presenting problems, behaviorists have been able to develop an impressive array of effective techniques. Even such relatively intractable problems as delinquent behavior in children and severe sexual dysfunctions have yielded to behavioral technology. On the other hand, behavior is only part of the person, and the problem person is only part of the family. Any form of therapy must deal with the whole person, who not only acts but also thinks and feels. Different therapies may concentrate on only one of these three human functions—psychoanalysts concentrate on thinking, just as behaviorists concentrate on action—but to be successful a therapy must affect all three.

You can't simply teach people to change if unrecognized conflict is keeping them stuck.

Unhappiness may center around a behavioral complaint, but resolution of the behavior may not resolve the unhappiness. Treatment may succeed with the symptom but fail the family. Attitudes and feelings may change along with changes in behavior, but not necessarily. And teaching communication skills may not be enough to resolve real conflict. Mere behavior change may not be enough for family members whose ultimate goal is to feel better. "Yes, he's doing his chores now," a parent may agree. "But I don't think he *feels* like helping out. He still isn't really part of our family." Behavior is not all that family members in distress are concerned about, and to be responsive to all their needs behavioral family therapists need to deal with cognitive and affective material, as well as behavioral.

Although behavioral family clinicians recognize the need to modify interpersonal interactions, they generally limit their attention to interactions between units of two, and they tend to accept the family's definition of one person (or couple) as *the* problem. Virtually no consideration is given to the role of marital problems in behavioral treatment of children, and behavioral couples therapists rarely discuss the role that children or extended family members play in marital distress.

Behaviorists hardly ever treat whole families. Instead they bring in only those subsystems that they consider central to the targeted behaviors. Unfortunately, failure to include—or even consider—whole families in treatment may be disastrous. A therapeutic program to reduce a son's aggressiveness toward his mother can hardly succeed if the father wants an aggressive son, or if the father's anger toward his wife is not more directly addressed. Moreover, if the whole family is not involved in change, new behavior will not be reinforced and maintained.

Despite these shortcomings, behavioral family therapy offers impressive techniques for treating problems with children and troubled marriages. Furthermore, its weaknesses can be corrected by broadening the focus of conceptualization and the scope of treatment to include whole families as systems. Although some behavior therapists may be naive about circular interactions and systemic structure, there is nothing inherently limiting in the usefulness of their technology.

Perhaps the greatest strength of behavior therapy is its insistence on observing what happens and then measuring change. Behaviorists have developed a wealth of reliable and valid assessment methods and applied them to initial evaluation, treatment planning, and monitoring progress and outcome. A second important advance has been the gradual movement from eliminating or reinforcing discrete "marker" behaviors to the teaching of general problem-solving, cognitive, and communicational skills. A third major advance in current behavioral family therapy is modular treatment interventions organized to meet the specific and changing needs of the individual and the family.

REFERENCES

Ables, B. S., and Brandsma, S. J. 1977. *Therapy for couples.* San Francisco: Jossey-Bass.

Alexander, J. F., and Barton, C. 1976. Behavioral systems therapy with families. In *Treating relationships*, D. H. Olson, ed. Lake Mills, IA: Graphic Publishing.

Alexander, J. F., and Parsons, B. V. 1973. Short-term behavioral intervention with delinquent families: Impact on family process and recidivism. *Journal of Abnormal Psychology. 51*:219–225.

Anderson, C. M., and Stewart, S. 1983. *Mastering resistance.* New York: Guilford Press.

Arrington, A., Sullaway, M., and Christensen, A. 1988. Behavioral family assessment. In *Handbook of behavioral family therapy*, I. R. H. Falloon, ed. New York: Guilford Press.

Azrin, N. H., Naster, J. B., and Jones, R. 1973. Reciprocity counseling: A rapid learning-based procedure for marital counseling. *Behavior Research and Therapy. 11*:365–383.

Baer, D. M., and Sherman, J. A. 1964. Reinforcement control of generalized imitation in young children. *Journal of Experimental Child Psychology. 1*:37–49.

Bancroft, J. 1975. The behavioral approach to marital problems. *British Journal of Medical Psychology. 48*:147–152.

Bandura, A. 1969. *Principles of behavior modification.* New York: Holt, Rinehart & Winston.

Bandura, A., and Walters, R. 1963. *Social learning and personality development.* New York: Holt, Rinehart & Winston.

Barton, C., and Alexander, J. F. 1975. Therapist skills in systems-behavioral family intervention: How the hell do you get them to do it? Paper presented at the annual meeting of the Orthopsychiatric Association, Atlanta.

Barton, C., and Alexander, J. F. 1981. Functional family therapy. In *Handbook of family therapy*, A. S. Gurman and D. P. Kniskern, eds. New York: Brunner/Mazel.

Beck, A. T. 1976. *Cognitive therapy and the emotional disorders.* New York: International Universities Press.

Birchler, G. R. 1988. Handling resistance to change. In *Handbook of behavioral family therapy*, I. R. H. Falloon, ed. New York: Guilford Press.

Birchler, G. R., and Spinks, S. H. 1980. Behavioral-systems marital therapy: Integration and clinical application. *American Journal of Family Therapy. 8*:6–29.

Boardman, W. K. 1962. Rusty: A brief behavior disorder. *Journal of Consulting Psychology. 26*:293–297.

Christophersen, E. R., Arnold, C. M., Hill, D. W., and Quilitch, H. R. 1972. The home point system: Token reinforcement procedures for application by parents of children with behavioral problems. *Journal of Applied Behavioral Analysis.* 5:485–497.

Crowe, M. 1988. Indications for family, marital, and sexual therapy. In *Handbook of behavioral family therapy*, I. R. H. Falloon, ed. New York: Guilford Press.

DiGiuseppe, R. 1988. A cognitive-behavioral approach to the treatment of conduct disorder children and adolescents. In *Cognitive-behavioral therapy with families*, N. Epstein, S. E. Schlesinger, and W. Dryden, eds. New York: Brunner/Mazel.

Eisler, R. M., and Hersen, M. 1973. Behavior techniques in family-oriented crisis intervention. *Archives of General Psychiatry.* 28:111–116.

Ellis, A. 1962. *Reason and emotion in psychotherapy.* New York: Lyle Stuart.

Ely, A. L., Guerney, B. G., and Stover, L. 1973. Efficacy of the training phase of conjugal therapy. *Psychotherapy: Theory, Research and Practice.* 10:201–207.

Epstein, N., Schlesinger, S. E., and Dryden, W. eds. 1988. *Cognitive-behavioral therapy with families.* New York: Brunner/Mazel.

Falloon, I. R. H. ed. 1988. *Handbook of behavioral family therapy.* New York: Guilford Press.

Falloon, I. R. H. 1985. *Family management of schizophrenia: A study of the clinical, social, family and economic benefits.* Baltimore: Johns Hopkins University Press.

Falloon, I. R. H., and Liberman, R. P. 1983. Behavioral therapy for families with child management problems. In *Helping families with special problems*, M. R. Textor, ed. New York: Jason Aronson.

Falloon, I. R. H., and Lillie, F. J. 1988. Behavioral family therapy: An overview. In *Handbook of behavioral family therapy*, I. R. H. Falloon, ed. New York: Guilford Press.

Ferster, C. B. 1963. Essentials of a science of behavior. In *An introduction to the science of human behavior*, J. I. Nurnberger, C. B. Ferster, and J. P. Brady, eds. New York: Appleton-Century-Crofts.

Follette, W. C., and Jacobson, N. S. 1988. Behavioral marital therapy in the treatment of depressive disorders. In *Handbook of behavioral family therapy*, I. R. H. Falloon, ed. New York: Guilford Press.

Forehand, R., and McDonough, T. S. 1975. Response-contingent time out: An examination of outcome data. *European Journal of Behavioural Analysis and Modification.* 1:109–115.

Forehand, R., Roberts, M. W., Doleys, D. M., Hobbs, S. A., and Resnick, P. A. 1976. An examination of disciplinary procedures with children. *Journal of Experimental Child Psychology.* 21:109–120.

Friedman, P. H. 1972. Personalistic family and marital therapy. In *Clinical behavior therapy*, A. A. Lazarus ed. New York: Brunner/Mazel.

Fuchs, K., Hoch, Z., Paldi, E., Abramovici, H., Brandes, J. M., Timor-Tritsch, I., and Kleinhaus, M. 1973. Hypnodesensitization therapy of vaginismus: Part I. "In vitro" method. Part II. "In vivo" method. *International Journal of Clinical and Experimental Hypnosis.* 21:144–156.

Gill, H., and Temperly, J. 1974. Time-limited marital treatment in a foursome. *British Journal of Medical Psychology.* 47:153–161.

Goldiamond, I. 1965. Self-control procedures in personal behavior problems. *Psychological Reports. 17*:851–868.

Goldstein, M. K. 1971. Behavior rate change in marriages: Training wives to modify husbands' behavior. *Dissertation Abstracts International. 32*:(1-8), 559.

Goldstein, M. K., and Francis, B. 1969. Behavior modification of husbands by wives. Paper presented at the National Council on Family Relations, Washington, DC.

Gordon, S. B., and Davidson, N. 1981. Behavioral parent training. In *Handbook of family therapy*, A. S. Gurman and D. P. Kniskern, eds. New York: Brunner/Mazel.

Gottman, J., Markman, H., and Notarius, C. 1977. The topography of marital conflict: A sequential analysis of verbal and nonverbal behavior. *Journal of Marriage and the Family. 39*:461–477.

Graziano, A. M. 1977. Parents as behavior therapists. In *Progress in behavior modification*, M. Hersen, R. M. Eisler, and P. M. Miller, eds. New York: Academic Press.

Guerin, P. J., Fay, L., Burden, S. L., and Kautto, J. B. 1987. *The evaluation and treatment of marital conflict: A four-stage approach*. New York: Basic Books.

Gurman, A. S., and Kniskern, D. P. 1978. Research on marital and family therapy: Progress, perspective and prospect. In *Handbook of psychotherapy and behavior change: An empirical analysis*, S. L. Garfield and A. E. Bergin eds. New York: Wiley.

Gurman, A. S., and Kniskern, D. P. 1981. Family therapy outcome research: Knowns and unknowns. In *Handbook of family therapy*, A. S. Gurman and D. P. Kniskern, eds. New York: Brunner/Mazel.

Gurman, A. S., and Knudson, R. M. 1978. Behavioral marriage therapy: A psychodynamic-systems analysis and critique. *Family Process. 17*:121–138.

Hawkins, R. P., Peterson, R. F., Schweid, E., and Bijou, S. W. 1966. Behavior therapy in the home: Amelioration of problem parent-child relations with a parent in the therapeutic role. *Journal of Experimental Child Psychology. 4*:99–107.

Heiman, J. R., LoPiccolo, L., and LoPiccolo, J. 1981. The treatment of sexual dysfunction. In *Handbook of family therapy*, A. S. Gurman and D. P. Kniskern, eds. New York: Brunner/Mazel.

Hickman, M. E., and Baldwin, B. A. 1971. Use of programmed instruction to improve communication in marriage. *The Family Coordinator. 20*:121–125.

Hogan, D. R. 1978. The effectiveness of sex therapy: A review of the literature. In *Handbook of sex therapy*, J. LoPiccolo and L. LoPiccolo, eds. New York: Plenum Press.

Jacobson, N. S. 1977. Problem solving and contingency contracting in the treatment of marital discord. *Journal of Consulting and Clinical Psychology. 45*:92–100.

Jacobson, N. S. 1978. Specific and nonspecific factors in the effectiveness of a behavioral approach to the treatment of marital discord. *Journal of Consulting and Clinical Psychology. 46*:442–452.

Jacobson, N. S. 1981. Behavioral marital therapy. In *Handbook of family therapy*, A. S. Gurman and D. P. Kniskern, eds. New York: Brunner/Mazel.

Jacobson, N. S., and Margolin, G. 1979. *Marital therapy: Strategies based on social learning and behavior exchange principles.* New York: Brunner/Mazel.

Jacobson, N. S., and Martin, B. 1976. Behavioral marriage therapy: Current status. *Psychological Bulletin.* 83:540–556.

Jones, M. C. 1924. A laboratory study of fear: The case of Peter. *Journal of Geriatric Psychology.* 31:308–315.

Kanfer, F. H., and Phillips, J. S. 1970. *Learning foundations of behavior therapy.* New York: Wiley.

Kaplan, H. S. 1974. *The new sex therapy: Active treatment of sexual dysfunctions.* New York: Brunner/Mazel.

Kaplan, H. S. 1979. *Disorders of sexual desire and other new concepts and techniques in sex therapy.* New York: Brunner/Mazel.

Katkin, E. S. 1978. Charting as a multipurpose treatment intervention in family therapy. *Family Process.* 17:465–468.

Keefe, F. J., Kopel, S. A., and Gordon, S. B. (1978). *A practical guide to behavior assessment.* New York: Springer.

Kimmel, C. and Van der Veen, F. (1974). Factors of marital adjustment in Locke's Marital Adjustment Test. *Journal of Marriage and the Family,* 36:57–63.

Knox, D. 1971. *Marriage happiness: A behavioral approach to counseling.* Champaign, IL: Research Press.

Knox, D. 1973. Behavior contracts in marriage counseling. *Journal of Family Counseling.* 1:22–28.

Lazarus, A. A. 1965. The treatment of a sexually inadequate male. In *Case studies in behavior modification*, L. P. Ullmann and L. Krasner, eds. New York: Holt, Rinehart & Winston.

Lazarus, A. A. 1968. Behavior therapy and group marriage counseling. *Journal of the American Society of Medicine and Dentistry.* 15:49–56.

Lazarus, A. A. 1971. *Behavior therapy and beyond.* New York: McGraw-Hill.

LeBow, M. D. 1972. Behavior modification for the family. In *Family therapy: An introduction to theory and technique.* G. D. Erickson and T. P. Hogan, eds. Monterey, CA: Brooks/Cole.

Lederer, W. J., and Jackson, D. D. 1968. *The mirages of marriage.* New York: Norton.

Liberman, R. P. 1970. Behavioral approaches to family and couple therapy. *American Journal of Orthopsychiatry.* 40:106–118.

Liberman, R. P. 1972. Behavioral approaches to family and couple therapy. In *Progress in group and family therapy*, C. J. Sager and H. S. Kaplan, eds. New York: Brunner/Mazel.

Liberman, R. P., Levine, J., Wheeler, E., Sanders, N., and Wallace, C. (1976). Experimental evaluation of marital group therapy: Behavioral vs. interaction-insight formats. *Acta Psychiatrica Scandinavia* Supplement.

Lobitz, N. C., and LoPiccolo, J. 1972. New methods in the behavioral treatment of sexual dysfunction. *Journal of Behavior Therapy and Experimental Psychiatry. 3*:265–271.

Locke, H. J., and Wallace, K. M. 1959. Short-term marital adjustment and prediction tests: Their reliability and validity. *Journal of Marriage and Family Living. 21*:251–255.

LoPiccolo, J., and LoPiccolo, L. 1978. *Handbook of sex therapy*. New York: Plenum.

Lovibond, S. H. 1963. The mechanism of conditioning treatment of enuresis. *Behavior Research and Therapy. 1*:17–21.

Mahoney, M. J. 1977. Reflections on the cognitive learning trend in psychotherapy. *American Psychologist. 32*:5–13.

Markman, H. J. 1979. Application of a behavioral model of marriage in predicting relationship satisfaction of couples planning marriage. *Journal of Consulting and Clinical Psychology. 47*:743–749.

Masters, W. H., and Johnson, V. E. 1970. *Human sexual inadequacy*. Boston: Little, Brown.

McCauley, R. 1988. Parent training: Clinical application. In *Handbook of behavioral family therapy*, I. R. H. Falloon, ed. New York: Guilford Press.

McGuire, R. J., and Vallance, M. 1964. Aversion therapy by electric shock: A simple technique. *British Medical Journal. 1*:151–153.

Meichenbaum, D. (1977). *Cognitive behavior modification*. New York: Plenum.

Minuchin, S. 1974. *Families and family therapy*. Cambridge, MA: Harvard University Press.

Minuchin, S., Rosman, B. L., and Baker, L. 1978. *Psychosomatic families*. Cambridge, MA: Harvard University Press.

Mischel, W. 1973. On the emprirical dilemmas of psychodynamic approaches: Issues and alternatives. *Journal of Abnormal Psychology. 82*:335–334.

Morris, S. B., Alexander, J. F., and Waldron, H. 1988. Functional family therapy. In *Handbook of behavioral family therapy*, I. R. H. Falloon, ed. New York: Guilford Press.

Morton, T. L., Twentyman, C. T., and Azar, S. T. 1988. Cognitive-behavioral assessment and treatment of child abuse. In *Cognitive-behavioral therapy with families*, N. Epstein, S. E. Schlesinger, and W. Dryden, eds. New York: Brunner/Mazel.

O'Dell, S. 1974. Training parents in behavior modification: A review. *Psychological Bulletin. 81*:418–433.

O'Leary, K. D., O'Leary, S., and Becher, W. C. 1967. Modification of a deviant sibling interaction pattern in the home. *Behavior Research and Therapy. 5*:113–120.

O'Leary, K. D., and Turkewitz, H. 1978. Marital therapy from a behavioral perspective. In *Marriage and marital therapy*, T. J. Paolino and B. S. McCrady, eds. New York: Brunner/Mazel.

O'Leary, K. D., and Wilson, G. T. 1975. *Behavior therapy: Application and outcome*. Englewood Cliff, NJ: Prentice-Hall.

Patterson, G. R. 1971a. Behavioral intervention procedures in the classroom and in the home. In *Handbook of psychotherapy and behavior change:*

An empirical analysis, A. E. Bergin and S. L. Garfield, eds. New York: Wiley.

Patterson, G. R. 1971b. *Families: Application of social learning theory to family life*. Champaign, IL: Research Press.

Patterson, G. R. 1986. The contribution of siblings to training for fighting; A microsocial analysis. In *Development of antisocial and prosocial behavior: Research, theories, and issues*, D. Olweus, J. Block, and M. Radke-Yarrow, eds. Orlando, FL: Academic Press.

Patterson, G. R. 1988. Foreword. In *Handbook of behavioral family therapy*, I. R. H. Falloon, ed. New York: Guilford Press.

Patterson, G. R., and Hops, H. 1972. Coercion, a game for two. In *The experimental analysis of social behavior*, R. E. Ulrich and P. Mountjoy, eds. New York: Appleton-Century-Crofts.

Patterson, G. R., Hops, H., and Weiss, R. L. 1973. A social learning approach to reducing rates of marital conflict. In *Advances in behavior therapy*, R. Stuart, R. Liberman, and S. Wilder, eds. New York: Academic Press.

Patterson, G. R., and Reid, J. 1970. Reciprocity and coercion; two facets of social systems. In *Behavior modification in clinical psychology*, C. Neuringer and J. Michael, eds. New York: Appleton-Century-Crofts.

Patterson, G. R., Weiss, R. L., and Hops, H. 1976. Training in marital skills: Some problems and concepts. In *Handbook of behavior modification and behavior therapy*, H. Leitenberg, ed. Englewood Cliffs, NJ: Prentice-Hall.

Pavlov, I. P. 1932. Neuroses in man and animals. *Journal of the American Medical Association. 99*:1012–1013.

Pavlov, I. P. 1934. An attempt at a physiological interpretation of obsessional neurosis and paranoia. *Journal of Mental Science. 80*:187–197.

Pendergrass, V. E. 1971. Effects of length of timeout from positive reinforcement and schedule of application in suppression of aggressive behavior. *Psychological Record. 21*:75–80.

Pierce, R. M. 1973. Training in intepersonal communication skills with the partners of deteriorated marriages. *The Family Coordinator. 22*:223–227.

Premack, D. 1965. Reinforcement theory. In *Nebraska symposium on motivation*, D. Levine, ed. Lincoln, NB: University of Nebraska Press.

Rappaport, A. F., and Harrell, J. A. 1972. A behavior-exchange model for marital counseling. *Family Coordinator. 21*:203–213.

Rimm, D. C., and Masters, J. C. 1974. *Behavior therapy: Techniques and empirical findings*. New York: Wiley.

Rinn, R. C. 1978. Children with behavior disorders. In *Behavior therapy in the psychiatric setting*, M. Hersen and A. S. Bellack, eds. Baltimore: Williams & Wilkins.

Risley, T. R. 1968. The effects and side effects of punishing the autistic behaviors of a deviant child. *Journal of Applied Behavior Analysis. 1*:21–34.

Risley, T. R., and Wolf, M. M. 1967. Experimental manipulation of autistic behaviors and generalization into the home. In *Child development: Readings in experimental analysis*, S. W. Bijou and D. M. Baer, eds. New York: Appleton.

Romanczyk, R. G., and Kistner, J. J. 1977. The current state of the art in behavior modification. *The Psychotherapy Bulletin. 11*:16–30.

Schwitzgebel, R. 1967. Short-term operant conditioning of adolescent offenders on socially relevant variables. *Journal of Abnormal Psychology. 72*:134–142.

Schwitzgebel, R., and Kolb, D. A. 1964. Inducing behavior change in adolescent delinquents. *Behaviour Research and Therapy. 9*:233–238.

Semans, J. H. 1956. Premature ejaculation: A new approach. *Southern Medical Journal. 49*:353–357.

Skinner, B. F. 1953. *Science and human behavior.* New York: Macmillan.

Spinks, S. H., and Birchler, G. R. 1982. Behavior systems marital therapy: Dealing with resistance. *Family Process. 21*:169–186.

Stuart, R. B. 1969. An operant-interpersonal treatment for marital discord. *Journal of Consulting and Clinical Psychology. 33*:675–682.

Stuart, R. B. 1971. Behavioral contracting within the families of delinquents. *Journal of Behavior Therapy and Experimental Psychiatry. 2*:1–11.

Stuart, R. B. 1975. Behavioral remedies for marital ills: A guide to the use of operant-interpersonal techniques. In *International symposium on behavior modification,* T. Thompson and W. Docken, eds. New York: Appleton.

Stuart, R. B. 1976. An operant interpersonal program for couples. In *Treating relationships,* D. H. Olson, ed. Lake Mills, IA: Graphic Publishing.

Stuart, R. B. 1980. *Helping couples change: A social learning approach to marital therapy.* New York: Guilford Press.

Thibaut, J., and Kelley, H. H. 1959. *The social psychology of groups.* New York: Wiley.

Umana, R. F., Gross, S. J., and McConville, N. T. 1980. *Crisis in the family: Three approaches.* New York: Gardner Press.

Vincent, J. P., Weiss, R. L., and Birchler, G. R. 1975. A behavioral analysis of problem solving in distressed and nondistressed married and stranger dyads. *Behavior Therapy. 6*:475–487.

Watson, J. B., and Raynor, R. 1920. Conditioned emotional reactions. *Journal of Experimental Psychology. 3*:1–14.

Weiss, R. L. 1978. The conceptualization of marriage from a behavioral perspective. In *Marriage and marital therapy,* T. J. Paolino and B. S. McCrady, eds. New York: Brunner/Mazel.

Weiss, R. L., and Birchler, G. R. 1978. Adults with marital dysfunction. In *Behavior therapy in the psychiatric setting,* M. Hersen and A. S. Bellack, eds. Baltimore: Williams & Wilkins.

Weiss, R. L., Hops, H., and Patterson, G. R. 1973. A framework for conceptualizing marital conflict, a technology for altering it, some data for evaluating it. In *Behavior change: Methodology, concepts and practice,* L. A. Hamerlynch, L. C. Handy, and E. J. Marsh, eds. Champaign, IL: Research Press.

Weiss, R. L., and Isaac, J. 1978. Behavior vs. cognitive measures as predictors of marital satisfaction. Paper presented at the Western Psychological Association meeting, Los Angeles.

Williams, C. D. 1959. The elimination of tantrum behavior by extinction procedures. *Journal of Abnormal and Social Psychology. 59*:269.

Wills, T. A., Weiss, R. L., and Patterson, G. R. 1974. A behavioral analysis of the determinants of marital satisfaction. *Journal of Consulting and Clinical Psychology. 42*:802–811.

Wolpe, J. 1948. An approach to the problem of neurosis based on the conditioned response. Unpublished M.D. thesis. University of Witwatersrand, Johannesberg, South Africa.

Wolpe, J. 1958. *Psychotherapy by reciprocal inhibition.* Stanford, CA: Stanford University Press.

Wolpe, J. 1969. *The practice of behavior therapy.* New York: Pergamon Press.

8

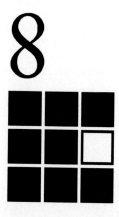

Bowenian Family Therapy

The pioneers of family therapy recognized that people are products of social context, but usually limited their attention to the nuclear family. They had the same kind of fervor as the first behavior therapists, who discovered the power of reinforcement to modify behavior, and they had the same kind of narrowness. Yes, our actions are powerfully influenced by what goes on in our immediate families, and often one person's symptoms can be resolved by altering interactions in the nuclear family. But what about the forces, past and present, that generate those patterns? What makes a husband react with a reflex to distance himself from the emotional demands of family life? And what makes a wife neglect her own life to the extent that she has such a need to regulate her children's lives? Murray Bowen sought answers—and solutions—to such questions in the larger network of family relationships.

Bowenian family therapy has by far the most comprehensive view of human behavior and human problems of any approach to family treatment. It extends the focus deeper—into the hearts and minds of family members—and broader—into the wider family context that shaped, and continues to shape, the life of the family.

While no one doubts the formative influence of family on molding personality, many people imagine that once they leave home they are grown-up: independent adults, free at last of their parents' influence. Some people prize individuality and take it as a sign of growth to separate from their parents; others wish they could be closer to their families but find visits home too painful, and so they stay away to protect themselves from disappointment and hurt. Once out of range of the immediate conflict, they forget and deny the discord. But as Bowen discovered, the family remains within us. Wherever we go, we carry unresolved emotional reactivity to our parents, in the form of vulnerability to repeat the same old patterns in every new intense relationship we enter into. As we shall see, unresolved relationships with our original families are the most important unfinished business of our lives.

SKETCHES OF LEADING FIGURES

Bowenian Family Systems therapy is a theoretical-clinical model directly descended from psychoanalytic principles and practice. Murray Bowen, M.D., its originator and major contributor, has been a dominant force in the family therapy movement; since the early 1950s, his influence has continued to grow and his stature as a commanding figure in the field is now firmly established. His preeminent position is due not only to the fact that he was one of the parent figures in the field, but also to the innovative and comprehensive nature of his ideas.

Bowen was the oldest child in a large, cohesive family living in rural Tennessee. After medical school and internship, he served for five years in the military. There he saw widespread psychopathology, matched by equally widespread ignorance about how to deal with it, which inspired him to seek a career in psychiatry. Here, Bowen felt, he could chart a course through largely unknown territory.

Once in psychiatry Bowen turned his attention to the enigma of schizophrenia. Thoroughly trained in psychoanalysis, including undergoing thirteen years of personal analysis, Bowen, not surprisingly, sought to apply psychoanalytic concepts to schizophrenia. He began by expanding his focus from the schizophrenic patient to the mother-child dyad. The goal of this work was to further the understanding of "mother-child symbiosis." These studies began at the Menninger Clinic where Bowen trained and remained on staff until 1954. From Menninger he moved to the National Institutes of Mental Health (NIMH) where he became the first director of the Family Division. One of the major observations to come out of the "mother-child symbiosis" research was the observation of repetitive relationship patterns: alternating cycles of closeness and distance, exquisitely sensitive to shifts in emotional tension within either mother or child, or the relationship between them. Separation anxiety coupled with incorporation anxiety was believed to be the underlying dynamic. From these observations Bowen focused on the notion of "anxious attachment," a pathological form of attachment driven by anxiety and emotionality that subverted reason and self-control. Anxious attachment is the opposite of "functional attachment," which is a central aspect of *differentiation*.

When Bowen moved to NIMH he expanded the scope of his studies to include fathers, and began to work out the concept of *triangles* as the central building block of relationship systems. From NIMH Bowen moved to Georgetown University's Department of Psychiatry in 1959. His plan was to transfer the NIMH family research team to Georgetown in order to continue and expand their work. Unfortunately the chairman of psychiatry who recruited Bowen, George Raines, died in 1959, and the team never got the chance to join Bowen. During the NIMH days Bowen had begun two additional projects. One was the development of a model of family psychotherapy for use with a less disturbed population; the second was the application of his newly discovered concepts to the study of his own family. Now at Georgetown, but without his research team, he concentrated on theory building, personal family study, and teaching and supervision of psychiatric residents.

During the past thirty years at Georgetown Bowen has developed his comprehensive theory of family therapy, inspired an entire generation of students, and become an internationally renowned leader of the family therapy movement.

Among the most prominent and influential of Bowen's students are Philip Guerin and Thomas Fogarty. Both trained by Bowen, they joined together on the faculty of the Einstein Family Studies Section where Israel Zwerling and Andrew Ferber attempted to bring together a faculty representative of the diversity of thinking and practice in the field of family therapy. While at Einstein they trained Betty Carter, Monica McGoldrick (then Orfanidis), Ed Gordon, Eileen Pendagast, and Katherine Guerin, all of whom, along with Peggy Papp, joined Guerin and Fogarty in 1973 to form the Center for Family Learning in New Rochelle, New York. Under Guerin's leadership, the Center for Family Learning has become one of the major and very best centers of family therapy training and practice.

While working on her M.S.W. at Hunter College, Elizabeth (Betty) Carter was unable to find a field placement in group therapy and so settled for something new called "family therapy" at the Ackerman Clinic. There, with fellow student Olga Silverstein, she learned about technique from Nathan Ackerman, but not much about how families function. Then she read Murray Bowen and felt a whole new world of understanding open up. From that moment she became an avid student of Bowen's approach, attending as many workshops as she could find, and then studying with Phil Guerin and Marilyn Mendelsohn at Einstein.

In 1977 Carter left the Center for Family Learning to become the founding director of the Family Institute of Westchester. She was joined by Monica McGoldrick, Fredda Herz, Ken Terkelson, and others. An ardent and articulate feminist, she is also Codirector of the Women's Project in Family Therapy with Peggy Papp, Olga Silverstein, and Marianne Walters. Today, in addition to being a respected leader in the field of family therapy and a very popular teacher, Betty Carter is an active clinician who specializes in marital therapy and therapy with remarried couples.

Monica McGoldrick is another therapist in the Bowenian tradition who, like her friend and colleague Betty Carter, has become one of the most respected voices in the field. McGoldrick cofounded the Family Institute of Westchester and is also Director of Family Training for the Department of Psychiatry, UMDNJ-Robert Wood Johnson Medical School. She is a popular teacher and writer, and a leader in the field of family therapy. Among her clinical special interests are ethnicity, genograms, family therapy with one person, remarried families, and dual-career families.

Many of Bowen's students continued to work with him for a long time, among them Michael Kerr, Edward Beal, Edwin Friedman, Jack Bradt, Joseph Lorio, Charles Paddock, and Daniel Papero. Each is an important representative of the extended family systems tradition, and all have helped transmit Bowen's ideas in their teaching and through papers presented at the annual Georgetown Family Symposium.

Edwin Friedman, who works in the Washington, D.C. area, is both a rabbi and a family therapist. Trained by Murray Bowen, he brings an extended family systems perspective to bear on religious life. One of his most important contributions has been introducing a sophisticated understanding and competence in family systems theory to ancillary professionals, especially pastoral counselors. Friedman transmits his version of the Bowenian tradition in his excellent writings and his very humorous speeches.

Michael Kerr, M.D., has been a long-time student and colleague of Bowen's, and since 1977 the director of training at the Georgetown University Family Center. Kerr is probably the most scholarly, informed, and faithful to the original theory of all Bowen's students, as his masterful account of Bowen theory in the book *Family Evaluation* (Kerr and Bowen, 1988) richly demonstrates.

Finally, we should mention James Framo, for many years one of the leading figures in family therapy. Although Framo is often thought of either as an independent practitioner or as a colleague of Ivan Boszormenyi-Nagy, he incorporates many of Murray Bowen's ideas in his own work. Framo is perhaps most well-known for his steadfast advocacy of couples groups.

Several key publications over the years are markers in the development of Bowenian family systems theory. Bowen's first major paper outlining the concepts of his new theory was "The Use of Family Theory in Clinical Practice," published in 1966. A year later at a Philadelphia conference organized by James Framo, Bowen delivered his first organized presentation of the application of his theory to his own personal family system (Anonymous, 1972). In 1976 Guerin edited a classic anthology of original papers, one of the most valuable books in the family therapy literature (Guerin, *Family Therapy: Theory and Practice*). In 1978 Bowen assembled all of his own papers from various professional journals and published them in *Family Therapy in Clinical Practice*. In 1987 Guerin and his colleagues at The Center for Family Learning's "marital project," Judith Kautto, Susan Burden, and Leo Fay, published *The Evaluation and Treatment of Marital Conflict*, one of the best and most useful books ever written in family therapy. In the following year Carter and McGoldrick (1988) published a revised edition of their acclaimed book on the family life cycle. Finally, the publication of *Family Evaluation* by Michael Kerr and Murray Bowen in 1988 represents the mature and comprehensive flowering of Bowen's theoretical ideas.

Murray Bowen died after a long illness in October, 1990, just as this book was going to press. The day before he died, he delivered an address to the annual AAMFT meeting in Washington, D.C. It was a fitting end to a long and productive life. He was and then he wasn't. And now family therapy has lost a giant.

THEORETICAL FORMULATIONS

Most of the early family therapists were pragmatists, more concerned with action than insight, and more interested in technique than theory. Murray Bowen was the exception to this rule. Bowen, among the most cerebral of all family therapists, has always been more committed to family as an orientation rather than a method, and more interested in theory than in technique. From his point of view most mental health professionals are too caught up in narrow questions of technique to ever fully grasp what systems theory is all about. Bowen's own theory is among the most carefully worked out and influential of family systems.

Although Bowenian theory has evolved and expanded, it has always centered around two counterbalancing life forces: those that bind personalities in family *togetherness*, and those that fight to break free toward *individuality*. Ideally these two forces are in balance. Unbalance in the direction of togetherness is called variously "fusion," "stuck-togetherness," and "undifferentiation" (Kerr and Bowen, 1988). *Differentiation*, the capacity for autonomous functioning, helps people avoid getting caught up in reactive polarities. Otherwise emotional reactivity results in polarized positions: *pursuer-distancer, overfunctioning-underfunctioning*, and so on. The concepts Bowen has used to express this central tension of the human condition have evolved from *mother-child symbiosis*, to *undifferentiated family ego mass*, to *fusion/differentiation*. However phrased, the central premise is that unresolved emotional attachment to one's family must be resolved, rather than passively accepted or reactively rejected, before one can differentiate a mature, healthy personality.

Bowen articulated the core concepts of his theory in two major papers: "The Use of Family Theory in Clinical Practice" (1966) and "Theory in the Practice of Psychotherapy" (1976). In the 1966 paper Bowen cited six interlocking concepts that make up his theory: *differentiation of self, triangles, nuclear family emotional process, family projection process, multigenerational transmission process,* and *sibling position.* He added two additional concepts in the 1970s (Bowen, 1976): *emotional cutoff* and *societal emotional process.*

Differentiation of Self

Differentiation of self, the cornerstone of Bowen's theory, is both an intrapsychic and interpersonal concept. Intrapsychic differentiation is the ability to separate feeling from thinking. Undifferentiated people hardly distinguish thoughts from feelings; their intellects are so flooded with feelings that they are almost incapable of objective thinking. Their lives are governed by an accretion of feelings from those around them, either blindly adhered to or angrily rejected. The differentiated person, on the other hand, is not a cold fish who only thinks and never feels. Instead, he or she is able to balance thinking and feeling: capable of strong emotion and spontaneity, but also capable of the restraint and objectivity that comes with the ability to resist the pull of emotional impulses.

Lack of differentiation between thinking and feeling occurs in concert with lack of differentiation between oneself and others. Because they are less able to think clearly, undifferentiated people react emotionally—positively or negatively—to the dictates of family members, or other authority figures. These people have little autonomous identity. Instead they tend to be fused with others. They find it difficult to separate themselves from others, particularly on important issues. Asked what they think, they say what they feel; asked what they believe, they echo what they've heard. They either conform or assume pseudo-independence through counter-conformity. In contrast, differentiated people are able to take definite stands on issues because they are able to think things through, decide what they believe, and then act on those beliefs. This enables them to be in intimate contact with others without being reflexively shaped by them.

Guerin defines differentiation as the process of partially freeing oneself from the emotional chaos of one's family. Getting free takes analyzing one's own role as an active participant in relationship systems, instead of blaming problems on everyone but oneself (Guerin, Fay, Burden, and Kautto, 1987). Guerin uses the concept of *adaptive level of functioning* to define and evaluate the ability to continue functioning in the face of stress. Adaptive level of functioning is the capacity to make the conscious effort to be objective and behave rationally in the face of pressures of emotionality.

Triangles

Triangles are the molecules of interpersonal systems. Three people are the smallest stable relationship in families, at work, or in social groups. Significant relationships made up of two persons are unstable and go through cycles of closeness and distance. When anxiety is high during a distancing cycle, a third person or thing is triangled in to the relationship. Two lovers may have a stable relationship as long as anxiety is low; however, should anxiety and tension arise, one of the lovers will feel so uncomfortable that he or she will tend to triangle in a third person or thing, by drinking, let us say, or consulting a psychotherapist, or confiding in a friend. In each of these cases, triangling cools off tension but freezes the conflict in place. The classic instance of triangling occurs when tension between a husband and wife is defused, though not resolved, by focusing on the children. Instead of fighting with each other, the parents devote their energy and attention to the kids. Unhappily, the greater the unresolved tension, the more likely this triangulation will lead to an overly intense attachment between one of the parents and the children; and this tends to produce symptoms in the most vulnerable child.

Emotional triangles are not limited to three separate persons, but may involve any three-sided system. Thus a common family triangle consists of father at point A, relatively distant from mother at point B, who in turn is relatively close to several children, all clustered at point C. Similarly, in work settings there is often a conflicted relationship between the two most powerful authority figures, who remain relatively distant from each other at points A and B. The rest of the work group will tend to form overlapping triangles, with most of them more closely allied with one of the major figures. Usually there's a good deal of talk and gossip about the "others," which tends to prevent genuine contact or resolution of problems between the major figures.

To understand triangles, it's helpful to remember that relationships aren't static. Any two people in a relationship go through cycles of closeness and distance; it's when they are distant that triangles are most likely to develop. Guerin points out that these cycles reflect not only good times and bad in relationships, but also people's needs for autonomy and connectedness (Guerin, Fay, Burden, and Kautto, 1987). He suggests that two basic mechanisms operate in the formation of marital triangles: In the first, the spouse experiencing the most discomfort moves away from the other and connects with someone else as a way of calming down and gaining an ally. Thus a wife upset with her husband's distance may increase her preoccupation with one or more of the children. In the second process, a third person (perhaps a friend or a child), who is sensitized either to one spouse's anxiety or the conflict between them, moves in to offer reassurance or calm things down. "For example, an older daughter may attempt to reduce intense marital conflict by talking individually to each parent or to the parent with whom she has the most influence. Meanwhile, her younger brother may absorb the tension of his parents or handle it by acting in an antisocial way. The acting-out behavior also serves the function of pulling the parents together to try to solve the common problem of the son's acting out" (Guerin, Fay, Burden, and Kautto, 1987, p. 62).

Nuclear Family Emotional Process

This concept deals with the emotional forces in families that operate over the years in recurrent patterns. Bowen originally used the term "undifferentiated family ego mass" to describe emotional oneness or fusion in families. Lack of differentiation in the family of origin leads to an emotional cutoff from parents, which in turn leads to fusion in marriage. The less the differentiation of self prior to marriage, the greater the fusion between spouses. Since this new fusion is unstable, it tends to produce one or more of the following: (1) reactive emotional distance between the spouses; (2) physical or emotional dysfunction in one spouse; (3) overt marital conflict; or (4) projection of the problem onto one or more children. The intensity of these problems is related to the degree of undifferentiation, extent of emotional cutoff from families of origin, and level of stress in the system.

Family Projection Process

This is the process by which parents transmit their immaturity and lack of differentiation to their children. Emotional fusion between spouses creates tension which leads to marital conflict, emotional distance, or reciprocal over- and under-functioning. A common case is one in which the husband, who is cut off from his family of origin, relates only in a very cool and distant way to his wife. This predisposes her to a relatively intense focus on the kids. Kept at arm's length by her husband, she devotes her emotional energy to the children, usually with the greatest intensity toward one particular child. This child may be the oldest son or daughter, the youngest son or daughter, or perhaps one who looks like one of the parents. Projection is different from caring concern; it's anxious, enmeshed concern.

The child who is the object of the projection process becomes the one most attached to the parents (positively or negatively) and the one with the least differentiation of self. Since it relieves his own anxiety, the husband supports the wife's overinvolvement with the children. He may do so directly, or indirectly by virtue of his own lack of involvement.

The emotional fusion between mother and child may take the form of a warm, dependent bond, or an angry, conflictual struggle. As the mother focuses her anxiety on the child, the child's functioning is stunted. This underdevelopment enables the mother to overcontrol the child, distracting her from her own anxieties but crippling the child emotionally. Thus infantilized, the child eventually develops symptoms of psychological impairment, necessitating further parental concern and solidifying the family pattern.

Multigenerational Transmission Process

This concept describes the transmission of the family emotional process through multiple generations. In every generation the child most involved in the family's fusion moves toward a lower level of differentiation of self, while the least involved child moves toward a higher level of differentiation.

We like to think that after we leave home we will marry someone who will make us happy. We expect to keep the good stuff from our families and get rid of the bad. It doesn't work that way. We may fight against our inheritance, but it catches up with us.

Bowen's multigenerational transmission concept takes emotional illness not only beyond the individual to the family, but also beyond the nuclear family to several generations. The problem in the identified patient is a product of the relationship of that person's parents, which is a product of the relationship of their parents, continuing back for several generations. The problem doesn't reside in the child and it's not the child's fault; nor are the parents to blame. Instead the problem is the result of a multigenerational sequence in which all family members are actors and reactors.

Sibling Position

This concept is similar to Toman's (1969) ten personality profiles of children who grow up in different sibling positions. Bowen concurs that children develop certain fixed personality characteristics based on the sibling position in their families. So many variables are involved that prediction is complex, but knowledge of general characteristics plus specific knowledge of a particular family is helpful in predicting what part a child will play in the family emotional process, and in predicting family patterns in the next generation.

Emotional Cutoff

Emotional cutoff describes the way people manage undifferentiation (and emotional intensity associated with it) between the generations. The greater the emotional fusion between generations, the greater the likelihood of cutoff. Some people seek distance by moving far away from their parents; others do so emotionally by, for example, avoiding personal subjects of conversation or always insulating themselves with the presence of third parties.

Here's how Mike Nichols (1986, p. 190) described how some people mistake emotional cutoff for emotional maturity: "We take it as a sign of growth to separate from our parents, and we measure our maturity by independence of family ties. Yet many of us still respond to our families as though they were radioactive and capable of inflicting great pain. Only one thing robs Superman® of his extraordinary power: kryptonite, a piece of his home planet. A surprising number of adult men and women are similarly rendered helpless by even a brief visit to or from their parents."

Societal Emotional Process

This is a concept Kerr and Bowen discuss in their 1988 book, *Family Evaluation*. But they don't discuss it much. The term refers to the fact that the emotional process in society influences the emotional process in families—like a background influence affecting all families. The concept of social emotional process describes how a prolonged increase in social anxiety can result in a gradual lowering of the functional level of differentiation in society. Kerr and Bowen cite the example of the high crime rate that results in communities with great social pressure. Bowen acknowledges that sexism and class and ethnic prejudice are examples of unhappy social emotional process, but he tends to downplay the importance of these concerns for family evaluation and therapy. Feminists don't agree; they believe passionately that sexism is a societal emotional process that infects families—and one that should be fought, and fought hard.

Fogarty (1976a) has described individuals as having four dimensions, and relating to others in three channels. The four dimensions of self are: depth, movement toward objects, movement toward persons, and time. The depth dimension includes much that we generally think of as intrapsychic, including thoughts, feelings, dreams, and aspirations. In addition to these attributes of personality, people vary according to the nature and degree of their proclivity for involvement with things—such as possessions, work, or games—as opposed to other people. Finally, Fogarty says, people vary in being fast or slow to think, act, and feel, and in being committed to the status quo or to change. This is the time dimension.

Fogarty's four-dimensional people are linked to one another by three systems: the thinking system, the emotional system, and the operating system. The thinking system of facts, judgements, and opinions functions in proportion to knowledge and information; it dysfunctions in proportion to which fact is confused with feeling. The emotional system provides color and vitality to relationships. Neither good nor bad, right nor wrong, the emotional system either works effectively or it does not. The third system by which people are connected is the operating system. This defines the ways in which people communicate their thoughts and feelings. Silence, withdrawal, talking, or yelling may all be used to convey essentially the same thought or feeling.

To the theoretical concerns of Bowenian therapists, Monica Mc-Goldrick and Betty Carter have added gender and ethnicity. Their point is that to open closed systems it isn't possible to ignore gender inequalities without ignoring some of the primary forces that keep men and women trapped in inflexible roles. Moreover, they might point out that the previous sentence itself is naive in implying that men and women alike are victims of gender bias. Women are victims of limiting social conditions *and* victims of the men who perpetuate them.

McGoldrick has also been a leader in calling attention to ethnic differences in families. Her book *Ethnicity and Family Therapy* (McGoldrick, Pearce, and Giordano, 1982) was a landmark in family therapy's developing sensitivity to this issue. Without understanding how cultural norms and values differ from one ethnic group to the next, the danger is of therapists imposing their own ways of looking at things on families whose perspectives are not "dysfunctional" but legitimately different. Some readers might be concerned that lengthy descriptions of how families of various ethnic groups differ (e.g., McGoldrick, Preto, Hines, and Lee, 1990: "Trying to talk the Irish out of their sense of guilt and need to suffer is a futile effort") fosters ethnic stereotyping. McGoldrick believes that it's important to sensitize family therapists to ethnic diversity, and that the most important thing is not to learn what characterizes one group or another, but rather to be open to differences.

NORMAL FAMILY DEVELOPMENT

In Bowen's system there is no discontinuity between normal and abnormal family development. When he began studying normal families in the late 1950s, he discovered many of the same mechanisms he had previously observed in schizophrenic families. This convinced him that there are no discrete categories of families (schizophrenic, neurotic, or normal), but that all families vary along a continuum from emotional fusion to differentiation. The fact that most of Bowen's clinical contact in recent years has been with families of professionals probably reinforces his belief that families are more alike than different.

Optimal family development is thought to take place when family members are relatively differentiated, when anxiety is low, and when the parents are in good emotional contact with their own families of origin. Most people leave home right in the midst of transforming relationships with their parents from an adolescent to an adult basis. Thus the transformation is not complete, and most of us, even as adults, continue to react with adolescent sensitivity to our parents—and anyone else who pushes the same buttons. Normally, but not optimally, people reduce contact with their parents and siblings to avoid the anxiety and conflict of dealing with them. Once out of contact with their families, people assume they've put the old difficulties behind them. However, they carry around unfinished business in the form of unresolved sensitivities that flare up in intense relationships wherever they go. Having learned to ignore their own role in family conflicts, they are unable to prevent recurrences in new relationships. Therefore people with greater differentiation who remain in contact with previous generations are more stable than people from enmeshed or splintered families. Although problems may not surface immediately in cut-off families, they will eventually occur in future generations.

Another heritage from the past is that the emotional attachment between spouses is identical to the one each had in the family of origin. People who were relatively undifferentiated in their original families will continue to be undifferentiated when they form a new family. Those who handled anxiety by distance and withdrawal will do the same in their marriages. Therefore Bowen is convinced that differentiation of autonomous personalities accomplished primarily in the family of origin is both a description of normal development and a prescription for therapeutic improvement. This inescapable link to the past, stressed more strongly in Bowen's approach than in any other, is the prevailing feature of functional family development.

In "Systems Concepts and the Dimensions of Self," Fogarty (1976a) elaborates the characteristics of well-adjusted families: (1) They are balanced and can adapt to change; (2) Emotional problems are seen as existing in the whole group, with components in each person; (3) They are connected across generations to all family members; (4) They use a minimum of fusion and a minimum of distance to solve problems; (5) Each dyad can deal with problems between them; (6) Differences are tolerated, even encouraged; (7) Each person can deal on thinking and emotional levels with the others; (8) They are aware of what each person gets from within and from others; (9) Each person is allowed his or her own emptiness; (10) Preservation of a positive emotional climate takes precedence over doing what is "right" or what is popular; (11) Each member thinks it's a pretty good family to live in; and (12) Members of the family use each other as sources of feedback and learning, not as emotional crutches.

In Bowen's system the hallmark of the well-adjusted person is rational objectivity and individuality. A differentiated person is able to separate thinking from feeling, and remain independent of, though not out of contact with, the nuclear and extended family. The degree of differentiation of self depends largely on the course of one's family history, which is a relatively deterministic position. However, as we shall see, it is possible to achieve higher levels of differentiation through the process of family treatment.

Betty Carter and Monica McGoldrick have done more than anyone else in family therapy to study and disseminate information about normal family development (Carter and McGoldrick, 1980). They are also in the vanguard of those calling for sensitivity to and corrective action for the inequality between men and women in American families (Carter and McGoldrick, 1988). Like others in the Bowenian tradition, Carter and McGoldrick stress that to understand the family it is necessary to understand what's going on in at least three generations. This is the operative emotional field at any one time.

Following up on the work of Rodgers (1960), Hill (1970), Solomon (1973), and Duvall (1977), Carter and McGoldrick have described the *family life cycle* as a process of expansion, contraction, and realignment of the relationship system to support the entry, exit, and development of family members in a functional way. Transitions from one stage of the family life cycle to the next require *second-order change*—change in the system itself—while problems within stages can usually be handled with *first-order change*—rearranging without restructuring the system.

In the *leaving home stage* the primary task for young adults is to separate from their families without cutting off or fleeing reactively to a substitute emotional refuge. This is a time to become an autonomous self before joining with another person to form a new family. In the *joining of families through marriage* stage the primary task is commitment to the new couple, but it is not simply a joining of two individuals; it is rather a changing of two entire systems and an overlapping to develop a third. While problems in this stage may seem to be primarily between the couple, they may also reflect a failure to separate from families of origin or an extreme cutoff that puts too much pressure on the twosome. *Families with young children* must adjust to make space for children, cooperate in the tasks of parenting, keep the marriage from being submerged in parenting, and realign relationships with the extended family. Both parents are challenged to fulfill the children's needs for nurture and control—and they are challenged to work together as a team. As anyone who's been through it knows, this is an extremely stressful stage, especially for young mothers, and it is the life cycle phase with the highest divorce rate.

The reward for those parents who survive the preceding stages is to have their children turn into adolescents. *Adolescence* is a time when children no longer want to be like Mommy and Daddy; they want to be themselves. They struggle to become autonomous individuals, and they struggle to open family boundaries. And they struggle however much it takes. Parents with lives of their own and a certain amount of flexibility welcome (or at least tolerate) the fresh (pun intended) air that blows through the family at this time. Those who insist on controlling their children as though they were still little ones, provoke painful escalations in the rebelliousness that is normal for this period. In the *launching children and moving on* stage, parents must let their children go, and they must take hold of their own lives. This may be a liberating time of fulfillment, but it is also notoriously the time of the *midlife crisis* (Nichols, 1986). Parents must not only deal with changes in their children's and their own lives, but also with changes in their relationship with their own parents who may need increasing support—or at any rate don't want to act like parents anymore. *Families in later life* must adjust to retirement, which not only means a sudden loss of vocation but also a sudden gain in proximity of the couple. With both husband and wife home all day, the house may suddenly seem a lot smaller. Later in life families must cope with declining health, illness, and then death, the great equalizer.

The one major variation in the life cycle, too common to still be considered a deviation, is *divorce*. With the divorce rate at 50 percent and the rate of redivorce at 61 percent (Glick, 1984), divorce now strikes the majority of American families. The major tasks of the divorcing couple are to end the marriage but maintain cooperation as parents. Some post-divorce families become single-parent families—consisting in the majority of cases of mothers and children, and in the vast majority of those cases facing terrible financial strain. The other alternative is remarriage and the formation of stepfamilies, in which, often, loneliness is swapped for conflict.

Carter and McGoldrick's work on the life cycle bridges Bowen's emphasis on multigenerational emotional processes and various ahistorical approaches to the family (e.g. structural and strategic) which emphasize the developmental stage of the moment. Guerin's clinical model emphasizes stress more than stages of development. Life cycle changes within individuals, dyadic relationships, and the family as a whole are seen as producing an increasing demand on both functioning and vulnerability. For purposes of clinical work Guerin suggests that developmental stress be viewed as "transition times." Transition times are defined as any addition, subtraction, or change in status of a family member. In this paradigm, a piling up of transition times is "cluster stress." Periods of cluster stress are by their nature times of increased vulnerability for individual family members and the family as a whole. It is during these times that symptom formation is most likely to occur.

DEVELOPMENT OF BEHAVIOR DISORDERS

In the Bowenian system, disorders of behavior in children, adolescents, and adults are viewed as an outgrowth of an increased level of anxiety and emotional arousal, which exceeds the family system's ability to bind or neutralize it. In this model the most vulnerable individual (in terms of isolation and lack of differentiation) is most likely to develop symptoms or be at the center of relationship conflict. The mechanism for this selectivity is the multigenerational transmission process. For example, a child of ten who presents with a conduct disorder manifested both at home and at school, is placed in the context of a three-generational genogram. From the theory it is assumed that the symptomatic child is the most triangled child in the family and, thereby, the one most emotionally caught up in the tension between the parents or affected most by the external tension in a particular parent. The multigenerational process behind this symptom complex is viewed as a byproduct of the parental level of differentiation from their families of origin, played out and exacerbated first within the marriage, then transmitted usually through the relationship between the parents (according to Bowen, usually the mother) and symptomatic child.

The clinical methodology tied to this formulation calls for: (1) lowering anxiety in the family, primarily by lowering the parents' anxiety; (2) increasing the parents' ability to monitor and manage their own anxiety within the nuclear family and thereby better able to handle their child's problematic behavior; and (3) fortifying the parents' level of emotional functioning by increasing their ability to operate with less anxiety in their families of origin. In this approach the child may or may not be seen. Calming down the parents and coaching them to deal more effectively with the problem is the primary approach taken by Bowen and his staff at the Georgetown Center.

In the modification of these methods taken by Guerin and Fogarty, more emphasis is put on establishing a relationship with the symptomatic child, and working with the dysfunctional struggle and reactive emotional process in the nuclear family triangles. Extended family work is put off unless it is directly and explicitly linked to symptom formation and maintenance. In other words, where Bowen generally went straight for the family of origin, second-generation Bowenians pay more attention to the nuclear family, and are likely to wait to institute work on the family of origin as a way to reinforce gains and to enhance individual and family functioning.

Behavior disorders in adults—such as repeated job loss, uncontrollable anger, and compulsions of substance, sex, or acquisition—are viewed in the context of either dysfunctional spouse- or adult-child triangles, and clinical interventions are planned accordingly.

According to Bowen, behavior disorders, mild or severe, result from *emotional fusion* transmitted from one generation to the next. Emotions flood the intellect, impairing rational functioning and competence. The greater the degree of fusion, the more life is programmed by primitive emotional forces, despite rationalizations to the contrary (Bowen, 1975). Furthermore the greater the fusion between emotions and intellect, the more one is fused to the emotional reactions of other people. Emotional fusion consists of tense interconnection and dependent attachment, overtly expressed or reactively rejected. Both the clinging, dependent person and the aloof, isolated one are equally caught up in emotional fusion; they merely manifest it in different ways. As long as they are emotionally stuck in the positions they occupied in their families of origin, their personal growth is stunted.

Emotional fusion is the reciprocal of differentiation. The fused person has few firmly held convictions and beliefs; he or she seeks acceptance and approval above any other goal, and makes decisions based primarily on feelings rather than rational thought. The undifferentiated person may have few or many opinions, but in either case the opinions are received, not thought out. Creating a good impression is all important, and the undifferentiated person is likely to be either dogmatic or compliant, but rarely able to calmly state his or her own beliefs without trying to inflate self or attack others.

Symptoms are a product of emotional reactivity, acute or chronic. They can be generated by an anxiety-driven togetherness pressure to conform, or by disruption of a fused relationship that has sustained someone's functioning (Kerr and Bowen, 1988). In undifferentiated people, symptoms can be relieved (though not necessarily resolved) by retreat to the safety of a dependent relationship, or by fleeing intimacy through distancing. The symptom patterns that develop from emotional fusion are: unhappy marriages, either combative or emotionally distant; dysfunction in one of the spouses (with reciprocal overfunctioning in the other); or projection of problems onto one or more children. The following clinical vignette illustrates how emotional fusion in the family of origin is transmitted.

After his father died, Mr. Klein and his older sister were reared by their mother. This woman was a relatively mature and thoughtful person, but following the death of her husband she increasingly devoted all her attention to her children. They were her chief preoccupation, and shaping their lives became the major project of her life. Throughout their childhood she insisted that they conform to her standards; she was persistent in correcting their manners, energetic in demanding high performance in school, and highly critical of anything they sought to do outside the home. She discouraged contact with neighbors and school friends, who were engaged in such "frivolous" pastimes as playing ball or going to school dances.

In late adolescence Mr. Klein began to realize the powerful control his mother exerted over him and his sister. The sister was never able to break free from her mother's influence, and remained single, living with her mother for the rest of her life. Mr. Klein, however, was determined to leave home and become independent. Since he had always been told what to think, where to go, and how to behave, it was difficult to move out and be on his own. However, he was strong-willed and energetic; finally, in his mid twenties, he left home and turned his back on his mother. He moved to a distant city, started working, and eventually married.

The woman he married, Liza, came from a large, closely knit, and affectionate family. She and her four sisters were very much attached to each other and remained best friends throughout their lives. Their relationship with their parents was warm and close; none of the sisters ever questioned this model of family structure.

After she graduated from high school, Liza announced to the family that she wanted to go to college. This was contrary to the family norm that daughters remain at home and prepare themselves to be wives and mothers. Hence a major battle ensued between Liza and her parents; they were struggling to hold on, and she was struggling to break free. Finally she left for college, but she was ever after estranged from her parents. They had forgiven, but not forgotten, her violation of the family tradition.

When Liza and Mr. Klein met, they were immediately drawn to one another. Both were lonely and cut off from their families. After a brief, passionate courtship, they married. The honeymoon didn't last long. Never having really differentiated himself from his domineering mother, Mr. Klein was exquisitely sensitive to any effort to direct him. He became furious at his wife's slightest attempt to change his habits or get him to accommodate to her way of doing things. After years of grating against his dictatorial mother, his patience for control had long since worn thin. Mrs. Klein, on the other hand, sought to re-establish in her new marriage the closeness she had in her family. But in order to be close, she and her husband had to do things together and share similar interests and routines. When she moved toward him, suggesting that they do something, he was angry and resentful, feeling his individuality impinged upon. After several months of conflict and argument, the two settled into a period of relative equilibrium. Mr. Klein put most of his energy into his work, where he felt free and autonomous, leaving his wife to adjust to the distance between them. A year later their first child, David, was born.

Both parents were delighted to have a baby, but what was for Mr. Klein a pleasant addition to the family was for Mrs. Klein the means to fulfill her desperate need to be close to someone. The baby meant everything to her. While he was an infant she was the perfect mother, loving him tenderly and caring for his every need. When he was hungry she fed him; when he was wet she changed him; and when he cried—whenever he cried—she held him. When Mr. Klein tried to become involved with his infant son, his wife hovered about making sure he didn't do anything "wrong" with her precious baby. Naturally this infuriated Mr. Klein, and after a few bitter arguments he gradually left David more and more in his wife's care.

As he learned to walk and talk, David got into mischief, as all little children do. He grabbed things that he wasn't supposed to, refused to stay in his playpen, and fussed whenever he didn't get his way. His crying was unbearable to his mother. She found herself unable to set limits or establish control on this precious baby whose love she needed so badly. When she put him in his crib for a nap, he cried. Although she desperately needed some time by herself, and little David also needed his nap, she was so unable to stand the crying that after five minutes she went and brought him downstairs. This was the beginning of a lifelong pattern.

David grew up with a distant father and a doting mother, thinking he was the center of the universe. Whatever he wanted, he expected to get; whenever he was frustrated, he threw a tantrum until he got what he wanted. Bad as things were at home, at least the family existed in a kind of equilibrium. Dad was cut off from his wife and son, but he had his work. Mother was cut off from her husband, but she had her baby. Although he was willful and disobedient, he gave her the affection she craved. David's difficulties began when he went off to school. Used to getting his own way, he found it impossible to share with other children, or to abide by the rules. His disobedience and tantrums did nothing to endear him to his schoolmates or teachers. The other children avoided him, and he grew up having few friends. With teachers he acted out his father's battle against any efforts to control him. When Mrs. Klein heard complaints about David's failure to conform to the school's demands, she sided with her son and saw these complaints as resulting from a failure to recognize David's specialness. ("These people just don't know how to deal with a creative child.") So she moved him from school to school. But everywhere the conflicts were the same.

David grew up with a terrible pattern of adjustment to school and friends, but retained his extremely close relationship with his mother. The crisis came with adolescence. Like his father before him, David tried to develop independent interests outside the home. However, he was far less capable of separating than his father had been, and his mother was equally incapable of letting him go. The result was the beginning of chronic conflicts between David and his mother. Even as they argued and fought, though, they remained centered on each other. David spent more time battling his mother than doing anything outside the family.

Although he eventually left home at twenty-five, David remained a severely limited person. He hadn't learned the knack of looking after himself, and so had to settle for a series of unrewarding and uninteresting jobs. Never having learned to compromise or adjust to other children, he found it extremely difficult to make friends. He spent the rest of his life as a lonely, isolated, and marginally adjusted person. Worst of all, he didn't even have the consolation of the warm relationship with his mother.

David's history illustrates the components of Bowen's theory of behavior disorder. Both of his parents grew up relatively undifferentiated in emotionally fused families. As dictated by their own emotional needs, Mr. and Mrs. Klein's parents held their children too close, too long. This fusion sharply limits independent thinking and acting. Smothered by parents, it's hard to do other than reflexively accept or oppose them.

As Betty Carter explains it (personal communication), problems break out when the "vertical" problems of anxiety and toxic family issues, that come down through the generations, intersect with the "horizontal" stresses that come at transition points in the family life cycle. Thus David's time of greatest vulnerability came when the unresolved fusion he inherited from his mother intersected with the stress of his adolescent urge for independence.

Except in unusual cases, even emotionally fused children reach a point where they try to break away. But breaking away in such instances tends to be accomplished by emotional cutoff rather than by mature resolution of family ties. In childhood we relate to our parents as children. We depend on them to take care of us, we uncritically accept many of their attitudes and beliefs, and we behave in ways that are generally effective in getting our way with them. This usually means some combination of being quiet and good, patiently waiting to be rewarded, and being upset and demanding. A good deal of this childish behavior just doesn't work in the adult world. However, most of us leave home before ever changing to an adult-to-adult pattern with our parents. We—and they—only begin to change before it's time to leave.

A meek, patient child may become a bit more assertive and demanding in adolescence. Predictably, parents react with disappointment and anger. But instead of weathering the storm and patiently persisting with an adult stance, most people get hurt and withdraw. This is the *emotional cutoff*. Instead of persisting long enough to transform the relationship to an adult basis, most people decide that the only way to deal with their parents is to move away. Unhappily, this only gives the illusion of independence.

The girl who didn't get past meek patience with her parents will probably adopt a similar stance outside the home. When it doesn't work, she may react with temper—which also won't work. Those who cut themselves off from their parents to minimize tension carry with them their childish ways, which break out to spoil intimacy.

According to Bowen, people tend to choose mates with equivalent levels of undifferentiation. They may be manifest in quite different ways—perhaps extreme dependence in one, with extreme independence in the other—but, underneath, the level of immaturity is the same. Observations of sharp increases in problems after nuclear families cut off from extended families (Kerr, 1971) tend to corroborate Bowen's view. When inevitable conflict develops, each spouse will be aware of the contribution of emotional immaturity—in the other one. Each will be prepared for change—in the other one. He will discover that her treating him like a father entails not only clinging dependence, but also emotional tirades and temper tantrums. She will discover that he withdraws the closeness she found so attractive in courtship as soon as she makes any demands. He fled from his parents because he needs closeness but cannot handle it. Faced with conflict, he again withdraws. Sadly, what turned them on to each other carries the switch that turns them off.

What follows is marital conflict, dysfunction in one of the spouses, debilitating overconcern with one of the children, or various combinations of all three. When families come for help, they may present with any one of these problems. Whatever the presenting problem, the dynamics are similar; undifferentiation in families of origin is transferred to marital problems, which are in turn projected onto a symptomatic spouse or child. Thus the problems of the past are visited on the future.

GOALS OF THERAPY

Most people can accept that unresolved family problems, passed down through the generations, continue to plague us here in the present. But most people also get hopelessly confused trying to ferret out the basic pattern of those problems. They take elaborate genograms and discover that Great Uncle Fred was this and Great Grandmother Harriet did that. So?

Tracing the pattern of family problems means paying attention to two things: process and structure. These are also the keys to therapy from a Bowenian perspective. Process refers to patterns of emotional reactivity; structure refers to patterns of interlocking triangles.

The goal of Bowenian therapy is to decrease anxiety and increase differentiation of self—nothing else lasts. Genuine change in the family system requires reopening of closed family ties and detriangulation, which creates the conditions for individual autonomy and growth. Symptoms are de-emphasized in a treatment that resembles "in vivo" psychoanalysis. Problems are presumed to inhere in the system, not the person; and change in the self is sought through changing in relationship to others. In order to change the system, and enable family members to achieve higher levels of differentiation, modification must take place in the most important triangle in the family—the one that involves the marital couple. To accomplish this the therapist creates a new triangle, with him or herself and the two primary members of the family. If the therapist stays in contact with the spouses, while remaining emotionally neutral, then the spouses can begin the process of detriangulation and differentiation which will profoundly and permanently change the family system.

Defining specific goals for therapy seems to become progressively more vague as the unit of treatment gets larger. Changes sought in individuals need to be spelled out in rather specific detail (cf., Ford and Urban, 1963); goals for nuclear families are somewhat less specific. When Bowen describes goals for the extended family (as opposed to the individual goal of differentiation) it seems enough for him to speak of developing one-to-one relationships and avoiding triangles. The point is not that the goals of extended family work are naive or less well thought-out than those for individuals, but that they are relatively self-evident. Once the point is conceded that people are embedded in a larger social context, it seems obvious what needs to be done; open the system.

Guerin's sophisticated clinical approach has led to a more differentiated set of therapeutic goals. These goals are derived from highly articulated clinical models developed to deal with problems of children and adolescents, marital conflict, and dysfunctional adults. Guerin's goals are both general and specific. General goals are: (1) placing the presenting problem in the context of the multigenerational system by doing a thorough and accurate genogram; (2) connecting with key family members and working with them to calm their own anxiety and level of emotional arousal and, thereby, lower anxiety throughout the system; and (3) define the parameters of the central symptomatic triangle, as well as important interlocking triangles. More specific goals are determined by the presenting problem and which unit of the family (mother and child, nuclear family, marital couple, individual) is the primary clinical focus.

In working with marital conflict, Guerin and his colleagues (1987) evaluate the progress of their work by looking for specific areas of improvement. The areas evaluated correspond to the criteria used by Guerin to measure the severity of conflict. These criteria are divided into: family system criteria, which include emotional climate, cluster stress, and intensity of triangulation; marital dyad criteria, which include communication, "critical index," "credibility index," relationship time and closeness, pursuer-distancer synchrony, and tracking of the interactional sequence; and individual criteria, which include degree of projection versus self-focus, and neutralization of resentment and bitterness. In working with individuals, using a family systems format, the goals proposed by Guerin are management of anxiety and depression, with an increase in functional attachment and operational freedom throughout the multigenerational unit.

Monica McGoldrick, speaking from a committed feminist perspective, argues that it isn't enough to approach marital relationships with neutrality—to help couples negotiate compromises with each other in their own terms. As long as marital relationships are based on inherent imbalances, conscientious therapists must be aware of inequality and actively work to redress it. That means introducing the subject of gender inequality, even if it isn't an active part of a couple's agenda:

> Most men have trouble with intimacy. It's part of how they were socialized. We've got to admit it to ourselves, and help men change. We need to help them see the detrimental impact of the dominant value system that makes it difficult for them to relate effectively to their families. At the same time we need to help women to become effective in the areas where they are lacking: dealing with money, anger, and effective participation in the world of paid work and success (McGoldrick, 1990).

McGoldrick believes that economic inequality between men and women is a powerful and neglected context of marriage, making it harder for women to insist on change because it's harder for them to be financially self-sufficient. Money means options. McGoldrick therefore believes that it is important to encourage women to develop their earning power. In short, "gender-sensitive therapy" extends the goals of treatment beyond the expressed complaints of families to include the context within which these complaints develop. This means attending to the wider family context *and* to the inequalities of gender and class:

> If the wife is not in an economically viable position, marital therapy may be impossible. If she does not have the power to negotiate the relationship from a position of equality, the pretense of negotiation may be a farce. Beware of urging her to leave before having some awareness of the limitations and her options.
>
> HIS therapy may involve attention to his dreams, keeping a journal, learning to be intimate with his children or his friends.
>
> HER therapy may involve focusing on her resume, a Dale Carnegie course, or a consultation with a financial planner, and taking a vacation from family responsibilities (McGoldrick, 1990).

Betty Carter puts the case for gender sensitivity in therapists this way: "Marital therapy that ignores sexism is like rearranging the deck chairs on the Titanic."

CONDITIONS FOR BEHAVIOR CHANGE

Bowen believes that change occurs when anxiety is low, and that understanding, not behavior, is the critical vehicle for change. Most family therapists subscribe to the notion that emotional tension leads to processes that are reflected in the structure of family relationships, and that tension is maintained or resolved by the nature of those relationships. But there are clear differences between Bowen and other systems theorists as far as conceptions of what conditions are necessary for change. Strategic and structural therapists believe that behavior change, not understanding, is critical, and that such change is most likely to occur when anxiety is high and conflicts are allowed to surface. Bowen, on the other hand, believes that anxiety breeds emotional fusion, and that lasting change requires understanding and differentiation in a calm, unheated atmosphere.

Bowenian therapists lessen emotional reactivity by lowering anxiety. Therapists must learn to tolerate the inevitable emotionality in families, *without becoming reactive themselves*. "The learning depends on having the courage to engage emotionally intense situations repeatedly and to tolerate the anxiety and internal emotional reactivity associated with that engagement. This is anxiety associated with trying to become more of a self, an anxiety of progression rather than regression" (Kerr and Bowen, 1988, pp. 130–131). Therapists must avoid automatically accommodating or rebelling, dominating, submitting, or scapegoating. In other words, just as family members must learn to overcome emotionally driven automatic reactions—appeasing, controlling, or shifting focus—so must therapists.

Guerin suggests that if a family comes in during a crisis they should be encouraged to discuss it until their agitation is relieved. Guerin calls this "cooling down the affective overload" (Guerin and Pendagast, 1976). Beginners often make the mistake of trying too quickly to divert new families from their initial concerns to those with more theoretical interest to the therapist. If they do this with hostility or abruptly, they may cause families to drop out prematurely.

Bowen also differs from most systems therapists in believing that meaningful change does not require the presence of the entire family. Instead he believes that change is initiated by individuals or couples who are capable of affecting the rest of the family. His program of treatment can be described as proceeding from inside to out. Differentiation of self, which begins as a personal and individual process, is the vehicle for transforming relationships and the entire family system. For most family therapists treating individuals doesn't make much sense; after all, their fundamental premise is that individuals are products of their social context. Although he also believes this, Bowen's work is predicated on the idea that well-motivated individuals are more capable of change than are larger family groups. The therapeutic process is a cycle in which the individual differentiates a self, which transforms the family system, which in turn leads to further differentiation in the individual.

Therapy may not require the presence of the entire family, but it *does* require an awareness of the entire family. Looking at the nuclear family isn't enough. Bowen stresses the importance of a broad assessment, saying, for example, "A family therapist may treat two parents and their schizophrenic son, but not attach much importance to the fact that the parents are emotionally cut off from their families of origin. The parents' cut off from the past undermines their ability to stop focusing on their son's problems; once again, the therapy will be ineffective" (Kerr and Bowen, 1988, p. vii).

Part of the process of differentiating a self is to develop a personal relationship with everyone in the extended family. The power of these connections may seem mysterious at first—particularly for people who don't think of their strength or well-being as dependent on family ties. A little reflection reveals that increasing the number of important relationships will enable an individual to spread out his or her emotional energy. Instead of concentrating all emotional energy in one or two family relationships, it is defused into several. Freud had a similar notion on an intrapsychic level. In "The Project for a Scientific Psychology," Freud described his neurological model of the mind. The immature mind has few outlets ("cathexes") for channeling psychic energy and, hence, little flexibility or capacity to delay responding. The mature mind, on the other hand, has many channels of response, which permits greater flexibility. Bowen's notion of increasing the emotional family network is, like Freud's model, writ large.

Since we learn how to relate to the family during childhood, we learn to relate as children. Because most of us leave our families before we have established adult personalities, we continue to react childishly to our parents, brothers, and sisters. Furthermore, we react similarly in any new relationship that restimulates the unmodified sensitivities. Returning to the family—as adults—enables us to understand and modify old habits. This in turn frees us from acting out childish reactions in future relationships.

Bowen maintains that his treatment approach follows from his theory rather than from his personal style (Anonymous, 1972). Yes and no. Undoubtedly his highly reasoned and self-disciplined approach has its roots in the core of Bowen's personality. But be that as it may, his techniques of treatment do seem to follow from his theory more than other approaches in the field. The theory postulates fusion in grandparents transmitted to parents and projected onto children; the therapy prescribes differentiation, reversing this process in overlapping stages. Opening closed relationships and resolving triangles in the extended family results in greater differentiation, which then leads to a reduction in problems in the nuclear family. This emphasis on the extended family is one of the unique and defining features of Bowen's system.

Unresolved tensions in families are described as leading to a series of overlapping triangles (Andres, 1971). Conflict between two people is detoured to a third person who is triangled in. With additional tension, a fourth person may be brought in, leaving out the third. In a family with a great deal of tension and an equivalent tendency toward emotional cutoff, the available triangles will eventually be exhausted and the family will triangle in an outsider. The outsider may be a friend, minister, colleague, or psychotherapist. If a stranger comes into contact with two parts of the triangle (for instance, a mother and father), the stranger will either become triangulated or withdraw (Bowen, 1976). If the stranger is a family therapist, he or she can remain in contact with the twosome, but avoid becoming emotionally triangulated.

Therapy with couples is based on the premise that tension in the dyad will dissipate if they remain in contact with a third person (in a stable triangle)—if that person remains neutral and objective rather than emotionally entangled. This therapeutic triangle can reverse the insidious process of problem-maintaining triangulation. Furthermore, change in any one triangle will change the entire family system.

Family therapy with individuals is based on the premise that if one person in the family achieves a higher level of differentiation of self, this will enable (or cause) other members of the family to do the same. Bowen teaches individuals about triangles, and then coaches them to return to their families of origin where they work to detriangle themselves, develop greater objectivity, and thus achieve a permanent reduction in their emotional reactiveness. This in turn has a therapeutic impact on all systems of which these individuals are a part.

Some family therapists rely on insight to change behavior; others believe that behavior change can precede—even be independent of—insight. Bowen and Haley are representative examples of these different viewpoints.

TECHNIQUES

Bowenian therapists believe very strongly that understanding how family systems operate is far more important than this or that technique. In fact, Bowen speaks of "technique" with disdain, especially eclecticism uninformed by theory. While it is obviously true that, regardless of how involved with theory they are, every therapist must *do* something—that is, all therapists use techniques—Bowenians insist that it is important not to become preoccupied with specific techniques, not to look for the magic bullet.

If there *were* a magic bullet in Bowenian therapy—one essential technique—it would be asking questions. The questions are designed to help clients think about, rather than react to, their dilemmas, and discover how to modify their own role in troubled relationships. Bowen himself was a very laid-back therapist: all he did was ask questions. (Incidentally, Bowen's questions were always circular questions: questions designed to tease out patterns of relationship.)

Those who have followed Bowen ask questions, too, but also move in occasionally to challenge, confront, and explain. Betty Carter, for example, asks questions designed to help couples understand their situation, but then tries to intensify the process and speed it up a little by explaining what works or doesn't work and by assigning tasks. Most of the tasks she assigns are calculated to move people out of triangles. She might, for example, encourage a wife to visit her mother-in-law, or a husband to begin calling his own mother on the phone. Another favorite device of Carter's is to encourage people to write letters, addressing unresolved issues in the family. One way to prevent such letter writing from degenerating into telling people off is to have clients bring in the letters and then help them edit out the anger and emotional reactivity.

Guerin, perhaps more than any other Bowenian, has worked to develop clinical methodologies and models of intervention that feature specific techniques. His categorizing marital conflict into four stages of severity and detailed suggestions for treating each stage (Guerin, Fay, Burden, and Kautto, 1987) is the most elaborate demonstration of his well-worked-out technique.

Bowen advocates a variety of methods all aimed at the same goals. Whether treatment involves nuclear families, couples, individuals, or multiple family groups, the effort is directed at modifying the family system.

Family is the conceptual unit, though not necessarily the group to be included in treatment sessions. Guerin (Guerin and Pendagast, 1976) recommends accommodating to the family's view of deciding who to include in treatment. If they see the problem as a marital one, the husband and wife may wish to come in without the children. Where one of the children is described as the problem, parents and children should be included. A single family member can be seen individually, but the treatment will still affect the entire family.

Family Therapy with Couples

Whenever possible, Bowen prefers to work with both parents or spouses. When the therapist joins the couple, a therapeutic triangle is formed. If the therapist avoids being emotionally triangulated, the couple will be forced to deal with each other. The emotional tone of sessions should be lively enough to be meaningful, but cool enough to be objective. This is accomplished by asking more, and less, provocative questions, and by regulating the amount of interaction between the spouses. When things are calm, conflicting feelings can be dealt with more objectively, and the spouses can talk rationally with each other. But when feeling outruns thinking, it's best to ask questions which get the spouses to think more and feel less, and to talk to the therapist rather than to each other. Fogarty (1976b) stresses the need for the therapist to maintain control when there is open conflict; otherwise the couple's interaction will be destructive. If they simply fight in therapy the way they do at home—or worse—they will become convinced that change is impossible. One way to minimize conflict with a battling couple is to change the subject. If they attack each other, switch to a discussion about the kids or the extended family. If they still cannot talk calmly, control the fighting by having each talk directly to the therapist. Couples who have argued for years about the same subject are often amazed to discover that the first time they ever really hear the other's position is when they listen as the other talks to the therapist. It's so much easier to hear when you aren't busy planning your own response. If all else fails to cool things down, Fogarty (1976b) recommends seeing the spouses in separate sessions.

Contrary to popular belief, couples don't solve problems just by talking about them. Left to their own devices they tend to argue unproductively, project all responsibility onto the other one, and attack instead of negotiate. Change requires talk *and* willingness to listen, so that each can begin to change personally rather than endlessly demand change of the other. Because of the universal tendency to see only others' contributions to problems, special techniques are required to help family members see the process, not just the content, of interactions; to see their part in the process, instead of just blaming others; and finally to change.

Guerin (1971) recommends the "displacement story" as a device for helping family members achieve sufficient distance to see their own roles in the family system. The displacement story is about other families with similar problems. For example, a couple too busy attacking to listen to each other might be told: "It must be terribly frustrating not getting through to each other. Last year I saw a couple who just couldn't seem to stop arguing long enough to listen to each other. Only after I split them up and they blew off steam for several sessions individually with me did they seem to have any capacity to listen to what the other one was saying."

Guerin also uses films as displacement materials. If the proper aesthetic distance is maintained, people can become emotionally involved with a movie so that it has an impact but at the same time remain sufficiently removed to be objective. Underdistancing, in therapy sessions or in some highly provocative movies, results in an emotional experience devoid of reflection. Overdistancing, such as may occur in a lecture or uninteresting film, may lead to a lack of involvement and impact. Guerin selects films like *Kramer Versus Kramer, The War of the Roses, I Never Sang for My Father, Scenes from a Marriage,* and *Breaking Away* to use as displacement materials for teaching family dynamics to trainees and to families in therapy.

Therapists should always strive to remain detriangled. A major axiom of Bowen's theory is that emotional tension between two people results in their trying to draw a third person into the emotional issues between them (Bowen, 1975). Successful therapy requires that the therapist relate meaningfully to the couple without becoming entangled in the family system. Armed with a knowledge of triangles, the therapist endeavors to remain neutral and objective. This requires an optimal level of emotional distance, which Bowen says (1975) is the point where the therapist can see both the tragic and the comic aspects of the couple's interactions. Keeping detriangled requires a calm tone of voice and talking about facts more than feelings. This calm objectivity on the part of Bowenian therapists is expressed and enhanced by the use of process questions—questions aimed to get through emotional reactivity and make contact with family members' reasonableness.

As the spouses talk, the therapist concentrates on the process of their interaction, not on the details under discussion. Becoming overly concerned about the content of the discussion is a sign that the therapist is emotionally entangled in the couple's problems. It may be hard to avoid being drawn in by issues as controversial as money, sex, or discipline of children, but the therapist's job is not to settle disputes—it is to help the couple do so. The aim is to get husband and wife to express ideas, thoughts, and opinions to the therapist in the presence of the other spouse. Should one break down in tears, the therapist remains calm and inquires about the thoughts that touched off the tears. If the couple begins arguing, the therapist becomes more active, calmly questioning one, then the other, and focusing the issue on their individual thoughts.

Although strict neutrality is considered essential by Bowen, those of his followers with feminist convictions believe that it's important to address problems of sexual inequality, even if couples don't bring them up. Betty Carter, for example, introduces issues of gender inequality by asking questions about who does what in the family, and how much time does each parent spend with the kids. She asks each spouse how much money they make. And when the usual discrepancy emerges, she asks, "What role do you think this plays in the decision-making process?"

Descriptive labels are helpful devices for seeing the process underlying the content of family interactions. For example, Fogarty (1976b) has described the "pursuer-distancer" dynamic among couples. The more one pursues, and asks for more communication, time, and togetherness, the more the other distances—watches TV, works late, or goes off with the kids. Frequently, spouses alternate pursuing and distancing in different areas. Husbands commonly distance themselves emotionally, but pursue sexually. The trick, according to Fogarty, is, "Never pursue a distancer." Instead, help the pursuer explore his or her own inner emptiness. "What's in your life other than the other person?" It is also important that the therapist not pursue the distancer. When no one is chasing, the distancer will be able to move toward the family.

Bowen betrays a certain indecisiveness about the relative merits of thinking versus feeling, as well as togetherness versus individuality. Sometimes he states that thinking and feeling are equally valid (Bowen, 1976); but he also says that intellectual functioning is uniquely human and represents the apogee of human accomplishment (Bowen, 1975). A similar ambivalence is evident in his discussions of togetherness and individuality. He writes in one place (Bowen, 1975) that relationship systems maintain their equilibrium from two forces, togetherness and individuality, which implies that both are equally valid and worthwhile. On the other hand, he also extols the virtues of individuality and denigrates togetherness. Although his writing may overemphasize thinking and individuality, his therapy does not suffer from it. Just as emotive therapy is a useful antidote to the intellectualized ramblings that often characterize individual therapy (Nichols and Zax, 1977), so does Bowen's rational approach offer an effective counter to the emotional haranguing so common in couples therapy. It may be that, just as emotive treatment fosters greater rationality, Bowen's emphasis on reason and separateness creates the conditions necessary for couples to become more loving and affectionate at home.

To underscore the need for objectivity and emotional neutrality, Bowen speaks of the therapist as a "coach" or "consultant." He does not mean to imply coldness or indifference on the therapist's part, but rather to emphasize the calm rationality required to avoid triangulation. In traditional terms this is known as "managing transference and countertrans-ference reactions." And just as analysts are analyzed themselves so they can recognize their own countertransference, so Bowen considers differ-entiating a self in one's own family necessary to avoid being emotionally triangled by couples. Furthermore Guerin suggests that the best way to develop a genuine understanding of family concepts is to try them out in your own family (Guerin and Fogarty, 1972).

In order to help each spouse define a position as a differentiated self, it's useful for the therapist to establish an "I-position" (Guerin, 1971). The more the therapist defines an autonomous position in relation to the family, the easier it is for family members to define themselves to each other. Gradually family members learn to calmly state their own beliefs and con-victions, and to act on them without attacking others in the family, or becoming overly upset by their responses. When one partner begins dif-ferentiating, the other is discomfited and presses for a return to the status quo (Carter and Orfanidis, 1976). If this emotional counterreaction is weathered calmly, with neither one giving in to opposition or becoming hostile, then both partners move toward a higher level of differentiation. The process takes place in small steps, with spouses alternating between separateness and togetherness. Eventually, when each has a sufficiently well-articulated self, they can come together in mutual caring and respect, rather than in clinging dependency.

After sufficient harmony has been purchased with progress toward self-differentiation, Bowen teaches the couple how emotional systems op-erate, and encourage them to explore their own families of origin (Bowen, 1971). He prepares them for this by first making occasional references to their families of origin. Once they begin to recognize the relevance of their prior family experience to their current problems, transition to the focus on their families of origin will be smooth. Kerr (1971) suggests that when relationship problems in the nuclear family are being discussed, therapists should occasionally ask questions about similar patterns in the family of origin. If they can see that they are repeating earlier patterns, family mem-bers are more likely to recognize their own emotional reactivity. Recently, one of us (M.P.N.) saw a couple who were unable to decide what to do with their severely disturbed teenaged daughter. Although the daughter was seriously disturbed and virtually uncontrollable, her mother found it very difficult to consider hospitalization. When she was asked what her own mother would have done, without hesitating she replied that her long-suffering mother would have been too guilt-ridden ever to consider place-ment, no matter how much she and the rest of the family might suffer. Little more needed to be said.

More didactic teaching occurs in the transition from brief to long-term therapy. Knowledge of family systems theory enables family members to analyze their own problems, and gives them a framework in which they can continue to change. Such information is useful when tensions have abated, but trying to impart it can be risky during periods of conflict and anxiety. At such times battling family members are liable to distort any statements about how families function as support for one or the other opposing position. So primed are warring spouses to make the other "wrong" in order for them to be "right," that they "hear" much of what the therapist says as being for them or against them. But when they are calm, they abandon the idea that if one is right the other must be wrong, and they can profit from didactic sessions. As they learn about systems theory, both spouses are sent home for visits, to continue the process of differentiation in their extended families. During this phase of treatment— coaching—Bowen believes that infrequent sessions are not only possible, but desirable (1976). Meeting with the therapist only once a month or so forces families to become more responsible and resourceful. It also dissolves a great deal of dependency on the therapist.

Family Therapy with One Person

Bowen's personal success at differentiating himself from his family convinced him that a single, highly motivated person can be the fulcrum for changing an entire family system (Anonymous, 1972). Subsequently he made family therapy with one person a major part of his practice. He uses this method with one spouse when the other refuses to participate, or with single adults who live far from their parents or whose parents won't come for treatment. Aside from these cases, in which Bowen has made a virtue out of necessity, he uses this approach extensively with trainees and other mental health professionals. Extended family work with spouses is also the focus of couples treatment after the presenting anxiety and symptoms subside.

The goal of working with individuals is the same as working with larger units: differentiation. With individuals the focus is upon resolving neurotic emotional relationships in the extended family. This means developing person-to-person relationships, seeing family members as people rather than emotionally charged images, learning to observe one's self in triangles, and finally, detriangling one's self (Bowen, 1974).

The extent of unresolved emotional attachment to parents defines the level of undifferentiation. More intense levels of undifferentiation go hand in hand with more extreme efforts to achieve emotional distance, either through internal mechanisms or physical distance. A person may handle mild anxiety with parents by remaining silent or avoiding personal discussions; but when anxiety rises he or she might find it necessary to walk out of the room or even leave town. However, the person who runs away is as emotionally attached as the one who stays home and uses psychological defenses to control the attachment. The one who runs away needs closeness but can't handle it. In marriage and other intense relationships, when tension mounts the person will again withdraw.

Two sure signs of this emotional cutoff (Bowen, 1974) are denial of the importance of the family, and an exaggerated facade of independence. Cut-off people boast of their emancipation and infrequent communication with their parents. The opposite of emotional cutoff is an open relationship system, in which family members have genuine, but not confining emotional contact. Bowen's therapy is designed to increase the frequency and intimacy of emotional contact with the extended family. In fact, Bowen finds the results of extended family work superior to working directly on the nuclear family (Bowen, 1974). He believes that it is easier to observe emotional forces in the context of one's parental family, where one's needs are no longer as intimately imbedded (Anonymous, 1972). Perhaps the essentially cognitive and directive nature of his procedure lends itself better to coaching individuals than to working directly with nuclear family groups. Families have a culture and life of their own, and it's more effective to enter into families and influence them from within than to remain outside and attempt to direct them. Bowen's success with individuals, and he really focuses on individuals, whether he sees them alone or with their spouses, is, at least in part, a function of his intellectual approach.

Prerequisites to differentiating a self in the extended family are: (1) some knowledge of how family systems function; and (2) strong motivation to change. It's difficult to sustain the energy to work on the family in the absence of current distress, and many people often work only in spurts from one crisis to the next (Carter and Orfanidis, 1976). When things are calm they relax, and only when problems arise again do they continue their efforts to change.

The actual process of change is begun by learning about one's larger family—who made up the family, where they lived, what they did, and what they were like. Most people are surprisingly ignorant of their family's history. A basic working knowledge of family, as far back as grandparents, is an adequate beginning. A useful device for organizing this material is the *genogram.*

Genograms are schematic diagrams of families, listing family members and their relationships to one another. Included are ages, dates of marriage, deaths, and geographical locations. Men are represented by squares and women by circles, with their ages inside the figures. Horizontal lines indicate marriages with dates written on the line, and vertical lines connect parents and children. (For more detailed suggestions see McGoldrick and Gerson, 1985.) Let us say, in constructing a typical genogram, that I (M.P.N.) am forty-five (actually, I'm ninety-seven, but let's say forty-five), my wife is forty-seven, and we were married in 1968 (Figure 8.1).

FIGURE 8.1

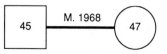

FIGURE 8.2

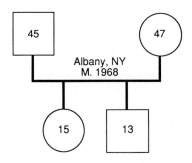

The next diagram shows that we have two children—a daughter aged fifteen and a son aged thirteen, and that we live in Albany, New York (Figure 8.2).

Next the genogram is expanded to include the extended family, beginning with my family of origin (see Figure 8.3). My father, aged seventy-six, and my mother, aged seventy-three, live in Washington, D.C.; my brother and his wife live in Ridgefield, Connecticut, and they have three children.

My wife's family of origin, shown by Figure 8.4 on page 394, consists of her parents, who live in Chicago, and her brother who lives in New Jersey. The double slash in the line joining her brother and his ex-wife indicates that they are divorced; she remarried in 1988 and is living in Philadelphia; he is living with his fiance who has a twenty-two-year-old daughter by a previous marriage.

FIGURE 8.3

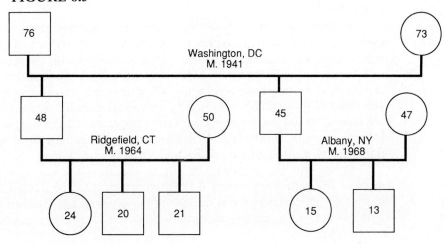

FIGURE 8.4

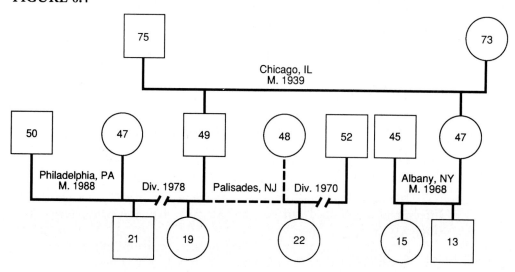

Dates of important events such as deaths, marriages, and divorces deserve careful study. These events send emotional shock waves throughout the family, which may open lines of communication and foster personal contact, or may close off channels; in the latter case issues may get buried and family members progressively more cut off. A divorce may bring the family together or divide it. In some cases, news of the divorce reminds the family that the people divorcing are separate individuals with emotional needs, rather than a self-sufficient unit. Furthermore, family members may discover that it's easier to be with the divorcing spouses one at a time, when they are freed from the chronic tension of being together. In other cases, families take sides after a divorce. One side is "right," the other is "wrong"; the divorce between two people becomes a divorce between two segments of the family.

Another significant piece of information on the genogram is the geographical location of various groups in the family system. Clusters of family groups in one location suggest strong family bonds. In more explosive families, the emotional cutoff is graphically illustrated by extreme distances separating family subunits. Of course it's possible to live in the same community and be separated by emotional distance. Also, many people choose to live where there are career opportunities, a reason that has little to do with family feeling. Nevertheless, the geographical spread of the family is a good clue of underlying emotional patterns.

Filling out the genogram is not an end in itself, nor is it a simple matter. The genogram is only a skeleton which must be fleshed out with important information about the family. In order to put meat on the skeleton's bones, it is necessary to know what to look for. Dates, relationships, and localities are the framework for exploring emotional boundaries, fusion, cutoffs, critical conflicts, amount of openness, and the number of current and potential relationships in the family.

Family members may know some of these things, but not all. For, as recent work by Nisbett and Wilson (1977) suggests, people's reports about their experience often reflect their personal theories of attribution (what's *supposed to be*) rather than accurate observation (what *is*). Sometimes a "good relationship" with parents turns out to be one in which fusion and tension are managed by distancing tactics, such as infrequent contact, superficial conversation, or gossiping about other family members. Therefore it's important to ask for descriptions of family relationships, rather than conclusions about them. Not "Do you have a good relationship with your parents?" but "Where do your parents live? How often do you see them, write, or call? What do you and your mother talk about when you're alone together? Do you ever go out to lunch, just you and your dad?" This more detailed kind of inquiry reveals the nature of personal relationships and the existing triangles in the system.

Other kinds of information that help to explain the family include cultural, ethnic, and religious affiliations; educational and economic levels; relationships with the community and social networks; and the nature of the work that family members do. Just as an individual cut off from his extended family is liable to be fused in his nuclear family, a family cut off from social and community ties is liable to be enmeshed in its own emotions, with limited outside resources for dissipating anxiety and distress.

The person who embarks on a quest of learning more about his or her family usually knows where to look. Most families have one or two members who know a great deal about the family—perhaps a maiden aunt, a patriarch, or a cousin who is very family-centered. Phone calls, letters, or, better yet, visits to these family archivists, will yield much information, some of which will produce startling surprises.

Gathering information about the family is also an excellent vehicle for the second step in the differentiation project, which is establishing person-to-person relationships with as many family members as possible. This means getting in touch with people and speaking personally with them, not about other people or impersonal topics. If this sounds easy, try it. Few of us can spend more than a few minutes talking personally with certain family members without getting a bit anxious. When this happens, we're tempted to withdraw physically or emotionally, or triangle in another person. Gradually extending the time of real personal conversation will improve the relationship and help differentiate a self.

There are profound benefits to be derived from developing person-to-person relationships with members of the extended family, but they have to be experienced to be understood. In the process of opening and deepening personal relationships you will learn about the emotional forces in the family. Some of the family triangles will immediately become apparent; others will emerge only after more careful examination. Usually we notice only the most obvious triangles because we're too emotionally engaged to be rational and astute observers. Few people can be objective about their parents. They are either comfortably fused or uncomfortably reactive. Making frequent short visits will help control emotional reactiveness so that you can become a better observer.

Many of our habitual emotional responses to the family impede our ability to understand and accept others; worse, they make it impossible for us to understand and control ourselves or the situation. It's perfectly natural to get angry and blame people when things go wrong. The differentiated person, however, is capable of stepping back, controlling emotional responsiveness, and reflecting on the best strategies for improving things. Bowen (1974) calls this "getting beyond blaming and anger," and says that, once learned in the family, this ability is useful for handling emotional snarls throughout life.

Ultimately, differentiating a self requires that you identify interpersonal triangles you participate in, and detriangle from them. The goal is to relate to the other people without gossiping or taking sides, and without counterattacking or defending yourself. Bowen suggests that the best time to do this is during a family crisis, but it can be begun at any time.

A common triangle is between one parent and a child. Suppose that every time you visit your folks your mother takes you aside and starts complaining about your father. Maybe it feels good to be confided in. If you're a mental health professional, maybe you'll have fantasies about rescuing your parents—or at least your mother. In fact, the triangling is destructive to all three relationships: you and Dad, Dad and Mom, and, yes, you and Mom. In triangles, one pair of poles will be close and two will be distant (Figure 8.5). Sympathizing with Mom alienates Dad. It also makes it less likely that she will do anything about working out her complaints with him.

Finally, although this triangle may give you the illusion of being close to your mother, it is at best an ersatz intimacy. Nor is defending your father a solution. That only moves you away from Mom towards Dad, and widens the gulf between them. As long as the triangulation continues, personal and open one-to-one relationships cannot develop.

FIGURE 8.5

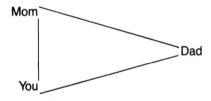

Once the triangle is recognized for what it is, you can make a plan of action so you stop participating in it. The basic idea is to do something, anything, to get the other two people to work out their own relationship. The simplest and most direct approach is to suggest that they do so. In the example just given, you can suggest that your mother discuss her concerns with your father, *and* you can refuse to listen to more of her complaints. Less direct, but more powerful, is to tell Dad that his wife has been complaining about him, and you don't know why she doesn't tell him about it. She'll be annoyed, but not forever. A more devious ploy is to overagree with Mom's complaints. When she says he's messy, you says he's a complete slob; when she says he's not very thoughtful, you say he's a monster. Pretty soon she'll begin to defend him. Maybe she'll decide to work out her complaints with him; or maybe she won't. But either way you will have removed yourself from the triangle.

Once you become aware of them, you'll find that triangles are ubiquitous. Some common examples include griping with colleagues about the boss; telling someone that your spouse doesn't understand you; undercutting your spouse with the kids; and watching television to avoid talking to your family. Breaking free of triangles may not be easy, but the rewards are great. Bowen believes that differentiating an autonomous self requires opening relationships in the extended family, and then ceasing to participate in triangles. The payoff comes not only from enriching these relationships, but also from enhancing your ability to relate to anyone—friends, fellow workers, patients, and your spouse and kids. Furthermore, if you can remain in emotional contact, but change the part you play in the family and maintain the change in spite of family pressure to change back, the family will have to change to accommodate to your change.

Some degree of rejection is expectable when one embarks on a direction for oneself that is not approved of by spouses, parents, colleagues, or others. The rejection, which is triggered by the threat to the relationship balance, is designed to restore the balance (Kerr and Bowen, 1988).

Some useful guidelines to resisting the family's attempts to get you to change back to unproductive, but familiar, patterns of the past have been enumerated by Carter and Orfanidis (1976), and by Guerin and Fogarty (1972). You can read about how to work on family tensions by resolving your own emotional sensitivities in two marvelous books by Harriet Lerner: *The Dance of Anger* (Lerner, 1985) and *The Dance of Intimacy* (Lerner, 1989).

Although differentiation in the family can be accomplished on your own, it is best to work with a coach who has successfully guided others through the process. A coach, trained in Bowen's theory, recognizes that the main work of differentiation must be accomplished outside therapy sessions in relationships with the family, rather than during sessions in relationship to the therapist. Therefore, the therapist recognizes the diminished importance of his or her relationship to the client and strives to minimize and discourage transference.

If you do attempt this work, an important rule of thumb is to keep your own counsel. A professional coach can give neutral and objective advice; family members and friends cannot. Keep in mind that the changes you make are for yourself. Arm yourself with a plan to handle the family's counterreactions. As you move in and out of the family system, distinguish between planned and reactive distance. Distance is useful when you want to think, but interpersonal problems are never resolved at a distance.

When a problem arises in the family, examine your own behavior. Problem behavior is an expression of a family process, and you have responsibility for part of that process. The only change anyone can really make is change of self. If you're confused about what you're doing to maintain the status quo, try simply reversing what you were doing. Instead of pleading with your mother to visit you, try ignoring her. Instead of yelling at the kids, back off and let your spouse do it. Such reversals often have an immediate and dramatic impact on the system. But to see any real results, you may have to persist in the face of the family system's resistance to change.

Re-entry into your family of origin is necessary to open the closed system. Sometimes all that's required is visiting. Other times, buried issues must be raised, activating dormant triangles by stirring up emotions in the system. If you can't move directly toward your father without his withdrawing, move toward other people to whom he is close, thus activating a triangle. If your father is tense about being alone with you, spend some time alone with your mother. This is likely to make him want to have equal time.

In re-entry, it's advisable to begin by opening closed relationships before trying to change conflictual ones. Don't start by trying to resolve the warfare between yourself and your mother. Begin by looking up a sibling or cousin with whom you've long been out of touch. In all contacts deal with personal issues, but avoid stalemated conflicts. If your contacts with some sections of the family are routine and regular, make them more irregular and unpredictable.

Those who continue working on their family relationships beyond the resolution of a crisis, or beyond the first flush of enthusiasm for a new academic interest, can achieve profound changes in themselves, in their family systems, and in their own clinical work. Extended family systems therapy is never finished. Coaching sessions may be spaced at more infrequent intervals, but even when these sessions are discontinued, it is usually with the understanding that the client will continue applying the principles in family, social, and work relations. If the client feels stuck or faces a new crisis, the process can always be renewed. Clients may request refresher appointments after a couple of years, and extended family systems therapists often consult each other if they have difficulty at home or at work.

EVALUATING AND VERIFYING THERAPY THEORY AND RESULTS

The status of extended family systems therapy and theory rests not upon empirical research but upon the elegance of Murray Bowen's theory, clinical reports of successful treatment, and the personal profit experienced by those who have worked at differentiating a self in their families of origin.

Bowen's original research with schizophrenic families was more clinical observation than controlled experimentation. In fact, Bowen is decidedly cool to empirical research (Bowen, 1976), preferring instead to refine and integrate theory and practice. For Bowen, there is a distinction between "science" and "methodology"; research directed toward "facts" is encouraged, but this isn't usually the same kind of empirical research favored in the social sciences. The little empirical work that has been done in the field is reported at the annual Georgetown Family Symposia. There, evaluations of various programs and occasional research reports have been presented. One of these, a study by Winer, was of sufficient interest to be published in *Family Process* (Winer, 1971). Winer reported on observations of four families in multiple family therapy led by Murray Bowen. Over the course of treatment, the experimenter tracked the ratio of self references to other references, and the number of differentiated-self references. Statements considered as differentiated-self references included: speaking for self without blaming, dealing with change or desired change in self rather than in others, distinguishing thoughts from feelings, and showing awareness and goal-directedness. There were two significant findings, both of which supported Bowen's position. First, in early sessions there were fewer self statements; the greatest number referred to "we" and "us," indicating that the spouses did not differentiate separate positions. Second, there was an evolution toward more differentiated "I" statements over the course of treatment. Initially these occurred less than half the time, but after a few sessions differentiated statements predominated.

Although it does support the effectiveness of Bowen's therapy in increasing differentiation, the Winer study did not test the premise that differentiation of self is synonymous with positive therapeutic outcome. In fact that is an article of faith with Bowen, and it points to a certain circularity in this theory: symptoms indicate emotional fusion, and fusion is demonstrated by the presence of symptoms (Bowen, 1966). These contentions may both be correct and useful, but they are circular.

Bowen repeatedly stresses the importance of theory in clinical practice (Bowen, 1976), and so invites judgement on the basis of his theory. Therefore, it should be noted that although his theory is thorough, consistent, and useful, it is largely a series of constructs based on clinical observation. The basic tenets are not supported by empirical research and, in fact, are probably not amenable to confirmation or disconfirmation in controlled experimentation. Bowen's theory, like psychoanalysis, is probably best judged not as true or false, but as useful or not useful. On balance, it seems eminently useful.

The theory is a blueprint for therapy, and the therapy is consistent with the theory. This is not as banal as its sounds, for Bowen's theory is more complex than most and his treatment is faithful to his theory, more so than the techniques of other family therapists to their theories.

Evidence for the effectiveness of extended family systems therapy rests largely on personal experience and clinical reports. Bowenian therapists apparently do at least as well as the standard figures; that is, one-third of the patients get worse or no better; one-third of the patients get somewhat better; and one-third get significantly better.

People who develop systems of therapy are influenced by their personal and emotional experiences, and Bowen is more aware and candid than most about this (Anonymous, 1972). His family was middle-class, symptom-free, and relatively enmeshed; and his techniques seem most relevant for this sort of family. Like Bowen, most of the other therapists considered in this chapter also work in private practice with primarily middle-class patients.

Phil Guerin and Tom Fogarty have made notable contributions, not only in keeping alive and teaching Bowenian theory, but also in refining techniques of therapy. Both are master therapists. Betty Carter and Monica McGoldrick have made more of a contribution in studying how families work: the normal family life cycle, ethnic diversity, and the pervasive role of gender inequality. Because they are students of the family as well as therapists, some of their interventions have a decidedly educational flavor. In working with stepfamilies, for example, Betty Carter takes the stance of an expert and teaches the stepparent not to try to assume an equal position with the biological parent. Stepparents have to earn moral authority; meanwhile what works best is supporting the role of the biological parent. Just as Bowen's approach is influenced by his personal experience, it seems that both Carter and McGoldrick infuse their work as family therapists with their own experience as career women and their own convictions about the price of inequality.

All these therapists are fine clinicians; and they and their students have the advantage of working with theories that are sufficiently specific to provide clear strategies for treatment. Particularly now when family therapy is so fashionable, most people who see families use an eclectic hodgepodge of unrelated concepts and techniques; they are not apt to have a clear theory or a consistent strategy. The unhappy result is that most family therapists are drawn into the families' emotional processes and absorbed in content issues. The treatment that results tends to be haphazard and ineffectual.

Second-generation family therapists, like Guerin and Fogarty, are well-grounded enough in a theoretical system (for them, Bowen's) that they are able to diverge from it and add to it without losing focus. However, third-generation family therapists (students of students) are often left with no clear theoretical underpinning, and their work suffers from it. Interestingly, students of the pioneer family therapists have not been particularly innovative. None of them has surpassed their teachers. These observations underscore the plight of graduate students who are exposed to a variety of approaches, all of which are presented with more criticism than sympathetic understanding. Consequently they are left with no one coherent approach. Probably the best way to become an effective clinician is to begin as a disciple of one particular school. Apprentice yourself to an expert—the best you can find—and immerse yourself in one system. After you have mastered that approach and practiced it for a few years, then you can begin to modify it, without altogether losing focus and direction.

SUMMARY

Bowen's conceptual focus is wider than most family therapists', but his actual unit of treatment is smaller. His concern is always with the multigenerational family system, even though he usually meets with individuals or couples. Since he first introduced the "three-generational hypothesis" of schizophrenia, he has been aware of how interlocking triangles connect one generation to the next—like threads interwoven in a total family fabric. Although Bowenian therapists are unique in sending patients home to repair their relationships with parents, the idea of intergenerational connections has been very influential in the field.

According to Bowen, the major problem in families is emotional fusion; the major goal is differentiation. Emotional fusion grows out of an instinctual need for others, but is an unhealthy exaggeration of this need. Some people manifest fusion directly as a need for togetherness, while others mask it with a pseudo-independent facade. The person with a differentiated self need not be isolated, but can stay in contact with others and maintain his or her own integrity. Similarly, the healthy family is one that remains in viable emotional contact from one generation to another.

In Bowenian theory the triangle is the universal unit of analysis—in principle and in practice. Like Freud, Bowen stresses the pivotal importance of early family relations. The relationship between the self and parents is described as a triangle and considered the most important in life. Bowen's understanding of triangles is one of his most important contributions and one of the central ideas in family therapy.

For Bowen, therapy is a logical extension of theory. Before you can make any significant inroads into family problems, you must have a thorough understanding of how family systems operate. The cure is to go backwards, to visit your own parents, grandparents, aunts, and uncles, and learn to get along with them.

Bowen's theory espouses a balance between togetherness and independence, but the practice has a distinctly intellectual and emotionally distanced character. As a family therapist, Bowen seems more scientific than humanistic, more theoretical than practical. He sees anxiety as a threat to psychic equilibrium, consequently his approach to treatment often seems dispassionate. Bowen moves away from the heat of family confrontations in order to contemplate the history of family relationships. Like moving from the playing field into the stands, patterns become more visible, but it may be more difficult to have an immediate impact.

Bowen's model defocuses on symptoms in favor of systems dynamics. The treatment discourages therapists from trying to "fix" relationships, and instead encourages clients to begin a lifelong effort at self-discovery. This is not, however, merely a matter of introspection, but of actually making contact with the family. Clients are equipped for these journeys of self-discovery with cognitive tools for understanding their own patterns of emotional attachment and disengagement.

Seven techniques are most prominent in the practice of Bowenian family systems therapy:

1. *Genogram.* From his earliest NIMH days, Bowen used what he termed a "family diagram" to collect and organize important data concerning the multigenerational family system. In a 1972 publication Guerin renamed the family diagram "the genogram," a name that stuck. The main function of the genogram is to organize data during the evaluation phase and to track relationship processes and key triangles over the course of therapy. The most comprehensive guide to working with genograms is Monica McGoldrick's and Randy Gerson's book, *Genograms in Family Assessment* (McGoldrick and Gerson, 1985).

2. *The Therapy Triangle.* This technique is based on the theoretical assumption that conflictual relationship processes within the family have activated key symptom-related triangles in an attempt to re-establish stability; and the family will automatically attempt to include the therapist in the triangling process. If they succeed, therapy will generally be stalemated. On the other hand, if the therapist can remain free of reactive emotional entanglements—in other words, stay detriangled—the family system and its members will calm down to the point where they can begin to work out solutions to their dilemmas.

In the treatment of couples, each spouse is asked in turn a series of process questions aimed at toning down anxiety and emotional arousal, and fostering objective observation and thought. Some effort is made to slow down the overfunctioner in the dyad, while engaging and making it safe for more distant underfunctioners to open up and get involved. This same technique can be used with child-centered families by having the therapist place himself or herself at the point of a potential triangle with the symptomatic child and each parent, as well as between the parents. (Notice how similar this is to structural family therapists' attempts to get enmeshed mothers to pull back, and disengaged fathers involved. See Chapter 10.)

3. *Relationship Experiments.* Relationship experiments are carried out around structural alterations in key triangles. The goal here is to help family members become aware of systems processes—and learn to recognize their own role in them. Perhaps the best illustration of such experiments are those developed by Fogarty for use with emotional pursuers and distancers. Pursuers are encouraged to restrain their pursuit, stop making demands, and decrease pressure for emotional connection—and to see what happens, in themselves and in the relationship. This exercise isn't designed to be a magic "cure" (as some people have hoped), but to help clarify the emotional processes involved. Distancers are encouraged to move toward the other person and to communicate personal thoughts and feelings—in other words to find an alternative to either avoiding or capitulating to the other's demands.

4. *Coaching.* Coaching allows therapists to work openly and directly to help patients work on their family problems. Coaching is the Bowenian alternative to a more personal and emotionally involved role common to most other forms of therapy. By acting as coach, the Bowenian therapist hopes to avoid taking over for patients or becoming embroiled in family triangles. Coaching does not mean telling people what to do. It means asking process questions designed to help clients figure out family emotional processes and their role in them. The goal is increased understanding, increased self-focus, and more functional attachments to key family members.

5. *The "I-Position."* Taking a personal stance—saying what you feel, instead of what others are "doing"—is one of the most direct ways to break cycles of emotional reactivity. It's the difference between saying "You're lazy" and "I wish you would help me more"; or between "You're always spoiling the children" and "I think we should be stricter with them." It's a big difference.

Bowenian therapists not only encourage clients to take I-positions, they also do so themselves. An example would be when after a family session the mother pulls the therapist aside and confides that her husband has terminal cancer, but she doesn't want him or the children to know. What to do? Take an I-position: Say to the mother: "I believe your husband and children have a right to know about this." What she does is, of course, still up to her.

Another assumption in Bowenian therapy is that confrontation increases anxiety and decreases the ability to think clearly and see options. Therefore, displacing the focus, making it less personal and less threatening, is an excellent way to increase objectivity. This forms the basis for two related techniques, multiple family therapy and displacement stories.

6. *Multiple Family Therapy.* In his version of multiple family therapy, Bowen works with couples, taking turns focusing on first one then another and minimizing interaction. The idea is that one couple may learn more about emotional process by observing others—others in whom they are not so invested as to have their vision clouded by feelings. James Framo uses a similar approach.

7. *Displacement Stories.* This is Guerin's technique, showing films and videotapes and telling stories, to teach family members about systems functioning in a way that minimizes their defensiveness.

Finally, although students of family therapy are likely to evaluate different approaches according to how much sense they make and how useful they promise to be, Bowen himself considers his most important contribution to be showing the way to make human behavior a science. Far more important than methods and techniques of family therapy, Murray Bowen has made profound contributions to our understanding of how we function as individuals, how we get along with our families, and how these are related.

REFERENCES

Andres, F.D. 1971. An introduction to family systems theory. In *Georgetown Family Symposium*, vol. 1. F. Andres and J. Lorio, eds. Washington, DC: Department of Psychiatry, Georgetown University Medical Center.

Anonymous. 1972. Differentiation of self in one's family. In *Family interaction*, J. Framo, ed. New York: Springer.

Bowen, M. 1966. The use of family theory in clinical practice. *Comprehensive Psychiatry.* 7:345–374.

Bowen, M. 1971. Family therapy and family group therapy. In *Comprehensive group psychotherapy*, H. Kaplan and B. Sadock, eds. Baltimore: Williams and Wilkins.

Bowen, M. 1972. Being and becoming a family therapist. In *The book of family therapy*, A. Ferber, M. Mendelsohn, and A. Napier, eds. New York: Science House.

Bowen, M. 1974. Toward the differentiation of self in one's family of origin. In *Georgetown Family Symposium*, vol. 1, F. Andres and J. Lorio, eds. Washington, DC: Department of Psychiatry, Georgetown University Medical Center.

Bowen, M. 1975. Family therapy after twenty years. In *American handbook of psychiatry*, vol. 5, S. Arieti, ed. New York: Basic Books.

Bowen, M. 1976. Theory in the practice of psychotherapy. In *Family therapy: Theory and practice*, P.J. Guerin, ed. New York: Gardner Press.

Carter, B., and McGoldrick, M. 1980. *The family life cycle*. New York: Gardner Press.

Carter, B., and McGoldrick, M. 1988. *The changing family life cycle: A framework for family therapy*. 2nd ed. Boston: Allyn & Bacon.

Carter, E., and Orfanidis, M.M. 1976. Family therapy with one person and the family therapist's own family. In *Family therapy: Theory and practice*, P.J. Guerin, ed. New York: Gardner Press.

Duvall, E.M. 1977. *Marriage and family development*. 5th ed. Philadelphia: Lippincott.

Fogarty, T.F. 1976a. Systems concepts and dimensions of self. In *Family therapy: Theory and practice*, P.J. Guerin, ed. New York: Gardner Press.

Fogarty, T.F. 1976b. Marital crisis. In *Family therapy: Theory and practice*, P.J. Guerin, ed. New York: Gardner Press.

Ford, D.H., and Urban, H.B. 1963. *Systems of psychotherapy*. New York: Wiley.

Glick, P. 1984. Marriage, divorce and living arrangements. *Journal of Family Issues*. 5 (1):7–26.

Guerin, P.J. 1971. A family affair. *Georgetown Family Symposium*. vol. 1, Washington, DC.

Guerin, P.J. 1972. We became family therapists. In *The book of family therapy*, A. Ferber, M. Mendelsohn, and A. Napier, eds. New York: Science House.

Guerin, P.J., ed. 1976. *Family therapy: Theory and practice*. New York: Gardner Press.

Guerin, P.G., Fay, L., Burden, S., and Kautto, J. 1987. *The evaluation and treatment of marital conflict: A four-stage approach*. New York: Basic Books.

Guerin, P.J., and Fogarty, T.F. 1972. Study your own family. In *The book of family therapy*, A. Ferber, M. Mendelsohn, and A. Napier, eds. New York: Science House.

Guerin, P.J., and Pendagast, E.G. 1976. Evaluation of family system and genogram. In *Family therapy: Theory and practice*, P.J. Guerin, ed. New York: Gardner Press.

Hill, R. 1970. *Family development in three generations*. Cambridge, MA: Schenkman.

Kerr, M. 1971. The importance of the extended family. *Georgetown Family Symposium*. vol. 1, Washington, DC.

Kerr, M., and Bowen, M. 1988. *Family evaluation*. New York: Norton.

Lerner, H.G. 1985. *The dance of anger: A woman's guide to changing patterns of intimate relationships*. New York: Harper & Row.

Lerner, H.G. 1989. *The dance of intimacy: A woman's guide to courageous acts of change in key relationships*. New York: Harper & Row.

McGoldrick, M., 1982. Through the looking glass: Supervision of a trainee's trigger family. In *Family therapy supervision*, J. Byng-Hall and R. Whiffen, eds. London: Academic Press.

McGoldrick, M. 1990. Gender presentation. Article in progress.

McGoldrick, M., and Gerson, R. 1985. *Genograms in family assessment.* New York: Norton.

McGoldrick, M., Pearce, J., and Giordano, J. 1982. *Ethnicity in family therapy.* New York: Guilford Press.

McGoldrick, M., Preto, N., Hines, P., and Lee, E. 1990. Ethnicity in family therapy. In *The handbook of family therapy.* A.E. Gurman and D.P. Kniskern, eds. 2nd ed. New York: Brunner/Mazel.

Nichols, M.P. 1986. *Turning forty in the eighties.* New York: Norton.

Nichols, M.P., and Zax, M. 1977. *Catharsis in psychotherapy.* New York: Gardner Press.

Nisbett, R.E., and Wilson, T.D. 1977. The halo effect: Evidence for unconscious alteration of judgments. *Journal of Personality and Social Psychology. 35*:250–256.

Papero, D. 1990. *Bowen family systems theory.* Boston: Allyn & Bacon.

Rodgers, R. 1960. Proposed modification of Duvall's family life cycle stages. Paper presented at the American Sociological Association Meeting, New York.

Solomon, M. 1973. A developmental conceptual premise for family therapy. *Family Process. 12*:179–188.

Toman, W. 1969. *Family constellation.* New York: Springer Publishing Company.

Winer, L.R. 1971. The qualified pronoun count as a measure of change in family psychotherapy. *Family Process. 10*:243–247.

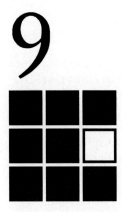

9

Strategic and Systemic (Milan) Family Therapies

The models of therapy that have been most directly influenced by Gregory Bateson's version of cybernetics (see Chapter 2) fall under the rubrics of strategic and systemic therapies. As a result of this common heritage, these models, while containing major differences, share elements which have strongly influenced the field of family therapy. These models also continue to thrive, although in the case of the systemic (Milan) model, in a form that is quite different from the original.

In this chapter we will look most closely at three models: (1) the Mental Research Institute (MRI) group, (2) the strategic approach of Jay Haley and Cloe Madanes, and (3) the Milan model. These models share a systemic (circular) view of problem-maintenance and a strategic (planned) orientation to change. They organize therapy around creative strategic interventions designed to bypass resistance, and to do so as quickly as possible. They focus on resolving problems and don't worry much about the intrapsychic processes of individual family members.

Haley (1973) coined the term "stategic therapy" when describing Milton Erickson's work. In many ways the strategic approaches of both the MRI group and Haley can be seen as different applications of Erickson's methods to work with families. To make this translation to family interaction, these theorists added cybernetics and, in Haley's later work, the structural framework.

SKETCHES OF LEADING FIGURES

The leading strategic family therapists include: Jay Haley and Cloe Madanes in Washington, DC; and members of the Mental Research Institute (MRI) in Palo Alto, including Paul Watzlawick, John Weakland, and Richard Fisch.

Haley's development is unique among family therapists in that he learned from and with the three people who had the most influence on the evolution of family therapy: Milton Erickson, Gregory Bateson, and Salvador Minuchin. The impact of each of these pioneers is apparent in Haley's model which, more than any other in this chapter, integrated divergent trends as family therapy developed. Haley's work with the Bateson project and subsequently with Don Jackson at the MRI has been described in Chapter 1. His influential book *Strategies of Psychotherapy* (Haley, 1963), summarizes his thinking at that time.

In 1967 Haley left MRI to join Minuchin and Braulio Montalvo at the Philadelphia Child Guidance Clinic. For approximately ten years he was director of family therapy research there, as well as a clinical member of the University of Pennsylvania's Department of Psychiatry. His association with Minuchin was productive for both men. Minuchin credits Haley for helping him articulate many of the principles elaborated in *Families and Family Therapy* (Minuchin, 1974), and Haley gives Minuchin credit for helping him understand the structure of families. In Haley's later work (Haley, 1976, 1980), he uses the structural view of family organization as the context within which to apply his strategic techniques. Haley's example may serve to help bridge the gap between competing approaches in the field.

In 1976 Haley left Philadelphia for Washington, DC, to join the faculty of the University of Maryland Medical School and to establish his own family therapy clinic with Cloe Madanes. Madanes, known as one of the most creative therapists in the field, started at the Philadelphia Child Guidance Clinic, where she worked with Haley, Minuchin, and Montalvo. In 1976 Haley and Madanes opened the Family Therapy Institute of Washington, DC, which is now one of the major training institutes in the country. In addition many therapists have been exposed to their ideas by attending one of the many workshops they do together across the country.

The Mental Research Institute (MRI) led the way in research and training in family therapy's first decade. MRI began in 1959 when its founding director, Don Jackson, who was a consultant to the Bateson project, assembled an energetic and creative staff interested in communication, therapy, families, and schizophrenia. Among them in the early 1960s were Jules

Riskin, Virginia Satir, Jay Haley, John Weakland, Paul Watzlawick, and Janet Beavin. Haley and Weakland brought to MRI both the exciting cybernetic ideas of Bateson and the revolutionary clinical ideas of Erickson, with whom they were visiting and studying periodically in Phoenix.

This group started one of the first formal training programs in family therapy, did much of the first family interaction research, and made some of the most important contributions to the family therapy literature during those early years, including Satir's (1964) *Conjoint Family Therapy*, Watzlawick, Beavin, and Jackson's (1967) *Pragmatics of Human Communication*, and Haley's (1963) *Strategies of Psychotherapy*.

Later MRI was also home to several other influential strategic writers, including: Carlos Sluzki, who was its director for several years and editor of *Family Process* through much of the 1980s, James Coyne, who used the model to understand and treat depression, and Steve de Shazer, who expanded on the original MRI model to create his solution-focused approach described in Chapter 11.

In 1967 the Brief Therapy Center of MRI opened under the directorship of Richard Fisch. The staff included John Weakland, Paul Watzlawick, and Arthur Bodin. Their mission was to develop the briefest possible treatment for psychiatric disorders. What emerged was a very active approach, focused on the presenting symptoms and limited to ten sessions. It is this approach that has come to be identified as the MRI model. This approach was described in Watzlawick, Weakland, and Fisch's (1974) book, *Change: Principles of Problem Formation and Problem Resolution*, which popularized strategic therapy, and later in a follow-up volume, *The Tactics of Change: Doing Therapy Briefly* (Fisch, Weakland, and Segal, 1982).

The MRI model and Haley's work had an impact on the Milan Associates, Mara Selvini Palazzoli, Luigi Boscolo, Gianfranco Cecchin, and Guiliana Pata, who developed the Milan model.

Selvini Palazzoli was a prominent Italian psychoanalyst, specializing in eating disorders, when, out of frustration with the results of her individual orientation (Selvini Palazzoli, 1981), she began exploring the writings of many of the theorists mentioned above and began to develop her own approach to families. In 1967 she led a group of eight psychiatrists who, originally, tried to apply psychoanalytic ideas to working with families. Later they discovered the ideas of Bateson, Haley, Watzlawick, and others, which in 1971 led the systemic faction of the group (Selvini Palazzoli, Boscolo, Cecchin, and Prata) to form the Center for the Study of the Family in Milan, where they developed the "Milan model."

In 1980 the Milan Associates underwent another split, with Boscolo and Cecchin moving in the direction of training and Selvini Palazzoli and Prata more interested in research. Each group formed separate centers with new staffs and their approaches also diverged; the men became increasingly less strategic and more interested in changing family belief systems through the questioning process, and the women pursued their interest in understanding and interrupting the games they believed severely disturbed families were caught up in.

In addition to these primary developers of the strategic and Milan models, there are other people who have contributed to both. Lynn Hoffman's evolution as a therapist parallels that of the strategic-systemic branch of family therapy. In the 1960s she collaborated with Haley and, in 1977, joined the Ackerman Institute in New York where she experimented with strategic approaches and later became a major proponent of the Milan model in the United States (Hoffman, 1981). Subsequently she left Ackerman for Amherst, Massachusetts and left the Milan model for her own approach based on constructivist principles (see Chapter 3).

The Ackerman Institute has been an incubator for both the strategic and Milan models. Prominent contributors from the Ackerman faculty include: Peggy Papp (1980, 1983), who has been a creative contributor to strategic work; Joel Bergman (1985), who developed many original strategies for dealing with difficult families; Peggy Penn (1982, 1985), who elaborated on the Milan innovation of circular questioning; and Olga Siverstein, who is known for her clinical artistry.

Karl Tomm (1984a, 1984b, 1987a, 1987b), a psychiatrist in Calgary, Canada, had been the most prominent interpreter and elaborator of the Milan model in North America, but recently, with the influence of Michael White's work (see Chapter 11), has been developing his own ideas about the impact of the therapist on families.

Finally Richard Rabkin (1977), a literate and eclectic social psychiatrist practicing in New York City, was influenced by and influenced all the developers of strategic therapy.

THEORETICAL FORMULATIONS

Strategic therapists are more interested in generating changes in behavior than changes in understanding; consequently they write mostly about technique rather than theory. The hallmark of the strategic approaches is designing novel strategies for solving problems. Like most clinicians', their theories are simpler and more pragmatic than those of scholars and academicians. Haley has often remarked that clinicians need simple maps to guide their action, while researchers can entertain complex ones because they have the luxury of not having to change things.

Because Milton Erickson's work had such a strong impact on the thinking of the strategic theorists, we will present first the aspects of Ericksonian theory that are replicated in strategic formulations. Erickson boldly broke with the prevailing psychiatric traditions of his time, which were based on elaborate theories for explaining and categorizing human behavior but provided little direction for how to change it. For example, unlike psychoanalysts who held that symptoms should not be focused upon because they were only the tip of the intrapsychic iceberg, Erickson was highly symptom- or problem-focused. He tried to learn details regarding the impact and context of a symptom in order to find leverage for changing it (Haley, 1981).

Rather than viewing a person's unconscious as being full of destructive or aggressive impulses, Erickson saw it as containing a great deal of wisdom that, if unfettered by the conscious mind, could solve problems or heal symptoms. Thus he found little value in traditional attempts to give patients insight through interpretation or through taking them on historical fishing expeditions. He assumed that patients already knew what to do; they just didn't have access to that wisdom. One way to get access was to break out of habitual patterns of behavior or thinking, so Erickson developed many ways of getting people to do something different in the context of the old behavior, or to do the old behavior in a new context.

In addition, at a time when therapy was considered a laborious, multi-year proposition, Erickson believed that people could change quickly, and tried to make therapy as brief as possible. He also took responsibility for changing his patients rather than assuming that patients had to take that responsibility for themselves. Thus, failures could not be explained away as being due to the patient's resistance, because Erickson saw his job as finding ways to bypass or use "resistance." Many of what have been called paradoxical techniques came out of Erickson's application of hypnotic principles to resistant patients (Haley, 1981).

Erickson initiated the revolution in understanding and treating people that strategic family therapy elaborated and made popular. He believed that people had the resources to change quickly once a therapist could get the process of change started. He eschewed interpretation and focused on changing action and context. Through Haley and Weakland's translations of Erickson's work, all of these assumptions became theoretical underpinnings of strategic family therapy.

These radical ideas about the nature of therapy and change were combined with the cybernetic concepts that Bateson introduced to the remarkable group of theorist-clinicians that were in Palo Alto during the late 1950s and 1960s. These included Haley and Weakland, as well as Don Jackson, Virginia Satir, Paul Watzlawick, Richard Fisch, and Arthur Bodin. All of these people contributed to the development of the strategic approach and, with the exception of Satir, remain identified with it. Other prominent contributors to strategic theory include Richard Rabkin, Lynn Hoffman, Carlos Sluzki, James Coyne, and Steve de Shazer.

From cybernetics, strategic theorists borrowed the concept of the *positive feedback loop*, and applied it to problematic family interaction (see Chapter 2 for more on cybernetics and family therapy). For the MRI group (particularly Watzlawick, Weakland, Fisch, and Bodin) that translated into a simple yet powerful principle of problem formation. They concluded that all families encounter many difficulties over the course of their lives, but whether or not a difficulty becomes a "problem" (that needs outside intervention), depends on how family members respond to it (Watzlawick, Weakland, and Fisch, 1974).

That is, family members may make commonsensical but misguided attempts to solve their difficulties and, upon finding that the problem persists or gets worse, often apply more-of-the-same attempted solutions. This, in turn, results in a corresponding escalation of the problem which provokes more of the same, and so on—in a vicious cycle. For example, Johnny feels threatened by the arrival of his baby sister and so he pouts and becomes temperamental. When Johnny acts this way, his father thinks he is regressing and tries to get him to act his age by punishing and criticizing him. Father's harshness confirms Johnny's belief that his sister is displacing him, so he regresses more often and more severely. Father, in turn, becomes more critical and punitive, and Johnny becomes increasingly sullen and alienated from the family. This is an escalating positive feedback loop: The family system is reacting to a deviation in the behavior of one of its members with feedback designed to dampen that deviation (*negative feedback*), but it actually has the effect of amplifying the deviation (*positive feedback*).

What is needed is to get father to reverse his attempted solution. If he could comfort rather than criticize Johnny and help him see that he wasn't being displaced, then Johnny would calm down. The system is governed, however, by unspoken rules which allow for only one interpretation of Johnny's behavior—as being disrespectful. For father to reverse his attempted solution, this rule would have to change.

Thus MRI theorists, Don Jackson in particular, also borrowed from cybernetics an interest in the *rules*—the underlying premises that govern the operation of systems. A thermostat, as an example of a cybernetic system, has settings (rules) that govern the range of deviation the system will tolerate before positive feedback in the form of heat or air conditioning is activated. In most families, there are unspoken rules governing all sorts of behavior, most of which serve them well. Where a rule promotes the kind of rigid attempted solutions described above, it isn't just the behavior (father's critical discipline), but the rule governing that behavior (father's interpretation of Johnny's behavior) that must change. When only the behaviors or interactions within a system change, this is *first-order change*, as opposed to *second-order change*, which occurs when the rules of the system that govern those interactions change (Watzlawick, Weakland, and Fisch, 1974). How does one change the rules? One way that the MRI group emphasized is the technique of *reframing* the problem—that is, changing father's interpretation of Johnny's behavior from disrespect to fear of displacement; from bad to sad.

Thus the MRI approach to problems is quite simple: first, identify the more-of-the-same, positive feedback loops that surround problems; second, find the rules or frames that maintain those interactions; and third, find a way to change those loops or rules. Their interest, then, is limited to problem-centered, short-term sequences of interaction; they do not look beyond these sequences at other potential problems in a family, unless the family identifies them as problems. With this minimalistic ethic, the MRI group, unlike Haley or the Milan team, doesn't speculate about the function that a family member's symptoms may be serving for the family or about problematic family boundaries or coalitions.

Haley, on the other hand, added to the Ericksonian and cybernetic influences a functionalist (see Chapter 2) emphasis, with his interest in the interpersonal payoff of behavior. Later he added many structural concepts picked up in the ten years he spent working with Minuchin and his colleagues in Philadelphia. Haley lengthened the duration of sequences he considered important in understanding problems from those immediately surrounding a problem, often involving only two people, to sequences involving at least three people and lasting longer periods of time (Breunlin and Schwartz, 1986). For example, Haley might notice that whenever Johnny and his father fight, mother protects Johnny by criticizing father for being so harsh. He might also see Johnny becoming more agitated when mother criticizes father, trying to get his parents' attention off their conflicts and onto him.

From this interest in larger and longer sequences, Haley also considers a different level of rules that govern them. He believes that the rules around the *hierarchy* in the family are crucial and finds a malfunctioning family hierarchy lurking behind most problems. Indeed, Haley (1976, p. 117) suggests that, "an individual is more disturbed in direct proportion to the number of malfunctioning hierarchies in which he is embedded." It may be obvious that Johnny's parents don't work together effectively to discipline and nurture Johnny, and so Johnny is embedded in one malfunctioning hierarchy, but it may also be the case that Johnny's grandparents undermine his father too. In this case, two generational boundaries would be violated.

Haley (1980) also identifies long-term sequences within families of troubled young adults. In these sequences, which might take place over months or years, the parents start to argue, which distresses the young adult to the point that he or she becomes symptomatic; the parents unite to try to deal with the strange symptoms and, perhaps, hospitalize the now-identified patient; the patient gets better in the hospital and begins to take steps toward autonomy; without being able to focus on the patient, the parents are distressed and begin to argue; so the patient's symptoms return; and so on and on. The rule governing this disabling sequence is that the parents' marriage cannot survive if they are left to face each other. Haley tries to change this rule by showing parents that if they work together they can control and help their troubled child. The good feeling produced by successfully improving the family hierarchy sets the stage for challenging their belief that they cannot face the differences between them.

Thus Haley's assessment of problems and his goals, generally, are structural: to improve the family's hierarchical and boundary problems that support dysfunctional sequences. It is his calculated approach and step-by-step tactics that are strategic.

Along these lines, the book *Problem-Solving Therapy* contains one of Haley's (1976) unique contributions: the idea that families cannot simply move from a dysfunctional structure directly to a functional one. Instead he believes that families must proceed through several stages, some of which may be dysfunctional, before reaching a healthy structure—much as a broken arm must remain in a cast for a period of time and then be exercised before it can heal. For example, Haley might suggest that before Johnny's parents feel good about each other and work together to deal with him, the family may have to go through a stage in which father and son get closer and exclude mother from their relationship; or the parents may need to go through a stage in which they work only on cooperating on discipline, putting aside their marital resentments, before reaching a stage in which they can address those issues.

With this therapy-in-stages perspective, Haley's approach could be called "plan-ahead therapy." He helped therapists consider the importance of developing game plans for the overall course of therapy, as well as anticipating a family's reaction to events in their lives, and in therapy. He also encouraged the planning of each session and developed a how-to model of a first session with families that consisted of several stages (Haley, 1976).

Finally Haley differed from his MRI colleagues, who tried to avoid imputing motives to the behavior they observed, because he viewed human interactions as interpersonal struggles for control and power. He kept a functionalist eye on family patterns, looking for the purpose that the problem behavior served for the individual or for the family. To counter the problem's payoff, he often borrowed Erickson's technique of prescribing an ordeal so that the price for keeping the problem came to outweigh that of giving it up. To illustrate this technique, consider Erickson's famous maneuver of prescribing that an insomniac set his alarm every night to wake up and wax his kitchen floor for several hours. Haley even tried to explain all therapy based on his theory for using ordeals (Haley, 1984).

Cloe Madanes (1981, 1984) also emphasized this function-of-the-system aspect of problems, particularly the *incongruous hierarchy* created when children use their symptoms to try to change their parents. For example, when a daughter sees her mother looking depressed, the daughter can provoke a fight which prods the mother from being sad and helpless to acting strong and competent. Much of Madanes' approach involved finding creative ways for symptomatic children to help their parents openly and directly so that they wouldn't have to resort to symptoms as the only way to help their parents.

In her most recent book, Madanes' (1990) formulations have become more elaborate. As an overview, she states, "All problems brought to therapy can be thought of as stemming from the dilemma between love and violence" (p. 5), and the rest of the book describes strategies for transforming violence into love. She categorizes family problems according to four basic intentions of the family members involved in them. The first of these is the desire to dominate and control, and she sees symptoms like delinquency and behavioral problems as related to this kind of family. The second intention is to be loved, and she associates psychosomatic symptoms, depression, anxiety, and eating disorders with this kind of family. The third desire is to love and protect others, and related symptoms include suicide threats, abuse and neglect, obsessions, and thought disorders. The final category of intention is to repent and forgive, and she finds that these families have problems like incest, sexual abuse, and sadistic acts.

For each of these categories of families, Madanes recommends certain strategies for helping them change. For example, for the first category of domination and control, she suggests that therapists get parents to work together to take charge of their problem children, whereas if the problem was more related to the third category, love and protection, the child might be asked to find a different way to protect or care for his or her parents. In generating these guidelines, Madanes offers a more comprehensive framework for using strategic interventions than has been previously available.

Mara Selvini Palazzoli and her associates in Milan (1978) had read the work of Bateson, the MRI group, and Haley and were working with families of schizophrenic and anorexic patients. Like Haley, they also focused on the power-game aspect of family interaction and, relatedly, on the protective function that the symptom served for the whole family. The Milan Associates (Selvini Palazolli, Gianfranco Cecchin, Luigi Boscolo, and Giuliana Prata) extended the length of family sequences that therapists considered in their assessments, even beyond the months-long sequences that Haley (1980) described in *Leaving Home* (Breunlin and Schwartz, 1986). They interviewed families about their history, sometimes over several generations, searching for evidence to confirm their hypotheses about how the children's symptoms came to be necessary. These hypotheses often involved elaborate networks of covert family alliances and coalitions, including extended family. They generally concluded that the patient had to use her symptoms to protect one or more other family members so as to maintain the delicate network of family alliances.

It appears that while the various strategic or systemic models had some theoretical elements in common, each model covered a different range of family phenomena and focused on a different length of family sequence

(Breunlin and Schwartz, 1986). The MRI model focused exclusively on the brief, more-of-the-same, interactions surrounding the problem and had little concern for structural formulations. Haley included those short sequences, but was also interested in longer ones that last months or years and reflect chronic structural problems. The Milan Associates were interested in some of those longer sequences, but also in the way a family evolved over generations that led to the network of alliances which necessitated a symptom.

NORMAL FAMILY DEVELOPMENT

The MRI group is vehemently opposed to setting up standards of normality, or as they say, "nonnormative." "By nonnormative, we mean that we use no criteria to judge the health or normality of an individual or family. As therapists, we do not regard any particular way of functioning, relating, or living as a problem if the client is not expressing discontent with it" (Fisch, 1978). Thus by limiting their task to eliminating problems presented to them, the MRI group avoids taking any position regarding how families *should* behave. This relativism has deep roots. As early as 1967 Don Jackson wrote an essay called "The Myth of Normality" in which he argued that because there is no one model of health or normality, it is a mistake to impose one on clients.

Despite their disdain for normative goals, it is clear that MRI therapists believe that healthy families are flexible enough to shift their attempted solutions when they find they are not working. This flexibility is needed not only with everyday difficulties, but also to navigate transitional points in the family's development (Weakland, Fisch, Watzlawick, and Bodin, 1974). In addition it is implied that successful families will not over- or underreact to difficulties and will avoid the kind of utopian thinking that makes people try to change things that don't need changing—like the "generation gap."

The Milan associates also adopted a nonnormative stance (Selvini Palazzoli, Boscolo, Cecchin, and Prata, 1978b). Their hypotheses about systems of relationships that maintained problems usually involved any number of covert, cross-generational alliances; thus one could infer that they believed families should have clear generational boundaries. Normality is not the converse of abnormality, however, so one cannot always make that extrapolation.

They also, however, strove to maintain an attitude that was originally called "neutrality" (Selvini Palazzoli et al., 1980) and later came to be known as "curiosity" (Cecchin, 1987) regarding families. Therapists who successfully adopt this attitude don't have preconceived goals or normative models for their client families. Instead, by raising questions that help a family examine itself and that expose hidden power games, they trust that the family will reorganize on its own in a better way, even if that way doesn't conform to some normative map.

In contrast to the relativism of these other two approaches, Haley's thinking about families was based on assumptions about normal family functioning. His therapy was designed to get families out of a dysfunctional structure and into what he considered to be a functional one (Haley, 1976). The normative map that he uses in this endeavor is basically the same one that Minuchin and the structuralists use, with its clear generational boundaries and hierarchy (see Chapter 10). Haley (1973) also emphasized the impact of life cycle stages on a family's structure.

DEVELOPMENT OF BEHAVIOR DISORDERS

Among the strategic and systemic models there are three basic explanations for the way problems develop. The first, described earlier, is cybernetic: Difficulties are turned into chronic problems by the persistence of misguided attempted solutions, forming positive feedback escalations (Watzlawick, Weakland, and Fisch, 1974). The second is structural: Problems are the result of flaws in a family's hierarchy or boundaries. The third is functional: Problems result when people try to protect or control one another indirectly, such that their problems come to serve a function for the system. The MRI group limits itself to the first explanation, while the other strategic or systemic models embrace all three, although each model emphasizes one explanation over the others. Haley emphasizes the structural, while Madanes often focuses on the functional. The Milan Associates consider both structural and functional ideas in their hypothesizing.

To clarify these differences, consider the following example: sixteen-year-old Tommy recently began refusing to go outside his house. An MRI therapist might ask his parents about how they had been trying to get him to go outside. This MRI therapist would focus on the parents' attempted solutions, believing that these were maintaining Tommy's refusal, and on the parents' explanation or "frame" for why Tommy was behaving this way, believing that their frame for Tommy's problem may be maintaining their attempted solutions.

A Haley-style strategic therapist also might be interested in the parents' attempted solutions, but would try to infer from those behaviors information about the parents' marriage, and about the ways in which Tommy was involved in struggles between his parents. This therapist would be acting on the assumption that Tommy's behavior was part of a sequence of behavior in a dysfunctional triangle consisting of mother, father, and Tommy, that was maintaining Tommy's symptoms. This therapist might further assume that this triangular sequence was fueled by unresolved conflicts between the parents. A Madanes-style strategic therapist might also be interested in this triangle, but, in addition, would be particularly curious about how Tommy's behavior might be protecting one or the other parent from having to face some threatening issue. This protecting would be seen as the maintaining factor.

A Milan-style, systemic therapist would not focus so much on attempted solutions but, instead, would ask questions about a variety of past and present relationships in the family. In doing this, the Milan therapist would be trying to uncover an elaborate network of power alliances, often running across generations, that constituted the family's "game." This game left Tommy in the position of having to use his symptoms to protect another family member or to help that member win. Through this process the family might disclose, for example, that if Tommy were to grow up and leave home, mother would be sucked back into a power struggle between her parents, which she avoided only by having a child on whom to focus. Also, by not succeeding in life, Tommy might be protecting father from the shame of having a child who exceeded him in occupation, just as he had done for his father.

From the above discussion we can see that, while all of these approaches view problems as embedded in interactional sequences among family members, they differ in terms of the number of family members included and the length of time over which the sequence takes place, beginning with the MRI model, in which the focus is on short, present-day sequences involving only a few family members, and ending with the Milan model, which examines long-term, historical sequences involving many family members. Haley and Madanes fall between these two positions, using both short and some longer sequences and involving at least three family members (cf., Breunlin and Schwartz, 1986).

GOALS OF THERAPY

For all of these strategic and systemic therapies, the primary goal of therapy is the resolution of the presenting problem. They differ considerably, however, on how best to achieve this goal, how much must happen for the changes in the problem to last, and how much responsibility the therapist should take for creating these changes.

The MRI group is proudly minimalistic in goals. Once the presenting problem is resolved to the client's satisfaction, therapy is over. Even where other problems in a family are apparent to the therapist, if the family doesn't ask for help with those problems, they are not targeted. MRI therapists justify this minimalist position by asserting that, because they view people who have problems as stuck rather than sick, their job is to simply help people get unstuck and moving, not to change their personalities or family structures.

They disdain more open-ended forms of family therapy in which the goals are less clear. Fisch and colleagues (1973) wrote sarcastically of such therapies: "By no means should the therapist encourage any discussion about concrete goals of treatment, since the family would then know when to stop treatment" (p. 601). In contrast, MRI therapists pride themselves on helping families define clear and reachable goals so that everyone knows when to stop treatment. They often find that much of the therapy takes place simply in the process of pushing clients to set such clear, behavioral goals, because in doing so, clients are forced to clarify vague ambitions or dissatisfactions. Also, in getting clients to define achievable goals, MRI therapists help clients let go of the utopian goals with which they often enter therapy and, thereby, diminish their sense of frustration or hopelessness.

Like the behaviorism that dominated psychology at the time the MRI model was developing, the MRI model is behavioral in both its goals and its primary assessment of observable patterns of interaction, preferring not to speculate about intrapsychic states or intentions. In trying to achieve the larger goal of problem-resolution, the immediate goal is to change the behavioral responses of people to their problems. More specifically, as described earlier, MRI therapists try to interrupt (often to reverse) the more-of-the-same vicious feedback loop. To achieve this behavioral change they may try to "reframe the problem," and, in that sense, are not strictly behavioral. But any conceptual change still is in the service of the primary goal of behavior change.

Haley was also quite behavioral and, even more than the MRI group, downgraded the importance of insight or awareness as a goal. He has always been scornful of therapies that helped clients understand why they did things, but did little to get them to do something different.

Haley's ultimate goal often was a structural reorganization of the family, particularly its hierarchy and generational boundaries, but since he approached therapy in stages, he had intermediate goals along the way. Unlike structural family therapy, however, all of these structural goals were directly connected to the presenting problem. For example, to improve the relationship between the polarized parents of a rebellious teenager, a structural family therapist might get the parents to talk to each other about their marital issues, where Haley would have them talk instead about their difficulty working together to deal with their rebellious son. Only after the problems with their son had improved would Haley allow their discussions to shift to their marriage.

Unlike the MRI group, who focused exclusively on the presenting problem because that was all they wanted to change, Haley's problem-focus was a strategy. He shared strategic therapists' general goal to avoid having to deal directly with client resistance. He found that if therapists make the presenting problem the center of their interventions, a family's motivation to change the problem will keep them engaged even while they change their structure.

To continue contrasting structural and strategic, structural therapists don't shy from and sometimes deliberately provoke conflict or tension in sessions, and rely on their personal relationship with each family member to keep them engaged. Strategic therapists, who tend to be more distant, less personal than structuralists, rely on strategies rather than their personalities to minimize resistance or conflict while people change. One of these strategies is to focus on the problem until it's resolved and then explore other, often more threatening, family issues, after the family has more trust in the therapist and in each other because of their previous success. Unlike the MRI group then, Haley doesn't necessarily believe that therapy should end with the resolution of the presenting problem, but instead therapy should continue until the structural problems that produced it are resolved.

Haley's inclination to divide therapy into stages extended to individual sessions. Haley (1976) recommended that therapists follow a clear first session format that included several stages: a social stage in which the goal is to make the family feel comfortable, a stage in which the problem is defined and family members' opinions about it are solicited, and a stage in which family members interact about the problem.

Haley's interest in stages and his formulaic approach reflects the strategic therapists' ethic that responsibility for change rests with the therapist rather than the client. They believe that there should be a strategy to deal with any kind of resistance, so therapists shouldn't blame treatment failures on their clients' lack of readiness. With this conviction comes the responsibility on strategic theorists, like Haley, to develop and clearly describe specialized techniques for all kinds of problems or resistances, as well as the steps and stages of therapy. Thus the writing of strategic therapists tends to be short on theory and long on technique.

Recently Madanes (1990) has expanded the goals of her version of strategic therapy well beyond the problem-focused or even the structural goals to include growth-oriented areas like balance, harmony, and love. She states that, "A goal of therapy is to bring harmony and balance into people's lives. To love and to be loved, to find fulfillment in work, to play and enjoy: All are part of a necessary balance" (p. 13). Despite the fact that her practice of therapy is still quite strategic, this is a big departure from the standard goals of strategic therapy and brings her closer to the goals of people like Satir and other experientialists.

It is in this area of goals of and responsibility for therapy that the strategic and systemic therapies eventually diverged. The early work of the Milan group (Selvini Palazzoli, Boscolo, Cecchin, and Prata, 1978b) was heavily influenced by the MRI and Haley models. The Milan Associates, as described above, expanded the network of people involved in maintaining the problem, but were still primarily interested in finding powerful techniques to interrupt family games. The techniques they developed differed from those of the strategic schools in that they were not so behavioral and, instead, were designed to expose games and reframe motives for strange behavior. Thus while being less problem-focused and more interested in changing a family's awareness or beliefs than strategic therapists, the original Milan approach was no less manipulative: the responsibility for change rested on the therapist whose job it was to outwit resistance.

When the Milan associates split into two groups in the early 1980s, this strategic emphasis remained with Selvini Palazzoli and the groups she subsequently formed. She, however, took a low profile during the 1980s while she researched her hypotheses and developed a new strategic approach (Selvini Palazzoli, 1986). The goal of her new therapy remains to disrupt and expose the "dirty games" that severely disturbed family members play with each other.

Luigi Boscolo and Gianfranco Cecchin drifted in a different direction, away from strategically manipulating families and toward collaborating with them to form systemic hypotheses about their problems. For this branch of the Milan group, therapy became more of a research expedition which the therapist entered without specific goals or strategies, trusting that this process of self-examination would allow families to better choose whether or not they wanted to keep their problems. The therapist was released from responsibility for any certain outcome and took an attitude of curiosity (Cecchin, 1987) toward families rather than the adversarial, controlling attitude of strategic therapists.

In moving in this direction, Boscolo and Cecchin took a position, relative to therapist goals and attitudes, directly opposite to that of their strategic predecessors. This illustrates the pendulum-swinging process described in Chapter 2; it also echoes the polarization around the issue of power and control that existed in the original Bateson group. Bateson, the anthropologist, wanted to understand families, but was strongly opposed to tampering with them, whereas Haley and the others influenced by Erickson thought that this systemic wisdom should be used to find the most effective ways to fix families. The strategic schools remain committed to that belief, while Boscolo and Cecchin have tried to translate the spirit of Bateson's noninterventionist ethic into therapy.

CONDITIONS FOR BEHAVIOR CHANGE

As we have discussed, for the MRI strategic school the primary condition for resolving a problem is to change the behaviors associated with it. It is believed that through seeing the results of altering rigid behavioral responses, clients will become more flexible in their problem-solving strategies. When this happens, clients will achieve second-order change—a change in the rules governing their response to problems—as opposed to first-order change, which might involve doing more of the same.

For example, Jill argues with her father about her curfew and father grounds her. She then runs away and stays with a friend. A first-order intervention at this point might be to help father find a more effective punishment to tame this out-of-control child. A second-order strategic intervention might be to direct father to act distracted and sad around his daughter and to imply to her that he has given up trying to control her. This shifts Jill from feeling trapped by father to feeling concerned about him, and she becomes more reasonable. Father learns that when attempted solutions aren't working, try something different.

Thus clients do not need to be educated about the problem, nor do they need insight into why they have needed it or how it arose. They also don't need to reorganize other family relationships. They simply need to do something different, even if it runs against common sense, as father's directive did. Second-order change in families often seems to arise out of apparently illogical new attempts. This is because many logical or common-sense solutions have been tried by families before they come to treatment. What they don't need is more of the same. What they do need is flexibility—to have the illogical as well as the logical in their repertoire of responses.

This means that therapists must be able to get clients to do something completely different. To achieve this, strategic therapists give directives that clients are to follow between sessions. To get clients to comply with their directives, since these directives often require behavior that is counterintuitive or a reversal of habit, therapists must be able to maximize clients' motivation and minimize resistance. Thus many of the techniques discussed in the next section are designed to enhance the chances that directives will be followed.

Along these lines, MRI therapists try to find out who is the "customer" in the family. That is, who has the most motivation for the problem to change. They often find that the customer isn't the person with the problem, and sometimes isn't even someone in the family, but might be the person who made the referral. Frequently they will work primarily, or even exclusively, with the customer, believing that it is most efficient to work with the most motivated person in the system, and that frequently the problem will change even if only one person in the system surrounding it changes.

On many of these points, Haley would agree. Haley (1976) believed that telling people what they are doing wrong doesn't help them change, it only mobilizes resistance. The same is true, Haley believed, of cathartic expression of feeling. He believed changes in behavior alter feelings and perceptions, rather than the other way around. Madanes (1980) said, "If a problem can be solved without the family's knowing how or why, that is satisfactory" (p. 79). It may seem curious, then, that Madanes, Haley and the MRI group relied heavily on the technique of reframing, in which the therapist tries to change the way clients perceive or understand the problem. The strategic theorist's response to this inconsistency is likely to be that reframing is in the service of behavior change, which is what really changes client perception or feeling. Until people have a different experience with a problem, they will not be able to see it differently.

Over time the Milan group turned this behavioristic position on its head. From the beginning, the Milan associates were more interested in getting a family to see things differently (through a reframing technique called "positive connotation" to be discussed later) than in getting family members to behave differently. Increasingly, they (Boscolo and Cecchin, in particular) moved toward a meaning-changes-behavior position as they found that helping people examine the systemic evolution of their problems allowed them to relate differently. This led to a style of therapy that contained very few directives and mostly involved asking questions designed to help family members re-examine their predicaments. This shift from behavior to meaning paved the way for the constructivist movement, described in Chapter 3, which pivoted on meaning changes.

TECHNIQUES

Strategic therapy is the most technique-driven of all family therapies. Strategic therapists have maintained Erickson's tradition of trying to tailor interventions to the idiosyncrasies of person and problem. As a result, rather than presenting a method that is to be adapted to different contexts, the strategic literature is full of unique interventions, customized to fit specific problems. For example, in surveying the strategic literature up to 1980, Duncan Stanton (1981) found references that describe interventions for over forty different syndromes or types of problems, covering everything imaginable, from adolescent problems to schizophrenia to thumb-sucking. In the eighties, the flow of problem-specific interventions has not slowed, even though fewer of these articles appear in mainstream family therapy journals. Because of the emergence of their own journal, the *Journal of Strategic and Systemic Therapies*, strategic and systemic writers, while no less productive, have become more insular and reach a smaller audience.

While this parade of articles and books describing customized techniques has continued since the basic strategic theory and techniques were described in the midseventies (most notable among these: Fisch, Weakland, and Segal, 1982; Papp, 1983; Coyne, 1987; Coyne, Kahn, and Gotlib, 1987; Haley, 1984, Madanes, 1984; Stanton, Todd, and Associates, 1982), there have not been major (second-order) shifts in strategic concepts or method since then. We will describe the basic methods for the MRI, Haley, and Milan models.

The MRI Approach

Members of the MRI's Brief Therapy Center follow a six-step treatment procedure:

1. Introduction to the treatment setup
2. Inquiry and definition of the problem
3. Estimation of the behavior maintaining the problem
4. Setting goals for treatment
5. Selecting and making behavioral interventions
6. Termination

Upon arrival, clients fill out a form covering basic demographic data. Next the therapist explains that sessions are recorded and observed, and points out the advantages of having several professionals involved in the case. The therapist also explains that treatment is conducted within a maximum of ten sessions, thereby setting up a powerful expectation of change.

Once the preliminaries are concluded, the therapist asks for a clear definition of the major problem. The MRI group believe that clients must be able to define a single major problem for therapy to succeed. When the problem is stated in vague terms, such as "We just don't seem to get along," or in terms of presumptive causes, "Dad's job is making him depressed," the therapist helps translate it into a clear and concrete goal, asking questions like "What will be the first small sign that things are getting better?"

When the problem and goals are defined clearly and behaviorally, MRI therapists begin to ask about the clients' attempted solutions that may be maintaining the problem. For example, the husband who nags at his wife to spend more time with him may succeed only in driving her further away; the parents who criticize their son in an attempt to get him to quit fighting with his sister may perpetuate his sense that they like her better; or the husband who does everything his wife asks to reassure her of his love may feel so resentful that he begins to hate her.

In general the solutions that tend to perpetuate or exacerbate problems fall into one of three categories:

1. The solution is simply to deny that a problem exists; action is necessary, but not taken. For instance, parents do nothing despite growing evidence that their teenage son is heavily involved with drugs.

2. The solution is an effort to solve something which isn't really a problem; action is taken when it shouldn't be. For example, parents severely punish a child for masturbating.

3. The solution is an effort to solve a problem within a framework that makes a solution impossible; action is taken, but at the wrong level. A husband, for instance, buys increasingly expensive gifts for his unhappy wife when what she wants is his affection (Watzlawick, Weakland, and Fisch, 1974).

Each of these three classes of problem-maintaining attempted solutions imply therapeutic strategies: in the first, clients need to act; in the second, to stop acting; and in the third, to act in a different way. Once the therapist conceives of a strategy for changing the problem-maintaining sequences, the clients must be convinced of the value of following this strategy. To sell their directives to clients, MRI therapists will reframe the problem (provide a new meaning for problem behaviors) to increase the likelihood of compliance. Thus MRI reframes are different from psychodynamic interpretations in that the goal of a reframe is not to produce insight or to educate, but simply to induce compliance. The MRI therapist is not constrained to only use reframes he or she believes are true. Instead, these pragmatists feel free to use any plausible rationale that might bolster their directives. The therapist tells an angry, disengaged teen that when his father calls him worthless and locks him out of the house it is the only way father knows to show love to him.

As we described earlier, in order to change problem-maintaining sequences, strategic therapists often try to get family members to do or believe things that are counterintuitive, the opposite of common sense. Such counterintuitive techniques have been called *paradoxical interventions* because it seems paradoxical that people must sometimes do things that are in apparent opposition to the goals of therapy in order to reach those goals (Frankl, 1960; Haley, 1973, 1976; Hare-Mustin, 1975; Watzlawick, Weakland, and Fisch, 1974).

For example, Watzlawick and his colleagues (1974) describe a young couple who were bothered by their parents' tendency to treat them like children by doing everything for them. Despite the husband's adequate salary, the parents continued to send money and to lavish gifts on them, refused to let them pay even part of a restaurant check, and so on. The strategic team helped the couple solve their difficulty with their doting parents by having the couple become less rather than more competent. Instead of trying to show the parents they didn't need help, the couple was told to act helpless and dependent, so much so that the parents got disgusted and finally backed off. This form of paradox is an *outpositioning* strategy (Rohrbaugh, Tennen, Press, and White, 1981) in the sense that the couple took their parents' position that they were dependent and exaggerated it to an absurd extreme, at which point the sequence must change.

The techniques most commonly thought of as paradoxical are symptom prescriptions in which the family is told to continue or expand the behavior that they complain about. In some contexts such a prescription might be made with the hope that the family will try to comply with it, and thereby be forced to reverse their attempted solutions. If sad Johnny is told to try to become depressed several times a day and his family is asked to encourage him to be sad, then they will no longer try ineffectively to cheer him up and he won't feel guilty for not being happy. Michael Rohrbaugh and his colleagues (1981), in their useful taxonomy of paradoxical techniques, called this a *compliance-based* paradox because the therapist wants the family to comply with the directive.

At other times a therapist may prescribe the symptom, while secretly hoping that the clients rebel against this directive. The therapist may encourage Johnny to continue to be depressed because, in doing so, he is helping his brother (with whom Johnny is competitive) feel superior. This is called a *defiance-based* intervention because the therapist wants the clients to defy the directive, and reframes the reason for the directive in terms that will maximize Johnny's defiance.

Still other times the therapist may *prescribe the symptom* with the hope that in doing so the network of family relationships that maintain the problem will be exposed. The therapist says that Johnny should remain depressed because that way he can continue to keep his mother's attention, which will keep her from looking to father for affection, since father is still emotionally involved with his mother, and so on. Since Rohrbaugh didn't include this category, we will call it an *exposure-based* paradox, which is most frequently associated with the Milan, rather than the MRI, model.

From this discussion, we can see that the reframe or rationale that accompanies the paradoxical directive is quite important. It will include different content and use different language depending on whether the therapist wants to maximize compliance, defiance, or exposure.

Rohrbaugh described another class of paradoxical directives that is also designed to manipulate resistance. Most families enter therapy with a certain amount of ambivalence regarding the problem and the changes required to improve it. When the therapist encourages the family to make these changes, family members are likely to respond with the fearful side of their ambivalence and increase their resistance. If the therapist, instead, were to preempt these fears by warning the family of the dangers of change and restraining them from trying to change too fast, the family may react with the side of their ambivalence that wants the changes. Thus MRI therapists will frequently use such *restraining techniques* as asking about the negative consequences of change and warning family members to go slow, or worrying about the relapse when improvements occur.

Haley and Madanes Approach

In many ways Jay Haley's work is a cross between the MRI approach and the structural approach of Minuchin and his colleagues. In terms of the actual moves in a session, Haley tends to be strategic and may use many of the paradoxical techniques described above. His goals, however, are usually structural, with an emphasis on the family hierarchy. Haley (1976) believes that if therapy is to end well, it must begin properly. Therefore he devotes a good deal of time and attention to the opening moves of treatment. Regardless of who is presented as the official patient, Haley begins by interviewing the entire family, or as much of it as can be assembled. His approach to this initial interview is highly structured and regularly follows four stages: a social stage, a problem stage, an interaction stage, and finally a goal-setting stage. These stages, with clear-cut instructions for each, provided a secure structure for a generation of novice family therapists who wanted to know just what to do in their first session.

Families are often quite uncomfortable and defensive when they come to therapy for the first time. Family members often don't know why they are there or what to expect, and fear that the therapist will blame them for the problem. Therefore Haley has therapists use the initial minutes of a first session to help everyone relax. He makes a point of greeting every family member and trying to make sure they are comfortable. He acts as though he were a host, making sure that his guests feel welcome. While making small talk, Haley observes how each family member behaves and how they all interact.

After this brief *social stage*, Haley gets down to business in the *problem stage*. Before asking for the family's position, he introduces himself, repeats what he knows about the family, and explains why he has asked the entire family to come—that is, because he wants everyone's opinions and ideas. Haley then asks each person to give their perspective on the problem. His clear and practical suggestions even address such specific questions as whom to speak to first. Since mothers are usually more central and fathers less involved, Haley recommends that the therapist speak first to the father in order to increase his concern and involvement. This suggestion nicely illustrates Haley's strategic maneuvering, which begins with the first contact, and characterizes the course of all subsequent meetings.

Haley listens carefully to the way each family member defines the problem and their involvement in it, making sure that no one interrupts until each has had a turn. During this phase, Haley is observing the reactions of each family member for clues to the family's triangles and hierarchy; but he discourages therapists from making any interpretations or comments regarding these observations which might make the family defensive. Instead, these observations are filed away, awaiting further confirmation, and providing the basis for further interventions. He does "interactionalize" problems that are being presented as belonging only to one member. For example, mother says that Johnny is just a depressed person. In listening to everyone's report, Haley noticed that the parent's disagreed regarding the best way to help Johnny; thus he can list this disagreement as another aspect of the problem, which certainly doesn't help Johnny.

Once everyone has had a chance to talk, Haley encourages them to discuss their various points of view among themselves. In this, the *interactional stage*, Haley can observe, rather than just hear about, the sequences that surround the problem. As they talk, Haley looks for alliances between family members against others. How functional is the hierarchy? Do the parents work well together or do they undercut each other? How does the patient respond to conflict between others? During this stage, the therapist is like an anthropologist, watching for patterns in the family action.

Sometimes Haley ends the first session by directing the family to carry out a task. In subsequent sessions, directives play a central role in his problem-solving therapy. Effective directives are not in the form of simple advice. Advice is rarely helpful, unless clients happen to be ignorant of some piece of information or unless problems are minor. As Haley says, advice generally doesn't help because people don't have rational control over what they do.

To design an effective directive, the therapist has to learn what solutions have already been tried and failed. Asking families what they've tried that hasn't worked not only gains information, but also underscores the fact that they haven't been successful and need the therapist's help. To persuade family members to do a task, they must be convinced that each one will gain something by complying. This effort to get families to feel their past failures so as to elevate the therapist's credibility illustrates an important difference between the strategic approach and the more collaborative approaches that emerged in the eighties (described in Chapter 11). These later models strive to help families feel like they have been successful in the past and only need to expand that success.

The following two tasks are taken from Haley's *Problem-Solving Therapy*. A couple who were out of the habit of being affectionate with each other were told to behave affectionately in order to teach their child how to show affection. In another case, a mother who was unable to control her twelve-year-old son had decided to send him away to military school. Haley suggested that since the boy had no idea how tough his life would be at military school, it would be a good idea for the mother to help prepare him. They both agreed. Haley directed her to teach him how to stand at attention, be polite, and wake up early every morning to make his bed. They followed these instructions as if playing a game, with mother as sergeant and son as private. But after two weeks the son was behaving so well that his mother no longer felt it necessary to send him away.

Madanes (1981) has used the observation, illustrated by the second case above, that people will often do something they wouldn't ordinarily do if it is framed as play or pretend, to develop a whole range of *pretend techniques*. One such strategy is to ask a symptomatic child to pretend to have the symptom, and encourage the parents to pretend to help. The child can give up the actual symptom now that pretending to have it is serving the same family function. The following two case studies summarized from Madanes (1981) illustrate the pretend technique.

In the first case, a mother sought therapy because her ten-year-old son had night terrors. There were also two older daughters and a baby brother. Madanes suspected that the boy was concerned about his mother, who was poor, spoke little English, and had lost two husbands.

Since the boy had night terrors the therapist asked all the members of the family to describe their dreams. Only the mother and the son had nightmares. The mother's nightmare was that someone would break into the house, and the boy's was that he was being attacked by a witch. When Madanes asked what the mother did when the boy had nightmares, she said that she took him into her bed and told him to pray to God. She explained that she thought his nightmares were the work of the devil.

The treatment team's conjecture was that the boy's night terrors were both a metaphorical expression of the mother's fears, and an attempt to help her. As long as the boy was afraid, his mother had to be strong in order to help him; thus she could not be afraid herself. Unfortunately, while she tried to protect him, she frightened him further by talking about God and the devil. Both mother and child were helping each other in unproductive ways.

The family members were told to pretend that they were home and mother was afraid that someone might break in. The son was asked to protect his mother. In this way the mother had to pretend to need the child's help instead of really needing it. At first the family had difficulty playing the scene because the mother would attack the make-believe thief before the son could help. Thus she communicated that she was capable of taking care of herself; she did not need the son's protection. After the scene was performed correctly, with the son attacking the thief, they all discussed the performance. The mother explained that it was difficult for her to play her part because she was a competent person who could defend herself. Madanes sent the family home with the task of repeating this dramatization every evening for a week. If the son started screaming during his sleep, his mother was to wake him up and play the scene again. They were told that this was important to do no matter how late it was or how tired they were. The son's night terrors completely disappeared.

In the second case, a mother sought psychiatric treatment for her five-year-old son because he had uncontrollable temper tantrums. After talking with the family for a few minutes Madanes asked the son to pretend to have a tantrum to show her what it was like. They boy said, "Okay, I'm the Incredible Hulk®!" He puffed out his chest, flexed his muscles, made a monstrous face, and started screaming and kicking the furniture. Madanes then asked the mother to do what she usually did in such circumstances. The mother responded by telling her son, in a weak and ineffective way, to calm down. She tried to pretend to send him to another room as she tried to do at home with little success. Next Madanes asked the mother if the boy was doing a good job of pretending. She said that he was.

Madanes asked the boy to repeat the scene. This time he was Frankenstein and his tantrum was performed with a more rigid body posture and a face more appropriate to Frankenstein's monster. Then Madanes talked with the boy about the Incredible Hulk® and Frankenstein and congratulated the mother for rearing such an imaginative child.

Following this discussion, mother and son were told to pretend that he was having a tantrum while she was walking him to his room. The boy was told to act like the Incredible Hulk® and to make lots of noise. Then they were told to pretend to close the door and hug and kiss. Next Madanes instructed the mother to pretend that she was having a tantrum, and the boy was to hug and kiss her. Madanes instructed mother and son to perform both scenes every morning before school, and every afternoon when the boy came home. After every performance the mother was to give the boy milk and cookies if he did a good job. Thus the mother was moved from a helpless position to one of superiority in which she was in charge of rewarding his make-believe performance. The next week the mother called to say that they did not need to come for therapy because the boy was behaving very well and that his tantrums had ceased.

Both of these cases contain the hallmarks of strategic therapy: tracking the sequences around the problem and giving directives that change those sequences. Like Haley, Madanes is primarily interested in the sequences that relate to the family's hierarchy. Unlike Haley, however, her directives are usually aimed less at getting parents back in control through power plays and more through structuring new, enjoyable opportunities for parents and children to care for or protect each other in direct ways.

Haley's preference is often to get parents to work together to control their out-of-control children. This preference is clearly illustrated in the strategies he recommends for dealing with severely disturbed young adults in the book *Leaving Home*. Parents are to put aside their personal resentments and collaborate in planning and implementing a highly structured, rather authoritarian regimen of discipline for their young adult, treating him or her younger-than-age until the child is back on track toward normality. Haley speculates that by forcing the parents to cooperate for the good of their child, he is interrupting the sequence in which the tension from their marital conflicts precipitates their child's crazy behavior as a way to distract them.

While Haley believed that a problematic marriage often lurks behind a child's problem, he also warned therapists to not target these marital issues too soon or, in some cases, at all. He believed that families were often protective of and threatened by disturbances in that relationship. Instead, by getting parents to work together to help their child, the couple may make simultaneous changes in their relationship without it ever being overtly addressed. If marital issues do come up, the parents will feel less fear of dealing with them if they have had success in cooperating to help their child. All of this reinforces Haley's commitment to remain focused on the presenting problem until it improves.

Later Haley (1984) returned to his strategic, Ericksonian roots in a book called *Ordeal Therapy*, a collection of case studies in which ordeals were prescribed which made the clients' symptoms more trouble than they were worth. Haley's general approach is based on this premise: "If one makes it more difficult for a person to have a symptom than to give it up, the person will give up the symptom" (p. 5). For example, a standard ordeal is for a client to have to get up in the middle of the night and exercise strenuously whenever he or she had symptoms during that day. Another example might be for the client to have to give a present to someone with whom he or she has a poor relationship—e.g., a mother-in-law or ex-spouse—each time the symptoms occur. As these examples illustrate, the ordeal should be something that clients do not want to do, but would be good for them or would improve their health or relationships.

Since Haley also subscribed to structural goals in therapy, he also used ordeals to restructure families. For example, a sixteen-year-old boy put a variety of items up his behind and then expelled them, leaving his stepmother to clean up the mess, while his father remained peripheral. Haley (1984) arranged that after each such episode the father had to take his son to their backyard and have the boy dig a hole three feet deep and three feet wide, in which he was to bury all the things he was putting up his rear end. After a few weeks of this, Haley reported that the symptoms stopped, the father became more involved with his son and the stepmother became closer to the father.

As we mentioned earlier in this chapter, Madanes (1990) has developed a classification system for families that provides guidelines describing which strategic techniques to use with which kind of family. In this system she suggests when to use her own favorite methods, like pretend techniques or finding ways that children can be appropriately helpful to their parents; when to use Haley's ordeals or hierarchical techniques; and when to use techniques more associated with the MRI, like prescribing the symptom.

In addition she developed a sixteen-step model for the reparation of families in which there has been sex abuse. Many of these steps revolve around getting the abuser to apologize, on his knees, to the victim; getting the family also to apologize for not protecting the victim; and making sure that the abuse doesn't recur. Madanes (1990) doesn't accompany her cookbooklike model for sex abuse with outcome data. Therefore, and because sex abuse is a difficult and complex problem, we advise that her model be viewed as suggestive until it is further tested.

The Milan Model

The techniques of the Milan model are difficult to summarize because there are several very different Milan models.

The original model was highly strategic and formulaic. Families were treated by male-female cotherapists, while being observed by other members of a therapy team. Sessions were held, on the average, once a month and, initially, were limited to ten sessions in emulation of the MRI model. The monthly sessions were an artifact of the long distances many families had to travel to the center in Milan; however, the team came to believe that the long interval between sessions was beneficial. If families were seen weekly, the effects of the previous session's paradoxical prescription might be diminished because families seemed to take longer to fully react.

The standard session format had five parts: the presession, the session, the intersession, the intervention, and the postsession discussion. As Boscolo, Cecchin, Hoffman, and Penn (1987, p. 4) describe:

> During the presession the team came up with an initial hypothesis about the family's presenting problem . . . During the session itself, the team members would validate, modify, or change the hypothesis. After about forty minutes, the entire team would meet alone to discuss the hypothesis and arrive at an intervention. The treating therapists would then go back to deliver the intervention to the family, either by positively connoting the problem situation or by a ritual to be done by the family that commented on the problem situation and was designed to introduce change . . . Finally, the team would meet for a postsession discussion to analyze the family's reactions and to plan for the next session.

As indicated in that description, the main intervention was either a ritual or a positive connotation.

The *positive connotation* was the most distinctive innovation to emerge from this original Milan model. Derived from the MRI technique of reframing the symptom as serving a protective function for the family—for example, Johnny needs to continue to be depressed to distract his parents from their marital issues—the positive connotation eliminated the implication inherent in such reframes that some family members wanted or benefited from the patient's symptoms. This implication made for resistance that the Milan team found could be circumvented if the patient's behavior was construed, not as protecting specific people or relationships, but as preserving the family's homeostasis or rigid rules. Indeed, every family member's behavior was often connoted in this system-serving way.

In this way, through a session the treatment team would hypothesize about the way that the patient's symptom fit into the family system, and after the mid-session break the therapists would turn this hypothesis into a statement and give it to the family, along with the injunction that the situation should not change. Johnny should continue to sacrifice himself by remaining depressed as a way to reassure the family that he will not become an abusive man like his grandfather. Mother should also maintain her overinvolvement with Johnny as a way to make him feel valued while he sacrifices himself. Father should continue to criticize mother and Johnny's relationship so that mother will not be tempted to abandon Johnny and become a wife to her husband.

Rituals were used to engage the whole family in a series of actions which run counter to, or exaggerate, rigid family rules and myths. For example, one family of four was highly enmeshed with their large extended family. They were told to hold family discussions behind locked doors every other night after dinner during which each family member was to speak for fifteen minutes about the family. Meanwhile they were to redouble their allegiance and courtesy to the other members of the clan. By exaggerating the family's loyalty to the extended family while simultaneously breaking that loyalty rule by meeting apart from the clan and talking about it, the family could examine and break the loyalty rule that perpetuated their dysfunctional system.

Rituals were also used to dramatize the positive connotation. For example, each family member might have to express their gratitude each night to the patient for having his or her problem (Boscolo, Cecchin, Hoffman, and Penn, 1987). The Milan group also devised a set of rituals based on an "odd and even days" format (Selvini Palazzoli, Boscolo, Cecchin, and Prata, 1978b). For example, a family in which the parents are deadlocked over parental functions might be told that on even days of the week father will be in charge of the patient's behavior and mother is to act as if she was not there. On odd days, mother is in charge and father is to stay out of the way. Here, again, the family's rigid sequences are interrupted and they must react differently to each other.

These positive connotations and rituals are powerful and provocative interventions. To keep families engaged while using such methods, the therapist-family relationship becomes crucial. Unfortunately, the Milan team originally portrayed therapy as a struggle for power between therapists and families. Their main advice to therapists was to remain neutral in the sense of avoiding the appearance of taking sides with one family member or another. This *neutrality* was often interpreted by practitioners of the model as distance, so that therapists often delivered these dramatic interventions while seeming aloof and, not surprisingly, families often became angry or didn't return.

In the late 1970s and early 1980s, the original Milan team began to split around the nature of therapy. Selvini Palazzoli maintained the model's strategic and adversarial bent, although she stopped using paradoxical interventions. Instead she and Giuliana Prata and some new colleagues experimented with a specific kind of ritual called the *invariant prescription*, which they assigned to every family they treated.

Selvini Palazzoli (1986) believes that psychotic or anorexic patients are caught up in a *"dirty game"*: a power struggle originally between their parents that these patients are pulled into and, ultimately, wind up using their symptoms in an attempt to defeat one parent for the sake of the other.

Her invariant prescription method begins in much the same way the original Milan model did, using circular questions to build hypotheses. But this time the questioning and hypothesizing center around the family's presupposed dirty game.

At the end of the third assessment session, by which time a sense of the family's game should be established, the invariant prescription begins (Gelcer and Schwartzbein, 1989). The parents are directed to tell their children and select members of the extended family that they have a secret. They are also supposed to observe and record the reactions of family members to their keeping a secret. During ensuing sessions, the therapist and the parents meet to discuss the family's reaction and the parents are instructed to not only continue keeping the secret but to go out together for varying periods of time, and to do so mysteriously, without warning other family members. Therapy continues this way until the patient's symptoms abate.

This invariant prescription can be seen as a variant of structural or Haley-style strategic therapy in that by getting parents to share a secret and go out together, the therapist is shoring up the boundary around their subsystem. Plotting together and mysteriously eloping adds a sense of playfulness and connectedness to a stultified marriage which might ease the power struggle underlying a dirty game. Children or other family members who watch the parents keeping a secret and eloping may initially fear and try to break this new alliance between the parents but, if they are unsuccessful, may feel relieved to see an end to the parents' chronic cold war and to be out of the middle of it. In addition as the parents carefully observe, record, and discuss the family's reactions to their new behavior, they become more aware of the network of dysfunctional family alliances and more aware of the process of change in those patterns.

One can see how, if parents can be convinced to follow this invariant prescription, it might be effective. One should not, however, underestimate the difficulty of getting parents to follow such a directive. Chronically conflicted parents fear each other, and those allied with each parent fear the end of their alliance. The skill in this approach is not so much in the directive itself, but in the therapist's ability to sell it.

In contrast to Selvini Palazzoli, Boscolo and Cecchin drifted away from this kind of strategic intervening and toward a collaborative, non-striving style of therapy. This therapy grew from their increasing impression that the value in the Milan model was not so much in the directives (positive connotations or rituals), which had been the model's centerpiece, but in the interview process itself. Their therapy came to center around *circular questioning*, an interviewing technique aimed to elicit family members' opinions regarding differences of several kinds:

> . . . differences in perception of relationships ("Who is closer to Father, your daughter or your son?"); questions about differences of degree ("On

a scale of one to ten, how bad do you think the fighting is this week?");
now/then differences ("Did she start losing weight before or after her
sister went off to college?"); and hypothetical or future differences ("If
she had not been born, how would your marriage be different today? If
you were to divorce, which parent would the children stay with?") (Boscolo, Cecchin, Hoffman, and Penn, 1987, p. 11).

By asking about differences like these, the circular nature of problems
becomes apparent as family members are lifted out of their limited and
linear perspectives. Circular questions have been further refined and cat-
alogued by Penn (1982, 1985) and Tomm (1987a, 1987b).

As an example, let's return to Johnny's family and imagine the following conversation (adapted from Hoffman, 1983):

QUESTION   Who is most upset by Johnny's depression?

ANSWER   Mother.

QUESTION   How does mother try to help Johnny?

ANSWER   She talks to him for hours and tries to do things for him.

QUESTION   Who agrees most with mother's way of trying to help
Johnny?

ANSWER   The psychiatrist who prescribes his medication.

QUESTION   Who disagrees?

ANSWER   Father. He thinks Johnny shouldn't be allowed to do what
he wants.

QUESTION   Who agrees with father?

ANSWER   We all think Johnny is babied too much. And grandma too.
Grandpa would probably agree with mother but he died.

QUESTION   Did Johnny start to get depressed before or after grandfather's death?

ANSWER   Not long after, I guess.

QUESTION   If grandfather hadn't died, how would the family be different now?

ANSWER   Well, mother and grandma probably wouldn't fight so much
because grandma wouldn't be living with us. And mother wouldn't
be so sad all the time.

QUESTION   If mother and grandma didn't fight so much and mother
wasn't so sad, how do you think Johnny would be?

ANSWER   Well, I guess he might be happier too. But then he'd probably be fighting with father again.

Just by asking questions, the frame for Johnny's problem gradually shifts from a psychiatric one to being symptomatic because of difficult changes in the family structure.

Boscolo and Cecchin became aware that the spirit in which these questions are asked determined the usefulness of this technique. If a therapist maintains a strategic mind-set—uses the questioning process to strive for a particular outcome—the responses of family members will be constrained or inhibited by their sense that the therapist is after something. If, on the other hand, the therapist asks circular questions out of genuine curiosity (Cecchin, 1987), as if joining the family in a research expedition regarding their problem, an atmosphere can be created in which the family can arrive at new understandings of their predicament on their own.

Other Contributions

Up to this point we have described the techniques developed by the major schools of strategic or systemic therapy: the MRI group; Haley and Madanes; and the Milan Associates. There are many other people who have added innovations.

Strategic therapy has pioneered the *team approach* to therapy. Originally the MRI group used teams behind one-way mirrors to help brainstorm strategies, as did the Milan group. Peggy Papp (1980) and her colleagues at the Ackerman Institute brought the team more directly into the therapy process by turning the observers into a kind of "Greek chorus" that reacted to events in the therapy session. For example, the team might, for strategic purposes, disagree with the therapist. In witnessing this staged debate between the team and their therapist over whether a family should change, family members might feel that both sides of their ambivalence were appreciated and represented in the therapy session. Having the team interact openly with the therapist or even with the family during sessions paved the way for later approaches in which the team might enter the treatment room and discuss the family while the family watched (Andersen, 1987).

Jim Alexander was a behaviorist who, out of frustration with limits of his exclusively behavioral orientation, incorporated strategic ideas. The result is *functional family therapy* (Alexander and Parsons, 1982) which, as the name implies, is concerned with the function that family behavior is designed to achieve (see also Chapter 7). Functional family therapists assume that most family behaviors are attempts to become more or less intimate and through "relabeling" (another word for reframing) help family members see each other's behaviors in that benign light. They also help family members set up behavioral contingency management programs to help them get the kind of intimacy they want more directly. Functional family therapy, then, represents an interesting blend of strategic and behavioral therapies and, unlike many strategic schools, retains the behaviorist ethic of basing interventions on sound research.

Carlos Sluzki has made a number of contributions to strategic theory and technique, including an innovative approach to marital therapy, a topic rarely addressed by strategic writers (Sluzki, 1978). He provided a series of concrete guidelines such as: "If A and B concur in defining A as victim and B as victimizer, then find a way of reversing the roles/labels and state the reversal forcefully" (p. 368). For example, Sluzki was treating a couple who were locked in a relationship in which the wife's nagging, complaining negativism was complemented by the husband's appeasing optimism. Both of them agreed that she was the victimizer and he was the victim. Sluzki praised her for taking on the burden of being the villain, but added that making her husband good while she remained the "mean one" must have given her some satisfaction. But he said, there are no kicks like being the "good guy," and he selfishly monopolizes this role.

Then Sluzki assigned them the following task: He told the husband to respond to any of his wife's statements by being as pessimistic as possible, regardless of his true feelings. Sluzki then directed the wife to remain as pessimistic as always, "in order to make the task more difficult for her husband."

The task served the following purposes:

1. the prescription acknowledged that he could be genuinely pessimistic
2. her habitual behavior was being relabeled as a gesture of good will
3. if they followed instructions, they would quite quickly reach a deadlock that would force her to extricate the positive side of the matter
4. nobody—but the therapist—would be blamed for any escalation into pessimism between them, totally eliminating any label of victim and victimizer
5. they were being granted a humorous way out of confrontations, which they continued to use thereafter on occasions

In fact both expressed a remarkable reduction of the conflicts and a general improvement in the relationship from then on, while Sluzki, in typical MRI form, expressed concern about their unexplainable and too dramatic change.

Some authors have combined the strategic and structural approaches. Duncan Stanton (1981) begins with straightforward structural techniques and resorts to strategic interventions only when a family strongly resists his restructuring attempts. After the often paradoxical strategic interventions have reduced resistance, he returns to the structural approach. Maurizio Andolfi (1979; Andolfi and Zwerling, 1980) does it the other way, starting strategically and ending structurally. He restrains severely dysfunctional families from changing until the identified patient improves and the family members are more accessible to him, at which point he becomes more structural.

EVALUATING THERAPY THEORY AND RESULTS

More than any of the other models in this book, information about strategic therapy is exchanged through the case report format. Nearly all of the hundreds of articles and books on strategic therapy include at least one description of a successful technique or therapy outcome. Thus strategic therapy appears to have a great deal of anecdotal support for its efficacy (although people tend not to write about their cases that fail).

Some strategic groups have tracked their outcome more systematically. In the book *Change* that launched the MRI model, Watzlawick and colleagues (Watzlawick, Weakland, and Fisch, 1974) conducted follow-up phone interviews with ninety-seven consecutive cases treated at their Brief Therapy Center approximately three months after treatment was terminated. Interviewers asked clients if their behavior had changed as planned and whether their complaints were relieved. The interviewers also asked if the patients had sought additional treatment elsewhere and, to check for possible symptom substitution, they asked if any new problems had developed. To minimize the possibility that patients might exaggerate the benefits of treatment to please their therapists, all interviews were conducted by members of the team who were not involved in treatment.

The average length of treatment for this sample of cases was seven sessions. Forty percent reported achieving complete relief; 32 percent achieved considerable but not complete relief; and 28 percent reported no change. In none of the complete relief cases were there any signs of symptom substitution.

Haley, who is interested in family structure as well as problem behavior, has said that evaluations should be based not just on the presence or absence of symptoms, but also on changes in the system (Haley, 1976). This point of view is consistent with the mainstream view of the family therapy movement, but was sharply criticized by Richard Fisch (1978) of the MRI. Fisch rebuked Haley for using what he considers a variant of the old psychoanalytic "iceberg" formulation—a symptom is merely a manifestation of a deeper, underlying disturbance and unless the basic conflict is altered the symptom will reappear or be displaced.

Oddly, when Haley (1980) did report on the outcome of his "leaving home" model with schizophrenic young adults, he used rehospitalization as his only criterion. Fourteen such patients, each of whom had been hospitalized for the first time, were treated by different therapists for an average of fourteen sessions. The therapists of these patients followed up on their treatment between two and four years after terminating. In that time three of the fourteen had been rehospitalized, while another patient had committed suicide. Interestingly this rehospitalization rate is comparable to rates obtained by psychoeducational models described in Chapter 11, although Haley's is a very different approach.

There are some studies of the outcome of family therapies that are based on, or similar to, the methods of strategic therapy. In their classic study, Langsley, Machotka, and Flomenhaft (1971) studied the effectiveness of their family crisis therapy, which has some similarities with both the MRI and Haley models. Patients who were seen as needing hospitalization were randomly assigned to either a psychiatric hospital or to crisis family therapy on an outpatient basis. Eighteen months later, the group who received family therapy had spent less than half the number of days in the hospital than the group who had previously been hospitalized. Furthermore the cost of treatment during this period was six times as high for the hospitalized group.

In another carefully controlled study, Alexander and Parsons found their functional family therapy (described earlier in this chapter) to be more effective in treating a group of delinquents than a client-centered family approach, an eclectic-dynamic approach, or a no-treatment control group (Parsons and Alexander, 1973). Recidivism was cut in half by the functional approach, in contrast to the other three groups which did not differ significantly from each other. Furthermore a three-year follow-up showed that the incidence of problems in the siblings was significantly lower for the functional treatment.

Stanton, Todd, and Associates (1981) have convincingly demonstrated the effectiveness of an approach combining structural and Haley's strategic family therapies for treating heroin addicts. The results of this study are particularly impressive because family therapy resulted in twice as many days of abstinence from heroin than a methadone-maintenance program.

The Milan group's early work was filled with anecdotal case reports of amazing outcome with anorexia nervosa, schizophrenia, and delinquency (Selvini Palazzoli, Boscolo, Cecchin, and Prata, 1978b, 1980). Later, however, members of the original team expressed reservations about the model and implied that it wasn't as effective as they originally suggested (Selvini Palazzoli, 1986; Selvini Palazzoli and Viaro, 1988; Boscolo, 1983).

Some who have studied the Milan model more systematically concur with these less enthusiastic impressions. Sandra Coleman (1987) compared a group of families treated with the Milan approach to another group treated with a structural/strategic model. The results with the Milan model were far inferior to those obtained with the structural/strategic approach. Another study (Machal, Feldman, and Sigal, 1989) found that only a little over half of the parents in families treated by their Milan team reported positive changes in their family at follow-up, half reported disliking the therapy, and about two-thirds had at least one member who went on for further treatment.

In discussing their disappointing results with the Milan model, the authors of both of these studies cited clients' negative reactions to the therapist or team. Families frequently felt that the therapists were cold and distant and the team was impersonal. It seems that sometimes the attitude of adversarial strategizing recommended in *Paradox and Counterparadox* showed through the therapists' attempts to positively connote family members. It would be interesting to replicate these studies using the same techniques, but with therapists who were influenced by the recent trends in family therapy to feel less adversarial and more empathetic toward the families. We seem to have to learn the same lesson over and over: people have trouble changing if they don't feel cared about.

These studies question the effectiveness of the original Milan model. The fact that none of the founders of this model continues to practice it also indicates that, despite its initial appeal and popularity, it had problems. There is a lesson somewhere in family therapy's initial infatuation and later disillusionment with the Milan model.

The studies of strategic therapy provide some support for its efficacy with some kinds of problems. It is difficult to generalize these results too far, in part because the strategic therapy is far from a homogeneous approach. The forms used in these different studies differ considerably from each other. Also, the number of rigorous studies is quite small.

SUMMARY

Derived from a combination of Ericksonian hypnotherapy and Batesonian cybernetics, strategic therapy has developed a body of powerful procedures for treating psychological problems. Strategic approaches vary in the specifics of theory and technique, but share a problem-centered, pragmatic focus on changing behavioral sequences, in which therapists take responsibility for the outcome of therapy. Insight and understanding are eschewed in favor of directives designed to change the way family members relate to each other. Because strategic therapists prefer to circumvent rather than deal directly with resistance, their directives are often paradoxical.

There are two main strategic camps: the MRI group on the West Coast, and Haley and Madanes on the East. The MRI model tries to remain strictly interactional—observing and intervening into sequences of interaction surrounding a problem rather than speculating about the feelings or intentions of the interactants. Haley and Madanes are interested in motives—Haley mainly in the desire to control others, and Madanes in the desire to love and be loved. In addition, unlike the MRI group, Haley and Madanes incorporate many structural concepts in their model and don't limit their goals to simple problem resolution. They believe successful treatment often requires structural change, with an emphasis on improving family hierarchy.

Like Haley, the Milan Associates originally saw power in the motives of family members and tried to understand the elaborate multigenerational games that surrounded symptoms. They designed powerful interventions—positive connotations and rituals—to expose or disrupt these games, and to change the meaning of the problem. Later the original group split, with Selvini Palazzoli and new colleagues maintaining their games-orientation and experimenting with a method they call the invariant prescription, and Cecchin and Boscolo moving away from the power of single interventions and becoming more interested in the questioning process as a way to help families to new understandings.

While these models seem to have retained their popularity, the MRI and Haley-Madanes strategic family therapies as well as Selvini Palazzoli's version of the Milan model are all based on a therapist-family relationship that the field seems to be moving away from (see Chapter 11). These schools have developed unquestionably powerful techniques that are applied by a therapist who, in the role of expert, assesses the family and comes up with a creative directive, without much input from the family. Currently family therapy is experimenting with approaches that are far more collaborative in the sense of working with family members to help them find their resources. If this trend continues, it will be interesting to see how these strategic schools react since they are based so strongly on the noncollaborative, authority position of the therapist.

REFERENCES

Alexander, J., and Parsons, B. 1973. Short-term behavioral intervention with delinquent families: Impact on family process and recidivism. *Journal of Abnormal Psychology.* 81:219–225.

Alexander, J., and Parsons, B. 1982. *Functional family therapy.* Monterey, CA: Brooks Cole.

Andersen, T. 1987. The reflecting team: Dialogue and meta-dialogue in clinical work. *Family Process.* 26:415–417.

Andolfi, M. 1979. *Family therapy: An international approach.* New York: Plenum Press.

Andolfi, M., and Zwerling, I., eds. 1980. *Dimensions of family therapy.* New York: Guilford Press.

Bergman, J. 1985. *Fishing for barracuda: Pragmatics of brief systemic therapy.* New York: Norton.

Boscolo, L. 1983. Final discussion. In *Psychosocial intervention in schizophrenia: An international view,* H. Stierlin, L. Wynne, and M. Wirsching, eds. Berlin: Springer-Verlag.

Boscolo, L., Cecchin, G., Hoffman, L., and Penn, P. 1987. *Milan systemic family therapy.* New York: Basic Books.

Breunlin, D., and Schwartz, R. 1986. Sequences: Toward a common denominator of family therapy. *Family Process. 25*:67–87.

Cecchin, G. 1987. Hypothesizing, circularity and neutrality revisited: An invitation to curiosity. *Family Process. 26*:405–413.

Coleman, S. 1987. Milan in Bucks County. *Family Therapy Networker. 11*:42–47.

Coyne, J. 1987. Depression, biology, marriage and marital therapy. *Journal of Marital and Family Therapy. 13*:393–408.

Coyne, J., Kahn, J., and Gotlib, I. 1987. Depression. In *Family interaction and psychopathology*, T. Jacob, ed. New York: Plenum Press.

Fisch, R. 1978. Review of *Problem-solving therapy* by Jay Haley. *Family Process. 17*:107–110.

Fisch, R., Watzlawick, P., Weakland, J., and Bodin, A. 1973. On unbecoming family therapists. In *The book of family therapy*, A. Ferber, M. Mendelsohn, and A. Napier, eds. Boston: Houghton Mifflin.

Fisch, R., Weakland, J., and Segal, L. 1982. *The tactics of change*. San Francisco: Jossey Bass.

Frankl, V. 1960. Paradoxical intention: A logotherapeutic technique. *American Journal of Psychotherapy. 14*:520–535.

Gelcer, E., and Schwartzbein, D. 1989. A Piagetian view of family therapy: Selvini Palazzoli and the invariant approach. *Family Process. 28*:439–456.

Haley, J. 1963. *Strategies of psychotherapy*. New York: Grune and Stratton.

Haley, J. 1973. *Uncommon therapy*. New York: Norton.

Haley, J. 1976. *Problem-solving therapy*. San Francisco: Jossey Bass.

Haley, J. 1980. *Leaving home: The therapy of disturbed young people*. New York: McGraw-Hill.

Haley, J. 1981. *Reflections on therapy*. Chevy Chase, MD: The Family Therapy Institute of Washington DC.

Haley, J. 1984. *Ordeal therapy*. San Francisco: Jossey Bass.

Hare-Mustin, R. 1975. Treatment of temper tantrums by a paradoxical intervention. *Family Process. 14*:481–485.

Hoffman, L. 1981. *Foundations of family therapy*. New York: Basic Books.

Hoffman, L. 1983. A coevolutionary framework for systemic family therapy. In *Diagnosis and assessment in family therapy*, J. Hansen and B. Keeney, eds. Rockville, MD: Aspen Systems.

Jackson, D. D. 1967. The myth of normality. *Medical Opinion and Review. 3*:28–33.

Langsley, D., Machotka, P., and Flomenhaft, K. 1971. Avoiding mental hospital admission: A follow-up study. *American Journal of Psychiatry. 127*:1391–1394.

Machal, M., Feldman, R., and Sigal, J. 1989. The unraveling of a treatment program: A follow-up study of the Milan approach to family therapy. *Family Process. 28*:457–470.

Madanes, C. 1980. Protection, paradox and pretending. *Family Process. 19*:73–85.

Madanes, C. 1981. *Strategic family therapy*. San Francisco: Jossey-Bass.

Madanes, C. 1984. *Behind the one-way mirror*. San Francisco: Jossey-Bass.

Madanes, C. 1990. *Sex, love, and violence: Strategies for transformation.* New York: Norton.

Minuchin, S. 1974. *Families and family therapy.* Cambridge, MA: Harvard University Press.

Papp, P. 1980. The Greek chorus and other techniques of paradoxical therapy. *Family Process. 19*:45–57.

Papp, P. 1983. *The process of change.* New York: Guilford.

Parsons, B., and Alexander, J. 1973. Short term family intervention: A therapy outcome study. *Journal of Consulting and Clinical Psychology. 41*:195–201.

Penn, P. 1982. Circular questioning. *Family Process. 21*:267–280.

Penn, P. 1985. Feed-forward: Further questioning, future maps. *Family Process. 24*:299–310.

Rabkin, R. 1977. *Strategic psychotherapy.* New York: Basic Books.

Rohrbaugh, M., Tennen, H., Press, S., and White, L. 1981. Compliance, defiance, and therapeutic paradox: Guidelines for strategic use of paradoxical interventions. *American Journal of Orthopsychiatry. 51*: 454–466.

Satir, V. 1964. *Conjoint family therapy.* Palo Alto: Science and Behavior Books.

Selvini, M., ed. 1988. *The work of mara selvini palazzoli.* Northvale, NJ: Aronson.

Selvini Palazzoli, M. 1981. *Self-starvation: From the intrapsychic to the transpersonal approach to anorexia nervosa.* New York: Aronson.

Selvini Palazzoli, M. 1986. Towards a general model of psychotic games. *Journal of Marital and Family Therapy. 12*:339–349.

Selvini Palazzoli, M., Boscolo, L., Cecchin, G., and Prata, G. 1978a. A ritualized prescription in family therapy: Odd days and even days. *Journal of Marriage and Family Counseling, 4*:3–9.

Selvini Palazzoli, M., Boscolo, L., Cecchin, G., and Prata, G. 1978b. *Paradox and counterparadox.* New York: Jason Aronson.

Selvini Palazzoli, M., Boscolo, L., Cecchin, G., and Prata, G. 1980. Hypothesizing—circularity—neutrality: Three guidelines for the conductor of the session. *Family Process. 19*:3–12.

Selvini Palazzoli, M., and Prata, G. 1983. A new method for therapy and research in the treatment of schizophrenic families. In *Psychosocial intervention in schizophrenia: An international view*, H. Stierlin, L. Wynne, and M. Wirsching, eds. Berlin: Springer-Verlag.

Selvini Palazzoli, M., and Viaro, M. 1988. The anorectic process in the family: A six-stage model as a guide for individual therapy. *Family Process. 27*:129–148.

Sluzki, C. 1978. Marital therapy from a systems theory perspective. In *Marriage and marital therapy: Psychoanalytic, behavioral and systems therapy perspectives*, T. J. Paolino and B. S. McCrady, eds. New York: Brunner/Mazel.

Stanton, D. 1981. Strategic approaches to family therapy. In *Handbook of Family Therapy*, A. Gurman and D. Kniskern, eds. New York: Brunner/Mazel.

Stanton, D., Todd, T., and Associates. 1982. *The family therapy of drug abuse and addiction*. New York: Guilford.

Tomm, K. 1984a. One perspective on the Milan systemic approach: Part I. Overview of development, theory and practice. *Journal of Marital and Family Therapy. 10*:113–125.

Tomm, K. 1984b. One perspective on the Milan systemic approach: Part II. Description of session format, interviewing style and interventions. *Journal of Marital and Family Therapy. 10*:253–271.

Tomm, K. 1987a. Interventive interviewing: Part I. Strategizing as a fourth guideline for the therapist. *Family Process. 26*:3–13.

Tomm, K. 1987b. Interventive Interviewing: Part II. Reflexive questioning as a means to enable self-healing. *Family Process. 26*:167–184.

Watzlawick, P., Beavin, J., and Jackson, D. 1967. *The pragmatics of human communication*. New York: Norton.

Watzlawick, P., Weakland, J., and Fisch, R. 1974. *Change: Principles of problem formation and problem resolution*. New York: Norton.

Weakland, J., Fisch, R., Watzlawick, P., and Bodin, A. 1974. Brief therapy: Focused problem resolution. *Family Process. 13*:141–168.

10

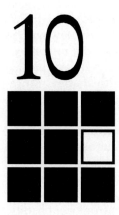

Structural Family Therapy

In the 1970s structural family therapy emerged as perhaps the most influential approach in the field. This predominance came about, not only because of the effectiveness of the approach, but also because of the stunning virtuosity of its primary exponent, Salvador Minuchin. Known initially as a clinician rather than a theoretician, Minuchin first established his reputation in dramatic and compelling teaching demonstrations; but he also described families as having an underlying organization in terms that provide clear guidelines for diagnosis and treatment.

One of the reasons family therapy is so difficult is that families often appear as collections of individuals who affect each other in powerful but unpredictable ways. Beginning therapists are usually puzzled by the complex transactions that make up family life. Structural family therapy offers a clear framework that brings order and meaning to those transactions. The consistent, repetitive, organized, and predictable patterns of family behavior are what allow us to consider that they have a structure, although, of course, only in a functional sense. The emotional boundaries and coalitions that make up family structure are abstractions; nevertheless, using the concept of family structure enables therapists to intervene in a systematic and organized fashion.

Salvador Minuchin began seeing families of institutionalized children in the late 1950s. Unlike other family therapists, he didn't have to make the transition from sitting in an office listening and talking to doing family therapy; as a child psychiatrist working with delinquents, he always had to use action and pressure. And he had to understand people in context, because even the hard-core toughs he worked with were always pushed and pulled by the pressures of the gang and pressures of the family. Moreover, given where he chose to start his career, it should come as no surprise that Minuchin has always been passionately concerned with social issues.

When he first burst onto the scene, Minuchin's immediate galvanizing impact was as a clinician, an incomparable master of technique. But perhaps his most lasting impact will prove to be the development of a theory of family structure and a set of guidelines for treatment to organize his therapeutic techniques: Families who come for treatment are seen as stuck for lack of alternatives; therapy is designed to unfreeze them from rigid habits, creating the opportunity for new structures to emerge. This approach was so successful that it captivated the field of family therapy in the 1970s, and Minuchin helped build the Philadelphia Child Guidance Clinic into a world-famous complex, where thousands of family therapists have been trained in structural family therapy.

SKETCHES OF LEADING FIGURES

Minuchin was born and raised in Argentina. He served as a physician in the Israeli army, then came to the United States, where he trained in child psychiatry with Nathan Ackerman at the Jewish Board of Guardians in New York City. After completing his studies, Minuchin returned to Israel in 1952 to work with displaced children—and to become absolutely committed to the importance of families. He moved back to the United States in 1954 to begin psychoanalytic training at the William Alanson White Institute, where he was imbued with the interpersonal psychiatry of Harry Stack Sullivan. After leaving the White Institute, Minuchin took a job at the Wiltwyck School for delinquent boys, where he suggested to his colleagues that they start seeing families. Other family therapists during this period, such as Nathan Ackerman and Don Jackson, were working with middle-class families; their approaches hardly seemed suitable to multi-problem, poor families with children at Wiltwyck. Therefore Minuchin had to develop new concepts and techniques applicable to these families, one of which was of the idea of *enactment*—that is, bringing problematic sequences into the treatment room by having families act them out so that the therapist can observe and change them. Most of Minuchin's techniques were concrete and action-oriented, developments that have continued to characterize structural family therapy ever since.

At Wiltwyck, Minuchin and his colleagues—Dick Auerswald, Charlie King, Braulio Montalvo, and Clara Rabinowitz—taught themselves to do family therapy, inventing it as they went along. To do so, they built what may have been the first one-way mirror and took turns observing each other work. In 1962 Minuchin made a hajj to what was then the Mecca of family therapy, Palo Alto. Here he met Jay Haley and began a friendship that was to bear fruit in an extraordinarily productive collaboration. A couple of years later Minuchin renewed his contact with Nathan Ackerman, who from 1950 to 1952 had guided his early development as a child psychiatrist. Minuchin credits Ackerman with demonstrating the personal power of a therapist passionately engaged with the families he treats. While most family therapists are observers, Minuchin, like Ackerman, joins the families he treats, becoming for a time one of them.

The clinical and conceptual success of Minuchin's work with the families at Wiltwyck led to a book, *Families of the Slums*, written with Montalvo, Guerney, Rosman, and Schumer. Minuchin's reputation as a practitioner of family therapy grew, and he became the Director of the Philadelphia Child Guidance Clinic in 1965. The Clinic, located in the heart of Philadelphia's black ghetto, then consisted of less than a dozen staff members. From this modest beginning Minuchin created one of the largest and most prestigious child guidance clinics in the world. When he stepped down ten years later, there were three hundred people on the staff and the clinic had become part of an elaborate modern complex along with the Children's Hospital of Philadelphia adjacent to the University of Pennsylvania campus.

Among Minuchin's colleagues in Philadelphia were Braulio Montalvo, Jay Haley, Bernice Rosman, Harry Aponte, Carter Umbarger, Marianne Walters, Charles Fishman, Cloe Madanes, and Stephen Greenstein, all of whom have had an important role in shaping structural family therapy. Many other therapists associated with the Philadelphia Child Guidance Clinic as students and staff members have also influenced structural family therapy with their own ideas and styles; these second-generation structuralists are now dispersed throughout the country. By the late 1970s structural family therapy had become, perhaps, the most influential and widely practiced of all systems of family therapy.

When he was working with poor people at Wiltwyck, Minuchin says he got no flack for doing family therapy. The flack came when he turned the Philadelphia Child Guidance Clinic into a family therapy center. Both the APA and AMA raised serious questions: Was family therapy proper for the training of child psychiatrists? Could Minuchin's unorthodox notion that family therapy and child psychiatry should be synonymous be right? Accused of heresy and summoned to constant meetings to defend his point of view, Minuchin responded strategically: He didn't show up at the meetings. But even more important than his refusal to take the defensive was the fact that the influential institution he created gave him a power base from which he was able to fight and win a place for family therapy in the medical establishment.

In 1975 Minuchin stepped down as Director of the Philadelphia Child Guidance Center, but stayed on as the head of its training until 1981. He now directs his own clinic, Family Studies, Inc., and travels around the world teaching and demonstrating his uniquely charismatic brand of family therapy. Perhaps less widely known, but also perhaps closer to his heart, is Minuchin's dedication to reforming the social welfare system in New York City, especially the foster care process that continues to separate children from their parents.

Like players on the same team with a superstar, some of Minuchin's colleagues are not as well known as they might be. Chief among these is Braulio Montalvo, one of the great and underrated geniuses of family therapy. Born and raised in Puerto Rico, Montalvo, like Minuchin, has always been committed to treating minority families. He is also like Minuchin in being a brilliant therapist, though he favors a gentler, more supportive approach. Montalvo was instrumental in building the Philadelphia Child Guidance Clinic, but his contributions are less well known because he is a quiet man who usually works behind the scenes.

THEORETICAL FORMULATIONS

The prominence of structural family therapy is due in part to Minuchin's renown as a clinician, and to the excellent training programs offered at the Philadelphia Child Guidance Clinic, but also to the fact that Minuchin's theory is both simple and practical.

Most therapists are impatient with theories: They see them as abstractions, which they are eager to bypass in order to learn techniques. But all the clever techniques and impressive interventions that one can pick up from books and supervisors are nothing but tactical maneuvers. Without a map you're lost—caught up in the detailed content of family discussions with no overall plan. This often occurs in individual psychotherapy, where therapists become experts at passivity: You can sit back and listen impassively, week after week, as Mr. Jones bitches about his wife. As long as he gets some relief from just complaining there's no need to do much but listen and nod sympathetically. In family work it's harder to be passive. Family members aren't confirmed into the status of patienthood and they won't put up with a passive therapist. They want action! They want solutions! They want a therapist to solve their problems. Families present problem after problem, crisis after crisis, and demand that therapists *Do Something!*

Beginners tend to get caught up in the content of family problems because they don't have a theory to help them see the process of family dynamics. Structural family therapy is a blueprint for analyzing the process of family interactions. As such, it provides a basis for consistent strategies of treatment, which obviates the need to have a specific technique—usually someone else's—for every occasion.

Three constructs are the essential components of structural family theory: *structure*, *subsystems*, and *boundaries.*

Family structure, the organized pattern in which family members interact, is a deterministic concept, but it doesn't prescribe or legislate behavior; it *describes* sequences that are predictable. When they are repeated, family transactions establish enduring patterns. These repeated patterns determine how, when, and to whom family members relate. When a mother tells her daughter to pick up the toys and the daughter refuses until the father shouts at her, an interactional pattern is initiated. If it's repeated, it creates a structure in which father is competent as a disciplinarian, mother is incompetent. In addition, mother is likely to be more affectionate to her daughter, while father, the disciplinarian, remains on the outside.

Family structure involves a set of covert rules which govern transactions in the family. For example, a rule such as "family members must always protect one another" will be manifested in various ways depending on context and which family members are involved. If an adolescent son has to be up early for school, mother wakes him; father does all the shopping if driving makes the mother nervous; the kids intervene to diffuse conflict between the parents; and the parents' preoccupation with the kids' problems keeps the couple from spending time together. All of these sequences are isomorphic; they are structured. Changing any of them may or may not affect the underlying structure, but altering the basic structure will have ripple effects on all family transactions.

Family structure is shaped partly by universal and partly by idiosyncratic constraints. For example, all families have some kind of hierarchical structure, with parents and children having different amounts of authority. Family members also tend to have reciprocal and complementary functions. If one parent is supercompetent and responsible, the other will be less so; if the supercompetent one gets "sick" or less competent in some other way, the other will take over.

Transactional patterns foster expectations that determine future patterns. Often these become so ingrained that their origin is forgotten, and they are presumed necessary rather than optional. If a young mother, burdened by the demands of her infant, gets upset and complains to her husband, he may respond in various ways. Perhaps he'll move closer and share the heavy demands of childrearing. This creates a united parental team. On the other hand, if he decides, and his wife concurs, that she is "depressed," she may be sent into psychotherapy to get the emotional support she needs. This creates a structure where the mother remains distant from her husband, and learns to turn outside the family for emotional support. Whatever the chosen pattern, it tends to be self-perpetuating and resistant to change. Although alternatives are available, families are unlikely to consider them until changing circumstances produce stress and dysfunction in the system.

Family structure is not easily discerned. Two things are necessary: a theoretical system that explains structure, and seeing the family in action. The facts are not enough. Knowing that a family is a single-parent family with three children, or that two parents are having trouble with a middle child doesn't tell you what the family structure is. Structure only becomes evident when you observe the actual interactions among family members over time. Single interactions are affected by specific circumstances; repeated sequences reveal structural patterns.

Consider the following example. A mother calls the clinic to complain of misbehavior in her 17-year-old son. She is asked to bring her husband, son, and their three other children to the first session. When they arrive, the mother begins to describe a series of minor ways in which the son is disobedient around the house. He responds angrily, saying nobody understands him and he never gets any sympathy from his mother. This spontaneous dialogue between mother and son reveals an intense involvement between them—an involvement no less real or intense simply because it is conflictual. This dyadic sequence doesn't tell the whole story, however, because it doesn't include the father or the other three children. They must be engaged in interaction to observe their role in the family structure. If the father sides with his wife, but seems unconcerned, then it may be that the mother's preoccupation with her son is related to her husband's lack of involvement. Further, if the three younger children tend to agree with the mother and describe their brother as bad, then it becomes clear that all the children are close to the mother—close and obedient up to a point, then close and disobedient.

Families are differentiated into *subsystems* of members who join together to perform various functions. Every individual is a subsystem, and dyads or larger groups make up other subsystems, determined by generation, gender, or common interests. Obvious groupings such as the parents or the teenagers are sometimes less significant than covert coalitions. A mother and her youngest child may form such a tightly bonded system that others are excluded. Another family may be split into two camps, with Mom and the boys on one side, and Dad and the girls on the other. Though certain patterns are common, the possibilities for subgrouping are endless.

Every family member plays many roles in several subgroups. Mary may be a wife, a mother, a daughter, and a niece. In each of these roles she will be required to behave differently and exercise a variety of interpersonal options. If she's mature and flexible, she will be able to vary her behavior to fit the different subgroups in which she functions. Scolding may be okay from a mother, but it causes problems from a wife or a daughter.

Individuals, subsystems, and whole families are demarcated by *interpersonal boundaries*, invisible barriers that surround individuals and subsystems, regulating the amount of contact with others. Boundaries serve to protect the separateness and autonomy of the family and its subsystems. A rule forbidding phone calls at dinner time establishes a boundary which protects the family from outside intrusion. When small children are permitted to freely interrupt their parents' conversation at dinner, the boundary separating the parents from the children is minimal. Subsystems that aren't adequately protected by boundaries limit the development of interpersonal skills achievable in these subsystems. If parents always step in to settle arguments between their children, the children won't learn to fight their own battles and will be impaired in their dealings with peers.

Interpersonal boundaries vary from being rigid to diffuse (Figure 10.1). Rigid boundaries are overly restrictive and permit little contact with outside systems, resulting in *disengagement*. Disengaged individuals or subsystems are relatively isolated and autonomous. On the positive side, this permits independence, growth, and mastery. If parents don't hover over their children, telling them what to do and fighting their battles, then the children will be forced to develop their own resources. On the other hand, disengagement limits warmth, affection, and nurturance; and disengaged families must be under extreme stress before they mobilize mutual support. If parents keep their children at a distance, affection is minimized, and the parents will be slow to notice when the children need support and guidance.

Enmeshed subsystems offer a heightened sense of mutual support, but at the expense of independence and autonomy. Enmeshed parents are loving and considerate; they spend a lot of time with their kids and do a lot for them. However, children enmeshed with their parents learn to rely on the parents and tend to be dependent. They're less comfortable by themselves, and may have trouble relating to people outside the family.

Minuchin described some of the features of family subsystems in his most accessible work, *Families and Family Therapy* (Minuchin, 1974). Families begin when two people join together to form a spouse subsystem. Two people in love agree to share their lives and futures and expectations, but a period of often difficult adjustment is required before they can complete the transition from courtship to a functional spouse subsystem. They must

FIGURE 10.1   Interpersonal Boundaries

Rigid Boundary	Clear Boundary	Diffuse Boundary
_____	- - - - - - - - -	. . . .
Disengagement	Normal Range	Enmeshment

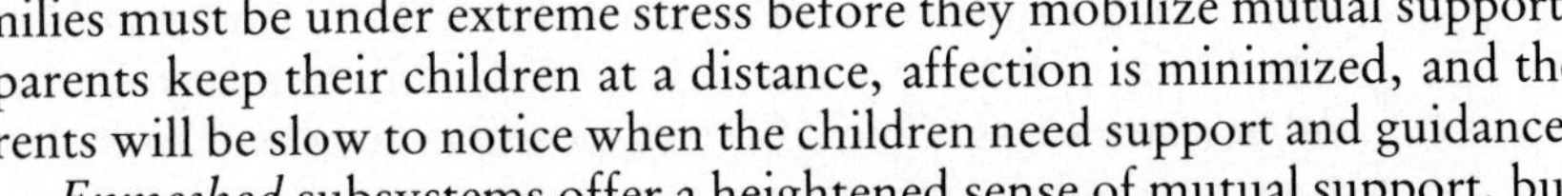

learn to *accommodate* to each other's needs and preferred styles of inter-action. In a normal couple, each gives and gets. He learns to accommodate to her wish to be kissed hello and goodbye. She learns to leave him alone with his paper and morning coffee. These little arrangements, multiplied a thousand times, may be accomplished easily or only after intense struggle. Whatever the case, this process of accommodation cements the couple into a unit.

The couple must also develop complementary patterns of mutual sup-port. Some patterns are transitory and may later be reversed—perhaps, for instance, one works while the other completes school. Other patterns are more stable and lasting. Traditional sex-role stereotypes may allow couples to achieve complementarity, but at the expense of fully rounded functioning for each spouse. A traditional woman may not have to open doors, earn a living, or mow the lawn; on the other hand, she may have to deny her own intelligence, submerge her independence, and live in the shadow of her husband. A traditional husband may get to make all the decisions, not have to change dirty diapers, and be waited on hand and foot around the house; however, the price for these "masculine" prerogatives may be that he's not allowed to cry, never learns the pleasure of cooking a special meal, and doesn't share the joy of caring for his children.

Exaggerated complementary roles can detract from individual growth; moderate complementarity enables spouses to divide functions, to support and enrich each other. When one has the flu and feels lousy, the other takes over. One's permissiveness with children may be balanced by the other's strictness. One's fiery disposition may help to melt the other's icy reserve. Complementary patterns, such as pursuer-distancer, active-passive, dominant-submissive, exist in most couples. They become pathological when they are so exaggerated that they create a dysfunctional subsystem. Therapists must learn to accept those structural patterns that work, and challenge only those that do not.

The spouse subsystem must also have a boundary which separates it from parents, from children, and from the outside world. All too often, husband and wife give up the space they need for supporting each other when children are born. A rigid boundary around the couple deprives the children of the support they need; but in our child-centered culture, usually the boundary separating parents and children is extremely diffuse.

The birth of a child instantly transforms the family structure; the pattern of interaction between the parental and child subsystems must be worked out and then modified to fit changing circumstances. A clear bound-ary enables the children to interact with their parents, but excludes them from the spouse subsystem. Parents and children eat together, play to-gether, and share much of each others' lives. But there are some spouse functions which need not be shared. Husband and wife are sustained as a loving couple, and enhanced as parents, if they have time to be alone together—alone to talk, alone to go out to dinner occasionally, alone to fight, and alone to make love. Unhappily, the demands of small children often make parents lose sight of their need to maintain a boundary.

In addition to maintaining some privacy for the couple, a clear boundary establishes a hierarchical structure in which parents exercise a position of leadership. All too often this hierarchy is disrupted by a child-centered ethos, which influences family therapists as well as parents. Parents enmeshed with their children tend to argue with them about who's in charge, and misguidedly share—or shirk—the responsibility for making parental decisions. Offering a child the choice in picking out clothes or choosing friends is respectful and flexible. Asking children whether they want to go to school, or trying to convince a toddler to agree that it's dangerous to play in the street simply blurs the line of authority.

In his most recent book, *Institutionalizing Madness* (Elizur and Minuchin, 1989), Minuchin makes a compelling case for a systems view of family problems that extends beyond the family itself to encompass the entire community. As long as they confine their attention to the nuclear family, family therapists themselves suffer from a myopia that may produce solutions that don't work. Minuchin points out, forcefully, that unless family therapists learn to look beyond the limited slice of ecology where they work, to the larger social structures within which their work is embedded, their efforts may amount to little more than spinning wheels.

NORMAL FAMILY DEVELOPMENT

The prevailing view is that normal family life is happy and harmonious. This is an idealized myth. Normal families are constantly struggling with problems in living. What distinguishes a normal family is not the absence of problems, but a functional family structure. Normal husbands and wives must learn to adjust to each other, rear their children, deal with their parents, cope with their jobs, and fit into their communities. The nature of these struggles changes with developmental stages and situational crises. Normal family life is neither static nor problem free. Nevertheless, as Minuchin put it, "the myth of placid normality endures, supported by hours of two-dimensional television characters" (1974, p. 50).

When two people marry, the structural requirements for the new union are *accommodation* and *boundary making*. The first priority is mutual accommodation to manage the myriad details of everyday living. Each spouse tries to organize the relationship along familiar lines, and pressures the other to accommodate. Each must adjust to the other's expectations and wants. They must agree on major issues, such as where to live and if and when to have children; less obvious, but equally important, they must coordinate daily rituals, like what to watch on television, what to eat for supper, when to go to bed, and what to do there. Often the little things are the most irksome and problematic, and the couple may argue heatedly about who will take out the garbage, or wash the clothes.

In accommodating to each other, the couple also must negotiate the nature of the boundary between them, as well as the boundary separating them from the outside. A vague, diffuse boundary exists between the couple if they call each other at work frequently; if neither has separate friends or outside independent activities; and if they come to view themselves only as a pair rather than also as two separate personalities. On the other hand, they've established a rigid boundary between them if they spend little time doing things together, have separate bedrooms, take separate vacations, have different checking accounts, and each is considerably more invested in careers or outside relationships than in their marriage. While none of these markers by itself defines enmeshment or disengagement, each of them suggests the pattern that will develop.

Typically spouses come from families with differing degrees of en-meshment or disengagement. Each spouse tends to be more comfortable with the sort of proximity that existed in the family of origin. Since these expectations differ, a struggle ensues that may be the most difficult aspect of a new marriage. He wants to go play poker with the boys; she feels deserted. She wants to hold hands and whisper in the movies; he wants to concentrate on the picture. His major attention is on his career; her major attention is on the marriage. Each thinks the other wrong, unreasonable— and terribly hurtful.

Couples must also define a boundary separating them from their orig-inal families. Rather suddenly the families that each grew up in must take second place to the new marriage. This, too, is a difficult adjustment, both for newlyweds and their parents. Families of origin vary in the ease with which they accept and support the new union.

The addition of children transforms the structure of the new family into an *executive parental subsystem* and a *sibling subsystem*. It's typical for spouses to have different patterns of commitment to the babies. A woman's commitment to a unit of three is likely to begin with pregnancy, since the child inside her belly is an unavoidable reality. Her husband, on the other hand, may only begin to feel like a father when the child is born. Many men don't accept the role of father until the infants are old enough to begin to respond to them. Thus, even in normal families, children bring with them great potential for stress and conflict. The woman's life is usually more radically transformed than the man's. She sacrifices a great deal and typically needs more support from her husband. The husband, meanwhile, continues his job, and the new baby is far less of a disruption. Though he may try to support his wife, he's likely to resent some of her demands as inordinate and unreasonable.

The family takes care of the psychosocial needs of the children and transmits the culture to them. Children develop a dual identity within the family; a sense of belongingness and a sense of being separate. John Smith is both a Smith and also John; part of the family, yet a unique person.

Children require different styles of parenting at different ages. Infants primarily need nurturance and support. Older children need guidance and control; and adolescents need independence and responsibility. Good parenting for a two-year-old may be totally inadequate for a five-year-old or a fourteen-year-old. Normal parents adjust to these developmental challenges. The family modifies its structure to adapt to new additions, to the children's growth and development, and to changes in the external environment.

Minuchin (1974) warns family therapists not to mistake family growing pains for pathology. The normal family experiences anxiety and disruption as its members adapt to growth and change. Many families seek help at transitional stages, and therapists must keep in mind that they may be in the process of modifying their structure to accommodate to new circumstances.

All families face situations that stress the system. Although no clear dividing line exists between normal and abnormal families, we can say that normal families modify their structure to accommodate to changed circumstances; pathological families increase the rigidity of structures that are no longer functional.

DEVELOPMENT OF BEHAVIOR DISORDERS _____

Family systems must be stable enough to insure continuity, but flexible enough to accommodate to changing circumstances. Behavior disorders arise when inflexible family structures cannot adjust adequately to maturational or situational challenges. Adaptive changes in structure are required when the family or one of its members faces external stress and when transitional points of growth are reached.

Structural family therapists use a few simple symbols to diagram structural problems, and these diagrams usually make it clear what changes are required. Figure 10.2 shows some of the symbols used to diagram family structure (see page 456).

One problem often seen by family therapists arises when parents who are unable to resolve the conflicts between them divert the focus of concern onto a child. Instead of worrying about each other, they worry about the child (see Figure 10.3). Although this reduces the strain on father (F) and mother (M), it victimizes the child (C) and is therefore dysfunctional.

An alternate but equally common pattern is for the parents to continue to argue through the children. Father says mother is too permissive; she says he's too strict. He may withdraw, causing her to criticize his handling of the child, which in turn causes further withdrawal. The enmeshed mother responds to the child's needs with excessive concern and devotion. The

FIGURE 10.2   Symbols of Family Structure

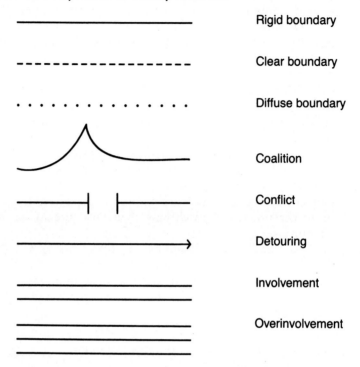

disengaged father tends not to respond even when a response is necessary. Both may be critical of the other's way, but both perpetuate the other's behavior with their own. The result is a *cross-generational coalition* between mother and child, which excludes the father (Figure 10.4).

Some families function quite well when the children are small, but are unable to adjust to a growing child's needs for discipline and control. Parents may be particularly solicitous of children if they have had reason to worry about the children's health, if they had to wait a long time before they had them, or if they have few interests outside the family to give

FIGURE 10.3   Scapegoating as a Means of Detouring Conflict

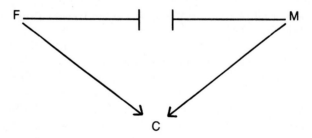

FIGURE 10.4   Mother-Child Coalition

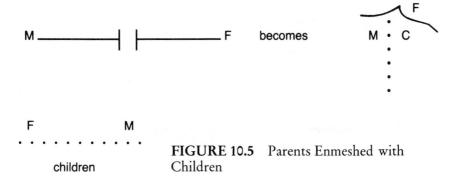

F   M

children

FIGURE 10.5   Parents Enmeshed with Children

meaning to their lives. Parents who are unable to have children of their own, and finally decide to adopt, may find it very difficult to set appropriate limits. They're too invested and enmeshed with their children to be able to exercise appropriate control (Figure 10.5).

Infants in enmeshed families receive wonderful care: their parents hug them, love them, and give them lots of stimulation. Although such parents may be too tired from caring for the children to have much time for each other or for outside interests, the system may be moderately successful. However, if these doting parents don't teach the children to obey rules and respect adult authority, the children may be unprepared to successfully negotiate their entrance into school. Used to getting their own way, they may be unruly and disruptive. Several possible consequences of this situation may bring the family into treatment. The children may be afraid to go to school, for instance, and their fears may be covertly reinforced by "understanding" parents who permit them to remain at home (Figure 10.6). Such a case may be labeled as school phobia, and may become entrenched if the parents permit the children to remain at home for more than a few days.

The children of such a family may go to school; but since they haven't learned to accommodate to others they may be rejected by their schoolmates. These children may become depressed and withdrawn. In other cases, children enmeshed with their parents become discipline problems at school, and the school authorities may initiate counseling.

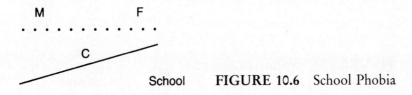

School   **FIGURE 10.6**   School Phobia

FIGURE 10.7   Divorce and Remarriage

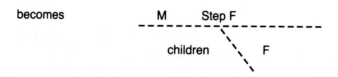

A major change in family composition that requires structural adjustment occurs when divorced or widowed spouses remarry. Such "blended families" either readjust their boundaries or soon experience transitional conflicts. When a women divorces, she and the children must first learn to readjust to a structure that establishes a clear boundary separating the divorced spouses, but still permits contact between father and children; then if she remarries, the family must readjust to functioning with a new husband and stepfather (Figure 10.7). Sometimes it is hard for a mother and children to allow a stepfather to participate as an equal partner in the new parental subsystem. Mother and children have long since established transactional rules and have learned to accommodate to each other. The new parent may be treated as an outsider who's supposed to learn the "right" (accustomed) way of doing things, rather than a new partner who will give as well as receive ideas about childrearing (Figure 10.8). The more mother and children insist on maintaining their familiar patterns without adjusting to the modifications required to absorb the stepfather, the more frustrated and angry he'll become. The result may lead to child abuse or chronic arguing between the parents. The sooner such families enter treatment, the easier it is to help them adjust to the transition. The longer they wait, the more entrenched the structural problems become.

An important aspect of structural family problems is that symptoms in one member reflect not only that person's relationships with others, but also the fact that those relationships are a function of still other relationships in the family. If Johnny, aged sixteen, is depressed it's helpful to know

FIGURE 10.8   Failure to Accept a
Stepparent

that he's enmeshed with his mother. Discovering that she demands absolute obedience from him and refuses to let him develop his own thinking or outside relationships helps to explain his depression (Figure 10.9). But that is only a partial view of the family system, and therefore an incomplete guide to treatment.

Why is the mother enmeshed with her son? Perhaps she's disengaged from her husband; perhaps she's a widow who hasn't found new friends, a career, or any other outside interests. Helping Johnny resolve his depression may best be accomplished by helping his mother satisfy her needs for closeness with her husband or friends.

Because problems are a function of the entire family structure, it's important to include the whole group for assessment. For example, if a father complains of a child's misbehavior, seeing the child alone won't help the father to state rules clearly and enforce them effectively. Nor will seeing the father and child together do anything to stop the mother from undercutting the father's authority. Only by seeing the whole family interacting is it possible to get a complete picture of their structure.

Sometimes even seeing the whole family isn't enough. Structural family therapy is based on recognition of the importance of the context of the social system. The family may not be the complete or most relevant context. If one of the parents is having an affair, that relationship is a crucial part of the family's context. It may not be advisable to invite the lover to family sessions, but it is crucial to recognize the structural implications of the extramarital relationship.

In some cases, the family may not be the context most relevant to the presenting problem. A mother's depression may be due more to her relationships at work than at home. A son's problems at school may be due more to the structural context at school than to the one in the family. In such instances, structural family therapists work with the more relevant context to alleviate the presenting problems.

Finally, some problems may be treated as problems of the individual. As Minuchin has written, "Pathology may be inside the patient, in his

FIGURE 10.9

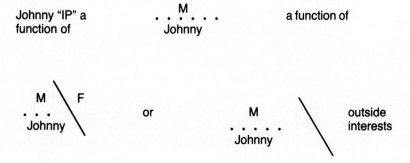

social context, or in the feedback between them" (1974, p. 9). Elsewhere Minuchin (Minuchin, Rosman, and Baker, 1978, p. 91) referred to the danger of "denying the individual while enthroning the system." Family therapists should therefore not overlook the possibility that some problems may be most appropriately dealt with on an individual basis. The therapist must not neglect the experience of individuals, although this is easy to do, especially with young children. While interviewing a family to see how the parents deal with their children, a careful clinician may notice that one child has a neurological problem or a learning disability. These problems need to be identified and appropriate referrals made. Usually when a child has trouble in school, there's a problem in the family or school context. Usually, but not always.

GOALS OF THERAPY

Structural family therapists believe that problems are maintained by dysfunctional family structures. Therefore therapy is directed at altering family structure so that the family can solve its problems. The goal of therapy is structural change; problem-solving is a by-product of this systemic goal.

The structural family therapist joins the family system in order to help its members change their structure. By altering boundaries and re-aligning subsystems, the therapist changes the behavior and experience of each of the family members. The therapist doesn't solve problems; that's the family's job. The therapist helps modify the family's functioning so that family members can solve their own problems. In this way, structural family therapy is like dynamic psychotherapy—symptom-resolution is sought not as an end in itself, but as a result of lasting structural change. The analyst modifies the structure of the patient's mind; the structural family therapist modifies the structure of the patient's family.

Symptomatic change and enhanced family functioning are seen as inextricably interrelated goals. The most effective way to change symptoms is to change the family patterns that maintain them. An effectively functioning family is a system that supports its members. The goal of structural family therapy is to facilitate the growth of the system in order to resolve symptoms and encourage growth in individuals, while also preserving the mutual support of the family.

Short-range goals may be to alleviate symptoms, especially life-threatening symptoms such as anorexia nervosa (Minuchin, Rosman, and Baker, 1978). At times behavioral techniques, suggestion, or manipulation may be used to provide temporary surcease. However, unless structural change in the family system is achieved, short-term symptom-resolution may collapse.

The goals for each family are dictated by the problems they present and by the nature of their structural dysfunction. Although every family is unique, there are common problems and typical structural goals; some aspects of family structure are thought to be generally important for all families.

Most important of the general goals for families is the creation of an effective hierarchical structure. Parents are expected to be in charge, not to relate as equals to their children. A general goal is to help parents function together as a cohesive executive subsystem. When only one parent is present, or when there are several children, one or more of the oldest children may be encouraged to be a parental assistant. But this child's needs must not be neglected, either.

With enmeshed families the goal is to differentiate individuals and subsystems by strengthening the boundaries around them. With disengaged families the goal is to increase interaction by making boundaries more permeable.

CONDITIONS FOR BEHAVIOR CHANGE

Structural family therapy changes behavior by opening alternative patterns of family interaction which can modify family structure. It's not a matter of creating new structures, but of activating dormant ones. If, once activated, the dormant sequences are functional, they will be reinforcing; and family structure will be transformed. When new transactional patterns become regularly repeated and predictably effective, they will stabilize the new and more functional structure.

The therapist produces change by joining the family, probing for areas of possible flexibility and change, and then activating dormant structural alternatives. *Joining* gets the therapist into the family; *accommodating* to their accustomed style gives him or her leverage; and *restructuring* interventions transform the family structure. If the therapist remains an outsider or uses interventions that are too dystonic, the family will reject him or her. If the therapist becomes too much a part of the family or uses interventions that are too syntonic, the family will assimilate the interventions into previous transactional patterns. In either case there will be no structural change.

For change to occur, the family must first accept the therapist, and then respond to his or her interventions as though to a novel situation. This increases stress, which in turn unbalances family homeostasis, and thus opens the way for structural transformation.

Joining and accommodating to the family is considered prerequisite to restructuring. To join the family the therapist must convey acceptance of family members and respect for their way of doing things. Minuchin (1974) likened the family therapist to an anthropologist who must first join a culture before being able to study it.

To join the family's culture the therapist makes accommodating overtures—the sort of thing we usually do unthinkingly, although often unsuccessfully. If parents come for help with a child's problems, the therapist shouldn't begin by asking for the child's views. This conveys a lack of respect for the parents and may lead them to reject the therapist.

Only after the therapist has successfully joined with a family is it fruitful to attempt restructuring—the often dramatic confrontations that challenge families and force them to change.

Structural family therapy changes behavior by reframing the family's presentation of their problems into a systemic model. Families define problems as a function of individuals or outside forces; structural family therapists redefine these problems as a function of the family structure. The first task is to understand the family's view of their problems. The therapist does this by tracking their formulation, in the content they use to explain it, and in the sequences with which they demonstrate it. Then the family therapist reframes their formulation into one based on an understanding of family structure.

In fact, all psychotherapies use reframing. Patients, whether individuals or families, come with their own views as to the cause of their problems—views that usually have not helped them solve their problems—and the therapist offers them a new and potentially more constructive view of these same problems. What makes structural family therapy unique is that it uses enactments within therapy sessions to make the reframing happen. This is the *sine qua non* of structural family therapy: observing and modifying the structure of family transactions in the immediate context of the session. Although this sounds simple, it has important implications for treatment. Structural family therapists work with what they see going on in the session, not what family members describe about what happens outside, nor with the content of family discussions. Action in the session, family dynamics in process, is what structural family therapists deal with.

There are two types of live, in-session material on which structural family therapy focuses—*enactments* and *spontaneous behavior sequences*. An enactment occurs when the therapist stimulates the family to demonstrate how they handle a particular type of problem. Enactments commonly begin when the therapist suggests that specific subgroups begin to discuss a particular problem. As they do so, the therapist observes the family process. Working with enactments requires three operations. First the therapist defines or recognizes a sequence. For example, the therapist observes that when mother talks to her daughter they talk as peers, and little brother gets left out. Then the therapist directs an enactment. For example, the therapist might say to the mother, "Talk this over with your kids." Third and most important, the therapist must guide the family to modify the enactment. If mother talks to her children in such a way that she doesn't take appropriate responsibility for major decisions, the therapist must guide her to do so as the family continues the enactment. All the therapist's moves should create new options for the family, options for new behavior sequences. A common mistake made by many family therapists is to simply criticize what they see by labeling it, without offering options for change.

Once an enactment breaks down, the therapist intervenes in one of two ways: commenting on what went wrong, or simply pushing them to keep going. For example, if a father responds to the suggestion to talk with his twelve-year-old daughter about how she's feeling by berating her, the therapist could say to the father: "Congratulations." Father: "What do you mean?" Therapist: "Congratulations; you win, she loses." Or the therapist could simply nudge the transaction by saying to the father: "Good, keep talking, but help her express her feelings more. She's still a little girl; she needs your help."

In addition to working with enacted sequences, structural family therapists are alert to observe and modify spontaneous sequences of behavior that are the illustrative processes of family structure. Creating enactments is like directing a play; working with spontaneous sequences is like focusing a spotlight on action that occurs without direction. In fact, by observing and modifying such sequences very early in therapy sessions the therapist avoids getting bogged down in the family's usual nonproductive ways of doing business. Dealing with problematic behavior as soon as it occurs in the first session enables the therapist to organize the session, to underscore the process, and to modify it.

An experienced therapist can develop formulations about probable family structure even before the first interview. For example, if the therapist knows nothing more than that a family is coming to the clinic because of a "hyperactive" child, it's possible to guess something about the family structure and something about sequences that may occur as the session begins, since "hyperactive" behavior is often a function of the child's enmeshment with the mother. Mother's relationships with the child may be a product of a lack of hierarchical differentiation within the family; that is, parents and children relate to each other as peers, not as members of different generations. Furthermore, mother's overinvolvement with the "hyperactive" child is likely to be both a result of and a cause of emotional distance from her husband. Knowing that this is a common pattern, the therapist can anticipate that early in the first session the "hyperactive" child will begin to misbehave, and that the mother will be inadequate to deal with this misbehavior. Armed with this informed guess the therapist can spotlight (rather than enact) such a sequence as soon as it occurs, and modify it. If the "hyperactive" child begins to run around the room, and the mother protests but does nothing effective, the therapist might say, "I see that your child feels free to ignore you." This powerful confrontation may force the mother to behave in a more competent manner. The therapist may have to push further, saying, "Come on now, do something about it." Once such a theme is focused on, the therapist needs to pursue it relentlessly.

TECHNIQUES ——————————————————————————

In *Families and Family Therapy*, Minuchin (1974) taught family therapists to see what they are looking at. Through the lens of structural family theory, previously puzzling family interactions suddenly swam into focus. Where others saw only chaos and confusion, Minuchin saw structure: families organized into subsystems with boundaries. This enormously successful book (over 200,000 copies in print) not only taught us to see *enmeshment* and *disengagement*, but also let us hope that changing them was just a matter of *joining*, *enactment*, and *unbalancing*. Minuchin made changing families look simple, and we believed it was. It isn't.

Anyone who watched Minuchin at work ten or fifteen years after the publication of *Families and Family Therapy* would see a creative therapist still evolving, not someone frozen in time back in 1974. There would still be the patented confrontations ("Who's the sheriff in this family?") but there would be fewer enactments, less stage-directed dialogue. We would also hear bits and pieces borrowed from Carl Whitaker ("When did you divorce your wife and marry your job?") and Maurizio Andolfi ("Why don't you piss on the rug, too?"), and others. Minuchin embraces parts of many other approaches and combines many things in his work. To those familiar with his earlier work, all of this raises the question: Is Minuchin still a structural family therapist? The question is, of course, absurd; we raise it to make one point: Structural family therapy is not a set of techniques; it's a way of looking at families.

In the remainder of this section, we will present the classic outlines of structural family technique, with the caveat that once family therapists master the basics of structural theory, they must learn to translate the approach in a way that encompasses as many techniques as they can usefully employ, and in a way that suits their own personal styles.

Those who claim that psychotherapy is a science maintain that its techniques are specifiable and teachable. Those who contend that it's an art insist that theories are teachable, but techniques are not. Minuchin believes that implementing the specific techniques of therapy is an art, and that therapists must discover and create techniques that fit each family's transactional style and therapist's personality. Since every therapeutic session has idiosyncratic features, there can be no interpersonal immediacy if the specific context is ignored. Imitating someone else's technique is stifling and ineffective—stifling because it doesn't fit the therapist, ineffective because it doesn't fit the family.

Although the details of therapy are a matter of personal style, Minuchin believes that the large movements of therapeutic strategy can be specified and taught.

In *Families and Family Therapy*, Minuchin (1974) listed three overlapping phases in the process of structural family therapy. The therapist 1) joins the family in a position of leadership; 2) maps their underlying structure; and 3) intervenes to transform this structure. This program is simple, in the sense that it follows a clear and specifiable plan, but immensely complicated because it is difficult to accomplish these tasks, and furthermore because there is an endless variety of family patterns.

Observed in practice, structural family therapy is an organic whole, created out of the very real human interaction of therapist and family. If they are to be genuine and effective, the therapist's moves cannot be preplanned or rehearsed. Competent family therapists are more than technicians. The strategy of therapy, on the other hand, must be thoughtfully planned. In general, the strategy of structural family therapy follows these steps:

1. Joining and accommodating
2. Working with interaction
3. Diagnosing
4. Highlighting and modifying interactions
5. Boundary making
6. Adding cognitive constructions

The first three strategies constitute the opening phase of treatment. Without carefully planning and skillfully accomplishing the critical opening moves, therapy usually fails. When we begin, we're often too anxious or eager to consider opening wisely. Only after we get started and the jitters calm down, do we look around, assess the situation, and then act accordingly. Unfortunately this sort of catch-up strategy results in the loss of much valuable ground. The therapist who neglects the opening moves of treatment may lose all chance of having a significant impact.

Genuine preparation and an effective opening must be distinguished from obsessional rituals which do nothing but bind anxiety and use up energy. Habitually arriving ten minutes early for sessions, arranging and rearranging the furniture, and endlessly reading charts or books on technique—as many of us do—should not be confused with careful planning.

Joining and Accommodating

Because families have firmly established homeostatic pattens, effective family therapy requires strong challenge and confrontation. But assaults on a family's habitual style will be dismissed unless they are made from a position of leverage. Family therapists earn this leverage by performing competently, and by demonstrating acceptance and understanding of family members.

The need for leverage is even more important in family treatment than in individual therapy. Individual patients generally enter treatment already predisposed to accept the therapist's authority. By seeking therapy, the individual tacitly acknowledges suffering, need for help, and willingness to trust the therapist. So familiar is the doctor-patient model that most patients accept its assumptions; many even welcome it. Not so with families.

The family outnumbers the therapist, and they have mutually agreed-upon and long-practiced ways of seeing and doing things. Their set is to treat the family therapist as an unwelcome outsider. After all, why did the therapist insist on seeing the whole family rather than just the official patient? They expect to be told that they're doing things all wrong, and they're prepared to defend themselves. The family is thus a group of non-patients who feel guilty and anxious; their set is to resist, not to cooperate.

First the family therapist must disarm defenses and ease anxiety. This is done by generously conveying understanding and acceptance to every single member of the family. The therapist greets each person by name and makes some kind of friendly contact.

These initial greetings convey respect, not only for the individuals in the family, but also for their hierarchical structure and organization. The therapist shows respect for the parents by taking their authority for granted. They, not their children, are asked first to describe the problems. If a family elects the mother as their speaker, the therapist notes this but does not initially challenge it.

Children also have special concerns and capacities. They should be greeted gently and asked simple, concrete questions, "Hi, I'm so-and-so; what's your name? Oh, Johnny, that's a nice name. Where do you go to school, Johnny?" Those who wish to remain silent should be "allowed" to do so. They will anyway, but the therapist who reflects their feelings of fear or anger and conveys acceptance of their reticence will have made a valuable step toward keeping them involved. "And what's your view of the problem?" (Grim silence.) "I see, you don't feel like saying anything right now? That's fine; perhaps you'll have something to say later."

Failure to join and accommodate produces tense resistance, which is often blamed on the family. It may be comforting to blame others when things don't go well, but it doesn't improve matters. Family members can be called "negative," "rebellious," "resistant," or "defiant," and seen as "unmotivated"; but it is more useful to make an extra effort to connect with them.

It's particularly important to join powerful family members, as well as angry ones. Special pains must be taken to accept the point of view of the father who thinks therapy is hooey or of the angry teenager who feels like a hunted criminal. It's also important to reconnect with such people at frequent intervals, particularly as things begin to heat up.

A useful beginning is to greet the family and then ask for each person's view of the problems. Listen carefully, and acknowledge each person's position by reflecting what you hear. "I see, Mrs. Jones, you think Sally must be depressed about something that happened at school." "So Mr. Jones, you see some of the same things your wife sees, but you're not convinced it's a serious problem. Is that right?"

Working with Interaction

Family structure is manifest in the way family members interact. It cannot be inferred from their descriptions, nor from reconstructing previous discussions. Therefore, asking questions like "Who's in charge?" "Do you two agree?" or "Can you show me what happened in yesterday's argument?" tend to be unproductive. Families generally describe themselves more as they think they should be than as they are.

Family dynamics are what happens when the family is in action, not what they *say* happens, or what the therapist *imagines* must happen. They have to talk among themselves for the dynamics to emerge. When they do, the therapist observes: Who talks to whom? when? in what way?

Structural family therapists work with two sorts of interactions, *enactments* and *spontaneous sequences*. Getting family members to talk among themselves runs counter to their expectations, and they resist doing it. They expect to present their case to an expert, and then be told what to do. If asked to discuss something in the session, they'll say: "We've talked about this many times"; or "It won't do any good, he (or she) doesn't listen"; or "But you're supposed to be the expert."

If the therapist begins by giving each person a chance to speak, usually one will say something about another which can be responded to as a springboard for an enactment. When, for example, one parent says that the other is too strict, the therapist can develop an enactment by saying: "She says you're too strict; can you answer her?" Picking a specific point for response is more likely to stimulate a dialogue than a vague request, such as "Why don't you two talk things over?"

Once an enactment is begun, the therapist can discover many things about the family's structure. How long can two people talk without being interrupted—that is, how clear is the boundary? Does one attack, the other defend? Who is central, who peripheral? Do parents bring children into their discussions—that is, are they enmeshed?

In addition to creating enactments, structural therapists also work with spontaneous sequences of behavior. In the first instance they are like theatrical directors, telling the actors what to do. In the second case, they are like lighting experts, focusing the spotlight of attention on some particular action.

Families may demonstrate enmeshment by frequently interrupting each other, speaking for other family members, doing things for children that they can do for themselves, or by constantly arguing. In disengaged families one may see a husband sitting impassively while his wife cries; a total absence of conflict; a surprising ignorance of important information about the children; a lack of concern for each other's interests.

If, as soon as the first session starts, the kids begin running wildly around the room while the parents protest ineffectually, the therapist doesn't need to hear descriptions of what goes on at home to see the executive incompetence. If a mother and daughter rant and rave at each other while the father sits silently in the corner, it isn't necessary to ask how involved he is at home. In fact, asking may yield a less accurate picture than the one revealed spontaneously.

Diagnosing

It's necessary to have a formulation to organize strategies of change. Clinicians must steer a course between the Scylla of unorganized experience and the Charybdis of rigid characterizations which don't capture the reality of the family's experience. Structural diagnostic categories organize what otherwise may be a confusing welter of impressions, without arbitrarily distorting the dynamic aspects of family interaction.

Families usually conceive of problems as located in the identified patient and as determined by events from the past. They hope the therapist will change the identified patient—with as little disruption as possible to the family homeostasis. Family therapists regard the identified patient's symptoms as an expression of dysfunctional transactional patterns affecting the whole family. A structural diagnosis broadens the problem beyond individuals to family systems, and moves the focus from discrete events in the past to ongoing transactions in the present. A family diagnosis is predicated on the goal of transforming the family in a way that benefits all of its members.

Even many family therapists categorize families with constructs that apply more to individuals than to systems. "The problem in this family is that the mother is smothering the kids," or "These parents are defiant," or "He's a placater." Structural family therapists diagnose in such a way as to describe the systemic interrelationships of all family members. Using the concepts of boundaries and subsystems, the structure of the whole system is described in a way that points to desired changes.

These diagnoses are based on observed interactions that take place in the first session. In later sessions the formulations are refined and revised so that they are increasingly more accurate. Although there is some danger of bending families to fit categories when they're applied early, the greater danger is waiting too long.

We see people with the greatest clarity and freshness during the initial contact. Later, as we come to know them better, we get used to their idiosyncrasies and soon no longer notice them. Families quickly *induct* therapists into their culture. A family that initially appears to be chaotic and enmeshed soon comes to be just the familiar Jones family. For this reason, it is critical to make structural formulations as quickly as possible.

In fact, it's helpful to make some guesses about family structure even before the first session. This starts a process of active thinking which sets the stage for observing the family. For example, suppose you're about to see a family consisting of a mother, a sixteen-year-old daughter, and a stepfather. The mother called to complain of her daughter's misbehavior. What do you imagine the structure might be, and how would you test your hypothesis? A good guess might be that mother and daughter are enmeshed, excluding the stepfather. This can be tested by seeing if mother and daughter tend to talk mostly about each other in the session—whether positively or negatively. The stepfather's disengagement would be confirmed if he and the girl are unable to converse without the mother's intrusion.

The structural diagnosis takes into account both the problem that the family presents and the structural dynamics that they display. And it includes all family members. In this instance, knowing that the mother and daughter are enmeshed is not enough; you also have to know what role the stepfather plays. If he's reasonably close with his wife but distant from the daughter, finding mutually enjoyable activities for stepfather and stepdaughter will help increase the girl's independence from her mother. On the other hand, if the mother's proximity to her daughter appears to be a function of her distance from her husband, then the marital pair may be the most productive focus.

Without a diagnostic formulation and a plan, the therapist is defensive and passive. Instead of knowing where to go and moving forcefully, the therapist lays back and tries to cope with the family, put out brush fires, and help them through a succession of incidents. Consistent awareness of the family's structure and focus on one or two structural changes helps the therapist see behind the various content issues that family members bring up.

Highlighting and Modifying Interactions

Once families begin to interact, problematic transactions emerge. Noticing them demands focus on process, not content. Nothing about structure is revealed by hearing who is in favor of punishment or who says nice things about others. Family structure is revealed by who says what to whom, and in what way.

Perhaps a husband complains, "We have a communication problem. My wife just won't talk to me; she never expresses her feelings." The therapist then stimulates an interaction to see what actually does happen. "Your husband says it's a communication problem; can you respond to that? Talk with him." If, when they talk, the husband becomes domineering and critical while the wife grows increasingly silent and withdrawn, then the therapist sees what goes wrong: The problem isn't that she doesn't talk, which is a linear explanation. Nor is the problem that he nags, also a linear explanation. The problem is that the more he nags, the more she withdraws, and the more she withdraws, the more he nags.

The trick is to highlight and modify this pattern of interaction. This requires forceful intervening. It's usually necessary to use therapeutic dynamite to break families loose from their patterns of equilibrium. Structural therapists use *intensity* to make these interventions.

Minuchin himself frequently speaks to families with dramatic and forceful impact. He regulates the intensity of his messages to exceed the threshold that family members have for not hearing challenges to the way they perceive reality. When Minuchin speaks, families listen.

Minuchin is forceful, but his intensity is not merely a function of his personality; it reflects his clarity of purpose. Knowledge of family structure and a serious commitment to help families change make powerful interventions possible. Families will usually respond to messages delivered with the kind of intensity that comes from being clear about the goal.

Structural therapists achieve intensity by selective regulation of affect, repetition, and duration. Tone, volume, pacing, and choice of words can be used to raise the affective intensity of statements. It helps if you know what you want to say. Here's an example of a limp statement: "People are always concerned with themselves, kind of seeing themselves as the center of attention and just looking for whatever they can get. Wouldn't it be nice for a change if everybody started thinking about what they could do for others? I mean, thinking about other people and the country before themselves." Compare that with, "Ask not what your country can do for you—ask what you can do for your country." John Kennedy's words had impact because they were carefully chosen and clearly put. Family therapists don't need to make speeches or be clever phrasemakers, but they do occasionally have to speak forcefully to get the point across.

Affective intensity is not simply a matter of crisp phrasing. You have to know how and when to be provocative. For example, one of us (M.P.N.) was recently working with a family in which a twenty-nine-year-old woman with anorexia nervosa was the identified patient. Although the family maintained a facade of togetherness, it was rigidly structured; the mother and her anorectic daughter were enmeshed, while the father was excluded. In this family, the father was the only one to express anger openly, and this was part of the official rationale for why he was excluded. His daughter was afraid of his anger, which she freely admitted. What was less clear, however, was that the mother had covertly taught the daughter to avoid him, because she, the mother, couldn't deal with his anger. Consequently, the daughter grew up afraid of her father, and men in general.

At one point the father described how isolated he felt from his daughter; he said he thought it was because she feared his anger. The daughter agreed, "It's his fault all right." The therapist asked the mother what she thought, and she replied, "It isn't his fault." The therapist said, "You're right." She went on denying her real feelings to avoid conflict, "It's no one's fault." The therapist answered in a way that got her attention, "Like hell it isn't!" Startled, she asked what he meant. "It's your fault!" the therapist said.

This level of intensity was necessary to interrupt a rigid pattern of conflict-avoidance that sustained a pathogenic alliance between mother and daughter. The content—who really is afraid of anger—is less important than the structural goal: freeing the daughter from her position of over-involvement with her mother.

Therapists too often dilute their interventions by overqualifying, apologizing, or rambling. This is less of a problem in individual therapy, where it's often best to elicit interpretations from the patient. Families are more like the farmer's proverbial mule—you sometimes have to hit them over the head to get their attention.

Intensity can also be achieved by extending the duration of a sequence beyond the point where the dysfunctional homeostasis is reinstated. A common example is the management of severe temper tantrums. Temper tantrums are maintained by parents who give in. Most parents try to not to give in; they just don't try long enough. Recently a four-year-old girl began to scream bloody murder when her sister left the room. She wanted to go with her sister. Her screaming was almost unbearable, and the parents soon were ready to back down. However, the therapist demanded that they not allow themselves to be defeated, and suggested that they hold her to "show her who's in charge" until she calmed down. She screamed for one solid hour! Everyone in the room was frazzled. But the little girl finally realized that this time she was not going to get her way, and so she calmed down. Subsequently, the parents were able to use the same intensity of duration to break her of this highly destructive habit.

Sometimes intensity requires frequent repetition of one theme in a variety of contexts. Infantilizing parents may have to be told not to hang up their child's coat, not to speak for her, not to take her to the bathroom, and not to do many other things that she is able to do for herself.

Shaping competence is another method of modifying interactions, and it is a hallmark of structural family therapy. Intensity is generally used to block the stream of interactions. Shaping competence is like altering the direction of the flow. By highlighting and shaping the positive, structural therapists help family members use functional alternatives that are already in their repertoire.

A common mistake made by beginning family therapists is to attempt to foster competent performance by pointing out mistakes. This is an example of focusing on content without due regard to process. Telling parents that they're doing something wrong, or suggesting they do something different has the effect of criticizing their competence. However well-intentioned, it's still a put-down. While this kind of intervention cannot be completely avoided, a more effective approach is to point out what they're doing right. Generous praise for competent performance uses both content and process to boost confidence and effectiveness.

Even when people do most things ineffectively, it's usually possible to pick out something that they're doing successfully. A sense of timing helps the therapist punctuate sequences while they're going well. For example, in a large chaotic family the parents were extremely ineffective at controlling the children. At one point the therapist turned to the mother and said, "It's too noisy in here; would you quiet the kids?" Knowing how much difficulty the woman had controlling her children, the therapist was poised to comment immediately on any step in the direction of effective management. The mother had to yell "Quiet!" a couple of times before the children momentarily stopped what they were doing. Quickly—before the children resumed their usual uproar—the therapist complimented the mother for "loving her kids enough to be firm with them." Thus the message delivered was "You're a competent person, you know how to be firm." If the therapist had waited until the chaos resumed before telling the mother she should be firm, the message would be "You're an incompetent parent, you need to be more firm."

Wherever possible, structural therapists avoid doing things for family members that they're capable of doing themselves. Here, too, the message is "You are competent, you can do it." Some therapists justify taking over the family's functions by calling it "modeling." Whatever it's called it has the impact of telling family members that they are inadequate. Recently a young mother confessed that she hadn't known how to tell her children that they were coming to see a family therapist and so had simply said she was taking them for a ride. Thinking to be helpful, the therapist then explained to the children that "Mommy told me there were some problems in the family, so we're all here to talk things over to see if we can improve things." This lovely explanation tells the kids why they came, but confirms the mother as incompetent to do so. If instead the therapist had suggested to the mother, "Why don't you tell them now?" then the mother, not the therapist, would have had to perform as an effective parent.

Boundary Making

Dysfunctional family dynamics are developed from and sustained by overly rigid or diffuse boundaries separating subsystems in the family. Structural therapists intervene to realign the boundaries by increasing either the proximity or distance between family subsystems.

In highly enmeshed families the therapist's interventions are designed to strengthen the boundaries between subsystems and to increase the independence of individuals. Family members are urged to speak for themselves, interruptions are blocked, and dyads are helped to finish conversations without intrusion from others. A therapist who wishes to support the sibling system and protect it from unnecessary parental intervention may say, "Susie and John, talk this over, and everyone else will listen carefully." If children frequently interrupt their parents, a therapist might challenge the parents to strengthen the hierarchical boundary by saying, "I can't believe you let them horn in on your conversation! Why don't you get them to butt out so that you two grown-ups can settle this."

Although structural family therapy is begun with the total family group, subsequent sessions may be held with individuals or subgroups to strengthen the boundaries surrounding them. A teenager who is overprotected by her mother is supported as a separate person with individual needs by participating in some separate sessions. Parents so enmeshed with their children that they never have private conversations may begin to learn how if they meet separately with a therapist.

When a forty-year-old woman called the clinic for help with depression, she was asked to come in with the rest of the family. It soon became apparent that this woman was overburdened by her four children, and received little support from her husband, either as a husband or a father. The therapist's strategy was to strengthen the boundary between the mother and the children, and help the parents move closer toward each other. This was done in a series of stages. First the therapist joined the oldest child, a sixteen-year-old girl, and supported her competence as a potential helper for her mother. Once this was done, the girl was able to assume a good deal of responsibility for her younger siblings, both in the sessions and at home.

Freed from some of the preoccupation with the children, the parents now had the opportunity to talk more with each other. They had very little to say to each other, however. This was not the result of hidden conflict or anger, but instead it reflected the marriage of a relatively nonverbal husband and wife, with different interests. After several sessions of trying to get the pair to enjoy talking with each other, the therapist realized that while talking may be fun for some people, it may not be for others. So to support the bond between the couple the therapist asked them to plan a special trip together. They chose a boat ride on a nearby lake. When they returned for the next session, the spouses were beaming. They reported having had a wonderful time, being apart from the kids and enjoying each other's company. Subsequently they decided to spend a little time out together each week.

Disengaged families tend to avoid or detour conflict, and thus minimize interaction. The structural therapist intervenes to challenge conflict-avoidance, and to block detouring in order to help disengaged members increase contact with each other. The therapist creates boundaries in the session which permit family members to discuss their conflicts without being interrupted. In addition, the therapist prevents escape or avoidance, so that the disagreements can be resolved.

Without acting as judge or referee, the structural therapist creates conditions in which family members can face each other squarely and struggle with the difficulties between them. When beginners see disengagement, they tend to think first of ways to increase positive interaction. In fact, disengagement is usually a way of avoiding arguments. Therefore, spouses isolated from each other typically need to fight before they can become more loving.

Most people underestimate the degree to which their own behavior influences and regulates the behavior of those around them. This is particularly true in disengaged families. Problems are usually seen as the result of what someone else is doing, and solutions are thought to require that the others change. The following complaints are typical: "We have a communication problem; he won't tell me what he's feeling." "He just doesn't care about us. All he cares about is that damn job of his." "Our sex life is lousy—my wife's frigid." "Who can talk to her? All she does is complain about the kids." Each of these statements suggest that the power to change rests solely with the other person. This is the almost universally perceived view of linear causality.

Whereas most people see things this way, family therapists see the inherent circularity in systems interaction. He doesn't tell his wife what he's feeling, because she nags and criticizes; *and* she nags and criticizes because he doesn't tell her what he's feeling.

Structural therapists move family discussions from linear to circular causality by stressing the complementarity of family relations. The mother who complains that her son is naughty is taught to consider what she's doing to stimulate or maintain his behavior. The one who asks for change must learn to change his or her way of trying to get it. The wife who nags her husband to spend more time with her must learn to make increased involvement more attractive. The husband who complains that his wife never listens to him may have to listen to her more, before she's willing to reciprocate.

Minuchin emphasizes complementarity by asking family members to help each other change. When positive changes are reported, he's liable to congratulate others, underscoring family interrelatedness.

Adding Cognitive Constructions

Although structural family therapy is not primarily a verbal or cognitive treatment, its practitioners use words and concepts to alter the way family members perceive reality. Reality, Minuchin says, is a perspective. Changing the way family members relate to each other offers alternative views of reality. The converse is also true: Changing the way family members view reality enables them to change the way they relate to each other.

Structural family therapists have a more flexible and functional view of reality than those who believe in immaculate perception. Cognitive constructions may be veridical interpretations, pragmatic fictions, or paradoxes.

Sometimes the structural family therapist acts as a teacher, offering information and advice based on training and experience. Information may be imparted to reassure anxious family members, to help them behave more competently, or to restructure their interactions. When family members feel embarrassed because they fight over little things, it may be helpful to tell them that most people do. Sometimes young parents will profit from a simple suggestion that they hire a baby-sitter and get out once in a while.

Minuchin occasionally teaches families about structure. Doing so is likely to be a restructuring maneuver and must be done in a way that minimizes resistance. He does this by delivering first a "stroke," then a "kick." If Minuchin were dealing with a family in which the mother speaks for her children, he might say to her, "You are very helpful" (stroke). But to the child, "Mommy takes away your voice. You can speak for yourself" (kick). Thus mother is defined as helpful, but intrusive (one stroke and one kick).

Structural therapists also use constructions, which are pragmatic fictions, to provide family members with a different frame for experiencing. This aim is not to educate or to deceive, but to offer a pronouncement which will help the family to change. For instance, telling children that they are behaving in a way that is consistent with being younger than they are is a very effective means of getting them to change. "How old are you?" "Seven." "Oh, I thought you were younger, because when you really get to be seven, you won't need Mommy to take you to school anymore."

Paradoxes are cognitive constructions which frustrate or confuse family members into a search for alternatives. Minuchin himself makes little use of paradox, but it can be an effective means of stimulating new transactional patterns (see Chapter 9).

EVALUATING THERAPY THEORY AND RESULTS

While he was Director of the Philadelphia Child Guidance Clinic, Minuchin developed a highly pragmatic commitment to research. As an administrator he learned that research demonstrating effective outcomes is the best argument for the legitimacy of family therapy. Both his studies of psychosomatic children and Stanton's studies of drug addicts show very clearly how effective structural family therapy can be.

In *Families of the Slums*, Minuchin and his colleagues (1967) at Wiltwyck described the structural characteristics of low socioeconomic families, and demonstrated the effectiveness of family therapy with this population. Prior to treatment mothers in patient families were found to be either over- or undercontrolling; either way their children were more disruptive than those in control families. These observations were the basis of Minuchin's classification of families as either *enmeshed* or *disengaged.* After treatment mothers used less coercive control, yet were clearer and more firm. Treatment was found to be more successful with enmeshed than with disengaged families.

Studies demonstrating the effectiveness of structural family therapy with severely ill psychosomatic children are convincing because of the physiological measures employed, and dramatic because of the life-threatening nature of the problems. Minuchin, Rosman, and Baker (1978) reported one study which clearly demonstrated how family conflict can precipitate ketoacidosis crises in psychosomatic-type diabetic children. The investigators compared three groups of families—psychosomatic, behavior disorder, and normal—in terms of their response to a sequence of stress interviews. In the baseline interview parents discussed family problems with their children absent. Normal spouses showed the highest levels of confrontation, while psychosomatic spouses exhibited a wide range of conflict-avoidance maneuvers. Next, a therapist pressed the parents to increase the level of their conflict, while their children observed behind a one-way mirror. As the parents argued, only the psychosomatic children seemed to be really upset. Moreover, these children's manifest distress was accompanied by dramatic increases in free fatty acid levels of the blood, a measure which is related to ketoacidosis. In the third stage of these interviews, the patients joined their parents. Normal and behavior-disorder parents continued as before, but the psychosomatic parents detoured their conflict, either by drawing their children into their discussions or by switching the subject from themselves to the children. When this happened, the free fatty acid levels of the parents fell, while the children's levels continued to rise. The study provided strong confirmation of the clinical observations that psychosomatic children are used (and let themselves be used) to regulate the stress between their parents.

The first outcome study of structural family therapy was conducted at Wiltwyck by Minuchin and his colleagues (1967). In this study, seven of eleven families were judged to be improved after six months to a year of family therapy. Although no control group was used, the authors compared their results favorably to the usual 50 percent rate of successful treatment at Wiltwyck. The authors also noted that none of the families rated as disengaged improved.

By far the strongest empirical support for structural family therapy comes from a series of studies with psychosomatic children and adult drug addicts. Minuchin, Rosman, and Baker (1978) summarized the results of treating fifty-three cases of anorexia nervosa with structural family therapy.

After a course of treatment which included hospitalization followed by family therapy on an outpatient basis, forty-three of these anorectic children were "greatly improved," two were "improved," three showed "no change," two were "worse," and three had dropped out. Although ethical considerations precluded using a control treatment with these seriously ill children, the 90 percent improvement rate is extremely impressive, especially compared with the usual 30 percent mortality rate for this disorder. Moreover, the positive results of termination have been maintained at follow-up intervals of up to several years. Structural family therapy has also been shown to be extremely effective in treating psychosomatic asthmatics and psychosomatically complicated cases of diabetes (Minuchin, Baker, Rosman, Liebman, Milman, and Todd, 1975).

Finally, Duke Stanton has shown that structural family therapy can be an effective form of treatment for drug addicts and their families. In a well-controlled study, Stanton and Todd (1979) compared family therapy with a family placebo condition and individual therapy. Symptom reduction was significant with structural family therapy; the level of positive change was more than double that achieved in the other conditions, and these positive effects persisted at follow-up of six and twelve months.

SUMMARY

Salvador Minuchin may be best known for the artistry of his clinical technique, yet his structural family theory has become one of the most widely used conceptual models in the field. The reason that his theory is popular is that it is simple, inclusive, and practical. The basic structural concepts—boundaries, subsystems, alignments, and power—are easily grasped and applied; they take into account the individual, family, and social context. And the structural model provides a clear organizing framework for understanding and treating families.

Minuchin first created his technique while working with disorganized families from inner city slums. In order to gain entrance to these families he developed techniques of joining, and in order to change them he developed concrete and powerful restructuring techniques. It is therapy of action, directed at the here-and-now interactions of families, but designed to alter the basic structure underlying those interactions.

The single most important tenet of this approach is that every family has a structure, and that this structure is revealed only when the family is in action. According to this view, therapists who fail to consider the entire family's structure, and intervene in only one subsystem, are unlikely to effect lasting change. If a mother's overinvolvement with her son is part of a structure that includes distance from her husband, no amount of therapy for the mother and son is likely to change the family.

Subsystems are units of the family based on function. If the leadership of a family is taken over by a father and daughter, then they are the executive subsystem, not the husband and wife. Subsystems are circumscribed and regulated by emotional boundaries. In normal families boundaries are clear enough to protect the separateness and autonomy of individuals and subsystems, and permeable enough to insure mutual support and affection. Enmeshed families are characterized by diffuse boundaries; disengaged families have very rigid boundaries.

Structural family therapy is designed to resolve the presenting problem by reorganizing the family structure. Assessment, therefore, requires the presence of the whole family, so that the therapist can observe the structure underlying the family's interactions. In the process, therapists should distinguish between dysfunctional and functional structure. Families with growing pains should not be treated as pathological. Where structural problems do exist, the goal is to create an effective hierarchical structure. This means activating dormant structures, not creating new ones.

Structural family therapists work quickly to avoid being inducted as members of the families they work with. They begin by making concerted efforts to accommodate to the family's accustomed ways of behaving, in order to circumvent resistance. Once they have gained a family's trust, structural therapists promote family interaction, while they assume a decentralized role. From this position they can watch what goes on in the family and make a diagnosis, which includes the problem and the structure that supports it. These diagnoses are framed in terms of boundaries and subsystems, which are easily conceptualized as two-dimensional maps that can be used to suggest avenues for change.

Once they have successfully joined and diagnosed a family, structural therapists proceed to activate dormant structures using techniques that alter alignments, and shift the power within and between subsystems. These restructuring techniques are concrete, forceful, and often highly dramatic. However, their success depends as much on the joining and assessment as on the power of the techniques themselves.

Structural family therapy's popularity is based on its theory and techniques of treatment; its central position in the field has been augmented by its research and training programs. There is now a substantial body of research which lends considerable empirical support to this school's approach. Moreover, the training programs at the Philadelphia Child Guidance Clinic have influenced an enormous number of family therapy practitioners throughout the world.

Although structural family therapy is so closely identified with Salvador Minuchin that they once were synonymous, it may be a good idea to differentiate the man from the method. When we think of structural family therapy, we tend to remember the approach as described in *Families and Family Therapy* published in 1974. That book adequately represents structural theory, but emphasizes only the techniques Minuchin favored at that time. Minuchin, the thinker, has always thought of families in organizational terms. He read Talcott Parsons and Robert Bales and George Herbert Mead; and in Israel he saw how children from unstructured Moroccan families often became delinquents, while those from organized Yemenite families did not. Minuchin the therapist has always been an opportunist, using whatever works. In the 1990s, you can see Carl Whitaker and constructivism in Minuchin's work. From Whitaker, he took the idea of challenging families' myths and engaging with them from a position of passionate involvement. The young Minuchin followed families and watched them in action; that's why he made such use of enactments. The older Minuchin, who has seen thousands of families, now sees things faster; he uses enactment much less, and is likely to confront one family on the basis of what he has seen in hundreds of similar cases. Should we follow him in this? Yes, as soon as we have the same experience.

Minuchin has always been a constructivist, though he comes by it intuitively, not from reading books. He challenges families, telling them, essentially, that they are wrong; their stories are too narrow. And he helps them rewrite stories that work. Minuchin has always been interested in literature and story telling; perhaps he likes the doctrine of constructivism simply because it legitimizes his story telling. But, he cautions, when constructivism is not grounded in structural understanding or when it neglects the emotional side of human beings, it can become an arid intellectualism. Minuchin has moved toward eclecticism in technique, but not in theory. Although Minuchin the therapist has changed since 1974, his basic perspective on families, described in structural family theory, still stands, and continues to be the most widely used way of understanding what goes on in the nuclear family.

REFERENCES

Elizur, J., and Minuchin, S. 1989. *Institutionalizing madness: Families, therapy, and society.* New York: Basic Books.

Minuchin, S. 1974. *Families and family therapy.* Cambridge, MA: Harvard University Press.

Minuchin, S., Montalvo, B., Guerney, B., Rosman, B., and Schumer, F. 1967. *Families of the slums.* New York: Basic Books.

Minuchin, S., Baker, L., Rosman, B., Liebman, R., Milman, L., and Todd, T.C. 1975. A conceptual model of psychosomatic illness in children. *Archives of General Psychiatry.* 32:1031–1038.

Minuchin, S., Rosman, B., and Baker, L. 1978. *Psychosomatic families: Anorexia nervosa in context.* Cambridge, MA: Harvard University Press.

Minuchin, S., and Fishman, H.C. 1981. *Family therapy techniques.* Cambridge, MA: Harvard University Press.

Stanton, M.D., and Todd, T.C. 1979. Structural family therapy with drug addicts. In *The family therapy of drug and alcohol abuse,* E. Kaufman and P. Kaufmann, eds., New York: Gardner Press.

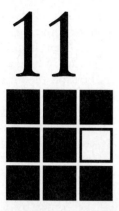

11

The Cutting Edge of Family Therapy

As family therapy moves into the nineties, a number of promising models are emerging (several of which were introduced in Chapter 3) that don't fit easily into one of the schools described in the preceding chapters and haven't yet blossomed to the point of qualifying as a separate new school. To handle these models, we've added this chapter which will differ from the previous chapters in that we will not use the general outline they follow (Introduction, Sketches of Leading Figures, Theoretical Formulations, etc). While all these new models have some elements in common, their diversity makes squeezing their concepts and methods into these general outline categories more confusing than useful.

These new models include: the *solution-focused* model developed by Steve de Shazer and colleagues and expanded by Bill O'Hanlon and Michele Weiner-Davis; Michael White's *externalization* model; the *psychoeducational* model pioneered by Carol Anderson and others; and Richard Schwartz's *internal family systems* model. Another new approach, known as the *post-Milan* movement, has gained considerable following and was described briefly in Chapter 3. We can't go into more depth on this approach, however, because the leaders, who include Lynn Hoffman, Harry Goolishian, and Harlene Anderson, have yet to clearly describe what they do in therapy.

SOLUTION-FOCUSED THERAPY ————————————————

The solution-focused model grows from the soil of strategic therapy (particularly from the MRI model), and yet it also represents a departure from that tradition. It maintains the strategic school's de-emphasis of history and underlying pathology, and their commitment to brevity, but it moves away from their focus on problems. Where strategic family therapists talk with families or individuals about the sequences that surround their problems— with an eye toward discovering attempted solutions that aren't working, and may even be prolonging the problem—solution-focused therapists get clients to focus exclusively on solutions that have worked or might work. At first glance, this shift may seem trivial, but it isn't.

Most of the leading figures in this movement worked together at one time or another at the Brief Family Therapy Center in Milwaukee. This private training and treatment institute was started in the late 1970s when a group within a Milwaukee community agency, who were drawn to the MRI model, became dissatisfied with the agency's constraints and broke out on their own. The initial group included the married couple of Steve de Shazer and Insoo Berg. De Shazer, who had worked earlier in Palo Alto with the MRI group, devoted much of his time to researching, theorizing, and writing, while Berg pursued her interest in training therapists.

Other notable clinician/theorists associated with this center include Eve Lipchik, who was particularly interested in the development of therapeutic questions, and Michele Weiner-Davis who converted another agency in Woodstock, Illinois to the solution-focused model. Both of these women are currently in private practice and present the solution-focused approach in workshops around the country. Bill O'Hanlon, who practices in Omaha, Nebraska, was never formally associated with the Milwaukee center but, having been trained by Milton Erickson and having become a prominent translator of Erickson's ideas, the step toward the solution-focused approach was an easy one. He and Weiner-Davis (O'Hanlon and Weiner-Davis, 1989) have collaborated to expand upon the groundwork laid by de Shazer.

Because solution-focused therapists set their sights on solutions rather than problems, they have little to say about how problems arise. They contend that therapists don't need to know a great deal about the nature of the problems that bring people to therapy. Instead they need to know about the nature of solutions that can apply across people (de Shazer, 1985). Like the MRI model, they believe that people are constrained by their narrow, pessimistic views of their problems or their lives which generate rigid sequences of more-of-the-same attempted solutions. As O'Hanlon and Weiner-Davis (1989, p. 48) put it:

> So, the meanings people attribute to behavior limit the range of alternatives they will use to deal with a situation. If the methods used do not

produce a satisfactory outcome, the original assumption about the meaning of the behavior is generally not questioned. If it were, new meanings might be considered, which in turn might prompt a different, perhaps more effective, approach. Instead, people often redouble their efforts to solve the problem in an ineffective way, thinking that by doing it more, harder, or better (e.g., more punishments, more heart-to-heart talks, and so on) they will finally solve it.

Solution-oriented therapists also take a strong position against the idea that problems serve ulterior functions for individuals or families, or that people are ambivalent about their problems. They assume that clients *really do* want to change. De Shazer (1984), in fact, has declared the death of resistance as a concept, suggesting that when clients don't follow directives, it's their way of "cooperating" by teaching the therapist the best way to help them.

Solution-focused therapists also believe that people are quite suggestible, and that therapists may, unwittingly, create or maintain problems that to solution-focused therapists do not exist (O'Hanlon and Weiner-Davis, 1989, p. 54):

> If the client walks into a behaviorist's office, he or she will leave with a behavioral problem. If clients choose psychoanalysts' offices, they will leave with unresolved issues from childhood as the focus of the problem. If a client seeks help from a Jungian analyst, he or she is likely to get a problem that can be treated most effectively by examining symbolism in the client's dreams.

Thus much of the work for solution-focused therapists lies in the negotiation of a goal that is achievable and isn't related to the therapist's preconceptions about what lies behind the problem.

With this orientation, then, there is no model of normal family or individual development. Solution-focused therapists borrow from constructivists the idea that there is no true reality, so therapists shouldn't impose what they think is normal on clients. Instead, therapy should concern itself only with the complaints that clients present.

> Solution-oriented therapists don't believe that there is any single "correct" or "valid" way to live one's life. We have come to understand that what is unacceptable behavior in one family or for one person is desirable behavior in another. Therefore clients, not therapists, identify the goals to be accomplished in treatment (O'Hanlon and Weiner-Davis, 1989, p. 44).

Thus like MRI therapists, the goals of solution-focused therapists are to resolve the presenting complaints by helping a client do or think something different so as to become more satisfied with his or her life. More than MRI therapists, however, solution-focused therapists trust and use the resources of clients to help them reach their goals. They believe that people already have the skills to solve their problems but, often, have lost sight of these abilities because the problems loom so large to them that their strengths are crowded out of the picture. Sometimes a simple shift in focus from what is not going well to what they are already doing that works can remind them of, and expand their use of, these resources. Other times people may have to search for abilities that they aren't currently using and bring those dormant skills to bear on their problems.

The orientation toward solutions, then, is an attempt to create an atmosphere in therapy in which people's strengths can move out of the shadows and into the foreground. De Shazer (1985, 1986) found these strengths lurking in the spaces between problems—in the "behaviors, perceptions, thoughts, feelings, and expectations that are outside the complaint's constraints. These exceptions . . . can be used as building blocks in the construction of a solution . . . solutions involve determining what 'works' so that the client can do more of it" (de Shazer, 1986, p. 48).

To illustrate this process, de Shazer (1986) uses the metaphor of a man whose problem is that he wants to leave Chicago. To solve this problem much of the following information has little relevance: how he got to Chicago, how long he's been there, what's kept him from leaving earlier, or the nature of Chicago. Instead, the traveler need only focus on where he wants to go, and on the resources at his disposal for getting there.

It may be, however, that in discussing his desires, he remembers some good days in Chicago, and that while these exceptions had seemed insignificant, in thinking about what made them exceptional, he realizes that those were days when he was having fun with other people. He decides that he doesn't really have to leave Chicago after all, and instead directs his energy toward spending more time with people he enjoys. It is this focus on goals, resources, and exceptions to the problem that characterizes solution-focused models. With that focus people will either find a solution to their original problem (leaving Chicago) or decide that their problem is something else (not enough time with friends) and find a solution to it.

In the early 1980s de Shazer's team began experimenting with this orientation toward solutions by giving all clients the same assignments that they called "formula tasks." They found that some of these assignments were universally effective regardless of the kind of problem they were targeting. One of these tasks, given in the first session, was to ask clients to observe what happens in their life or relationships that they want to continue (de Shazer, 1985). They found that this assignment helped reorient clients from focusing on the bad things in their lives to thinking about and expecting the good. They also found that this shift in perspective seemed to build on itself—to create a more positive outlook that led to a more competent approach to life.

With the success of these formula tasks, it began to dawn on the team that the process of change could be initiated without much knowledge of the problem or the personalities of those suffering from it. They began to focus on ways to initiate and maintain this problem-solving facility in people, which they believed was inhibited by a focus on their problems or deficits. This thinking led to the development of the "miracle question" and the "exception question," two mainstays of the solution-focused approach (de Shazer, 1985).

The *miracle question* is: "Suppose one night, while you were asleep, there was a miracle and this problem was solved. How would you know? What would be different?" This question seems to activate the problem-solving process in people by giving them a clear vision of their goal, perhaps in the same way that visualization of the perfect serve helps a tennis player. It also helps clients look beyond the problem to see that what they really want may not be the eradication of the problem per se, but instead to be able to do the things that the problem is obstructing. When this is the case the therapist can encourage them to begin doing those things despite the problem and, suddenly, the problem doesn't loom as large. For example, Mary, who suffers from bulimia, says that if not for her symptoms, she'd get closer to people and have more fun. If, with her therapist's encouragement, Mary begins to take interpersonal risks and has more fun, then her bulimia may become less of a problem, less of an obstacle in her life, which might also increase her ability to control it.

The *exception question* ignores the snapshot of the problem clients hold up and, instead, directs their attention to the negative of that picture—to times in the past or present when a client did not have the problem when, ordinarily, he or she would have. By exploring these times and what was different about them, clients find clues to what they can do to expand those exceptions. In addition, clients may find that in light of the fact that they were able to control the problem sometimes, their outlook towards it changes. It seems less oppressive and omnipresent, more controllable. Mary remembers several times the previous week when she had the urge to binge and purge but didn't. She discovers that at those times she was away from her parents and didn't feel like she was disappointing them. She decides that it's time to become more independent.

Solution-focused therapists claim that if both client and therapist can reorient themselves in the direction of strengths—exceptions to the problem, clarified goals, and strategies to achieve them—then therapy can be quite brief. Two assumptions justify this belief. The first draws once again from constructivism and the power of expectation and suggestion. As O'Hanlon and Weiner-Davis (1989, p. 34) explain,

Since what you expect influences what you get, solution-oriented therapists maintain those presuppositions that enhance client-therapist cooperation, empower clients, and make our work more effective and enjoyable. We hold assumptions which focus on strengths and possibilities; fortunately, these assumptions also help create self-fulfilling prophecies.

If one perspective is as valid as the next, then why not assume that solutions can be found easily and quickly.

The second assumption is borrowed from the MRI model—that a small change is usually all that is needed because it can snowball into bigger changes. O'Hanlon and Weiner-Davis (1989, p. 42) state,

> Once a small positive change is made, people feel optimistic and a bit more confident about tackling further changes. Couples seeking treatment often provide clear examples of this phenomenon. Blaming and withholding typically characterize these relationships. However, when person A undertakes one small gesture which pleases person B, person B reciprocates, which in turn stimulates person A to respond in kind, and so on.

With these two assumptions about change, the solution-focused theorists have fashioned a collection of questions and tasks that are designed to create an optimistic reality and start the snowball rolling. They not only have drawn many assumptions and techniques from the MRI group, but they also back up their claims with the same kind of research.

In 1988 David Kiser followed the outcome of 164 clients treated at the Brief Family Therapy Center for six, twelve, and eighteen months after therapy (Wylie, 1990). He used a questionnaire similar to the one used by the MRI group in 1974, where they reported that about 75 percent of their cases had at least some relief from their presenting complaint (Watzlawick, Weakland, and Fisch, 1974). Kiser found even better results.

> Of 69 cases receiving 4 to 10 sessions, 64 clients, or nearly 93 percent, felt they had met or made progress on their treatment goal (about 77 percent of the 64 met the goal, and more than 14 percent made progress). At the 18-month follow-up, of all 164 clients (94 percent of whom had had 10 or fewer sessions), about 51 percent reported the presenting problem was still resolved, while about 34 percent said it was not as bad as when they had initiated therapy. In other words, about 85 percent of the clients reported full or partial success (Wylie, 1990, pp. 34–35).

While this kind of research isn't rigorously scientific, it does indicate that solution-focused therapists have a sizable number of satisfied customers, despite the brevity of the work.

The solution-focused movement epitomizes several trends within family therapy. Its growing popularity is related, in part, to the increasing pressure from insurance companies and mental health administrators on therapists to be brief. In contrast to other brief models, this focus away from problems and onto strengths and solutions produces a more pleasant form of therapy that can help therapists avoid burnout. In addition, the procedure for doing solution-oriented therapy is quite clearcut and formulaic; so much so that de Shazer and his team have devised a computer program that can tell therapists exactly what to do depending on a client's response.

This approach, like the others in this chapter, also reflects the field's shift away from searching within families or individuals for the cause of their problems to empowering people to improve their lives. With an increased trust in clients' abilities comes an increased emphasis on the use of questions to elicit them, a trend begun by the Milan model and shared with Michael White's approach. Finally, this solution-orientation seems a logical extension of the field's interest in constructivism, the idea that people create their own realities. If all realities are merely personal constructions, then why not help people construct the reality that their problems aren't so bad or are solvable?

Critics of the solution-focused approach have targeted its briefness and the credibility of its outcome claims (Wylie, 1990). While at times the approach has been portrayed modestly—as a way to start therapy on a positive note, with the option to switch to other methods if the problem perseveres (de Shazer, 1987; O'Hanlon, 1990)—other writing is less modest and conveys the impression that almost any problem can be treated successfully with a few solution-focused sessions. Such claims raise the concern that, in some cases, the therapist's need for the clients to think positively or feel strong may induce denial or minimizing of problems. If people are as suggestible as solution-focused therapists say they are, what prevents therapists, caught up in their enthusiasm for quick cures, from suggesting away problems that should be addressed?

In conclusion, solution-focused theorists have contributed an orientation toward therapy and a set of questions and tasks that can empower clients. As with many new schools, enthusiasm for the approach may have led to some overstating of its effectiveness (which probably will be tempered with experience). The solution-focused school reflects, and has helped to create, a new period of empowerment of family therapy that will serve the field well.

PSYCHOEDUCATION

The psychoeducational model shares with the other approaches discussed in this chapter an antipathy for blaming families for the problems of their children and an eagerness to collaborate with family members to overcome obstacles. It differs with these other models, primarily, in its ambitions. Instead of setting up cure as a goal, psychoeducators hope only to maximize the functioning and coping abilities of patients and their families, and to prevent relapse. This difference in goals can be explained by the fact that the psychoeducational model has as its primary focus the treatment of schizophrenia. As described in Chapter 1, it was the search to find a cause and cure for schizophrenia within families that launched the field of family therapy in the 1950s. Ironically it is this psychoeducational model, developed thirty years later, which doesn't attempt to find a cause or cure, that may help schizophrenics the most.

The psychoeducational model was born from dissatisfaction with both the traditional family therapy and psychiatric approaches to schizophrenia. As Carol Anderson, Douglas Reiss, and Gerald Hogarty (1986, p. vii) lament,

> We have blamed each other, the patients themselves, their parents and grandparents, public authorities, and society for the cause and for the too often terrible course of these disorders. When hope and money become exhausted, we frequently tear schizophrenic patients from their families, consigning them to the existential terror of human warehouses, single room occupancy hotels, and more recently to the streets and alleys of American cities.

Family therapists, in their attempts to get at the reputed function of the schizophrenic's symptoms or to get family members to express bottled up feelings, created sessions full of highly charged emotion which often generated blame and defensiveness. After noticing the frequent decline in functioning of patients and increased anxiety in their families after such sessions, Anderson and her colleagues (1986, p. 2) "began to wonder if most 'real' family therapy was in fact antitherapeutic."

Psychiatry, on the other hand, had put all its eggs in the medication basket and hardly bothered with the patient's family. Psychiatrists believed that the high relapse rate for schizophrenics was mainly due to patients who stopped taking medication. As studies of relapse rates emerged, demonstrating that compliance with medication regimens didn't prevent relapse, the patient's environment was reconsidered. Several studies concluded that the schizophrenic patients who fared best after being hospitalized were those who returned to the least stressful households. A British group including George Brown, John Wing, Julian Leff, and Christine Vaughn had focused on what they called "expressed emotion" (EE) in the families of schizophrenics—particularly criticism, hostility, and emotional overinvolvement (Brown, Birley, and Wing, 1972; Brown, Monck, Carstairs, and Wing, 1962). Studies suggested that patients returning to high EE households had much higher rates of relapse than those returning to low

EE homes (Brown, Birley, and Wing, 1972; Vaughn and Leff, 1976; Vaughn, Snyder, Jones, Freeman, and Falloon, 1984).

These observations pointed to the view that schizophrenia was a thought disorder involving a biological vulnerability of unknown origin that makes people highly reactive to and easily overwhelmed by stress in their environment. The idea is that when family members are hypercritical or intrusive, the schizophrenic patient cannot process these communications adequately and becomes overloaded, leading to decompensation.

With this view in mind, three different groups in the late 1970s and early 1980s began experimenting with ways to reduce stress in the most common environments for schizophrenic patients, their parents' homes. Michael Goldstein led a group at UCLA (Goldstein, Rodnick, Evans, May, and Steinberg, 1978) who designed a brief, concrete model focused on anticipating and circumventing the stresses the family was likely to face and reducing conflict with or among those around the patient. The Goldstein group demonstrated that this family program, in combination with medication, could achieve an impressive decrease in relapse rates. Following the Goldstein study, groups headed by Ian Falloon at USC (whose model is highly behavioral) and Carol Anderson at the Western Psychiatric Institute and Clinic in Pittsburgh experimented with psychoeducational models. Rather than trying to describe all of these models, we will focus on Anderson's because it is clearly articulated and, despite the psychoeducational antipathy for what family therapists have done to schizophrenics and their families, it contains many concepts and methods derived from family therapy.

Anderson and her colleagues (1986) focus their interest on the devastating impact of schizophrenia on a family system, rather than on the possible effects of pre-existing family characteristics on either the onset or maintenance of the syndrome. They see the isolation and enmeshment of many families of schizophrenics as an inevitable consequence of the embarrassment, frustration, and concern that family members feel.

> During an acute illness in any family member, of course, it is necessary for the rest of the family to focus their attentions and their energies on the patient. However, in any long-term illness (like diabetes, heart disease, *or* schizophrenia), patients must learn to live with their limitations and life must go on for those around them. If this does not happen, the impact of illness can become debilitating to families. In fact, family members may experience so much stress that they will be unable to offer ongoing support to patients, and may even incur additional problems of their own making (p. 125).

Thus, while family members may be contributing to a less than optimal course of their child's schizophrenia, it isn't because their system needs symptoms; it is because the illness has drained the family's resources and initiated dysfunctional patterns both within the families and with those whose attempts to help are making things worse.

Thus, psychoeducators not only try to help families change their ideas about and interactions with patients but they also try to reverse the damage that may have been done to families by the insensitive professionals they encountered. Instead of providing the information, support, structure, and sense of control that these families need when in crisis, many mental health professionals ignore family members except to gather information about the patient and the family—information about what went wrong. The implications of this line of questioning add to the sense of guilt, shame, and confusion that family members already feel. It's no wonder that many families either give up and hand their patients over to these authoritarian professionals, or get into antagonistic battles with them.

Instead, psychoeducators seek to establish a collaborative partnership with families in which family members feel empathized with, supported, and also empowered to deal with the patient. Families should leave their contacts with professionals with a sense of their importance in the treatment process but also a sense that they are not alone—that a caring group is involved with them. To achieve this kind of partnership, Anderson and colleagues find that they must re-educate professionals to give up ideas that the family caused or wants the schizophrenia, to scan for and emphasize family strengths rather than deficits, and to share what information exists about schizophrenia rather than keeping families in the dark.

It is this information-sharing that constitutes the education of psycho*education*. Anderson and her colleagues believe that information about the nature and probable course of schizophrenia helps family members develop a sense of mastery—a way to understand and anticipate the often chaotic and apparently uncontrollable process. Too often in the past this information was withheld out of neglect of or antagonism toward families, or because schizophrenia's less than rosy prognosis might discourage them. Since families are usually the principal caretakers, however, it makes sense that they should be the most, rather than the least, informed members of the team.

In a one-day "survival-skills workshop," Anderson and her colleagues teach groups of family members the history and epidemiology of schizophrenia, and current knowledge about its etiology, prognosis, psychobiology, and treatment. They discuss in some depth the EE findings regarding the impact of the social environment on patients, and they suggest how families can reorganize to deal with these special needs. Research demonstrating the importance of medication in preventing relapse is also presented.

The goal of these workshops is to translate what's known about schizophrenia into a framework that allows family members to understand

and not feel bad about their behavior, the patient's behavior, and the behavior of professionals. Family members are also given the sense that, compared to the history of approaches to schizophrenia, they are part of a special turning point in that history when schizophrenics and their families are treated with compassion and understanding. They are given hope that life can be better, although psychoeducators are careful not to give what they consider to be the false hope of a complete cure.

Families are encouraged to provide an atmosphere of low stimulation and expectation, but not without structure or limit-setting. While patients are to be given a lot of latitude regarding their desire to withdraw from stimulation or other idiosyncrasies, they aren't to be allowed to engage in strange or irritating behavior that upsets others in the house. Family members are to minimize conflict or criticism among themselves or toward the patient so that when parents set limits they are to do so in a matter-of-fact, rather than angry, manner. If necessary they are to set up chores and rules around the house as they might for a much younger child so that the patient has the structure he or she might need.

One of psychoeducation's key interventions is to lower expectations, so as to reduce pressure on the patient to perform normally. For example, the goals for the first year following an acute episode are primarily the avoidance of another episode and the gradual taking on of some responsibilities in the home. Family members are to view the patient as they might someone who's had a serious physical illness and needs a long recuperation. Patients may need an excessive amount of sleep, solitude, and limited activity for some period following an episode, and may seem restless, with trouble concentrating. By predicting these characteristics psychoeducators try to prevent conflicts between the patient and family members due to impatience or frustration with lack of movement toward unrealistic goals.

These recommendations are quite a contrast to the general family therapy attitude of "treat people as if they are normal and they will behave normally." Haley's (1981) *Leaving Home* model encouraged parents to expect normal behavior from schizophrenics and to work together to get the patient to pursue a normal life as soon as possible. The Milan Associates (Selvini Palazzoli, Boscolo, Cecchin, and Prata, 1978) implied that schizophrenics could be cured after a few sessions. As we shall see, Michael White (1989) gets families and patients to fight against, rather than to expect, the schizophrenic person's "in-the-corner lifestyle." The psychoeducational shift in goals away from cure or normality and towards coping with illness and prevention of relapse is a radical and difficult one for family therapists, and represents one of their biggest and most controversial departures from the family therapy mainstream.

Anderson and her group (1986, p. 131) can point to the apparent results of these workshops in responding to concerns that they are criticism of their methods.

Whether it is the information itself, the decreased sense of blame and guilt that is communicated by the absence of an emphasis on family etiology, the conveying of respect and equality, or the increase in hope generated by a new approach, the response to these workshops has been dramatic. The climate between staff and families seems to become less polarized, less tense and resistant family members become more cooperative. Family and professionals both become less isolated, and less subject to burnout.

This workshop and the initial sessions or contacts with the family that may have preceded it are only a part of the psychoeducational regimen. Regularly scheduled outpatient family sessions and crisis support is likely to last for a year or more after an acute episode. These sessions include the assignment to the patient of small tasks and the monitoring performance on them. But it's in these sessions that the Anderson group allows the focus to stray from the patient and on to problems in the family's structure, which may have arisen as a result of the schizophrenia, or even on to problems that family members are facing that aren't directly related to the patient.

That is, from this point on, Anderson's psychoeducational approach looks very much like structural family therapy, except that the family's structural flaws are construed as the *result* of rather than the *cause* of the presenting problem.

> During the chronic course of a schizophrenic illness, generational and interpersonal boundaries within families often become blurred. When the patient is an adolescent or young adult, one or both parents may become involved with the patient to the detriment of their relationship with one or another of the children. Wives or husbands come to treat their ill spouses as children, and children come to perform parental roles to fill in for ill parents. Often, the patient's illness dominates the household, so that all decisions and plans are made on the basis of what the patient needs, wants, or will tolerate. This, in effect, puts the patient in control of the rest of the family. These confused generational boundaries are a problem for everyone, as is the central position the patient occupies within the family. The familial structure becomes skewed in such a way that the normal needs of its members cannot be satisfied or attended to properly (p. 173).

Thus much of the therapy follows the familiar themes of reinforcing generational boundaries by getting parents to work together on discipline and getting children out of parental roles, opening up the family's boundary to the outside world and developing support networks, getting parents to reinvest in their marriage, and getting family members to not speak or do for the patient.

In addition, as we mentioned, the Anderson model doesn't shy away from dealing with problems in family members' lives that aren't obviously related to the schizophrenia. They find that marital conflict, problems with the patient's siblings, and depression are common, and can interfere with the family's ability to reorganize to help the patient. They are careful, however, to address these problems only when the family asks for help on them, or when the problems are clearly impeding progress relative to the patient. The danger in going after problems without an invitation from the family is that they may feel blamed and defensive—as if the therapist suspected that those problems were behind the schizophrenia. Anderson et al. (1986) report that frequently these other problems improve without direct attention as the family reorganizes to help the patient.

Is the psychoeducational model effective? The answer to that question depends on one's definition of success. By psychoeducational standards of lowering relapse rates for the first year following an acute schizophrenic episode, all psychoeducational studies show comparably dramatic success. For example, in the Anderson et al. (1986) study,

> Among treatment takers ($n = 90$), 19% of those receiving family therapy alone experienced a psychotic relapse in the year following hospital discharge. Of those receiving the individual behavioral therapy, 20% relapsed, but *no* patient in the treatment cell that received both family therapy and social skills training experienced a relapse. These relapse rates constitute significant effects for both treatments when contrasted to a 41% relapse rate for those receiving only chemotherapy and support (p. 42).

The other major studies showed at least equally impressive results (Falloon et al., 1985; Leff et al., 1982). There seems to be little question that psychoeducation can delay relapse and readmission to a hospital better than other approaches to schizophrenia that have been studied. The question that remains for family therapy is whether it is willing to settle for that kind of limited goal.

If, as is true of other family therapy models (e.g., Haley, 1981; Selvini Palazzoli, Boscolo, Cecchin, and Prata, 1978), one's goal is to return the patient to normal functioning through the resolution of family problems that are hypothesized to maintain the need for the schizophrenic symptoms, then the psychoeducator's success in delaying relapse would be interpreted differently. Psychoeducators would be seen as stabilizing dysfunctional families by helping them to focus on their child as the sick one and, thereby, continue to avoid issues that maintain their dysfunctional system and the need for the symptoms.

This criticism is less relevant for the Anderson model because the kinds of family structural problems that might create a need for symptoms are dealt with as they emerge. Indeed families are more likely to ask therapists for help with those kinds of scary issues if they don't think the therapist sees them as responsible for the schizophrenia.

In this sense, then, Anderson's version of psychoeducation can be seen as a nonantagonistic, less intense, form of structural family therapy. The consistent message to families is that they are in no way responsible for the patient's illness, and the consistent empathy and support for the family's struggle with the illness creates a nondefensive, collaborative therapeutic atmosphere in which the therapist can help families address structural problems without having to coerce or trick them into it. Whether the structural problems predate the schizophrenia or were caused by it seems irrelevant as long as they are addressed.

Anderson and her colleagues (1986) suggest that this model need not be limited to the treatment of schizophrenia, but may be applied to any chronic problem, and Anderson (1988) has also described its application to depression. Much of the work with addictions based on Alcoholics Anonymous or on the Adult Children of Alcoholic models can be seen as fitting this psychoeducational mold. Alcoholism is viewed as a disease; families are educated, empathized with, and supported regarding its effects on them (Steinglass, Bennett, Wolin, and Reiss, 1987). The codependence movement, on the other hand, implies that family members are culpable in the alcoholism and, consequently, would not be consistent with psychoeducation's attempts to clear family members of any implication.

The work of John Rolland (1984, 1987, 1988) with chronic medical illness also has much in common with the psychoeducational approach. Rolland tracks and tries to counter the effects of the illness on the family. This work is less controversial within family therapy than psychoeducation because fewer people would assert that illnesses like MS, diabetes, and stroke are caused by family patterns, should not be medicated, or could be totally cured by family therapy. Thus, the families that Rolland works with are less ashamed and defensive to begin with, and less polarized with helping professionals than families of schizophrenics.

Rolland adds two emphases to the psychoeducational model. One emphasis is on the stages that families go through and can get stuck in when dealing with a chronic illness. The other is a multigenerational exploration with families of the beliefs that family members have about illness in general, about the patient's particular illness, and about the degree to which they can do something to improve their lives. Rolland finds that these belief systems often determine a family's response and, if left unchallenged, can undermine the best educational efforts. Peter Steinglass has also applied psychoeducational methods to chronic illness recently (Steinglass and Horan, 1988).

In conclusion, these psychoeducational models are both reflective of recent trends in family therapy and also represent a unique departure. As with the other models in this chapter, there is a strong move away from an antagonistic view of and relationship with families, and toward a collaborative partnership. As with these new models, therapists look for the family's strengths rather than their deficits, and find ways to lift families out of the guilt and blame that accompany problems. Unlike the other models, however, the Anderson group creates this kind of collaborative, nonblaming relationship by accepting the current psychiatric position on schizophrenia as being a chronic illness with which the family will probably have to struggle indefinitely. It remains to be seen whether family therapy can accept this aspect of psychoeducation.

MICHAEL WHITE AND EXTERNALIZATION

The work of Michael White contains elements that are remarkably similar to aspects of both the solution-focused and the psychoeducational approaches. Like them, White doesn't assume that symptoms serve functions in families—in fact he believes that people feel oppressed by their problems—and he forms collaborative, strength-oriented therapy relationships. Like the psychoeducators, he focuses on the effect that problems have on families. Like the solution-focused therapists, he gets families to explore and expand times where the problem didn't dominate the family—the effect that people have had on their problems—that de Shazer calls *exceptions* and White calls *unique outcomes.*

Michael White is a family therapist living in Adelaide, Australia. He and Cheryl White are based at the Dulwich Center, out of which comes training, clinical work, and publications related to Michael White's approach. White has had a powerful impact on the family therapy scene in Australia and New Zealand for many years and, since he and Cheryl have been travelling internationally over the past several years, his influence has become widespread in Europe and in this country. He has collaborated closely with New Zealander David Epston who has contributed literary metaphors to their work (White and Epston, 1990). Recently Karl Tomm, who has been an advocate and translator of the Milan model, has expanded that role to include White's work.

Particularly in his early writing, White's view of people and their problems drew heavily from Bateson (see Chapter 2), and from political philosopher Michel Foucault (1965, 1973). More recently the social constructionists (e.g., Goffman, 1961; Gergen and Gergen, 1984) seem to have an increasing impact. With this combination of influences, White has constructed a model designed to help free people from the oppression of their problems, much as a populace might be freed from an oppressive state. To do this people must begin to see themselves and their situations differently.

Consequently the meanings or stories that people carry about themselves and their views of the world, and the use of language to construct those stories, are central to White's thinking and therapy, as they were a central focus of Bateson, Foucault, and the constructionists.

White (1989) is not interested in what caused problems, but he is quite interested in the evolving effects of problems on families over time. His belief is that through their interpretation of their life events, people with problems often develop what he calls "problem-saturated descriptions" of their lives. For people with a problem-saturated story, the negative events in their lives and negative aspects of their personalities are constantly in the foreground, making them feel powerless and, consequently, easy prey of problems. As family members try and fail to solve the problem, this story comes to dominate the family (White, 1989, p. 5).

> Although the problem was usually defined as internal to the child, all family members were affected by it, and often felt overwhelmed, dispirited and defeated. In various ways they took the ongoing existence of the problem, and their failed attempts to solve it, as a reflection on themselves, each other and/or on their relationships. The continuing survival of the problem, and the failure of corrective measures, served to confirm, for family members, the presence of various negative personal and relationship qualities or attributes.

Therapy helps people "locate, generate or resurrect alternative stories. . ." (p. 7) that offer a different sense of self and a different relationship with problems.

So far this is not so different from the constructivist thinking of the post-Milan theorists like Harlene Anderson and Harry Goolishian (1988), who also try to change families' stories in their "conversations" with clients. White's unique contribution is in the way he uses language to achieve this "re-storying." Rather than having loose, directionless conversations with families as the post-Milan groups claim to, in hopes that through that process a new and better story will emerge, White has a specific type of story that he wants people to achieve. This new story highlights the person's or family's past, present, and future agency over the course of their lives and problems. People, not problems, are in charge.

The first step toward adopting a new story is to get some distance from the old one. To separate people from their problem-saturated stories, White *externalizes* their problems. That is, in conversing with families about their problem, White (1989) speaks of the problem as if it were a separate entity, existing outside of any family member—an entity with a will of its own, which is to dominate the person or family. This externalizing helps family members see that it is not the person who is, or the family relationships that are, the problem. Rather, it is the problem, or the person's relationship with it, that is the problem.

With the problem externalized, White can ask a series of questions regarding the person's or family's relationship with it. As people separate from their problem and examine their relationship with it, they can see that, perhaps, there have been times when they had some control over it—times that White calls *unique outcomes*—times that had been obscured by their problem-saturated story. In addition, once family members no longer blame each other or themselves for the problem, they can work together to fight it. In this sense White is like an exorcist who casts the devilish problem out of the bodies or minds of family members and then helps them organize to tame it.

White (1989, p. 6) suggests that externalizing has the following beneficial effects:

1. Decreases unproductive conflict between persons, including those disputes over who is responsible for the problem;

2. Undermines the sense of failure that has developed for many persons in response to the continuing existence of the problem despite their attempts to resolve it;

3. Paves the way for persons to cooperate with each other; to unite in a struggle against the problem and to escape its influence in their lives and relationships;

4. Opens up new possibilities for persons to take actions to retrieve their lives and relationships from the problem and its influence;

5. Frees persons to take a lighter, more effective, and less stressed approach to "deadly serious" problems; and

6. Presents options for dialogue, rather than monologue, about the problem.

Therapy becomes a series of questions. One set of questions examines the influence that the problem has had over family members' lives, and, in turn, a second set maps the influence that family members have had over the problem (the unique outcomes, e.g., "Can you recall an occasion when you/your son/your relationship/etc., could have given in to the problem but didn't?"). These questions not only introduce a new story to the family by helping them see that they haven't been as dominated by the problem as they thought, but the therapist's questions also reinforce the externalizing process because, in answering, family members have to talk of the problem as if it were separate from them.

In this interest in and reliance upon questions in therapy, White follows the tradition in family therapy begun by the Milan Associates (see

Chapters 3 and 9) and expanded by others like Karl Tomm (1987a, 1987b). There is one major difference, however, between the circular questioning that those theorists developed and White's use of questions. Circular questions are to be asked without a particular outcome in mind so that the family is not constrained in their responses by the agenda of the therapist (Cecchin, 1987). The idea is to use circular questions to loosen up family discussions and focus them on the level of relationship, which allows the family to examine themselves and reorganize in any way they want.

Most of White's questions, on the other hand, are rhetorical. They are designed to elicit specific responses. White's questions help people realize that: (1) they are separate from the problem, (2) they have power over the problem, or (3) they are not who they thought they were. Thus, White's work unabashedly leads people to certain conclusions, with the trust that, rather than being constraining, those conclusions will liberate them from the constraints of their previous beliefs, and they will have a far greater range of alternatives. This difference in therapist agenda—leading clients to empowering conclusions versus allowing families to generate their own, new (and, one hopes, empowering) conclusions—represents the major difference between the Milan and post-Milan approaches and White's approach.

Due perhaps to the influence of Foucault who analyzes comtemporary society through a lens of power, wherein the state oppresses people through its ability to keep them divided and make them think they are responsible for their own problems, White's metaphors consistently convey the relationship between people and their problems as a struggle for control or survival—as if the problem were a live adversary. Originally the problem takes advantage of the family's divisiveness and hopelessness to oppress and "feed off" of them. Gradually they begin refusing to submit to it, and instead, begin to undermine, turn the tables on, or "starve it." White suggests that the problem is dependent on its effects for its survival so that by not allowing it to affect them in the old way, clients cut off the problem's "life support system."

As people begin to perceive their relationship with the problem differently and begin to come out from under its oppression, White asks questions regarding how this change affects their stories about themselves and each other (e.g., "What does this tell you about yourself/your relationship/your son/etc., that it is important for you to know?"). This ties the subjugation of the problem to the larger goal of the "re-authoring" of the client's self or family story.

White's therapy comes to life in his case descriptions, so we present excerpts below from his (1989, pp. 10–11) description of a family with an encopretic child that illustrates many of these concepts and methods.

When mapping the influence of family members in the life of what we came to call "Sneaky Poo", we discovered that:

1. Although Sneaky Poo always tried to trick Nick into being his playmate, Nick could recall a number of occasions during which he had not allowed Sneaky Poo to "outsmart" him. These were occasions during which Nick could have cooperated by "smearing," "streaking" or "plastering," but he declined to do so. He had not allowed himself to be tricked into this.

2. There was a recent occasion during which Sneaky Poo could have driven Sue into a heightened sense of misery, but she resisted and turned on the stereo instead. Also, on this occasion, she refused to question her competence as a parent and as a person.

3. Ron could not recall an occasion during which he had not allowed the embarrassment caused by Sneaky Poo to isolate him from others. However, after Sneaky Poo's requirements of him were identified, he did seem interested in the idea of defying these requirements . . .

4. . . . it was established that there was an aspect to Sue's relationship with Nick that she thought she could still enjoy, that Ron was still making some attempts to persevere in his relationship with Nick, and that Nick had an idea that Sneaky Poo had not destroyed all of the love in his relationship with his parents.

After identifying Nick's, Sue's, and Ron's influence in the life of Sneaky Poo, I introduced questions that encouraged them to perform meaning in relation to these examples, so that they might "re-author" their lives and relationships.

How had they managed to be effective against the problem in this way? How did this reflect on them as people and on their relationships? . . . Did this success give them any ideas about further steps that they might take to reclaim their lives from the problem?

In response to these questions, Nick thought that he was ready to stop Sneaky Poo from outsmarting him so much, and decided that he would not be tricked into being its playmate any more. . .

White met with the family two weeks later and found that Nick had fought Sneaky Poor valiantly, having only one minor episode, and he seemed happier and stronger. Sue and Ron had also done their parts in the battle. In her effort to not cooperate with Sneaky Poo's requirements for her to feel guilty, Sue had begun to "treat herself" when Sneaky Poo was getting her down and Ron had fought Sneaky Poo's attempts to keep him isolated by talking to friends about the problem.

I encouraged the family to reflect on and to speculate about what this success said about the qualities that they possessed as people and about the attributes of their relationships. I also encouraged them to review what these facts suggested about their current relationship with Sneaky

Poo. In this discussion, family members identified further measures that they could take to decline Sneaky Poo's invitations to them to support it (p. 11).

White reports that the family expanded these efforts in the interim and by the third session they felt confident that Sneaky Poo had been defeated. At a six-month follow-up they were still doing well.

We're not aware of any systematic efforts to study the outcome of White's approach. In nearly all of his writing, he sprinkles descriptions of successful cases, like the one above. White (1989) has applied his model to such difficult problems as anorexia nervosa, schizophrenia, uncontrolled children and adolescents, encopresis and enuresis, and mourning and loss. In each of these areas he has developed innovative twists of his technique to accommodate to the problem's idiosyncrasies and we are given the impression that his approach works quite well.

This issue of outcome is an elusive one, however. For example, if we examine White's writing on schizophrenia and compare it to the psycho-education of Anderson, Reiss, and Hogarty (1986), described above, we find that despite many apparent contradictions between the two models, including the kind of outcome families struggling with schizophrenia should expect, there are remarkable similarities in both technique and expected outcome.

The most striking contradiction between these models is that, unlike Anderson and her colleagues, who accept and use the psychiatric definition of schizophrenia, White (1989) believes the psychiatric understanding of schizophrenia limits people's ability to counter it. "If schizophrenia constructs rigid and implicit beliefs about chronicity and deterioration; if scientific classification produces docile subjects; . . . then the socially constructed nature of schizophrenia must exert a powerful influence on its course" (p. 48).

As he does with other problems, White externalizes schizophrenia, or what he calls the "in-the-corner lifestyle" that it produces, and thereby reduces the guilt and recrimination that surrounds it, and he unites family members to fight it. The Anderson model, by calling schizophrenia a disease, is also, in a sense, externalizing it and achieves a comparable atmosphere of collaboration.

Maybe the difference is in what is expected of the patient in terms of the pace at which he or she can return to normal functioning or even be cured. Don't the psychoeducators collaborate with the "in-the-corner life style" by telling family members to let the patient withdraw when he or she wants to, and by suggesting that change in the patient's functioning will be extremely slow? Like the psychoeducators, White (1989) does not claim that his model can cure schizophrenia; only that it can help alter the "in-the-corner lifestyle" that the whole family submits to, and can reduce relapse rates.

He also has learned to lower family members' expectations for quick change. "Throughout this process, the therapist's stance remains mildly conservative. S/he is enthusiastic about the successful steps that family members take in their escape from the in-the-corner lifestyle, but always encourages them to consider shortening future steps and to take them one at a time" (p. 55). With questions like, "Do you think you have let ambition push you into doing too much too soon?" White restrains families and patients from expecting too much of the patient, much as the psycho-educators do.

In juxtaposing Anderson and White this way we were struck by the similarity of the two approaches in practice, in contrast to the major contradictions in their views of schizophrenia. It seems that sensitive therapists will take similar lessons from the families they treat, and adjust their theories to accommodate this learning. If the two approaches achieve comparable results, this would imply that the power of both of them lies in their ability to counter the blame/recrimination cycles in families and pull family strengths together. It does seem preferable that families are drawn together to battle with an in-the-corner lifestyle than with a chronic disease. White, however, has yet to demonstrate the effects of his externalizing of schizophrenia.

In conclusion, Michael White has constructed an approach that has much in common with the other models in this chapter, yet presents a unique and powerful view of and language about problems and people that have great appeal. He uses constructivism to explain how people can reauthor their life stories, but instead of constructivism leading him to the value-free, "anything goes" position we criticized in Chapter 3, White, with Foucault's influence, retains strong values for helping people organize to escape the oppression of problems or other people. These convictions produce a highly focused and methodical therapy with specific techniques (most of which are in the form of questions) and goals.

THE INTERNAL FAMILY SYSTEMS MODEL

As we have discussed, family therapy originally focused on action—on behavioral sequences—and then in the eighties the field became interested in the belief systems that drove people's actions. As family therapy became more interested in meaning, one might expect that intrapsychic process would be re-examined using the systemic principles and techniques that have been applied so effectively to families. For much of family therapy such an exploration was detoured by the field's traditional aversion to intrapsychic speculation—what might be called "psyche-phobia"—and by its adoption of constructivism which attended only to consciously held and verbalized attitudes or beliefs.

In the early 1980s, however, Richard Schwartz (1987, 1988) did begin this kind of systemic exploration of internal process. Schwartz has been with the Family Systems Program of the Institute for Juvenile Research in Chicago for the past ten years, where he conducts training and research. He wrote extensively on the training and supervision of family therapists and on treating eating disorders, before the latter interest led to his exploration of internal systems. His doctorate is in marital and family therapy so that, not being steeped in traditional intrapsychic models, he entered the world of internal process relatively naively, with few preconceptions as to what he would find.

While conducting an outcome study of structural-strategic family therapy and bulimia that, overall, achieved good results (Schwartz, Barrett, and Saba, 1985), Schwartz worked with some cases in which family therapy alone didn't seem to be enough. Frustrated with the limits imposed by the exclusion of internal process, he broke this "external only" tradition by asking clients about what went on inside them before, during, and after a binge.

He discovered that each client described a similar sequence of interaction among what they called internal "voices" or "parts" of them. "A part of me attacks me for being so fat, then another part feels hurt and lonely, and then still another takes over and makes me binge. . ." Their descriptions made it seem as if each of these parts or voices was more than just habitual thought patterns or feeling states—as if these parts were autonomous internal personalities. Schwartz wondered if the same systemic principles and techniques that had been so effective in working with families might also apply to his clients' internal systems. He continued to interview clients, tracking the interaction patterns among their competing voices, trying to understand the relationships among them, and experimenting with ways to intervene systemically in this inner ecology.

Schwartz found that not only did systemic principles and methods apply to internal process, but when they were applied, family members began to understand themselves and each other in ways that allowed them to change more easily than other intrapsychic models predicted. With these techniques clients could tap into previously obscure inner resources and change their relationship with parts of themselves that were contributing to problems.

He also found that the language of the model by itself was a powerful tool to help families understand each other and their problems in more empowering ways. It is easier to consider changing a small part of yourself or of another family member than to have to change the whole personality.

Despite being the only model in this chapter that explores internal process, Schwartz's internal family systems (IFS) model, like these new models, fosters a collaborative relationship with clients, and a blame-free atmosphere for family sessions. Like Anderson's psychoeducation and White's externalization, the IFS model unites family members to counter the effects of entities that are contributing to the problem. By extending systems thinking to the level of internal process, however, the IFS affords a richer understanding of people and their problems than models that exclude internal systems, and broadens the therapist's ability to move fluidly between internal and external levels, allowing an understanding of each level to inform the work with the other.

The IFS model rests on relatively simple basic assumptions which, although developed independently, correspond with some of the assumptions of other models that have explored this subpersonality phenomena (Assagioli, 1965; Jung, 1956; Hillman, 1975; Stone and Winkelman, 1985; Watkins and Watkins, 1979; Watanabe, 1986).

The first of these assumptions is that the mind consists of a multitude of specialized subminds, each of which has unique talents and intentions, and a certain range of emotion and expression. Schwartz found that these subpersonalities (or what he calls "parts" because that's a term people are comfortable with), interact internally like members of a tribe or large family. They organize into alliances, vie for control, and, at times, go to war against each other.

To make this seem less foreign to the reader, consider a time in your life when you were facing a difficult decision. You probably experienced internal debates among conflicted thoughts or feelings regarding the right move to make. If you had focused exclusively on one of those thoughts or feelings and asked it questions, you might find that it was more than just a transient thought or feeling. You might find that it had a lot to say, that it had been saying similar things to you all of your life, and that it commonly fought with the same parts it was fighting with at that point.

In tracking the sequences among these parts, Schwartz found that they often protect or distract each other much as happens in distressed families. He also found that most people habitually favor and listen to some parts while disliking and shutting out others. From these observations, he became interested in the parallels between a person's internal system and their external family system.

Take the example of Jane who grew up in a family that strongly feared overt expressions of anger and taught girls to take care of others and disregard or neglect themselves. Jane, like most of us, has a part of her that wants to help her stand up for and assert herself, but because of her family background, she was "cut off" from that assertive part of her. Instead she listened to her fearful and selfless parts' warnings that bad things would happen if she asserted herself.

Since Jane's assertive part was forced to watch helplessly while people continuously exploited her, it became extremely angry. On the rare occasions when Jane couldn't contain this angry part, it seized control and made her suddenly fly into a rage, surprising and scaring people around her who were used to her passivity. These outbursts only reconfirmed to her fearful and selfless parts how dangerous the assertive part was, increasing their conviction to keep it out of the system, which, of course, made it more extreme, and so on. Thus, Schwartz found the same positive feedback loops that family therapists had described as characterizing escalations among family members (Watzlawick, Weakland, and Fisch, 1974; and see Chapter 2), characterizing the polarizations within "internal families" as well.

He also found frequently that when these internal positive feedback sequences were reversed, the formerly polarized parts quickly returned to their natural state, which was always valuable—just as happens when polarizations among family members are reversed. To achieve this kind of depolarization among a person's parts, Schwartz gained access to the person's inner system through Gestalt therapy "open-chair" technique or through imagery, and then he began experimenting with a variety of family therapy techniques. He found that by using a simple boundary-making technique from structural family therapy he could help a person get their polarized parts to deal with each other while blocking the interference of other parts.

During this experimenting, Schwartz found that when he tried to get a client to interact with one part (we'll call it part A), frequently another part or parts that were polarized with A would interfere by making the client feel something extreme about part A—perhaps fear, anger, envy, or hopelessness. To counter this Schwartz asked clients to find the interfering parts and get them to stop interfering, much as a family therapist gets interfering family members to respect a boundary around a family subsystem. Most clients could do this and when they did their perception of part A, which had been extreme, suddenly shifted to compassion for or curiosity about part A.

For example, when Jane, using imagery, first saw her angry part, she felt frightened by it and it looked like a monster. After she moved her fearful and selfless parts into imaged rooms and asked them to not interfere, she suddenly felt sorry for the angry part and it looked younger and less fierce. She could listen to it describe how it felt isolated and abandoned by her. At that point she could negotiate a new relationship with this part— she would try to listen to and speak for it more, and, in return, it would not try to take over. The more Jane used her assertive part, the less she was exploited by people, and the less extreme the part became. In this way, internal changes create external changes, and vice versa.

Schwartz also tried guiding clients to separate from not just a few, but all the parts they could identify. He consistently discovered that, when separated from their parts, everyone had a similar experience described variously as "feeling calm," "lighthearted," "confident," and "in the present." He found, in addition, that once they had achieved this state, people could change their relationships with their parts with relative ease. He called this differentiated entity the *Self,* and discovered that while in this Self-mind, people could lead their internal families quite effectively.

In the IFS model, then, the Self is not a passive, observing state of mind, but instead is an active internal leader, who helps the system of parts continuously reorganize to relate more harmoniously. In this leadership role the Self listens to each part and what it really wants, nurtures or comforts some parts, helps change the role of others, and negotiates with polarized parts to resolve their differences. For example, the Self may comfort and soothe frightened or sad parts, calm rageful defenders, or get striving achiever parts to compromise with parts that demand more relaxation. In this sense, then, the person's Self becomes a therapist to their internal family.

Schwartz found that once he helped a person differentiate their Self from their parts, they could do a great deal of work on their own, between sessions. In doing that work, people achieved new insights or perspectives regarding themselves and their problems on their own, without having been given reframes or interpretations by the therapist. Thus, the IFS therapist is taken out of the position of having to construct and sell new realities to people about their problems. The therapist structures an environment in which people change themselves and, consequently, feel less dependent on therapists and learn to trust their own resources.

One goal of the IFS model, then, is to help people achieve "Self leadership." Schwartz (1987) used the metaphor of an orchestra, in which the parts were analogous to the musicians and the Self to the conductor. A good conductor values each musician's talents and knows his or her limitations. He or she knows the best point in a symphony to draw out one section and mute another. Each musician, despite wanting to spotlight his or her own talent or have the piece played in a way that emphasizes his or her section, respects the conductor's judgement and follows the conductor's direction, while playing as well as possible.

If each section were to choose its own tempo, phrasing, or volume, the result would be cacophonous; sections would compete against each other, and no one would be happy. Similarly, one part of a person might insist that he or she get to work, while another demands a playful diversion, and still another pleads for intimacy with a lover. Without a respected leader, who each part trusts will see that their needs are met, the parts would fight for control and sabotage each other, resulting in constant internal conflict or in the domination of one part and the oppression of the others.

When a person's Self is differentiated from the parts and elevated to a position from which it can provide this kind of fair, strong leadership the internal system depolarizes—the orchestra is (literally) harmonious. Within this harmony, the Self leads and the parts advise, lend feelings or talents, and otherwise assist the Self.

In working with a family, the goal is for the Self of each family member to be in the lead when they interact with each other. When someone in a family has a problem that frustrates others, usually parts of one family member struggle to change parts of another, leading to positive feedback loop escalations between parts of different family members, and also within each family member.

For example, Johnny has been fighting at school and rebelling at home. The therapist asks him about the parts that make him do that and Johnny describes a conflict between a rebellious part of him and a part that worries about displeasing his parents and criticizes him for rebelling. He thinks that things might go better for him if he could resolve this internal conflict, but he doesn't know how. The therapist asks father what parts of him are activated by Johnny's rebellion. Father describes a frustrated and furious part, and agrees that things don't get better when this part of him takes over; he feels ashamed afterward, but he can't seem to control his "temper." Mother says that father's temper part triggers scared parts of her that try to protect Johnny from father's temper.

Thus, the therapist asks each family member to describe the parts of them that are involved in the problem and may ask questions like: How difficult is it for them to control their parts? How might the problem be affected if they could stay their Selves rather than letting their parts take over? And how do they want to change their relationship with these parts that interfere in their life? People respond naturally and nondefensively to this language. Admitting that a little part of yourself contributes to the problem feels less shameful and overwhelming than implicating your whole personality.

In addition, the model's language alters people's view of themselves and each other. Instead of having a rebellious, disrespectful child, the parents find they have a son who has some trouble with a few of his parts, but also has a Self that wants to work on those parts. Father is transformed from being a dangerous tyrant to being a good man struggling with his angry part. The view of mother is likewise changed by this multiplicity perspective of personality, which is more benevolent and holds more potential for change than the idea that people have a unitary personality. Therapy consists of getting all the family members' Selves to work together to help each person deal with the parts that are interfering in their family's life. "It is in such an atmosphere, free of coercion or recrimination and full of empowerment and hope, that a family's resources surface" (Breunlin, Schwartz, and Karrer, in press).

Finally, the IFS model provides an ecological understanding of therapy that enables therapists to be more sensitive to the impact of their interventions, at both the internal and family levels. For example, an IFS therapist who encounters "resistance" believes he or she has interacted with the family in ways that activated protective parts of family members. Since the therapist expects parts of a person, family, or any ecology, to react protectively when threatened with being made vulnerable, the therapist views this as a natural reaction.

Rather than trying to overpower or to outwit this resistance, the therapist respects those protective parts as holding important information regarding the therapist's impact on this delicate ecology, and may suggest that the clients ask their parts what they are upset about. Once protective parts disclose their fears, the therapist and clients can negotiate ways to accommodate or reassure those parts. When protective parts are shown this kind of respect and consideration, therapists encounter less "resistance."

In addition, Schwartz and his colleagues have gradually learned about the common relationship patterns among people's parts, so that they are better able to avoid triggering these protective reactions. For example, many people are like fifteen-year-old Ben who grew distant and defensive when, in an early session, the therapist asked him if he ever felt sad about his parents' divorce. The therapist later learned that, like many people, Ben feared and avoided his sad part because it had overtaken him in the past, making him feel helpless and fragile. Many other parts of Ben had organized to keep him away from the sad part, and had to be convinced that Ben could approach that sad part without being overcome by it before they would allow his Self any access to it. Thus, therapists' awareness of common relationships among parts helps them act so as to minimize the provoking of any system's protective parts.

The techniques of the IFS have been refined over the past seven years and are well defined but also quite involved. Out of fear of publishing them prematurely and without sufficient guidelines, Schwartz has delayed publication until he and colleagues complete a comprehensive manual in the near future.

The model can be applied effectively, however, in a general way by simply using the language and concepts. The therapist asks about the problem, and then asks each family member what they say to themselves about it. In reiterating any family member's response to that question, the therapist might ask, "So a part of you says _____ about the problem, is that right?" And then, "How do you think the problem would be affected if this part of you didn't take over?"; "Ask the part to let your Self lead the discussion about the problem this time and see how it goes."

Through this process, people become increasingly aware of when their parts are interfering, and then increasingly able to lead with their Selves. Families then can find their own solutions because the full resources of each family member are available to the group rather than being squandered in rigid polarizations within and between family members. When a person is able to remain his or her Self in the face of extreme parts of another person, the other person's Self gradually emerges and their interaction becomes more productive. This is similar to Bowen's technique of getting people to remain differentiated in the face of their family's emotional field (see Chapter 8).

Aspects of IFS therapy are similar to Bowen and structural family therapies as well as the other models covered in this chapter, and the IFS provides an alternative understanding of how those models are effective. With the absence, at this point, of more than anecdotal documentation of its effectiveness, however, the IFS model's acceptance will be based on its intuitive appeal. In family therapy that appeal is limited by the field's long-standing psychephobia and by the general difficulty people have accepting the multiplicity of the mind.

SUMMARY

The four models presented in this chapter, plus the post-Milan, constructivist movement, and the feminist movement (see Chapter 3), represent the wave that carries family therapy into the nineties. Despite their differences, these models and movements share an ethic of collaborating with, rather than directing or coercing, people. This common interest in collaboration is no accident—it reflects the maturing of the field.

The pioneers saw families as powerful, resistant adversaries, in part, because they themselves felt weak; they lacked the conceptual frameworks or techniques that could give them confidence while working with highly distressed families. It's taken family therapists time to develop these frameworks and methods, and as therapists felt stronger relative to the families they treat, their need to control or outwit families has diminished. Family therapists have learned that they don't have to *make* families change. Indeed therapists are finding that when they don't try to make families change, but instead create a climate in which problems can be explored in less defensive or polarized ways, families are able to change themselves.

This shift in the therapist-family relationship hasn't made inactive observers of therapists. Therapists are still leaders in therapy, but their style of leadership is shifting from the authoritative director who points out or reframes problems, to the confident partner who elicits strengths. These models are the harbingers of a new era in the history of family therapy in which therapists search for ways to help people discover their own resources, instead of trying to impose solutions.

REFERENCES

Anderson, C.M., Reiss, D., and Hogarty, B. 1986. *Schizophrenia and the family.* New York: Guilford.

Anderson, C.M. 1988. Depression and families. In *Chronic disorders and the family*, F. Walsh and C. Anderson, eds. New York: Haworth Press.

Anderson, H., and Goolishian, H.A. 1988. Human systems as linguistic systems: Preliminary and evolving ideas about the implications for clinical theory. *Family Process. 27*:371–393.

Assagioli, R. 1965. *Psychosynthesis.* New York: Penguin Books.

Breunlin, D., Schwartz, R., and Karrer, B. *Metaframeworks.* San Francisco: Jossey-Bass. In press.

Brown, G.W., Birley, J.L.T., and Wing, J.K. 1972. The influence of family life on the course of schizophrenic disorders: A replication. *British Journal of Psychology. 121*:241–258.

Brown, G.W., Monck, E.M., Carstairs, G.M., and Wing, J.K. 1962. Influence of family life on the course of schizophrenic illness. *British Journal of Preventive and Social Medicine. 16*:55–68.

Cecchin, G. 1987. Hypothesizing, circularity, and neutrality revisited: An invitation to curiosity. *Family Process. 26*:405–413.

de Shazer, S. 1984. The death of resistance. *Family Process. 23*:11–21.

de Shazer, S. 1985. *Keys to Solutions in Brief Therapy.* New York, Norton.

de Shazer, S. 1986. An indirect approach to brief therapy. In *Indirect Approaches in Therapy*, S. de Shazer and R. Kral, eds. Rockville, MD: Aspen.

de Shazer, S. 1987. Minimal elegance. *Family Therapy Networker.* September/October, 59.

de Shazer, S. 1988. *Clues: Investigating solutions in brief therapy.* New York: Norton.

de Shazer, S., Berg, I.K., Lipchik, E., Nunnally, E., Molnar, A., Gingerich, W., and Weiner-Davis, M. Brief therapy: Focused solution development, *Family Process. 25*:207–222.

Falloon, I.R.H., Boyd, J.L., McGill, C.W., Williamson, M., Razani, J., Moss, H.B., Gilderman, A.M., and Simpson, G.M. 1985. Family management in the prevention of morbidity of schizophrenia: Clinical outcome of a two-year longitudinal study. *Archives of General Psychiatry. 42*:887–896.

Foucault, M. 1965. *Madness and civilization: A history of insanity in the age of reason.* New York: Random House.

Foucault, M. 1973. *The birth of the clinic: An archeology of medical perception.* London: Tavistock.

Gergen, M.M., and Gergen, K.J. 1984. The social construction of narrative accounts. In *Historical social psychology*, K.J. Gergen and M.M. Gergen, eds. New Jersey: Erlbourn Associates.

Goffman, E. 1961. *Asylums: Essays in the social situation of mental patients and other inmates.* New York: Doubleday.

Goldstein, M.J. ed. 1981. *New Developments in interventions with families of schizophrenics.* San Francisco: Jossey-Bass.

Goldstein, M.J., Rodnick, E.H., Evans, J.R., May, P.R., and Steinberg, M. 1978. Drug and family therapy in the aftercare treatment of acute schizophrenia. *Archives of General Psychiatry. 35*:1169–1177.

Haley, J. 1981. *Leaving Home.* San Francisco: Jossey-Bass.

Hillman, J. 1975. *Re-visioning psychology.* New York: Harper and Row.

Jung, C. 1956. *Two essays on analytical psychology.* Cleveland, OH: Meridian.

Leff, J.P., Kuipers, L., Berkowitz, R., Eberlein-Vries, R., and Sturgeon, D. 1982. A controlled trial of social intervention in the families of schizophrenic patients. *British Journal of Psychology. 141*:121–134.

Lipchik, E. 1986. Purposeful interview. *Journal of Strategic and Systemic Therapies,* 5, 88–99.

O'Hanlon, W.H. 1990. Debriefing myself: When a brief therapist does long-term work. *Family Therapy Networker. 14*(2):48–49, 68–69.

O'Hanlon, W.H., and Weiner-Davis, M. 1989. *In search of solutions: A new direction in psychotherapy.* New York: Norton.

Rolland, J.S. 1984. Toward a psychosocial typology of chronic and life-threatening illness. *Family Systems Medicine.* 2:245–263.

Rolland, J.S. 1987. Chronic illness and the life cycle: A conceptual framework. *Family Process.* 26:203–221.

Rolland, J.S. 1988. Family systems and chronic illness: A typological model. In *Chronic disorders and the family,* F. Walsh and C. Anderson. New York: Haworth Press.

Schwartz, R. 1987. Our multiple selves. *Family Therapy Networker. 11*:25–31, 80–83.

Schwartz, R. 1988. Know thy selves. *Family Therapy Networker. 12*: 21–29.

Schwartz, R., Barrett, M.J., and Saba, G. 1985. Family therapy for bulimia. In *The handbook of psychotherapy for anorexia nervosa and bulimia,* D. Gardner and P. Garfinkel, eds. New York: Guilford.

Selvini Palazzoli, M., Boscolo, L., Cecchin, G., and Prata, G. 1978. *Paradox and counter paradox.* New York: Aronson.

Steinglass, P., Bennett, L., Wolin, S., and Reiss, D. 1987. *The alcoholic family.* New York: Basic Books.

Steinglass, P., and Horan, M.E. 1988. Families and chronic medical illness. In *Chronic disorders and the family,* F. Walsh and C. Anderson. New York: Haworth Press.

Stone, H., and Winkelman, S. 1985. *Embracing ourselves.* Marina del Rey, CA: Devross & Co.

Tomm, K. 1987a. Interventive interviewing: Part I. Strategizing as a fourth guideline for the therapist. *Family Process.* 26:3–14.

Tomm, K. 1987b. Interventive interviewing: Part II. Reflexive questioning as a means to enable self-healing. *Family Process.* 25:167–184.

Vaughn, C.E., and Leff, J.P. 1976. The influence of family and social factors on the course of psychiatric illness. *British Journal of Psychiatry. 129*:125–137.

Vaughn, C.E., Snyder, K.S., Jones, S., Freeman, W.B., and Falloon, I.R.H. 1984. Family factors in schizophrenic relapse: Replication in California of British research on expressed emotion. *Archives of General Psychiatry. 41*:1169–1177.

Watanabe, S. 1986. Cast of characters work. *Contemporary Family Therapy.* 8:75–83.

Watkins, J., and Watkins, H. 1979. Ego states and hidden observers. *Journal of Altered States of Consciousness.* 5:3–18.

Watzlawick, P., Weakland, J., and Fisch, R. 1974. *Change*. New York: Norton.

White, M. 1989. *Selected papers*. Adelaide, Australia: Dulwich Center Publications.

White, M., and Epston, D. 1990. *Narrative means to therapeutic ends*. New York: Norton.

Wylie, M.S. 1990. Brief therapy on the couch. *Family Therapy Networker*. *14*:26–34, 66.

12

Comparative Analysis

The exponential growth of family therapy has crowded the field with competing schools, every one of which has made important contributions. This diversity has produced a rich and varied literature, which bears witness to the vitality of the field. But these different approaches also constitute a confusing array of concepts and techniques, creating a dilemma: with the bewildering variety of family therapies, how is one to choose among them?

A therapist's theoretical orientation is no accident. The choice is over-determined and rooted in personal experience. For some the choice of which approach to follow is dictated by what is available from their teachers and supervisors. Others pick and choose concepts and techniques from here and there, hoping to mold their own eclectic approach. Unfortunately, with no anchor to insure coherence, this strategy may be intellectually satisfying, but clinically ineffective. Finally, there are those who pledge allegiance to a single approach; this provides them with a consistent, but often incomplete model.

In this chapter we will offer a comparative analysis of systems of family therapy to sharpen the reader's appreciation of the separate approaches, and to serve as a guide to understanding the similarities and differences among the systems. Each system proclaims a set of "truths," yet despite some overlap there are notable conflicts among these "truths."

This chapter will highlight the conflicts and examine the competing positions. Our aim is to examine different solutions to some of the most significant problems of family therapy.

THEORETICAL PURITY AND TECHNICAL ECLECTICISM

Systems of family therapy are most clearly distinguished by their conceptual positions. Whether they claim to be based entirely on theory (behavioral family therapy) or to be atheoretical (experiential family therapy), each of the systems is supported by a set of beliefs about families and how to change them. Moreover, these theories relate to practice in a circular and mutually reinforcing manner. Practice generally precedes theory; thereafter progress in theory and practice proceeds in leapfrog fashion. Developments in one lead to developments in the other, in a continuing process.

The systematizers of family therapy are methodologists first, theoreticians second. The facts of their clinical observations and experience come before the hypotheses and speculations of their theories. Originally these theories were like maps drawn by explorers of new territories; but for those who came afterwards, students and colleagues, the theories offered preset guidelines for viewing the terrain.

Because they offer a preset way of looking at clinical data, theories have a biasing effect on observation. Students undoubtedly "see" what the theories they have studied prepare them to see. This is easily demonstrated by showing a videotape of the opening minutes of a family therapy session to a group of students. Even if the family conducts itself in a perfectly unremarkable fashion, students will "see" evidence of pathology, phrased in terms of whatever concepts they have learned.

Theories can bias observation and stultify creative thinking; but they also bring order out of chaos. They enable us to organize our observations, and to make sense out of what families are doing. Instead of seeing a "blooming, buzzing confusion," we begin to see patterns of interaction. Moreover, these patterns are organized in conceptual categories that are directly relevant to therapeutic intervention.

Theories also serve a political purpose. They demarcate one system from the others, and announce their unique points of view. For this reason, theoretical positions tend to be stated in doctrinaire terms that maximize their distinctions. While this makes interesting reading, it is somewhat misleading. The truth is that the different systems of family therapy are more alike in practice than their theories suggest. Moreover, each new approach tends to become more eclectic over time. Practitioners start out as relative purists, but eventually discover the validity of theoretical concepts from other approaches and the usefulness of other people's techniques.

The result is that, with increasing experience, most family therapists gradually become more eclectic.

Practice is the expected consequence of theory, but it doesn't always work out that way. Theory is molded by the requirements of logical consistency and elegance, and often reflects a desire to be seen as original and clever. Practice is molded in the pragmatic arena of clinical treatment; it's shaped by encounters with real people, who often turn out to be more complicated than abstract models. Clinicians trained in one school are often forced by the complexity of the task to incorporate methods from other schools. In everyday practice the schools of family therapy tend to become synthetic and integrative. Therapists from technique-oriented schools, which focus on small sequences of interaction (behaviorists and strategists), have begun to adopt the organizing frameworks of schools with more comprehensive understanding of family dynamics (Bowenian and structural). At the same time, certain techniques that have proven their potency have been adopted by many of the schools of family therapy. Family therapists of all persuasions are now likely to clarify communications, direct enactments, and express skepticism about some clients' ability to change, no matter what their approach.

FAMILY THERAPIST—ARTIST OR SCIENTIST?

Theories are modified in practice to suit the personal styles of therapists as well as the practical needs of families. Expertise requires a body of operative knowledge, but it is not synonymous with expertness. Accomplished therapists begin with a grounding in theory; beyond that they must learn to extemporize. The therapist is not the system; just because Minuchin cures anorexia nervosa doesn't mean that anyone can, simply by joining, unbalancing, and boundary-making.

The phrase, "the art and science of psychotherapy," implies that the therapist assumes a dual role, that of artist and scientist (Jasnow, 1978). On the surface, this seems innocuous, even banal. We all agree that a practitioner is first required to master the general principles and proven techniques in the field. Later these principles and techniques must be applied skillfully in a way that is appropriate to each case and in a manner that is congruent with the therapist's personality. There is, however, much room for disagreement about the degree to which the family therapist is more like an artist or more like a scientist.

Techniques do not make a family therapist. The therapist's personal qualities, respect for patients, and reverence for life are also important. Techniques are the tools, but human qualities are the supreme qualification of the good psychotherapist. Compassion—a deeply felt understanding of other people's sufferings—and sensitivity—an appreciation of people's inner world—can be lost in preoccupation with theoretical concepts. Without understanding and respect for individuals, family therapy remains a technical operation, instead of becoming a living human experience.

Behavioral and strategic therapists emphasize the technical role of the therapist, while experiential and constructivist therapists stress the artistic side of the person. We believe that the best way to become an effective family therapist is to first learn to be a "scientist" and then become an "artist." A beginner should concentrate on learning theory and technique, and subject himself or herself to a tutorial program of supervision. During this training it is reasonable, even wise, to adopt or copy outright technique, style, and even language from one's mentors. Furthermore, it may be necessary to identify and modify or subdue certain types of responses that come naturally.

> Mr. C. was a straight-A student in a psychiatric social work program, who came to a well-known family therapy institute with very strong references. His previous supervisors rated him as an outstanding young therapist, and stressed his warmth and ability to empathize with clients. When he began to see families it was immediately apparent that he had a natural gift for understanding and communicating his acceptance of people. His families liked him and they tended to remain in treatment with him.
>
> Unhappily, his natural warmth and compassion for people made him respond to family problems by expressing sympathy and then taking over. Although many of his families were happy to become dependent upon him, they failed to learn how to solve their own problems. Moreover, since they experienced no pressure to resolve their own problems, the therapist was left with very little leverage to influence them in significant ways.
>
> In supervision Mr. C. was helped to recognize and restrain his well-meaning but counterproductive tendency to rescue his clients. The immediate result was a long and painful period of self-imposed restraint, but this eventually enabled him to become a better therapist.

Most young therapists come equipped not only with some innately helpful qualities but also with a number of nontherapeutic impulses. Common among these are: assuming an overly central and controlling position with families; paying more attention to family members' feelings (or behavior, or thinking) than to other aspect of their experience; taking on the families' dilemmas as problems to be solved by the therapist; getting angry at resistant families; and identifying only with adolescents (or small children, or parents). Because most of these tendencies are automatic reflexes of character, it is unlikely that young therapists will be able to identify them without supervision. The only other way to detect troublesome lack of objectivity in a therapist is to recognize repeated failures or stalemates with certain types of families. Once these clues to problems in the therapist are identified, self-analysis, consultation, or supervision will help to determine if the problem stems from inadequate skill or from unrecognized emotional reactivity.

THEORETICAL FORMULATIONS

All schools of family therapy have theories. Some are elaborate (psychoanalytic), some simple (experiential); some are developed from other disciplines (behavioral); others are developed directly from family work (structural, strategic). Theories are ideas abstracted from experience and observation. Their purpose is to simplify and order the raw data of family life as an aid to understanding. In this chapter we will evaluate theories for their pragmatic function—understanding families in order to better treat them. The schools of family therapy will be compared on the basis of their theoretical positions on a sample of key conceptual dimensions: families as systems; stability and change; past or present; communication; content/process; monadic, dyadic, or triadic points of view; the nuclear family in context; and boundaries.

Families as Systems

Communications family therapists introduced the idea that families are systems. More than the sum of their parts, systems are the parts *and* the way they function together. Family group therapists also treated families as more than collections of individuals; but their idea of a superordinate group process was a more limited concept that refers to something that happens when a group of people interact, rather than to an organizing principle that governs a family's entire life.

All family therapists now accept the idea that families are systems; not believing in systems theory is like not believing in the flag, apple pie, and motherhood. Schools of family therapy vary, however, in the degree to which they actually incorporate systems thinking in their practice, and in the kind of systems thinking they use. Behavioral family therapists say very little about systems, and treat individuals as separate entities who influence each other only by acting as stimuli and reinforcers. Most of the mainstream family therapy models, on the other hand—Bowenian, communications, strategic, Milan, and structural—base their approach to families on some version of systems thinking.

Stability and Change

Communications theorists describe families as rule-governed systems with a tendency toward stability or homeostasis (Jackson, 1965). If a family member deviates from the family's rules, this constitutes feedback, and if the family reacts to it as *negative feedback*, they try to force that person to change back. Families, like other living systems, maintain their inter-actions within a relatively fixed range in order to remain stable in the face of normal environmental stresses. In structural family theory the same point is made by saying that families have a relatively stable structure which enables them to function effectively as a system, with various subsystems each fulfilling part of the family's overall task.

Families must also change to adapt to changing circumstances. To do so they must be capable of revising their rules, and modifying their struc-ture. Dysfunctional families are distinguished by their rigidity and inflex-ibility; when circumstances change, they do not.

The dual nature of families—homeostatic and changing—is best ap-preciated by family therapists from the communications, structural, and strategic schools; they expect families to come to treatment because they failed to adapt to changing circumstances. They do not presume that the families they see are inherently pathological.

Anyone who ignores this principle runs the risk of placing an undue emphasis on pathology. If a therapist sees a family that is having trouble, but fails to consider that they may be stuck at a transitional impasse, then he or she is apt to think that they need an overhaul, when a tune-up might do. The therapies that emphasize long-range goals are all susceptible to this therapeutic overkill. Although they emphasize growth rather than pathol-ogy, psychoanalytic, experiential, and extended family practitioners are inclined to assume that the families they see are basically flawed and need fundamental reorganization. Since they have the equipment for major sur-gery—long-term therapy—they tend to see the patient as needing it. Some-times the patient doesn't.

In the 1970s most family therapists (with the notable exception of Virginia Satir) tended to overestimate homeostatic forces in families and underestimate their flexibility and resourcefulness. This viewpoint encour-aged therapists to act as provokers, controllers, and strategizers. The cor-ollary of the family held fast by systemic forces they cannot understand was the oh-so-clever therapist who would do the understanding for them. Many of the newer approaches to family therapy (discussed in the previous chapter) are designed to elicit family resources, rather than struggle with their fears. These models encourage therapists to collaborate with families to help them work out solutions, rather than to assume they won't change unless provoked.

Past or Present

When it was inaugurated, family therapy was heralded as a treatment which emphasizes the present, in contrast to individual therapies which emphasize the past. Psychoanalysis was the chief whipping boy of family therapists eager to define themselves as different in every way. Psychoanalysis was portrayed as a monadic theory which focused on past traumas as the cause of problems, and tried to cure people by helping them remember the past. While this picture accurately describes Freud's treatment in 1895, modern psychoanalysis is quite a bit more complicated.

That people are influenced by past experiences is an unarguable fact. The question is, how necessary is it to think about the past in order to understand the present? All family therapists work in the here-and-now; some see residues of the past, others do not.

Emphasis on the past is correlated with concern for individuals. Psychoanalytic practitioners view the determinants of behavior as resting with individuals. Theirs is a personality-trait model, in which family life is seen as a product of enduring dispositions, internalized from early object relations. This viewpoint affects practice, but not in the obvious way. Psychoanalytic therapists use their knowledge of past influences to inform their understanding of the present. They don't concentrate on helping people remember the past; instead they use psychoanalytic theory to help them understand what's going on in the present. The present may be understood in terms of transference and projection from the past, but it's still the present.

Surprisingly, the therapists who spend the most time talking with their patients about the past are the very ones who accentuate the here-and-now in their writings. Experiential therapists believe that unfinished business from the past interferes with full experiencing in the present. For this reason they spend a lot of time talking with patients about old preoccupations in order to help them let go of the past (Pierce, Nichols, and DuBrin, 1983). An example of this approach is Paul's (1967) technique of *operational mourning*.

The past also plays a prominent role in Bowenian theory. Present family relationships are assumed to be products of relationships within the original family. Problems with a child, for example, are presumed to result from the parents' unresolved conflicts with their own parents. Unlike psychoanalytic therapists, who deal with the residuals of those relationships by pointing out their influence in the current family, Bowenian therapists send patients back to their families. Is this a return to the past? In practice, that is impossible; conceptually it is a return to the past.

The schools of family therapy that view the determinants of behavior as being outside—that is, between—individuals stress the present, in theory and practice. Family group therapists, communicationists, strategists, and structuralists have little to say about the past. They're less interested in how or why problems get started than what maintains them. They often see families as stuck in transition between one developmental phase and another, but their concern is with contemporary interactions, not with events fixed in time.

Behavior therapists once explained all behavior as a result of past learning history. Pavlov's dogs salivated at the sound of a bell because they had been conditioned to do so; parents had trouble with their children because they had trained them improperly. Today behavior therapists rely on operant conditioning as the model to explain most human behavior. According to this model, behavior is maintained by its consequences. Parents have trouble with their children because of the way they respond to them in the present. Therapy derived from this model deals with how people currently reinforce maladaptive behavior. The classical conditioning model is still used to explain certain anxiety disorders, especially sexual dysfunction, but treatment is designed to relax anxiety in the present.

Most of the newer models try to strike a balance between past and present. Michael White helps families explore the historical evolution of how the problem got the upper hand over them, but then tries to empower family members to deal with the problem in the present. Richard Schwartz finds that parts of people carry outmoded or irrational beliefs and feelings from the past, but he helps clients change their relationship with these parts in the present—they learn about the past, but stop living there.

Communication

Working with communication no longer distinguishes one school of family therapy from the others. All behavior is communicative, and all family therapists deal with verbal and nonverbal behavior. Although they all think about communication, they do so in very different ways.

Family group therapists have the most straightforward and simple view of communication. For them communication is the medium of exchange through which members of families interact. Their treatment is to help transform blocked, incomplete, and covert communication into clear and open expression. They take what is conscious but unexpressed (except perhaps nonverbally) and bring it out into the open.

Behaviorists also think of communication in simple terms; for them communication is a skill that can be taught. In addition they understand something less obvious about communication; namely that the message received may not be the one intended. They distinguish reinforcement from aversive control, and have, for example, pointed out that yelling at a child may be reinforcing, even though it's intended to be punishing. On the other hand, angrily berating a spouse for not spending more time with you may be more punishing than informing.

In psychoanalytic psychotherapy, communication is taken as metaphor, with the manifest content conveying derivatives of hidden needs and feelings. The therapist's job is to decode these latent meanings in order to help patients better understand themselves. In psychoanalytic family therapy the therapist not only brings these hidden meanings to light but also helps family members express their latent emotions to each other. The therapist uses a knowledge of defenses, especially displacement and symbolization, to understand the unconscious content of family members' communications, and a knowledge of family dynamics to help complete these communications in the family.

Communications therapists also deal with communication on two levels, but instead of conscious and unconscious content, they deal with content and intent. Every communication is treated as conveying not only a message but also a statement about the relationship. For communications therapists this second communication, or metacommunication, is the more significant because it is the relationship that concerns and controls people.

Structural and strategic therapy both may be considered offshoots of communications theory (Madanes and Haley, 1977), and each emphasizes a particular aspect of communications in family relations. According to structural family theory, patterns of communications are what create family structure. Family organization develops from repeated sequences of interaction—communication; therapists detect the family's underlying structure by observing who speaks to whom and in what way. If a mother complains that she "can't communicate" to her teenaged daughter, the structural therapist will enact a sequence where they try to talk to each other in the session. If they talk for only a few moments before breaking off, the therapist will conclude that they are disengaged; if they argue back and forth like peers or siblings, the therapist may conclude that there is no hierarchical distinction, they are enmeshed; or if their conversation is repeatedly interrupted by the father, the therapist may conclude that interpersonal boundaries are blurred, and that the communication problem between the mother and daughter is a product of the father's enmeshment.

In Madanes and Haley's version of strategic therapy the main purpose of communication is to gain power in interpersonal relationships. From this point of view symptoms are percevied as communications designed to manipulate other family members. For instance, a child's phobic fear of going to school may be a covert way to communicate that he is afraid that his parents might separate; the symptom serves to keep them together to take care of him. Family members' responses to problems are thought to create symptoms. In this case the parents' decision to stay home to take care of the child only makes matters worse. A strategic therapist would not try to help the family understand the meaning of these symptoms, but would instead try to provoke them to relate—communicate—in a way that makes the symptoms unnecessary. If the parents, together, took the child to school and, together, helped him with his homework, the improvement of the child could be divorced from whether or not the parents stay together.

The experientialists' interest in communication is also two-layered; what they consider important are unexpressed feelings, lying beneath the surface content of family members' communications. Like psychoanalytic therapists, they consider it important to reduce defenses so that people can communicate what's really on their minds; unlike psychoanalysts, they look in the present for relatively conscious feelings. Instead of interpreting defenses, they confront them in order to help people break out of their inhibitions. Because they work with families, they are concerned not only with uncovering feelings but also with helping family members communicate their feelings honestly and openly within the family. Satir, in particular, focused on communication style as reflective of a person's level of self-esteem. She encouraged straight talk as a way to straighten out relationships—and to make people feel better about themselves for being honest.

Extended family systems therapists foster communication as a vehicle for opening up relationships with the wider kinship group. In emotional cutoffs there is a breakdown in communication; in emotional reactivity communication comes from an undifferentiated stance in which people lose sight of their own thoughts and feelings; and in triangulated relationships communication is diverted from unresolved conflict in a dyad to third person. Therapy is designed to help people re-establish communication with extended family members, teach them to communicate "I-position" statements, and redirect communication from a triangulated third party to the person for whom it was originally intended.

Content/Process

A system is the parts of a whole plus the way they function; process is the way families and groups function. Family and group therapists learn to attend to process and attempt to change it. When a mother and her teenaged daughter discuss the daughter's curfew, the mother and daughter are interested in *what* the other one says; the mother listens to when the daughter wants to come home and the daughter listens to her mother's response. A family therapist, listening to the same conversation, will be more interested in *how* the mother and daughter talk to each other. Does each state her point of view directly? Do they listen to each other? Is the mother clearly in charge? These questions have to do with the process of the conversation; they may not determine when the daughter comes home, but they reveal how the dyad functions.

When families come for treatment, they are usually focused on a content issue; a husband wants a divorce, a child refuses to go to school, a wife is depressed, and so on. The family therapist talks with the family about the content of the problem, but thinks about the process of discussion by which they try to solve it. While the family discusses what to do about a child's refusal to go to school, for instance, the therapist notices whether the parents seem to be in charge and if they support each other. If the therapist tells the parents to solve the problem by making the child go to school, then he or she is working with content, not process. The child may go to school, but the parents will not have improved the process of their decision-making.

All schools of family therapy have a theoretical commitment to working with the process of family interaction. Psychoanalytic and experiential clinicians try to reduce defensiveness and foster open expression of thoughts and feelings; family group and communications therapists increase the flow of interactions and help family members reduce the incongruence between different levels of communication; Bowenians block triangulation and encourage family members to take differentiated, "I-position" stances; strategic therapists ferret out and interdict problem-maintaining sequences of interaction; behaviorists teach parents to use positive control, and couples to eliminate coercive communication; structural therapists realign emotional boundaries and strengthen hierarchical organization.

Despite their theoretical commitment to process concepts, family therapists sometimes get distracted by content issues. Sometimes content is important. If a wife is drinking to drown her worries or a husband is molesting his daughter, a therapist needs to know and do something about it. But to the extent that therapists focus exclusively on content, they are unlikely to help families change to become better functioning systems. Psychoanalytic therapists sometimes lose sight of process when they concentrate on individual family members and their memories of the past. Similarly, experientialists are prone to becoming overly central while working with individual family members to help them overcome emotional defensiveness. The danger is that by so doing therapists will neglect the interactional processes in the family that affect individual expression.

Behavioral family therapists generally neglect process in favor of content. They do so when they isolate a particular behavioral sequence from its context in the family, ignoring the process that maintains it. They also interfere with the process of family interaction by assuming a directive, teaching role. As long as the teacher stands in front of a class and lectures, there is little opportunity to observe how the students behave on their own.

Process concepts are so central to extended family systems therapy that there is little danger that therapists in this school will forget them. Only naive misunderstanding of Bowenian therapy would lead someone to think merely of re-establishing family ties, without also being aware of processes of triangulation, fusion, and differentiation. The same is true of structural family therapy, family group therapy, and communications therapy; process issues are always at center stage.

Strategic family therapists have a dual focus—their goals are content-oriented, but their interventions are directed at process. As in behavioral therapy, the goal is in terms of content—solving the presenting problem. To understand what maintains the problem, however, strategic therapists shift their attention to process. Usually this involves discrete sequences of interaction, which they try to block by using directives. The goal, though, is not to improve the process of family functioning, but merely to interdict a particular sequence in order to resolve the content of the presenting problem.

Monadic, Dyadic, or Triadic Model

Family therapy was initiated when clinicians recognized that the identified patient's behavior is a function of the whole family; all family practitioners now subscribe to this systems viewpoint. In practice, however, family therapists sometimes think in terms of units of one, two, or three persons. Some clinicians (psychoeducational therapists, for example) think of one person in the family as the patient, and bring in the family to help deal with the patient. When these therapists work with families they emphasize the individual's thoughts and feelings. Their aim is to help family members become more aware of how they feel about and deal with the identified patient.

Psychoanalytic therapists tend to think about intrapsychic dynamics, whether they meet with people alone or with their families. They see current family relations as a product of internalized relationships with the previous family, and they are often more concerned with these mental ghosts than with flesh-and-blood families. Child behavior therapists use a monadic model when they accept a family's definition that their symptomatic child is the problem, and set about teaching the parents to change the child's behavior. Experiential therapists also work with individuals to help them uncover and express their feelings.

Actually, no living thing can adequately be understood in monadic terms. A bird's egg may be the closest thing in nature to a self-contained monad. The fetus is locked away inside its shell with all the nutrients it needs to survive. Even this view is incomplete, however, for there is an exchange of heat between the egg and the surrounding environment. Without the mother's warmth, the baby bird will die.

A dyadic model is necessary to understand the fact that people are always in relationships. Even the psychoanalytic patient, free-associating on the couch, is filtering memories and dreams through reactions to the analyst. Most of the time family therapists operate with a dyadic model; they usually work on relationships between two people at a time. Even when a large family is in treatment, the focus is usually on various pairs of family members, considered in sequence.

Helping two people learn to relate better does not always mean that the therapist thinks in dyadic terms. Behavioral couples therapists work with two spouses, but treat them as separate individuals, each of whom is deficient in the art of communicating. A true dyadic model is based on the understanding that two people in a relationship are not separate monads interacting with each other; they each define the other. Using this model a wife's agoraphobia would be understood as a reaction to her husband and as a means of influencing him. Likewise, his decision to send her for behavior modification reflects his refusal to accept his relationship to the symptom.

Family therapists of all schools use some dyadic concepts; unconscious need complementarity, expressive/instrumental, projective identification, symbiosis, intimacy, quid pro quo, double-bind, symmetrical, complementary, pursuer/distancer, and behavioral contract. Some terms are based on dyadic thinking even though they may involve more than two people: compliant (referring to a family's relationship to a therapist) or defiant; some seem to involve only one: countertransference, dominant, and supercompetent. Still other concepts are capable of encompassing units of three or more, but are often used to refer to units of two: boundary, coalition, fusion, and disengagement.

Most of the time family therapists think in dyadic terms, and most schools of family therapy do not take triadic relationships into account. Murray Bowen introduced the concept of emotional triangles into the family therapy literature, and has done more than anyone else to point out that human behavior is always a function of triadic relationships. Structural family therapists have also consistently been aware that enmeshment or disengagement between two people is always a function of reciprocal relationship with a third. Communications therapists wrote about triadic relationships, but tended to think in terms of units of two. The same is true of most strategic therapists, although Haley, Selvini Palazzoli, and Lynn Hoffman are consistently aware of triadic relationships.

The advantage of triadic thinking is that is permits a more complete understanding of behavior in context. If a boy misbehaves when his mother does not use firm discipline, teaching her to be firm will not work if her behavior is a function of her relationship with her husband. Perhaps she subtly encourages her child to misbehave as a way of undermining her husband's authority; or she and her husband may have worked out a relationship where her incompetence reassures him that he is the strong one.

The fact that triadic thinking permits a more complete understanding does not mean that family therapists must always include all parties in treatment. The issue is not how many people are in treatment, but whether or not the therapist considers problems in their full context.

The Nuclear Family in Context

Just as all family therapists espouse the ideas of systems theory, they also all regard families as open systems. The family is open in that its members interact, not only with each other, but also with extra familial systems in a constant exchange of information, energy, and material. Family therapy is a treatment of people in context; the most significant context for most people may be the nuclear family; but even to understand the nuclear family properly it is necessary to consider its context.

Communications family therapists introduced the concept of open systems to family therapy, but actually treated families as though they were closed systems. They paid little attention to sources of stress outside the family and rarely considered the impact of friends or extended family on the nuclear unit. The first clinicians to take the extrafamilial into account (and into treatment) were Murray Bowen and Ross Speck. Bowen has always stressed the critical role of extended family relationships, and Speck mobilized the patient's network of family and friends to aid in treatment.

Bowenian therapists and network therapists virtually always include people outside the nuclear family in treatment; psychoanalytic, group-oriented, behavioral, and communications therapists almost never do. Among experientialists, Whitaker has begun to routinely include members of the extended family in treatment for one or two sessions. Including extended family members or friends in treatment is often useful and sometimes essential. It is not, however, the same thing as thinking of the family as an open system. An open system is not a larger system; it is a system that interacts with its environment.

Nowhere is the idea of families as open systems better articulated than in Minuchin's (1974) *Families and Family Therapy.* Writing about "Man in His Context," Minuchin contrasts family therapy with psychodynamic theory. The latter, he says, draws upon the concept of man as a hero, remaining himself in spite of the circumstances. On the other hand, "the theory of family therapy is predicated on the fact that man is not an isolate. He is an acting and reacting member of social groups" (p. 2). He credits Gregory Bateson with erasing the boundary between inner and outer space, and goes on to say that just as the boundary separating the individual from the family is artificial, so is the boundary separating the family from the social environment. "Theories and techniques of family therapy lend themselves readily to work with the individual in contexts other than the family" (p. 4).

Structural family therapists recognize that families are embedded in a social context, and they often include teachers, school administrators, and other social agents in family diagnosis and treatment. If a single mother is enmeshed with her children, a structural family therapist might help her get more involved with friends or community activities as a way of helping her loosen her grip on the children.

Strategic family therapists may not treat families as open systems, but they do not confine their search for problem-maintaining sequences to the nuclear family. Selvini Palazzoli's work illustrates that in close-knit Italian families, grandparents are often directly involved in sequences of behavior that support symptoms, and members of the MRI group often work with problem-maintaining sequences that involve someone outside the family, like a supervisor at work or a neighbor. Routinely including grandparents or friends in family therapy is useful but not essential; however, to gain a full understanding of families you must consider the forces outside the family acting and interacting with them.

Feminist therapists have challenged us to face our culture's gender inequality and to recognize reflections of this inequality in the families we treat. In addition, clinicians like Evan Imber Black have expanded our view to include the impact of institutions and agencies, and encouraged us to deal directly with these larger systems.

Boundaries

Family practitioners study and treat people in context—individuals in context of their families, and families in context of their extended families and communities. One of the most useful concepts in family therapy is that of boundaries, a concept that applies to the relationship of all of these systems within systems in terms of the nature of their interface. The individuality and autonomy of each subsystem (individual, siblings, parents, nuclear family) is regulated by a semipermeable boundary between it and the suprasystem.

The clearest and most useful concepts of interpersonal boundaries are in the works of Murray Bowen and Salvador Minuchin. Bowen is best at describing the boundaries between individuals and their families; Minuchin is best at describing the boundaries between various subsystems within the family. In Bowen's terms, individuals vary on a continuum from fusion to differentiation, and Minuchin describes boundaries as diffuse or rigid, with resultant enmeshment or disengagement.

Bowen's thinking reflects psychoanalytic sources. Psychoanalytic theory emphasizes the development of interpersonal boundaries while describing how individuals emerge from the context of their families. Beginning with the separation and individuation from symbiosis with the mother that characterizes the psychological birth of the human infant (Mahler, Pine, and Bergman, 1975), psychoanalytic clinicians describe repeated and progressive separations that culminate first in the resolution of oedipal attachments and then eventually in leaving home.

Bowen's thinking about boundaries continues the somewhat one-sided emphasis on poorly defined boundaries between self and other. He pays little attention to the problems of emotional isolation stemming from rigid boundaries, and describes this as an artifact—a defense against a basic lack of psychological separateness. Bowen uses a variety of terms—togetherness, fusion, undifferentiation, emotional reactivity—which refer to the danger he is most concerned with, that people will lose themselves in relationships.

Minuchin offers a more balanced view of boundaries, describing the problems that result when they are either too rigid or too diffuse. Diffuse boundaries allow too much outside interference into the functioning of a subsystem; rigid boundaries allow too little communication, support, and affection between different segments of the family. Bowen describes only one boundary problem—fusion—and only one goal—differentiation; Minuchin speaks of two possibilities—enmeshment or disengagement— and his therapy is designed to fit the specific case.

Minuchin (1974) explains the function of boundaries, their reciprocal relationship, and how a knowledge of boundaries can be used to plan therapy. Boundaries protect individuals and subsystems from intrusion so that they can function autonomously. Newlyweds, for instance, need to establish a clear boundary between themselves and their parents in order to work out their own independent relationship. A diffuse boundary will leave them overly reliant on their parents, preventing them from developing their own autonomy and intimacy. If a wife calls her mother whenever she is upset, she will not learn to work things out with her husband; if she borrows money from her father whenever she wants to make a large purchase, she will not develop her own potential to earn a living.

In Bowenian theory people tend to be either emotionally fused or differentiated. Fusion is like a disease—you can have a bad case or a mild one. In structural family theory the enmeshment-disengagement distinction plays two roles. Some families are described as either enmeshed or disengaged; but more often families are described as made up of different subsystems with the enmeshment of some producing the disengagement of others. For example, a mother and child may be described as enmeshed (Bowen would say fused); this will be seen not in isolation but as a product of the woman's disengaged relationship with her husband. Using this understanding of the interlocking nature of subsystem boundaries, it is possible to design therapy to fit a specific family and to coordinate change among its subsystems.

Bowen's "fusion" and Minuchin's "enmeshment" both deal with the consequences of blurred boundaries, but they are not alternate vocabularies for the same thing. Fusion is a quality of individuals and it is the counterpart of the psychoanalytic concept of individuation. Both are intrapsychic concepts for a person's *psychological* embeddedness—undifferentiation— within a relationship context. The dynamics of fusion have an impact on other relationships (especially in the form of triangulation), but fusion is *within* the person. Enmeshment is strictly a social systems concept; enmeshment is *between* people. These conceptual differences are also related to differences in treatment. Bowen coaches individuals to stay in contact and maintain an "I-position"; success is measured in individual differentiation. Minuchin joins the system and realigns coalitions by strengthening *or* weakening boundaries; success is measured by change in the whole system. Bowen's conceptualization may lead to lasting individual personality change, which may affect the whole family system; Minuchin's conceptualization permits greater leverage and quicker change. The difference is between working with individuals to change the system, and working with the system to change individuals.

NORMAL FAMILY DEVELOPMENT

As a rule family therapists have less to say about developmental issues than do individual psychotherapists. One of the distinguishing characteristics of family therapy is its focus on the here-and-now interactions that maintain family problems. Normal family development involves the past and what is healthy and, therefore, has been underemphasized.

Many family therapists have pointed out that normality and abnormality are not discrete, that there is a wide range of functional and dysfunctional behavior (Watzlawick, Beavin, and Jackson, 1967; Minuchin, 1974). This point is well taken, but it has been made often enough; it is no longer a valid excuse for failing to develop models of normal, or functional, family behavior.

Most therapists do have implicit models about what is normal, and these assumptions influence their clinical assessment and treatment. The problem is that these unarticulated models are based largely on personal experience; as long as these remain unexamined they are apt to reflect personal bias. Many people assume that healthy families are just like their own—or just the opposite. However, the fact that a therapist comes from a relatively disengaged, upwardly striving, intact nuclear family does not make this the only, or the best, model of family life. When it comes to setting goals for family treatment, the choice is not between using a model of normality or having no model, but between using a model that has been spelled out and examined, or operating on the basis of ill-defined and personal standards.

Among family therapists, those concerned with the past, especially members of Bowenian and psychoanalytic schools, have had the most to say about normal development. These two schools share an evolutionary, developmental perspective. Whereas most other family therapists explain problems in terms of ongoing interactional difficulties, Bowen and the psychoanalysts are interested in the developmental history of problems. Although their main interest in development is to understand how problems arise, their analyses also describe normal development.

Whereas most schools of family therapy are not concerned with how families get started, the Bowenian and psychoanalytic schools have a great deal to say about marital choice. Bowen speaks about differentiation, fusion, and triangles, while the psychoanalytic writers speak of unconscious need-complementarity, projective identification, and idealization; but they seem to be using different terms to describe similar phenomena. Psychodynamic therapists speak of marital choice as an object of transference from the family of origin, and of people choosing partners with the same level of maturity; Bowen says that people pick partners who replicate familiar patterns of family interaction, and select mates at the same level of differentiation as in the family of origin.

These are descriptions of significant ways in which people marry partners with similar underlying personality dynamics. Both of these schools also discuss ways in which people choose mates who appear to be different—at least on the surface—in ways that are exciting and that seem to make up for deficiencies in the self. Obsessives tend to marry hysterics, and according to Bowen togetherness-oriented people often marry distancers. This brings up another way in which the Bowenian and psychodynamic schools are similar to each other and different from the others. Both have an appreciation of depth psychology; both recognize that personalities have different strata. Both think that the success of a marital relationship depends not only on the partners' shared interests and values but also on the nature of their internal, introjected object images. Spouses will perceive and relate to each other in terms of their inner (unconscious) object worlds.

Psychoanalysts emphasize the critical importance of good object relations in early childhood. The infant's ability to develop a cohesive self-image and good internal objects depends upon "good-enough mothering" in an "average expectable environment." With a cohesive sense of self the child will grow up able to be with others and be independent; without a coherent self, being with others may feel like being engulfed, and being alone may feel like being abandoned. Early object relations are not just memories, they actually form psychic structures of the mind which preserve early experiences in the form of self-images and object-images. These internalized object-images, in turn, determine how people in the environment will later be experienced. Thus the child's future—and the future of his or her family development—is laid down at a very early age.

Bowen's description of normal family development is highly deterministic. Parents transmit their immaturity and lack of differentiation to their children; emotional fusion is passed on in a multigenerational transmission process. A family's fate is a product of relationships worked out in preceding generations.

Bowenian and psychoanalytic therapists also describe the triangular relationship between mother and father and child as a crucial determinant of all later development. The psychoanalytic writers describe this oedipal situation in terms of conflicting drives, and believe that their resolution affects all future relationships. Bowenians describe this triangle in terms of stabilizing unresolved emotional tension in the marital dyad, and see it as the prototype of all subsequent relationships.

Clinicians are most likely to see people from families in which the triangular family romance was not resolved, but these theories include the possibility of successful resolution. Both theories, Bowenian and psychoanalytic, hold up visions of ideal functioning toward which people can strive but which they can never fully achieve. The result can be either a utopian model which condemns patients to dissatisfaction with their lives, or a standard used to guide people toward an enriched but not perfect life.

The clearest statement of such a standard is Bowen's (1966) description of families with "moderate to good differentiation." In these families the marriage is a functioning partnership in which spouses can be intimate without losing their autonomy. They permit their children to develop autonomous selves without becoming unduly anxious or trying to mold the children to their own images. Everyone in these families is responsible for himself or herself and neither credits others for personal success nor blames them for failure. They are able to function well with other people or to be alone, as the situation requires. Their intellectual functioning is not infused with emotionality at times of stress; they are adaptable, flexible, independent, and able to cope with good times and bad.

While they do not emphasize the past, most of the other schools of family therapy have a few isolated concepts for describing processes of normal family development. For example, communications therapists speak of the *quid pro quos* (Jackson, 1965) which are exchanged in normal marriages. The behaviorists describe the same phenomenon in terms of social exchange theory (Thibaut and Kelley, 1959).

Although all family therapists have a few concepts for dealing with normal family development, Minuchin is one of the few (other than Bowen and the psychodynamic therapists) who say that it is important to know what is normal in order to recognize what is abnormal. According to Minuchin (1974), clinicians need to have both an intellectual and emotional appreciation of the facts of ordinary family life in order to become effective family therapists. First, it is necessary to recognize that normal family life is not a bed of roses. When two people marry they must learn to accommodate to each other; each succeeding transition in the family life cycle requires further modifications of the family structure. Clinicians need to be aware of this, and able to distinguish functional from dysfunctional structures, as well as pathological structures from structures that are simply in a transitional process. Moreover, Minuchin adds, it is hard to be truly effective as a therapist without having personally experienced some of the problems that families in treatment are struggling with. This is a point that older and more experienced therapists are more sympathetic with than are young ones.

Because structural family therapy begins by measuring the adequacy of the client family's structure, it sometimes appears to have an ideal standard. In fact, however, normality is defined in terms of functional accomplishment, and structural family therapists recognize that diverse patterns may be functional. Functional families may be somewhat enmeshed or disengaged. The clarity of subsystem boundaries is far more important than the composition of the subsystem. For example, a parental subsystem made up of a father and oldest child can function effectively if the lines of responsibility and authority are clearly drawn. Patterns of enmeshment and disengagement are viewed as preferred styles, not necessarily as indications of abnormality.

The other schools of family therapy describe concepts of normality by mentioning specific mechanisms that are missing in dysfunctional families. Strategic therapists, for example, portray dysfunctional families as creating symptoms out of normal problems by failing to adjust their functioning to meet the demands of changing circumstances, and then trying to solve the problem by doggedly doing more of the same.

Bowenian and psychoanalytic family clinicians have developed elaborate models of normal development partly because they have an intrinsic interest in theory building. Both schools value understanding for its own sake. But what are the practical consequences of building models of normal family development? To begin with it is important to realize that the goals of these two approaches are different from the goals of most other family therapies. They are designed not merely for solving problems but for lifelong structural reorganization—intrapsychic and interpersonal. To recognize the dynamic residues of a family's past, it is necessary to have a model of how the past was—and should be—organized.

Most family therapists do not think in terms of restructuring the past, and therefore believe they have little need for models of normal family development. Instead, they intervene around specific sequences of problem-maintaining behavior, which are conceptualized in terms of function. The sequences they observe are dysfunctional, and, therefore, by implication, what is functional must be just the opposite. Communication therapists use discrete concepts of family functioning, like rules and metarules. That is what they think about, that is what they see, and that is what they intervene to alter.

While it may not be necessary to have a way of understanding a family's past in order to help them, it is necessary to have a way of understanding the family's organization of the present, using a model of normal behavior to set goals for treatment. Such a model should include a design for the present and for change over time. Among the ideas presented in this book the ones most useful for a basic model of normal family functioning include structural hierarchy, effective communication, and family life cycle development.

The issues involved in whether or not to hold up normative maps as goals are thorny. If therapists adhere too strongly to a normative model, they may impose it on families for whom it doesn't fit—families from other cultures, for example—and they are more likely to take an authoritarian stance regarding the proper ends of treatment. On the other hand, therapy without a model of healthy family functioning can degenerate into a directionless exercise. Any normative model must be taken as a rough guideline and used flexibly rather than taken as a Procrustean bed onto which families must be forced to fit.

DEVELOPMENT OF BEHAVIOR DISORDERS

In the early days of family therapy, patients were seen as scapegoats on whom families projected their conflicts and whose deviance maintained family stability. Much of the literature emphasized how parents with serious but covert conflict unite in concern for their emotionally disturbed child, who then becomes the identified patient. This was a theory of how family conflict causes behavior disorders in children. Many of the concepts put forward at that time were about dysfunctional ways of keeping the peace: scapegoating, pseudomutuality, rubber fence, family projection process, double-bind, disqualification, mystification, and so on. These mechanisms may have driven young people crazy, but they helped keep their families together.

Initially, the patterns of disturbed function observed in schizophrenic families were thought to cause schizophrenia. Eventually, etiological models gave way to transactional ones. Instead of causing schizophrenia, these disturbed family interactions came to be seen as patterns of family relationship in which schizophrenia is embedded. Neither the family nor the symptomatic member is the locus of the problem—the problem is not *within* people, it is *between* them.

Today family therapists do not think about what causes problems; they think about how families unwittingly maintain their problems. Each of the systems of family therapy have unique ideas about how pathological families fit together, but the following themes are useful to define some of the important differences of opinion in the field: inflexible systems, function of symptoms, underlying dynamics, and pathological triangles.

Inflexible Systems

Inflexibility is the characteristic of pathological family systems most frequently indicted. Chronic inflexibility is a striking feature of families with disturbed members; these families are so rigid that it is virtually impossible to grow up in them healthy and normal. Acute inflexibility explains why other families become dysfunctional at transitions in the life cycle; disorder breaks out in these families when they fail to modify their organization in response to growth or stress.

Early observers of schizophrenic family interactions emphasized the rigid inflexibility of these families. Wynne coined the term *rubber fence* to dramatize how psychotic families resist outside influence, and *pseudomu-*

tuality to describe their rigid facade of harmony. R.D. Laing showed how parents, unable to tolerate their children's healthy strivings, used *mystification* to deny and distort their experience. Communications theorists thought that the most striking disturbance in schizophrenic families was the extreme inflexibility of their rules. According to this systems analysis, these families were unable to adapt to the environment because they had no mechanisms for changing their rules; they were rigidly programmed to negative feedback, treating novelty and change as deviations to be resisted. Forces of homeostasis overpower forces of change, leaving these families stable but chronically disturbed.

This tradition of viewing families of schizophrenics and other severely disturbed patients as rigidly homeostatic had been taken into the 1980s and 1990s by Selvini Palazzoli in the form of her concept of "dirty games." Carol Anderson and Michael White, on the other hand, have tried to counter this negative way of looking at families with disturbed members by suggesting that their rigidity may be the result of living with serious problems—and being attacked by mental health professionals.

Explaining family problems in terms of rigid homeostatic functioning is today one of the cornerstones of the strategic school. Strategists describe dysfunctional families as responding to problems within a limited range of solutions. Even when the attempted solutions do not work, these families rigidly keep trying; thus the attempted solutions, rather than the symptoms, are the problem. Behaviorists use a similar idea when they explain symptomatic behavior as a result of faulty efforts to change behavior. Often when parents think they are punishing their children, they are actually reinforcing them with attention.

Psychoanalytic and experimental clinicians have identified pathological inflexibility in individuals and couples, as well as in whole families. According to these two schools, intrapsychic rigidity, in the forms of conflict, developmental arrest, and emotional suppression, are the individual's contribution to family pathology. Psychoanalysts consider pathological families as closed systems that resist change. According to this line of thought, symptomatic families are rigid in that they treat the present as though it were the past. When faced with a need to change, dysfunctional families regress to earlier levels of development where unresolved conflicts left them fixated.

Experientialists often describe pathological families as chronically resistant to growth. The symptom-bearer is seen to be signaling a family pattern of opposition to life forces. Unfortunately this model makes the family the villain, and the individual the victim. The experiential model of inflexibility is fairly simple, and is primarily useful with minor forms of psychic difficulty.

Structural family therapists locate the inflexibility of dysfunctional families in the boundaries between subsystems. Disturbed families tend to be either markedly enmeshed or markedly disengaged. Young therapists who have trouble diagnosing family structure are at first happily surprised when confronted with a profoundly disturbed family. The structure is so easy to see. Unfortunately, families with an unmistakably clear structure are extremely deviant and very difficult to change.

Structural family therapy also identifies inflexibility in symptomatic families. Rigidity was one of the most prominent characteristics found in psychosomatic families, for example. Minuchin (1974) stresses that otherwise normal families will develop problems if they are unable to modify a previously functional structure to cope with an environmental or developmental crisis. Family therapists should be very clear on this point: symptomatic families are often basically sound, they simply need help adjusting to a change in circumstances.

The Function of Symptoms

Early family therapists described the identified patient as serving a critical function in disturbed families, detouring conflict and, thus, stabilizing the family. Vogel and Bell (1960) portrayed emotionally disturbed children as family scapegoats, singled out as objects of parental projection on the basis of traits which set them apart from other members of the family. Thereafter their deviance promotes cohesion. Communications theorists thought that symptoms were fraught with meaning—functioning as messages—and with consequences—controlling other family members.

Today many family therapists deny that symptoms have either meaning or function. Behavioral and MRI therapists do not assume that symptoms are necessary to maintain family stability, and so they intervene to block the symptom without being concerned about restructuring the family. Behaviorists have always argued against the idea that symptoms are a sign of underlying pathology or that they serve any important function. Behavioral family therapists treat problems as the uncomplicated result of faulty efforts to change behavior and lack of skills. Restricting their focus to symptoms is one of the reasons why they are successful in discovering the contingencies that reinforce them; it is also one of the reasons why they are not very successful in cases where a child's behavior problems function to stabilize a conflicted marriage, or where a couple's arguments protect them from dealing with unresolved personal problems. MRI strategic family therapists recognize that symptoms may serve a purpose, but deny that it is necessary to consider that purpose when planning therapy. Instead of trying to figure out what function may be served by symptoms, they concentrate on understanding how the pieces of the system fit together in a coherent fashion. Members of this school take the modest position that if they help to free families from their symptoms, then the families can take care of themselves.

The psychoeducational approach and that of Michael White take a strong stand against the symptoms-serve-a-purpose idea. They argue that this thinking blames the victims and that families feel oppressed by, not grateful for, the symptoms of their members. Richard Schwartz takes the position that there may sometimes be parts of family members that fear change, but the parts of them that want relief often can be activated without having to confront them about their fearful parts.

Some of the schools of family therapy continue to believe that symptoms signal deeper problems, and that they function to maintain family stability. In families that cannot tolerate open conflict, a symptomatic member may serve as a smokescreen and a diversion. Just as symptomatic behavior preserves the balances of the nuclear family, so many problems in the nuclear family preserve the balance in the extended family. In psychoanalytic, Bowenian, and structural formulations, a couple's inability to form an intimate bond may be ascribed to the fact that one or both of them are still being used to mediate the relationship between their parents. In this way symptomatic behavior is transmitted across generations, and functions to stabilize the multigenerational family system.

Many times it is possible to see how systems function to arouse a depressed or disengaged parent to become more involved with the family. Two examples will illustrate this frequent observation. The first is from Jay Haley's (1976) *Problem-Solving Therapy*. According to Haley, a child's misbehavior is often part of a repetitive cycle that serves to keep the parents involved. In a typical sequence, father becomes unhappy and withdraws; the child misbehaves; mother fails to discipline the child; father steps in, reinvolving himself with the mother through the child. The second example is from an interview conducted by Harry Aponte (a noted structural family therapist), quoted in Hoffman (1981, p. 83).

> The interview is with a poor black family that fully answers to the description "multiproblem." Everybody—the mother, six grown or nearly grown children, and two grandchildren—is at risk, from breakdown, illness, nerves, violence, accident, or a combination of all these factors. In addition, the family members are noisy, disruptive, and hard to control.
>
> At a certain point Aponte asks the mother, "How do you handle all this?" The mother, who has been apathetic and seemingly unconcerned as the therapist tries to talk with the children, says, "I put on my gorilla suit." The children laugh as they describe just how terrible their mother is when she puts on her gorilla suit.
>
> An incident occurs shortly after this conversation which suggests that a circular causal sequence is at work, one of those redundancies that may have to do with family balance. Mother is still apathetic and looks tired, and the therapist begins to ask about her nerves. At first the children are somewhat quiet, listening. As she begins to admit that she has had

bad nerves and that she is taking pills, they begin to act up. One boy pokes the baby; another boy tries to restrain the baby from kicking back; the baby starts to yell. The therapist asks the twenty-year-old daughter (the baby's mother) if she can control him; she says no. At this point the mother gets up and smacks her daughter's baby with a rolled-up newspaper, rising out of her lethargy like some sleeping giant bothered by a gnat. She sits the baby down with a bump, and he makes no further trouble. During this sequence the rest of the children jump and shriek with joy, causing their mother to reprimand them, after which they calm down and the mother sits back, more watchful now and definitely in control.

Here a mother overwhelmed by stress becomes depressed; as she describes her depression the children become anxious and misbehave; the misbehavior triggers a reaction in the mother, rousing her from withdrawal to control the chaos. The children's symptomatic misbehavior functions as cause and cure of the mother's depression, in a recurring cycle.

Underlying Dynamics

The idea that there are hidden dynamics underlying observable behavior is reminiscent of the individual psychodynamic theory that family therapy developed in opposition to. In the 1950s family therapists challenged the psychoanalytic belief that symptoms are only surface phenomena and that the real problems are inside. Instead, they showed how observations limited to the surface of family interactions were sufficient to understand and treat behavioral problems.

Today there are still many family therapists who deny that it is necessary or valid to look for underlying dynamics in order to explain or treat symptomatic behavior. These clinicians believe that it is sufficient to observe patterns of interaction in the family. Some strategic therapists, like the MRI group, confine the field of focus to interactions surrounding symptomatic behavior; others, like the Milan group, take a broader view of the whole family. Behaviorists maintain that in order to account for unwanted behavior it is necessary only to observe its reinforcing consequences.

Despite the family therapy tradition of explaining problem behavior without bringing in underlying dynamics, many family therapists believe that neither the presenting symptoms nor surrounding interactions are the real problem; the real problem is some form of underlying family pathology. When families come in, these therapists look beneath—or beyond—behavioral sequences for some hypothesized basic flaw in the family. Minuchin's concept of family structure is the leading example of such a concept. Structural family therapists listen to families describe problem behavior, but they look for underlying structural pathology to explain and resolve these problems.

Structural pathology is conceptually different from the intrapsychic conflict in psychodynamic theory. Intrapsychic conflict is an inferred psychological concept; structural pathology is an observed interactional concept. (Constructivists would disagree. They believe every "observation" about reality is really a construction of reality.) Nevertheless, in practice, structural family therapists shift their attention from the family's complaints to a different level of analysis.

Family structure is now one of the central concepts in family therapy, and the field can be divided into those that include structure in their analyses and those that do not. Haley (1980) does, and for this reason many people consider him a structuralist as much as a strategist. Selvini Palazzoli and Lynn Hoffman bring in structural concepts in terms of systemic conflict and "too richly cross-joined systems" (Hoffman, 1981). John Weakland of the MRI group emphatically denies the need to include structural concepts in family assessment, and he considers doing so a species of discredited psychodynamic theorizing. Others in the family field, including behaviorists (Patterson) and some experientialists (Whitaker), accept the utility of structural concepts; their doing so shows a growing convergence among competing systems.

Neither psychoanalytic nor Bowenian therapists use Minuchin's structural family theory, but both schools have their own concepts of underlying dynamics. Psychoanalysts originated the idea of underlying dynamics; present-day psychoanalytic family therapy practitioners use this idea in concepts of intrapsychic structural conflict (id, ego, superego); developmental arrest; internal object relations; and interlocking psychopathological structures among family members. According to the psychoanalytic model, problems may develop in interactions, but it is the interacting individuals who have have the basic flaws.

In Bowen's theory, fusion, family projection process, and interlocking triangles are the major concepts of underlying family dynamics. So much are these underlying issues emphasized that Bowenians probably spend less time than anyone else dealing directly with presenting symptoms or even with symptom-bearers.

Bowenian theory uses a *diathesis-stress* model of mental disorder. This is a model from genetic research in which a person develops a disorder when a genetic weakness is sufficiently stressed by an event in the environment. In Bowenian theory, people who develop symptoms in the face of anxiety-arousing stress have low levels of differentiation and are emotionally cut off from support systems, especially in the extended family. The diathesis may not be genetic, but it is passed on from one generation to the next.

The psychoeducational therapists have brought the diathesis-stress model into family therapy through their view of schizophrenia as a disease that is powerfully affected by environmental (family) stress. The goal becomes to reduce stressful "expressed-emotion" in families. Richard

Schwartz, by extending systems thinking into the realm of internal process, offers a resolution of the issue of whether it is internal (intrapsychic) or external (interactional) dynamics that underlie problems. He sees problems embedded in imbalances at both levels, each affecting the other. Both are important and so therapists can effectively address either.

Pathological Triangles

The double-bind theory was a landmark in the shift from an individual to a systems unit in the analysis of the development of behavior disorder. Current concepts of pathology sometimes refer to individuals—fusion of emotion and intellect, repressed affect, developmental arrest; and sometimes to dyads—fusion in a relationship, mystification, unresolved symbiotic attachment. However, the most sophisticated thinking in the field is triadic.

Pathological triangles are at the heart of several family therapy explanations of behavior disorder. Among these, Bowen's theory is perhaps the most elegant and well known. Bowen explains how when two people are in conflict, the one who experiences the most anxiety will triangle in a third person. This model not only provides a beautiful explanation of systems pathology, but also serves warning to therapists. As long as a therapist remains fused with one party to an emotional conflict, then he or she is part of the problem, not part of the solution.

In psychoanalytic theory, oedipal conflicts are the root of neurosis. Here the triangle is stimulated by family interactions, but formed and maintained in the individual psyche. Mother's tenderness may be seductive and father's jealousy threatening, but the wish to destroy the father and possess the mother is a figment of fantasy. Pathological fixation of this conflict may be caused by developments in the outer space of the family, but the conflict is harbored in the inner space of the mind.

The psychoanalytic model of the individual is that of a divided self at war within. But psychoanalytic family practitioners treat family problems as disorders in relationships. The cause of the problem may be a function of individual personalities, but the result is in the interaction. *Pathological need complementarity* is the core psychoanalytic concept of interlocking pathology of family relationships. A person with a strong need to be submissive, for instance, will marry someone with a strong need to be dominant. These needs are based on early identifications and introjections. The husband who has a sense of himself as a victim has internalized pathogenic introjections that revolve around aggressive conflicts, but his needs are acted out in pathological relationships—that is, his unconscious need for an aggressor will lead him to select a mate who can act this role, allowing him to project his repressed or split-off aggression onto his wife. Divided selves thus become divided spouses.

Structural family theory of disorder is based on triangular configurations where a dysfunctional boundary between two people or subsystems is a reciprocal product of a boundary with a third. Father-and-son's enmeshment reflects father-and-mother's disengagement; a single mother's disengagement from her children is the counterpart of her overinvolvement outside the family. Structural family theory also uses the concept of pathological triangle to explain *conflict-detouring triads*, where parents divert their conflict onto a child. Minuchin, Rosman, and Baker (1978) have even demonstrated that physiological changes occur when parents in conflict transfer their stress to a psychosomatic child. Using this model, therapy is designed to disengage the child from the parents' struggle and to help the parents work out their conflicts directly.

Most strategic family therapists work with a dyadic model—one person's symptoms are maintained by others' (taken as a single group) efforts to resolve them. Haley and Selvini Palazzoli, however, use a triangular model in the form of *cross-generational coalitions*. These "perverse triangles," as Haley (1977) calls them, occur when a parent and child, or grandparent and child, collude to form a bastion of covert opposition to another adult. Failure to recognize these cross-generational coalitions dooms to failure any attempt to help parents resolve "their" problems with a symptomatic child. For this reason, behavioral parent training probably will not work when there is significant unrecognized conflict between the parents. Teaching a father how to reward respectful behavior from his son will not get very far if mother subtly reinforces the son's disrespect.

Triangular functioning seems less central to the newer models described in Chapter 11 because they are less focused on the way families create or even maintain problems and more on how to help them out of whatever predicaments they're in.

GOALS OF THERAPY

The goal of all psychological treatment is to help people change in order to relieve their distress. This is true of individual therapy, group therapy, and family therapy. Why then is so much written about the differing goals of various schools of therapy? Some of it has to do with differing ideas about how people change; some of it merely has to do with alternate vocabularies for describing change. When Bowenians speak of "differentiation of self" and psychoanalytic therapists speak of "increased ego strength," they mean pretty much the same thing.

If we strip away the semantic differences, there are two major dimensions of goals on which the schools of family therapy vary. First, the schools differ with respect to the form of their intermediate goals; they seek change through different aspects of personal and family functioning. Second, the schools differ in terms of how much change they seek. Some are content with symptom resolution, others aspire to transform the whole family system.

The variations in the form of intermediate goals among the systems are based upon theoretical differences about which aspects of personal and family functioning it is most necessary to change. One of the goals of experiential family therapy is to help families become more emotionally expressive. Experientialists believe that emotional stagnation is a primary problem, and that increased expressiveness will make people more alive and happy. To a large extent, therefore, the differences in the form of intermediate goals among different schools reflects theoretical differences of opinion about how behavior change is best accomplished. We will discuss these distinctions more fully below in *Conditions for Behavior Change*.

The second difference in goals—how much change—has to do with how the schools differ with respect to their aims about the resolution of presenting problems or the overhauling of family systems. All family therapists are interested in resolving problems and decreasing symptomatology. But they vary along a continuum from being exclusively concerned with symptom resolution to being more concerned with ultimately changing the entire family system. Strategic and behavioral therapists are least concerned with changing the whole system; psychoanalytic and Bowenian therapists are most concerned with systems change. In addition, psychoanalysts and Bowenians are particularly interested in fundamental changes in individual personalities (intrapsychic structural change or differentiation), and they are unique among family therapists in this respect.

The goal of structural family therapy is both symptom resolution and structural change. But the structural change sought has the modest aim of reorganizing that particular part of the family structure which has become dysfunctional and problematic by failing to change to meet changing circumstances. Structural family therapists do not have the more ambitious goal of remaking the whole family. Group, communications, and experiential family therapists also aim midway between symptomatic improvement and systematic family reorganization. Practitioners from these schools focus neither on presenting complaints nor on the overall family system. Instead they pay special attention to discrete processes which they think underlie symptoms: group dynamics, patterns of communication, and emotional expressivity. Improvements in these processes are thought to resolve symptoms and promote growth and health, but neither symptom resolution alone nor systems change per se is the goal.

In our view, one goal of family therapy must be to resolve the problems that clients come in with. If a family asks for help with a specific problem and the therapist helps them express their feelings better, but does not help them solve the problem, then he or she has failed the family in an important way. One of the virtues of the behavioral and strategic approaches that focus narrowly on presenting complaints is that they do not fool themselves or their clients about whether or not these problems get solved. Some of the other approaches with grander aspirations run the risk of losing sight of this first responsibility of family therapists. For example, if a mother complains that her small daughter is disobedient and does not do well in school, and a therapist bypasses these problems to get to the "real issues," which may be defined as the woman's relationship with her parents or conflicts with her husband, there is a real danger of the therapist's failing the family. If success is defined as accepting the therapist's point of view and working toward his or conceptual goal, then therapy becomes a power struggle or an indoctrination. To some extent this happens in all therapies, but is justified only when achieving the therapist's conceptual goals also meets the family's goals.

The advantage of working toward symptom change is that it's directly responsive to the family's request and eliminates much obfuscation about whether or not therapy is successful. The disadvantage is that working only at the level of symptomatic or symptom-maintaining behavior may produce changes that do not last. This fundamental debate about the effects of symptomatic improvement must ultimately be answered empirically. In the meantime it seems clear that changing symptom-maintaining behavior—even without worrying much about underlying family dynamics—can produce a positive spiral, or "runaway," increasing change that leads to increasingly satisfactory family functioning. On the other hand, there is the danger that symptom resolution will succeed but not last, especially when interventions are designed to effect monadic or dyadic change without taking into account how individuals or pairs are affected by the whole family context.

We do not agree with psychoanalysts who say that without insight into unconscious motivation, behavioral changes will not last, or with Bowenians who say that problems in the nuclear family will not change until relationships with extended family are repaired. But it does seem that to insure that symptom resolution will last, successful interventions must take into account triangular patterns of relationships in the nuclear family.

As a final note on goals, problem resolution or cure has been family therapy's trademark, emblematic of the optimism of its practitioners, proud problem solvers. Now, however, by embracing the disease model (Yes, Virginia, there is such a thing as schizophrenia), some family therapists, notably those who practice psychoeducation, advocate coping with serious psychopathology as a worthy goal. This modest but realistic goal has been hard for some family therapists to accept and has generated a great deal of controversy. What appears to be at stake is a question of which is more powerful: family therapy or schizophrenia.

CONDITIONS FOR BEHAVIOR CHANGE

Once it was necessary to contrast family therapy with individual therapy in order to establish family treatment as a distinct and legitimate approach.

Family therapists used to emphasize their differences with individual therapists; today they emphasize differences among themselves. Now that family therapy is an established force in the helping field, family therapists are competing among themselves for recognition and patronage.

The various family therapists share a consensus about broad principles of change, but differ on many specific issues. The core principle of family therapy is treating people in their natural environment. What divides the field into competing camps are differences of opinion about how best to bring about change. In this section we will compare and contrast the different systems of family therapy in terms of action or insight; change in the session or change at home; duration of treatment; resistance; family-therapist relationship; and paradox.

Action or Insight

One of the early distinctions between family therapy and individual therapy had to do with action and insight. Individual therapists stressed intellectual and emotional insight; family therapists stressed action. Although they emphasized action in their writing, many of the techniques of early family therapists were designed to change action through understanding. Actually, since people think, feel, and act, no form of therapy can succeed without affecting all three of these aspects of the human personality. Different approaches may concentrate on different modes of experience, but they inevitably deal with the total—thinking, feeling, and acting—person.

Action and insight are the primary vehicles of change in family therapy. Most family therapists use both mechanisms, but some schools emphasize either action (strategic) or insight (psychoanalytic).

The case for action is based on the observation that people often do not change even though they understand why and how they should. The truth of this is familiar to anyone who has ever tried and failed to lose weight, stop smoking, or spend more time with the kids. Behaviorists make the case for action by pointing out that behavior is often reinforced unwittingly; explanations, they say, do not change behavior, reinforcement does. Parents are taught to change their children's behavior by rewarding desired actions and ignoring or punishing undesirable actions. Likewise, married couples are taught that actions speak louder than words; it does not matter so much what you tell your spouse, what matters is that you reward pleasing behavior. Behavioral family therapists do not, however, practice what they preach. They tell clients that reinforcement is the way to change behavior, but they rely on simple explanations to bring about those changes. Action may be the message, but understanding is the medium.

Like behaviorists, strategic therapists focus on behavior, and are not concerned with insight. However, they differ from behaviorists in one important respect—behaviorists rely on the power of rational instruction; strategic therapists eschew understanding altogether. They do not believe in insight, and they do not believe in teaching; instead they believe that the way to change behavior is through manipulation. They box stuck families into a corner, from which the only way out is to become unstuck.

The case for insight is based on the belief that if people understand themselves they will be free to act in their own best interest. Psychoanalytic clinicians believe that people are blind to their real motives and feelings. Without insight into hidden conflicts, they believe, action is self-defeating, even dangerous. Unexamined action is considered self-defeating because symptomatic relief without insight fosters denial and repression; it is considered dangerous when repressed impulses are acted on precipitously.

Many actions are regarded in the psychoanalytic school as symptomatic—that is, such actions are protective devices designed to bind the anxiety that signals impulses whose expression might lead to punishment. Only by understanding their impulses and the dangers involved in expressing them can people change. Moreover, since the important conflicts are unconscious, only methodical interpretation of the unconscious brings about lasting change. In psychoanalytic therapy, unanalyzed action initiated by families is called "acting out"; unanalyzed action initiated by therapists is considered manipulation. Insight can only be achieved if families verbalize their thoughts and feelings rather than act on them, and therapists interpret unconscious meaning rather than suggest or manipulate action.

Discussions of insight are often divisive, because insight is a buzz-word; proponents extol it, opponents ridicule it. Advocates of insight use the concept as a pseudomedical idea—insight, like medicine, cures. Actually, insight doesn't cure anything; it's something through which cure occurs. To say that a family acquires insight means that family members learn what they intend by their actions, and also what they want from each other; how they act on their insight is up to them.

Do people change when they are propelled into action, or when they develop understanding? Both. People change for a variety of reasons; the same person may change one day because of being forced into action, and another day because of some new understanding. Some individuals may be more or less responsive to either action or insight, and these people will be more or less successful in therapies that emphasize insight or action. People change when they are ready *and* when the right stimulus is applied.

In contrast to the polar positions taken by these three schools, the other systems work with action *and* insight. In structural family therapy, change is initiated in action and then supported by understanding. According to Minuchin (Minuchin and Fishman, 1981), family structure and family beliefs support and reinforce each other; the only way to achieve lasting change is to challenge both. Action comes first because it leads to new experiences which then make insight possible. In Bowenian theory, interventions also affect both levels—action and understanding; but the order of effect is reversed. Bowenians begin by calming people down, so that they will be receptive to learning extended family systems theory. Once family members are armed with this new understanding, they are sent into action—back to their families to re-establish ties based on differentiation of self.

The Milan model and the later work of Cecchin, Boscolo, and Hoffman have elevated the importance of working with systems of meaning. Thus, systems-oriented family therapists are becoming less limited in their focus on action.

Change in the Session or Change at Home

All family therapists aim to transform interactions among family members, but they differ as to where they expect these transformations to take place. In structural family therapy, transformation occurs in the session, in the present, and in the presence of the therapist. Action is brought into the consulting room in the form of enactments, and change is sought then and there. The same is true in experiential family therapy; emotional breakthrough comes in session, in response to the therapist's provocations. In both of these therapies, changes wrought in the session are believed to transfer to the family's life outside.

Other family therapists promote change that they expect to occur, not in the session but at home. Strategic therapists are relatively inactive in the session. They use sessions to gather information that they use to formulate interventions, which they often deliver in the form of directives to be carried out at home. Bowenians also plan changes that will take place outside the consultation room. Family members are encouraged to return to their families of origin, and coached to respond in new and more productive ways. Most forms of behavior therapy are planned to influence interactions that take place at home. Parents are sent home to reward their children's positive behavior, and spouses are taught to please each other, or to have sex without anxiety. Some behaviorists, however, supervise parents playing with and disciplining their children in the session, usually behind a one-way mirror.

The goal of family therapy is to solve problems so that people can live better. The ultimate test of success comes at home after therapy is over. But since therapists take on the job of creating change, utilizing the context of the session, first to promote interactions and then to observe and change them, gives maximum impact. Just as live supervision is preferred because it teaches therapists what to do while they do it, so supervised change in the session seems more effective than unsupervised change at home.

Duration of Treatment

Most family therapy is brief. Families generally seek treatment at a time of crisis and are motivated only to solve their immediate problems. Usually they only reluctantly agree to come in as a family, and generally they are not interested in personal growth. Because family therapists only have the leverage necessary to work with families as long as they are in distress, family treatment tends to be pragmatic and symptom-focused. This is especially true in strategic family therapy.

Some strategic therapists limit treatment to about ten sessions, and announce this at the outset as a means of motivating families to work for change. Haley (1976) says that change occurs in stages and he plans therapy accordingly, but many strategic therapists believe that change occurs in sudden shifts (Hoffman, 1981; Rabkin, 1977). Strategists do not reason with families, they give them a sudden jolt. These jolts—usually paradoxical directives—provoke families stuck in dysfunctional homeostasis to change with or without their willing cooperation. Success in this operation requires that lasting change be achieved on the impact of a few interventions, and that it can occur without any understanding on the part of the family.

Other schools of family therapy believe that lasting change requires understanding, and that it occurs gradually over the course of several months of treatment. The duration of therapy is related both to the goal of treatment and the question of who is considered to be responsible for change. Strategists and behaviorists limit their goals to solving the presenting problem, and they assume responsibility for change. Psychoanalytic and experiential practitioners seek profound personal changes in their clients, and they place the responsibility for change with the clients. These therapists take responsibility only for providing a therapeutic atmosphere in their sessions; change is up to the clients.

Structural family therapists are interested in solving problems, not in personal growth; however, the problems that they are concerned with are structural. They believe that it is necessary to restructure dysfunctional families for lasting benefit to occur. MRI therapists, on the other hand, say that it is not necessary to change the whole family; all that is required is to interrupt the vicious feedback cycles that maintain present symptoms.

Bowenian therapy can be a lifelong enterprise. The goal is personal growth *and* change in the entire extended family system. Since change is the responsibility of the client and occurs during visits home, the process may take years.

If the family's goal is growth and enrichment, then therapy must be protracted; but if the goal is relief, then therapy should be brief. Problems arise when therapists try to hold on to families. The motives for doing so are many and complex, including pursuit of utopian goals, money, guilt over not having done more, and unresolved emotional attachments. For some mental health professionals, being in therapy is a way of life. These therapists may convey exaggerated expectations of improvement, with the result that family members are bound to suffer disillusionment. Fortunately, therapy is expensive, time-consuming, and stressful; this puts pressure on families to get it over with and get on with their lives.

In brief prescriptive therapy, termination is initiated by the therapist when there is a change in the presenting problem or when the agreed-upon number of sessions is up. With compliant families, strategic therapists acknowledge progress and give the family credit for success; with defiant families, they express skepticism and predict a relapse. (The idea of giving families credit for success may have a hollow ring, when families have no idea what they did to bring it about.) In longer, elicitory therapy, termination is initiated by the clients, either directly or indirectly. It is time to consider termination when family living becomes more enjoyable, when family members run out of things to talk about in therapy, or when they begin to complain about competing obligations. Part of successful termination is helping families accept the inevitability of the normal problems of everyday life. Successful therapy partly changes behavior and partly changes expectations. Therapy *can* go on forever, but by keeping it brief, therapists prevent families from becoming dependent on outside help and teach them to rely on their own resources.

Resistance

Families are notoriously resistant to change. In addition to the combined resistances of individual family members, the system itself resists change. Where there is resistance, therapy cannot succeed without overcoming it. Behavior therapists minimize the importance of resistance and succeed only where their clients are willing and able to follow instructions. The other schools of family therapy consider resistance the major obstacle to treatment, and have devised various ways to overcome it.

Psychoanalytic practitioners believe that resistance is motivated by unconscious defenses, which first must be made manifest and then resolved through interpretation. This is an intrapsychic model, but it does not ignore conscious and interactional resistances. Instead, psychoanalytic therapists believe that interactional problems—among family members or between the family and therapist—have their roots in unconscious resistance to basic drives. Experiential therapists have a similar model; they see resistance to emotional expression, and they blast away at it using personal confrontations and emotive exercises. Experientialists believe that breaching defenses automatically releases natural, healthy strivings; change occurs from the inside out.

People do avoid knowing painful things about themselves, but even more strenuously conceal painful truths from other members of the family.

It is one thing to tell a therapist that you are angry at your spouse; it is another thing to tell your spouse. Therapies that are more interactive and systems-oriented focus on conscious withholding and on the system's resistance to changing its rules.

Minuchin's solution to the problem of resistance is straightforward: he wins families over by joining and accommodating to them. This gives him the leverage to utilize powerful confrontations designed to restructure the pattern of family interactions. Resistance is seen as a product of the interaction between therapist and family; change is accomplished by alternately challenging the family and then rejoining them to repair breaches in the therapeutic relationship.

Strategic family therapists expect resistance, but avoid power struggles by going with resistance rather than opposing it head on. They assume that families do not understand their own behavior and will oppose attempts to change it. In response, strategic practitioners try to gain control by provoking families to resist. Once the family begins to respond in opposition to therapeutic directives, the therapist can manipulate them to change in the desired direction. In practice, this can result in either doggedly pursuing reverse psychology, or in a creative form of therapeutic jujitsu. The creative response to resistance is illustrated by the Milan group, who, for example, routinely ask a third person to describe interactions between two others ("gossip in the presence") in order to minimize defensiveness.

Finally, under the heading of resistance, we should consider the phenomenon of *induction*. Induction is what happens when a therapist is drawn into the family system—and abides by its rules. When this happens the therapist becomes just another member of the family; this may stabilize the system, but it reduces therapeutic mobility and prevents systems change. A therapist is inducted when he or she is sucked in to fulfill a missing family function—disciplining children when the parents do not or cannot, sympathizing with a husband whose wife does not, or coaxing a reticent teenager to open up to the therapist instead of to his parents; or when the therapist does what everybody else does—avoids challenging the fragile patriarch, minimizes a drinking problem, or sees a mother as just a nag.

Minuchin describes the danger of induction, and teaches structural family therapists how to recognize and avoid it (Minuchin and Fishman, 1981). Part of the value of live supervision is helping to avoid induction. Working with colleagues helps to avoid induction, either with cotherapists (Whitaker) or with a team (Selvini Palazzoli). Bowenians avoid induction by remaining calm and objective; they stay in contact but keep themselves detriangled and outside of the family projection system.

Induction is so subtle that it is hard to see, so seductive that it is hard to resist. As helpers and healers, therapists are especially prone to take over for people, doing for them what they do not do for themselves. But taking over—being inducted—precludes real change. As long as families have someone to do for them, they do not have to learn to do for themselves.

Rigidly stuck families are run by their fears, and therapists, eager to be liked, are vulnerable to those fears. Families quickly teach therapists what's safe and what's threatening: "Don't look in there"; "Don't ask *him* about *that*." The art of therapy is understanding and sympathizing with those fears, but avoiding induction enough to be able to challenge them. As in so many things, progress takes doing what you're afraid to do.

Family-Therapist Relationship

Individual psychotherapists have argued that the fundamental pillar of treatment is the patient-therapist relationship. Carl Rogers even claimed that certain qualities of the therapist are necessary and sufficient to produce successful outcomes. Family therapists tend to be more technically oriented and they de-emphasize the therapeutic relationship in their writing. Systems thinkers run the risk of losing sight of the individuals that make up the system. Furthermore, whether or not they consider the human qualities of the participants in therapy, all family therapists have an implicit model of patient-therapist relationship.

The variations of patient-therapist relationships—including subject-object, interpersonal, phenomenological, and encounter—are a function of individual practitioners, but they also tend to characterize different schools of treatment. The hallmark of the *subject-object* paradigm is the therapist's objective observation of the family. In this model the therapist is a natural scientist, who makes observations and carefully tailored interventions. Personal and emotional reactions are regarded as confounding intrusions. The assumption is that therapist and family are separate entities. This is not an attractive description, and few family therapists would describe themselves in these terms; nevertheless there are aspects of behavioral, psychoanalytic, strategic, and structural therapy that fit this model.

Behavioral family therapists think of themselves as objective observers and rational scientists; without a doubt they fit this paradigm. Psychoanalytic practitioners operate within this model when they think of themselves as neutral and objective, as blank screens upon whom patients project their distorted perceptions and fantasies. Although many psychoanalytic clinicians still maintain this assumption, it is not consistent with the best and latest psychoanalytic thinking. No therapist is neutral and objective; the blank screen is a metaphor and a myth. Therapists reveal themselves in a thousand ways, and patients' reactions are always influenced by the reality of the therapist's behavior as well as by personal distortions. The strategic school has produced some of the most sophisticated concepts of the intricate relationship between therapists and families (Hoffman, 1981). The subject-object paradigm is not a basic feature of this school, but it creeps in when therapists think of themselves as outsiders, locked in contest with families. The adversarial stance of some therapists in this system assumes that the therapist and family can and should be separate. The structural emphasis on mapping a family's structure can lead some therapists to see themselves as simply mapmakers, rather than mapmakers who are also part of the map.

The *interpersonal* paradigm treats therapy as a two-way interaction. This model acknowledges that therapists and families are related and that they constantly influence each other. Psychoanalytic clinicians employ this idea in their concepts of transference/countertransference, projective identification, and introjection; the model of influence here is interactive and transversal. In fact, this paradigm describes most family therapists most of the time. However, the constructivist movement in the 1980s represents an attempt on the part of some systems-oriented family therapists to include the effects of the therapist's presuppositions and behavior on the families they treat.

The *phenomenological* paradigm is one in which the therapist tries to adopt the patient's frame of reference. It is what happens when psychoanalytic practitioners try to identify with their patients, when structuralists join families, and when therapists of any persuasion try to understand and accept that families are doing the best they can. Stanton, Todd, and Associates (1981) use this concept in their technique of "ascribing noble intention" to families. This tactic fits the phenomenological model when it is done sincerely; it does not when it is used merely as a strategic ploy—for example, in most reframing. Selvini Palazzoli's positive connotation is far more effective when done with sincerity; Boszormenyi-Nagy's recognition that symptomatic behavior is an act of unconscious loyalty to the family is definitely sincere. Experientialists speak of accepting the patient's frame of reference, but sometimes they follow an encounter paradigm, in which they loudly proclaim their own honest feelings and challenge families to do the same.

The *encounter* paradigm is an encounter between the therapist's total personality and the client's. It involves mutual sharing, honesty, openness, and self-disclosure, and its use in family therapy is primarily restricted to experientialists. During an encounter the therapist becomes a full participant, which is something that most family therapists do not let happen. However, it is possible to let yourself go and confront a family if you do so with clear therapeutic indications and not simply because you feel like it. Minuchin engages in genuine encounters from time to time, but he shows good timing and the ability to recover his professional objectivity. Honest encounters are perhaps useful when done occasionally, for a good reason, and by someone with enough experience and insight to keep from losing perspective.

The 1980s brought a shift in the therapist-family relationship. The field began moving away from the directive, hierarchical, adversarial position of many of the original models, and toward a *collaborative* relationship, exemplified by the models described in Chapter 11. In a collaborative relationship, the therapist not only empathizes with a family's predicament, but also empowers them to use their own strengths to find solutions, from a position of partnership, rather than as The Great Expert.

Paradox

The use of paradox is a central and controversial topic in family therapy. Paradoxical instructions encourage rather than attack symptoms and objectionable behavior. They are designed to block or change dysfunctional sequences using indirect and seemingly illogical means. Paradoxical interventions are used instead of direct attempts to introduce change by therapists who assume that families cannot or will not comply with advice or persuasion.

Paradoxical interventions are associated with the newer strategic forms of therapy, but they are not confined to this group and they are not new. Behavior therapists have used paradoxical interventions for over fifty years, as negative practice or conditioned inhibition. Dunlap (1928) advised patients who wished to get rid of certain undesirable habits to practice them. He called this "negative practice," and reported success with tics, typing errors, stammering, and thumb sucking. Learning theorists believe that negative practice works through "conditioned inhibition," which has been described as fatigue induced by mass practice (Kendrick, 1960).

Frankl's (1960) "paradoxical intention" was an early version of what communications family therapists later called "prescribing the symptom." In all of these applications the idea is the same: if you deliberately practice a symptom, it will go away. Following Milton Erickson's influence, the MRI group reasoned that since family pathology was a function of paradoxical communication, it could be cured by "therapeutic double-binds." According to Haley (1963) the person with a symptom gains power by controlling those around him or her. He interpreted the effectiveness of paradoxical directives as a result of the therapist's gaining control over the symptoms by ordering them to occur on command. If symptoms are a tactic in interpersonal power struggles, the therapist can take control by prescribing them. Rabkin (1977) suggests that while some symptoms serve such devious purposes, others are simply habits reinforced by trying too hard not to do something and anxiously worrying about it. For example, worrying about being self-confident and trying too hard to be it may cause a lack of self-confidence. When a therapist prescribes the symptom, however, the patient may stop worrying about the problem and family members may stop trying to solve it.

Strategic therapists use paradox in two ways: as directives and as reframing, which is really interpretation and subtle direction. Reframing not only gives a new label for behavior, it also acts as an indirect message to change. Strategic therapists think of symptoms as part of self-reinforcing sequences; symptoms are maintained by attempts to suppress them. Paradoxical directives provoke change by altering the attempted solutions and thus resolving the symptoms. Hoffman (1981) cites an example of a wife whose constant jealous questioning of her husband only reinforced his reticence, which in turn reinforced her jealousy. The strategy to disrupt this sequence was to use a paradoxical directive to the wife to redouble her jealous questioning. The expected result was that the wife rebelled against the task and so solved the problem. Strategic therapists claim that it is usually unnecessary to look at the context or history of a symptom in order to resolve it.

There are two problems with provoking people to change by telling them not to. The first is obvious. This paradoxical device implies that families are oppositional; many are, but many are not. The second problem is that intervening only around a symptom neglects the broader family context. Ignoring the family context is like going to London without an umbrella; you won't get wet unless it rains. Symptoms may be maintained by attempts to suppress them, but many symptoms also serve a purpose in the family structure. Among strategic therapists, Haley and Selvini Palazzoli are the most aware that symptoms sometimes fit into the larger field of the family. The key is to be flexible; not to see symptoms as always or never playing a role in the family's psychic economy.

Minuchin's structural concepts have been carried into the strategic camp by Jay Haley, whose approach is a hybrid of structural and strategic methods. Haley (1976) recognizes that problem-maintaining sequences may be rooted in the family's dysfunctional structure. He doesn't advocate using paradoxical directives with highly disturbed families (Haley, 1980) and has become more concerned with shifting triadic sequences and with establishing appropriate hierarchical structure in families.

Selvini Palazzoli and her Milan cohorts relied on paradox as an explanatory concept and a treatment device, but they also looked beyond symptom-maintaining sequences to the context of the whole family. Since disturbed families sustain their pathology through an intricate network of paradoxes, Selvini Palazzoli (1978) reasoned that the best way to break these pathological networks was through therapeutic counterparadox. The Milan group not only prescribed the problem behavior but also the whole configuration of interactions surrounding it. Usually this took the combined form of "positive connotation" and assignment of a paradoxical family ritual. In this way, they tried to deal with the problem and its larger context at the same time. This seems to us the best and most appropriate use of therapeutic paradox. Best, because it deals with the family structure as well as with the symptom; and most appropriate, because the Milan group works with severely disturbed families. Paradoxical interventions keep the therapist distanced from the family; it's not a technique for therapists who need to be liked, but it does help to avoid the suction of families with serious disturbed members.

Paradoxical directives can break a family pattern, but why should such changes last? They will if the change also effects a change in the total family structure. Many examples of paradoxical instructions are insulting. (Madanes' (1980) pretend techniques avoid this insulting quality, and allow the therapist to avoid emotionally distancing himself or herself from the family.) Hoffman (1981), for example, describes a therapist telling a depressed wife to become more subservient to her husband. Not surprisingly, the woman rebels to defy the therapist. According to Hoffman, this technique worked because the paradoxical directive unbalanced a complementary balance, which then became symmetrical. Previously, the husband and wife were balanced in a relationship where he was one-up and she was one-down. By trying to push her further down, the therapist provoked a rebellion and the couple then established a relationship based on equality. Why that should happen is not at all clear. Why don't they simply re-establish the same complementarity they had before?

Paradoxical techniques are so appealing that they seem like a magic solution to entrenched family problems. Actually, the way to resolve problems is to understand their context. In structural terms, this means understanding the family's dysfunctional structure; in systemic terms, it means understanding the circular patterns and relational context. The real key is the understanding; whether the therapist intervenes directly or indirectly is far less important. Indeed, it is possible to make paradoxical remarks in the form of a warm and sincere skepticism about a rigid family ability to change. "I don't know, you've been operating this way for a long time, perhaps you will not be able to change." The family that hears such a comment may try to change or may not; either way they're likely to feel understood, not confronted.

TECHNIQUES

Comparing techniques by reading about them is difficult because clinicians often describe techniques as abstract concepts rather than as concrete actions. Modeling, for example, is a concept invoked by behaviorists for telling or showing parents how to speak to their children; by experientialists for talking about their own feelings; and by structural family therapists for speaking sharply to children who interrupt their parents. Are all these techniques modeling? Actually, modeling is not a technique; it is a hypothetical construct to explain how people learn through observation. Often, techniques are described in the jargon of a particular school—restructuring, therapeutic double-binds, differentiating—and it is not clear precisely what is meant. In this section, we will treat issues of technique as a series of practical questions about how to conduct therapy, and we will describe techniques as specific actions.

Much of what is written about the techniques of family therapy is about the middle game of treatment. This reflects a tendency among family practitioners to differentiate among themselves by describing their definitive and unique interventions; and it caters to the reader's wish to get on with therapy and get to the problem-solving part. Families come for treatment anxious and eager for direction, and they communicate their anxiety to the therapist. "Help us," they say, and in so doing they pass some of their anxiety on to the practitioner. Because they are the most anxious, young therapists are the most eager to discharge it by acting—by doing something definitive. Although family therapy is a therapy of action, the way must be prepared for the action to be effective. Before a therapist can know what is wrong with a particular family and gain the leverage to change it, he or she must make emotional contact and establish a therapeutic climate within which the family will be receptive to treatment. This involves such practical considerations as: who to invite to the first session, what kind of treatment team to use, how to enter into the family system, what sort of therapeutic stance to take, and how to assess the family.

Who to Invite

Most family therapists invite everyone living under the same roof to the first session. This reflects the belief that everyone in the family is involved in any problem (or at least can contribute to its solution), even if it is manifest in only one member. It also reflects the principle that in order to change the presenting symptom it is necessary to change the family inter-actions that create or sustain it.

Inviting the whole family to the first consultation is a powerful re-structuring and reframing move in and of itself. Whether or not it is ex-plicitly stated or openly acknowledged, the presence of the whole family in the assessment of a psychological problem implies that they are all in-volved. In many cases, the act of assembling the entire family to discuss a problem is the single most effective step toward solving it. Most experienced family practitioners are convinced of this, and they do not waste much time worrying about how to get the family in. They are positive that it is essential; they know that it is how they work; and so they calmly state this to the family. When the request that the whole family attend at least once is put in a straightforward, matter-of-fact way to families, most comply. Occasionally it is necessary to explain that the therapist would like everyone to attend in order to get all their points of view, but if the therapist is comfortable with the idea most families will also accept it.

Sometimes, however, one or two family members will not attend the consultation. When this happens most family therapists work with whoever is available. In such cases the failure of key family members to participate in treatment seems like a problem; it may be *the* problem. If a father, for instance, refuses to participate in treatment designed to help his daughter overcome her shyness, his absence from treatment is a sign that his unavailability may be a significant element in the problem. Working with the mother and children to get him involved may be the most important step in solving the presenting problem. On this matter, sensitive family therapists are like psychoanalysts who consider resistance not as an impediment to treatment, but as the object of treatment.

Members of some schools of family therapy do not insist upon seeing the entire family. Practitioners of behavioral parent training focus on teaching the parents—usually the mother—how to deal with the identified patient. For this reason, some invite only the parents and child to the first session, while others (Gordon and Davidson, 1981) recommend interviewing both parents in the child's absence. Strategic family therapists vary in whom they include in the first session. Haley (1976) recommends seeing the whole family, but many of his MRI colleagues will see individuals, parents, or couples alone as the situation seems to require. This determination is based on who in the family is "the customer"—who asks for help and who seems to be unhappy enough to do something about the problems.

Bowenian therapists usually work with individuals or couples. If a child is presented as the problem, members of this school see the parents; if a couple complains of marital problems, Bowenian therapists will see them together; and if only one person is willing to attend, the Bowenian therapist will see that person.

Finally, most family therapists (whether they specialize in couples therapy or not) will see a marital couple without their children if the couple complains of problems in their relationship. This is not, however, universally true. Structural, experiential, psychoanalytic therapists often ask that the children attend the first session, and exclude them only if and when the couple needs to discuss private matters, such as their sexual relationship. Milan therapists often find they get the most useful information from family members who are most peripherally involved, because they can speak the most openly.

Instead of seeing less than the whole family, some therapists insist on seeing more. Network therapists convene large groups of family and friends; some therapists try to include grandparents as well as the nuclear family. Inviting members of the extended family is a practice that cuts across the different schools. Many family therapists invite the grandparents in if they live in the nuclear family's household or if they seem particularly involved; some—for example, Whitaker and Selvini Palazzoli—invite grandparents as a matter of course. Another variant on the composition of therapy is seeing several families or couples together in a group. We have some reservations about the use of this procedure. Group therapy with individuals who are strangers is a useful method because it creates a naturalistic imitation of life. In family therapy there is no need to imitate life; convening the family brings life into the treatment room. However, group therapy with couples and families can be useful after a couple or family has made progress on overcoming their difficulties—in the focused way that private therapy allows. Then, meeting with other families or couples can be useful by helping people see how others solve similar problems. Sometimes it's easier to learn something when you're watching than when you're on the hot seat.

Although each of these variations on who is initially invited into treatment is supported by a rationale, we believe that the best practice is to include all members of the same household in the initial meeting. Later there may be good reasons for meeting with a subset of the family, but at the outset it is best to see everyone. Sometimes deviations from this format may be due more to anxiety than to good clinical judgment. Families are anxious about meeting together and airing their problems, and so, naturally, many are reluctant to come as a whole group. This is understandable, and should be dealt with calmly by insisting that everyone attend. Therapists, too, are anxious about convening families, particularly when the family indicates that one of its members does not want to come. The therapist's anxiety is sometimes the real reason for meeting with less than the whole family; in other words, some of the variations in composition of family meetings are probably due more to countertransference than to sound principles of family treatment.

There are times when it makes sense to work with a subset of the family—when, absolutely, only some will attend, or when the therapist thinks some people should be blocked. The main thing is not to be pressured into such a decision, and certainly not to drift into it without thinking.

Treatment Team

Family therapists frequently work in groups, either with a cotherapist or with a team of observers. Family interactions are so complex that it is difficult for one person working alone to see all that goes on. Moreover, the emotional pull on therapists who work with families is so strong that it is easy to be drawn in, to take sides, and to lose balance and objectivity. Working with colleagues helps because it provides additional observations and makes any loss of perspective obvious. In general, cotherapy seems to be favored by those schools of family therapy that emphasize intense emotional involvement (especially the experiential school); observation teams are favored by those schools that emphasize tactical planning (strategic, Milan), or who train therapists through live supervision (structural).

Whitaker has taken a strong position in favor of cotherapy; Minuchin and Haley take the opposite point of view. Whitaker's brand of experiential therapy is intensely personal and interactive. Because of this, he advocates (Whitaker and Keith, 1981) using cotherapists to counterbalance one another; while one is actively involved in a freewheeling interchange with the family, the other acts to limit partiality and to counteract the intrusion of countertransference-based interventions.

Minuchin and Haley have both argued that a solo therapist is more able to act decisively and is therefore preferable to cotherapists. Haley's position is consistent with his directive style, and it is shared by most strategic therapists (with the notable exception of the original Milan therapists who worked in mixed-gender teams of cotherapists). Minuchin, on the other hand, is controlling but less central and directive than most strategic therapists. His goal is to change families by manipulating their interactions with each other in the session. To this end he uses family members as his cotherapists. If a small child is shy, Minuchin will prod someone in the family to draw the child out; if a teenager is disobedient, Minuchin will goad the parents to become disciplinarians. By using family members as cotherapists, structural family practitioners avoid being induced to take over a function that is missing in the family.

None of the other schools of family therapy takes as clear a stand about cotherapy. Those who advocate cotherapy teams frequently cite the desire to provide male and female role models or advocates; this is especially true for sex therapists. Psychoanalytic therapists emphasize privacy and tend to work alone, as do Bowenian therapists. Network therapists work in teams of four or more simply as a matter of practical necessity, since they have to manage large groups. Behavioral therapists tend to work in cotherapy pairs while they are graduate students, and then work alone after they finish their training.

Most uses of cotherapy are probably based on economic and teaching considerations. In training settings, where there are more trainees than families, cotherapy may be a way to give everyone a chance to act as therapist. Beginners are often asked to work together as a way of helping each other. Although having a cotherapist may ease a beginner's initial anxiety, it can lead to confusion about who is in charge and where to go.

A solution favored by many family clinicians is to work alone backed up by a team of observers behind a one-way mirror. For research and training this method is invaluable; for everyday clinical practice it is a useful adjunct to the therapist's power of observation. Teams of observers are most commonly used by structural, Milan, and strategic therapists; the observers comment after a session is over, and also may enter or consult while the session is in progress. This is done programatically by the MRI group and by the Milan Associates. The advantages of this format are that observers can provide additional information, advice, and feedback. By contacting the family either by entering and speaking directly to them, or by sending a message through the therapist, observers can say something that is provocative or critical without the therapist's having to share responsibility for their statements.

The use of videotape adds another dimension to the treatment team. It enhances the observers' ability to see small movements and repetitive patterns, and it enables the therapist to observe him or herself interacting with the family. Videotaping equipment is expensive and not usually found outside of training clinics; its use is thus more an economic than a theoretical or technical issue. The same is true of one-way mirrors, observers, and cotherapists, which are usually used more often in clinics and training centers than in private practice. Cotherapy is, however, not uncommon among private practitioners, and its use may be partly a way of assuaging loneliness. To some extent, then, cotherapy is a little like a marriage: it works well if the partners are well matched and flexible, but if they are not, it can be a disaster.

Entering the Family System

Family clinicians think of the family in terms of a system—a collection of parts interacting as a single entity. Whether they realize it or not, therapists themselves are part of a larger system, one that includes the family and the therapist. This is true for therapists who keep their emotional distance (Bowenian, behavioral) as well as for those who become emotionally involved (experiential). All schools of family therapy have a more or less consistent style of making contact with families and of maintaining a particular therapeutic stance.

In structural family therapy the process of entering families is considered a critical determinant of therapeutic success, and it has been described more fully by this school than by any other. Minuchin (1974) uses the terms *joining* and *accommodation* to describe how the therapist relates to a family and adjusts to accept the family's organization and style. Most families come to treatment anxious and mistrustful; they expect their viewpoint to be challenged, and they expect to be blamed for causing their own problems. Fearing criticism and worried about having to change, they are set to resist. Recognizing this, structural family clinicians begin by trying to put the family at ease: they greet each member of the family separately; ask each for his or her point of view; and accept what they have to offer, even if at first it is only angry silence. "Okay, right now you're angry and don't want to talk."

The restructuring moves that come later—often as dramatic and forceful confrontations—require a great deal of leverage; this is achieved by joining. From a structural point of view, some of the other schools that emphasize the resistant properties of families (especially the strategic school) probably do an inadequate job of joining. In addition to joining, therapists gain leverage by establishing their status as experts. Minuchin does not emphasize this point in writing, but when he introduces himself as Director of the Clinic he immediately establishes himself as an expert and a figure of authority. Not all therapists have impressive sounding titles, but most make some effort to establish themselves as authorities, whether it is by hanging diplomas on the wall or by demonstrating competence through their actions.

Among strategic therapists, Haley has written the most about the process of entering the family system. His position (Haley, 1976) is similar to Minuchin's; he describes the therapist as a host who must make the family comfortable and put them at ease, while at the same time maintaining a businesslike demeanor. He also uses the idea of accommodating to the family's organization by suggesting that therapists speak first to the parents; but his recommendation that the less-involved parent be addressed first is not consistent with accommodating, and it is the first clue to Haley's stance as a therapist.

Like most strategic therapists, Haley is an expert manipulator. Members of this school relate to families from an emotionally distant position; they do not say what they really think and feel, but speak for a calculated effect—depending on the nature of resistance encountered. Whether they take a one-up or one-down position, their stance is that of experts who coolly assess family problems and prescribe solutions. Perhaps the best illustration of this stance is the way the Milan Associates consulted with their observers and returned to present the family with a written prescription. Members of the MRI group often adopt a one-down position; they demonstrate humility, confusion, and pessimism in order to avoid provoking resistance with optimistic pressure to change. To be successful with this strategy, therapists must be able to forgo the need to look good or be seen as in command.

In sharp contrast to the strategic approach, experiential family therapists enter fully into emotional life of the family and work from a stance that is open and close. Experientialists begin by greeting families and getting acquainted. In the process, they are likely to speak of their own feelings and attitudes, and to develop a warm, empathic relationship. Such intimate emotional engagement makes it difficult to be objective; it is hard to understand the patterns in the whole family system when you are actively engaged in emotional dialogues with individual family members. This is one of the reasons why Whitaker insists upon working with a cotherapist.

Psychoanalytic practitioners scrupulously refrain from active involvement with their clients. They do so by design, to avoid directing or becoming actors in a drama that they believe should unfold spontaneously. In psychoanalytic psychotherapy the therapist's stance is the most important ingredient in the method. Not interpretation, not analysis of the unconscious, but silent observation is the key to getting at hidden issues in the family.

The father of psychoanalytic family therapy, the late Nathan Ackerman, was an exception; he engaged in active dialogue with families, aggressively confronting them, "tickling their defenses," and even sharing some of his own feelings. He did so in part because he was more of a psychoanalyst inventing family therapy than a practitioner of psychoanalytic therapy with families. He followed the dictates of his own style and personality as much as he did his training. Perhaps this is a good place to make the point that the way that therapists relate to families—whether they are more or less active, more or less emotionally close—reflects their personality styles and personal preferences as well as the stance favored by the systems they follow. All therapists learn that using an approach that is congenial to personal style avoids unnecessary conflict. It is also true, however, that practitioners within the various schools tend to have similar stances.

Bowenian therapists take a position midway between the emotional intimacy of experientialists and the controlled technical mastery of strategists. Their byword is objectivity; their goal is to make contact with families but to remain detriangled. Learning is thought to occur in a calm atmosphere, so the Bowenian therapist tries to reduce anxiety and create a climate of rational understanding. He or she begins by inquiring about the symptoms and their clinical course. Once this is done the therapist begins to act as a teacher, explaining family systems theory, and as a coach, encouraging family members to make contact with the rest of the family and to work toward defining a self.

Behavioral therapists take over in the role of expert. Their stance is that of teachers; they take a central position, ask questions, explain principles, and assign homework. Their centrality, activity, and directiveness make it difficult for them to observe the natural and spontaneous interactions of the families they work with. It is an approach that controls and limits the field of observation. They can thus bring a great deal of technical expertise to dealing with part of the problem, but they run the risk of isolating that part from the whole family context.

Those who treat families as though they were conducting therapy groups vary in the intensity of their emotional engagement. Some, following the Tavistock model, are disengaged observers; other, influenced by the human potential movement, are active and interactive. Whether engaged or detached, family group therapists treat families as collections of individuals; they do not join families, they conduct family meetings.

When communications family therapy began, the family was treated as an opposing team—a confused and confusing opponent whose power to destroy meaning had to be controlled from the outset. Members of this school paid a great deal of attention to the structure and management of sessions; they were afraid to let things unfold naturally, because they thought that they would never be able to regain control. They began with explicit statements of their belief that the whole family was involved in the patient's symptoms, and they laid down the rules for how therapy would be conducted: "Speak for yourself"; "Don't interrupt."

As they gained experience, communications therapists realized that families tend to resist so direct an approach. They began to use more indirect means of establishing control, largely through paradoxical interventions, and so changed communications therapy into strategic therapy. But the general model is still a cerebral attempt to outwit families. Therapists are considered to be well motivated and rational; families are treated as stuck and liable to resist direct advice. The result is an emotionally distanced stance and a treatment imposed on families for their own good.

Assessment

Systems of family therapy vary in their emphasis on assessment and in the methods they use to make assessments. Each school has a theory about families that determines where they look for problems and what they see. Some look at the whole family (Milan, structural, Bowenian); some look at individuals and dyads (psychoanalytic, experiential); and some focus narrowly on sequences that maintain symptoms (strategic, behavioral). Strategic therapists think small to keep their clients from being overwhelmed, and to help them achieve immediate success.

Behavioral family therapists place the greatest importance on assessment and use the most formal and standardized procedures. In this approach assessment is separated from treatment and is the first order of business. Behaviorists also assess the effectiveness of their interventions, so it is more proper to say that their initial diagnostic assessment is separate from treatment. The great advantage of the behavioral emphasis on assessment is that it provides clear data, definite goals, and a reliable way to determine whether or not therapy succeeds. The disadvantage is that by using standardized interviews and questionnaires, behaviorists do not see the family in natural interaction. By looking only at a part of the family (mother and child, or marital couple), they miss the total context; by structuring the assessment, they see only how the family reacts to the therapists.

Strategic family therapists also make careful assessments, but they do so in a more naturalistic fashion. They begin by inquiring about problems, and then listen to discover how the problems are maintained by attempted solutions. The critical questions in this approach are: What is the problem? Who is involved? What are they doing to make a symptom out of a problem? These questions are answered by what the family says, and what the therapist concludes; there is less emphasis on observing actual interactions than in the experiential or structural schools. On the other hand, strategic practitioners are quite sensitive to the interactions between themselves and families, and they take these interactions into account as part of their evaluation. They frequently give directives in the first session to discover whether families are compliant or resistant. This emphasis is consistent with the centrality of the patient-therapist relationship and with the limited utilization of in-session interactions among family members.

Structural family therapists also emphasize assessment, but their evaluations are based on observation of family members interacting among themselves. These interactions take place either spontaneously or at the therapist's direction. Enactments give the therapist a chance to observe patterns of enmeshment and disengagement, which are the principal components in a structural family diagnosis. The positive aspects of this school's assessment procedure are that it utilizes the family's patterns of interaction among themselves, it includes the entire family, and it is organized in simple terms that point directly to desired changes. If the therapist enacts a discussion between two parents, but they are frequently interrupted by their child, the structural family evaluation would be that the boundary around the marital subsystem is too diffuse. The goal of therapy in such a case would be to increase the parent's involvement with each other, while strengthening the boundary between the parents and the child. A potential disadvantage to structural assessment is that it may lose sight of individuals while focusing on their roles in the family. This does not necessarily happen, but it is an error made by many beginning family clinicians.

The Bowenian school also does an excellent job of considering the whole family in its assessment procedure. Unlike structuralists, however, Bowenians rely on what they are told instead of what they see, and they are interested in the past as well as the present. Their evaluations consist of extensive clinical interrogatories, which are guided by Bowenian theory. The theory says that symptoms are a function of anxiety-provoking stressors, the level of differentiation of family members, and the degree of emotional cutoff from support systems, especially the extended family.

An extended family systems assessment begins with a description and history of the presenting problem. Exact dates are noted and later checked for their relationship to events in the extended family life cycle. Next comes a history of the nuclear family, including information about when the parents met, what their courtship was like, their marriage, and childbearing. Particular attention is also paid to where the family lived and when they moved, especially in relation to where their extended families live. The next part of the evaluation is devoted to the history of both spouses' birth, sibling position, significant facts of childhood, and about the past and current functioning of their parents. All of this information is recorded on a genogram, covering at least three generations. This assessment provides a panoramic view of the whole family and its history; it also provides detailed information about the individuals in the family.

The psychoanalytic and experiential schools also pay a good deal of attention to individuals. Their assessments focus on individual family members and their dyadic relationships within the family. Evaluations in these two schools are unstructured and take place in the ongoing process of treatment. An exception to this rule is that some psychoanalytic clinicians (Nadelson, 1978) meet with each spouse separately before proceeding to evaluate the family together. As in other approaches, the data that psychoanalytic and experiential therapists examine are not always the same as those that they are ultimately interested in. Behaviorists are interested in behavior, but they accept verbal reports; psychoanalysts are interested in latent ideas and experientialists are interested in latent feelings, but they both look carefully at behavior in the sessions for clues as to what is being withheld.

Although the form of evaluation is similar in psychoanalytic and experiential therapy, the content is quite different. These two schools occupy extreme ends on a continuum of the elaborateness of theory; psychoanalytic theory is extensive and complex, experiential theory is limited and simple. The breadth of psychoanalytic theory enables practitioners in this school to theorize well ahead of their data; a little information suggests a great deal. The advantage is that the theory organizes the data and provides valuable leads to uncovering hidden meanings. The danger is that the theory may distort the data, leading the clinician to see what is not there. Experientalists do not have these advantages or disadvantages. Their evaluations are guided by a simple theory about feelings and how they are suppressed; they tend not to uncover much that is hidden, but they also tend not to see things that are not there.

Just as there are many ways to conduct therapy, there are many assessment procedures; what works in one system may not work in another. We believe, however, that there are two general principles of assessment that are valid for all family therapists. First, it is best not to rely on formal structural evaluation procedures. The introduction of this much structure early in treatment produces an artificial atmosphere; instead of learning how the family behaves naturally, the clinician who makes a formal assessment learns what they say and how they interact with him or her. Moreover, once a therapist becomes a formal evaluator, it is difficult to move into a decentralized position and become an observer of family dynamics. Furthermore, once a family is treated with the structure of a formal assessment, they may forever resist freely interacting in therapy.

Although it seems to contradict our first point, we also believe that most family practitioners pay too little attention to assessment. There is a tendency to treat all families the same, especially by therapists with powerful techniques but limited conceptual schemes. For example, paradoxical directives are useful but are not necessary with compliant, well-motivated families. "Speak for yourself" is a good suggestion for enmeshed families, but not necessary for disengaged ones. Quid-pro-quo contracts may not be appropriate for couples with a complementary structure. Using pet techniques unguided by an assessment of the whole family may do some good, but without an evaluation of the family's structure such techniques are unlikely to change the basic configuration that creates and maintains family problems.

Once a therapist has assembled the family, joined with them, established a therapeutic stance, and assessed their structure and functioning, the stage is set for the powerful techniques that constitute the decisive interventions of family therapy.

Decisive Interventions

Members of every school of family therapy use a wide variety of techniques; some are dictated by the approach, others by the therapist's personality and experience. Even if we limit our attention to the techniques common to all members of each of the schools, the list would be long and confusing. Some techniques are used by virtually everyone who practices family therapy—reflecting feelings, clarifying communication; this common list has been growing as the different approaches have become more integrated. Each approach, however, relies on one or two techniques that are relatively unique and decisive. In this section we will highlight and compare these definitive interventions.

In psychoanalytic family therapy there are two decisive techniques. The first of these, *interpretation*, is well known, but not well understood. Properly used, interpretation refers to elucidating unconscious meaning. It does not mean statements of opinion—"You need to express your feelings to each other, before you can really be close"; advice—"As long as you continue writing to him, the affair isn't over"; theory—"Some of the reasons you were attracted to him are based on unconscious needs"; or confrontations—"You said you didn't care, but you were really angry." Interpretations are explicit statements of the therapist's conjecture about the unconscious meaning of certain behaviors or utterances. "You've been talking about your son's unpleasant habit of arguing with you all the time. Based on what you've said previously, I think that some of this anger is deflected from your husband. He does the same thing, but you are afraid to tell him so, and that's why you get so mad at your son."

By refraining from asking questions, giving advice, or directing what people should talk about, the psychoanalytic practitioner maintains a consistent stance of listening and fostering understanding. By limiting his or her interventions to interpretations, the therapist makes it clear that treatment is designed for learning; whether families take advantage of this atmosphere and whether they change their behavior as a result of what they learn is up to them.

The second decisive technique in psychoanalytic family treatment is *silence*. The therapist's use of silence permits him or her to discover what is on the patients' minds and to test the family's resources; it also lends force to the eventual interpretations. When the therapist is silent, family members talk, following their own thoughts rather than responding to the therapist's interests. If they know that the therapist will not often interrupt, they react and respond to each other. This produces a wealth of information that would not otherwise emerge. If a father begins the first session by saying, "The problem is my depression," and the therapist asks, "How long have you been depressed?" he or she may not discover what thoughts are associated in the man's mind with his depression, or how the man's wife responds to his complaint.

The therapist's silence tends to prolong the dialogues among family members. This enables the therapist to learn more about how they talk, and it forces the family members to find constructive ways to resolve their own interactional impasses. With an active therapist, families get in the habit of waiting for suggestions when they get stuck; with a silent therapist, they struggle to get themselves unstuck. The therapist's silence also enhances the impact of his or her interventions. Words weigh more when they are punctuated by long silences. (Unfortunately, with chaotic and extremely emotional families, therapists cannot always afford the luxury of silence, but must intervene actively to keep things under control.)

Many family group therapists use a number of active and manipulative techniques, including giving advice and making suggestions. The essence of this approach, however, is encouraging free and open discussions so that family members will improve their ability to communicate and learn to solve their own problems. The decisive technique in this approach is *confrontation*: family group therapists confront quiet family members and prod them to open up; they confront domineering members and encourage them to be quiet and listen.

Confrontation is also a decisive technique in experiential family therapy. In this school, confrontations are designed to provoke emotional reactions and are often aggressively blunt. It is not unusual for experiential therapists to tell clients to shut up, or to ridicule people for expressing themselves insincerely. Confrontations are often combined with *personal disclosure* from the therapist, which is the second major technique of this school. Experientialists use themselves as spontaneous, emotionally expressive, freewheeling models. Finally, most experiential therapists make use of a number of *structured exercises*. These include role-playing, psychodrama, sculpting, and a family drawing. The rationale for these techniques is that they are a quick way to provoke emotional experiencing in the session; their obvious drawback is that, because they are artificial, the reactions they provoke may be divorced from ordinary family experience.

Family members may get something off their chests in a structural exercise, but may not transfer this to their everyday interactions at home.

Most people associate reinforcement with behavior therapy, but reinforcement is not a technique used in behavioral family therapy; *observation* and *teaching* are the major techniques in this approach. Behavioral family practitioners begin by observing very carefully the contingencies of reinforcement in the families they work with. Their aim is to discover the antecedents and consequences of problem behavior. Once they have completed a functional analysis of behavior, they become teachers, teaching families how they inadvertently reinforce undesirable behavior. As teachers, their most useful lesson is how to use positive control. They teach parents that it is more effective to reward children for good behavior than to punish them for bad behavior; they teach married couples to substitute being nice to each other for their usual bickering.

Positive control—rewarding desirable behavior—is one of the most useful principles in family therapy. It is a valuable lesson for families and therapists. Therapists, like parents, tend to chide their charges for mistakes; unfortunately, if you are told that you are suppressing your feelings, spoiling your children, or using coercive control, you are most often apt to feel stupid and inadequate. Although it may be necessary to point out people's mistakes, it is more effective to concentrate on praising the positive aspects of their behavior. Among practicing family therapists this point seems to be best understood by structuralists, who speak of working with the family's strengths, and by strategists and Milan therapists, who use reframing and positive connotation to support families' efforts to do the right thing.

Extended family therapists are also teachers, but they follow a different curriculum. They teach people to be responsible for themselves, and how by doing so they can transform their entire family systems. Being responsible for yourself means getting clear about what you think and feel—not what your mother says or what you read in *The New York Times* but what you really believe—and then being true to your beliefs in your interactions with other people. You do not have to change others or even wish they were different; you do have to speak for yourself and maintain your own values. The power of this position is tremendous. If you can accept that you are you, and that other people are different and themselves, then you no longer have to approach relationships with the idea that either you or the other person has to change. This enables you to be in contact with people without becoming unduly upset or emotionally reactive.

In addition to teaching differentiation, Bowenian therapists have two corollary lessons—avoiding triangulation and reopening cut-off family relationships. Taken together these three lessons enable a single person to transform the whole network of his or her family system. If your spouse nags, if your kids are disobedient, if your mother never comes to visit, *you* can create a change. Other schools of therapy exert leverage for change by including the entire family in treatment sessions; Bowenians teach individuals to be themselves, to make contact with others, and to resolve conflicts with the people they are in conflict with. This lesson gives a person leverage for change that is more portable and lasting than family therapy sessions.

Communications family clinicians contributed so much to the theoretical base of the family therapy movement that it is difficult to separate out their techniques or to single out their principal interventions. Perhaps their greatest achievement was to point out that communication is multilayered and that often the most important things being said are said covertly. Therapy was designed to make the covert overt. Initially this was done by pointing out hidden messages; when this direct approach met with resistance, therapists began using directives to make the rules of family functioning explicit, and to provoke changes in the rules.

Strategic therapy is an offshoot of communications theory, and the techniques used by strategists are refinements of those used by communicationists. Principal among these are *reframing, directives*, and *positive connotation*. Strategic practitioners begin by getting detailed descriptions of problems and attempts to solve them. In the process, they pay particular attention to the family's language and expectations. They try to grasp the family's point of view and acknowledge it—which is positive connotation; then they use reframing to shift the family's point of view, and directives to interrupt their problem-maintaining behavior. Using this general outline, members of this school plan on a general method; but as many others do, they tailor their intervention to fit each case.

In most cases the single most powerful intervention is probably the use of a directive. These directives are designed to break up rigid homeostatic patterns; these are assigned to be carried out when the family is at home; and they are often paradoxical. Although strategic therapists emphasize fitting the treatment to the patient, they consistently assume that indirect interventions are necessary to outwit resistance. This is sometimes but not always necessary. It is not so much that some families are resistant and others are not, but that resistance is not a property *in* families; it is a quality of interaction between therapist and family. A therapist who proceeds on the assumption that families are unable and unwilling to follow advice is likely to encounter the expected resistance.

Structural family therapy is also a therapy of action, but in this approach the action occurs in the session. The decisive technique in this system is *boundary making* between family members while they are in the process of interacting. Rigid boundaries are softened when the therapist gets people to talk with each other and blocks attempts to detour or interrupt them. Likewise, diffuse boundaries are strengthened when the therapist works to realign boundaries in the whole family. Blocking a parent's intrusion into the children's functioning will not last unless that parent is helped to get more involved with the spouse.

Several promising techniques emerged in the 1980s around which whole models of therapy were built. Steve de Shazer and his colleagues expanded the technique of focusing on successful solutions to problems that family members had already tried but abandoned into a whole new approach—solution-based therapy. Michael White did the same with the technique of externalizing problems—getting families to view their problems as separate from them, and then working together to "defeat" these alien enigmas.

CONTEXT AND APPLICABILITY OF THE SCHOOLS OF FAMILY THERAPY

The predominant influence of social context, emphasized in family therapy, also applies to family therapists themselves and to the systems of treatment they develop. The pioneers of family therapy worked in different settings and with different patient populations. They did not set out to invent family therapy. They were working on other problems—analyzing communication, discovering the etiology of schizophrenia, treating delinquent children—and family therapy turned out to be part of the solution. But, as we have seen, "family therapy" is not one approach, it is many. The variation in setting, population, and intent of the developers combined to influence the nature of the various family therapies, and also helps to determine the type of patients that each method is most suited to. In this section we will briefly examine the context from which the different sects of family treatment emerged, and then consider which approaches are best for which problems.

The contextual roots of psychoanalytic family therapy are less easy to locate than those of other systems. Ackerman was certainly the originator of this approach, but his death in 1971 left this school without a leader. Since then contributing influences to psychoanalytic family therapy have come from many different quarters. Until recently most of the major figures in this school, including Ackerman himself, have been psychoanalytically trained clinicians who abandoned psychoanalysis for family therapy; their analytic training was reflected in their theoretical papers, but not in their clinical methods. These early psychoanalytic family practitioners worked in a variety of settings—child guidance, social welfare, and marriage and family clinics; but for the most part, the families they worked with were members of the middle class with mild to moderate problems.

Today more and more psychoanalytically trained clinicians are practicing family therapy using methods that are consistent with their training (Nadelson, 1978; Nichols, 1987). These practitioners tend to work in the same settings and with similar patients as do individual psychoanalytic therapists, namely, medical school outpatient clinics and private practices, with verbal, intelligent, middle-class patients who are not seriously disturbed. Psychoanalytic treatment—individual or family—is a method of self-discovery that relies heavily on words; and it works best with verbal patients who are motivated to learn about themselves. The more educated and sophisticated, the more readily they accept this approach.

The specific methods of family group therapy were developed by John E. Bell, but the general model of group therapy was used by most practitioners who treated families before family systems models of treatment were available. For this reason it is not possible to describe a specific context of family treatment in which this approach was developed. On the contrary, since this approach was developed for treating groups of strangers, it is probably more applicable to such groups than to families.

Carl Whitaker, the most prominent experiential family therapist, worked with delinquents and schizophrenics early in his career; later he shifted toward less seriously disturbed patients. This transition, from more to less serious psychopathology, tends to come with experience as a psychotherapist. Poverty and problems go together. The most seriously troubled people are often poor and are usually treated by young clinicians in public clinics.

The concepts and methods of experiential psychotherapy were developed in the human potential movement to treat people with normal problems of everyday life. The cathartic techniques of this approach may not be as useful for people struggling with serious psychopathology or situational stress, but for repressed neurotics these techniques are like an elixir that infuses new life into their days of anxiety and apathy.

Behavioral marriage therapy was developed in university departments of psychology and applied primarily to members of the academic community. These couples tend to be young, educated professionals, whose relationships are symmetrical and whose problems are not severe. They are usually well motivated and willing to follow instructions in an educational format. Behavioral parent training was also developed in academic training centers, but has been applied to seriously disturbed children in institutions as well as to mildly disturbed children in university clinics. The concrete symptomatic focus of this treatment makes it a popular approach for dealing with severely symptomatic children. For this reason, behavior therapy is often used as an adjunct to other forms of treatment for hospitalized children (Minuchin, Rosman, and Baker, 1978). In hospital settings, behavioral treatment is usually applied not by the parents but by the staff; in fact, much of the behavioral parent training is conducted by graduate students in university counseling centers and psychological training clinics.

Murray Bowen developed his ideas about family therapy while he was at NIMH, studying middle-class families that had a psychotic member. This may help account for two of the main emphases in his work: differentiation of self and working with extended families. In psychotic families there is often a blurring of psychological boundaries—what

Bowen called the undifferentiated family ego mass. These families exhibit an intense clinging interdependence in which individual identities get diffused in an amorphous family togetherness. Bowen concluded that this lack of differentiation, or fusion, is the major source of pathology in all families. The goal of his treatment is to help family members differentiate themselves, which in turn will have a beneficial effect on the entire system. The process of differentiation begins with the therapist, who must remain emotionally neutral and avoid being drawn into the emotional quicksand of the undifferentiated family. This stance must have been necessary to avoid being engulfed by the psychotic families that Bowen started out with.

Bowen distingushed between differentiation and emotional cutoff, which is common in the middle-class suburban families he studied in Washington, DC. Emotional cutoff is a reactive flight from fusion, masquerading as genuine independence.

Although he first developed his ideas about families while studying a psychotic population, Bowen was more successful at understanding these families than he was at treating them. He no longer believes that family therapy is effective with schizophrenic families, and most of his work now is with middle-class professional families. Bowenian therapy may be most useful for young couples who have not yet successfully separated from their original families, including not only those who are obviously still dependent on their parents, but also those whose pseudoindependence is based on reactive distance. While Bowenian therapy may be ideally suited for middle-class couples in their twenties and thirties, its applicability is certainly not limited to this group. Bowen has an exquisite appreciation of triangular processes, and his therapeutic concepts are useful in any situation where two people form a coalition against a third.

Communications family therapists were scientists first, healers second. Their original intent was to study communication in schizophrenic families; only later did they decide to treat these unhappy people. At first they saw patients as victims of a family conspiracy to keep them sick, and tried to protect identified patients from the scapegoating of their relatives. Later they realized that in schizophrenia there are no victims and victimizers; the whole family is stuck.

The feature of family life that captured their attention was the strange and puzzling ways families with schizophrenic members communicate. Conversation in these families is often permeated with paradoxes, disqualifications, and double-binds. Analyses of these patterns of pathological communication were illuminating, and the findings cast doubt on traditional views of mental illness. Having discovered what they felt was the family's role in creating and perpetuating psychological disorders, communications theorists began to criticize traditional individual psychotherapy. Jay Haley was the most outspoken critic, and his writing helped prepare the way for a new form of treatment based on the family's role in mental illness.

Among these theorists, Jackson, Haley, and Weakland were the most interested in therapy, and they were the pioneers of communications family treatment. It is a tribute to their optimism that they thought that schizophrenia could be cured by bringing together patients with their families and somehow talking them out of their strange and destructive patterns of communication. When they found that the direct approach did not work, they developed an indirect one. In place of interpretation they began to use manipulation. When communications therapists became strategists, they took a more emotionally distanced position, conducting therapy like generals outside the fray.

Jackson and Haley were the pivotal figures in the transition from communications theory to strategic therapy. Haley took the core concept of communications theory—that messages cannot be taken at face value because they are always qualified by other messages on different levels—and derived the notion that all communication is part of a struggle for power in relationships. This position reflects Haley's personality and the context he was working in. Haley is an intellectual and an outsider; some of his major contributions have been critiques and attacks against psychoanalysis, the human potential movement, and experiential family therapy. His therapy is about power and control—how to wrest power in order to gain control of families through ingenious manipulation. Psychiatric symptoms are seen as perversions of the normal struggle for control. Instead of openly fighting for control, families of psychiatric patients deny that there is any conflict. They do not honestly refuse to participate; they "can't" because they are "sick." Strategic therapy forces patients into a corner from which they can escape only by giving up their symptoms. Haley's concept of ordeal therapy, derived from Milton Erickson, illustrates this way of thinking.

Emotional distance, struggle for power, and manipulation—none of these sounds very nice. To understand how these positions were developed it's necessary to consider where they were developed. Communications therapists worked with acute schizophrenics whose families, they thought, were capable of driving people crazy with baffling responses and maddening double-binds. Perhaps conducting therapy from a distance seemed to be the only way to avoid getting completely entangled in such families. Perhaps if therapists don't struggle for power, they will be defeated by these families; and if they don't use manipulation, they will be manipulated. Today's strategic therapists still work with seriously disturbed cases, many of whom have tried and failed with other straightforward approaches. But today's therapists are rarely as combative as in the past, and are likely to be genuinely sympathetic to the problem of living with a seriously disturbed member.

Structural family therapy was first developed with families of delinquents from the inner-city slums. These families are poor and often disorganized. Some are enmeshed—chaotic and tightly interconnected; others are disengaged—isolated and seemingly unrelated. Both types lack clear hierarchical structures. Creating functional structures by differentiating subsystems and realigning their boundaries is the object of structural family therapy.

Another characteristic of the ghetto families that Minuchin worked with at Wiltwyck is that they are outside the mainstream of American culture and feel alien in relation to middle-class helping professionals. In order to work with these families it is first necessary to get their attention and then to gain their confidence; this helps to account for Minuchin's active, directive style, and his emphasis on joining.

Structural family therapy's focus on the whole family is different from some of the other approaches that tend to work with subsets of the family. Strategic and Bowenian practitioners, for instance, move quickly to the adults, even when the presenting problem is about a child. Minuchin, however, was trained as a child psychiatrist, and he has always believed that it is important to include children in treatment.

Understanding the contexts in which the different systems of family therapy were developed makes it easier to see why they have the form that they do. However, it doesn't tell us which therapy to use with which problem. There is little hard evidence that one system is more effective than the others, nor do we know much about which is best with any particular problem.

There are, however, a growing number of researchers beginning to add hard evidence to long-standing debates, which in the past were thought to be primarily matters of opinion and personal choice. There is now a substantial and growing body of evidence about effective methods for treating schizophrenic patients and their families as well as chemically dependent persons and their families. There are numerous studies, some of which relate to specific models and others that deal with meta-analyses of family therapy clinical trials. Among the most informative discussions of the empirical literature are: Gurman, Kniskern, and Pinsof's (1986) review chapter in the third edition of the *Handbook of Psychotherapy and Behavior Change*; Hazelrigg, Cooper, and Borduin's (1987) paper "Evaluating the Effectiveness of Family Therapies: An Integrative Review and Analysis"; Burlingame et al.'s review article in the 1989 edition of the *Annual Review of Psychology*; and Kazdin's (1987) *Psychological Bulletin* article, "Treatment of Antisocial Behavior in Children: Current Status and Future Directions."

In the final analysis, the best treatment is given by the best therapist. If the best therapist in town is an experientialist, the best therapy in town is experiential.

SELECTION OF A THEORETICAL POSITION: RATIONAL AND IRRATIONAL FACTORS

How do students go about selecting a therapeutic orientation, and how should they? Deliberate choice probably exerts less influence than the personality and values of the student, or the training milieu. Having selected and been selected by a graduate program, students are pressured to conform to the models offered by their teachers and supervisors. While the idea of conformity may not be appealing, it is probably a good idea to embrace the model offered by your teachers. Learning whatever you can from every teacher or supervisor does not destroy your independence any more than rejecting and arguing protects it.

Except in the most homogeneous settings, students are liable to be exposed to a variety of different approaches during their graduate education; their interests are based on a series of fluid identifications with faculty members. While this may be confusing, it helps innoculate beginning clinicians against dogmatic thinking. Moreover, it provides the necessary breadth of information upon which to base an informed choice of a specialty. Once you leave academic coursework to begin practical training, it is too late to shop around. During your clinical training, you should concentrate on learning one method well—that is, becoming thoroughly immersed in it. It may seem more creative to blend elements from a variety of systems in a personal integration, but this is better done after you master one single approach.

Selecting a system of family therapy to specialize in is not simply a question of which one is best. For one thing, we still don't know which is the best form of treatment (though there have been several reports published in *The Journal of Marital and Family Therapy*, by Hetherington in 1987, Kolevzon and Green in 1982, and Kolevzon, Sowers-Hoag, and Hoffman in 1989, that deal with therapist selection of orientation). The choice depends upon what is available, what suits your clientele, and what suits you. The methods and techniques of therapy are never wholly separate from the qualities of the person applying them. Therefore, it is wise to choose an approach that is congruent with your style as a person.

Far too many people discontinue their training before they have mastered their craft. Training can be expensive; job offers beckon; and nobody wants to be a student forever. Because most people discontinue their training before they become expert, the field is filled with many so-called family therapists who are equipped with little more than a basic understanding of systems theory and a rudimentary knowledge of techniques.

After training (whether it is pursued to conclusion or prematurely terminated), there is a transition from student to full-fledged therapist. This can be a very gratifying time. Freed from the constraints of a beginner's status and removed from the watchful eyes of supervisors, practicing therapists become more spontaneous and fluid. Instead of being anxious about following the model or pleasing a supervisor, the therapist is free to get more involved with families and incorporate some of his or her natural style along with techniques that by now have become almost second nature. After you have gained experience in applying your model of therapy to the treatment of families, you are liable to experience the limitations of the model or your skill as therapist, or both. Many people then take refresher courses or look for workshops in new treatment approaches. Although we do believe strongly in mastering one particular model of therapy, we do not think it matters whether an experienced practitioner returns for a brush-up in the original model or seeks out some new ideas. Experienced practitioners will be able to—will have to—integrate whatever they learn with their personal styles.

However, being able to integrate a variety of family therapy models with your own personality only works for those who have a thorough background of training and supervision in some form of family therapy. Therapists who substitute periodic attendence at workshops and training conferences for a protracted period of indoctrination and training in one particular school of family therapy tend not to be competent family therapists. A series of workshops can stimulate and enhance the skills of experienced practitioners but cannot substitute for the necessary apprenticeship.

SUMMARY

The theme of the first edition of this book was the proliferation of competing schools, each portrayed as unique and uniquely effective. That was how family therapy entered the 1980s. Now, as family therapy enters the 1990s, the theme of this attempt to describe the field should perhaps be integration. So many dedicated family therapists have been working for so long that the field has accumulated a significant number of useful ways of looking at and treating families. Today it no longer makes sense to study one and only one model and to neglect the insights of the others. Family therapists are not only cross-fertilizing across models of family therapy, they are also adding concepts and methods from psychology and individual psychotherapy.

Neither of the authors likes to use tired clichés (unless we make them up), but one familiar metaphor is that of family therapy moving out of its adolescence and into adulthood. We trot out this old chestnut because it's true. Once, like adolescents trying to define our identities, we were proud to be special and different; and we were a little snotty about the accomplishments of the older generation: individual psychotherapists. Now we seem to have less and less need to prove we're unique and special and different, and we seem to be developing more respect for those "others" who practice different versions of family therapy—and even those who practice altogether different forms of psychotherapy. Family therapy may have rediscovered psychodynamic psychotherapy in the 1980s; in the 1990s perhaps we will rediscover behavior therapy and begin to utilize its enormous technology for changing behavior.

Before we say goodbye to the family-therapy-growing-up metaphor, one more point: When the field was young we often got by on enthusiasm and promise. But that may not work in maturity. Now when we promise a therapy that works, we're expected to deliver. An important aspect of this is that empirical research demonstrating what we claim to accomplish will be one of the most important requirements in the 1990s. If family problems cause psychological problems, we should be able to demonstrate it; and, perhaps more important, if we say we can resolve problems with family therapy, we'll probably have to prove it.

Underlying each approach is a view of human nature. Differences among schools in their view of what it means to be human account for many of the differences in concepts and methods that we have discussed. If people are power-game players, therapists will devise indirect strategies to outwit them. If the feelings and behavior of people depend primarily on the network of relationships (or family structure) in which they are embedded, therapists will use their relationship to restructure families. If people are undifferentiated from their irrational emotionality, therapists will use their own rationality and knowledge of how systems work to teach people how to differentiate. If people contain untapped inner resources, therapists will collaborate with them to bring out those strengths. We're pleased to see this last way of thinking gaining ground, especially, for example, in the work of the late Virginia Satir, Salvador Minuchin, Luigi Boscolo and Gianfranco Cecchin, Steve de Shazer, Bill O'Hanlon and Michele Weiner-Davis, Carol Anderson, Richard Schwartz, and Michael White.

In the past, each of the rival systems of family therapy proclaimed its unique way of understanding and treating families. However, as we have seen, the differences are more sharply drawn in theory than in practice. The success of new developments in one school often lead to their adoption by others, shrinking the gaps among the various therapeutic orientations. The trend toward convergence will be the story of family therapy in the 1990s. In what follows we will offer some very subjective comments about picking and choosing some of the more useful concepts and methods that have proven themselves classics of family therapy.

Theories of family functioning have both a scientific and a practical purpose. The most useful theories treat families as systems; have concepts to describe forces for stability and change; consider the past, but concentrate on the present; treat communication as multileveled and complex; recognize the process underlying the content of family discussions; recognize the triadic nature of human relationships; remember to consider the context of the nuclear family, rather than viewing it as a closed system isolated from its environment; and recognize the critical function of boundaries in protecting the cohesiveness of individuals, subgroups, and families.

Clinicians are more concerned with pathology and change than with normality, but it is useful to have a model of normal family functioning, both to mold treatment goals and to distinguish what is pathological and needs changing from what is normal and does not. Some of the most useful concepts of normal family functioning are: Minuchin's structural model of families as open systems in transformation; the communications theory model of direct, specific, and honest communication in a family system with rules clear enough to ensure stability and flexible enough to allow change; the behavioral model of equitable exchange of interpersonal costs and benefits, the use of positive control instead of coercion, and mutual and reciprocal reinforcement between spouses; the family group theory which points out that groups function best when they are cohesive, when there is a free flow of communication, and when members' roles are clearly defined and appropriate to their needs; the strategic model of systemic flexibility, which allows adjustment to changing circumstances and the ability to find new solutions when old ones don't work; and the Bowenian model which explains how differentiation of self enables people to be independent at times, intimate at others.

Most family therapy concepts of behavior disorder focus on systems and interactions, but the psychoanalytic, Bowenian, Schwartz's parts model, and experiential models add intrapersonal depth to the interactional view, bridging the gap between private, inner experiences and outward public behavior. The clinical observation that many divorced people repeat the mistakes of their first marriages supports these schools' position that some of what goes on in families is a product of individual character. Some of the most valuable concepts of personality dysfunction in families are: Bowen's concept of fusion; the experiential concepts of repressed affect and stifled growth; and psychoanalytic concepts of developmental arrest, internal object relations, and instinctual conflict. These concepts of individual psychopathology are useful adjuncts, but the guiding ideas in the field explain behavior disorder in terms of systems theory. The most influential of these are about inflexible systems, too rigid to accommodate to individual strivings or to adjust to changes in circumstances; symptomatic family members promoting cohesion by stabilizing the nuclear and extended families; inadequate hierarchical structure; families that are too tightly or too loosely structured; and pathological triangles.

The broad goals of family therapy are to solve presenting problems and to reorganize families. Behaviorists and strategists aim for the former, Bowenians and psychoanalysts aim for the latter; most of the other schools aim for both. As we have seen, some family practitioners expect therapy to be prolonged, while others keep it brief. These diverse strategies reflect differences of opinion about how much change families need to accomplish.

In our opinion, that question should be left to the family. Therapists should accept the family's goal to solve their immediate problems, and design therapy to reorganize only that aspect of the family that has become dysfunctional. If families want more, they should say so.

Some of the specific goals of family therapy are practically universal—clarifying communication, solving problems, promoting individual autonomy—and some are unique. Some of the schools take the presenting problem at face value, while others treat it as a metaphor and a sign. In either case, goals should not be so broad as to neglect symptom resolution, or too narrow to insure the stability of symptom resolution. Incidentally, values are seldom discussed in the family therapy literature. The one exception is Boszormenyi-Nagy, but he considers the ethical dimension only in terms of the patient. There is too little consideration of a practicing therapist's ethical responsibilities, including the possibility of conflicting responsibilities to individuals, families, and the larger community.

Some of the major differences among family therapists about how behavior is changed are focused on the following issues: action or insight; change in the session or change at home; duration of treatment; resistance; family-therapist relationship; and paradox. Even though there is a general consensus about some of the issues—for example, once most family therapists believed that action is primary and insight is useful but secondary—there have always been divergent opinions on every one of these points. Strategic therapists, for example, flatly denied that insight is necessary or useful.

We have discussed some of the major methodological issues and tried to separate out the decisive techniques of the different systems. As is always the case when a number of variables are involved in a final result, it is not easy to know to what degree each variable contributes to that result, or how important each one is. Furthermore, the more we talk about techniques, the greater the danger of seeing family therapy as a purely technological enterprise. Studying families is like solving a riddle; the art of treating them is to relieve suffering and anguish. The job of the theoretician is to decode or decipher; it requires theory and ingenuity. The job of the therapist is to help relieve suffering; it requires theory, but also conviction, perseverance, and caring. Treating families is not only an act of science and technology; it is also an act of love.

REFERENCES

Bowen, M. 1966. The use of family theory in clinical practice. *Comprehensive Psychiatry.* 7:345–374.

Dunlap, K.A. 1928. A revision of the fundamental law of habit formation. *Science.* 67:360–362.

Frankl, V. 1960. Paradoxical intention: A logotherapeutic technique. *American Journal of Psychotherapy.* *14*:520–535.

Gordon, S.B., and Davidson, N. 1981. Behavioral parent training. In *Handbook of family therapy*, A.S. Gurman and D.P. Kniskern, eds. New York: Brunner/Mazel.

Gurman, A.S., Kniskern, D.P., and Pinsof, W. 1986. Research on the process and outcome of marital and family therapy. In *Handbook of psychotherapy and behavior change*, S.L. Garfield and A.E. Bergin, eds. 3rd ed. New York: Wiley.

Haley, J. 1963. *Strategies of psychotherapy.* New York: Grune and Stratton.

Haley, J. 1976. *Problem-solving therapy.* San Francisco: Jossey-Bass.

Haley, J. 1977. Toward a theory of pathological systems. In *The interactional view*, P. Watzlawick and J. Weakland, eds. New York: Norton.

Haley, J. 1980. *Leaving home: The therapy of disturbed young people.* New York: McGraw-Hill.

Halleck, S. 1978. *The treatment of emotional disorders.* New York: Jason Aronson.

Hazelrigg, M.D., Cooper, H.M., and Bourdin, C.M. 1987. Evaluating the effectiveness of family therapies: An integrative review and analysis. *Psychological Bulletin.* *101*:4228–4442.

Hoffman, L. 1981. *The foundations of family therapy.* New York: Basic Books.

Jackson, D.D. 1965. Family rules: The marital quid pro quo. *Archives of General Psychiatry.* *12*:589–594.

Jasnow, A. 1978. The psychotherapist—artist and/or scientist? *Psychotherapy: Theory, Research and Practice.* *15*:318–322.

Kazdin, A.B. 1987. Treatment of antisocial behavior in children: Current status and future directions. *Psychological Bulletin.* *102*:187–203.

Kendrick, D.D. 1960. The theory of "conditioned inhibition" as an explanation of negative practice effects: An experimental analysis. In *Behavior therapy and the neuroses*, H.J. Eysenck, ed. New York: Pergamon.

Luborsky, L. 1972. Research cannot yet influence clinical practice. In *Changing frontiers in the science of psychotherapy*, A.E. Bergin and H.H. Strupp, eds. New York: Aldine-Atherton.

Madanes, C. 1980. Protection, paradox and pretending. *Family Process.* *19*:73–85.

Madanes, C., and Haley, J. 1977. Dimensions of family therapy. *Journal of Nervous and Mental Disease.* *165*:88–98.

Mahler, M.S., Pine, F., and Bergman, A. 1975. *The psychological birth of the human infant.* New York: Basic Books.

Matarazzo, J.D. 1972. Interview: J.D. Matarazzo. In *Changing frontiers in the science of psychotherapy*, A.E. Bergin and H.H. Strupp, eds. New York: Aldine-Atherton.

Minuchin, S. 1974. *Families and family therapy.* Cambridge, MA: Harvard University Press.

Minuchin, S., and Fishman, H.C. 1981. *Family therapy techniques.* Cambridge, MA: Harvard University Press.

Minuchin, S., Rosman, B., and Baker, L. 1978. *Psychosomatic families: Anorexia nervosa in context.* Cambridge, MA: Harvard University Press.

Nadelson, C.C. 1978. Marital therapy from a psychoanalytic perspective. In *Marriage and marital therapy*, T.J. Paolino and B.S. McCrady, eds. New York: Brunner/Mazel.

Nichols, M.P. 1987. *The self in the system*. New York: Brunner/Mazel.

Paul, W.L. 1967. The use of empathy in the resolution of grief. *Perspectives in Biology Medicine*. *11*:153–169.

Pierce, R., Nichols, M.P., and DuBrin, J. 1983. *Emotional expression in psychotherapy*. New York: Gardner Press.

Rabkin, R. 1977. *Strategic psychotherapy*. New York: Basic Books.

Rogers, C.R. 1957. The necessary and sufficient conditions of therapeutic personality change. *Journal of Consulting Psychology*. *21*:95–103.

Selvini Palazzoli, M., Boscolo, L., Cecchin, G., and Prata, G. 1978. *Paradox and counterparadox*. New York: Jason Aronson.

Selvini Palazzoli, M., Boscolo, L., Cecchin, G., and Prata, G. 1980. Hypothesizing-circularity-neutrality: Three guidelines for the conductor of family interviews. *Family Process*. *19*:3–12.

Stanton, M.D., Todd, T.C., and Associates. 1981. *The family therapy of drug addiction*. New York: Guilford.

Thibaut, J.W., and Kelley, H.H. 1959. *The social psychology of groups*. New York: Wiley.

Vogel, E.F., and Bell, N.W. 1960. The emotionally disturbed child as the family scapegoat. In *The family*, N.W. Bell and E.F. Vogel, eds. Glencoe, IL: Free Press.

Watzlawick, P., Beavin, J., and Jackson, D.D. 1967. *Pragmatics of human communication*. New York: Norton.

Whitaker, C.A., and Keith, D.V. 1981. Symbolic-experiential family therapy. In *Handbook of family therapy*, A.S. Gurman and D.P. Kniskern, eds. New York: Brunner/Mazel.

Appendix A:
RECOMMENDED READINGS

Note: Recommended readings are categorized first by chapters of this book, and then a second list of our overall recommendations.

_____ Chapter 1. The Historical Context of Family Therapy

Ackerman, N.W. 1958. *The psychodynamics of family life.* New York: Basic Books.

Boszormenyi-Nagy, I. 1962. The concept of schizophrenia from the point of view of family treatment. *Family Process. 1*:103–113.

Bowen, M. 1960. A family concept of schizophrenia. In *The etiology of schizophrenia*, D.D. Jackson, ed. New York: Basic Books.

Greenberg, G.S. 1977. The family interactional perspective: A study and examination of the work of Don D. Jackson. *Family Process. 16*:385–412.

Guerin, P.J. 1976. Family therapy: The first twenty-five years. In *Family therapy: Theory and practice*, P.J. Guerin, ed. New York: Gardner Press.

Haley, J. 1959. The family of the schizophrenic. *American Journal of Nervous and Mental Diseases. 129*:357–374.

Haley, J., and Hoffman, L., eds. 1968. *Techniques of family therapy.* New York: Basic Books.

Jackson, D.D. 1957. The question of family homeostasis. *The Psychiatric Quarterly Supplement. 31*:79–90.

Jackson, D.D. 1965. Family rules: Marital quid pro quo. *Archives of General Psychiatry. 12*:589–594.

Lidz, T., Cornelison, A., Fleck, S., and Terry, D. 1957. Intrafamilial environment of schizophrenic patients. II: Marital schism and marital skew. *American Journal of Psychiatry. 20*:241–248.

Weakland, J.H. 1960. The "double-bind" hypothesis of schizophrenia and three-party interaction. In *The etiology of schizophrenia*, D.D. Jackson, ed. New York: Basic Books.

Whitaker, C.A. 1958. Psychotherapy with couples. *American Journal of Psychotherapy. 12*:18–23.

Wynne, L.C., Ryckoff, I., Day, J., and Hirsch, S.I. 1958. Pseudo-mutuality in the family relationships of schizophrenics. *Psychiatry. 21*:205–220.

_____ Chapter 2. The Conceptual Context of Family Therapy

Bateson, G. 1971. *Steps to an ecology of mind.* New York: Ballantine.

Bateson, G. 1979. *Mind and nature.* New York: E.P. Dutton.

von Bertalanffy, L. 1950. An outline of General System Theory. *British Journal of the Philosophy of Science. 1*:134–165.

von Bertalanffy, L. 1967. *Robots, men and minds.* New York: George Braziller.

Breunlin, D.C., and Schwartz, R.C. 1986. Sequences: Toward a common denominator of family therapy. *Family Process. 25*:67–88.

Breunlin, D.C., Schwartz, R.C., and Karrer, B.M. *Metaframework for systemic therapy.* San Francisco: Jossey-Bass. In press.

Carter, E., and McGoldrick, M., eds. 1989. *The changing family life cycle: A framework for family therapy.* 2nd ed. Boston: Allyn & Bacon.

Davidson, M. 1983. *Uncommon sense: The life and thought of Ludwig von Bertalanffy.* Los Angeles: J.P. Tarcher.

Dell, P.F. 1982. Beyond homeostasis: Toward a concept of coherence. *Family Process. 21*:21–42.

Falicov, C. J., ed. *Family transitions.* New York: Guilford.

Haley, J. 1985. Conversations with Erickson. *Family Therapy Networker. 9*(2):30–43.

Hoffman, L. 1981. *Foundations of family therapy.* New York: Basic Books.

Simon, R. 1982. Reflections on family therapy: An interview with Jay Haley. *Family Therapy Networker. 6*(5):18–26.

Simon, R. 1984. Stranger in a strange land: An interview with Salvador Minuchin. *Family Therapy Networker. 8*(6):21–31, 66–68.

Sluzki, C. 1983. Interview on the state of the art. *Family Therapy Networker. 7*(1):24.

Weiner, N. 1948. *Cybernetics or control and communication in the animal and the machine.* Cambridge, MA: Technology Press.

———— Chapter 3. The Contemporary Context of Family Therapy

Bloch, D.A., and Weiss, H.M. 1981. Training facilities in marital and family therapy. *Family Process. 20*:133–146.

de Shazer, S. 1984. The death of resistance. *Family Process. 23*:11–16.

Eiduson, B.T. 1979. Emergent families of the 1970s: Values, practices, and impact on children. In *The American family: Dying or developing,* D. Reiss and H. Hoffman, eds. New York: Plenum Press.

Goldner, V. 1985. Feminism and family therapy. *Family Process. 24*:31–48.

Goldner, V. 1988. Generation and gender: Normative and covert hierarchies. *Family Process. 27*:17–33.

Gurman, A.S., Kniskern, D.P., and Pinsof, W.M. 1986. Research on marital and family therapies. In *Handbook of psychotherapy and behavior change,* S.L. Garfield and A.E. Bergin, eds. 3rd ed. New York: Wiley.

Hare-Mustin, R.T., and Marecek, J. 1988. The meaning of difference: Gender theory, postmodernism and psychology. *American Psychologist. 43*:455–464.

Hare-Mustin, R.T., and Marecek, J., eds. 1990. *Making a difference: Psychology and the construction of gender.* New Haven: Yale University Press.

Keeney, B.P. 1983. *The aesthetics of change.* New York: Guilford Press.

Leupnitz, D. 1988. *The family interpreted: Feminist theory in clinical practice.* New York: Basic Books.

McGoldrick, M., Anderson, C., and Walsh, F., eds. 1989. *Women in families: A framework for family therapy.* New York: Norton.

Schwartz, R.C., and Breunlin, D.C. 1983. Research: Why clinicians should bother with it. *Family Therapy Networker.* 7(4):22–27, 57–59.

Schwartz, R.C., and Perrotta, P. 1985. Let us sell no intervention before its time. *Family Therapy Networker.* 9(4):18–25.

Walsh, F., ed. 1982. *Normal family processes.* New York: Guilford.

_____ Chapter 4. Early Models: Group and Communications Family Therapy

Bell, J.E. 1961. *Family group therapy.* Public Health Monograph No. 64, Washington, DC: U.S. Government Printing Office.

Bell, J.E. 1975. *Family therapy.* New York: Jason Aronson.

Bion, W.R. 1961. *Experience in groups.* London: Tavistock Publications.

Haley, J. 1963. *Strategies of psychotherapy.* New York: Grune and Stratton.

Hoffman, L. 1971. Deviation-amplifying processes in natural groups. In *Changing families,* J. Haley, ed. New York: Grune and Stratton.

Jackson, D.D. 1961. Interactional psychotherapy. In *Contemporary psychotherapies,* M.T. Stein, ed. New York: Free Press of Glencoe.

Jackson, D.D. 1967. *Therapy, communication and change.* Palo Alto, CA: Science and Behavior Books.

Laqueur, H.P. Multiple family therapy. In *The book of family therapy,* A. Ferber, M. Mendelsohn, and A. Napier, eds. Boston: Houghton Mifflin.

Lederer, W., and Jackson, D.D. 1968. *Mirages of marriage.* New York: Norton.

MacGregor, R., Richie, A.M., Serrano, A.C., Schuster, F.P., McDonald, E.C., and Goolishian, H.A. 1964. *Multiple impact therapy with families.* New York: McGraw-Hill.

Satir, V. 1964. *Conjoint family therapy.* Palo Alto, CA: Science and Behavior Books.

Sluzki, C.E. 1978. Marital therapy from a systems theory perspective. In *Marriage and marital therapy,* T.J. Paolino and B.S. McCrady, eds. New York: Brunner/Mazel.

Speck, R.V., and Attneave, C.A. 1971. Social network intervention. In *Changing families,* J. Haley, ed. New York: Grune and Stratton.

Watzlawick, P., Beavin, J.H., and Jackson, D.D. 1967. *Pragmatics of human communication.* New York: Norton.

Wynne, L.C. 1970. Communication disorders and the quest for relatedness in families of schizophrenics. *American Journal of Psychoanalysis.* 30:100–114.

_____ Chapter 5. Psychoanalytic Family Therapy

Ackerman, N.W. 1966. *Treating the troubled family.* New York: Basic Books.

Boszormenyi-Nagy, I. 1972. Loyalty implications of the transference model in psychotherapy. *Archives of General Psychiatry.* 27:374–380.

Boszormenyi-Nagy, I. 1987. *Foundations of contextual therapy*. New York: Brunner/Mazel.

Dicks, H.V. 1967. *Marital tensions*. New York: Basic Books.

Meissner, W.W. 1978. The conceptualization of marriage and family dynamics from a psychoanalytic perspective. In *Marriage and marital therapy*, T.J. Paolino and B.S. McCrady, eds. New York: Brunner/Mazel.

Nadelson, C.C. 1978. Marital therapy from a psychoanalytic perspective. In *Marriage and marital therapy*, T.J. Paolino and B.S. McCrady, eds. New York: Brunner/Mazel.

Nichols, M.P. 1987. *The self in the system*. New York: Brunner/Mazel.

Sander, F.M. 1989. Marital conflict and psychoanalytic theory in the middle years. In *The middle years: New psychoanalytic perspectives*, J. Oldham and R. Liebert, eds. New Haven: Yale University Press.

Scharff, D., and Scharff, J.S. 1987. *Object relations family therapy*. New York: Jason Aronson.

Stern, D.N. 1985. *The interpersonal world of the infant*. New York: Basic Books.

Vogel, E.F., and Bell, N.W. 1960. The emotionally disturbed child as the family scapegoat. In *The family*, N.W. Bell and E.F. Vogel, eds. Glencoe, IL: Free Press.

Zinner, J., and Shapiro, R. 1976. Projective identification as a mode of perception of behavior in families of adolescents. *International Journal of Psychoanalysis. 53*:523–530.

Chapter 6. Experiential Family Therapy

Duhl, B.S., and Duhl, F.J. 1981. Integrative family therapy. In *Handbook of family therapy*, A.S. Gurman and D.P. Kniskern, eds. New York: Brunner/Mazel.

Duhl, F.J., Kantor, D., and Duhl, B.S. 1973. Learning, space and action in family therapy: A primer of sculpture. In *Techniques in family therapy*, D.A. Bloch, ed. New York: Grune and Stratton.

Greenberg, L.S., and Johnson, S.M. 1988. *Emotionally focused therapy for couples*. New York: Guilford.

Kaplan, M.L., and Kaplan, N.R. 1978. Individual and family growth: A Gestalt approach. *Family Process. 17*:195–205.

Keith, D.V., and Whitaker, C.A. 1977. The divorce labyrinth. In *Family therapy: Full length case studies*, P. Papp, ed. New York: Gardner Press.

Kempler, W. 1981. *Experiential psychotherapy with families*. New York: Brunner/Mazel.

Laing, R.D., and Esterson, A. 1970. *Sanity, madness and the family*. Baltimore: Penguin Books.

Napier, A.Y., and Whitaker, C.A. 1978. *The family crucible*. New York: Harper & Row.

Neill, J.R., and Kniskern, D.P., eds. 1982. *From psyche to system: The evolving therapy of Carl Whitaker*. New York: Guilford.

Satir, V.M. 1988. *The new peoplemaking*. Palo Alto, CA: Science and Behavior Books.

Satir, V.M., and Baldwin, M. 1983. *Satir step by step: A guide to creating change in families.* Palo Alto, CA: Science and Behavior Books.

Whitaker, C.A. 1967. The growing edge. In *Techniques of family therapy,* J. Haley and L. Hoffman, eds. New York: Basic Books.

Whitaker, C.A., and Keith, D.V. 1981. Symbolic-experiential family therapy. In *Handbook of family therapy,* A.S. Gurman and D.P. Kniskern, eds. New York: Brunner/Mazel.

_____ Chapter 7. Behavioral Family Therapy

Alexander, J.F., and Barton, C. 1976. Behavioral systems therapy with families. In *Treating relationships,* D.H. Olson, ed. Lake Mills, IA: Graphic Publishing.

Barton, C., and Alexander, J.F. 1981. Functional family therapy. In *Handbook of family therapy,* A.S. Gurman and D.P. Kniskern, eds. New York: Brunner/Mazel.

Birchler, G.R., and Spinks, S.H. 1980. Behavioral-systems marital therapy: Integration and clinical application. *American Journal of Family Therapy.* 8:6–29.

Epstein, N., Schlesinger, S.E., and Dryden, W. 1988. *Cognitive-behavioral therapy with families.* New York: Brunner/Mazel.

Falloon, I.R.H. 1988. *Handbook of behavioral family therapy.* New York: Guilford.

Gordon, S.B., and Davidson, N. 1981. Behavioral parent training. In *Handbook of family therapy,* A.S. Gurman and D.P. Kniskern, eds. New York: Brunner/Mazel.

Graziano, A.M. 1977. Parents as behavior therapists. In *Progress in behavior modification,* M. Hersen, R.M. Eisler, and P.M. Miller, eds. New York: Academic Press.

Jacobson, N.S., and Margolin, G. 1979. *Marital therapy: Strategies based on social learning and behavior exchange principles.* New York: Brunner/Mazel.

Kaplan, H.S. 1979. *The new sex therapy: Active treatment of sexual dysfunctions.* New York: Brunner/Mazel.

Liberman, R.P. 1972. Behavioral approaches to family and couple therapy. In *Progress in group and family therapy,* C.J. Sager and H.S. Kaplan, eds. New York: Brunner/Mazel.

Masters, W.H., and Johnson, V.E. 1970. *Human sexual inadequacy.* Boston: Little, Brown.

O'Leary, K.D., and Turkewitz, J. 1978. Marital therapy from a behavioral perspective. In *Marriage and marital therapy,* T.J. Paolino and B.S. McCrady, eds. New York: Brunner/Mazel.

Patterson, G.R. 1971. *Families: Application of social learning theory to family life.* Champaign, IL: Research Press.

Stuart, R.B. 1980. *Helping couples change: A social learning approach to marital therapy.* New York: Guilford Press.

Weiss, R.L. 1978. The conceptualization of marriage from a behavioral perspective. In *Marriage and marital therapy*, T.J. Paolino and B.S. McCrady, eds. Brunner/Mazel.

———— **Chapter 8. Extended Family Systems Therapy**

Anonymous. 1972. Differentiation of self in one's family. In *Family interaction*, J. Framo, ed. New York: Springer.

Bowen, M. 1978. *Family therapy in clinical practice*. New York: Jason Aronson.

Carter, E., and Orfanidis, M.M. 1976. Family therapy with one person and the family therapist's own family. In *Family therapy: Theory and practice*, P.J. Guerin, ed. New York: Gardner Press.

Fogarty, T.F. 1976. Systems concepts and the dimensions of self. In *Family therapy: Theory and practice*, P.J. Guerin, ed. New York: Gardner Press.

Fogarty, T.F. 1976. Marital crisis. In *Family therapy: Theory and practice*, P.J. Guerin, ed. New York: Gardner Press.

Guerin, P.J., Fay, L., Burden, S., and Kautto, J. 1987. *The evaluation and treatment of marital conflict: A four-stage approach*. New York: Basic Books.

Guerin, P.J., and Pendagast, E.G. 1976. Evaluation of family system and geogram. In *Family therapy: Theory and practice*, P.J. Guerin, ed. New York: Gardner Press.

Kerr, M.E., and Bowen, M. 1988. *Family evaluation*. New York: Norton.

———— **Chapter 9. Strategic Family Therapy**

Boscolo, L., Cecchin, G., Hoffman, L., and Penn, P. 1987. *Milan systemic therapy*. New York: Basic Books.

Cecchin, G. 1987. Hypothesizing, circularity and neutrality revisited: An invitation to curiosity. *Family Process*. 26:405–413.

Fisch, R., Weakland, J.H., and Segal, L. 1982. *The tactics of change: Doing therapy briefly*. San Francisco: Jossey-Bass.

Haley, J. 1973. *Uncommon therapy*. New York: Norton.

Haley, J. 1976. *Problem-solving therapy*. San Francisco: Jossey-Bass.

Haley, J. 1980. *Leaving home*. New York: McGraw-Hill.

Hoffman, L. 1976. Breaking the homeostatic cycle. In *Family therapy: Theory and practice*, P.J. Guerin, ed. New York: Gardner Press.

Madanes, C. 1981. *Strategic family therapy*. San Francisco: Jossey-Bass.

Madanes, C. 1984. *Behind the one-way mirror*. San Francisco: Jossey-Bass.

Madanes, C. 1990. *Sex, love and violence: Strategies for transformation*. New York: Norton.

Papp, P. 1980. The Greek chorus and other techniques of paradoxical therapy. *Family Process*. 19:45–57.

Rabkin, R. 1972. *Strategic psychotherapy*. New York: Basic Books.

Rohrbaugh, M., Tennen, H., Press, S., and White, L. 1981. Compliance, defiance, and therapeutic paradox: Guidelines for strategic use of paradoxical interventions. *American Journal of Orthopsychiatry*. 51:454–456.

Selvini Palazzoli, M. 1986. Towards a general model of psychotic games. *Journal of Marital and Family Therapy. 12*:339–349.

Selvini Palazzoli, M., Boscolo, L., Cecchin, G., and Prata G. 1978. *Paradox and counterparadox*. New York: Jason Aronson.

Tomm, K. 1987. Interventive interviewing: Part 1. Strategizing as a fourth guideline for the therapists. *Family Process. 26*:3–14.

Watzlawick, P., Weakland, J., and Fisch, R. 1974. *Change: Principles of problem formation and problem resolution*. New York: Norton.

_____ Chapter 10. Structural Family Therapy

Minuchin, S. 1974. *Families and family therapy*. Cambridge, MA: Harvard University Press.

Minuchin, S., Baker, L., Rosman, B., Liebman, R., Milman, L., and Todd, T.C. 1975. A conceptual model of psychosomatic illness in children. *Archives of General Psychiatry. 32*:1031–1038.

Minuchin, S., and Fishman, H.C. 1981. *Family therapy techniques*. Cambridge, MA: Harvard University Press.

Minuchin, S., Montalvo, B., Guerney, B., Rosman, B., and Schumer, F. 1967. *Families of the slums*. New York: Basic Books.

Minuchin, S., Rosman, B.L., and Baker, L. 1978. *Psychosomatic families: Anorexia nervosa in context*. Cambridge, MA: Harvard University Press.

Stanton, M.D., and Todd, T.C. 1979. Structural family therapy with drug addicts. In *The family therapy of drug and alcohol abuse*, E. Kaufman and P. Kaufmann, eds. New York: Gardner Press.

_____ Chapter 11. The Cutting Edge

Anderson, C.M., Reiss, D., and Hogarty, B. 1986. *Schizophrenia and the family*. New York: Guilford.

Anderson, H., and Goolishian, H.A. 1988. Human systems and linguistic systems: Preliminary and evolving ideas about the implications for clinical theory. *Family Process. 27*:371–393.

de Shazer, S. 1988. *Clues: Investigating solutions in brief therapy*. New York: Norton.

O'Hanlon, W.H., and Weiner-Davis, M. 1989. *In search of solutions: A new direction in psychotherapy*. New York: Norton.

Rolland, J.S. 1987. Chronic illness and the life cycle: A conceptual framework. *Family Process. 26*:203–221.

Schwartz, R.C. 1987. Our multiple selves. *Family Therapy Networker. 11*: 25–31.

White, M., and Epston, D. 1990. *Narrative means to therapeutic ends*. New York: Norton.

Wylie, M.S. 1990. Brief therapy on the couch. *Family Therapy Networker. 14*:26–34, 66.

—————— **Chapter 12. Comparative Analysis**

Gurman, A.S. 1978. Contemporary marital therapies: A critique and comparative analysis of psychoanalytic, behavioral and systems theory approaches. In *Marriage and marital therapy*, T.J. Paolino and B.S. McCrady, eds. New York: Brunner/Mazel.

Madanes, C., and Haley, J. 1977. Dimensions of family therapy. *Journal of Nervous and Mental Diseases.* 165:88–98.

Sluzki, C.E. 1983. Process, structure and world views: Toward an integrated view of systemic models in family therapy. *Family Process.* 22:469–476.

Sluzki, C.E. 1987. Family process: Mapping the journey over 25 years. *Family Process.* 26:149–153.

The following are among the best and most useful books about families and family therapy.

—————— **General Principles of Family Systems**

Carter, B., and McGoldrick, M. 1988. *The changing family life cycle: A framework for family therapy.* 2nd ed. Boston: Allyn & Bacon.

Hoffman, L. 1981. *The foundations of family therapy.* New York: Basic Books.

Kerr, M.E., and Bowen, M. 1988. *Family evaluation.* New York: Norton.

Minuchin, S. 1974. *Families and family therapy.* Cambridge, MA: Harvard University Press.

Nichols, M.P. 1988. *The power of the family.* New York: Fireside/Simon & Schuster.

Paolino, T.J., and McCrady, B.S., eds. 1978. *Marriage and marital therapy.* New York: Brunner/Mazel.

Watzlawick, P., Beavin, J., and Jackson, D. 1967. *Pragmatics of human communication.* New York: Norton.

—————— **Marriage**

Dicks, H.V. 1967. *Marital tensions.* New York: Basic Books.

Guerin, P.J., Fay, L., Burden, S., and Kautto, J. 1987. *The evaluation and treatment of marital conflict: A four-stage approach.* New York: Basic Books.

Lederer, W., and Jackson, D. 1968. *The mirages of marriage.* New York: Norton.

Lerner, H.G. 1985. *The dance of anger: A woman's guide to changing patterns of intimate relationships.* New York: Harper & Row.

Scarf, M. 1987. *Intimate partners: Patterns in love and marriage.* New York: Random House.

—————— **In-Laws and the Extended Family**

Guerin, P.J., ed. 1976. *Family therapy: Theory and practice.* New York: Gardner Press.

Lerner, H.G. 1989. *The dance of intimacy: A woman's guide to courageous acts of change in key relationships.* New York: Harper & Row.

McGoldrick, M., and Gerson, R. 1985. *Genograms in family assessment.* New York: Norton.

_____ Families With Babies and Small Children

Brazelton, T.B. 1983. *Infants and mothers: Differences in development.* Rev. ed. New York: Dell.

Faber, A., and Mazlish, E. 1974. *Liberated parents, liberated children.* New York: Grosset & Dunlap.

Ginott, H. 1969. *Between parent and child.* New York: Macmillan.

Patterson, G. 1975. *Families: Application of social learning theory to family life.* Champaign, IL: Research Press.

_____ Families With Older Children

Bank, S., and Kahn, M. 1982. *The sibling bond.* New York: Basic Books.

Blos, P. 1979. *The adolescent passage: Developmental issues.* New York: International Universities Press.

Faber, A., and Mazlish, E. 1987. *Siblings without rivalry.* New York: Norton.

Fishel, E. 1979. *Sisters: Love and rivalry inside the family and beyond.* New York: Quill/William Morrow.

Schlaadt, R., and Shannon, P. 1986. *Drugs of choice.* 2nd ed. Englewood Cliffs, NJ: Prentice-Hall.

_____ Divorce, Remarriage and Stepparenting

Ahrons, C., and Rodgers, R. 1987. *Divorced families: A multidisciplinary developmental view.* New York: Norton.

Vaughan, D. 1986. *Uncoupling: Turning points in intimate relationships.* New York: Oxford University Press.

Visher, E., and Visher, J. 1988. *Old loyalties, new ties: Therapeutic strategies with stepfamilies.* New York: Brunner/Mazel.

_____ Leaving Home and the Postchildrearing Years

Levinson, D. 1978. *The seasons of a man's life.* New York: Ballantine.

Nichols, M.P. 1987. *Turning forty in the eighties.* New York: Fireside/Simon & Schuster.

Viorst, J. 1986. *Necessary losses.* New York: Simon & Schuster.

_____ Family Therapy Technique

Anderson, C., and Stewart, S. 1983. *Mastering resistance: A practical guide to family therapy.* New York: Guilford Press.

Guerin, P.J., Fay, L., Burden, S., and Kautto, J. 1987. *The evaluation and treatment of marital conflict: A four-stage approach.* New York: Basic Books.

Isaacs, M.B., Montalvo, B., and Abelsohn, D. 1986. *The difficult divorce: Therapy for children and families.* New York: Basic Books.

Minuchin, S., and Fishman, H.C. 1981. *Family therapy techniques.* Cambridge, MA: Harvard University Press.

Pittman, F. 1988. *Turning points.* New York: Norton.

White, M., and Epston, D. 1990. *Narrative means to therapeutic ends.* New York: Norton.

Appendix B
GLOSSARY

accommodation. Elements of a system automatically adjust to coordinate their functioning; people may have to work at it.

anorexia nervosa. Self-starvation leading to loss of 25 percent or more of body weight, hyperactivity, hypothermia, and amenorrhea (in females).

aversive control. Using punishment and criticism to eliminate undesirable responses; commonly used in dysfunctional families.

basic assumption theory. Bion's concept that group members become diverted from the group task to pursue unconscious patterns of *fight-flight*, *dependency*, or *pairing*.

behavior exchange theory. Explanation of behavior in relationships as maintained by a ratio of costs to benefits.

black box metaphor. The idea that because the mind is so complex, it's better to study people's input and output (behavior, communication) than to speculate about what goes on in their minds.

blended families. Separate families united by marriage; stepfamilies.

boundary. A concept used in structural family therapy to describe emotional barriers that protect and enhance the integrity of individuals, subsystems, and families.

circular causality. The idea that events are related through a series of interacting loops or repeating cycles.

circular questioning. A method of interviewing developed by the Milan Associates in which questions are asked that highlight differences among family members.

classical conditioning. A form of respondent learning in which an unconditioned stimulus (UCS), such as food, which leads to an unconditioned response (UCR), such as salivation, is paired with a conditioned stimulus (CS), such as bell, the result of which is that the CS begins to evoke the same response; used in the behavioral treatment of anxiety disorders.

communications theory. The study of relationships in terms of the exchange of verbal and nonverbal messages.

complementary. Relationships based on differences which fit together, where qualities of one make up for lacks in the other; one is one-up while the other is one-down.

concurrent therapy. Treatment of two or more persons, seen separately, usually by different therapists.

conjoint therapy. Treatment of two or more persons in sessions together.

constructivism. A relativistic point of view that emphasizes the subjective construction of reality. Implies that what we see in families may be based as much on our preconditions as on what's actually going on.

contingency contracting. A behavior therapy technique whereby agreements are made between family members to exchange rewards for desired behavior.

countertransference. Emotional reaction, usually unconscious and often distorted, on the part of the therapist to a patient or member of a family in treatment.

cross-generational coalition. An inappropriate alliance between a parent and child, who side together against a third member of the family.

cybernetics. The study of control processes in systems, especially analysis of the flow of information in closed systems.

differentiation.   Psychological separation of intellect and emotions, and independence of self from others; opposite of fusion.

disengagement.   Minuchin's term for psychological isolation that results from overly rigid boundaries around individuals and subsystems in a family.

double-bind.   A conflict created when a person receives contradictory messages on different levels of abstraction in an important relationship, and cannot leave or comment.

dyadic model.   Explanations based on the interactions between two persons or objects: Johnny shoplifts to get his mother's attention.

emotional cutoff.   Bowen's term for flight from an unresolved emotional attachment.

enactment.   An interaction stimulated in structural family therapy in order to observe and then change transactions which make up family structure.

enmeshment.   Minuchin's term for loss of autonomy due to a blurring of psychological boundaries.

epistemology.   The branch of philosophy concerned with the study of knowledge. Used by Bateson to mean worldview or belief system.

expressive role.   Serving social and emotional functions; in traditional families, the wife's role.

extended family.   All the descendants of a set of grandparents.

externalization.   Michael White's technique of getting families to fight to control their problem, as if problems were external to persons.

extinction.   Eliminating behavior by not reinforcing it.

family drawing.   An experiential therapy technique where family members are asked to draw their ideas about how the family is organized.

family group therapy.   Family treatment based on the group therapy model.

family homeostasis.   Tendency of families to resist change in order to maintain a steady state.

family life cycle.   Stages of family life from separation from one's parents to marriage, having children, growing older, retirement, and finally death.

family structure.   The functional organization of families that determines how family members interact.

family myths.   A set of beliefs based on a distortion of historical reality and shared by all family members that help shape the rules governing family functioning.

family of origin.   A person's parents and siblings; usually refers to the original nuclear family of an adult.

family projection process.   In Bowenian theory, the mechanism by which parental conflicts are projected onto the children or a spouse.

family ritual.   Technique used by Selvini Palazzoli and her Milan Associates that prescribes a specific act for family members to perform, which is designed to change the family system's rules.

family rules.   A descriptive term for redundant behavioral patterns.

family sculpting.   A nonverbal experiential technique in which family members position themselves in a tableau that reveals significant aspects of their perceptions and feelings.

feedback.   The return of a portion of the output of a system, especially when used to maintain the output within predetermined limits (negative feedback), or to signal a need to modify the system (positive feedback).

first-order change.   Superficial change in a system which itself stays invariant.

functional analysis of behavior.   In operant behavior therapy, a study of a particular behavior, what elicits it, and what reinforces it.

function of the system.   The idea that symptoms are often ways to distract or otherwise protect family members from threatening conflicts.

fusion.   A blurring of psychological boundaries between self and others, and a contamination of emotional and intellectual functioning; opposite of differentiation.

general systems theory.   A biological model of living systems as whole entities which maintain themselves through continuous input and output from the environment; developed by Ludwig von Bertalanffy.

genogram.   A schematic diagram of the family system, using squares to represent men, circles to indicate women, horizontal lines for marriages, and vertical lines to indicate children.

group dynamics.   Interactions among group members that emerge as a result of properties of the group rather than merely their individual personalities.

hierarchical structure.   Family functioning based on clear generational boundaries, where the parents maintain control and authority.

homeostasis.   A balanced steady state of equilibrium.

identified patient.   The symptom bearer or official patient as identified by the family.

instrumental role.   Decision-making and task functions; in traditional families, the husband's role.

intensity.   Minuchin's term for changing maladaptive transactions by using strong affect, repeated intervention, or prolonged pressure.

internal family systems.   A model of the mind that uses systemic principles and techniques to understand and change intrapsychic processes.

introjection.   A primitive form of identification; taking in aspects of other people, which then become part of the self-image.

invariant prescription.   A technique developed by Mara Selvini Palazzoli in which parents are directed to mysteriously sneak away together.

invisible loyalties.   Boszormenyi-Nagy's term for unconscious commitments that children take on to help their families.

joining.   A structural family therapy term for accepting and accommodating to families in order to win their confidence and circumvent resistance.

linear causality.   The idea that one event is the cause and another is the effect; in behavior, the idea that one behavior is a stimulus, the other a response.

live supervision.   Technique of teaching therapy whereby the supervisor observes sessions in progress and contacts the therapist to suggest different strategies and techniques.

marital schism.   Lidz's term for pathological overt marital conflict.

marital skew.   Lidz's term for a pathological marriage in which one spouse dominates the other.

metacommunication.   Every message has two levels, report and command; metacommunication is the implied command or qualifying message.

mirroring.   Expression of understanding and acceptance of another's feelings.

modeling.   Observational learning.

monadic model.   Explanations based on properties of a single person or object: Johnny shoplifts because he is rebellious.

multigenerational transmission process.   Murray Bowen's concept for the projection of varying degrees of immaturity to different children in the same family; the child who is most involved in the family emotional process emerges with the lowest level of differentiation, and passes problems on to succeeding generations.

multiple family therapy.   Treatment of several families at once in a group therapy format; pioneered by Peter Laqueur and Murray Bowen.

multiple impact therapy.   An intensive, crisis-oriented form of family therapy developed by Robert MacGregor; family members are treated in various subgroups by a team of therapists.

mystification.   Laing's concept that many families distort their children's experience by denying or relabeling it.

network therapy.   A treatment devised by Ross Speck in which a large number of family and friends are assembled to help resolve a patient's problems.

neutrality.   Selvini Palazzoli's term for balanced acceptance of family members.

nuclear family.   Parents and their children.

object relations.   Internalized images of self and others based on early parent-child interactions which determine a person's mode of relationship to other people.

object relations theory.   Psychoanalytic theory derived from Melanie Klein and developed by the British School (Bion, Fairbairn, Guntrip, Winnicott) which emphasizes the object-seeking propensity of the infant, instead of focusing exclusively on libidinal and aggressive drives.

open system.   A system that exchanges information or material with its environment, as opposed to a closed system that does not. Living systems are, by definition, open systems.

operant conditioning.   A form of learning whereby a person or animal is rewarded for performing certain behaviors; the major approach in most forms of behavior therapy.

ordeals.   A type of paradoxical intervention in which the client is directed to do something that is more of a hardship than the symptom.

paradox.   A self-contradictory statement based on a valid deduction from acceptable premises.

paradoxical directive.   A technique used in strategic therapy whereby the therapist directs family members to continue their symptomatic behavior. If they conform, they admit control and expose secondary gain; if they rebel, they give up their symptoms.

parental child.   A child who has been allocated power to take care of younger siblings; adaptive when done deliberately in large or single-parent families, maladaptive when it results from unplanned abdication of parental responsibility.

positive connotation.   Selvini Palazzoli's technique of ascribing positive motives to family behavior in order to promote family cohesion and avoid resistance to therapy.

Premack principle.   Using high-probability behavior (preferred activities) to reinforce low-probability behavior (nonpreferred activities).

prescribing the symptom.   A paradoxical technique which forces a patient to either give up a symptom or admit that it is under voluntary control.

pretend techniques.   Madanes' playful paradoxical intervention in which family members are asked to pretend to engage in symptomatic behavior. The paradox is if they are pretending to have a symptom, the symptom cannot be real.

process/content.   Distinction between how members of a family or group relate and what they talk about.

projective identification.   A defense mechanism that operates unconsciously, whereby unwanted aspects of the self are attributed to another person and that person is induced to behave in accordance with these projected attitudes and feelings.

pseudohostility.   Wynne's term for superficial bickering that masks pathological alignments in schizophrenic families.

pseudomutuality.   Wynne's term for the facade of family harmony that characterizes many schizophrenic families.

psychoeducation.   A type of therapy developed in work with schizophrenics, which emphasizes educating family members to help them understand and cope with a seriously disturbed family member.

quid pro quo.   Literally, "something for something," an equal exchange or substitution.

reframing.   Relabeling a family's description of behavior to make it more amenable to therapeutic change; for example, describing someone as "lazy" rather than "depressed."

regression.   Return to a less mature level of functioning in the face of stress.

reinforcement.   An event, behavior, or object that increases the rate of a particular response. A positive reinforcer is an event whose contingent presentation increases the rate of responding; a negative reinforcer is an event whose contingent withdrawal increases the rate of responding.

reinforcement reciprocity. Exchanging rewarding behaviors between family members.

resistance. Anything that patients or families do to oppose or retard the progress of therapy.

restraining. A strategic technique for overcoming resistance by suggesting that a family not change.

role-playing. Acting out the parts of important characters to dramatize feelings and practice new ways of relating.

rubber fence. Wynne's term for the rigid boundary surrounding many schizophrenic families, which allows only minimal contact with the surrounding community.

scapegoat. A member of the family, usually the identified patient, who is the object of displaced conflict or criticism.

schizophrenic mother. Fromm-Reichmann's term for aggressive, domineering mothers thought to precipitate schizophrenia in their offspring.

second-order change. Basic change in the structure and functioning of a system.

self-object. Kohut's term for a person related to not as a separate individual, but as an extension of the self.

separation-individuation. Process whereby the infant begins, at about two months, to draw apart from the symbiotic bond with mother and develop his or her autonomous functioning.

shaping. Reinforcing change in small steps.

social learning theory. Understanding and treating behavior using principles from social and developmental psychology as well as from learning theory.

solution-focused. Steve de Shazer's term for a style of therapy that emphasizes the solutions that families have already developed for their problems.

structure. Recurrent patterns of interaction that define and stabilize the shape of relationships.

structured family interview. An assessment procedure, introduced by Watzlawick, in which families are given a series of tasks for discussion, and their interactions are observed and coded.

subsystem. Smaller units in families, determined by generation, sex, or function.

symmetrical. In relationships, equality or parallel form.

system, closed. A functionally related group of elements regarded as forming a collective entity that does not interact with the surrounding environment.

system, open. A set of interrelated elements that exchange information, energy, and material with the surrounding environment.

systems theory. A generic term for studying a group of related elements that interact as a whole entity; encompasses general systems theory and cybernetics.

theory of logical types. Bertrand Russell's theory of hierarchical levels of abstraction; a class is a different logical type than a member of the class.

three-generational hypothesis of schizophrenia. Bowen's concept that schizophrenia is the end result of low levels of differentiation passed on and amplified across three succeeding generations.

token economy. A system of rewards using points, which can be accumulated and exchanged for reinforcing items or behaviors.

transference. Psychoanalytic term for distorted emotional reactions to present relationships based on unresolved, early family relations.

triadic model. Explanations based on the interactions among three people or objects; Johnny shoplifts because his father covertly encourages him to defy his mother.

triangle.   A three-person system; according to Bowen, the smallest stable unit of human relations.

triangulation.   Detouring conflict between two people by involving a third person, stabilizing the relationship between the original pair.

unconscious.   Psychoanalytic term for memories, feelings, and impulses of which a person is unaware. Often used as a noun, but more appropriately limited to use as an adjective.

undifferentiated family ego mass.   Bowen's early term for emotional "stuck-togetherness" or fusion in the family, especially prominent in schizophrenic families.

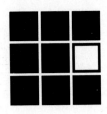

Name Index

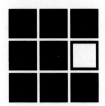

Subject Index

Accommodation, 453–54, 465–67, 546, 556–57
Ackerman Institute (Family Institute), 54, 164,
        227, 364, 410, 436
Action, 541–42
Action-oriented techniques, 113, 128, 446
Adaptive level of functioning, 367
Addictions, research on, 169, 173
Adolescence, 243–44, 374
Adolescent inpatient units, 14
Adult Children of Alcoholics, 493
Agoraphobia, behavioral treatments for, 311
Ahistorical model of group interactions, 190
Alcoholics Anonymous, 493
Alcoholism, 14–15, 155
Alienation from experience, 285
American Association for Marriage and Family
        Therapy (AAMFT), 160
American Association of Marriage Counselors, 37
American Family Therapy Association (AFTA),
        160–61
American Group Psychotherapy Association, 12
American Institute of Family Relations, 37
American Journal of Family Therapy, 162
American Orthopsychiatric Association, 18, 54,
        161
Anaclitic depression, 233
Analysis, 531–38
Annual Review of Psychology, 570
Anorexia nervosa, 139–40, 169, 243, 313, 460, 470,
        476–77, 499
Anxiety, 230, 310, 347–48, 383, 402
Anxious attachment, 363–64
Assertive training, 346
Assessment, 296, 332, 559–62
Atlanta Institute for Family Studies, 166–67
Atlanta Psychiatric Clinic, 59, 276, 295
Authenticity, 5
Autistic children, 312
Autistic phase of development, 232–33
Average expectable environment, 528
Aversive control in marriage, 323

Basic needs, unfulfilled, 3–4
Basic trust, 234
Battle fatigue mother syndrome, 284
Behavioral contracts, 313

Behavioral family therapy, 13, 170, 308–61, 521,
        541–42, 558, 559, 564
    marriage therapy, 338–46, 567
    parent training, 329–30, 337–38, 349, 567
Behavior change, conditions for, 202–6, 252–56,
        288, 325, 383–86, 421–23, 461–63, 540–51
Behavior disorders, development of, 197–201, 240–
        49, 283–86, 320–24, 375–80, 417–18, 455–
        60, 574
Behaviorism, 419
Behavior modification, 314
Behavior, relationship to feelings, 422–23
Behavior Research and Therapy, 311
Belief systems, 89
Bias, 88–96, 98–99, 512
Black box metaphor, 109, 191
Blended families, 458
Borderline personality disorders, 232, 244
Boston Family Institute, 63, 163, 277
Boundaries, 111, 112, 124, 135, 451, 525–27
Boundary making, 127–28, 472–74, 503, 565
Bowenian family therapy, 362–406, 544, 558, 560
Brief Family Therapy Center (Milwaukee), 167,
        481, 485
Brief therapy, 45–46
Brief Therapy Center (MRI), 409, 423–26, 438
Brooklyn State Hospital, 15
Brown University Family Therapy Newsletter, 162
Bulimia, 501

Career, influence on choice of, 3
Center for Family Learning, 63, 164–65, 364
Center for the Study of the Family (Milan), 409
Change, 196, 203–4, 515–16, 543
Change (Watzlawick, Weakland, and Fisch),
        86–87, 409, 438
Chestnut Lodge, 186
Child development, 38, 239
Child Guidance Clinic, 54
Child guidance movement, 17–20
Choreography, 9, 13
Chronic illness, 493–94
Circular causality, 28, 191, 195
Circularity, 108, 124–25, 399, 474
Circular questioning, 137, 140–41, 386, 434–36
Classical conditioning, 310